Henry Kurtz, Church of the Brethren

The Brethren's Encyclopedia

Henry Kurtz, Church of the Brethren

The Brethren's Encyclopedia

ISBN/EAN: 9783337217457

Printed in Europe, USA, Canada, Australia, Japan

Cover: Foto ©Suzi / pixelio.de

More available books at **www.hansebooks.com**

THE

𝕭rethren's Encyclopedia,

CONTAINING

The United Counsels and Conclusions of the Brethren,

AT THEIR

ANNUAL MEETINGS,

CAREFULLY COLLECTED, TRANSLATED (FROM THE ORIGINAL GERMAN IN PART) AND ARRANGED IN ALPHABETICAL AND CHRONOLOGICAL ORDER,

ACCOMPANIED WITH

NECESSARY AND EXPLANATORY NOTES, &c.

BY

ELDER HENRY KURTZ.

COPYRIGHT SECURED.

PUBLISHED BY THE AUTHOR, AT COLUMBIANA, OHIO.

Printed by W. S. Haven, cor. Wood and Third Sts., Pittsburgh.

1867.

INTRODUCTORY ADDRESS.

BELOVED BRETHREN IN THE LORD:—It is with the deepest feelings of gratitude to God, who has been pleased in mercy to spare my unprofitable life, and to enable me, though under severe afflictions, to pass this work through the press thus far. It is also with feelings of deep humility and self abasement, when I consider the object I had in view originally, namely, to put into the hands of my brethren of the present generation those words of peace and union which had been concluded upon by our beloved brethren of past generations under their own trials and difficulties, for our present and future benefit and instruction; and, on the other hand, perceive my imperfections and shortcomings in a great many ways. It was but a very humble task to be merely the interpreter of sayings of old, and I must confess my aim was a little higher; that is to say, to furnish my dearly beloved brethren, in the "Encyclopedia," a handbook to be consulted on any point or question that might occur to any conscientious brother in his private life, or to any church in her dealings with individual members, though it had not been presented or decided at a Yearly Council hitherto; but continued ill health prevented much scrutiny and revision, and so there was left out much which had been intended for insertion, and some few things may have slipped in which ought to have been left out, and for these things he earnestly pleads for indulgence and pardon of the dear reader.

A few words of explanation and caution seem to be necessary to those who will use this little collection of the united counsels and conclusions of our Annual Meetings, since there are different opinions about them even among brethren. Some perhaps esteem them somewhat too highly, taking them as rules and laws of equal authority as divine writ, and which, like the Persian laws, could not be altered. Others again put perhaps a too low estimate upon them, considering them as a bundle of human traditions, as they are sometimes called as *"traditions of elders,"* which we cannot too soon forget and lay aside, because, they think, they conflict with and are contrary to the word of God, as it is written. They object, when reference is made to these conclusions, and would have rather consigned them to destruction for fear they might obtain an undue influence. We honor both these opinions, for we believe, they are founded upon well intended, though perhaps mistaken views; at any rate we cannot take sides conscientiously with either of these two classes, and beg leave to lay here before our respected readers, whether they have belonged to either of said two classes, or whether they have like us occupied an impartial position, a few of our

REFLECTIONS

upon the subject, and we hope all will give them a fair and candid consideration, they being the result of a research at once deep and earnest for nearly forty years.

1. The fundamental principles of the Brethren, whether they lived in apostolic times eighteen hundred years ago, or in the Middle Ages, during the prevailing darkness of a corrupted church without a Bible, or since the Reformation and the art of Printing had given the Bible to every one who felt a desire for it, was, *to take the pure word of God, and that alone, as the infallible rule of their faith and practice.*

2. Guided by this principle, they rejected every form of doctrine, every practice, every custom and ordinance contrary to that divine and infallible rule, and united as a church with the sincere object to follow the apostles' converts on Pentecost : *" to continue steadfastly in the apostles' doctrine and fellowship, &c."* Acts 2 : 42.

3. But, as in the days of the apostles, there arose teachers who began to teach a different doctrine, and thus caused confusion and difficulties, we are informed how the apostles labored for union, and the Brethren even in our days have tried to follow their example, especially in our Yearly Meetings.

4. Now in any question that is presented, if there is an express word of God found to cover and decide this question, of course we would do very wrong to call such a decision a human tradition.

5. However, there also may be raised questions to which the word of God affords no direct answer. If they are mere matters of opinion, not inconsistent with true faith and morality, brotherly love will be liberal and forbearing, without insisting on others to be of our opinion. But if the expression of my opinions is offensive to others, brotherly affection, humility and prudence will teach me at once, at least not to give offense, and consequently to withhold the utterance of offensive opinions.

6. But if questions are of a practical nature, and as we are to be of one mind, and co-workers together, it becomes necessary to agree, "that there be no divisions among you;" and suppose the word of God, and especially the New Testament, is silent on the subject, but the brethren have come to a unanimous agreement in the matter, all one whether it was yesterday or a hundred years ago, by brethren representing the whole fraternity in Yearly Meeting, then such agreement is binding upon all, as the contract of a parent or of a duly authorized agent or attorney is binding upon the children or parties, their heirs and assigns, until it is either fulfilled or lawfully cancelled or recalled.

7. In this light, brethren, let us look upon the counsels and conclusions as solemn agreements or covenants upon which our fathers brake annually the bread of communion, and considered them as bonds of love, to bind them together in union of the spirit, so as " to be perfectly joined together in the same mind, and in the same judgment;" and on the other hand, they considered those who would act contrary to these articles of agreement as disturbers of the peace of the church, and covenant breakers, whom they could not fellowship, unless they repented indeed.

Such, my beloved brethren in the Lord, are our simple views of the Minutes of our Yearly Meeting. They are NOT *laws and rules* made and enacted by some legislative authority for the government of others, because we believe Christ to be our only legislator and lawgiver, and *his* laws, contained in the New Testament, are *perfect laws*, needing neither addition nor amendments, but nothing more than to be properly understood and faithfully applied. Oh, my brethren beloved, let us thank God daily for that perfect law of Christ, which we have, and let us try to be as faithful, as our brethren in times past tried to be faithful, in examining and obeying that perfect law, and setting forth in those Minutes a practical comment of this same law—the New Testament.

Neither can we call those Minutes mere traditions of men, in the sense of vain traditions, which the Saviour condemned, because they, the Pharisees, "transgressed the commandments of God by their traditions." Having said something on the subject of "Traditions" in the body of this work, we refrain from saying more here, and refer the dear reader to that article on page 179, and reference is there made to 2 Thess. 2 : 15, and 3 : 6, and 1 Cor. 11 : 2, where the observance of a different kind of traditions is earnestly recommended not only, but strongly inculcated and commanded. Let us, dear brethren, properly distinguish between traditions of Pharisaic Elders, which would make void the law of God, and between traditions of our Christian Elders, which only tend to the more perfect obedience of the law of Christ; prove all things by that law, and we will not be led astray by traditions.

Having said here what our Minutes, given in this work, are not; that is, neither laws, nor vain traditions, we may be asked again, what they really are in our humble estimation; and though we have intimated already more than once what we understood by them, we will try once more to elucidate and illustrate our simple ideas more fully. As in a judicial court there are judges, lawyers, the contending parties, the witnesses, and all the people that choose to attend, yet none of these parties, or all together. can bring in a verdict, but the twelve men specially selected, and called the JURY; so in the church of Christ none but those who are deemed to be impartial (we think,) will be able to give a true "Verdict," and such we deem the conclusions of our Yearly Meetings. Or, as when parties make an agreement, by which they are mutually bound to perform certain express conditions, not only they, but their heirs and assigns, are bound to observe the conditions in order to enjoy its benefits—so in the church of Christ, the brethren in Yearly Meeting assembled, agreeing on any point, bind not only themselves, but those who sent them, until released in the same manner. Or, as parties who have been at war with each other, in order to bring about a reconciliation, a treaty of peace is drawn, and signed, and confirmed, in which the conditions to be observed by each party are stated;—so when a party in the church of Christ has become estranged, and desires reconciliation, in such case the terms might be called a treaty of peace, as in the former case an agreement. In fact, we may say, every Yearly Meeting was a solemn act of renewing our covenant, into which each one of us had entered, when we made a public confession of our faith, renouncing Satan, the world, and all its sinful ways, and covenanting with God to be faithful even to the end, at our baptism in the name of the Father, and of the Son, and of the Holy Ghost. This covenant is renewed in every communion we attend, and, as to the whole body of the church, was renewed at every Annual Meeting by the articles agreed on, signed and sealed under the most solemn sanction of the divine presence, which had been sought by the most humble prayer of all the faithful, and by the influence of the Holy Spirit had again become united and "joined together in the same mind, and in the same judgment,"—and by celebrating a lovefeast, and partaking of the emblems of a Saviour's dying love, fear, and every erroneous, dividing and sinful sentiment was cast out by perfect love in every pious heart present. Would to God this latter feature of our Annual Meetings was restored again in these our days!!

Finally, brethren, after cautioning you thus to prove all things by the infallible test of the word of God, and asking pardon for anything amiss in this work, owing to our own shortsightedness or shortcoming, and particularly for not having been able to give at this time the "Appendix" often referred to in this work, on account of continued failing health (and even not being able to promise any thing further than this, that if the Lord would please to restore to us such a measure of health, that we could revise this work, and "set in order the things that are wanting" in this respect, we would with His help try to do so, and if possible without further expense to our subscribers); feeling every day more sensibly our approach to our dissolution, and we hope and trust to that home which our Saviour has prepared for us, scarcely hoping to see our beloved brethren any more in the flesh, that live away at any distance, but still rejoicing in the lively hope of once meeting where there shall be no parting any more forever,—with all these solemn feelings and impressions we bid our readers the kindest "Farewell." May the Lord, his wisdom and love be with us all. Amen.

Written in June, 1867.

BRETHREN'S ENCYCLOPEDIA.

ACKNOWLEDGMENT, or confession in case of a member committing a public fault or offence.

The discrimination between a public fault or offence and a public crime, is not as distinctly stated in the following cases as might be desirable, but probably will be in their proper place.

At the yearly meeting on Blackwater, Va., in 1797, "it was concluded in union, that when a brother or sister should commit a fault which was not between brother and brother, but public before the world, the church is to investigate the case, and if the fault was not so criminal as to compel the church to cut him off entirely, according to the word of the Lord, and the failing member sees it and is sorry for his sin, then he should make a public acknowledgment in the presence of the believers and the unbelieving. But if he should harden his heart, and would not obey the counsel of the church, then members could not have communion with such until the time when he becomes willing to acknowledge and to obey."

At the yearly meeting in Morrison's Cove, 1825, the question was presented, "In case members commit a public fault for which an acknowledgment is required, should it be made publicly, or only before the church? It was considered, in case the transgression was made without the church, and is deemed by the world a fault, and the transgressor should feel in himself urged to it (to make a public confession), in such case it might be good; but if it should be something that is not deemed a transgression by the world, and the conviction were not truly born from within or from the heart, then it would be no light before the world, and it would be better done before the membership."

At the Y. M. 1844, the following query came up, and was answered as follows: "Art 12. How is it considered, if a member makes an open transgression, and refuses to come before the church to acknowledge it, though he declares his willingness to make acknowledgment before some brethren? It was considered, that such private confession could not be deemed sufficient, since the word says, 1 Tim. 5: 20, 'Them that sin, rebuke before all, that others also may fear.'"

We cannot refrain from inserting the following letter treating on the same subject :

ROCKINGHAM, VA., March 6, 1833.

* * * " Now to come to your questions, whether we might require of a member an acknowledgment in public meeting according to the gospel and the Brethren's order ? According to the old Brethren's order as they kept house forty years ago, we might do so, but since we were helping to keep house, we have not required so much of a member, because we have no plain word in the Scripture for it. Paul says, 1 Tim. 5 : 20, ' Them that sin, rebuke before all, that others also may fear.' This is a good evidence for a public rebuke before the whole membership, and further we cannot understand it. We read in Numbers 5 : 6, ' When a man or woman shall commit any sin that men commit, to do a trespass against the Lord, and that person be guilty, then they shall confess their sin which they have done, and he shall recompense his trespass, &c.' And Lev. 6 : 5 we find, ' that he had to make restoration first, and then to bring his trespass-offering unto the priest, and the priest had to make an atonement for him before the Lord.' Now says Paul, ' Whatsoever things were written aforetime, were written for our learning;' and again it is said, ' If it be possible, as much as lieth in you, live peaceably with all men.' Rom. 12 : 18, and 15 : 4. Again, ' Follow peace with all men, and holiness, without which no man shall see the Lord.' Heb. 12 : 14. ' Now it seems to be quite plain, that when a brother commits a fault, or wrongs his neighbor, whether he is a member or not, he should first go with some brethren to the one he offended, and be reconciled with him, and then come to the church, and bring his trespass-offering, such as David says, Psalms 51 : 17, ' The sacrifices of God are a broken spirit; a broken and a contrite heart, O God, thou wilt not despise ;' that is, a repenting and humble heart he should bring to the church, and then the church can forgive him, as the Saviour had said to his disciples, John 20 : 23, ' Whosesoever sins ye remit, they are remitted unto them; and whosesoever sins ye retain, they are retained.' Now we must believe that the Saviour meant here the church, as he said to Peter, Matt. 16 : 18, ' Upon this rock I will build my church, and the gates of hell shall not prevail against it. And I will give unto thee the keys of the kingdom of heaven ; and whatsoever thou shalt bind on earth shall be bound in heaven ; and whatsoever thou shalt loose on earth shall be loosed in heaven.' This key is what we read of in Matt. 18 : 17, 'If he neglect to hear the church, let him be unto thee as an heathen man and a publican.' However, we have to be very careful to do to any one neither too much nor too little. In Matt. 23 : 23, the Saviour accuses the Pharisees to have ' omitted the weightier matters of the law, judgment, mercy and faith.' Now we read in Lev. 5 : 5, 'If a soul has sinned, though not against his fellow man, he shall confess that he has sinned, and shall bring his trespass-offering unto the priest (v. 8); and the priest shall make an

atonement for him, &c.' (v. 10.)   From this we learn that when a member has offended against God and 'the truth, it is his duty to come to the church, &c.; for Peter says to the believers, 'Ye are a royal priesthood (1 Peter 2: 9); and Paul says, 'If I forgave anything, I forgave it in the person of Christ.'   From this it is very clear, that when a church is keeping house right carefully, and upon true contrition and confession forgives a member, such will also be reconciled through Christ, the true High-priest, before God the heavenly Father.   But if a member were not truly repenting, it might be as we read, Lev. 13: 28, that when the priest had pronounced one clean, and it had still continued to spread, then the priest had still to pronounce him unclean, because it was leprosy.   Just so it may happen with a member; if he would continue in his old sinful course, the church would be compelled at last to put him without the camp, as the children of Israel had to do with all the leprous, else the whole church might fall into guilt.   The Saviour says, Luke 12: 42, 'Who then is that faithful and wise steward, whom his lord shall make ruler over his household, to give them their portion of meat in due season?'   Let this suffice on this point."

Two remarks we feel to make before we close this article. *First.* When we compare the above counsels carefully, we find that our brethren always endeavored to understand and carry out the word and will of God, according to the best light they had at the time; and so far from following blindly the views of their forefathers, as we are sometimes accused, they thought and acted for themselves, and felt free to pursue another course, if it seemed to them more in consonance with the word of God.

Our *second* remark is, that perhaps it would be desirable by some, that our old brethren should have clearly defined what kind of sins can be remitted by the church upon an acknowledgment or confession, and which could not be remitted, or rather must be *retained*, according to John 20: 23.   From this very passage it is plainly to be seen that there are some sins which can be remitted upon a confession or acknowledgment, and again other sins which the church cannot remit, but must retain even when confessed or acknowledged; but we must look elsewhere in the word of God for instructions about those different sins. To that word of God our old brethren always referred us, and in it they believed we could find all the necessary light and instruction for keeping house in the church of God.   They pointed us to Matt. 18: 15–18, as the divine rule for dealing with simple trespassers, and to 1 Cor. 5, as containing the law for those who had committed crimes, though at first in their simplicity they did not discriminate so fully between the two ordinances, and dealt with transgressors of the first class as rigorously as with those of the second.

Finally, let it be observed, that no bare acknowledgment or confession of having done wrong would be deemed sufficient. unless it was accompanied by a willingness to repair that wrong to the extent of our ability, or at least as far as the church may require of us.

ADMITTING STRANGERS (not members) to our church councils.

It would seem necessary to say a few words in explanation to those who may read the following, not being fully acquainted with our peculiarities.   In most denominations a church council meeting means only the meeting of the church officers for the transaction of the church business.   In such meetings no one, even no private member of the same church, is admitted, or will ask admittance without being specially invited.   But the case is different with us.   It is not only the privilege, but also the duty of every member to attend church council, whether official or private, male or female, and to assist in transacting business. Friends, seeing our members going to meeting, and being at leisure, may come also by mistake, expecting preaching.   Husbands, whose wives are members, may be induced by kindness to convey and accompany their companions to meeting, even if they are informed of its peculiar character. Some may come moved by curiosity or other motives, but all feel more or less mortified and offended when requested to withdraw. The reluctance of brethren to give that offence was the origin of the query following, we suppose.

At the yearly meeting in Ohio, 1822, the question was presented, whether such as were not members could be present in our church-councils, and the answer was, " Considered, as it was at all times considered, that it could not be allowed."

At the special yearly meeting in Indiana, 1845, question 6 was, " Whether in a council meeting of the church the gospel will allow such as are no members to be admitted ?" and the answer was, Considered, that inasmuch as our Saviour directs us, Matt. 18, the course we are to take with an offending brother, to tell it in the last step *unto the church*, it seemed to be obvious by (or in) the gospel, that those who do not belong to the church ought not to be in council.

ADMITTING STRANGE MINISTERS (not brethren, but from other denominations,) to preach in our meetings.

At a special meeting in Tennessee, 1846, query 5 was, " Whether we should give liberty to preachers of other denominations to speak in our stated meetings? Considered, that it could not be allowed according to the gospel. See John's 2d Epistle, verses 9 and 10."

At the Y. M. 1849. Art 18. reads thus : "Whether it is advisable to give preachers of other denominations privilege to speak at our regularly appointed meetings ? The answer was, Considered, it is not advisable."

ADMITTING TESTIMONY from strangers or outsiders.

Y. M. 1841. Art. 6. " Whether members may be brought before the council of the church, and be judged for a crime, only on testimony from without, *i. e.* from persons that are not members of the church ? Answer. Considered, that when there is some report abroad of a brother walking disorderly, or having committed a crime, it is the duty of the church to send some brethren to the place where the report has originated, to investigate the matter. If nothing be found establishing the charge, and the (accused) member denying the same after a close examination, nothing more can be done. However, if there should be created some suspicion in the members by the general conduct of the accused, the church may advise such a member not to approach the Lord's table until the matter is cleared up to the satisfaction of the church. But to disown entirely a member on testimony only from without, was not considered right and just according to the gospel."

Y. M. 1845. Art. 9. How is it considered, if brethren are accused by the mouths of two or three witnesses of honest, moral character, but not being members, and their testimony against those members agrees, that they were guilty of drunkenness or any other crime, and the church has cause to believe such testimony from other circumstances, but the brethren so accused deny the charge? Considered, as in the year 1841, Art. 6, that such members might be advised not to approach the Lord's table until the matter is cleared up to the satisfaction of the church; but to judge a brother on testimony from without alone, and without his own confession, would not be just, according to the gospel.

ADULTERY.

By this word the Brethren understand not only those gross acts of violation of the marriage vow, which even the world condemns, but also those acts as defined by our Saviour in Matt. 19 : 9, Luke 16 : 18, &c.

Y. M. 1797. The case was presented of married people separating from one another, and then the one party marrying again, thus committing adultery. Afterward the other party also marries again, and then the latter comes to the church, and desires to be received by baptism as a member in the church, and it was considered, that if the church was agreed, and the applicant should heartily repent, confess and acknowledge the fault (and especially if the first companion would be dead by this time), we might include such person within the (bounds of the) mercy and merits of Jesus, and receive as a member by baptism.

Y. M. 1812. Another case was presented of a woman who was deserted by her husband, and after being informed that he was dead, she married again; but the information proved to be untrue; her first husband made his appearance again, but without calling or claiming her he went away the second time, and now he is said again to be dead, and she (the woman) now makes application to be received into the church. The brethren decided that it could not be done according to the word of God, until there is evidence that her first husband be dead, and then only she might be received upon true repentance and confession.

Y. M. 1819. In a similar case of a woman marrying a man who had left his wife, both were considered adulterers while that first wife lives, according to the declaration of the Apostle Paul, Rom. 7 : 2, 3; and that the church could not receive them as members, until the first marriage was dissolved by death, and then only upon heartfelt sorrow and repentance. But if those who are in such condition would for the sake of God (and their salvation) firmly resolve, and actually (endeavor to) live separate (and apart from each other), with godly sorrow for their former transgression, they might find grace and be reconciled with God (through Christ).

Special Y. M. Miami, 1822. Art. 7. With regard to persons who live in adultery, it was considered, that they could not be received into the church as long as they live in such condition.

Y. M. 1842. Art. 8. "Whether a person, who was married, and whose partner broke the marriage vow by fornication, may marry again according to the gospel, after obtaining a bill of divorce? Considered, that according to the word of God (Matt. 5 : 31, 32, and 19 : 3–10; Mark

10 : 2–12 ; Luke 16 : 1⁸, and 1st Cor. 7 : 10, 11, 39), a person cannot marry again while the first companion lives, and that the gospel considers (declares) not only the person that would marry again after being divorced, but also the person who would marry the divorced party, as adulterers."

Y. M. 1850. Art. 12. In a similar case it was " considered, that such persons should not be received in the church under such circumstances, and that the brethren who received them have erred, and should make acknowledgments before the church in order to the reconciliation of the brethren who have been grieved at (by) their proceedings."

Y. M. 1856. Art. 18. " How are we to hold a brother and sister, who lived together for some years in lawful matrimony, but not very agreeably, and now they are separated, the brother being with his children in Iowa, and the sister with her friends in Ohio ? Answer.—The church, or churches, where such members lived, should investigate the matter, and judge according to the gospel and the circumstances or facts in the case, in the fear of the Lord."

Same Y. M. Art. 24. " If a man shall put away his wife for the cause of fornication, procuring a bill of divorcement and marrying another, has he committed the sin of adultery, or could he be received into the church, all the parties still living, if he in all other respects brings forth fruits meet for repentance ? Referred to next yearly meeting."

Y. M. 1857. Art. 8. " The 24th query on the minutes of 1856 being brought forward (again), it was concluded best for such churches as have occasion to act on such cases, to act in the fear of the Lord, according to their knowledge of the cases (and of course, according to the word of the Lord)."

Y. M. 1858. Art. 7. " What is to be done, when a man has put away his wife for the cause of adultery, and obtaining a bill of divorcement, marries again ; the church not knowing of this, nor he that the church disallows of such, for some two years after he has become a member ? Answer.—We have not light enough at present to give any advice different from what the brethren have formerly given."

Same Y. M. Art. 40. " Should the church receive a person that has been living in a state of matrimony awhile and apparently did not live in peace, then leaving his companion gets married to another one, and after some time leaving the second one for the same reason he left the first, and while his first companion was yet living ? Considered, that according to the gospel such a person should not be received into the church."

Y. M. 1859. Art. 17. " A man's wife leaves him for no just cause, and she then obtains a bill of divorcement ; after this she marries another man. And then in consequence of this the (first) husband (thus) left and divorced (by the action of his wife), also marries another woman after some time, with whom he is living. And he having become convinced of the truth, has made application for baptism. Can he be received into the church? Answer.—We think he cannot while living with the last woman as a husband. See 1st Cor. 7: 10, 11."

Same Y. M. Art. 21. "A man marries his uncle's wife (widow), but afterward thinks he discovers it forbidden in Lev. 18: 14, and 20: 20, and separates from her. He then marries another woman. He now desires to bo received into the church. Can he be received, as the first woman is still living, and in a married connection with another man? Answer.—According to the civil law the first marriage would be considered lawful, and, consequently, the second marriage is contrary to the gospel, and he cannot therefore be received into the church by baptism while he and the woman with whom he is living are living together in the relation of man and wife."

Y. M. 1862. Art. 3. If a sister is married to a man, who, after living with her awhile, leaves her, and she, not hearing from him for several years, marries again, can she be held as a member? Answer.—No; she could not be held as a member.

Same Y. M. Art. 28. "Can the church hold in fellowship persons living as husband and wife, while the husband's former wife is still living, from whom he was divorced, but not for the cause of fornication? Answer.—We consider, according to Matt. 19: 9, that the church cannot hold such in fellowship."

ADVANCING BRETHREN IN THE MINISTRY —(see also the articles of "*Choice for Ministers*" and "*Ministers*," &c.)

As our Saviour, when he deemed it necessary and expedient to call men to his assistance for the work he came from heaven to accomplish, did not go to Jerusalem, to the schools of those learned in the law, nor to the sects of the Sadducees or Pharisees, but made his selection from among his own followers; so it is a settled principle among the Brethren, when in any particular church the want of assistance in the ministry is felt, not to go to any high school, university or theological seminary, or even outside of that particular church, but there, from among themselves, under the counsel and direction of experienced elders, and more particularly under the guidance of the Holy Spirit, make a selection. And as Christ did not all at once entrust his disciples with the full powers of the ministry, but kept them for years under his own personal direction and instruction, more as disciples and learners than as teachers, so the Brethren try to follow his example, laying no greater burden on their newly elected ministers than they can bear, who perhaps before their election had never thought of such a thing. Hence such brethren are simply entrusted with the word, and if they, after a shorter or longer trial, have proved themselves humble, faithful and useful, they are, by counsel of the church, *advanced* to the administration of the holy ordinances of the Lord. And if in course of time the elder ministers have been removed, such of the second degree may be *advanced* by the unanimous voice of the church, and may take their places as rulers and overseers of the flock.

Y. M. 1848. Art 7. How to make arrangements that in every church brethren be authorized to baptize and serve at communion tables? Considered, to leave it to the judgment of the churches, with the advice of neighboring ordained elders, whether they think it necessary and expedient.

Y. M. 1850. Art. 19. Whether it would bo agreeable to the order of the church, where there is a bishop and two or more teaching brethren in one arm of the church, to elect a (second) bishop without the consent of the church? Considered necessary by all means to have the voice (and consent) of the church in such cases.

Y. M. 1856. Art. 20. Is it the rule and order among the Brethren to forward a brother to baptize at the same time he is put into the ministry? Answer.—No.

Y. M. 1858. Art. 19. What is the ancient and established order of the Brethren in advancing speakers to the second degree of office? Are they received with hand and kiss? Considered, that the proper way is to receive them with hand and kiss. ·

ALMS COLLECTING.

Y. M. 1788. Resolved unanimously, that hereafter no member of the church, whether brother or sister, under no pretext whatever, should go from church to church, or from house to house, to collect alms; but where there is any want or distress of a member (greater than the church to which he or she belongs is able to relieve), the church shall state the case in writing, and send it to the next church, if necessary by the member himself, and if in that church full relief could not be obtained, the writing should be renewed until relief is accomplished, if even it were necessary to call upon all the churches. And we deem it proper that every church should state on the writing how much is yet lacking.

Y. M. 1793. Inasmuch as God has commanded his ancient people Israel by Moses, and said, "There shall be no beggar among you (German translation), for the Lord shall greatly bless thee in the land which the Lord thy God giveth thee for an inheritance to possess it, &c." Deut. 15: 4. And says further, "If there be among you a poor man of thy brethren within any of thy gates in thy land which the Lord thy God giveth thee, thou shall not harden thy heart, nor shut thy hand from thy poor brother. But thou shalt open thy hand wide unto him, and shall surely lend him sufficient for his need, in that which he wanteth." And says again, "Beware that there be not a thought in thy wicked heart, saying, &c. Thou shalt freely give him, and thy heart shall not be grieved when thou givest unto him; because that for this thing the Lord thy God shall bless thee in all thy works, and in all thou puttest thy hand unto." And again says, "For the poor shall never cease out of the land; therefore I command thee, saying, Thou shalt open thy hand wide unto thy brother, to thy poor, and to thy needy, in thy land, &c." Deut. 15: 7–11. And the Apostle James says, "Hearken, my beloved brethren, hath not God chosen the poor of this world rich in faith, and heirs of the kingdom, &c." James 2: 5. And inasmuch it has happened by bad people, that such as were actually poor have been robbed of their gifts by men going about and pretending to be Brethren, have asked assistance, which they have afterward spent in taverns by drinking and gambling, now in order to prevent such deception, some years ago at a large meeting in Conestoga it was resolved unanimously, that hereafter no member should go from church to church, or from house to house, to collect alms, &c. And inasmuch as members have been imposed upon since in a deceitful manner, therefore, we have concluded again in this present great meeting unanimously, that hereafter no member shall be allowed to go himself to another church, but if there should be found a member in want or distress, the overseer in the church where such member lives is to hold counsel with the church in order to see whether they would relieve the want, and if so, it should not go any further. But if not, then the overseer, with the counsel of the church, should send a letter to the adjoining church with a brother of his church, and if there the want can be relieved it shall go no further. But if the want is not redressed then according to the finding of that church, it should be proceeded in the same manner from that to the next church, until relief is obtained, so that our loving brethren and members, who, according to the doctrine of Paul, are willing to do good unto all men, especially unto them who are of the household of faith (Gal. 6 : 10), may no longer be imposed upon in such deceitful manner. This is not to be understood that we should not do good also to those poor without the church, &c.

Y. M. 1852. Art. 18. " Whether members have a right by the gospel to go begging for money through the different churches? Considered, that they have no right according to the gospel, and where there are poor members that are in a suffering condition, it is the duty of the church in which they live to see to it, and to supply their wants; and if that church is not able to support them, the church has a right to apply to the neighboring churches for help, and not the brother that is in want.

ANNUAL MEETING.

This is an *ancient* institution, almost as old as our brotherhood in this our land America, though not exactly under that name ; or rather, more correctly speaking, it is an institution as ancient as the gospel. It is a *peculiar* institution, not at all like the synods, conferences, ecclesiastical associations, assemblies or conventions of the present day among the various denominations of Christian professors. It is a *highly prized and cherished* institution in our brotherhood, as a reunion not only of ministers and official members, but of the church at large, open to all the brethren and sisters who feel disposed and able to attend it. Hence multitudes from far and near, not only of members but also of outsiders, come together on such occasions. This latter feature threatening to defeat its original object, has been the frequent subject of thought and reflection of earnest and sober minded brethren, and has also been the cause of some changes in conducting the same, heretofore adopted, and still contemplated for the immediate future.

SCRIPTURAL FOUNDATION OF THE CHURCH AND HER AUTHORITY.

When our Lord and Saviour Jesus Christ had asked his disciples, Matt. 16: 13 –20, " Whom do men say that I, the Son of man, am?" they said, Some (say that thou art) John the Baptist; some, Elias; and others, Jeremias, or one of the prophets." " He saith unto them, But whom say ye that I am. And Simon Peter answered and said, Thou art the Christ (Messiah), the Son of the living God. And Jesus answered and said unto him, Blessed art thou Simon Bar-jona: for flesh and blood hath not revealed it unto thee, but my Father which is in heaven. And I say also unto thee, That thou art Peter (Greek, *petros*); and upon this rock (Greek, *petra*, *i. e.* not the man, but that confession made,) I will build my church; and the gates of hell shall not prevail against it. And I will give unto thee (the disciples, or the church as a unity) the keys of the kingdom of heaven: and whatsoever thou shalt bind on earth shall be bound in heaven; and whatsoever thou shall loose on earth shall be loosed in heaven."

That this authority was given to the church and not to the individual, is further evident from the express words of our Saviour on another occasion, Matt. 18: 15–18, where he gives direction how a brother is to deal with his brother in case of a private trespass against him personally, and says at last, "TELL IT UNTO THE CHURCH!" and adds presently after, "Whatsoever ye (as forming the church) shall bind on earth shall be bound in heaven; and whatsoever ye shall loose on earth shall be loosed in heaven."

How this authority was exercised not only toward private members, but also toward the ministers, and the apostles themselves, even Peter, when any thing was done that needed explanation and seemed to some wrong, we find an example, Acts 11: 3. (Please read all from the beginning of the chapter to v. 18.)

But the example related Acts 15: 1–35, appeared to our ancient brethren as the main foundation for holding such general councils or annual meetings, and this apostolic example was their avowed pattern; see hereafter, Y. M. 1837, Art. 3.

THE ORIGIN OF ANNUAL MEETINGS.

From our forthcoming History of the Brethren in America, which shall be published as soon as possible, if the Lord will spare us yet so long, we will find that the first company of our Brethren, having arrived in 1719, almost 150 years ago, held their *first* love feast in Germantown, Pa., on Christmas-day, December 25, 1723, and previous to this, we are informed, "*they had important work. They remembered difficulties, which had occurred in Crefeld* (Germany) *already. They were indeed a branch of a church, but not yet a church* (sufficiently organized and established) *that could assume* (the authority) *to administer the sacraments* (ordinances). *But the chief difficulty was, that there were still differences among themselves, and they only of late had commenced to come together. After all these difficulties had been worked through in the spirit, they at last agreed to gratify them* (the new converts, who desired baptism and being received into fellowship, and also to hold the love feast)." So then we have a record not only of the first church visit, the first meeting for public worship, the first baptism and the first love feast, but also of the first council meeting, and in fact the first general council or yearly meeting ever held in this country; and it is presumable that the love feasts were connected and preceded by such council meetings the day before love feast, and that these council meetings being attended by members and ministers from every church, were sufficient for every purpose during the first thirty or forty years, while the churches were confined at first within a territory bordered only by the Delaware river on the east and the Schuylkill on the west, and at a later date by the Susquehanna on the west. But as the churches multiplied, and extended into New Jersey on the east and beyond the Susquehanna on the west, and even into Maryland, &c., and it thus becoming impracticable for all the churches to be represented at every ordinary love feast, it became a necessity to set apart every year a certain time, and appoint from year to year a place for such a general council. This was done, as far as we can learn, a little after the middle of last century, and consequently a little over a hundred years ago. The first council meeting had been held, as we have seen, about Christmas, the presumed birthday of the Saviour, but now a more proper time was chosen in fixing Pentecost of every year, the birthday of the church, for the big meeting, as it was called even to a recent day of our own recollection. With regard to the place, it was concluded at a late day, that the big meetings should be held alternately, one year east of the Susquehanna, and the next year west of that river. The churches spreading further west and south, the Allegheny mountains were considered as the dividing line for a time in this respect, and still more recently the Ohio river was named as such line.

HOW THE YEARLY MEETINGS WERE HELD.

That they were at first held in the most simple manner, even as our ordinary council meetings have been held up to our own times, is evident from all the testimony we could gather. Brethren met on Friday morning before Pentecost, and opened as usual by singing, exhortation, prayer, and, perhaps, reading the Scriptures. Having met in the fear of the Lord, and invited him to preside over the meeting, and prayed for the Holy Spirit to guide and direct all hearts, they considered the meeting ready for business. Cases were presented and decided, questions asked and answered, all by word of mouth, as in ordinary council meetings; there was no clerk chosen nor minute taken, and hence it is that our records are so meagre for the first twenty-five or thirty yearly Pentecostal meetings. But as will be made to appear more at large in our forthcoming "History of the Brethren," when any important case or cases had been presented, it was answered afterward by letter to the church or churches that had presented them. Of these manuscript letters a goodly number yet extant have been collected with great care, and are embodied in this present work.

FIRST CHANGE.

When in course of time it came to pass, that among many questions also improper ones were asked in the presence not only of a great number of brethren and sisters, but also of strangers, it was counseled and concluded, that five, seven or more of the oldest ministers should, after opening the meeting, retire to a private place, where those who had questions to ask, or cases to present, might present them; while at the same time younger ministers might exercise themselves in preaching, and edify the people. This order prevailed up to our own time, as many elder brethren can testify as well as the writer. Some few of those questions were privately answered, others were answered by letter to the church concerned, and only questions of general interest were reserved for public discussion. There were some advantages, and some disadvantages in this change, and it is hard to tell on which side was the preponderance. Before the change, we believe, the council consumed but one day (Friday) in most cases; on Saturday was public worship during the day, and in the evening love feast, and on Lord's day (Pentecost) morning solemn worship, at the close of which the whole meeting was considered ended, and the people departed to their own homes about noon. Upon the whole this first change worked well, and was a judicious one. It seems to have given general satisfaction to the church for a great number of years even up to A. D. 1830 and 1831, where the writer was an eye and ear witness; to his certain knowledge, this improved yet simple manner of holding our yearly meetings still prevailed. Thus far no change or extension in the time has taken place. The meeting commenced Friday morning, and broke up on Lord's day noon. We will try to set before our readers a simple description of what we witnessed at those two first Y. M's. we ever attended, among, perhaps, more than thirty such meetings at which we were present within thirty-six years past.

On Friday morning at an early hour meeting commenced as usual. When worship was over, one of the oldest brethren made a brief statement, according to which it became the duty of the elders of the church where the Y. M. was held, to nominate those brethren who should receive the messages, &c., and conduct the business of the meeting. This nominating was done simply thus: the brother stepped up to what may be called the ministers' table, and with a sweep of his hand pointed out those seated behind that table as his and the church's choice, without naming them, and told them to follow him to a private place. When these arose in order to retire, some one mentioned that during their absence the congregation might be edified by preaching, which was done by those younger ministers who felt disposed or were called upon to do so, one by one, until the elder brethren returned to the congregation, and business meeting was commenced, and continued, if necessary, till Saturday noon. Then, after dinner, public worship began again, and in the evening the great love feast and communion was held, and on Lord's day morning (Pentecost) the solemn worship of God commenced at an early hour, and continued till noon, when the great congregation was dismissed, and dispersed after partaking of some refreshments. Thus the ordinary time consumed by those meetings had been only two days and a half, and if the brethren had continued in this way, many of the present difficulties and objections would have been entirely obviated. But we must close our remarks, as the many smaller and greater changes attempted afterward will be stated in the following extracts of private notes and of ordinary minutes of Y. M. Suffice it to say here, that already in 1830 and 1831 there was some talk about extending the meeting to Monday noon, in order that the Sabbath should not be desecrated by the breaking up and dispersing so large a congregation. This may seem but a small matter, but when we reflect, that adding one day, together with the care, labor and expense of providing for a multitude, making two-fifths more time, and adding another day, almost doubled the previous amount, we will all agree that it became eventually a great matter indeed.

Y. M. 1813. "It has been also again requested of, and counseled by the old brethren, that the great (annual) meeting should be continued in the order as it has been heretofore declared and laid down by the old brethren, namely, that the ministers and overseers of the churches, every one in his own district and church, should in good time lay it before the church, how some should be willing to go to the big (annual) meeting, and that the church should assist them if possible, that some may be able to go, so that from all parts, and if it could be from all churches, some may come to that meeting; and those that will come, should endeavor to arrive on Thursday evening so near to the place of meeting as to be able to be at the place Friday morning at 9 o'clock, that the business may go on without hindrance."

Y. M. 1832. "Change of the time of yearly meeting. Meeting to commence on Pentecost, with public meeting and love feast. Monday and Tuesday, council meeting."

Y. M. 1836. Art. 4. How is it deemed best at the yearly meeting, whether first to hold council, or first public meeting and communion? It was considered as expedient, to commence on Lord's day with public meeting, and in the evening to break the bread of communion, and afterward to hold counsel.

Y. M. 1837. Art. 3. "How is it considered, to make a better arrangement in holding annual meetings according to the pattern of the apostles (Acts 15)? The unanimous counsel of this meeting and desire of the old brethren is, to follow the track of the apostles as closely as possible. Therefore the council meeting ought to consist of the elders and all the members of that church which receives the meeting, and of such teachers, ministers or (private) members, who may be sent as delegates from other churches. It is considered necessary, that every church, or where the distance is too great, several churches together, should send two, three or more delegates to the annual meeting. The yearly meeting is to take place as heretofore on Pentecost or Whitsuntide, and the council meeting to be held on Friday and Saturday before, to which the delegates ought to arrive in the neighborhood on Thursday evening. The public meeting to begin on Sunday, when love feast will be held, and the church is at liberty to invite thereto also neighboring churches as usual. The proceedings of the council meeting should be immediately recorded in writing, and as much as possible communicated to all the churches." (The minutes of this meeting were printed and published for the first time this year by order of the brethren assembled.)

Y. M. 1842. Art. 5. "Whether the queries to be submitted to the yearly meeting should not be laid first before the individual church, and be sent with their consent? Considered, that queries in relation to a particular church ought to be brought in with the council of that church, but a brother should not be prevented thereby to present any question that may occur to him as important and necessary to be considered."

Y. M. 1845. Art. 13. "About the order of annual meetings, it was concluded to refer the consideration of his query to the next yearly meeting for the same reason as in Art. 11, and with the same recommendation to the consideration of all the churches."

Y. M. 1846. Art. 1. "As regards the way and manner of holding annual meetings, so as to enjoy more order, convenience and satisfaction, it was considered, in the fear of the Lord, that the counsel of the Y. M. in the year 1837 in this respect was proper and expedient, if observed, and that the best plan will not mend the matter, if not carried out. Different plans were proposed, and after a long discussion and mature reflection it was resolved to make no material change but this : that our western brethren shall have the privilege of taking the yearly meeting every other year, if they request it, and that our eastern brethren should not fail to attend the same—that it should be explicity understood and given out, that on Friday and Saturday there will only be private council meeting, all the ordained elders to form the committee to take in (receive) and bring before the meeting those matters to be considered. The public meeting should be on Sunday, and if possible not in the same place where the council meeting is held."

Y. M. 1847. Art. 1. "Whether we could not amend our plan in holding our yearly meetings, so that the business might be conducted more quietly and orderly? Concluded in regard to our yearly meetings, that the brethren meet on Saturday before Pentecost, and have public meeting till Sunday evening. Love feast to be held either on Saturday or Sunday evening, at the option of the church where the Y. M. is held. On Monday the council meeting to begin and continue until all the business is transacted or disposed of. The council to consist of delegates, not more than two to be sent from each church, with a written certificate, containing also the queries to be presented (by the church whom they represent) to the yearly meeting. The delegates to constitute a committee of the whole to receive and examine all matters communicated to the Y. M., and to arrange all the queries and questions for public discussion, and after they are publicly discussed, and the general sentiment heard, then the delegates are to decide, and if two-thirds or more of the delegates agree, let the decision thus made be final. But if the nature of the case be such that two-thirds do not give their consent, then let it be delayed (postponed) until it receives the voice of at at least two-thirds of the legal representatives. The yearly meeting to be attended by as many teachers and members as may think proper to do so, and the privilege in discussion to be free and open to all who may desire to participate in the same as heretofore."

Y. M. 1848. Art. 29. "The committee to whom the letters concerning our yearly meetings had been referred, reported as follows : No less than twelve letters from all parts of the church had been presented in regard to this important matter, and after reading and weighing them all, and taking also in view the general state of feeling and experience of this present meeting, we propose the following in the fear of the Lord: Considered, that this yearly meeting is as anxious and unanimous in the desire of following in the track of the apostles (Acts 15) as our beloved brethren were eleven years ago at the Y. M. in 1837. We find, however, by experience, that the change of the time of holding the council *after* public meeting doth work well, removing from us the great crowd of strangers. We are also satisfied, that the sending of delegates or messengers from all the churches is necessary and proper, as also, that all the elders who come to us, ought to be members of the meeting, whether sent or not. A general committee of five or seven elders is to be appointed as heretofore, and as many special committees as may be deemed proper or necessary, in order to dispatch business. But as to voting, we hold that it will be best to aim always at unanimity, and dispose of business as hitherto. Should the meeting not be able to agree in any one point, let it be postponed to a future meeting. In addition, it was proposed that all the churches should be admonished to use every diligence in sending each year two delegates, or at all events one, to yearly meetings."

" *The above was unanimously adopted* (by the whole meeting) *without a dissenting voice.*

Y. M. 1850. Art. 5. "Whether it is right for brethren in different arms of the church to go against the counsel of the yearly meeting? Considered, that it is wrong for brethren to go against the counsel of our great annual meeting; but should brethren not be satisfied with said counsel, they have liberty, with the consent of their church, to bring the matter before another yearly meeting for a reconsideration."

Art. 22. "Whether the committee could not be selected, and the questions taken in at our annual meetings, on Saturday as well as on Monday? Considered, to leave it as it is at present."

Art. 32. "Why the annual meeting was not conducted or carried out according to the order or plan laid down at the Y. M. 1847? Considered, that the querists shall be referred to the minutes of Y. M. 1818, Art. 29, where twelve letters are mentioned, which contained chiefly remonstrances against said plan."

Y. M. 1851. Art. 9. "Would it not be better to alter the plan of holding our annual meetings, so as to have no public preaching, but only a church council meeting? Considered, that at this time we could make no more alteration but this, that instead of meeting on Friday, and having public meeting on Saturday and Sunday, we will come together on Saturday evening, and meeting to commence on Sunday morning, and to be no communion meeting at the place of the annual meeting. The council meeting then to commence on Tuesday morning (after having prepared for business on Monday)."

Y. M. 1853. Art. 1. Whether it would not give more general satisfaction in the arrangement of the standing committee, to select them by ballot out of the whole number of ordained brethren present? Considered unanimously, to make no change in this matter from the ancient and present usage, viz. that the elders of the church where the yearly meeting is held, should have the privilege, as heretofore, to nominate said committee.

Art. 13. Could not the brethren adopt a plan to hold the yearly meetings in such a manner that public preaching might be held in the neighborhood around, and not at the place for counsel? Considered, to make no change for the present.

Y. M. 1857. Art. 21. Would it not be better in deciding upon all subjects brought before our annual meeting, to refer first to the word of God, instead of first referring to the old minutes? We think it always safest to refer first to the word of God. (So it is thought and believed that our old brethren also did, and by consulting them we may be directly led to the word of God on the point in question.)

Art. 24. Would it not be best for churches in selecting delegates to represent them in the annual council, to make choice of one deacon, or of one lay member, to serve as a delegate in connection with one ministering brother, and thus relieve the ministry from the responsible position of being the exclusive advisers of the churches? Answer.—We think it should be left to the churches to select such members for delegates as they may think proper.

Art. 31. Would it not be advisable to change the time of holding our annual meetings, as Whitsuntide comes too early some seasons, especially in some parts of the country? Answer.—We judge it best to make no change in the time of holding our annual council.

Y. M. 1858. Art. 15. Would it not be agreeable to the gospel and the order of the Brethren, when the standing committee appoints committees to go to other churches to settle difficulties, to authorize such brethren, whom circumstances will not permit to attend such council, to send some other ordained brethren in their places, so that there will be a full committee? Considered, that it is the duty of such brethren that cannot go to appoint others in their places, that the committee may be full.

Y. M. 1860. Art. 1. Inasmuch as we publicly denounce (human) church discipline, and claim the New Testament Scriptures as the only rule of our faith and practice, is it then consistent with our profession to make a direct observance of the minutes of the annual council a test of fellowship? Answer.—The decisions of the annual meetings are obligatory until such decisions shall be repealed by the same authority.

In our preliminary remarks at the head of this article, we have given the history of the origin and manner of conducting these meetings from the first, as far as, or rather, including the first change, which in fact could scarcely be called a change; for as we have shown already, there was no change in the time, nor in the manner of conducting the meeting, with the exception only of receiving the questions, which were formerly presented all *viva voce* in public meeting, and afterward more privately to a committee, which was entrusted with conducting the business, in order to make a proper selection from those questions, as to which were to be presented publicly, and which to be answered more privately by letter to those who sent the queries. We have already observed that this was a wise move in the right direction, a judicious and satisfactory improvement, in order to reduce the number of questions for public consideration, and finish the business within two days and a half. When our brethren could do so for over a hundred years, why cannot we? If it be objected, that there is so much more business now than then, granted; but there are more laborers too. While formerly one committee labored alone, we can have as many committees as we need, to divide themselves into the work. Let only every committee use the discretion our ancient brethren used, to make a proper distinction and selection among the questions presented to them. "Where the Spirit of the Lord is, there is liberty," and as there is liberty to ask, so there ought to be liberty to answer them. The first point to be considered by a committee upon any question, is this: Is it a fair, proper question, couched in a Christian spirit and in proper terms? If not, our Saviour has himself left the example, not to answer such. If a proper question, it is to be decided whether it should be answered privately or brought before the public council, and published in the minutes. Oh, if our dear brethren had continued to exercise the discretion and discrimination which our ancient brethren had used, there would have been no need of so many changes as have occurred within the last thirty-three years, and no need of adding to the original two and a half days other two or three days, as the case now is, and calls so loudly for another change.

Let us recapitulate the history of our annual meetings, as contained in the extracts of minutes given above. In 1813 the brethren declared to continue in the order heretofore declared and laid down by the old brethren (that lived before them). In 1832 was the last meeting according to the old order, and there it was concluded to change the time, commencing on Pentecost with worship, and to have Monday and Tuesday for counsel. Already in 1836 again another change was proposed, but not granted. In 1837 the time was changed back again to Friday and Saturday for counsel. In 1847, 1848, 1850, 1851, 1853, &c., changes were again proposed, as the careful reader himself may readily understand. But to what conclusion will he come after reading it over again? Does it not seem as if in this matter our ship had lost its chart and compass, and no one knew rightly which way to steer? Or is it not as if a person in the wilderness loses his way, the main road, the beaten track, after night, and finds himself in the woods, or in the open prairie, and in the moon or starlight, or even without it, left to his own reason and resources, he feels and knows he has lost his way, but at first thinks he will soon right himself; he tries one direction, and after a while turns round and tries another course, and thus goes on, until at last he becomes completely bewildered and exhausted, not knowing what to do? Well, we think the best thing he can do is to sit still, and wait till God sends him a guide or daylight. Brethren, let us do so too, and pray God for guidance and light, and if we ask in faith he will grant it in due time.

ANOINTING THE SICK.

On this head thus reads the word of God: " Is any sick among you? let him call for the elders of the church; and let them pray over him, *anointing him with oil* in the name of the Lord: and the prayer of faith shall save the sick, and the Lord shall raise him up; and if he have committed sins, they shall be forgiven him. Confess your faults one to another, and pray one for another, that ye may be healed. The effectual fervent prayer of a righteous man availeth much. Elias was a man subject to like passions as we are, and he prayed earnestly that it might not rain: and it rained not on the earth by the space of three years and six months. And he prayed again, and the heavens gave rain, and the earth brought forth her fruit, &c." James 5 : 14–18.

This " anointing of the sick," based on the Scripture given above, is, as far as our limited knowledge extends, not practiced by any of the modern denominations, except by the Roman and the Greek Churches under the name "Extreme Unction," and it is therefore necessary to explain our position as simple followers of Christ and primitive Christianity in respect to this matter. We find in the gospel evidences that our Lord and Saviour submitted himself no less than three times to an anointing by different persons. We find also that at least in one case the Saviour declared, that wheresoever his gospel should be preached it should be also mentioned what had been done to him in this respect. From this we infer that our Lord and Master deemed this an act worthy not only of remembrance, but also of imitation. He also instructed his disciples among other things to "anoint the sick," and we cannot doubt that they obeyed this instruction. And now, since we cannot exercise this act any more on the person of Christ himself, we simply obey what James has recorded, namely, when one of the very least of the members of Christ calls upon the elders of the church the member being sick, and desirous for that anointing. we feel it our duty to obey that call. We believe if it is done and received in faith, the Lord will accept it as if done unto himself. and he will bless it either to raise the sick again from his sick-bed, or, what is far better, raise him or her up to glory.

Y. M. 1797. Art. 5. From James 5 : 14, &c., the brethren testified unanimously, "that the sick who desire and call for it, should be anointed, according to the word of the holy apostle, in the name of the Lord."

Y. M. 1812. Art. 1. In case a brother or sister should desire in their sickness to be anointed, it might be administered to them, provided they would not seek further help from an earthly physician; and if it should so be that the Lord would raise them again to health, and they should fall sick again, and think the Lord would call them away, and they ask again to be anointed, we would have no right from the word of God to refuse them, and it should be left to those brethren's wisdom who are called to do as the anointing will teach them. (1 John 2 : 20.)

Y. M. 1827. Art. 1. About the ordinance of anointing the sick, the manner of proceeding has ever been, first to sing a few verses, and with a united prayer to turn to God. Then (there should always be two brethren) the one reaches forth his hand, and the other poureth the oil on it, and the first puts the same on the head of the sick, and says the words which the Apostle James teaches (chap. 5 : 14), "Thou art anointed in the name of the Lord," and thus three times, but the words only once said. Then both brethren lay their hands upon the head of the sick, and pray over him. For it is not considered to be intended only an inward unction, but an outward anointing, whereof the apostle speaks, as mentioned before.

From manuscript accounts of elder brethren concerning the same, and exhibiting it more particularly, we have the following : As regards the ANOINTING, it requires two brethren in order to perform it, according to the advice of the apostle, since he says, "Let him call for the elders of the church, and let them pray over him." These words require more than one. Now when we are going to perform the same, the first we do after singing a few appropriate lines, and briefly exhorting, is to turn to God unitedly, and to pray God for a blessing upon ourselves, upon the sick member and upon all, as we do in a meeting, and there is liberty to pray for all the brethren present. If time will permit, and strangers are present, the passage of James, chap. 5, may be read as far as relates to this matter, and briefly commented upon. Then the sick member is raised to a sitting position (if the state of the patient permits), and the elder brother reaches forth his hand, and the other brother pours the oil upon it, while he (the first) puts it upon the head of the sick, and thus three times, saying the words of the apostle : " Thou art anointed in the name of the Lord"—unto the strengthening of thy faith—unto the comforting of thy conscience—and unto a full assurance of the remission of thy sins, or as the Lord may give utterance, and then the brethren both put their hands upon the sick, even as it is done when a brother is ordained, and pray chiefly for the sick member. Such an example we have of the Sa-viour, as we see in Mark 6 : 15 and 16 : 18, and this is the order the brethren have administered the same. Brethren who are not ordained may administer it in cases of necessity. [Appendix to Min. 1814.]

Y. M. 1828. Art. 5. Whether a member might be anointed more than once, was considered and decided, that it may be done on request of the sick person.

Y. M. 1837. Art. 4. How it is considered, to administer the anoint-ing of the sick, or to hold an election without an ordained brother (elder) being present ? It is the advice, that the anointing of the sick should not be administered without an ordained brother, except in a case of ne-cessity when no such is to be had, for the word says, " Call for the elders of the church."

Y. M. 1844. Art. 9. What to do in case a member on a sick or death-bed requests to have the bread of communion broken unto him ? Con-sidered, that the word of God does not seem to us to justify the breaking of the bread of communion to an individual member (for where there is but one there can be no communion), and that therefore we would be more safe to direct such a member to the grace and mercy of God in Christ Jesus, and to the advice of the Apostle James (5 : 14) where he says, " Is any sick among you, let him call for the elders of the church, and let them pray over him, *anointing him with oil in the name of the Lord*," &c.

Y. M. 1850. Art. 30. Who are the proper persons in the church to administer the ordinance recorded James 5 : 14 ? Considered, the bish-ops or ordained elders.

Art. 31. Is there any second order of persons in the church, who may administer the above ordinance in cases of great and pressing necessity, when the proper administrators cannot be had in time for the urgency of the case ? Considered, in such case brethren in less office, if at least one of them is authorized to baptize, might serve.

Art. 32. May the above ordinance be administered to a person who is not a member of the church, although solemnly believing in the healing vir-tues of the above, both spiritually and bodily, and requesting it of the church, such persons being in a dangerous situation, having shown fruits of repentance, and perfect willingness, if spared, to bow under the order of the church? Considered, that it could not be done, but that we are to direct to the (abundant) grace and mercy of God.

Y. M. 1852. Art. 20. Are persons, who can be up and about, and go to meeting, proper subjects to receive the anointing; or, has the apostle only reference to such who are altogether confined? Considered, that the apostle has only alluded to those who are sick or in a decline of life.

Art. 21. Is it agreeable to the sense of the word, that the anointing should be performed more than once in the same illness or confinement? Considered, that no person should be anointed more than once in the same sickness, according to our understanding of the word of God.

Y. M. 1853. Art. 43. Concerning anointing the sick with oil. Considered, that it should be administered according to the manner laid down by the brethren in the minutes of 1844, to be reprinted now again if there is room left.

Y. M. 1860. Art. 5. How is it considered when members that are sick, call for the elders of the church, and are anointed according to the gospel, and then again resort to the use of medicine? Is it wrong to do so? Answer.—We do not consider it wrong according to the gospel to do so.

Art. 6. As we see a difference in the words used in anointing the sick, we therefore ask for the most proper ceremony and manner for observing the same, according to the gospel and practice of the old brethren? Answer.—As the difference is not stated in the query, we know of nothing better than that which the brethren have given us in the appendix to the minutes of 1853; (the same as given above from appendix of minutes, 1844.)

Y. M. 1862. Art. 54. Who are the elders spoken of by James that are to be sent to anoint the sick in the name of the Lord? Answer.—The ordained elders, if they can be obtained; if not, the next in office.

ANXIOUS BENCH.

Y. M. 1842. Art. 2. Whether it will be to the edification of the church of God to hold protracted meetings, and to introduce mourning benches, in imitation of the new measures adopted by different sects and denominations? The brethren generally considered, that it was advisable to be very cautious, and at all times to keep good order in accordance with the doctrine and example of the apostles, and not to introduce such innovations like mourning benches, &c.

APPEAL TO THE YEARLY MEETING.

Y. M. 1833. Art. 7. Whether a member has a right to appeal to the yearly meeting, when put back by the council of his church? The answer, not recorded, was similar to the following:

Y. M. 1849. Art. 26. When the church deals with a member or members, and they are not satisfied with the proceedings of the church, whether it is in their or the church's place to write to strange brethren for assistance ? Considered, that the church would have to write, if any strange brethren should be called on.

ARDENT SPIRITS, making, selling and using of.

Y. M. 1781. Art. 2. Concerning distilleries, we heartily counsel all brethren who have distilleries, that they should by all means endeavor to put them away, in order to escape from the evil so often arising from them, and to avoid offence, and in this the brethren are still entirely united with the conclusion made at Pipe Creek, three years ago.

Y. M. 1783. Art. 1. At this great meeting a unanimous conclusion was laid down with regard to the very offensive evil which has endeavored to gain ground in the church, and by which already much mischief has been done, while the brotherly counsel has been repeatedly given, that distilleries (of ardent spirits) in the church (among members) should be put away. And since there are still from time to time more erected, it has been at this time unanimously concluded, that those brethren who have distilleries should be earnestly admonished to put them out of the way, and when they have been admonished in sincere love once and again, and they would not obey the counsel of the church, and not put away this loathsome idol, we could not break the bread of communion with them, and have to withdraw also the kiss and church council from them, until they are willing again to hear the church, as they have promised also at first at their baptism, before God and many witnesses.

Y. M. 1789. Art. 1. At the council meeting of the brethren it was in union deemed good and necessary, and we feel it also to be our duty to counsel as follows : Inasmuch we deem it our duty, obligation and office to see to it that union, tranquility and peace be maintained, that all should be united and of one mind, so that we may, according to the commandment of our Lord and Saviour Jesus Christ, love one another sincerely, and be enabled to love as he has given us a commandment, by which it shall be known that we are his disciples; therefore, it is our desire, that every grievance and every offence might be put out of the way ; and inasmuch there is a grievance and offence on account of the dis- tilleries of ardent spirits, because the old brethren could not allow them, and sad experience has taught us that almost whole families are gone to destruction, and the children have fallen into drunkenness and a rowdy life, the brethren some years ago came to the conclusion that they should be done away. But this has not yet been done, but there have been more bought and established since, and the evil is still growing. This makes a grievance and offence, that hardly one church can break bread with the other, and as has happened already, that brethren out of love had come a considerable distance, but when they saw that brethren who had distille- ries went to communion, they had to remain away, and go home again in grief, because they had not been able to partake of the memorial of the death of our Lord Jesus Christ on account of this grievous and offensive thing. Thus grief, disunion and division are brought upon the church. For this cause we beseech earnestly all brethren who have distilleries, to be diligent to put them away; and hereby exhort in heartfelt and humble love, all our much beloved fellow laborers in God, to use herein diligence in admonishing earnestly each member to obey this counsel of love, so that peace, love and union may be planted and restored. But whosoever is not willing to deny himself, as it should be indeed, and cannot or will not out of love obey this our loving counsel,. then we cannot consider him otherwise but as such who has not yet died (to sin), and is not yet risen with Christ in newness of life, and that he seeks more the things temporal than eternal, more the things on earth than those in heaven, more the things that pass away than the things that remain, and that he is in great danger to lose the everlasting treasure.

Y. M. 1804. Art. 2. Further it has been unanimously concluded, that no brother or sister should be engaged, by or with a permit, to sell strong drink, wine or ardent spirits by the quart or larger quantity, because it is feared that disorder and harm will arise thereby. Therefore all members who are engaged therein should be earnestly and faithfully exhorted in love and long-suffering to abstain from it, in order that such example may not lead our youth and offspring into licentiousness and scandal. But if one or the other should not heed such counsel of love and admonition, and not hear the church, we could not look upon such act otherwise than as being disobedient according to an impartial judgment.

Y. M. 1821. Art. 5. Whether brethren may have distilleries or not? It was considered, to leave it by what was concluded some thirty years ago, that no brother would be allowed to have a distillery or to distill ardent spirits.

Y. M. 1822. Art. 7. With regard to distilleries (held or carried on) by members of the church, it was again testified that it could not be. permitted. They should be admonished to put them away, and if they would not heed the counsel of love, we could not have fellowship with them.

Art. 9. If a brother has a vendue, and gives freely strong drink, how is it considered? It was considered, that no brother should give strong drink at the sale of his property.

Y. M. 1825. Art. 1. Whether a brother may keep and sell strong drink, has been considered thus: because so often disorder is caused by strong drink, it is improper for a brother to sell it, and should not be at all suffered.

Y. M. 1827. Art. 5. Whether a brother holding an office in the church may distill ardent spirits, was considered, and concluded that it is not becoming for any brother to do so, much less for a brother in office.

Y. M. 1828. Art. 10. Whether brethren may have distilleries was considered, and concluded that it should not be, nor by their children, as far as the authority of the parents extends; and if such brother will not take (or obey) the advice, we could not commune nor have fellowship with him. Also, to sell grain to distilleries (especially) when grain is scarce, should indeed not be.

Y. M. 1832. Art. 3. Whether it could be allowed for brethren to engage in store keeping and selling strong drink? The first may in cases of necessity, where members cannot make their living otherwise, but the latter in no case.

Y. M. 1833. Art. 8. About the making and using of strong drink, a strong testimony was made at this meeting against it.

Y. M. 1835. Art. 8. About distilleries, like the foregoing.

Y. M. 1835, in Miami. Art. 9. How it is considered to sell grain to distilleries? Should not be, except in case of necessity.

Art. 11. How it is considered for brethren to keep tavern? Not proper.

Y. M. 1836. Art. 2. Whether a brother or sister could be allowed to sell strong drink? Considered, that it should absolutely not be.

Y. M. 1837. Art. 11. How it is considered, when a brother keeps a brewery, and makes strong beer? Considered, that it could not be directly forbidden to a brother, but ought to be left to his own conscience, and to advise him that the safest would be not to carry on such a business, from which may arise so many and great disorders.

Y. M. 1838. Art. 3. Whether it be proper for a member to build a distillery, or distill ardent spirits? Considered, as it has been considered these many years, that it ought not to be.

Y. M. 1840. Art. 11. What is to be done with a brother who is erecting a distillery, and makes and sells ardent spirits? Considered, that when a brother has been admonished once and again, and will not be obedient to the counsel of the church, we could not break the bread of communion with him. Besides, it is the advice of the old brethren to dissuade all the members from the common use of intoxicating drinks, particularly at raising buildings, hay-making and harvesting.

Y. M. 1841. Art. 14. Concerning the use of ardent spirits, it was considered, that it is a great evil, leading to vice and crime, to destruction of peace and property, and to the ruin of body and soul, and that members of the church of Christ ought to refrain from the use of it except as medicine.

Y. M. 1842. Art. 4. How it is considered, if a brother or sister signs the pledge of total abstinence? Considered, inasmuch as our churches have always testified against intemperance, and even against the free use, the making and selling of ardent spirits, it is not advisable for members to put their hands to the pledge, or to meddle with the proceedings and excitements of the world on the subject.

Y. M. 1845. Art. 10. How is it considered, when a brother is carrying on a distillery ? Considered in the same light as our ancient brethren did sixty-two years ago in an annual council meeting held on Pipe Creek, Maryland, June 7, 1783.   (See above.)

Y. M. 1846.   Art. 7. Whether a brother may work in distilleries for wages ? And whether a brother, who owns a mill, may buy, sell and chop grain for distilleries ? Considered, that as the use of ardent spirits is always dangerous to the wellbeing of society, and the brethren have frequently testified against the making and using of the same, it would be best for brethren not to have anything to do with it in any shape or form.

Y. M. 1853.   Art. 27. Whether it is allowed for brethren to distill fruit, or get it distilled and sell the liquor ?   We say, No, not at all.

Y. M. 1856.   Art 4. How is it considered, when a church unitedly agrees not to use ardent spirits, except for medical, mechanical or communion purposes, and a member of said church will not comply with the above decision ?   Considered, that such member should be dealt with as in other offences.

Y. M. 1857.   Art. 1. Concerning the use of ardent spirits among the Brethren.   Considered, that every brother that is entrusted with the oversight of the church, should exert his influence, by example and precept, to induce all the members of his congregation to abstain altogether from the use of ardent spirits as an article of luxury, or as a drink ; and not to give it to the working hands to drink, admitting it only for medical or mechanical purposes.   The same advice is given to all the officers in all the churches throughout our whole brotherhood.

Y. M. 1862.   Art. 26. What is to be done with a brother that buys whiskey by the barrel, and sells it to such as he thinks use it temperately ; and when admonished once and again not to sell, he says he will be more careful to sell to none but those who use it temperately ?   Answer.—Any brother dealing in intoxicating liquors, if he continues to do so after being admonished, cannot be fellowshiped as a brother.

ASSIGNING PROPERTY.

Y. M. 1822, at Canton.   Art. 8. How it is viewed when a brother assigns his property to another, with a view to defraud his neighbors (creditors).   It is considered, that we cannot hold him in fellowship.

ATTEST, TAKING THE.

To understand this term, we must go back to the time when the advice was given. The year 1778, in the history of our country was the second year of that revolutionary war by which struggle it was to be decided whether our country should continue under the government of England, or become an independent self-governing people. While this question remained undecided many God-fearing people would not conscientiously transfer their allegiance to the States, which was done by the "attest," while some did. Why our brethren could not approve of this taking the attest, was more fully explained in the following year, as it will appear in the minutes of that year, given also above. From this it will appear also, that our brethren always stood aloof from political strife.

Y. M. 1778. After much reflection in the fear of the Lord, it has been concluded in union, that the brethren who have taken the attest should recall it before a justice, and give up their certificate, and recall and apologize in their churches, and truly repent for the error. If they cannot do this, and will justify themselves, the apostle exhorts us we should withdraw ourselves from every brother who walketh disorderly, and such a brother will be deprived of the kiss of fellowship, of the counsel, and the breaking of bread, until he becomes obedient again. Ministers and elders who have taken the attest, and are sorry and grieved for it, confessedly recall the matter before the justice of the peace and in the public church, counsel shall be held about them in their churches in presence of one or more ministers or overseers, to consider in the fear of the Lord, whether he or such as before mentioned could serve again iu their office. But if such minister or elder should approve himself stubbornly, and justify his course, yea, even teach the same, then we cannot comprehend how he can be obedient to the Spirit of truth, which teaches we shall not touch the unclean thing, nor be unequally yoked together with unbelievers, because Christ has no concord with Belial. Therefore we decide that such laborers are unfit in the Lord's vineyard, and also unfit to be members in the church of the living God, until their minds are changed, and they speak again with new tongues, or find their hearts with David. May God have mercy upon us!

Y. M. 1779. On account of taking the attest, it has been concluded in union as follows: Inasmuch as it is the Lord our God who establishes kings and removes kings, and ordains rulers according to his own good pleasure, and we cannot know whether God has rejected the king and chosen the state, while the king had the government; therefore we could not with a good conscience repudiate the king, and give allegiance to the states. And it seems to us that those who have done so have committed a fault, on account of which fault we could not break bread with them, but bear with them in love. But if they would come moved by their own conviction, and would make acknowledgments, being truly repentant, then we might forgive them, and we believe God would also forgive them, and we might break bread with them. But in regard to the laborers (ministers), we think they should stand still in their labor, and not baptize or administer in the breaking of bread. Should they, however, come convinced in themselves to have erred, and show contrition, saying, " We are sorry," then we might forgive them, and be in full fellowship with them, yet so that the church to which he belongs should be satisfied with him, when he should continue in his office. But if such go still further in this matter, as holding office (political) and so forth, show no sorrow, and rather continue in such course, then they should be also deprived of the church council and holy kiss, and *nota bene*, not only the ministers, but all who have taken this course.

AUTHORITY OF A BISHOP. (See also, "*Bishop*.")

Y. M. 1822, Canton. Art. 3. How far should a brother keep house without counseling the church, or members without counseling the housekeeper? It was considered, that the brother who is housekeeper should always act in concert with the church, especially with his co-laborers in the church, and just so his co-laborers should always counsel with their elder brother, and a private brother should not undertake to teach or serve until the church calls him to it.

Y. M. 1846. Art. 4. Is in the churches of the Brethren any material difference among the bishops, so that one has more power (authority) than another? Considered, that according to the word of our Saviour, Matt. 23: 8, "One is your master, even Christ; and all ye are brethren;" there is no difference in the brotherhood or among bishops but that which a higher age and more wisdom and experience may give. See 1 Pet. 5: 5, "Ye younger, submit yourselves to the elder."

Y. M. 1848. Art. 20. Whether three or more ordained elders have the authority of liberating out of avoidance, independent of the church? Considered, that it cannot be done properly without the counsel and consent of the church.

Y. M. 1849. Art. 36. Has a bishop authority to request a deacon who moved into his church without a letter of recommendation from the church from which he came, to take his place at a meeting for worship, and to preach or exhort? Considered, that he has no such authority, and the members that move from one church to another, ought always to bring a certificate of their membership and standing.

Art. 37. If a member commits an open fault in the world, has the overseer authority to send brethren to investigate the matter before counseling the church? Considered, that the overseer has the authority to do so.

Y. M. 1850. Art. 17. How is it considered, when a sister has an unbelieving husband who gets drunk and abuses her, and attempts to kill her with an axe; she then leaves him, and returns to her father, who then goes to the housekeeper in the church for advice, upon whose advice a bill of divorce is obtained? Considered, that a housekeeper has no right to give such advice without counseling the church; neither had the sister a right to get divorced without such counsel. (See Matt. 19: 6–9, 1 Cor. 7 : 11.)

AVOIDANCE, OR EXCOMMUNICATION.

AVOIDANCE is a term not known or used in the ecclesiastic terminology of the greater part of so-called Christian professors of the present day, outside of our fraternity and a few other communities of a more ancient date. For this reason we have added another term, which is more in general use by ecclesiastical writers, though not strictly a scriptural term. We will give the definition of both terms by the lexicographer Webster: "AVOIDANCE: the act of avoiding or shunning. *To avoid* is to shun; to keep at a distance; to avoid the company of a certain person." EXCOMMUNICATION in an ecclesiastical sense, is defined by the same author as "the act of ejecting from a church; expulsion from the communion of a church and deprivation of its rights, privileges and advantages; an ecclesiastical penalty or punishment inflicted on offenders. Excommunication is an ecclesiastical interdict (or prohibition) of two kinds, the lesser and the *greater*. The lesser excommunication is a separation or suspension of the offender from partaking of the eucharist (communion); the greater is an absolute separation and exclusion from the church and all its rights and advantages."

Cruden in his Concordance defines excommunication as "an ecclesiastical censure whereby they who incur the guilt of any heinous sin, are separated from the communion of the church, and deprived of spiritual advantages; that they may be brought to repentance, and others, by their example, kept from the like enormities. Matt. 18: 15–17; 1 Cor. 5: 5–7; 2 Thess. 3: 14, 15." He is also speaking of a "lesser and greater excommunication." While we agree with these authors in the last mentioned point, that there must be different degrees of church censure, as there are different degrees of guilt, we are compelled to differ from them, when they speak of ejecting, expelling, which imply the use of physical force, as being so contrary to the spirit and law of Christ, that no Christian could entertain such an idea, much less perform such an act. Hence the Brethren prefer the simple term "avoidance" to the Jewish word "ban" or "anathema," or to the Roman term "excommunication." The reason is, because avoidance is a simple, plain word in our own language, readily understood by all, and not subject to misapprehension, as words taken from other languages, and having acquired a signification foreign to the letter and spirit of the gospel, and what is still more, because it is a scriptural term. True, the substantive noun does not occur in our common version of the Bible, but the verb and root of the substantive, AVOID, occurs in the following passages: 1 Sam. 18: 11, "David *avoided* out of his presence twice." Prov. 4: 15, "*Avoid* it, (*i. e.* the path of the wicked and the way of evil men,) pass not by it, turn from it, and pass away." Rom. 16: 17, "Now I beseech you, brethren, mark them which cause division and offences contrary to the doctrine which ye have learned, and *avoid* them." 1 Cor. 7: 2: "Nevertheless to *avoid* fornication, let every man have his own wife." 2 Cor. 8: 20, "*Avoiding* this, that no man should blame us." 1 Tim. 6: 20, "*Avoiding* profane and vain babblings and oppositions of science, falsely so-called." 2 Tim. 2: 23: "But foolish and unlearned questions *avoid*" Titus 3: 9, 10, "*Avoid* foolish questions, &c." And when in the next verse "reject" occurs, in Greek it is the same word as in 2 Tim. 2: 23, where it is translated "avoid."

From these passages it is sufficiently clear what the general idea of avoidance is, namely, to avoid, shun and keep at a distance from evil, from physical or moral evil, and from evil men; and from two of the passages, Rom. 16: 17, and Tit. 3: 10, it is evident that they refer expressly to the ordinance under consideration.

But we must bring our remarks to a speedy close. That the main law of Christ concerning avoidance is recorded in Matt. 18: 15–20, and in 1 Cor. 5 from beginning to end, but more particularly verses 9–13, has been mentioned already, and will be repeated again in the following articles of counsel of the Brethren at yearly meetings. A critical and prayerful examination of these and other passages, together with a careful study of the history of the churches and of mankind, has convinced the writer of the correctness of the views and practice of the brethren in this respect, and that they can be defended against every objection of a candid believer of the word of God. Our brotherhood was once a unit on the subject (of course, with exceptions, as there was one among the Twelve an exception), as the sequel of this article will show. For more than a century it was the universal belief among our brethren, that this was as much an institution of the Lord as baptism, or any other ordinance, and none could gainsay it. But times have changed; a whole generation of old and faithful and steadfast brethren has almost entirely passed away, and at least in some parts of our wide-spread fraternity a new generation has come up, "which knew not Joseph;" and of late, sad to tell, it has come openly to light, that we are no longer in such cordial union on this and some kindred subjects as our brethren once were. We love our dear brethren, even those who do not see alike with us; indeed we thank them that they have come out openly and willing for discussion, and thus caused others to think and reflect on the subject more seriously than they ever did. We hope that all are desirous to be in union and full, real fellowship on every practical question. The reason why we feel specially grateful to those brethren dissenting on this subject, is this, that we have investigated the same again more deeply than ever, and we hoped to be able by this time to lay before our brethren the result of our labors. In this we failed; it was impossible for us to accomplish that part yet; but it is yet our intention, if the Lord spares our life, and grants his blessing, to do so at a future day. To do the subject full justice, we feared that it would make a much greater work than we at first contemplated, and we desired also to give those documents of our older brethren or yearly meetings, which we have been collecting ever since we came to the church, many of which might finally have been lost altogether, if not put in print, the preference over our own work, which we would rather leave as a legacy to our dear brethren, to be published after we have departed this life, or at least wait until the brotherhood is more in union again on this subject. For more union among us, which is the bond of love, I wish myself and all our brethren and sisters to pray, and to labor and even to suffer with all our hearts. Let us consider what our nation has done and suffered, and thousands have prayed during the late conflict for a merely human instrument, called the constitution, and for an earthly and temporal union! Should we then not stand as one man for that constitution which is of a divine origin, and for that union which will last forevermore?

We now merely add to those above our definition and description, derived from the word of God and the once universal practice of our brethren.

The ordinance of AVOIDANCE is an institution of the Lord Jesus Christ for the preservation of the purity and unity of the church, and for the bringing to repentance and restoration of fallen members. In cases of private offences and minor faults, which upon acknowledgment and submission to the counsel of the church might be readily forgiven and remitted, if the offender obstinately refuses to do so, and thus will not "hear the church," then, if admonished once and again, the church has no choice but to submit herself to the necessity and duty to pronounce the sentence expressed in Matt. 18 : 17, i. e. she must *avoid in part* such stubborn members, by not admitting them to communion or church council, and not saluting them as members. This avoiding in part was called by some *suspending*, and Cyprianus of the second century called it *putting back*, and so do our brethren to this day. But in cases of crimes and such heinous sins as enumerated 1 Cor. 5: 11, and other places, a different course is to be pursued. Here confession and acknowledgment will not suffice, nor a putting back or avoiding in part would answer the purpose of justice and mercy; hence Love and Wisdom divine devised and ordained "not to keep company with such, no not to eat," and to this our ancient brethren from the time we have any record of them, and many that live to this day, without adding or taking away a single word (for they tremble at God's word, Rev. 22 : 18, 19) gave their most humble yet willing assent and obedience, took up the cross as cross-bearing children of God should do (and there is undoubtedly a cross in this ordinance, and not a pleasure), and this they called *full avoidance.* Why the Lord did not institute this while yet personally on earth, the answer may be, may it not have been one of those things which the Lord had to tell the disciples, but they could not bear it then. What Paul said and did, he did it in the name of Christ, and consequently as if the Lord had said and done it himself.

From the testimony of the Brethren in 1713 (fully 150 years ago). See "Groundsearching Questions" in Alexander Mack's writings, page 129. Where Qu. 22 reads thus: Whether the external ban (excommunication) is an essential part of (the constitution of) the church of Christ, since he himself did not enforce and exercise it, even upon the very wicked Judas? Ans.—The ban is an essential and necessary thing in the church of Christ, as long as it is at war in this wicked world with wolves and evil spirits. *No church of Christ could exist without it.* [This idea has been misunderstood and rejected, seeing that there are churches in existence, and some have been for a long time without the avoidance. But the main point with regard these is: Will Christ acknowledge them to belong to *his* church, if they do not observe all whatsoever Christ commanded them?] The devil, with his leaven of wickedness, would soon destroy all that is good. True believers, while they were steadfast in the faith, never could refuse it (the salutary restraints appointed in the gospel). They have always viewed them as divine means of grace, appointed by the great love and provident care of God, and used them as a strong tower and wall round about the church of the Lord.

With respect to Judas we say, that Christ has executed the ban sufficiently upon him, giving him over to Satan; for he hanged himself. But that he was not excommunicated before he committed the outward act, is not against excommunication, but rather in its favor. That this was the mind of God at all times, as we perceive in Adam, who may have had probably some intercourse with the tempter previous to his fall; but he was not driven out of Paradise until he had actually eaten of the forbidden fruit. So Judas may have entertained traitorous thoughts long before he carried them out; but the long-suffering of Jesus had borne with him, and patiently tried to bring him to repentance, until the evil obtained the supremacy, and became manifest in the deed. Then he was sufficiently excommunicated by Christ, and we think the ban was fully executed upon him.

Ibid. page 132. Qu. 25. Whether the apostles ever prohibited the necessary spiritual or temporal assistance of charity from being rendered to the excommunicated? Ans.—The apostles have never commanded to withhold from the excommunicated necessary spiritual or temporal assistance; moreover, they are to be admonished to repentance. and though they do not hear, or receive it, we are clear. So likewise in worldly things, if we abound in the things of this world, and the excommunicated is in want, we are to communicate according to his need. Qu. 26. Whether your, the new Baptists, excommunication ever had in any of its subjects such a divine effect and result as that of the apostles? Ans. We firmly believe that all those we excommunicate according to the word of the Lord, will feel an internal effect, and an impression already here; and if not repenting in this time of grace, it will become manifest in the great day of judgment. But that men should immediately fall dead to the ground like Ananias, such has not happened yet, and is only once recorded of the apostles? and however many were excommunicated by the apostles, no more died thus literally, yet we believe the power of excommunication was fully realized in them.

Y. M. 1794. Art. 6. Concerning the ban, we would very readily deny ourselves so much for our brethren's sake, so as to drop the Jewish word "ban." But the ordinance of the Lord Jesus and his holy apostles we cannot give up even for our brethren's sake, namely: "If any man that is called a brother be a fornicator, or covetous, or an idolater, or a railer, or a drunkard, or an extortioner; with such a one no not to eat," 1 Cor. 5:11. Here we see clearly that Paul does not mean only the eating in (the Lord's) supper, but all eating (in his company). This is shown in the foregoing verse very plainly, when it says, "yet not altogether with the fornicators of this world, &c." Otherwise we might eat the bread of communion with the fornicators of this world, which certainly he cannot have meant at all.

Y. M. 1805. Art. 1. Concerning those who are in avoidance. Since some think that we may or should not even give them the hand, while others would feel disposed at times to offer them the hand as a token that we would willingly assist them to be released and reconciled again, the unanimous conclusion was, that we should be of one mind, and follow the same rule in housekeeping, and it was so laid down, that it might be best to offer them in that view the hand, but to have no dealings with them nor any familiar intercourse until a reformation takes place in them.

Y. M. 1822, Canton. Art. 11. How shall the church conduct itself toward those members that have been separated from the church? Considered, first, when a member is separated from the church as far as from the kiss, breaking of bread and church council, such ought to be diligently exhorted according to the evidence of the apostle, but could not be called brother. But when such would not receive the admonition of love, and should fall into more grievous sins, the church has to put them in avoidance, and have no company with them, according to the word of the apostle.

Y. M. 1822, Miami. Art. 1. When a member is put in avoidance, how far is his companion in wedlock to be held as a member? It was considered, that she may be held as a member, yet so as not to break the bread of communion.

Y. M. 1825. Art. 8. Concerning separation or excommunication, being viewed of unequal degrees. It was considered, that according to apostolic doctrine, such having committed gross or vicious sins, must be put entirely in avoidance, while less transgressions only precluded from the kiss, brotherly counsel, and the breaking of bread.

Y. M. 1827. Art. 2. About the avoidance and restoration of members. When a member, on account of crimes committed, must be separated and put in avoidance, and should afterward become reformed in life and conduct, and apply for restoration, or for release from the avoidance, and the church could not yet feel satisfied to restore such entirely, they might be released; and should such fall again into crime, we would have a right to put them again into avoidance.

Y. M. 1837. Art. 6. Whether the sense of the words of the Saviour, Matt. 18, "Let him be unto thee as a heathen man and a publican!" is the same as the sentence of the apostle, 1 Cor. 5, "Have no company with him," &c. It is understood by the meeting almost unanimously, that the expression of the Saviour, "Let him be unto thee as a heathen man and a publican," excludes a member only so far as from the church council, from the kiss and from the breaking of bread, but that the intention of the apostle when he speaks of the vicious (gross sinner), "Have no company with him," and after noting the (sins, crimes) vices, adds yet, "with such a one (you ought) no not eat!" that we ought to avoid such altogether, according to the (obvious) sense of the word.

Y. M. 1838. Art. 1. Whether a congregation (church) has the right, according to the gospel, to put a member in avoidance or not? Considered, that the old brethren always have thought it right, and (we) still think it right, according to the gospel, to put members in avoidance in accordance with the word of the gospel, 1 Cor. 5 : 9–11.

Y. M. 1840. Art. 3. In case one that was a brother, but now is held in avoidance, lives some hundred miles from a brother to whom he owes a debt, and writes back to brethren, that he were willing to pay, if he knew how much (he owed); whether in such case the brother might take the liberty to write to him and ascertain what amount he owes him? Considered, that brethren might make out and send such accounts, inasmuch it was at all times allowed to settle accounts with such members that had been put in avoidance.

Y. M. 1840. Art. 4. About the difference among brethren in regard to avoidance; since some seem to know or observe nothing at all of an avoidance, others take the liberty to eat with and greet as brethren those that are put in avoidance, which causes oftentimes temptations and great grief in those who feel themselves in duty bound, according to the word, to observe the avoidance strictly? Considered, that it is truly to be lamented that such a want of uniformity has crept in by degrees among the brethren in such a most important matter, and that it should be the ardent desire and earnest endeavor of all brethren and members, and especially of all ministers and housekeepers, to come again into full union in observing this evangelical and apostolic ordinance, to accomplish which may the ever faithful Chief Shepherd and Bishop of our souls grant his grace and the assistance of his good and holy Spirit.

Y. M. 1842.   Art. 1. Whether the sense of the words of our Saviour, Matt. 18, " Let him be unto thee as a heathen man and a publican !" is the same with the expression of Paul the Apostle, when he says, " Have no company with him !" 1 Cor. 5? This same query had been before the yearly meeting in Virginia in the year 1837, and a similar one before the annual meeting in Morrison's Cove in the year 1840, and even in the year 1794 (almost fifty years ago) the brethren expressed their views on the subject, which were read, and the brethren now assembled generally agreed to the then expressed views, desiring with our departed brethren, that our dearly beloved members would seek (endeavor) to hold fast to the written word of truth, for we fear with them, that whosoever will depart from it is in great danger of being deceived in these much confused times. Now he that attends strictly to the word, will see plainly, that Matt. 18 is quite another case than is mentioned in 1 Cor. 5. There the Saviour speaks of sins (trespasses) and offences which a brother or sister may commit against a fellow member. Here the apostle treats of vices and crimes which may be committed against God and the truth. And as there is a difference in the sins, even so is there also a difference in the discipline (or penalty). Already under the law there were some sins unto death, where the sinner had to die without mercy under two or three witnesses. Heb. 10 : 28. But some sins were not unto death, and would be atoned for by offerings and sacrifices. Even as there is a difference in the discipline under the gospel, as we may plainly see from those passages before alluded to, viz. Matt. 18 : 15–18, and 1 Cor. 5 : 9–14, if we examine them somewhat more closely. Therefore the brethren have always considered, and we consider it so still, that the divine sense requires to disown a member who will not be admonished, when he has been overtaken in a fault, which might have been atoned for by an acknowledgment, for his refusing to acknowledge, only so far as from the church council, from the breaking of bread, and from the (holy) kiss. But a member that has fallen into gross sins and vices, should be dealt with according to the word of God, as expressed by the Apostle Paul, to wit: " Not to keep company with such, no not to eat."

Y. M. 1843. Art. 5. When a brother is put in avoidance, according to the words of Paul, 1 Cor. 5, and his wife and children, being members in the church, have company with him, as it happens in a family, how is the church to treat them, or whether there is a difference between the wife and the children, who are yet under the lawful ages, and how we are to do when there is a difference of opinion about the withdrawing of the hand from those that are in avoidance? Considered, though we are always truly sorry when such a case occurs where we must put a member in avoidance, and feel sincere compassion for those who suffer immediately under it; yet we cannot set aside this apostolic ordinance, and do really believe that the more strictly it is observed by all the members, and especially by the nearest relatives, the more powerful it would operate to the salvation of the fallen member. But in case a wife would not withdraw from fellowship with her husband (being) in avoidance, it was always considered, that such a member could not break the bread of communion while so doing; and we do consider, that the children are in the same predicament, either to withdraw fellowship with the parent in avoidance, or not to break bread. And in regard to withdrawing the hand, it was considered, that when the church concludes to withdraw even the hand, the members should all unite in observing the same.

Same Y. M. Art. 11. Whether a teacher that is not ordained can excommunicate a deacon or visiting brother, on but one brother's testimony, and with only twelve members in council? The view of the brethren assembled is, that in consideration of the words of the apostle, 1 Tim. 5: 19, " Against an elder " (which word seems to be used in the New Testament sometimes in a more limited, and at other times a more general sense, and apparently including all those to whom is entrusted an office in the church,) "receive not an accusation, but before two or three witnesses." In consideration again, that as a brother that is not (yet) ordained, ought not (has not authority) to hold an election or to install ministers or deacons, so there ought to be none excommunicated without ordained brethren being present; and lastly, because that in such a case all the members of the church, or as many as possible, ought to be present, we could not approve of such a proceeding.

Our ancient brethren have taught us by precept and example, and experience has confirmed their teaching to be true and according to the gospel, the less authority we try to assume the better we will get along as housekeepers in the church; hence, in such cases as the one stated in the above question, where a minister or deacon has fallen under the censure of the church, even where two ordained elders presided in such church, they should not undertake such a case concerning a co-laborer, but should call for some elders from other churches to act in the case, so as to "abstain from all appearance of evil," of exercising too much authority, or of acting with partiality, &c. The wisdom of this course is so obvious, that it needs no further comment.

Y. M. 1844. Art. 8. In a case where man and wife are both members, and it so happens that the church would have occasion to hold one or the other in avoidance, and after being held thus, say two or more years, without manifesting any fruits of sincere repentance—which would be the most prudent course to take in behalf of the companion of such thus held in avoidance? Considered, that though we sincerely pity the innocent party, if there has no change taken place in the state of the fallen member, there can be no change in the course of the church toward such a member. But of this each church must judge according to existing circumstances. See 2 Cor. 2 : 5.

It is a very delicate matter sometimes, to inquire too deeply into such a special case presented at yearly meeting, neither would there be time sufficient for such investigation; but it would be an interesting inquiry, and one that could not fail of good results, if properly conducted, namely this : Why it is that a member is held in avoidance for two or more years without manifesting any change? It seems to be almost impossible that a person could remain in such a condition without some change either for better or for worse, especially if the church and the family would observe the avoidance faithfully. There is cause for close self-examination, particularly of those who coming into more or less frequent contact with such an offender in avoidance, to see whether they are not in the fault, that this ordinance should be ineffective for any length of time.

Y. M. 1846. Art. 6. Whether one that is called a brother, and has committed any gross crime, such as drunkenness, blasphemy or fornication, &c., can continue to be a member of the body of Christ, if he confesses his fault, and promises to do better? whether the church may forgive him, or whether he ought not to be expelled, until he shows forth fruits meet for repentance? Considered, that we can conceive of extraordinary cases of such deep or thorough contrition of heart, similar to that kind of leprosy (see Lev. 13 : 12–17,) which broke out abroad in the skin, and the leprosy covered all the skin of him that had the plague, from his head even to his foot, and where the priest had to consider him clean—and so the church likewise may unanimously feel satisfied with such signs of genuine repentance, and may be willing to forgive at once on his full confession ; yet in most cases it is the safest way, in the first place to obey the instruction of the Apostle Paul (1 Cor. 5), and to excommunicate such a member "with the power of our Lord Jesus Christ, that the spirit may be saved in the day of the Lord Jesus."

Y. M. 1848. Art. 18. Whether we have any authority of liberating a person out of the avoidance without the person making application? Considered, that there is to our knowledge no such authority in the gospel.

Y. M. 1848. Art. 20. Whether three or more ordained elders have the authority of liberating out of avoidance, independent of the church? Considered, that it cannot be done properly without the counsel and consent of the church.

Y. M. 1848. (Indiana.) Art. 11. When the church disowns a member, so that he is set back from the salutation of the kiss and from church fellowship, how is the proper way to do with such members as come from other arms of the church, and knowing the standing of such disowned members, yet will still hold fellowship with such? Considered, that inasmuch the church of Christ is one body all over the world, and the word says, " Whatsoever ye shall bind on earth shall be bound in heaven, and whatsoever ye shall loose on earth shall be loosed in heaven;" hence, if one branch of this church disowns a member (legally, of course) then members from other (churches or) branches, knowing this, should hold them equally disowned.

Y. M. 1849. Art. 27. To how great a degree must a brother sin and be degraded, before the church can put him in avoidance according to the gospel? and whether all dealings and communications of a temporal nature between such an individual and the members of the church should cease? Considered, that this subject has been often before the Y. M., and the views of the brethren then were read. But on the particular points of the present query we would refer our dear brethren to the word of God, which is plain, explicit and sharper than a two-edged sword. Paul the Apostle says, Rom. 15 : 4, " Whatsoever things were written aforetime, were written for our learning ;" and he evidently refers in these words to the writings of the Old Testament. Now we find, Lev. 5 : 17, "If a soul sin, and commit any of these things which are forbidden to be done by the commandments of the Lord, though he wist it not, yet he is guilty, and shall bear his iniquity, and he shall bring a trespass-offering unto the priest, and it shall be forgiven him." From this we may learn, that when a member has trespassed against God and the truth, even in ignorance, it is his duty to come to the church, and bring his trespass-offering, such as David says, Ps. 51 : 17, " The sacrifices of God are a broken spirit: a broken and contrite heart, O God, thou wilt not despise ;" and the church, which according to 1 Pet. 2 : 9, is " a royal priest-hood," is to judge and receive his offering, and forgive him accordingly. Here are the words of Christ himself duly to be considered : " Whosesoever sins ye remit, they are remitted unto them ; and whosesoever sins ye retain, they are retained." John 20 : 23.

Should, however, such a member that has trespassed, be not willing to bring his offering of acknowledgment of his fault, nor be willing to hear the church, then we may consider this as a rising, a scab, or bright spot, which eventually may turn into moral leprosy, Lev. 13 : 2, and in this case the priest (the church) had to shut him up, or, as Paul says in Thess. 3: 6, " Now we command you, brethren, in the name of our Lord Jesus Christ, that ye withdraw yourselves from every brother that walketh disorderly, &c.;" and as our Lord taught us, Matt. 18 : 17, " If he neglect to hear the church, let him be unto thee as a heathen man and a publican." This withdrawing, or shutting up from close communion with the church in the salutation of the kiss, the breaking of bread and the secret counsel, is continued, until it appears to the satisfaction of the priest (or the church) whether that spot is leprosy or not. Now if on examination the priest found that white spot somewhat dark, and that the plague did not spread in the skin, he was to pronounce him clean. So when a member begins to see and acknowledge his fault, as something dark, he may be reinstated again into full communion.

3

" But when the raw flesh appeareth in him, and the leprosy is thus confirmed, notice, he shall not be shut up, for he is unclean. And the leper in whom the plague is, his clothes shall be rent, and his head bare, and he shall put a covering upon his upper lip, and shall cry, *Unclean, unclean.* He shall dwell alone; without the camp his habitation shall be." Lev. 13: 14, 45, 46. So our ancient brethren considered, when the moral leprosy in a member was confirmed by raw works of the flesh, such as are described 1 Cor. 5: 11; Gal. 5: 19–21, &c., that the direction (or command) of the (Lord and his) Holy Ghost by the mouth of the Apostle Paul was to be strictly and literally obeyed, namely, " *not to keep company with such a one, no not to eat.*"

Our brethren were well aware of some commentators explaining these words as if they meant only not to have fellowship with such in spiritual matters, and not to eat with them the bread of communion. But they (our brethren) found it impossible to believe that the church at Corinth should have continued in full fellowship such a person as is described in 1 Cor. 5: 1, so that they should have still broken the bread of communion with him, &c., even until the apostle reproved them by this epistle. They (the brethren) also thought of the awful words, Rev. 21: 18, 19, and so they adhered simply to the word as it reads, had no intercourse, no dealings of any kind with such persons, and did not eat with them at the same table, or out of the same dish, at any common meal, while they were in this state of avoidance. Only acts of charity toward them our brethren did not consider prohibited by the word of God. And these views we still hold in communion with our departed brethren.

Y. M. 1850. Art. 20. If a member commits a fault, whether the church has the power according to the gospel, to put that member in avoidance without the assistance of another church? Considered, that if there is a bishop in that church, they have the power in the case of a private member.

But whether it is best and expedient to undertake such a solemn work, where family connections might interfere much with a fair and impartial trial, without the assistance of another church and other bishops, the church should seriously consider and decide in the fear of the Lord—a church like that of Philadelphia (Rev. 3: 8), where true *brotherly love* dwells; where the door is open for her sister churches at any time to enter; where humility acknowledges of *but little strength*, and is therefore willing to avail herself of all the help her sisters, though they have but little strengh too, may afford.

Y. M. 1850. Art. 24. Can a member that is cut off and kept in avoidance, be afterward released again from the bonds of excommunication without acknowledging the fault, or without coming and requesting to be released? And in case members are released without confessing their faults, or desiring to be released, how shall other members conduct themselves toward them? Considered, that where a member has committed one of those faults mentioned by the Apostle Paul, 1 Cor. 6 (or 5), and has been put in avoidance, the church having sufficient evidence that he has ceased from those evils, and by his earnest request he may be released out of the bonds of avoidance.—Art. 33. Whether members who have been put in avoidance, can be released without their request? Considered, that they cannot.—Art. 35. If a brother transgress so as to be deemed guilty of avoidance, should he not be cited to appear before the church in the presence of the witnesses, to hear the testimony given? Considered, that he ought to be particularly requested to attend.—Art. 36. In case such member be found guilty, by whom should he be informed? Considered, that this is a duty incumbent on the ordained brethren.

Art. 37. If it is proved by two or three brethren (witnesses) that a brother has been drinking to excess, yet not so much as to disable him from keeping on his feet; but has often before been charged, and also before been set back or put in avoidance, and still denies the charge; would he not come under the class of drunkards, or would it be prudent to hold him as a brother, or should he be expelled by the proof of four or five witnesses, though not members of the church? Considered, that no member should be put in avoidance without positive proof from members that he or she has been guilty of one of those mentioned by Paul, 1 Cor. 5: 11.—Art. 38. Have we a sufficient right according to the gospel, to put a man in avoidance who has already been put back from the kiss, the communion and the council, and disowned as a brother? Considered, that the church has the power to do so.—Art. 40. Whether an ordained brother, who has been once in avoidance, can be restored again to his full office? Considered, that a brother can be restored again to his full office by the voice of the church (as in a choice).

Y. M. 1855. Art. 3. How is it considered, if a young brother and sister want to marry each other, and being opposed by their parents, members too, accomplish their design so late as to bring reproach upon themselves and the church? Considered, that the young members should be dealt with according to the circumstances, so as to prove that the church is not participating in evil; and the parents should also be admonished, if the church finds them in error.—Art. 23. How is it considered, if a church having no ordained elder, has a case of gross sin, such as is described 1 Cor. 5 : 11, and application is made to ordained elders to assist them, the elders making an appointment, and fail to attend; has the church a right to put such members back, or ought the church to hold such transgressors as full members, until they can get ordained elders? Considered, that the church may and ought to put them back provisionally, when the crime is sufficiently proved, until ordained elders can attend.

BAILSHIP FOR CRIMINALS.

Y. M. 1848. (Indiana.) Art. 4. How would it be considered, if a man be put into the county prison for safe keeping until court, and a brother goes his security for his appearance in court, and releases him out of prison? Considered, that a brother ought not to meddle with such matters without counseling the church.

Becoming bail or surety for another was never thought advisable by the Brethren, from a consideration of the warnings contained in the word of God. See Prov. 6 : 1–5, "My son, if thou be surety for thy friend, if thou hast stricken thy

hand with a stranger, thou art snared with the words of thy mouth, thou art taken with the words of thy mouth (or with the signing of thy name). Do this now, my son, and deliver thyself, when thou art come into the hand of thy friend; go, humble thyself, and make sure thy friend. Give not sleep to thine eyes, nor slumber to thine eye-lids. Deliver thyself as a roe from the hand of the hunter, and as a bird from the hand of the fowler." See also Prov. 11 : 15, "He that is surety for a stranger shall smart for it; and he that hateth suretyship is sure." Prov. 17 : 18, "A man void of understanding striketh hands, and becometh surety in the presence of his friends." Prov. 22 : 26. "Be not thou one of them that strikes hands, or of them that are *sureties for debts.*"

BAN. (See "*Avoidance or Excommunication.*")

BAPTISM.

We hold baptism, with the generality of Christian professors, as the initial ordinance appointed by our Lord Jesus Christ, Matt. 28 : 19, &c., but cannot baptize any but such who profess to have repented of their sins, and to believe in the Lord Jesus Christ, Mark 16 : 16, &c. With regard to the action, we believe that the word baptism means only immersion, as all Greek scholars are ready to admit, if they are candid and honest. The Greek term $\beta\alpha\pi\tau\iota\zeta\omega$, $\beta\alpha\pi\tau\iota\sigma\mu\alpha$ or $\beta\alpha\pi\tau\iota\sigma\mu o\varsigma$, means, however, being in the frequentative form, a repeated action. Hence, we adhere to TRINE IMMERSION as the most ancient and original action. We are confirmed in this respect by the fact, that single immersion was first introduced full 600 years after A. D., and that only in Spain, while trine immersion, even in the Roman Church, prevailed in all other countries till about the time of the Reformation, and is continued indeed to this day in the Roman Church at Milan; that the Greek Church, numbering more than sixty millions of professors, has always practiced it until now; and that the Church of England has trine immersion indicated in her Book of Common Prayer to this very day; and that we have evidence that trine immersion was also the action in baptism practiced in the Lutheran Church in the days of Reformation.

Whether such as had been baptized by single immersion among other denominations, could be received among us without that baptism, we believe fully required by the gospel.

Y. M. 1804. Art. 6. About persons, who are among the English Baptists, and have been baptized by them, and come now, and desire to be admitted (in our church); whether they ought to be baptized again, according to the true order of baptism, or if they should prefer it, whether we would receive them without being baptized again? In consideration of the Scripture, and especially because the Lord said to Moses, "Look that thou make them after their pattern, which was showed thee in the mount" (Exod. 25 : 40), it has been concluded with one accord, that when such come to us, we should give them in all things good instruction according to the gospel, yea, according to the Scriptures; and when they believe, and are willing to obey from the heart, that form of doctrine according to the counsel of God, they ought to be baptized in the proper order, because there have occurred different examples, that heretofore persons had been received by the Brethren, who thought then they could be satisfied with their single backward immersion, but afterward they were more enlightened, have deemed their baptism as imperfect, and to put their conscience at rest, they requested and had to be baptized in the name of the Father, and of the Son, and of the Holy Ghost, by a trine immersion.

Y. M. 1821. Art. 6. Whether members (persons) might be received into the church, who have been but once immersed (without baptizing them in the manner we believe it ought to be done according to the gospel)? It was considered, that a threefold immersion is the true baptism; but if such persons would be content with their baptism, and yet acknowledge the Brethren's order as right, we would leave it over to them, and receive them with the laying on of hands and prayer.

Y. M. 1828. Art. 6. Whether a person may be received into the church, having been immersed but once? it is the counsel to be better that they should be baptized again in the true order.—Art. 7. Whether we had a right to cause a candidate for baptism to make a vow? it was considered, that it is according to the gospel to receive them in the order of the Brethren as usual.

Y. M. 1833. Art. 1. Whether we are to immerse at baptism once or thrice? It was considered, that we cannot deem any other baptism as valid according to the word of God, but a threefold immersion.

Y. M. 1834. Art. 4. Whether we could receive into our church a person that has been immersed once backward, without baptizing him again? Considered, that though it has been done before, still we believe that the best and safest way is to baptize them right and according to the proper order (as we believe), and that hereafter it should not be done otherwise.—Art. 10. How it is considered, when a member who was received after having been baptized with only one immersion backward. without receiving baptism according to our order, moves into another church, and there is required to be baptized? Answer in foregoing article 4.

Y. M. 1835. Art. 1. How it is viewed to receive colored people (into our church)? Considered, to make no difference on account of color.

Y. M. 1835. (Miami.) Art. 13. What is the order to receive applicants for baptism? It is necessary that there should be self-knowledge, repentance and faith, together with scriptural instruction, and then that it may be done with the counsel of the church.

Y. M. 1837. Art. 8. When·persons desire to be received by baptism into the church, whether it be necessary to instruct them before baptism with regard to the swearing of oaths, to the going to war and the like, that according to our views are forbidden in the gospel? The advice is, that such persons ought,.if possible, to be visited before baptism, and by all means to be previously instructed in the following points, viz. of the taking of oaths, going to war or to muster, to use the power of the law contrary to the gospel, and to conform to the fashions of this world in apparel, and the like; and that they ought to state before their reception their willingness to refrain from all such things.—Art. 12. How it is viewed to receive persons into the church in case of sickness and bodily infirmity, without baptism? Considered, that we have no express word for it, and that it would be more advisable and more safe to direct them simply to the mercy of God in Christ. Yet in certain (extraordinary or) singular cases, we would not set bounds, but advise all teachers (ministers) to be careful to do nothing without the counsel of their fellow laborers, and if it can be possible, of their church.

Y. M. 1844. Art. 4. In regard to the difference in the form of words, which the Brethren use in baptism, it was after a free discussion considered, since in the practice of a threefold immersion of the kneeling candidate, and in the use of the words of our Saviour, Matt. 28 : 19, "IN THE NAME OF THE FATHER, AND OF THE SON, AND OF THE HOLY GHOST," we are all perfectly agreed to lay the matter down as heretofore, and to bear with one another in love, yet so that the teachers of one and the same church or district ought to use the same form. See 1 Cor. 1 : 10.

Y. M. 1845. Art. 4. Where is the proper place for asking the candidates for baptism concerning their faith in Christ—in or out of the water ? Considered, that the most proper place for making a public confession of our faith in Christ, is in the water, immediately before baptism. See 1 Tim. 6 : 12.

Y. M. 1848. (Ohio.) Art. 3. How are we to receive members into the church from their first application until they are baptized according to the gospel ? Considered, that inasmuch as there has been hitherto a difference in the practice and in the form of words used in this ordinance, and inasmuch it is desirable to be in all such matters of *one* mind, and do and speak the same things, this meeting has unanimously agreed upon the following course and form of words, and recommend the same for adoption in all the churches :

First, the applicant to be examined by two or more brethren ; then the case to be brought before the church council, before whom the applicant is to declare his agreement with us in regard to the principles of being (non-resistant) non-swearing, and non-conforming to the world; then in meeting or at the water to read from Matt. 18 : 10–22, in public, the candidates being asked if they will be governed by these gospel rules. Then prayer at the water, and in the water the following questions to be asked :

Dost thou believe that Jesus Christ is the Son of God, and that he has brought from heaven a saving gospel ? Answer—Yea.

Dost thou willingly renounce Satan and all his pernicious ways, and all the sinful pleasures of this world ? Answer—Yea.

Dost thou covenant with God in Christ Jesus to be faithful until death ? Answer—Yea.

(Then the administrator continues)—"Upon this thy confession of faith, which thou hast made before God and these witnesses, thou shalt —for the remission of thy sins—be baptized in the name of the Father, and of the Son, and of the Holy Ghost." After baptism, while in the water, the administrator to lay his hands upon the head of the candidate, and to offer up a prayer to God in his behalf; and then the member is to be received by hand and kiss (if a brother by the brethren, and if a sister by the sisters, and by the opposite sex only by the hand) into church fellowship.

Y. M. 1848. Art. 5. Ought we to receive any person into the church without baptism, having been baptized by any other order of people? Considered, that this yearly meeting advise to be very careful in this matter, and give it as their unanimous conclusion, that it would be better to admit no person into the church without being baptized by the Brethren.

Y. M. 1851. Art. 17. Whether the form of words used in the ordinance of baptism, as laid down in the annual meeting, A. D. 1848, could not be reconsidered? Considered, to leave it as the minutes of 1848 have it.

Y. M. 1853. Art. 45. Inasmuch as there had been a difference in the form of words in administering baptism, settled and brought to a union (?) some years ago, could we not also come to a full union and agreement with regard to feet washing, the Lord's supper, &c., so that a member from one section would find in every other section the same celebration in manner and form as at home? Considered, to refer this to the next yearly meeting.

Y. M. 1855. Art. 6. Is it consistent with the gospel to receive persons into the church with hand and kiss, when circumstances will not permit baptism to be performed? Considered, that it is not according to the gospel to consider persons as members of the church without baptism; yet they should be encouraged, and if they wish it, their cases may be taken into consideration by the church in council, and they be received as candidates for baptism, which is to be performed as soon as circumstances will permit.—Art. 26. How is it considered best to do with a brother or brethren, that will not use the words in administering baptism, as it was decided at the yearly meeting near Wooster, Ohio, in 1848, " for the remission or forgiveness of sin ?" Considered, that the decision of said council should be observed, as it was observed by many brethren from time immemorial, and that those brethren who will not submit to it should be admonished for love sake (for union's sake) and (more than all) for the word's sake, to comply.

Y. M. 1857. Art. 20. Do not those administrators of baptism, who make the candidates for baptism renounce *all the world*, require too much of the candidates, since we all have more or less to do with the world? Would it not be more proper to require of them to renounce only what is contrary to the gospel? Ans.—The third article of the minutes of 1848 contains the proper renunciation of the world. The passage in that article, referred to here, reads thus: " Dost thou renounce *all the sinful pleasures of this world ?*"

Y. M. 1858. Art. 1. Can a person be received into the church, who is uncle to his wife? Or do the brethren think the gospel will not allow of such a person becoming a member of the church? Considered, that if he is uncle to his wife by marriage, he may be received, if by blood relation, he should not be —Art. 31. Is it contrary to the gospel for brethren to hold meetings for a number of days in succession, in one place, in order to preach the pure word of God, and to administer the ordinance of baptism to those who believe the word and receive it? Considered, not contrary to the gospel, if the believer is proceeded with according to the gospel, and the order of the brethren as given by the annual meeting of 1848, Art. 3.—Art. 41. Inasmuch as there has been great confusion in various branches of the church during the past year relative to the manner of taking in members, as this has been done in many different ways, would brethren not consider it prudent and consistent with the gospel, to have a unity of practice throughout the church, and if so, what shall that practice be? Shall it be the order laid down in the minutes of 1848, or will the brethren draft a new order? Considered, that we will continue the order laid down in the minutes of 1848, which is as follows: (see page 38.)

Y. M. 1859. Art. 3. How is it considered if a minister would buplicly teach that water baptism is not for the remission of sins, but that a person must have an evidence within that his sins are pardoned before he is a fit subject for baptism; and also would differ with brethren in the mode of electing brethren to the ministry, and likewise claim that all members, both male and female, have a right to admonish and exhort? Ans.—Considered, that it is not according to Acts 2: 38, and 22: 16, to teach that a person must have an evidence within that his sins are pardoned before he is a fit subject for baptism; and that we know of no better way for the brethren to elect their ministers than that which has been practiced heretofore. And concerning members exhorting without being authorized by the church, we think they should not do so in the church in our public or general meetings, according to 1 Cor. 14: 33–35.

Art. 5. Inasmuch as the ceremony used by the brethren in receiving members into the church is thought by a large proportion of the brethren to be of too great length, might it not be shortened? And instead of the questions being asked in the water, would it not be more consistent to ask them in the house or on the bank of the river or stream? Ans.— We do not consider it good to make any alterations from the present practice of the brethren.

Y. M. 1860. Art. 4. Shall it be an order among the brethren, to receive persons into the church as members, when they are sick, without baptism, with the promise that they will be baptized when they get well? Ans.—Let persons who wish to be received into the church, and who are too sick to have the ordinance of baptism administered to them, be considered as candidates for baptism to receive the ordinance as soon as circumstances will permit, but not in full membership until they are baptized.

Art. 11. Is it consistent with the order of the brethren and the gospel, to receive a member into the church without the counsel of the church, when it is possible to have a council? Ans.—It is not consistent.

Y. M. 1862. Art. 21. Would it not be better, instead of asking the consent of each individual member concerning the reception of an applicant, to make the request general, that is, ask the church as a body whether they are willing to receive such applicant, and if they are, let silence give consent, and if not, that member who is not willing to receive such applicant shall have full privilege to state his or her objections? Answer.—This is left optional to each arm of the church.

Y. M. 1862. Art. 27. A person was baptized and thus became a member of the church; afterward thought he was not in the right state of mind when he had been baptized, and felt that if he would die in this state, he would be lost, and then made application to be re-baptized. The brethren in the congregation tried to reconcile him, and could not; and (they) also sent strange and elder brethren to talk with him, who also failed to satisfy him. After repeated and continued application for re-baptism, a brother, without the counsel of the church, baptized him over again, when he became reconciled. Now did the brother who re-baptized the person do his duty? Answer.—We think he did not do his duty; but did wrong.

Art. 63. Will the brethren in annual council consider it right for ministering brethren to receive members into the church without requiring them to lay off the fashions of the world in regard to apparel, and to conform to the order of the brethren? Answer.—We consider it would not be right to do so; see Romans 12: 3.

Art. 67. When a person, having received baptism in the same way that we perform it, but by a member of a different denomination, wishes to be united to the Brethren, must such a person be re-baptized in order to be received into our church? Answer.—We refer to the minutes of the annual meeting of 1848, Art. 5. ["Ought we to receive any person into the church without baptism, having been baptized by any other order of people? Considered, that this yearly meeting advise to be very careful in this matter, and give it as their unanimous conclusion, that it would be better to admit no person into the church without first being baptized by the brethren."]

Y. M. 1864. Art. 12. Inasmuch there is a difference of opinion relative to the applicant for baptism declaring his agreement with the church in regard to the principles of non-resistance, non-swearing and non-conformity to the world, whether this should be done in the presence of the whole congregation, or of the church only. We wish a decisive answer, and not only a reference to the minutes of 1848 and 1858, as we have referred to them, but still get into difficulty. Answer.—We think it should be done in the presence of the church only.

Such questions seem to proceed either from new churches or young members, who are somewhat unacquainted with the ancient established order of the church.

The answer is exactly according to that order; and the reason why the brethren would rather refer back to former occasions, is simply this, that our brethren, even the oldest, instead of loving and assuming authority for themselves, would rather submit to another authority.

Art. 17. Is it wrong to baptize or immerse sick persons in a house? Answer.—We consider it is not advisable to do so whenever it is possible to avoid it.

Art. 25. Is it in accordance with the gospel and the order of the brethren, for the church to receive and take candidates in with (or, by) hand and kiss previous to the reading of Matt. 18, and then baptize them upon their public confession? Answer.—We think it is neither in accordance with the gospel or the order of the brethren to do so.

Art. 20. Is it according to the gospel and the order of the brethren, to receive and baptize into the church such as are in the military service, bearing arms in this war, or to go into the camps and baptize such, and let them remain in the service; or, should they not first get a full discharge, before they can be received into the church by baptism? Answer.—We cannot encourage such proceedings; but in case of extreme sickness, and when there is a promise to shed no more blood, we will let the churches applied to decide what shall be done; but let the privileges of the church be acceded to by all candidates.

BAPTISM OF THE HOLY GHOST.

Y. M. 1858.   Art. 37. How is it when one brother preaches that there is no baptism of the Holy Ghost now, but that it is only the gift of the Holy Ghost which believers receive, while another brother prays for the Lord to baptize with the Holy Ghost? Answer.—We think it best for no brother to preach that there is no baptism of the Holy Ghost now, but in praying we should pray for the gift of the Holy Ghost.

It would be advisable for old and young ministers to heed the admonition of the Apostle Paul, 1 Cor. 1: 10, when he says, " Now I beseech you, brethren, by the name of our Lord Jesus Christ, that ye all speak the same thing, &c.," and to abide by the simple declaration of the word of God, and whatever truth can be fairly and directly educed from it. By this we might escape from all apparent jarrings and contradictions in our discourses. Most of our differences and disputes arise from not heeding said admonition of the apostle. When John the Baptist told the multitude, speaking of Jesus, "He shall baptize you with the Holy Ghost," Matt. 3: 11, Mark 1: 8, Luke 3: 16, and the Saviour just before his ascension promised the same thing, Acts 1: 5, and fulfilled it on Pentecost not only to the disciples, but not long after to those who had become believers, Jews in Jerusalem, Acts 4: 31, and Gentiles in Cesarea, Acts 10 : 44, and 11 : 15 ; and when we consider that God is unchangeable, and that Jesus Christ is the same yesterday, to-day and forever ; and that the Holy Ghost operates now as effectually in the conversion of sinners and sanctification of believers, though perhaps in a less degree—we believe that the promises of God belong to us and our children, as well as to the primitive age, and that if we were united in spirit, heart and soul, as the apostles were at Pentecost, we might expect similar Pentecostal blessings.

BEARDS.

On this head we give an extract from the history of the Greek Church, in which men, especially priests and bishops, always wore their beards, until the

Russian Emperor Peter, in the seventeenth century, forbade its use. "The beard was indeed one of the fundamental characteristics of the ancient Eastern faith. Michael Cerularius had laid it down in the eleventh century as one of the primary differences between the Greek and Latin Churches. To shave the beard was pronounced at the council of Moscow, in the seventeenth century, a sin which even the blood of the martyrs could not expiate. It was defended, it is still defended, by texts of Scripture, by grave precedents, by ecclesiastical history. The Levitical law commands us not to cut the hair or the beard. Man was made in the image of God; is the image of God to be defaced? Our Saviour was (undoubtedly) bearded." Stanley's Lectures on the History of the Eastern Churches, page 512, &c.

Y. M. 1804. Art. 4. Whether upon request a brother might be ordained as a bishop, who shaves off his beard? it was considered, that inasmuch God made man with a beard; and again, God commanded his people in the law not to cut off the beard; and it was especially required of the priests of God not to mar the corners of the beard; and also Christ, our Master and precursor, together with his disciples, has left us an example herein—in consideration of these and other scriptures and examples, it (the ordination) could not readily be done in a sound faith and with an unoffended conscience.

Y. M. 1822 Art 1. Whether a brother might be set forward to baptize and break bread, who does not wear his beard; it was considered, that according to the image of God (in which man was created), and according to the image of Christ, we ought to (leave our beard undisturbed or) wear our beard (at least in part), and that no brother should be so far advanced who could not deny himself in this matter.

Y. M. 1835. Art. 3. On same subject, and decided similarly.

Y. M. 1846. Art. 11. How it is considered by this yearly meeting, whether brethren, who do not wear their beard, are to be advanced to administer baptism and the breaking of bread, or may even be ordained? Considered, that we are much grieved, how also in this respect a deviation and want of self-denial is becoming apparent here and there, and it would be well and laudable if we would not only keep in remembrance, but put also in practice the example and advice of our beloved old brethren. In 1822—twenty-four years ago—the query had been asked; see in full above. In 1804—forty-two years ago—the query came up; as given also above.

Y. M. 1854. Art. 19. How will it be considered, if a brother serving in the office of a deacon does not let his beard grow, and when admonished, opposes and asks scripture on that question? Considered, that brethren should bear and forbear (one another) in love, and give him the best scripture ground they can.

Y. M. 1862. Art. 12. How it is considered for brethren to wear the beard on the upper lip, they being conscientious in doing so? Answer. If a brother does not shave any, we would leave it with his conscience; but if he lets it stand on his upper lip only, we consider it wrong.

BISHOP, OR ELDER.

By these terms we understand that officer in the church, who after having served as a minister, first simply as a preacher of the word, and secondly as an administrator of the ordinance of baptism and the communion for a longer or shorter term of years, as the church saw and sees fit, and doing so to the acceptance and satisfaction of the church—has been chosen by the unanimous choice of all the members of the church, present at the occasion, in presence of at least two elders from adjoining churches, to be overseer of his church, and also to exercise his office wherever he may come—the field is the world—for the converting of sinners and the building up of the church of Christ. Concerning unanimity, it was always considered prudent in such case (and would be also in other cases), if any valid objection would be raised and substantiated by at least two members of good standing, that the ordination had best be postponed, inasmuch as the word of God says, Acts 20: 28, "Over the which (all the flock) the Holy Ghost hath made you overseers to feed the church of God," &c. Now, since we could not know in case of a division in the church by a majority and a minority, whether "man" or "the Holy Ghost" had made the overseer (or in any other case the decision), we aim at unanimity. If, therefore, those who conduct the choice upon examination find that the objections presented are well founded in Scripture, in this case for instance on 1 Tim. 3: 1–7, Tit. 1: 6, &c., and in fact by sufficient evidence, then it is best to stop proceedings, and postpone until the objections may have ceased to exist. On the contrary, if not well founded, the objectors should be admonished to withdraw them, and unite with the church in consenting to the ordination, and if they should refuse to do so, the conductors of the choice must exercise their own best judgment, without partiality on either side and in the fear of the Lord, whether to go on with the ordination or not, and by taking no account of unfounded objections, declare the voice of the church unanimous in case of only one or two dissenters. The still better way would be, if the church would be informed of the case, and the church, in the absence of the objectors, would decide it unanimously, and then the ordination proceeded with in the usual way by the laying on of hands.

Y. M. 1804. Art. 4. (See "*Beard.*")

Y. M. 1821. Art. 1. Whether an ordained brother (bishop) may collect debts by the power of law? It was considered, that no brother, much less one ordained, has a right to do so according to the gospel doctrine, not even for another.

Y. M. 1821. Art. 2. Whether an ordained or private brother may serve as executor, when he knows before that the law must be used, was likewise considered, that according to gospel doctrine it should not be. But inasmuch many brethren are involved in this way, the counsel is to have patience with them, until they can extricate themselves, yet meanwhile not to break bread with them. But since an executorship is very burdensome, it has been deemed necessary to adopt a remedy to lessen the burden; and since every father has a right to make a will as he sees proper, without hindrance from the powers that be, to divide and distribute his property, and also to select his executors, and to charge them what and in what manner they should do—they might put in their wills something like the following clause, namely: I nominate and appoint A. B. to be sole executor of my estate (this my last will and testament), to settle, pay off, and collect, as far as the rules of our church and the gospel will admit of, &c.

Y. M. 1836. Art. 4. When a bishop is old and too feeble to serve in his office fully as he ought, whether (the church) would have a right to select another? the counsel is, to go to counsel with the nearest churches, and if, looking on the proposition favorably, and the old bishop and his church would be of one mind, then it might be done.

Y. M. 1846. Art. 11. (See under foregoing heading, page 43. See also, "*Authority of a Bishop.*")

Y. M. 1846, Tennessee. Art. 4. How is it considered for a bishop, with a few members, to expel a member without taking the counsel of the church? Considered, that in all such important matters the church must be counseled.

Art. 6. Whether a deacon can be ordained to the office of a bishop? Considered, that we have no authority for so doing. See 1 Tim. 3 : 1–7; ch. 5 : 22.

Y. M. 1849. Art. 9. What is the duty of a bishop toward his church, and the duty of the church toward the bishop or bishops, in case the bishop commits an error; is it to be overlooked more in him than in another brother in office, or in a private member? Considered, that elders who rule well should be counted worthy of double honor, and that overseers should not undertake anything of importance without counsel of the church; and if there should be a general complaint of the church against him, he is to acknowledge his fault before the church like another member, and should not be spared; for " if the eye be evil, the whole body shall be full of darkness." Still it was always the advice of our old brethren, that in any case where laboring (ministering) brethren were in fault, strange and impartial brethren of experience should be called to assist in the investigation and justification of the same.

Y. M. 1849. Art. 36. (See page 25.)

Y. M. 1850. Art. 40. Whether an ordained brother, who had been once in avoidance, can be restored again to his full office? Considered, that a brother can be restored again to his full office by the voice of the church (as in a choice).

Y. M. 1851. Art. 6. A query concerning the ordaining of elders. Considered, that the ordination of elders is of the utmost importance to the church, and should always be under the special guidance of the Holy Spirit, who will teach and remind a church of the right person and the proper time for ordination; that there should be a full union of the church and the elders present on the subject; and that where there is any serious objection according to the word of God (see 1 Tim. 3 : 1–7; Titus 1 : 7), the elders and the church should be cautious (not) to proceed, if the objection could not be removed.

Y. M. 1852. Art. 9. What is the duty of a bishop, who has the oversight of an adjoining congregation, in which there is no householder and only one speaker?—and has that church liberty to call elders, and have a bishop or speaker appointed? Considered, that it is the duty of a bishop to attend to the necessities of such church, and if he neglects his duty, such church, if unanimous, may call other elders to assist them.

Y. M. 1853. Art. 4. Is it consistent with the gospel and its principles, as professed by our brotherhood, when a brother is chosen to the ministry only, not being authorized to baptize, that the ordained elder of the congregation should forward such brother, without consulting the church?   Considered, that all power, under God, is vested in the church (composed of elders, ministers, deacons and private members), and that therefore the church should in all such cases be consulted.—Art. 11. What is the most proper or scriptural mode of ordaining an elder or bishop? By the voice of the church, over which the elder is to be ordained (or preside), or by the wish or declaration of the elders or bishops of neighboring churches?   Answered, by referring to the minutes of 1851, Art. 6. (See above.)

Y. M. 1855.   Art. 17. If two brethren were chosen at one and the same time as ministers in the first degree, and some time afterward advanced together to the second degree, and in course of time the church is in need of an overseer or bishop, can these two brethren both be ordained as such, or only one?   Considered, that in such a case both brethren may be ordained, provided there be no sufficient cause known to prevent it.

Y. M. 1858.   Art. 56. Is it advisable for ordained brethren to ordain a ministering brother to the office of elder or bishop, who permits his children, even while under lawful age, to wear all manner of jewelry, and to learn instrumental music at boarding schools, &c.?   Considered, not advisable. 1 Tim. 2 : 9; 3 : 4, 5.

BONDS OR NOTES, BUYING AND SELLING.

Y. M. 1810.   Art. 1. About brethren who intend selling bonds, it was considered, that it should not be done without the counsel of the church.

Y. M. 1817.   Art. 6. Whether we may sell a note (or bond) or not? Considered, that no member should sell a note without the consent of the debtor.

Y. M. 1827.   Art. 7. With regard to selling bonds, it was considered, that none should be sold by which poor people might be oppressed; but since circumstances are so different, the church should be counseled (asked for counsel in any case.)

Y. M. 1858.   Art. 21. Is it right according to the gospel for brethren to purchase notes from brethren or others, and shave them at fifteen per cent. or more?   Considered, that it is not according to the gospel for brethren to do so.—Art. 30. How is it considered, if a brother has a note against another poor brother, who cannot pay, and the brother who has the note sells it to his son, who is no member of the church, and he collects the debt by law, and causes the poor brother's property to be sold, the brother who sold the note justifying himself in doing as he did? What is to be done in such a case?   Considered, that the brother who did so, committed a great fault, and that he should make restitution to the poor brother to the satisfaction of the church.

Y. M. 1864. Art. 16. Is it right and according to the gospel for a brother to invest money in government bonds? Ans.—We consider it not wrong to do so.

BORROWING FROM BANKS.

Y. M. 1847. Art. 8. Whether it may be proper and agreeable with the gospel for a brother to borrow money from banks or speculating money-lenders, for the purpose of buying and droving cattle, sheep and horses, or for buying wheat or other produce, and transporting the same to the Atlantic cities or other public markets, for the purpose of making gain or profit? Considered, that we in general council (assembled) would advise any (and every) brother not to engage largely in trading, as there is great danger, both in a temporal and in a spiritual point of view. See 1 Tim. 5: 9, 10.

BREAKING OF BREAD. (See " *Communion.*")

BREWERY KEEPING.

Y. M. 1827. Art. 11. How it is considered, if a brother keeps a brewery, and makes strong beer? Considered, though it could not be directly forbidden to a brother, but ought to be left to his own conscience, and (yet we wish) to advise him, that the safest way would be, not to carry on such a business from which may arise so many and great disorders.

BUTCHERING.

Y. M. 1850. Art. 7. Is a brother, being a full member in the church, allowed to purchase cattle and other animals, and following butchering, hire or rent a stall in a market house, and attend market as a butcher every market morning? Considered, that a brother engaged in butchering in the manner stated in the question is surrounded with many difficulties and temptations, and that we would advise brethren not to do so.

CAMP MEETINGS, ATTENDING.

Y. M. 1848. Art. 11. Can it be considered prudent or profitable for members to frequent camp meetings or protracted meetings from time to time? Unanimously considered, not to be profitable for members to do so.

CARPETS.

Y. M. 1827. Art. 8. How it is considered to lay carpets in (our) houses? It was considered, that it belongs to the grandeur (highness) of this world, and that it will not become a follower of Jesus to garnish his house in this manner, but rather that he should adorn his house as may be consistent with lowliness.

Y. M. 1828. Art. 9. Whether brethren may have carpets in their houses, was considered, that it cannot and should not be, because it leads to elevation (pride).

While such improvements were yet new, and only found in the houses of the great and rich in the world, it was proper for brethren to advise as above; but after such improvement had become a common thing, and it was a convenience generally known, there was no further objection to their introduction. Thus it was almost in all cases.

CARRIAGES.

Y. M. 1828.   Art. 2. Whether we may conform ourselves to the world with unnecessary things on our carriages?   Considered, that it cannot be. (See foregoing note.)

CERTIFICATES OF MEMBERSHIP.

Y. M. 1788.   Art. 2. The next was almost equally inportant, inasmuch it has happened that members have moved from one section of the country to another, and improprieties had been committed by them in the place from whence they moved, which are such as reflect no honor on the doctrine of the Lord, nor either on (our) Christian profession, so that we had to withdraw from them the kiss of charity, and they concealed this at the place where they had moved to, and sometimes it was discovered afterward, so that offence of tender minds might result therefrom; we conclude likewise, and find it more proper and perfect, that such removing family or member should bring a certificate from the church where they leave, to the church to which they move.

Y. M. 1834.   Art. 5. Concerning a certain brother's certificate.—Art. 15. Whether a certificate could be given to a brother minister, who moves away from his church, without paying his debts?   Special advice given, but not noted.

Y. M. 1841.   Art. 12. What is to be done with a brother or member, who removes into another church without bringing a certificate of membership along, and upon being asked for it, is offended by the request? Considered, that, as it has been decided often heretofore, it is requisite for members that remove from one church into another, to bring a testimonial or certificate along of their standing in the church whence they came, and that they ought not to be offended at being asked for the same. Should they refuse still to procure a certificate, the church to which they came would have a right to (inquire further and) ascertain their standing, before receiving them to full membership.

Y. M. 1849.   Art. 12. Concerning the propriety and necessity of recommendations for members that move from one church to another? Considered, that the ministers in the various churches should see (to it) that none of their members should move away without a recommendation; that no church is bound to receive (such) a member without recommendation, and that the recommendation be signed by not less than two or three witnesses, according to the gospel.   That the apostles gave written recommendations, see Rom. 16: 1, 2; 1 Cor. 16: 10, 11; 2 Cor. 8: 23; Eph. 6: 21, 22; Col. 4: 7–9; 1 Thes. 3: 2, &c.

Y. M. 1853.   Art. 24. Is it right to give a certificate to a brother, when he moves out of the church district without paying his debts, or giving general satisfaction to his creditors? Considered, that if the church is satisfied of the brother's having been honest, and having done all he could to pay his debts and satisfy his creditors, he ought to have a certificate. But should the brother be able and not willing to pay his debts, or give, or try to give satisfaction to his creditors, he should by no means have a certificate of full membership in the church.

Y. M. 1862.   Art. 20. What shall be done in such a case as follows : There are a brother and sister living here who claim to have stood in full fellowship with a church called Dunkards, in Lycoming county, Pa. When asked for a certificate, the brother said the church 'from which they moved did not give certificates, allowing that their conduct should suffice, and this (conduct) has been quite satisfactory to the members of this church? Answer.—We consider it right in all cases, when members move from one arm of the church to another, that they shall present to the church wherein they wish to reside, a certificate to prove their membership in the church from whence they came, or give satisfaction to the church of which they wish to become members.

CHOICE AND INSTALLATION OF MINISTERS, &c.

Y. M. 1835.   Art. 2. How it is viewed to elect brethren for the ministry by lot?   Considered, to abide the manner of holding a choice hitherto observed.   (Given from memory, as a witness present.)

Y. M. 1837.   Art. 4. How it is considered to hold an election without un ordained brother (elder) being present? As to holding elections, it is considered, that no election ought to be held without the presence of (two or) at least one ordained brother.

Y. M. 1838.   Art. 12. Whether in case that brethren, who are called to some ministry, move from one church into another, and are received with their office by the church to which they have removed, whether the sisters, their wives, ought to be received with them, as in the case of an election?   Considered, that it would be good to receive the sisters also with them.

Y. M. 1838.   Art. 9. Whether we have the right to appoint deacons, without laying hands on them according to the example of the apostles, Acts 6 : 6?   Considered, and resolved to postpone the further consideration of this query to the next annual meeting.

Y. M. 1839.   Art. 8. With regard to the laying on of hands on deacons, it was concluded to leave it as heretofore.   See also Y. M. 1844 : 1 ; 1845 : 11 ; 1846 : 3 ; Tenn. 6.

Y. M. 1840.   Art. 1. Whether it be agreeable to the gospel, as the brethren do hold elections for teachers and deacons?   Considered, that our mode to hold elections is according to the gospel, and that we do not see how to improve it.

4

Y. M. 1848.   Art. 4. How to forward a brother to the ministry as speaker according to the gospel?   Considered, that the church is exhorted to prayer to guide them in a proper choice, not discussing the subject with each other, but keeping their thoughts before God only; two ordained elders to be invited by the church to hold the election, who shall preside (at the election) and declare the one having the highest number of votes as chosen; the brother so chosen, having declared his willingness to fulfill the duties laid on him, is then received with hand and kiss.

Art. 7. How to make arrangements that in every church brethren be authorized to baptize and serve at communion tables?   Considered, to leave this to the judgment of the churches, with the advice of neighboring ordained elders, whether they think it necessary or expedient.

Y. M. 1848.   Art. 16. About the laying on of hands on deacons, it was unanimously considered, to postpone the discussion of this subject indefinitely, until there is reason to hope that it may be done calmly and without prejudice.

Y. M. 1858.   Art. 42. How is it considered if a member moves off some distance and be absent a while, and then return on a visit, and then while at the place at which he formerly resided, conducting himself either becoming or unbecoming a follower of Christ, the church gives him permission to exhort or preach, by taking silence for consent?   Considered, not according to the order of the brethren to do so.

Y. M. 1862.   Art. 4. In installing official members into office in the church, is there to be any difference observed between near relations ? Answer.—There is no difference to be observed.

Y. M. 1862.   Art. 50. Is it advisable to hold an election for a minister or deacon in one part of a congregation, in that in which it is most needed, and none but the members in that part voting, it being too small to form a separate church, providing the whole church consents to hold such an election ?   Answer.—We consider it advisable to do so.

CHURCH COUNCIL.

Y. M. 1845.   Art. 8. How is it considered, if a brother will rebel against the counsel held at council meetings; and say it is an abomination to God?   Considered, that such a brother should be visited and exhorted, and if he would not hear and obey the admonition, he could not be held as a brother.

Y. M. 1848.   Art. 26. Whether it is proper in all cases to ask counsel before giving a letter of recommendation ?   Considered, to be best always first to take the counsel of the church.

Y. M. 1848, Indiana.   Art. 7. How it is viewed, when persons living in one district request to be baptized and received into church-fellowship in the other district, whether it is proper to receive them without counsel of the district in which they live ?   Considered, that we deem it advisable, and it has been the general course of the brethren, in a case where a person made application for baptism in a meeting out of the district in which the applicant lives, to hold counsel with the members of that church in whose bounds he resides.

Y. M. 1856. Art. 9. How is it considered, where there is a church with a bishop and two speakers, one authorized to baptize, &c., and the other not, and a case of difficulty occurs between two members, and is brought before the church, those three ministers being present; but the two first being relatives to the parties, they authorize the third to attend to the case, and present it before the church; the question is, would it be considered legal? Considered legal.

The apostle informs us, that though things may be lawful, they are not always expedient. The position of the old brethren was accordingly, and they would in such a case have called brethren from other churches to act in it.

Y. M. 1857. Art. 13. What right have any two or three churches to reconsider the action of another church, and that without an, representation from the church upon whose decision they sit in judgment, and then reinstate members which said church had excluded? Answer.—We consider that one branch of the church has no right to restore a member to his place in the church, when he had been excluded by another branch of the church, without the concurrence of the church which excluded him.

Y. M. 1862. Art. 14. How is it considered, when a church has several ministers of equal standing, and none of them ordained; has the housekeeper, or have the ministers a right to call to their assistance an ordained brother, without the counsel of the church? Answer.—They have not the right to do so without the counsel of the church.

Art. 55. Which is the most advisable in holding council meetings, to ask each individual member for his consent, or to take silence for consent? Answer.—In all weighty matters it is best for each member to answer.

CHURCHES, TOO LARGE, to be subdivided.

Y. M. 1810, or rather of a special meeting, we find the following record: " August 11, 1810. We, the undersigned brethren, upon request of some members and upon our own approbation have made a general visit and investigation of almost all the members in the Conococheague church, whether there could not an arrangement be made, that the visit in said church and other necessary things could be carried out better, inasmuch as the district of the church is rather extensive, and for the better satisfaction of the church than has been for some time done? To this end we have presented our views and judgment to all the members that had assembled in manner and form, as follows: have asked them whether they felt satisfied, if the church were divided in so far that bro Nicholas Martin should have the oversight on that side of the Conococheague, where he lives? The visit and all necessary things, such as baptizing and breaking of bread, &c., in said church on said side of the water should lay upon him, and he should also have the oversight over the members in M'Connell's Cove and those who live near where the beloved brother Ohlinger lives. Brother Ohlinger should undertake nothing of importance without seeking counsel with brother Nicholas Martin. Just so should brother David Long have the oversight on the other side of Conococheague, where he lives, as far as the district of said church extends, to attend to the visit and everything that is necessary, as baptizing and breaking of bread with the counsel of the church. But when important matters should occur to require the judgment of the church (in criminal cases) or otherwise, on either side, and the brother who was set as housekeeper thought, as also the members thought, that it would be better to call the other brother to be along with them in the counsel, they should have entire liberty to do so; and we think it would be proper, and also according to amity and love, that both brethren should stand on an equality in their office, and be considered as stewards in said church. Yet they should not divide the meetings (by this we apprehend is meant, that they should not have separate meetings on one and the same day), but should continue to hold the meetings together (as heretofore). Is the meeting on brother Nicholas' side, he should see to it, in case brother David had a call elsewhere, or for some other cause could not come, that the meeting is attended to as usual; and if the meeting is on brother David's side, he should be careful, in case brother Nicholas had another call or could not come, that the meeting is properly held and continued (by a new appointment). But when both brethren come to meeting, then the brother in whose district it is shall commence and also close the meeting, unless upon his request and urging the other brother relieve him of this duty, to the end that all things may be done decently and in order, to which the whole church have given their sanction (at least), as many as were present.

In testimony whereof, the following brethren signed (the paper).

. Henry Danner,
Herman Blaser,
Martin Garber, &c.

This, though not strictly an act of general counsel, contains such excellent advice for ministers even in our own day, that we could not refrain from inserting it here. Study it, my dear ministering brethren, and not only that, but practice it, and you will find that much of the jealousy, temptation, and often very severe trials might be obviated, if we were heeding such simple rules as here laid down, and especially the gospel principle, to esteem others more highly than our (so very dear, and still so very bad) selves!!

CLASS MEETINGS, &c.

Y. M. 1838. Art. 10. Whether it be right for members to take part in Sunday schools, class meetings, and the like (under the control of other denominations)?   Considered, most advisable to take no part in such like things.

COLLECTING ALMS.   (See "*Alms.*")

COLONIZATION SOCIETY.

Y. M. 1851.   Art. 14. Whether it would be contrary to our profession and the doctrine of Christ, to make contributions to, or become members of the American Colonization Society, with the view of the furtherance of the liberty of the African race ?   Considered, that a person may contribute to the Society, but not become a member. ·

This distinction was undoubtedly made from the consideration that the colonization of free persons of color from this country was rather calculated to enhance the value of poor slaves, and make their liberation more hopeless.

COLORED PERSONS.

Y. M. 1835.   Art. 1. How it is considered, to receive colored persons into the church?   (The object of the question was not, whether they should be received at all, but whether they could or must be received or treated altogether like white members.)   It was considered, that inasmuch the gospel is to be preached to all nations and races, and if they come as repentant sinners, believing in the gospel of Jesus Christ, and apply for baptism, we could not consistently refuse them.   But inasmuch we receive our fellow members with the holy kiss, and there is a repugnance in some of our white members to salute colored persons in this manner, the colored members should bear with that weakness, and not offer the kiss to such weak members until they become stronger, and make the first offer, &c.   Otherwise, if they (the colored members) prove faithful, they should be considered on an equality of full membership.

Y. M. 1845.   Art. 2. In regard to receiving colored members into the church, it was considered, to leave it to the counsel of every individual church, as it is done in all cases; but if colored persons are once received as members into the church, the members should be at liberty to salute them in like manner as (we do) white members; at the same time having patience with those who may be weak in the faith, and cannot do so.   The assembled elders, however, consider it as the more perfect way, to which we all should strive to come, namely, that love which makes no distinction in the brotherhood in this respect.   See James 2 : 1–10.

Y. M. 1849.   Art. 31. How are we to conduct with colored members at communion ?   Considered, that this ought to be left to the individual churches, in which such members are, only that they ought not to be debarred from the Lord's table on account of their color.

COMMUNING WITH OTHER DENOMINATIONS.

Y. M. 1821.   Art. 3. How far brethren have liberty to commune with men who do not strictly adhere to the truth, was considered in council thus: that it is very dangerous to commune with such people as do not hold entirely the doctrine of Christ, since the apostle says, "If there come any unto you, and bring not this doctrine, receive him not in your house, neither bid him God speed," (2 John 10); and the counsel is, to give them no liberty to speak in our meetings.

COMMUNION.

Y. M. 1819. Art. 3. Whether we could break the bread (of communion) without having a supper? We hold, that we ought by all means in all the exercises (ordinances) look to the testimony of Jesus and his example; for the Lord Jesus, shortly before his suffering, when he instituted the Lord's supper, &c., after he had washed his disciples' feet, he did eat the supper with them, where he also dipped the sop, and gave it to Judas; see John 13 : 26. And Mark 14 : 18, " And as they sat, and did eat, Jesus said, Verily I say unto you, One of you which eateth with me shall betray me." And v. 22, " And as they did eat, Jesus took bread, and blessed, and brake it, and gave to them, and said, Take, eat: this is my body, &c."

Y. M. 1830. Art. 1. Whether a minister may break the bread of communion and communicate the cup of thanksgiving to a sick person, who is not a member? Considered, as contrary to our faith and conscience, and as more advisable to point or direct the sick to Christ and inward communion.—Another question presented and answered, that sick persons, who wish to be baptized, but feel too weak, might be received under the promise, that if restored to health they would submit to the command and ordinance of Christ, and in case of their death they may find comfort in the reflection, that God sees their good intentions, and may accept them for the deed.

Y. M. 1831. Art. 2. Similar to the foregoing.

Y. M. 1834. Art. 12. How it is considered, when a brother, not yet ordained, should administer the communion in presence of ordained brethren? (If the ordained brethren desire him to do so, there can be no objection; on the contrary, it is desirable for young hands in any work to have more experienced friends near to advise or assist.)

Y. M. 1841. Art. 8. Whether a minister has a right to break the bread of communion to a sick person that is not a member of the church? Considered, that a minister has not any authority in the gospel to do so; but that he should direct such a soul to the mercy of God in Christ Jesus, and to the terms and promises of the gospel.

Y. M. 1844. Art. 9. What to do in case a member on a sick or deathbed requests to have the bread of communion broken unto him? Considered, that the word of God does not seem to us to justify the breaking of the bread of communion to an individual member, for where there is but one there can be no communion; and that therefore we would be more safe to direct such a member to the grace and mercy of God in Christ Jesus, and the advice of the apostle, James 5 : 14, where he says, "Is any sick among you, let him call for the elders of the church, and let them pray over him, anointing him with oil in the name of the Lord, &c." (This is the ordinance, it seems, specially instituted for the *sick*.) If they still insist upon partaking of the bread and wine in remembrance of their dying Saviour, they might be gratified, as it has been done heretofore, when there should be a love feast in the neighborhood, by sending to them of the blessed bread and wine, or by holding a small love feast at their houses, in the right time and in the proper order.

Y. M. 1851. Art. 12. Whether it is according to the gospel for brethren to administer the communion to a sick or disabled member in the day-time, and without celebrating the other ordinances connected with it? Considered, not to be according to the gospel.

Y. M. 1861. Art. 8. Is it according to the gospel for brethren to administer the communion to the sick or disabled members in the day-time, and without celebrating the other ordinances connected with it? Considered, not according to the gospel, because the Master instituted it in the night. However, there is no impropriety in attending to it, if done in the regular way, and at the proper time, in connection with the other ordinances instituted with it.

Y. M. 1862. Art. 68. How shall we proceed in case a sick member requests the communion? Will any time do? And must feet-washing and the supper accompany the communion? Answer.—We consider it best to administer it in the evening, according to the example of Christ. John 13.

COMPLAINT AGAINST A MEMBER.

Y. M. 1843. Art. 10. Whether a complaint against a member may be taken up in the church, that is of several years standing? Considered, that this depends in a great measure upon circumstances. In complaints of a private nature between brother and brother, the course which our Saviour prescribes, Matt. 18, ought to be pursued, and when we have taken the two first steps toward a reconciliation, without being satisfied, then "tell it unto the church" is the Saviour's command; and when the yearly visit has gone round, and the bread of communion has been broken, and we neglected to obey this command, the church is not bound afterward to take up our complaint. But in case a fault had been committed by a member, and was not known to the complaining member until after a length of time, it is still his duty to tell it unto the church, and the complaint is to be taken up by the church.

CONFESSION. (See "*Acknowledgment.*")

CONFORMITY TO THE WORLD.

Y. M. 1804. Art. 8. Further, it has been discussed about the evil, offensive to God and the holy angels in heaven, and also to the faithful souls on earth, namely, about the new fashions which are in vogue with the world, and there are here and there even believers who obey the lust of their eyes, and herein conform themselves to the world, especially the young, having gone so far astray that the Lord has cause to complain that almost all flesh have corrupted their way. Therefore, it has been deemed good, that the bishops and ministers, as well as all fathers and mothers of families, should use all diligence to resist such things, that they may not spread further, but rather might be done away; especially when there are persons desiring to be received into the church, it should be laid before them, that such is contrary to the doctrine of salvation, and that it is their duty to deny themselves, and when they are willing to lay such things aside, then we may baptize them cheerfully, hoping that they will continue to receive further instruction, &c.

Y. M. 1817.   Art. 2. Concerning conforming to the world in wearing fashionable clothing and everything that is high, without exception, it was considered, that when a member should herein be found guilty, he should be admonished, and if the admonition would not be heeded, we could not hold such in full fellowship, inasmuch the Saviour says, "That which is highly esteemed among men is abomination in the sight of God." Luke 16 : 15.

Y. M. 1822, Canton.   Art. 6. How it is considered, when members will not heed the counsel of love of the brethren, with regard to conforming to the world in clothing, &c.? It was considered, for the third time in the great council, that when a member has been admonished in love once and again, we would not break bread with such. But at this meeting it has been considered, that when they will not receive counsel in love, we could not hold such member in full fellowship according to the gospel. Also such who permit those high fashions in their children who are yet under their control, and especially the bishops and ministers in the church should be examples of the flock.

Y. M. 1834. Art. 11. Concerning high and fashionable clothing, &c., and conformity to the world, it was considered a great evil as heretofore, which is not to be tolerated in the church.

Y. M. 1840.   Art. 7. Concerning the lamentably prevailing evil, that members conform themselves so much to the world in building, house furniture, apparel, &c., and even in sleighing have bells upon their horses ? It was considered, that all brethren and members, and especially ministers, should withstand and labor against this growing evil, and that anything unbecoming for brethren should be avoided.

Y. M. 1845.   Art. 6. In regard to members conforming too much with the world in fashionable dressing, building and ornamenting houses in the style of those high in the world, it was considered, that it is a dangerous and alarming evil, and ought not to be among the humble followers of the lowly Jesus.

Y. M. 1846. Art. 10. About pride in its various forms, which is creeping into the church, it is thought highly necessary that the yearly meeting instruct and urge it upon all the overseers of the church to see especially to that matter, and protest strongly against all manner of superfluities and vanity, such as building fine houses, having paintings, carpeting and costly furniture, &c., together with the adorning of the body too much after the fashion of the world. We believe that we should deny ourselves, and abstain from these things, especially the laborers in the word, who are called to be examples of the flock.

Y. M. 1849. Art. 25. Whether it would not be agreeable to the gospel, to advise those members who have been in the church two or three years, and are still conformed to this world, not to come to communion, until they deny themselves and become transformed from the world, after being admonished thereto? Considered, that conformity to the world presents itself in such various ways, that we cannot erect a standard in regard to it, so as to authorize the church to prohibit such members from partaking of the communion, but such members should be admonished and reproved by the church again and again.

Y. M. 1861. Art 3. Inasmuch as the brethren have decided in conference, that members who would not conform to the order in dress as generally practiced by the old brethren and sisters, that they could not have the privilege to the communion. . But as this does not restrain them into the order, we wish to know whether the church has the right to deal with them as offenders, when they will not conform in dress or to wearing caps, and leave off wearing hoops? Considered, that such members should be admonished, and that warmly too, to lay aside all superfluities, and conform to the order of the church. Otherwise they must and will be regarded as disobedient members. See Rom. 12.

Y. M. 1862. Art. 22. How is it considered for sisters to wear hoops, and to conform themselves to the new fashions of the world? Shall we tolerate it or not? Answer.—The answer to the third query of last yearly meeting is re-adopted.

Y. M. 1863. Art. 3. How are we to deal with sisters who are wearing hoops? They should be admonished once and again, and if they will not heed the admonitions, they should be dealt with according to Matt. 18. (See Min. 1861, Art. 3.)

Y. M. 1864. Art. 7. When the apostles prohibited the wearing of gold and pearls (1 Tim. 2: 9, 1 Pet. 3: 3), are gold watches to be included? Answer.—As the carrying of gold watches may and is likely to lead to pride, we think it advisable not to wear them.

Art. 8. How is it considered by the brethren in yearly council assembled, in relation to the members who do not conform to the order of the brethren in the wearing of apparel, and in the wearing of their hair, but follow the fashions of the world? Answer.—We think that the ministering brethren should heartily admonish and urge the members to conform to the order of the brethren, and set them a good example, and if those who are admonished again and again, and that by the church too as well as by the ministers, will not hear, the word of God directs us what to do with them. Matt. ch. 18.

Art. 10. Is it considered right, according to the gospel, for a minister to wear a soldier's overcoat when in the pulpit, or at other times; and if it is not, how is such a brother to be dealt with, if he should continue to wear it after being admonished? Answer.—It is considered not advisable for any brother, whether a minister or private member, to wear military clothing, and if he is admonished, and still persists in being disobedient, he should be dealt with according to the 18th chap. of Matthew.

CONGREGATIONAL.

Congregationalism is defined by Webster "as that system of church government which vests all ecclesiastical power in the assembled brotherhood of each local church as an independent body." Charles Buck describes *Congregationalists*, "as a denomination of Protestants, so called from their maintaining that each particular church or congregation is authorized by Christ to exercise all the acts of ecclesiastical power and privilege within itself, without being subject to the jurisdiction or control of any bishop, synod, presbytery or council composed of delegates from different associated churches." Now it happened that nearly one hundred years ago a certain writer, Morgan Edwards by name, and an English Baptist minister, in his "Materials toward a History of American Baptists," made mention of our Brethren, and among other things, that our churches were "Congregational," and this was republished again and again in other works, without being contradicted.

There are three systems of church government in vogue among the Protestant denominations in this country: the *Episcopal*, the *Presbyterian* and the *Congregati nal*. Neither of these answers or corresponds with our system, which we will call the *primitive* system. True, we have bishops, though the title is not assumed by those who are intrusted with that office, but they are calling themselves simply elders, and they are nothing like the great prelates of the Protestant Episcopal Church, who exercise authority over all the churches of a whole State or other large district. Neither are our bishops like those of the *Methodist Episcopal Church*, who have power, every year or two, to transfer all their subordinate ministers from one place to another, according to their own personal judgment, so that after every conference a general moving takes place among their clergy, with few exceptions. Our bishops are simply overseers over that one church where they reside, and over the one or two churches that may be destitute of an overseer in their immediate neighborhood; but it was always considered, that they should exercise their duty only by and with the consent of the respective church. And though he has the privilege and duty to exercise his office any where he may come, in a properly established church, he can do so only by request or invitation of that church. So it is evident that we are not Episcopalians in the common acceptation, but only in the scriptural sense of the word.

The same is the case with regard to *Presbyterianism*. Whatever authority may be claimed by modern presbyteries (elderships) separate and apart from the church (membership), no number of presbyters or elders in our church can exercise any authority, lay down any rules for the church, without the consent of the church. So then we are not Presbyterians.

If any one will say now, Then of course you must be Independents or Congregationalists; are you not? To this we answer emphatically, No. So far from feeling ourselves being independent, we know we are dependent, as in our natural condition, upon God for our life and every thing we have and are, and unto our fellow mortals, who prepare for us those things we cannot prepare for ourselves; so we are dependent upon God for every spiritual blessing, and upon our fellow Christians to assist us in obtaining those blessings. And tha' our churches were *not* founded on the *Congregational* principle, as defined above, is evident from the following historical

FACTS.

1. The first and oldest of our churches in America is in Germantown, near Philadelphia, Pa. It was established in 1723, Peter Becker being the first minister. If they had wished to act upon the "Congregational" principle, they might have done so, without asking any person outside of their immediate neighborhood, and as yet there was no other church of our faith on this side of the Atlantic. But before they took any step in organizing themselves into a church, and establishing weekly meetings for public worship, or before they ever held a public meeting for worship in this country, we are informed, they visited all their dispersed brethren and fellow believers as far as Skippach, Falconer Swamp, Oley, &c., undoubtedly to seek their advice and consent to the important step they were to take, and only after they had got this, they commenced to hold weekly meetings, we are told, alternately, "at brother Peter Becker's and ——— Gomorry's." And this principle. that a local church should not undertake anything of importance without counsel and consent of the brethren generally, outside of that locality, has ever been upheld to this day, with very few exceptions, and these exceptions have most always proved calamitous to such churches as ventured upon such an exceptional course.

2. The second fact to prove that local churches among us do not pretend to act independently of other churches is this, that to every love feast that is held in any church (excepting where a sick member requests a little love feast to be held in his house), members and ministers are invited from other churches to this day.

3. No choice is held in any church, even only for a single deacon, without two or more elders being present from other churches to conduct the choice.

4. No case of censure against an elder, minister or deacon, is taken up in counsel before a local church, without the presence of elders and as many ministering and private members from other churches.

5. No case, of which avoidance may be probably the result, is undertaken in a local church without some elders from other churches.

Now these facts prove very evidently that a local church among us does not lay claim to possessing all power, unless in contradiction to the fundamental principles and practice of our brotherhood.

Y. M. 1863.   Art. 20.   Can an arm of the church (or a local church) be congregational, or act independent from all the churches of our fraternity, and still be in full union with the church?   Answer.—It cannot, according to the gospel and the order of the brethren.   See Rom. 12 : 4, 5; 1 Cor. 1 : 10; Ephes. 5 : 2, 4, &c.

COUNCIL OF THE CHURCH.

Y. M. 1846, Tennessee.   Art. 4.   How it is considered for a bishop, with a few members, to expel a member without taking the council of the church?   Considered, that in all such important matters the church must be counseled.

Y. M. 1848, Ohio.   Art. 26.   Whether it is proper, in all cases to ask counsel (of the church) before giving a letter of recommendation?   Considered, to be best always first to take the counsel of the church.

Same year, Indiana.   Art. 7.   How it is viewed, when persons living in one district request to be baptized and received into church fellowship in another district, whether it is proper to receive them without counsel of the district in which they live?   Considered, that we deem it advisable, and it has been generally the course of the brethren, in a case where a person made application for baptism in a meeting out of the district in which the applicant lives, to hold council with the members of that church in whose bounds he resides.

Y. M. 1856. Art. 9. How is it considered, where there is a church with a bishop and two speakers, authorized to baptize, &c., and the other not, and a case of difficulty occurs between two members, and is brought before the church, those three ministers being present; but the two first being relatives to the parties, they authorize the third to attend to the case, and present it before the church. The question is, would it be considered legal? Considered, legal.

Y. M. 1862. Art. 14. How is it considered, when a church has several ministers of equal standing, and none of them ordained, has the housekeeper, or have the ministers, a right to call to their assistance an ordained brother (to a church council) without the counsel of the church? They have not the right to do so without the counsel of the church. (Should this not be reconsidered?)

Art. 55. Which is the most advisable in holding council meetings, to ask each individual member for his consent, or to take silence for consent? In all weighty matters it is best for each member to answer.

COVERING OF THE HEAD.

Y. M. 1848, Ohio. Art. 6. Whether the Scriptures require that women praying or prophesying, should have any other covering than their hair, and whether it includes alike married or unmarried women? Considered, unanimously, that they all should have a covering on their heads (besides their own hair). Read 1 Cor. 11 : 2–15.

In cases like the present, which concern the female portion of the church, would it be out of the way or contrary to the gospel to appoint a committee of elderly sisters (perhaps with an aged brother elder), to consider such questions and report thereon? It would seem to be consistent with the principles of equality, see Gal. 3 : 28, and their verdict would perhaps have more weight with their younger sisters.

. Y. M. 1856. Art. 26. Would it be proper to reconsider the 6th query of 1848? Seeing it is admitted that sisters should wear a covering, what should that covering be according to the gospel? We are satisfied, with our ancient brethren, that the plain cap worn by our dear aged sisters is a covering, as required by the Scriptures according to Paul.

Y. M. 1862. Art. 19. Inasmuch it is the order of the brethren, that sisters should wear caps, what should be done with a sister in case of stubbornness? And should there be any allowance made for the unmarried? We consider it is the duty of all the sisters to have on a plain covering at the time of worship.

DEACONS, THEIR OFFICE AND DUTY.

Y. M. 1835, Ohio. Art. 4. What is the duty of a visiting brother? First, as visiting brethren and overseers of the poor in the church, they have to assist and attend to the yearly general visit from house to house;

and it is necessary and their duty, when the church is divided into different visit-districts, to take the lead in the visit as well as that of the ministers; and in case the ministers could not assist on account of sickness, it is
the duty of the deacons to carry out the visit with other brethren, and to
bring before the ministers and the church what they have found. Further, when anything of importance is to be investigated in the church,
the ministers have the right to request them (the deacons) to accompany
them, or if the case is not of special importance, to send them (the deacons) to investigate the matter and bring it before the ministry. Further,.it is their duty, inasmuch as they have been elected to be overseers
of the poor, to visit the sick, especially if they are poor, who may be in
distress by reason of sickness or other causes, to examine their case, and
to report to the ministry, and, if necessary, the ministers to hold a council with the church what is further to be done. When money or grain
is contributed in the church for the poor in the church, it is their duty
to keep a regular book account of what they receive, and what they lay
out for the poor or otherwise for the church, so that they are able at times
to render an account with and to the church. Upon the whole, all that
may occur in the church and is to be investigated, is committed to their
care, and if they hear of anything, to bring it before the ministers, to
counsel whether it is to be examined, and to see it done if found necessary.

Further, it is their calling to assist the ministers at meeting, by reading the Scriptures, by using freedom in prayer, and to bear testimony to
what was spoken; and if it should happen that no minister (of the word)
could come to meeting, it is their duty to lead the worship by·sing-
ing, prayer and reading the Scriptures, and if they feel so, to exhort to
the edification of the congregation; yet it was the counsel of the old
brethren that it is not their calling to rise on their feet in order to exhort; and thus to conclude the meeting in the usual order, and to make
the ordinary appointments for meeting. Again, when a minister is called to hold meetings in another district, and he requests the visiting brethren to give him company and assistance, it is their duty to assist, and
one or the other to go with him.

Further, it is their duty to serve at tables; when a love feast is held, to
make the necessary preparations, to call as many other brethren as they
need to assist, and at the time of the love feast to see to it that the sisters can get all things ready at the proper time, and themselves setting
the tables, and so in all things see to it that everything is done decently
and in order.

Y. M. 1841. Art. 9. Whether a deacon or visiting brother may give
testimony to what a deacon has said, while there is one or more ministers
present that have not spoken, and request him to speak? Considered,
that he may if requested.

Y. M. 1843.   Art. 1. Is it agreeable with the word of God for a deacon or visiting brother to stand up in public meeting and exhort, when sufficient time has been spent already?   Considered, that according to the word of God " all things shall be done decently and in order," and as teaching is the proper office of the teachers, and not of deacons, they ought not to go any further than their calling requires of them where it is not necessary, and it would not be advisable for a teacher to urge them— the deacons—any further than duty calls them.

Y. M. 1838.   Art. 9. Whether we have the right to appoint deacons, without laying hands on them according to the example of the apostles? Acts 6 : 6.   Considered and resolved, to postpone the further consideration of this query to the next annual meeting.

Y. M. 1840.   Art. 8. The question about laying on of hands on deacons, decided to leave the matter as heretofore.

Y. M. 1844.   Art. 1. About the laying on of hands on deacons.   This query has been before the annual meeting of 1838 and 1839, and the brethren generally considered, that since there is no direct command to do so in the New Testament, and on the contrary the apostle gives advice, 1 Tim. 5 : 12, " Lay hands suddenly on no man," it would be best to proceed in this matter as the brethren of old have done.   This is, however, laid down with this proviso, that if any brother could throw more light on the subject, it might be presented again at the next annual meeting.

Y. M. 1845.   Art. 11. The question about the laying on of hands on deacons having been brought again before the yearly meeting, and being of such consequence and importance, it was considered, that since our churches are not generally represented (at this time), not one brother from Pennsylvania or Maryland, and also not many of our elder brethren, whose counsel had been given last year on this article, being present at this time, it would be best to refer this question to the next annual meeting, recommending the same to the (prayerful) consideration of all the churches.

Y. M. 1846.   Art. 3. About the laying on of hands on deacons.   On this much and long agitated question it was finally laid down as the safest way to continue as heretofore.   The objection, that it was an apostolical order, which ought to be observed, was answered, that (even) supposing the apostles had laid their hands on the heads of the deacons, which in our apprehension cannot be made evident, as little as a single walk of a few men through a wilderness will make a road or beaten track, just as little a thing once done makes it an order ; and that if the example of the chosen seven (Acts 7) having had hands laid on them, would have to be observed, as some of our beloved brethren understand it, then we would also have to imitate the example of the same church, " who had all things common, and sold their possessions and goods, and parted them to all men, as every man had need." Acts 2 : 44, 45.   But since we do not find in any other church established by the apostles any thing similar, and since there is also no testimony that the apostles ever after practiced the laying on of hands on the heads of deacons, our beloved brethren will not think hard of us, if under these and other considerations we abide by that practice with which so many faithful brethren in our churches have been introduced to the office of deacons and (ministers) speakers of the word.

Y. M 1846. (Tennessee.) Art. 6. Whether a deacon can be ordained to the office of bishop? Considered, that we have no authority for so doing. See 1 Tim. 3 : 10 and 5 : 22.—Art. 7. Whether a deacon should fill up appointments in the absence of the minister? Considered, that he may by singing, praying, exhorting, and reading the Scriptures; but that he is not to preach until he is legally authorized by the church. Art. 11. Whether a deacon has a right to appoint meetings and preach without being authorized by the church? Considerod, that he has no authority for so doing, but that he should try to discharge the duties incumbent upon him in the office for which he has been set apart.

Y. M. 1847. Art. 4. A request that the present yearly meeting reconsider the third query as it stands on the minutes of Y. M. 1846, concerning the laying on of hands on the deacons. It was almost unanimously concluded, that it would be better for the present to leave this subject rest as it is.—Art. 5. Would it be considered expedient for a church to elect a brother for the office of deacon, whose wife is not a member? · Considered, that if he be a brother of good report, and one in whom the church may have confidence, this circumstance ought not to hinder the church from electing him to the office of deacon, provided there be no other objections. 1 Tim. 3:12.

Y. M. 1848. Art. 16. About the laying on of hands on deacons it was unanimously considered, to postpone the discussion of this subject indefinitely, until there is reason to hope that it may be done calmly and without prejudice.

Y. M. 1850. Art. 27. About the laying on of hands on deacons, when installed into office. Considered, that the brethren, after a long continued and attentive investigation of the word of God on this agitating subject in question, have come to the following

CONCLUSION.

Whereas. it is plain from the Acts and the proceedings of the apostles, that there must have been deacons in those days, and that these deacons must have been active in their office, before the seven teachers or evangelists were chosen and installed into their office; see Acts 2: 45, and 4: 35, " Distribution was made unto every man, according as he had need," from which we conclude, if distributions were made to every man, there must of course have been those that made them. Hence it is, the opinion of the brethren in this council assembled, that the seven chosen and set before the apostles (Acts 6 : 6), were selected from among, as we might say the first class of teachers, (see Acts 6: 3, 8; ch. 8: 6, 7, 36–38; ch. 21: 8), and hands laid on them by the apostles to establish them, to settle the difficulty that had arisen among the deacons about the daily ministration, and that the seven were not deacons in the restricted sense of the word, and were never called such, the word "deacon"* not once occurring in the whole book of the Acts. Therefore, the laying on of hands ought to be practiced on such old teachers that are set apart (for the office of overseers or bishops); and deacons ought to be received into their office by hand and kiss, as the practice has been hitherto with the brethren.

The following was added to the minutes of the same year in an appendix on the same subject:

Whereas, The brethren of the various churches have taken into serious consideration the subject of the laying on of hands on deacons, and could therefore come to no satisfactory decision, we have now come to the following

CONCLUSION.

First, that the seven brethren elected, Acts 6, were not elected from the common (private) members, but from the teachers and evangelists; see Acts 21: 8.

Second, the business for which they were elected must have been to settle the disputes that had arisen among the then existing deacons, as such must have been already among them, since we read that "there were distributions made, as every one had need," see Acts 4: 35. Therefore, as we have no evidence that hands were laid on deacons elected from among the common brethren, it is thought proper and good to proceed as the brethren have heretofore done in the election of deacons. That there were such (deacons) in the churches in the time of the apostles, see Phil. 1: 1; 1 Tim. 3: 8, 10, 12, 13; and we now have need of them in the church too, that is, if deacons are necessary in a church. That the church come together with the elders and bishops, and with prayer and fasting let the church proceed to choose such an one as may be pointed out to them by the Spirit of God, and receive him by the holy kiss and the right hand of fellowship. We hereby also exhort our brethren everywhere, no more after this to cite as authority for deacons the seven elected from among the evangelists, Acts 6, but only the office

---

*The word deacon (Greek, *διακονος*,) occurs about thirty times in the New Testament, and is rendered in the common English version twenty times *minister*, seven times *servant*, and only three times *deacon*. See Matt. 20: 26, 22: 13, 23: 11; Mark 9: 35, 10: 43; John 2: 5, 9, 12: 26; Rom. 13: 4 twice, 15: 8, 16: 1, 1 Cor 3: 5; 2 Cor. 3: 6, 6: 4, 11: 15 twice, and 23; Gal. 2: 17; Eph. 3: 7, 6: 21; Phil. 1: 1; Col. 1: 7, 23, 25, 4: 7; 1 Thess. 3: 2; 1 Tim. 3: 8, 12, 4: 6. The English version contains the word *deacon* twice more, namely, 1 Tim. 3: 10, 13; but the original Greek has not the same word, and the German translation is more correct in these two instances, saying literally, verse 10, "Then let them *serve*, being found faithful;" and in verse 13, "For they that *serve* well, purchase to themselves a good degree, &c."

itself. From this mistake has originated the vexatious question which has agitated our brethren (in some parts) so long and so grievously. This, or something similar, we desire our brethren in council to place on our minutes, so that the subject may once be settled.

In citing Acts 6 : 1–8, when a choice was to be held in a church for any officers, our ancient brethren were not mistaken, inasmuch as they referred simply to it as the first and in fact the only example of the apostles on record, how they proceeded in conducting the.choice; at the same time, they held the principle that the church had authority from the Lord to define the duties of every officer, and to hold them responsible in their respective office for neglecting or transgressing their duties. It was only from a misapprehension of some brethren, both as to the proper application of Scripture declarations and examples, and to the proper limits of every office as understood by the old brethren, that the vexatious question above alluded to originated. If brethren in every office are truly humble, they will be satisfied with that degree of authority intrusted to them, and the manner and form by which the church has inducted them into office, and indeed it is desirable such questions would remain settled for good, and 2 Tim. 2 : 23 and Titus 3 : 9 were more heeded, when queries are formed, and repeatedly presented to yearly meetings.

Y. M. 1858. Art. 16. Is it right for a brother that is a deacon to give out a hymn and sing it, ten or fifteen minutes before the time appointed for commencing the meeting, when the house or room is full of people, or is it more advisable to remain silent till the time for commencing meeting arrives ? Ans. Considered, that we see no impropriety in singing, when in the estimation of the church it is done to its own edification, and to the honor of God.

Y. M. 1862. Art. 6. Is it proper for the visiting brethren at our public meetings, when there are from three to six laboring brethren present, to rise to their feet, and line out a hymn and exhort in preference to the laboring brethren, or are they to keep their seats? Ans. The laboring brethren are to conduct the meeting, and it is the duty of the visiting brethren to exhort, when liberty is given them.

Same year. Art. 39. How is it considered, when visiting brethren will, in meeting, get up on their feet and speak, when there are elected speakers present, and sometimes speak thirty minutes or upward, and that without liberty from the speakers ? If that is not in order for visiting brethren, what is the order ? Is it to stand upon their feet when they have anything to say, or to keep their seats? Ans. We consider it out of order for visiting brethren to do so, without liberty being given by ministering brethren, if such are present.

Though there has been a good deal said above, at different times and on different occasions, on the office of "deacon," with which we feel agreed fully and cordially, a few thoughts, occurring to us while we transcribed the foregoing pages, may not be amiss, and we will try to put them in the form of a direct

ADDRESS TO THE DEACONS, OR VISITING BRETHREN, OF THE PRESENT TIME.

BELOVED BRETHREN—Allow us to say a few words concerning the importance of your office, and first of all, to lay before you the word of God concerning it as recorded in 1 Tim. 3 : 8–13, "Likewise must the deacons be grave (serious), not double-tongued, not given to much wine, not greedy of filthy lucre, holding the mystery of the faith in a pure conscience. And let these also first be proved; then let them use the office of a deacon, being found blameless. Even so must their wives be grave, not slanderers, sober, faithful in all things. Let the deacons be the husbands of one wife, ruling their children and their own houses well. For they that have used the office of a deacon well, purchase to themselves a good degree, and great boldness in the faith which is in Christ Jesus."

From the very first word of this passage, "*likewise*," you will perceive that your office, though different in its duties, is equally important in the church as the office of a bishop. If it may be said, that the bishop or overseer is or should be the right eye of the church, and he with the other ministers the mouth of the church, you are or should be the right ear and the right hand of the church. THE RIGHT EAR—to hear the faint lamentations of the poor, sick and otherwise distressed members and others—to give attention to evil reports of the moral conduct of members, which, if founded in truth, would injure the character and usefulness of the church; and "holding the mystery of the faith" and the established principles and order of the church "in a pure conscience"—to watch the public ministrations of the brethren, that none but sound doctrine may be preached by them in union, and that all public meetings may be conducted to edification, "decently and in order." THE RIGHT HAND—to dispense the charities of the church according to its direction discreetly and impartially—to act in all cases of complaints against members, investigating, visiting and reporting to the church—to support your faithful ministers in the legitimate exercise of their duties by your prayers, by your testimony and defense in their behalf in and out of meeting, and to present their case to the church not only for consideration, but also for active sympathy, when duty calls them too frequently from home, spending their strength, time and money in the service of the Lord, so that their families may suffer, seeing things going wrong at home, and feeling distressingly the absence of their husband and father. Such a state of things in the families of ministers should not be overlooked by thoughtful and loving brethren, especially not by you, dear brethren deacons, whose particular province and business it is to extend your right arm to those in distress.

These few thoughts might be sufficient, together with the word of God preceding them, which inculcates the qualifications required for your office, and the great reward for a faithful discharge of your duties promised therein, to convince you, dear brethren deacons, of the great importance of your office, and the high calling to which the church has called you. But there is a still higher duty, which you may have to exercise. We are all poor fallible beings, subject to like passions as other men are, whether we be preachers, deacons or private members. Already

in the primitive churches, planted by divinely inspired apostles, it happened
sometimes that even the ministers became involved in disputes and difficulties with each other, and that there were such "doting about questions
and strifes of words whereof cometh envy, strife, railings, evil surmisings,
perverse disputings of men of corrupt minds and destitute of the truth,
&c." (1 Tim. 6 : 4, 5.) If such a sad state of things should occur in
your church, that your ministers could not agree, would not speak the
same thing, and cause confusion and disunion in the church, then,
brethren deacons, you that stand right between the ministers and the
private members, by standing up unitedly and manfully and without
partiality for the right, for order and for union, may become mediators and
peace-makers by calling elders of other churches to assistance, and thus
restore union and good feeling; and you know the peace-makers have
been blessed with a special blessing by our Saviour.

DEALING WITH MEMBERS UPON COMPLAINTS BEFORE THE CHURCH

Y. M. 1841. Art. 13. Whether a brother or member could be judged
(dealt with) consistently with the gospel, without having a hearing before
the church with privilege to defend him(or her)self? Ans. Considered,
that no brother or sister ought to be brought before the council of the
church for any accusation, without having previous information thereof
and without having the privilege of being present at the examination of
the witnesses, and also of defending himself or herself according to the
gospel.

This answer is good and right as far as it goes; but the question again arises:
If the member has been properly notified and invited to come before the council,
and he refuses to come, or at least does not come at the time appointed, what
then? Is the course of righteousness on the part of the church to be stopped in
this case? We will try to answer in the fear of the Lord, according to the general practice in our churches. As the cases may be different, and the causes of
the non-appearance of the member to be dealt with may also be different, the
church where the case has occurred can best judge whether to go on with it or
not. We will suppose three cases, such as have actually occurred in our presence. An aged brother had committed a trespass against one of the principles
of the gospel to which we hold steadfastly, though other denominations do not,
and would call the act of the brother just and right; in this case, considering the
age of the brother, and not knowing whether he had been well enough in health
or not to attend, the matter was postponed to another time. In another case, a
crime had been committed, which brought scandal upon the church. When the
guilty member was visited and invited to come before the council, and elders had
been invited from a distance specially for assisting in this case, and the member
did not come for very shame, sending word that the church should deal with her
according to the word of the Lord, and the church did so after the crime was
established by two or three witnesses, and confessed by the member before the
visiting brethren. In a third case, a similar crime had been committed, but
much aggravated by the circumstances. Again and again efforts had been made
to bring the matter before the church; but for a considerable time justice was
baffled. At last the church felt compelled to bring it to an issue. Direct and cir-
cumstantial evidence had accumulated, brethren from a considerable distance were
invited, and brethren had specially been sent to the guilty member, but he would
not and did not come. However, the case went on, and the ends of justice were
attained to the almost unanimous, though sorrowful, satisfaction of the church;
thus deciding that when a member refuses the privilege of being present at the
examination of witnesses, and also of defending himself, the church cannot be
prevented of doing her duty.

DEBTS, ABOUT BRETHREN GETTING INVOLVED IN.

Y. M. 1804. Art. 3. About such brethren, who so easily and heedlessly involve themselves in debts, and do not seek counsel, until they do not know any more how to counsel or help themselves; then they want at last counsel, when they desire and need help. It has been unanimously deemed good, that every church where such brethren live should endeavor diligently to instruct such brethren also in temporal or bodily things, that they should act considerately, and make no more debts than they can pay; and when at times their circumstances should be such that they could not see through, they should seek counsel of prudent brethren, and even the whole church is in duty bound to give counsel when requested; and if the counsel of the church should not be sufficient, it is also her duty to assist as far as possible in a case of necessity. At the same time such should be informed that if they would not receive good counsel, they should not expect or hope that the church would feel bound or willing to assist much.

Y. M. 1825. Art. 5. Whether a brother minister, that involves himself in debts, and assigns his property to his children, could serve in the ministry of the word, was considered, that when the creditors should be defrauded thereby, he should give himself over to the (judgment of the) church, and without doubt ought not to serve (in the office of a minister).

Y. M. 1832. Art. 6. How to do when a brother is indebted to another, and becomes insolvent? Ans. The church should deal with him according to the circumstances or degrees of aggravation, according to the word.

Y. M. 1841. Art. 5. Whether a brother consistently with the gospel can take the benefit of the law for insolvent debtors? Ans. Considered, that there may be cases where the involving at first, and the consequences thereupon, are not at all compatible with the gospel, and where the church could not hold such as brethren; and that there may be cases where a brother by misfortune may be brought to such extremity, and, if he were honest in his declaration, his application for the benefit of the law might even be excusable. In all such cases, however, the church has to investigate the matter, and judge according to the circumstances and nature of the case, and if the church is at a loss (in the case), to call in, as in other cases, the assistance of elders from other churches.

Y. M. 1862. Art. 30. What shall we do with brethren, of whom the world complains to the church for neglecting to pay their debts, and for causing disappointment to their creditors? Ans. If the brethren can and will not pay their debts, they should be dealt with according to the gospel as offending members.

Same year. Art. 64. How is it considered, if members owe a just debt and suffer themselves to be sued? Has the church a right to bring such members before the church (council), and investigate the case, to see whether such members have done their duty? Ans. We consider it has.

DEFENDING OUR ORDER.

Y. M. 1862.   Art. 18.   The brethren assembled in council in (the district of) the Valley of Virginia, being impressed with the importance of having the public more fully enlightened upon (the subject of) the ordinances, have agreed to adopt the plan at our communion meetings, when it is expedient in the afternoon service, to occupy the time in discussing these subjects before the commencement of, the evening exercises.   Will the annual meeting approve of this plan, insert it on the minutes, and recommend it?   Ans. While we strongly recommend the defense of the ordinances, we leave it to the direction of the churches to decide the time and place of their defense.

It seems it would be always best not to infringe on the liberty of the ministering brethren to select their subjects, with which they may feel impressed at any time or place. "Where the spirit of the Lord is there is liberty." Any prescribed plan will curtail that liberty, and may prevent the utterance of such truths that might be timely, useful, and of the utmost importance.

DEVIL, HIS PERSONALITY, AND ANGELS.

Y. M. 1856.   Art. 14.   (1) The question concerning the reality of a devil was considered, and after comparing opinions and sentiments on the subject of the reality of such a being and his nature, we agreed upon the following view: that the Scriptures recognize a devil or an evil spirit that manifests itself in the flesh.

To assist the careful reader in forming a proper judgment in this matter, the word of the Lord is added here.   The name "devil" (Greek, $\Delta\iota\alpha\beta\circ\lambda\circ\varsigma$,) occurs no less than thirty-eight times in the New Testament, to wit:

Matt. 4: 1, 5, 8, 11. Here are the facts of Christ's temptation related. If there was no personal tempter there outside of Christ, and still the temptation is admitted, then the temptation must have manifested itself in the flesh of Christ, which would be blasphemy of our most holy and sinless Saviour, and destructive to our hope of salvation through him.

Matt. 13 : 39. The enemy that sowed them is the devil.

25 : 41. Depart . . . into everlasting fire, prepared for the devil, and his angels.

Luke 4: 2, 3, 5, 6, 13. Compare with Matt. 4: 1, 11.

8 : 12. Then cometh the devil, and taketh away the word out of their hearts.

John 6 : 70. Have not I chosen you twelve, and one of you is a devil.

8 : 44. Ye are of your father the devil.

13 : 2. The devil having now put into the heart of Judas, &c.

Acts 10 : 38. Healing all that were oppressed of the devil.

13 : 10. O full of all subtlety and all mischief, thou child of the devil.

Ephes. 4 : 27. Neither give place to the devil.

6 : 11. That ye may be able to stand against the wiles of the devil.

1 Tim. 3 : 6. Lest . . . he fall into the condemnation of the devil.

       7. Lest he fell into reproach and the snare of the devil.

      11. Not slanderers (Greek, Διαβολους, devils).

2 Tim. 2 : 26. Out of the snare of the devil.

      3 : 3. False accusers (Greek, devils).

Tit. 2 : 3. Not false accusers (Greek, as above).

Heb. 2 : 14. Destroy him that had the power of death, that is, the devil.

James 4 : 7. Resist the devil, and he will flee from you.

1 Pet. 5 : 8. Your adversary, the devil, as a roaring lion.

1 John 3 : 8. Here the word occurs three times.

      3 : 10. In this the children of God are manifest, and the children of the devil.

Jude, verse 9. Contending with the devil.

Rev. 2 : 10. The devil shall cast some of you into prison.

      12 : 9. And the great dragon was cast out, that old serpent, called the Devil, and Satan.

Rev. 12 : 12. The devil is come down unto you.

      20 : 2. The dragon, that old serpent, which is the Devil, and Satan.

      20 : 10. And the devil that deceived them was cast into the lake of fire.

.A close examination of the above passages, and many others relating to the same being—the name "Satan" occurring also some thirty times in the New Testament—will assist any sincere inquirer after truth to overcome every difficulty on this subject. The objection, that these appellations are sometimes applied to men in Scripture, will vanish as soon as the reader learns that the literal meaning of the term devil (Διαβολος) is an accuser, calumniator, slanderer, or an adversary, an enemy. A greater difficulty is to reconcile the existence of such an evil, malignant and powerful being with the goodness and perfect character of God the Father Almighty, the Creator of heaven and earth, and who made all things good. But even this difficulty is obviated in Scripture, and by the fact that evil, wicked men do exist, and that God permitted such monsters of iniquity as Nero, Caligula, &c., to exist in times past. If we have fallen from our first estate of purity, and become sinners, and God still permitted us to live, while we were still sinners, why should we find it unreasonable that even angels, though superior to us in wisdom and power, still finite creatures of God, should have fallen from their first estate and become devils, and God permits them to exist for wise purposes known only to himself? The fact that there are angels which kept not their first estate, is expressly declared in the word of God. See Jude 6 : 2; Peter 2 : 4.

But while some believe too little with regard to the existence and personality, or reality as it is above expressed, of a devil, there are others who beleve too much, making of him almost a second God, all powerful and everywhere present. True, he is called the "God of this world," 2 Cor. 4 : 4. Admitted, also, that he is very powerful, knows a great deal, is very cunning and crafty, and, what is more than all, immortal. His empire is far more extensive than our globe; for he is "the prince of the power of the air," the atmosphere which surrounds the earth, Eph. 2 : 2, and has under him "principalities—powers—the rulers of the darkness of this world," Eph. 6 : 12. Remember, also, that he is not alone, not a single individual, but a prince or chief of devils, Matt. 10 : 25; Luke 11 : 15, &c.; that he has under him other angels, Matt. 25 : 41—multitudes of them, for he "drew the third part of the stars of heaven" after him in his fall, Rev. 12 : 4, and when "thousand thousands ministered unto him, and ten thousand times ten thousand stood before him" (the great Judge on the throne), Dan. 7 : 10— we may surmise that the number of falen angells amounts to many millions, united under one head; and if mankind have been enabled, by their ingenuity and the help of electricity (the telegraph), to overcome time and distance in such a manner as to bring almost all the world into immediate correspondence and connection, then it does not seem unreasonable to suppose that the ingenuity of devils is sufficiently great, and "the power of the air" (electricity) enables them to be in constant rapport with one another and with their prince, and learning all human affairs of interest to them, not only as soon as they occur, but as soon as they are spoken of by mankind, the greater part of which being under the immediate control of evil spirits, with the exception of those who have really renounced the devil and all sin, and become truly the obedient subjects of Christ, the Almighty King of kings, to whom even devils are subject. Hence, great as the power of the devil and his hosts among angels and men is, Christians with Christ on their side need not fear that power of darkness, if they are children of the light, and always on their guard and prayerful. As Christ overcame the tempter by rejecting his temptations through the word of God, and through submission to the will of his heavenly Father, even unto death, even to the ignominious death of the cross, so even the weakest Christian, standing in union with Christ and his church, will be enabled to withstand the powerful enemy of souls, and to be faithful unto death, even through Christ, and through him alone. But to deny the existence and to despise the power of the devil, and to neglect the means to escape from this power, is dangerous and foolish indeed.

DIFFERENCE IN DOCTRINE.

Y. M. 1844. Art. 7. How is considered the difference in doctrine, that some teach faith before repentance, and others repentance before faith? Ans. This query had been before a council meeting some years ago, and was answered thus: "Considered, that the difference arises when the word is not rightly divided. The apostle teaches us that the righteousness of God is revealed in the gospel from faith to faith, Rom. 1 : 17; and again, That he who cometh to God must believe that he is, and that he is a rewarder of them that diligently seek him. Heb. 11 : 6. Out of this faith, when it is quickened, repentance will come, and when the repenting sinner hears and receives the blessed gospel, an evangelical and saving faith will issue therefrom, which worketh by love, and makes itself known by keeping the commandments." To which the brethren present fully assented.

DIFFICULTIES IN CHURCHES.

Y. M. 1799. Art. 1. Whereas, there has existed for a long time a great difficulty between brother C. L. and brother J. Z., the overseers of —————— church; and whereas, there have been expressed very grave accusations and hard sayings by C. L. against some brethren, who shall be named hereafter, it has come to pass that brother C. L. has selected six brethren, and J. Z. has also selected six brethren, and they (both) have agreed to obey or submit to the advice or united counsel of those brethren, to which also the members (of the church) have consented. So we have assembled ourselves, we trust, in the fear of the Lord, and with a fervent prayer to God that he would bless our hearts with wisdom and understanding in order to be enabled to counsel our dear brethren wisely, and to come to conclusions evangelical, or according to the doctrine of the gospel. And after having heard the complaints and accusations (of both sides), we have become entirely agreed, and believe all that brother

L. has done grossly wrong against brother Z., and also against brethren A. M. and M. U's. transactions, and against J. L. and J. St., and whatsoever else might have been done (of the same nature).

Further, we believe also that wrong has been committed by J. Z. against L., but not so grossly as brother L. has done. Hence it is our unanimous conclusion, that when C. L. believes in his heart and cordially makes acknowledgment before this present brotherly and member meeting, and also before —— (his own) meeting, and asks for pardon, and also makes heartfelt confession for the suspicious (and offensive) expressions against the old brethren, and against L. and J. St., then we will, and it is hoped the members will bear with him in patience, and he may continue to serve as overseer in W. church. And what concerns Z., we have agreed, that when he makes acknowledgment before the members that he has also done wrong, and asks pardon, he shall also serve as overseer with L., yet so that in important matters, such as baptism, breaking of bread, receiving and excluding (members), he should not go on without L's. knowledge and consent; but with regard to holding meetings, attending funerals, and solemnizing marriages, he shall have equal liberty with brother L. Now, whoever of them will not submit to this above stated counsel and conclusion shall stand still in his office, until he is willing to accept it, and when it is accepted of both, there shall be hereafter no more heard of those things which are past. Unanimously concluded by us, the subscribers: Martin Urner, Martin Gaby, Henry Danner, Peter Leibert, Jacob Danner, Philip Engler, Michael Pfoutz, Martin Garber, John Greib, Martin Garber, Daniel Utz, Philip Levy, Valentine Pressel, Stephan Ulrich.

Y. M. 1803. Our cordial and united greeting of love to all our beloved brethren and members of the W—— church. We wish much grace, mercy and blessing from God, the Father of our Lord and Saviour Jesus Christ, to all our fellow-members united with us in love and faith, as also especially to our dear brethren C. L. and J. Z. It is our hearts' desire that the good God would make us all faithful laborers in his vineyard; for all that were hired by that householder were hired to labor in his vineyard, to which we wish you all much grace, blessing and salvation from God. The cause of our present writing is this: Since we, or some of us, have been informed by our dear brother Martin Gaby, who, on his journey to us, passed through W——, and also had meeting there, that brother C. L., since the big meeting, has only been a few times at meeting, and now for a considerable time has not come any more at all to meeting, so that some brethren feel oppressed in their minds on account of the word or expression which is found in that conclusion made at the big meeting, namely, "that brother J. Z. should not go on with baptism, breaking of bread, receiving and excluding, without L's. knowledge and consent;" hereupon we, the undersigned brethren, have conversed on the matter, and are of one mind on it, and now the same as it was at that time (three years before), and is in part also expressed in said conclusion, though briefly, that we all considered that brother L. had done wrong grossly, and if he would believe it from the heart, and confess and make acknowledgment, we and hopingly the members would bear with him in patience, and then he should serve as overseer in W——, and thus should brother Z. in such important matters not go on without his knowledge and consent. But if brother C. L. withdraws from the service, or from the duty of his office, contrary to the doctrine of the apostle, when he says, "If any one has an office, let him attend to the same" (German translation, Rom. 12:7), if now brother L. withdraws himself from the service of the church as overseer, so as not to attend the meetings, then he deprives himself of this honor, that brother Z. cannot counsel with him if he (bro. L.) does not attend meetings according to his duty. So it is our unanimous mind, that on this account brother Z. should not be bound or hindered to go on in his office, and faithfully discharge its duties, and prove himself a faithful laborer. But if brother L. acknowledges according to said conclusion, and endeavors to be faithful in his office, then we desire and hope the members will receive him, and not lay obstacles in his way—we mean, on account of things that are past. (Signed by most of those that signed the foregoing.)

Y. M. 1814, May 28. It has been publicly treated at the big meeting, on Pipe Creek, about the lamentable disturbance and dissension which have arisen some time ago between bro. C. H. and some members of this church with him, of one part, and the old ministers and bishop, and especially P. E. and other members, of the other part. This disturbance and dissension have existed already several years, and after said old brethren and ministers and overseers in said church had made many efforts with the church to settle the difficulty with the assistance of God, the troublesome affair has got worse still, so that said old brethren and overseers of said church had no other prospect but to counsel with other or strange brethren, and have charged the beloved old brother Henry Danner to see to it, that the matter might be settled and put to rest.

Now the loving brother was concerned about it according to his duty, and has, with other strange brethren, paid a visit at Pipe Creek, and has bro. C. H. with his adherents invited to come to the council meeting. But bro. C. H. objected; he could not come on account of his sore hand, and they came not. To the loving brother Henry Danner, to whom as aforesaid was intrusted this important affair, it was a heavy burden; so he appointed another time, and requested old brethren from afar, and paid with them another visit at Pipe Creek, especially to bro. C. H. and some of his adherents, and invited them again to come to the (council) meeting. Bro. C. H. again would not consent to come, and they did not come again, with the objection that it was not yet the time to settle the matter, and secondly, that they had not had sufficient information about the council meeting, and so they had not prepared their testimony. Then the dear brethren that had come from afar, counseled with the loving brother Danner, that this case should not remain thus, while there were members suffering under it, and some even had to depart this life under this pressure and sorrow; under these considerations, and with the advice of some brethren (of the church probably), they appointed again another meeting some months hence, and at once wrote and signed a letter of information to bro. C. II., and appointed some brethren to bring the letter to bro. C. H., and to read the same to him.

When the appointed time of the meeting came near, that strange brethren should have come, at least twelve, then bro. C. H. before the time went and made reconciliation and settlement with bro. P. E. externally with hand and kiss before the church, so that many rejoiced over it, and the meeting and appointment for the strange brethren was recalled. But that settlement and peace, alas! did not last long, and bro. C. H. with his adherents began again to complain against the church, and brought not only new complaints against the church, but raised also again the dispute about the land here and there, and without counsel and investigation in the church of the new complaints, and without counsel of other old brethren and bishops, and entirely contrary to the word of God and to the order of our Chief Shepherd and Bishop of his church and Head of his members, caused a division, and tore himself with other members from the church and the members, whom he had brought into confusion and mistrust against the old brethren and church with the hard and suspicious complaints which he, and others, against the order of God, have scattered far and wide; while, with all the invitations when strange brethren came, they never came to this day, in order to prove them with sufficient testimony, as it is required by the holy Scriptures or God in his word.

He has now, with those members he led astray, formed a separate con. gregation, and broke bread with them, not at the proper time, inasmuch as we are not to keep the feast with the old leaven, neither with leaven of malice and wickedness, but with the unleavened bread of sincerity and truth. Bro. C. II., with the others, have known that he was not in peace with the church, and especially with the housekeepers, nor they with him; and the Lord Jesus teaches us in these his precious words, "If thou bring thy gift to the altar, and there rememberest that thy brother hath aught against thee, leave there thy gift before the altar, and go thy way; first be reconciled to thy brother, and then come and offer thy gift." (Matt. 5 : 23–24.) Those whose eyes are anointed can clearly see that the whole thing is perverse. For the Spirit of God leads into all truth and union, and "as many as are led by the Spirit of God, they are the sons (children) of God," and "by this shall all men know that ye are my disciples, if you have love one to another."

And not only this, but at said supper he has introduced strange exercises, which our dear old brethren have not had, who indeed, as we believe, walked in the light, and in the pure knowledge of the truth kept

house, and entered, as we hope, into blessed rest. And as some have
heard, there has been drawn a shallow reason from Christ's words to
that practice, whereby that practice cannot be established, and it is to be
feared that said new practice is more calculated to cause disturbance,
trouble and division within, and rejoicing without among other denominations, as if the old Baptists and brethren would have now to learn from
them, that they had opened our eyes, and thus seeking persons who
are yet in the twilight, may be confused, thinking the old brotherhood
must not have had the full light, else they would not begin new practices, and thus this would serve more to scatter than to gather, and more
to the dishonor than to the honor of God.

Now since this matter has thus worked from time to time, as has been
briefly related, we (the undersigned) upon the request of said church, and
more for the sake of God, have found it our duty to take the case in consideration at this occasion, namely, in said big meeting; and several
brethren have visited bro. C. H. and his wife, and others of his members,
before the meeting, and have invited him to come with his company, and
bring his testimonies to prove his heavy complaints or accusations, in
order that those members who might have committed a fault could be
convinced, that there was hope, if they would, that all could be brought
to rest and reconciliation. But he would not come to lay the case before
the big meeting, and said there were too many judges at the big meeting—it would be better to have too few judges than too many. However,
on the second day he came to the place of the meeting, and said if the
matter was to be settled, the land would have to be altogether measured,
and they would bear the expenses.

But the council of the big meeting considered, that with further de-
ferring the case could not be improved, and slowly or never be brought
to an end, and the measuring would scarcely contribute to that end. Yet
they shall have perfect liberty to have the land surveyed, as it has been
spoken about. And upon the whole of said case it has been mutually
concluded by the whole council of the big meeting, inasmuch as brother
C. H. was never willing to come and bring sufficient testimony to prove
said accusations, we will hear and accept the testimony of brother P. E.
and of all those who were accused, on their good conscience, in hope and
trust as being true, until sufficient testimony should come, as the Scriptures require; and if sufficient testimony should come against one or the
other, then shall he, who is concerned, submit to the council of the church,
which brother P. and the accused have agreed to and promised before
the big meeting. Upon this condition we declare the beloved brother P. E.
and the other accused, as absolved, and intend at this and other occasions
to break the bread of communion in confidence and love with them, and to
hold with them full fellowship, as the Gospel of Jesus requires, and we
wish them light, grace and power from God to hasten forward on the way
of peace to the land of blessed rest. Amen

Further, it was mutually concluded, that the case as above stated is wrong and contrary to God's order according to the example and testimonies of the Old and New Testament of the Lord. From these weighty causes the big meeting concludes, that impartial brethren should be selected, and they should give themselves up for God's sake, to pay the church a general visit from house to house, and before the meeting takes place to visit also brother C. H., and all those who have cut off themselves with him, in a friendly manner, and to urge them to take steps toward peace, concord and reconciliation with the church and with God, in as far as mistakes have been made, and all those who should thus come should be cordially forgiven by the whole church.

But if one or the other would *not* accept or receive counsel according to the doctrine of Christ and his apostles, and *not* abstain from their error, with such we could not break bread, and would have to deny to them the kiss and church council after a long-suffering and sufficient admonition; and if brother C. H., with all his adherents, should oppose themselves, we would have to hold them, as the Lord Jesus says, "If he shall neglect to hear the church, let him be unto thee as a heathen man and a publican." The whole big meeting, yea, all members should be engaged and prayerful, that God would meet us with his blessing and salvation. Amen. Signed, Samuel Garber, Benjamin Bowman, George Preiss, Daniel Stober, Nicholas Martin, Jacob Beshor, Samuel Arnold, Martin Garber, David Pfoutz, John Eby, Christian Long, John Schleifer, Daniel Long, Daniel Garber, Michael Etter, Henry Gibbel, Herman Blaser, George Petry, Daniel Arnold, David Albaugh, John Diel, Jacob Shenefelt, John Price, Isaac Long.

In the year 1814, November 17, the strange brethren have come again to us on Pipe Creek about the difficulties with C. H. and his adherents, and have visited and admonished them again to peace, and union, and acknowledgment; and with these lines we inform our dear members of Pipe Creek church, briefly, how we found it on our visit to C. H., and the members that have turned away from the church. What concerns brother C. H., the visiting brethren have proposed he or they should elect six brethren on their part whom they would, and they should search out their true testimonies; and the old brethren on Pipe Creek should also elect six brethren and prepare their testimonies, and then the difficulties should be settled with the help of God according to the testimonies.

Brother H. said he would have nothing to do with it, and that he would have no fellowship with the unfruitful works of darkness. This was the amount upon the whole, upon which we told him the conclusion made at the big meeting. Likewise we have told brother J. W., upon his insolent and untrue asseverations, said conclusion. The said conclusion is, that if after patient admonition they would not return to union according to the truth of Jesus, we must deny to them according to the gospel the communion, in so far as not to break bread with them, and to refuse the kiss and counsel, until they should become repentant. We must observe here, that we have not seen any more of brother Benjamin Bowman and Nicholas Martin, after they had visited their part, and know not whether they have told the conclusion to any members. As concerning the other members, who are with C. H., it was found different; yet several have declared, that they would not fall away or separate from the old brethren; still they are halting at several points. We have told some, by hearsay and suppositions, they had got off from the church thus far. Now they should only believe what can be testified; in this way they might be restored and put right again. In this manner all the members should labor in this case with prayer and supplication to God, that by his co-operating grace all, and especially those who long after peace, could come again to peace and union with the church according to the mind of the Spirit of God and his soul-saving truth, in hope that they will reflect and choose that, what is counseled them according to the gospel, namely, to strive after peace with the church. Thus we have told the other members we visited the conclusion only in this form, that those who would continue to adhere to C. H., and go on with him in his strange works, all such would be held as is expressed in the conclusion until they would return repentant; that is, all such who would continue to break bread with him, and justify his strange baptism. Signed, &c.

We have given the above two lengthy records of an interesting part of the history of the Brethren, showing with what care, patience and long-suffering they dealt with erring members; and what are the fearful consequences of a stubborn resistance to the counsel of the church and of God, became specially evident in the after life of said C. H., whom the writer saw personally some thirty years ago. One by one his adherents left him, and returned to the church. For a living he followed the distilling business, and at last he died in obscurity and poverty.

Y. M. 1815. In the big meeting of the Brethren's church, which was held in White Oak church with brother Joseph Hershe, May 13, 1815, the following was discussed, and held counsel on the complaints arising in different parts of the church of the Brethren concerning strange views of some members, which are deemed by us as erroneous and not founded on the holy Scriptures, which holy Scriptures indeed shall be the sole foundation of our faith. And since we live now in perilous times, in which arise many and manifold temptations, and also many errors, so that weak minds may be easily led astray and in confusion, not knowing what or how to do in order to salvation. And inasmuch now, at this time, among the many religious parties and denominations there are such whose doctrines on repentance, on baptism, and on the forgiveness of sins, through the atoning sacrifice of Jesus, and on sanctification through the Holy Spirit, seem to differ not much from those of the old brethren, only that they, according to our views, as the word teaches us, do not put every thing in the right place.

They require of a man, before he is to be baptized, that he should have passed entirely through repentance, and should have a lively expe-

rience of the forgiveness of sins, and that he should have obtained the
new birth completely before baptism, so that they must confess such and
be enabled to say how they came to it; and that only then they were fit
to be received by baptism into the covenant of the grace of God. There
should have been made even such expressions in public meeting, that a
man must have obtained complete sanctification first, else he would be baptized too soon, as has been credibly testified. Now for such a confession
or doctrine we see no foundation in holy writ, nor a single example in
the whole New Testament. Candidates for baptism were directed to repent, or to a change of mind; they were exhorted by John to bring forth
fruit meet for repentance, that is, to lead such a life as would be consistent
with a change of mind; and of Christ and his apostles we do not find
that any more was required of candidates than besides repentance, faith
in the gospel, item, faith in Jesus Christ as the Son of God. Hence we
find no authority to ask more of candidates but what is founded in the
word of God. We believe that baptism is the entrance into the new
covenant according to the Scriptures. We also believe that the foundation which was laid by Christ and the apostles is the only foundation
on which we have to build, and that we have no right to change or amend
anything. We believe also that the (individual) cases of repentance are
very different—that some have much greater difficulties to overcome
than others; therefore we make (establish) no rule herein, because the
Scripture does not give any.

And since we cannot agree in the above named points, with such who
hold those points as articles of their faith, inasmuch the word of God
does not teach us thus, it happens sometimes that harsh expressions are
made about the old brethren; for instance, " that they were a crowd of
dead men who had not yet come to a new life;" " unconverted, who knew
nothing yet of conversion;" " a dead heap of flesh;" " as laying all in
a heap in death;" that not one (of them) had come to a newness of
life, or he could not remain among them; and on account of their baptizing too soon, the life of God commenced in them was presently again
extinguished, so that they could not come to the (new) birth, and so forth.

Such expressions do not proceed from love, nor will they build love.
We would let these good people willingly (to enjoy their sentiments) in
peace, if they would also permit us to enjoy (ours) in peace. It does
not work unto union according to the command of Christ. It causes
schisms and divisions. It seems as if it was the object and purpose also
in our churches to fill weak members with their notions, and to cause
confusion, so that many members become doubtful of their old brethren,
since they are represented to them so cold and dead. And such we counsel and admonish out of heartfelt love, that they should hold fast to the
word of God, and not be carried about with every wind of doctrine.
And it is our advice to all overseers and householders to admonish all the
members to this, that they should take fast hold of the written word of

the gospel; and if it should happen that some of our members should unite with such, break the bread of communion with them, receive them in their houses to hold meetings, so long as those stand in such separation against us, they (our members) should be admonished, and if they would give heed to it, we ought to have patience with them; but if they would not hear or be advised, they could not stand in full fellowship with us. For the Lord Jesus and the apostles teach us that we should be one, of one mind, speak the same thing, and that there should be no division among us, and to this end we also labor to be obedient to the gospel of Jesus Christ by the grace of God.

Y. M. 1820. In the counsel of the assembled brethren at the big meeting in Lancaster county, Pa., in Conestoga church, at brother Joseph Royer's, May 19, 1820, was proposed for consideration in church council the disturbances or troubles arising in the State of Ohio, in Mill Creek church, by diverse doctrinal points, which have been there introduced, viz., it has been taught by brother A. M., who is a colaborer in the word, that a man must have a real experience of the forgiveness of sins, and that he must be entirely born anew before he is baptized, which has been credibly testified. And it was considered at this meeting, that there is no gospel evidence for such doctrine, and it was concluded with one accord and unanimity, that if a brother will preach and persist in such doctrine, he could not be permitted to teach; for it is not consistent with the teaching of the apostle, when he says, Acts 2: 38, "Repent, and be baptized every one of you, in the name of Jesus Christ, for the remission of sins, and ye shall receive the gift of the Holy Ghost." This is thus laid down until such brother will prove his or such doctrine on the ground of the word of God. It was also considered, that brother J. K. went too far with the harsh expressions he made against brother A. M. in presence of the brethren, and it is required of him to make acknowledgment for such hard expressions, or else we could not be well with him. N. B. The expressions were these, that he is to have said, from the teaching of brother M., there was apparent a spirit of Methodism and of the River Brethren, and an Antichrist, &c., &c.

Y. M. 1835 (Miami). Art. 1. Concerning the trouble between brother M. L. and the church, L. was earnestly admonished by the old brethren to amend his ways, not to creep into houses in order to bring members into confusion, and cause division in the church, inasmuch they (the old brethren) saw and understood what manner of spirit was in him. For if he should come so far as to speak in a traducing and railing spirit against the church, he would have to be put in avoidance.

Y. M. 1848 (Indiana). Art. 3. How is it considered, when a part, say a minority of a church, disowns the other part, or a majority of the members, without taking a legal or scriptural course, and without giving a legal notice to the body of the church, and not showing or informing the disowned members wherein they transgressed? The difficulties in this case occupied the greater part of Monday and Tuesday, and lastly were postponed for decision until Wednesday morning.—Art. 12. In regard to the third query of the difficulties of Bachelor's Run church with brother Oyman, Patton, and others, the brethren in general council considered, that there had been committed errors on both sides, in consequence of which many members on both sides made satisfactory acknowledgments before the meeting; and it was concluded, that with such all that is past be forgiven and forgotten, and with as many as may yet come and make satisfaction, and that they all should be received into full fellowship. and brother David Fisher in his office as a speaker; furthermore, this meeting considers and counsels, that brothers O. and P., and such others that hold yet with them, should have still time to reflect, and should they come also in a reasonable space of time, and make satisfactory acknowledgments, the church should also be willing to forgive them. But if they should persist in their contrary course, going on in holding meetings in opposition to the church, and even become railers of the church, there would be no other way than to put them into full avoidance, according to 1 Cor. 5.—Art. 13. A long letter about difficulties in the Eel River church, and requesting the assistance of this meeting. Considered, that this meeting feels a deep concern for our brethren on Eel river, who are aggrieved and distressed on account of those difficulties existing among them, and that we would, if possible, most willingly investigate their case fully and impartially. But having spent already three days in council, and many members having already left this meeting; being also assured that those difficulties could not be settled here, and that there would be a small hope of making a final settlement just now; and on the other hand, a hope being expressed that the time might soon come when they could be settled satisfactorily to all parties—a result most devoutly to be desired—it was concluded, to lay down this case with our most solemn warning and earnest advice to our beloved brethren on Eel river, that they should lay aside all uncharitableness, envy and evil speaking, and in all private matters of difference to take the gospel rule for a guide (Matt. 18 : 15, ff.); for while ill feeling and a neglect of the word of God exists, it will be impossible to restore peace. But when they have laid down all private and family and party affairs, and are willing again to walk together in the gospel road, yet do not feel confident of being able to get into it without assistance, let them choose those who are to assist them in the work of reconciliation. Should they, however, fail in this, let them apply to the next annual meeting for a reconsideration of their case.

Y. M. 1849. Art. 15. About the still existing difficulties in Bachelor's Run church, Carroll county, Indiana. Concluded in general council, that brother Peter Nead and Michael Moyer, of Montgomery, and brother Daniel Miller, of Preble, (all of) Ohio, with such other brethren as they may see proper to call to their assistance, should be a committee to visit said church, and try once more to settle the difficulties there existing.

Y. M. 1850. Art. 1. A request that counsel be given to the church on Eel river, Ind., in order that the difficulties there existing might be settled. Concluded, that inasmuch as the said church is in an unreconciled state toward one another, this meeting doth appoint brother Peter Nead, David Bowman, Jr., Daniel Miller, and Ab. Erbaugh, of Ohio, and Jacob Miller, James Tracey, and David Hartman, of Indiana, as a committee to visit said church, and assist in settling the existing difficulties.

Y. M. 1851. Art. 1. A letter from Knob Creek church, East Tennessee, concerning a confusion and division in that church. Concluded, that a committee should be appointed by the Y. M. to go to East Tennessee to assist the brethren there in adjusting their difficulties, and that this committee and others of the same character be appointed by the general committee. The following brethren were appointed for this business, viz.: B. Bowman, John Harshberger, John Kline, and Daniel Brower, all of Rockingham, and B. Moomaw, of Roanoke, Virginia. Art. 4. A request from brethren in Shelby county, Ohio, for a committee to examine into the proceedings of the Logan church in a case of excommunication. Concluded, that brethren George Shively and Joseph Showalter, of Stark, John Molsbaugh, of Knox, John Shoemaker, of Mohegan church, and Jacob Kurtz, of Wayne county, be a committee to visit said churches in Logan and Shelby.—Art. 5. A letter about the difficulties in Salamony church, Indiana. Concluded, that brethren John Miller, of Elkhart, Henry Neff, of Turkey Creek, David Shoemaker, of Huntingdon, Nich. Frantz, of Eel river, and Abraham Moss and John Bowman, of Wayne county, Ind., be a committee to visit said church. Art. 11. An appeal to this yearly meeting from Whiteoak church, in Lancaster county, Pa., to appoint a committee to investigate, and, if possible, to settle the difficulties existing there. Considered, to grant the request, and to appoint brother Andrew Spanogle, Peter Long and Samuel Lehman, of Pennsylvania, and brother Phil. Boyle and D. P. Sayler, of Maryland, to be the committee.

Y. M. 1852. Art. 1. See "*Far Western Brethren.*"—Art. 15. The committee appointed last year to visit Salamony church, in this State (Indiana), in order to settle the difficulties there, reported that they could not yet accomplish the object of their appointment; but that there was now a prospect of doing it, and request some more brethren to be added. Concluded, that the committee should be reappointed with the addition of James Tracey, of Elkhart, and Jacob Miller, of Portage.—Art. 16. Request of a committee to go to Tiffin church, Seneca county, Ohio (to examine and adjust a case), concerning a sister, whose husband left (deserted) her, and she remained thus forsaken for seven years, but has now got a bill of divorce, and is married again. The following brethren were proposed and appointed as a committee to investigate and settle this business: Joseph Showalter, of Stark, John Molsbaugh, of Knox, John Shoemaker, of Mohegan. Elias Dicky, of Ashland, and Jacob Kurtz, of Wayne county, all in Ohio.—Art. 25. A call for a committee to be sent to Jonathan's Creek church, Ohio. The following brethren were appointed for this business, viz.: John Molsbaugh, John Shoemaker, John P. Ebersole, Jacob Kurtz and Henry Davy.—Art. 26. A request for a committee to visit two church districts in Montgomery county, Ohio. The request (was) granted by nominating Benjamin Bowman and David Hardman, of Indiana, and Daniel Miller, of Preble, George Butterbaugh, of Miami, John Frantz, of Clarke, Michael Meyer, of Montgomery, and Abraham Miller, of Allen, all in Ohio.—Art. 28. A request from the church between Salem and Union, in Montgomery county, Ohio, for the assistance of a committee. This request was also granted by appointing George Hoover, of Henry, George W. Studebaker, Daniel Miller, of Fourmile, John Shively and Martin Cable, all of Indiana, to be said committee.—Art. 30. A petition signed by more than seventy members, for a committee to investigate the case of Daniel Zook, in Snakespring Valley, Pa. Granted, by appointing Peter Long, Andrew Spanogle and Jacob Meyer, of Pennsylvania, and Joseph Arnold and Jacob Biser, of Virginia, to be said committee.

Y. M. 1853. Art 10. A request from the church in Williams county, Ohio, for a visit in order to settle difficulties among the leading members of said church. It was concluded, to appoint a committee consisting of Jacob Miller, of Portage, Indiana, Ab. Miller, of Allen, John P. Ebersole, of Seneca, and Elias Dicky, of Ashland, all in Ohio (with the exception of the first).—Art. 40. Report from Jonathan's Creek church in Ohio, and repeated request for a new committee. Request granted, and brother George Shively (added to former committee, names given above already).

Y. M. 1854. Art. 17. A request for a committee to visit Upper Conewago church, Pennsylvania. Granted, and brethren Jacob Sayler, of Maryland, William Boyer, of Franklin, John Berkley, of Somerset, Isaac Myers, of Union, and Jacob Hollinger, of Dauphin county, Pa , nominated as such committee. Art. 26. A request from Coventry church, Chester county, Pa., for a committee to examine grievances and difficulties there existing. The request granted, and the following brethren appointed: Phil. Boyle and D. P. Sayler, of Maryland, John Kline, of Virginia, and Samuel Harley, Jacob Wenger and Christian Longenecker, of Pennsylvania. Art. 27. A similar request for a committee to visit the Lower Cumberland church in Pennsylvania. Also granted, and brethren Isaac Pfoutz, of Maryland, Samuel Miller, Peter Long, Andrew Spanogle and David Bosserman, of Pennsylvania, nominated for this committee.

Y. M. 1855. Art. 1. A request for a committee to visit Sugar Creek congregation in Tuscarawas county, Ohio. Granted, &c.—Art. 13. A request for a committee to visit the church in Tulpehocken, Lebanon county, Pa. Granted, &c.—Art. 16. A private letter requesting a committee to settle difficulties in Mahoning church, Ohio. Privately answered by the committee.—Art. 31. A request for a committee to visit the church in Owen county, Ind. Left over to Elder John Metzger, to go there with some more brethren (and at least one more elder) to investigate the case.

Y. M. 1856. Art. 7. A request by the church in Carroll county, Ill., for a committee to settle the difficulties existing there. Granted, &c. Art. 28. A request from the church in Fayette county, Pa., to have our dear brother. James Quinter, ordained for the office of an overseer at this yearly meeting. Concluded, that inasmuch this brother had not been able to be present here, brother Joseph Showalter, of Stark, and Henry Kurtz, of Mahoning, Ohio, be appointed as a committee to attend to this business.—Art. 30. Request from the church on Owl creek, Knox county, Ohio, for a committee to settle some difficulties.—Art. 31. Request from Hunterdon county, N. J., for a committee to investigate certain matters in the church there. (Both requests were granted)—Art. 32. In regard to the still existing difficulties in the Coventry church, Chester county, Pa., we could see no other remedy, than either the whole church unite sincerely to submit to the advice given by the Y. M. and the committee sent there in 1854, or to establish that part of the church which is so inclined as a separate body or church ; and in order to accomplish either a true reconciliation or peaceable separation, the last named committee be also appointed for this business, and likewise for that on Indian creek, referred to in Art. 21 above.—Art. 35. Concerning difficulties in Covington church, Miami county, Ohio, brethren were appointed as a committee.—Art. 36. A request from the church in Highland county, Ohio, for a committee to visit said church. Granted likewise.

Y. M. 1857.—Art. 7. A request for a committee to visit the church in Monroe county, Iowa. The request was granted, &c.—Art. 18. A request for a committee to visit the Swatara church, in Dauphin county, Pa. Also granted.—Art. 26. A request for a committee to visit the church in Clarion county, Pa., to settle difficulties. Likewise granted. Art. 27. A request for a committee to visit the Ridge church in Cumberland county, Pa.—Art. 23 A request for the committee to visit the Tulpehocken church in Lebanon county, Pa., to settle difficulties existing there.—Art. 35. A request for a committee to visit the Ashland church, Ohio. All granted.

Y. M. 1858. Art. 13. If the churches demand committees by the annual meeting to visit them and to settle difficulties among them, would it be advisable for such churches to defray the expenses of said committees? Ans. The churches calling committees should defray the traveling expenses. Art. 15. Would it not be agreeable to the gospel and the order of the brethren, when the standing committee appoints committees, to go to other churches to settle difficulties, to authorize such brethren that circumstances will not permit to attend such council, to send some other ordained brethren in their places, so that there will be a full committee? Considered, that it is the duty of such brethren that cannot go to appoint others in their places, that the committee may be full.—Art. 59. Requests for committees : 1st, to visit Conestoga church, Lancaster county, Pa.; 2d, to visit Painter Creek church, Miami county, Ohio; 3d, to visit the Owl Creek church, Knox county, Ohio. (They were all granted.)

Y. M. 1859. Art. 36. Requests for committees : 1st, to visit Sugar Creek church, Tuscarawas county, Ohio, to investigate grievances; 2d, to visit Upper Conewago church, Adams county, Pa. (The requests were granted.)

Y. M. 1860. Art. 13. Requests for committees : 1st, to visit the Limestone congregation in Washington county, Tenn., to settle existing difficulties; 2d, to visit the church in Cedar county, Mo.; 3d, to visit the Ridge church in Cumberland county, Pa., to investigate grievances therein existing. (All granted, and committees appointed.)

Inasmuch this practice of appointing special committees for settling difficulties in churches, and the minutes do not state either the difficulties, nor how they were settled, the mentioning of the above requests for the 10—12 years before 1860 has only so much of a general interest as to give the careful reader food for reflection, why it is that so many churches year after year have difficulties and grievances, for which they must have committees from afar, in order to have them settled, and that in some cases, after the committees have done all they could, the difficulties still continue to exist, and are as unsettled as before?

But in order to draw out from the above records some useful lessons, we will think, in the first place, of the most common

CAUSES OF SUCH DIFFICULTIES.

When a physician is called in a case of bodily sickness, it is of advantage to him to know the cause of the trouble, in order to perform a cure. He will say, "If I can remove the cause, it will be an easy matter to remove the disease by proper remedies and treatment." But not only to the physician, who desires to fulfill his highly responsible calling in the most faithful, most conscientious and most beneficial manner, but to every intelligent parent or child, nurse or patient, it is of advantage to know and understand the most common causes of disease, in order to guard themselves or others against them. Even so it will be highly proper and useful in church difficulties to trace them to their causes. And it is a remarkable fact, that the most difficult cases had the same origin, or proceeded from the same cause, as the first great difficulty in the Christian church did; see Acts 15 : 1, where we read, "And certain men who came down from Judea, taught the brethren : Except ye are circumcised after the custom of Moses, ye cannot be saved."

A CHURCH NOT TO BE BLAMED, WHERE A DIFFICULTY RISES.

The church where the first great difficulty arose was the first Gentile church at Antioch, of which we read, Acts 11 : 19–30, how some of those scattered abroad by the persecution came there, "preaching the glad tidings of the Lord Jesus, and the hand of the Lord was with them; and a great number believed, and turned to the Lord; "how Barnabas was sent forth from Jerusalem to go as far as Antioch, "who, when he came and saw the grace of God, rejoiced," and (as it seems, after his arrival) "a great multitude was added to the Lord." Then Barnabas went to Tarsus to seek for Saul, and brought him to Antioch, and they were there "a whole year," and such was their success, that "the disciples were first called Christians in Antioch." Here also the first move was made "to send relief to the brethren dwelling in Judea." Here in Antioch, also, the first move was made of sending out brethren from their midst (that would be called now-a-days missionaries) to spread the gospel in other lands and nations. See Acts 13 : 1, 2, 3. And it appears that while Paul and Barnabas were absent from Antioch on their mission, certain believing men from Judea had come there, and being strict Jews, and perhaps Pharisees, they preached Moses, as well as Christ, and thus caused disturbance and confusion. Who will now blame the church at Antioch for this? Or who would blame our brethren, when, soon after they had settled in this country, and were engaged in the same work like Paul and Barnabas, of spreading gospel truth and planting gospel churches, one of their new converts arose, and preached, "Except ye keep the seventh day, or Sabbath, after the custom of Moses, ye cannot be my brethren?"

NOR IS A CHURCH TO BE BLAMED, BECAUSE A DIFFICULTY CANNOT BE SETTLED AT ONCE.

Undoubtedly the church at Antioch had tried to oppose error, and maintain the truth, before Paul and Barnabas returned; but in restoring peace and union on the point urged by the Jewish brethren, they had not succeeded. Neither did Paul and Barnabas succeed to make an end of the "no small discussion and disputation" with those Judaizing brethren. "But they (who?—the brethren or church at Antioch) determined that Paul and Barnabas, and certain others with them, should go up to Jerusalem to the apostles and elders, about this question." Indeed, after the council in Jerusalem was held, and the question was settled to the satisfaction of all present, and of the church at Antioch especially, we find long after unmistakable signs, in the epistles of the apostle, of the continued existence of the same error. See Gal. 5 : 2 ; 6 : 13, &c.

THE GOSPEL PLAN FOR SETTLING DIFFICULTIES IN THE CHURCHES,

According to the example recorded, Acts 15, and according to the law of Christ by analogy and general application of Matt. 18 : 15–20, seems to be this:

1. The church of Christ is in the Scriptures represented as a unity, as a body, of which Christ is the head, as a bride, as the Lamb's wife, and particular churches or congregations are as individual members or parts of the body, consisting of all individual persons who have professed repentance for their sins, and faith in the Lord Jesus Christ, and obedience to his laws.

2. Now as all brothers and sisters are fallible, and liable to err and to commit trespasses, and consequently, according to the law of Christ, are bound to be open to conviction, and to take counsel not only from the church, and not only from a select part of it, but from the very least and most humble member that may feel offended, so each congregation, consisting of fallible men and women, must acknowledge to be bound by the same law of Christ, so that if a sister church should be grieved or offended by another sister church, it is her duty to take the same course as the private brother or sister has to take in such case.

3. That this gospel rule is perfectly practicable between churches, as well as between private members, there is no doubt, if the right spirit of faithfulness and humility in love prevails. Suppose the church in A—— gives offense to the neighboring church in B—— by tolerating things among her members which those in B—— deem hurtful, and contrary to the principles of the gospel. Now if the church, willing to obey the same law whose observance they require of every young member, as well as old, and inspired by the same spirit of love, humility and faithfulness toward their sister churches they inculcate to their members to cherish toward each other, then the church at B—— will select two of her ministering brethren to go to the church at A——, and tell her in private (first to the leading members, and, if required, to the membership altogether) what grieves their members at B——. If this first step is taken and received in the right spirit, as with individuals, no further step need be taken. But if the sister at A—— will not hear thee, then take with thee one or two (sister churches or their representatives) more, as the second step ; and if she (sister A——) shall neglect to hear them (her two or three sister churches), tell it unto the church (represented in a yearly meeting), who, as the bride of Christ, will see his laws obeyed and executed, "as it is written."

Alas! that this golden rule of Christ is so much neglected! If it were not so, if members and churches were all striving to carry it out faithfully, what glorious progress would we all make toward a still higher degree of purification, holiness and peace and union in love! How soon would every trouble vanish, every difficulty be overcome, and every schism be healed! But let us remember there is a condition *sine qua non*, and that is, we must follow strictly the apostolic example in settling difficulties, if we desire to meet with the same measure of success as they did. How do we read Acts 15 : 22, "*Then the apostles and the elders, with the whole church, resolved, &c.?*" Let us carefully and reverently contemplate every word of this brief part of a sentence. *Then*, when, after much discussion, Peter had spoken (v. 7–11), and "all the multitude became silent," satisfied with the views Peter had expressed, and now giving ear to "Barnabas and Paul narrating" what God had wrought among the Gentiles (v. 12), and "*then*," when James had given his testimony to Peter's discourse, and brought the question to a still more practical issue, thus confirming the people still more in their union of sentiment with the apostles, "*then*" resolved, who? —"*the apostles*" – not only the two that had spoken, or whose words were at least recorded; not only a minority, or even a majority; not only some of them, but we are compelled to believe that all the apostles present without an exception agreed in the resolution, and not the apostles only, for it is said, "*and the elders*," from which words we must also conclude that all those present of that character were united in the same "resolve," whether they were elders residing in Jerusalem, or elders sent as delegates from other cities or countries, "*with the whole church*" —not without the church, not with a part only, not with a little less than half of the church, or a minority, nor with a little more than half, which would be called a majority; no, no, it was with the *whole* church resolved; what they did was done "*with one accord;*" *they all agreed*, "*having become of one mind.*" And how did this happen? "*For it seemed good to the Holy Spirit, and to us*" (v. 28). This explains the mystery. The apostles and elders, with the whole church, tried to learn, first, not what seemed good to themselves, to their own spirits, but what seemed good to the Holy Spirit; and after learning that, they did not wish to entertain a different opinion, but what seemed good to the Holy Spirit seemed also good to themselves. Will our dear brethren of this latter age learn the solemn lesson inculcated by word and example of primitive Christianity?

DISCIPLINE OF CHILDREN.

Y. M. 1789. Art. 2. Inasmuch as many of our children and young people fall into a coarse life, and a great occasion of it seems to be a want that there is not sufficient diligence used in instructing the children according to the word of the Lord given by Moses in Deut. 6 : 7, where we read : "And thou shalt teach them (these words which I command thee this day) diligently unto thy children, and shalt talk of them when thou sittest in thy house, and when thou walkest by the way, and when thou liest down, and when thou risest up;" and also, the apostle Paul says, Ephes. 6 : 4, that parents should " bring them (their children) up in the nurture and admonition of the Lord;" it is our opinion (and advice) that there should be used more diligence to instruct our dear youth and children in the word of truth to their salvation, and that it is the special duty of the dear parents, as well as of the pastors and teachers, to be engaged herein, inasmuch as the apostle teaches, " Feed the flock of God which is among you, taking the oversight thereof" (1 Pet. 5 : 2); and inasmuch as the children of the faithful belong to the flock of Christ, just as naturally as the lambs belong to the flock of sheep ; and inasmuch as the word can be brought nearer to the hearts of children in a simple conversation or catechization, or however it may be called, than otherwise in a long sermon, so that they apprehend the word of divine truth, believe in Jesus Christ, and accept his doctrine and commandments, and walk therein to their eternal salvation—hence we admonish in heartfelt and humble love all our in God much beloved fellow members, dear fathers and mothers of families, as also pastors and teachers, our in God much loved fellow laborers, in the dear and worthy name of our Lord Jesus Christ, who has given himself unto death for us, that we should die to ourselves, and live to him forever, that they would use all possible diligence, that our dear youth might be provoked to love God, and to appreciate his word from their childhood. Do not spare any labor and toil to convince them by our teaching and by our life, not after the manner, which is almost too common now-a-days, where the young are made to learn something by heart, and then to rehearse it in a light (thoughtless) manner, and then are permitted to go on in a life as thoughtless as before—but that they may give themselves up to God in an earnest life. The great Rewarder of all good will undoubtedly well remunerate you; for those that have done right shall live forever, and the Lord is their reward, and the Most High provides for them; they will receive a glorious kingdom and a beautiful crown from the hand of the Lord. Sap. 17:17.

Y. M. 1831. Art. 1. Whether it was considered advisable for a member to have his son educated in a college? Considered, not advisable, inasmuch as experience has taught that such very seldom will come back afterward to the humble ways of the Lord.

Y. M. 1857. Art. 10. How is it considered for brethren, and especially ministering brethren, to adorn their children with ear-rings, breast pins, finger rings, and jewelry in general, and send them from home to have them taught music, and to procure pianos for them? Ans. Brethren should not do so.

Y. M. 1862. Art. 34. Can this annual meeting allow brethren, and especially the bishops and ministering brethren, to suffer their children, while under their control, to follow all the foolish fashions of this world, such as wearing of hoops and unnecessary ornaments of the body? Ans. We consider such things should not be tolerated by the brethren, where they can reasonably be prevented.

DISCIPLINE OF THE CHURCH. See "*Order of the Church.*"

DISTILLERIES. See "*Ardent Spirits.*"

DISTRICT MEETINGS.

Y. M. 1856. Art. 23. A proposal of forming districts of five, six or more adjoining churches for the purpose of meeting jointly at least once a year, settling difficulties, &c., and thus lessening the business of our General Y. M.; we believe this plan to be a good one, if carried out in the fear of the Lord.

Y. M. 1862. Art. 58. Inasmuch as the brethren in annual council of 1856 have recommended the churches to hold district or council meetings, and with this we have complied, now we wish to know whether we should take minutes of our proceedings? Ans. We consider that no question of importance acted on by the sub-district meeting should be confirmed until presented to the annual meeting for its sanction.

Y. M. 1863. Art. 23. Would it not be better for the church, if this Y. M. would adopt the district meetings, so that the different States may form their districts as they may see proper? Considered, to leave this matter as it stands on the minutes of 1856, Art 23.

Y. M. 1864. Art. 13. As the annual meeting has recommended the holding of district meetings, we wish to know from it, whether it would be advisable to make a record of the proceedings of such district meetings? Ans. We would advise to keep no record of proceedings but what is to be submitted to the annual meeting.—Art. 14. Does the decision of the annual meeting of 1862, Art. 58, prohibit us from taking the minutes of the proceedings of our district meetings for our own benefit? Ans. Yes; we consider that it does.—Art. 31. Since the yearly meeting favors district meetings for the purpose of adjusting local difficulties, and lessening the labor of the yearly meeting, would it not be advisable to form regular districts in each State, and close them with lines, that individual churches may know to what district they belong? And if so, should not this Y. M. appoint brethren in each State to form such districts in their respective States, and close them by making such lines? Ans. Yes, but we will leave the districting of the States to the churches in the respective States.

Y. M. 1866. We recommend that each State form itself into convenient district meetings. These meetings shall be formed by one or two representatives from each organized church, and we recommend that each church be represented in the district meeting, either by representatives or by letter. We think it best to hold those meetings in simplicity, and as much like the common council meetings are held as possible. A record of the district meetings may be kept, but not published. · They should endeavor to settle all questions of a local character. But those of a general character, or those that concern the brotherhood in general, should be taken to the annual meeting. And all questions that cannot be settled at the district meetings, should be taken to the annual meeting. In taking questions from the district to the annual meeting, they should be correctly and carefully formed. And all queries from district meetings should be accompanied with an answer. But in case those meetings cannot agree upon any questions, then they shall be referred to the standing committee, and this shall form answers to the questions before they be read before the general council. And it is considered very desirable, and indeed necessary, that in all cases, in answering questions both in district and annual meetings, some Scripture authority, or reason, be given for the decision, though it should be done as briefly as possible.

No business can come before district meetings until it has passed through the church in which it originated.   It is understood that any member falling under the council of the church, and being dissatisfied with the decision, may appeal to the annual meeting by presenting a petition signed by a number of the members of the church.   Nothing in this arrangement shall be so construed as to prevent any member from presenting himself before the standing committee of A. M. to offer anything that cannot be brought before it in the manner prescribed, and the committee shall hear his case, and dispose of it according to its judgment.

DIVISIONS.   See *"Difficulties in Churches."*

DIVORCE.   (See *"Adultery,"* where many counsels refer to this mat-ter.)   Here are some facts:

In the year 1865 eight hundred and thirty-seven divorces were granted in the single State of Ohio, and if we take this as a fair average of all the States, the number of divorces in the United States in that one year cannot have been less than ten thousand.   This fact is elicited from a respectable religious paper in Ohio.

A correspondent in another paper, either from Missouri or Kansas, as both names are given in the article incidentally, complains " that divorced persons marrying again are treated by the church (what church is not stated) as though they were not adulterous, and frequently aim at more than ordinary excellence. A pettish prude (woman), thrice divorced and four times married, seeks divorce again, with a view to (a fifth) marriage, and still retains her church connection. Should these things be ?"

That this evil of frequent divorces exists not only in the West, but also in the East, is evident from the report of a special committee of ministers in New England, appointed to inquire : "In what degree do the State laws of divorce deviate from the law of the New Testament?"   The result of this inquiry is given in a religious paper of New York, as follows :

" 1. According to the word of God, there is but one legal cause for divorce, namely, fornication, by which is here to be understood either adultery after marriage, or perhaps also fornication committed before marriage with a third person.   But when this latter sin was known to the other party before their marriage, it cannot afterward give a cause for divorce any more.

" 2. This so defined sin justifies the offended party to seek a dissolution of the marriage covenant, though in all cases where repentance appears, it is more becoming to the Christian to forgive and forget.

" 3. Christian churches in their discipline should acknowledge no other cause for divorce as legal.   They cannot be guided in this matter by the civil law, but must, notwithstanding all difficulties, obey the divine law.

" 4. According to the word of God, the innocent party may be allowed to separate from the guilty party in bed and board ; yet both parties remain in such case bound, and neither can marry again, while both shall be living, without committing adultery."

Without giving any more opinions of men, let us look up the word of the Lord on this delicate and important point at once.

1.   Matt. 5 : 31, 32. Here the Lord from heaven spoke in his sermon on the mount, thus : " It hath been said, Whosoever shall put away his wife, let him give her a writing of divorcement ; but I say unto you, That whosoever shall put away his wife, saving for the cause of fornication, causeth her to commit adultery ; and whosoever shall marry her that is divorced, committeth adultery."

2.   Matt. 19 : 3, 9. " The Pharisees also came unto him, tempting him, and saying unto him, Is it lawful for a man to put away his wife

for every cause? And he answered and said unto them, Have ye not read, that he which made them at the beginning, made them male and female; and said, For this cause shall a man leave father and mother. and shall cleave to his wife: and they twain shall be one flesh. Wherefore they are no more twain, but one flesh. What therefore God has joined together, let not man put asunder. They say unto him, Why did Moses then command to give a writing of divorcement, and to put her away? He saith unto them, Moses, because of the hardness of your hearts, suffered you to put away your wives: but from the beginning it was not so. And I say unto you, Whosoever shall put away his wife, except it be for fornication, and shall marry another, committeth adultery; and whoso marrieth her which is put away doth commit adultery."

3. Mark 10: 2–9, corresponds with Matt. 19: 3–6, above; vers. 10–12. "And in the house his disciples asked him again of the same matter. And he saith unto them, Whosoever shall put away his wife, and marry another, committeth adultery against her. And if a woman shall put away her husband, and be married to another, she committeth adultery."

4. Luke 16: 18. "Whosoever putteth away his wife, and marrieth another, committeth adultery; and whosoever marrieth her that is put away from her husband, committeth adultery."

5. Rom. 7: 1–3. "Know ye not, brethren (for I speak to them that know the law), how that the law hath dominion over a man as long as he liveth? For the woman which hath a husband, is bound by the law to her husband so long as he liveth; but if the husband be dead, she is loosed from the law of her husband. So then, if while her husband liveth, she be married to another man, she shall be called an adulteress; but if her husband be dead, she is free from that law; so that she is no adulteress, though she be married to another man."

6. 1 Cor. 7: 10–11. "And unto the married I command, yet not I, but the Lord, Let not the wife depart from her husband: but and if she depart, let her remain unmarried, or be reconciled to her husband: and let not the husband put away his wife."

From all the gospel teaches, as here stated, our brethren could not come to any other conclusion but the following: That in the New Testament there is no warrant at all for a divorce with a view to marriage, or to marrying again; that in the exceptional case, where fornication has been committed by the one party, the innocent party may separate from the guilty, but is "to remain unmarried, or be reconciled" again to the former companion, upon repentance shown by genuine fruits; that the church of Christ is bound by the above stated declarations of Christ and his apostles to guard and testify against the increasing evil of frequent divorces in our land, by discountenancing and disallowing any transgression of the law of Christ in this respect, as far as our own members are concerned. "But them that are without God judgeth." 1 Cor. 5: 13.

DOCTRINES, STRANGE AND ERRONEOUS.

Y. M. 1785. Our cordial and united wish and greeting of love and peace to the beloved members, brethren and sisters on South Branch, especially to the loving brethren Valentine Power and Martin Power, and all the members in your vicinity. We wish you all much grace and peace from God the Father through Jesus Christ, his dear Son, to be faithful to him from the bottom of the heart according to the guidance and direction of his holy and good Spirit, even unto a blessed and God-pleasing end. Amen. Inasmuch as we have in part seen, and also heard, that there has arisen some difference in several doctrines among some brethren of your church and others, and having also seen the letter of the loving brother Valentine Power, which he has written to the big meeting, and heard from it his views about "carrying on war," which are to be proved especially from the words of Peter (1 Peter 2 : 13. ff.), so we have considered and weighed the matter in union and, we trust, in the fear of the Lord; but yet, for the sake of the word of God, we could not agree with such view, because we do not see it so, and do not understand so the loving Peter in that self-same chapter, nor in his other discourses; but God grant that we may be directed, according to his good pleasure.

First, we do not understand at all from the words of Peter alluded to, that we can give ourselves up to do violence, or that we should submit to the higher powers in such a manner as to make ourselves their instruments to shed men's blood, however it might be done. It is indeed difficult to believe that Peter, what he teaches in one place, should have rejected in another place. Therefore we cannot understand him thus, but that his mind and admonition to "submit to every ordinance of man, &c.," is something different. The question arises, How far or wherein are we to submit ourselves? and this question the loving Peter may answer himself. We find (Acts 5 : 28) that the higher power to which Peter and John were subjects had commanded them straitly (in our German version, earnestly) that they should not teach in this name (the name of Jesus) any more, but they (the apostles) did not obey herein. And when they were asked again, " Did we not straitly command you, &c.," then Peter and the other apostles answered and said, " We ought to obey God rather than men." It will be well, when we attend always to the sense of Holy Writ strictly; and in the very same chapter of Peter alluded to, we see clearly that Peter exhorts for conscience toward God to endure grief and to suffer wrongfully, and says even that Christ became in this our example, that we should follow his steps. Now we see that Christ always in all his sufferings endured them, and that with great patience, and never resisted or defended himself, but, as Peter says, "he committed himself to him that judgeth righteously." We see further, that our loving Saviour, though innocent, was attacked in a murderous manner by just such men as brother B. has mentioned in his letter. But the Saviour stood fast in the covenant of faithfulness, as the brother stated. In a murderous manner he was attacked, and Peter was quick and ready to draw his sword according to the legal justice of God, and struck a servant, and smote off his ear. But what says the Saviour? "Put up again thy sword into his place; for all they that take the sword shall perish with the sword." Here indeed was the greatest necessity (for self-defense), but all this time the Saviour resisted not, but he suffered patiently, and even healed the one whose ear was smote off, acting as it is written: "The righteous shall live by faith," and again, "I believe, therefore I speak, &c." Thus our Saviour had said before, "That ye resist not evil," for so he believed, and thus he spake, and thus he did.

Further says the loving Saviour: "He that believeth on me, as the Scripture has said, &c." Now we will consider a little what already at that time the Scripture was teaching about Christ and his kingdom; so we see that the holy man of God, Isaiah, says of the time of Christ: "They shall beat their swords into plough shares, and their spears into pruning hooks; nation shall not lift up sword against nation, neither shall they learn war any more" (Isa. 2 : 4). Again says Isaiah (9 : 5, Ger. version): "All war, with confused noise and garments rolled in blood, shall be burnt with fire, &c." So we believe, where that fire which Christ came to kindle, where that fire burns, there will be burnt all war, as predicted ; for the love to God constrains to the obedience of his commandments, as John teaches, and as Christ requires and says, "If ye love me, keep my commandments ;" and his commandments aim throughout at non-resistance.

So we hope the dear brethren will not take it amiss, when we from all these passages of Scripture, and especially from the words of Peter, cannot see or find any liberty to use any (carnal) sword, but only the sword of the Spirit, which is the word of God, by which we cast down imaginations, and every high thing that exalteth itself against the knowledge of God, and bring into captivity every thought to the obedience of Christ, as Paul (2 Cor. 10 : 5) says.

But that the higher powers bear the sword of justice, punishing the evil and protecting the good, in this we acknowledge them from the heart as the ministers of God. But the sword belongeth to the kingdom of the world, and Christ says to his disciples: "I have chosen you from the world, &c." Thus we understand the beloved Peter, that we are to submit ourselves in all things that are not contrary to the will or command of God, and no further.

And as to the *swearing of oaths*, we believe the word of Christ, that in all things which we are to testify, we shall testify what is yea, or what is true, with yea, and what is nay, or not true, with nay; for whatsoever is more than these cometh of evil. And herewith we will conclude for this. This we intended to send you in writing with our dear brethren Daniel Leatherman, and Jacob Danner and Henry Danner. Written May 15th, 1785, at the big meeting on Big Conewago, from your brethren united in love, Jacob Saur, Valentine Pressel, Mich. Bosserman, Martin Reinhart, David Studebaker, Peter Dierdorff, Martin Urner, Jacob Stoll, Christian Longenecker, Henry Neff, Lorenz Beckner, Philip Lewig.

Y. M. 1790. Unanimously concluded, that we desire and pray that the beloved brother Valentine P. would desist from his strange notion, because he has renounced with us before God, angels and men, all things that are contrary to the wholesome doctrine, and we believe and confess that Christ has forbidden to his followers the swearing of oaths and partaking of war. Hence we must keep to his word and truth, and withdraw ourselves from every brother that returns again to swearing and war. It is impossible for us to break the bread of communion with such a brother who pretends the higher powers were requiring such of him. For they cannot compel us, if they would, because we are to obey God rather than men. But now, thanks to God, we have such a government, that will not require of us what is against our conscience. But should there be any among us having such a conscience as to be able to fight and to swear oaths, such a one would not be of us; neither would we break the bread of communion with a minister that would baptize backward contrary to our faith.

Y. M. 1794. We hear that there arises a strange doctrine, or rather opinion, among the brethren in Carolina, and that some brethren are grieved about this matter, because some believe, say and teach the following, viz.:

1. That there is no other heaven but that in man.

2. That there is no other hell but that in man.

3. That God has no form or shape; and if a person would worship God, and would conceive in his mind God as in a human form, would imagine or believe that God had an appearance like a man, such person · would do the same as one who would worship a horse or any other beast.

4. That God had no anger, and would punish no person on account of his sins.

5. That the dead rise not; for out of the grave nothing would come forth.

6. That they will have nothing to do with the ban (or excommunication.)

For this cause some brethren desire to hear the views or minds of the brethren (in general council), and therefore we inform the loving brethren, that the view or doctrine of the old brethren is, that we are to believe *as the Scripture has said.* For Christ says, "He that believeth on me, as the Scripture has said, out of his belly shall flow rivers of living water." John 7:38. Further he says, "The Scriptures cannot be broken." John 10:35. Again we see, that Christ in his whole life has looked upon the Scriptures, and has fulfilled it in all things. For when they came, and would take him, and Peter struck with the sword, the Lord said, "Put up again thy sword into his place, for all they that take the sword shall perish with the sword. Thinkest thou that I cannot now pray to my Father, and he shall presently give me more than twelve legions of angels? *But how then shall the Scripture be fulfilled,* that thus it must be?" Matt. 26:50-54.

Now, to come to the before mentioned points or propositions, our dear brethren will not think hard of us because we believe, as it is written, and believe also with David, that the word of the Lord is well refined, and a true doctrine, and that we also believe with Paul, that it is our duty to bring into captivity every thought (all reason, says the German) to the obedience of Christ, &c.

1. Now, to come to the word about *heaven*. Says Moses, Gen. 1:1, "In the beginning God created the heaven and the earth; and the earth was without form, and void." Then no man was created yet, and Moses calls something *heaven*, that is not in man. And Acts 1:9. If we read, "And when he had spoken these things, while they beheld, he was taken up; and a cloud received him out of their sight. And while they looked steadfastly toward heaven as he went up, behold, two men stood by them in white apparel, which also said, Ye men of Galilee, why stand ye gazing up into heaven? This same Jesus wh'ch is taken up from you into heaven, shall so come in like manner as ye have seen him go into heaven." Here we see that there is a *heaven* up on high.

2. "That there be no other hell but that in man." We read Luke 15:22, ff. about the rich man, that he died, and that he also was buried. Now it is without contradiction, that when he died his soul and spirit have departed from the body, and have found, it seems, according to the word, the hell in which he suffered torments. So we think it would be well for us if we would on this point or word "*hell*" apply the doctrine of Paul, not to dispute about words. For we can notice in holy writ, that the word hell is used for different things. But we believe, as it is written, that there is a lake of fire or place of torment, in many places mentioned, which according to the word is outside of man, as we read plainly, Matt. 25:41, where Christ says, "Depart from me, ye cursed, into everlasting fire, prepared for the devil and his angels." Here we see clearly that the lake of fire is not in man, because men are sent into the lake of fire, and it says not that the fire should go into the men.

3. "That God has no shape or form, and if a person would worship God, and would conceive in his mind and believe God having a form like a man, such person would do the same as if he worshiped a horse or any other beast." This, it seems to us, is speaking very derogatory of God, or against God, though we believe also from the heart, that God is a Spirit, as Christ himself says, and that the true worshipers worship God in spirit and in truth. But not at all contrary to this says John, "In the beginning was the Word, and the Word was with God, and the Word was God." And further on, "And the Word was made flesh, and dwelt among us, and we beheld his glory," &c. Here God has put on a visible form. Now to be sure, in his worship man should not imagine a form or likeness of God; but if it should happen, that a person or disciple would in his worship in simplicity and sincerity toward God look to God in the person or appearance of Christ, we consider it

far less culpable than for a man to worship a horse or some other beast, and deem this a very unbecoming expression.

4. "That God has no anger, and punishes no person for his sins." Now we believe also with John, "that God is love; and that he that dwelleth in love, dwelleth in God, and God in him;" and that God is not angry like an unconverted man, but that penal judgments proceed from love to the human family. Yet notwithstanding the Holy Scriptures or the men of God in holy writ call God's judgments God's wrath, as Psalm 90 : 11, "Who knoweth the power of thine anger? Even according to thy fear, so is thy wrath." Again, John the Baptist says, John 3 : 36, "He that believeth on the Son hath everlasting life; and he that believeth not the Son, shall not see life, *but the wrath of God abideth on him.*" And that the Lord would punish no man for his sin, we deem to be an error. Christ says himself, "Suppose ye, that these Galileans were sinners above all the Galileans, because they suffered such things?. I tell you, nay; but except ye repent, ye shall all likewise perish." Luke 13 : 2, 3.

5. "That the dead rise not, for out of the grave nothing would come forth." We believe, as Christ says, John 5 : 28, "The hour is coming, in the which *all that are in the graves* shall hear his voice, and shall come forth," &c. So we read Matt. 27 : 51, 52, "The earth did quake, and the rocks rent, and the graves were opened, and many bodies of the saints which slept arose, and came out of the graves," &c.

6. Concerning the ban, see "*Avoidance.*

Y. M. 1798. It has been made known to us, that last fall at the great council meeting of the brethren in Virginia there was some discussion on account of the different views of the brethren, especially those in Carolina, where a brother minister, by name John H., has defended himself in the name of his whole church before many brethren in public, and brought to light many of his own sentiments, in so far, that the brethren who still hold fast to the word of truth, according to their best knowledge, could not break the bread of communion with said John H.; would however in such serious circumstances not lightly make a full conclusion, without hearing first also the mind of their beloved old, and by many temptations, established brethren, hence this is to inform our dear brethren in North Carolina, that the case has been presented to the brethren by those brethren who have seen John H. himself, and have heard from him many of his what can scarcely be called doctrines, but rather perverse apprehensions of holy writ, and have quite unanimously concluded, that we cannot hold said John H. and all who are of his mind, as brethren, as long as they do not acknowledge the doctrine of Jesus and his apostles as a true doctrine, sent from God unto salvation, and publicly confess, according to which doctrine we are to prove all the spirits and powers operating in us, and necessarily must. For we believe and confess with David, that the word of the Lord is a true doctrine and well refined ; therefore we cannot acknowledge such as our brethren any more, while they contradict the Holy Scriptures in many points. This we the undersigned brethren confess and testify to hold them as other people out of the church, as long as they do not seek and keep house according to Scripture. Signed by the brethren.

P. S. (COPY.) This is to certify that I heard John H. say in his preaching, that it would be no more sin to him to get upon the top of the barn, that he was in and preaching in, and swear and blaspheme all the new found oaths and curses, than to pray to God to forgive him his sins, or to bless him in any respect; and he said, he had not served such a God that required the prayers of human creatures to forgive them their sins, or to bless them in any manner, these seven years, nor never would. Those are the words I heard, as near as I can remember.

Per me, SAMUEL VAN ETTEN,
JOHANNES KELLER.

Y. M. 1800. Art. 1. (On account of the brethren in Carolina.) It has been made known to us that the brethren in Carolina desire to be informed more plainly concerning the conclusion made at the big meeting on Little Conewago, May 26, 1798, where it was concluded in union about brother John H., and all who are of his mind, that we could have no fellowship with him (and them) as long as they persisted in their erroneous doctrine, contrary to Holy Scripture. And since it is requested to inform them why and for what cause it was done, we should specify by name the causes, for which we can have no more fellowship with John H. and his sympathizers—this is to further inform them, that the chief causes were already mentioned in a letter from the big meeting held on Shenandoah, Virginia, October 20, 1794, as follows, viz.: that there arises a strange doctrine or rather opinion among the brethren in Carolina, and that other brethren are grieved by the same. (The six points are given above, Y. M. 1794.) These six chief points have been specified in the above mentioned letter of the big meeting with the answer, as the old brethren have given their views and doctrine in refutation, which letter, as we presume, has been sent to the brethren in Carolina, and they are all desired to read the same at pleasure. Then again at the big meeting which was held on Little Conewago, May 26, 1798, the same case was once more viewed by the old brethren, and also the Germantown brethren have sent their opinion by letter from br. Sander Mack, wherein it is sorrowfully lamented, that among the little flock of the Taufs-Gesinnte in America there should arise men who deny the resurrection of the dead, and that among brothers and sisters some had to have the misfortune to have their eyes smeared by that old, mouldy and horribly stinking leaven of the Sadducees. And in addition a written testimony has come to hand about John H., that he should have said in his preaching, which two truthful men have heard him say it, and have testified to it. (See postscript above.)

Behold, much beloved brethren, in view of all the unscriptural doctrines and expressions, we have been moved (compelled) to exclude from the fellowship and membership of the Lord Jesus at that big meeting of May 26, said John H., and all that are in union with him in such views, and we confirm again that conclusion unanimously in our great meeting of the brethren to-day, renouncing all fellowship with each and all such persons as hold such doctrines and views, as are stated above, until they acknowledge their error and repent. Still we look upon this case with sadness and heartfelt grief, and wish them (grace) of God in Christ Jesus, whose mercy endureth forever, that they may earnestly reflect and consider what may make for their peace and everlasting salvation, while yet it is the accepted time, and the day of salvation. This we desire from the bottom of our hearts, that the good God through the tender mercy of Jesus Christ would give and bestow to them and us for his merciful love's sake. Amen. So much from us, the undersigned brethren, assembled with one accord, and delivered to the hands of our loving brethren, who also in words will make it known to you in the name of the whole fraternity.

Y. M. 1815. See under the heading of "*Difficulties in Churches.*"

Y. M. 1846. (Tennessee.) Art. 1. How would it be considered for any brother to declare in public that God did not foreknow all things, and that the plan of salvation was not laid before the fall of man? Considered, that no brother would preach that doctrine, in that it is dangerous and anti-gospel: "for known unto God are all his works from the beginning of the world." Acts 15 : 18.

Art. 12. How is it considered, if a brother, in preaching, declare that our Saviour in speaking to Nicodemus (John 3 : 8), where he says, "the wind bloweth where it listeth, and thou hearest the sound thereof, but canst not tell whence it cometh or whither it goeth: so is every one that is born of the Spirit," means a spirit of delusion or error? Considered, that it is an erroneous view, and that it ought not to be preached, and that Christ undoubtedly had reference to the same Spirit spoken of in the preceding verses, and that the things of the Spirit are spiritually discerned by those that are born of the Spirit.

Y. M. 1847. Art. 6. How is it considered, if a brother preaches up the doctrine that Jesus Christ himself baptized, and contends so hard for it, that it has already caused a division in the church? Considered, that the brethren present at this Y. M. unanimously believe that Jesus did not baptize, but his disciples, as recorded John 4 : 2; and they also admonish such a brother not to speak so any more, and if he should still persist in so doing, that he shall not do it in the name of the brethren.

Art. 7. How is it considered, if a brother preach a sentiment on a part of Scripture, that would not be in accordance with the general views of the brethren, yet made good doctrine; whether it would be agreeable to the rules of the brethren to make it a question at the general council meeting, and forbid him to preach it, or condemn him for it as erroneous, without first reasoning with him, or taking the counsel of the church wherein he lives? Considered by the brethren present, that no accusation should be brought before the general council meeting against a brother in such a case, unless he first have had a hearing before his own church.

Y. M. 1849. Art. 24. How is it considered, when a brother, who is a deacon of the church, holds and defends the views of the Romanists and other sects? Considered, that such a brother should be visited by the brethren, and admonished; and if he still persist to hold and defend such views and practices, contrary to the views of the brethren, he could not be continued as a brother.

Y. M. 1853. Art. 15. How would the brethren hold a teacher that had preached, "there was no such a being as a devil, and that there was no serpent that beguiled Eve in the garden of Eden; that it was only the lust that tempted her and every one;" but after being admonished, promised not to teach nor argue said doctrine, yet still harbors the same belief? Considered, that such a teacher was admonished right, that he should not preach such doctrine; and if he should still persist in holding such sentiments, the brethren could not hold him as a teacher or even as a member. He should be admonished to search the Scriptures, which are able to make him wise unto salvation.

Y. M. 1858. Art. 37. How is it considered, when one brother preaches that there is no baptism of the Holy Ghost now, but that it is only the gift of the Holy Ghost which believers receive, while another brother prays for the Lord to baptize with the Holy Ghost? Ans. We think it best for no brother to preach that there is no baptism of the Holy Ghost now, but in praying we should pray for the gift of the Holy Ghost.

Y. M. 1859. Art. 3. How is it considered, if a minister would publicly teach that water baptism is not for the remission of sins, but that a person must have an evidence within that his sins are pardoned before he is a fit subject for baptism; and also would differ with brethren in the mode of electing brethren for the ministry; and likewise claim that all members, both male and female, have a right to admonish and exhort? Ans. Considered, that it is not according to Acts 2:38, and 22:16, to teach that a person must have an evidence within that his sins are pardoned before he is a fit subject for baptism, and that we know of no better way for the brethren to elect their ministers than that which has been practiced heretofore. And concerning members exhorting without being authorized by the church, we think they should not do so in the church in our public or general meetings, according to 1 Cor. 14:33-35.

DUTIES, GENERAL, OF ALL MEMBERS, WHETHER OFFICIAL OR PRIVATE.

Inasmuch there is no minute of our yearly meetings extant, specifying the duties of members generally, we copy the word of God.

I. Matt. 22:37, 38; Mark 13:29, 30, "The *first* of all the commandments is, Thou shalt love the Lord thy God with all thy heart, and with all thy soul, and with all thy mind, and with all thy strength." Luke 21:36, "Watch ye, therefore, and pray always, that ye may be accounted worthy to escape all these things that shall come to pass, and to stand before the Son of man." Phil. 4:6, "Be careful for nothing, but in every thing, by prayer and supplication, with thanksgiving, let your requests be made known unto God." 1 Thess. 5:17, 18, "Pray without ceasing. In everything give thanks." Eph. 5:20, "Giving thanks always for all things unto God and the Father, in the name of our Lord Jesus Christ." Matt. 4:10, "Thou shalt worship the Lord thy God, and him only shalt thou serve." Matt. 6:6, "But thou, when thou prayest, enter into thy closet, and when thou hast shut thy door, pray to thy Father who is in secret; and thy Father who sees in secret will reward thee openly." Heb. 10:25, "Not forsaking the assembling of ourselves together, as is the custom of some, but exhorting, and so much the more as ye see the day approaching." Rev. 15:4, "All nations shall come and worship before thee."

II. Matt, 22:39, Mark 12:31, "And the *second* is like unto it, Thou shalt love thy neighbor as thyself." 1 Pet. 4:8, "Above all things, have fervent charity among yourselves." John 13:34, 35, "A new commandment I give unto you, That ye love one another; as I have loved you, that ye also love one another: by this shall all men know that ye are my disciples, if ye have love one to another." John 15:12, "This is my commandment, that ye love one another, as I loved you." Heb. 13:1, "Let brotherly love continue." 1 Pet. 1:21, "See that ye love one another from the heart fervently." 1 John 4:20, 21; Mark 9:50, "Be at *peace* with one another." 2 Cor. 13, 11, "Be of one mind, live in peace." 1 Thess. 5:13, James 5:16, "*Pray* one for another." Eph. 6:18, "Praying always, for all saints." 1 Thess. 4:18, "*Comfort* one another." 1 Thess. 5:11, "*Edify* one another." Heb. 3:13, "*Exhort* one another daily." Rom. 15:14, "*Admonish* one another." Matt. 18:15, "If thy brother shall trespass against thee, go and tell him his fault.' Luke 17:3, "If thy brother trespass against thee, rebuke him." Eph. 4:2, "Forbearing one another in love." Eph. 4:32, "Forgive one another." Heb. 13:16, "To do good, and to communicate, forget not." Matt. 5:44, "Love your enemies." Let this suffice as a very imperfect sketch of Scripture precepts of duty.

ELECTIONEERING AND ELECTIONS (POLITICAL).

Y. M. 1813. Art. 2. Further, it has been considered in union concerning electioneering, namely, giving votes for officers or men for the assembly or congress, in order to elect them to their several offices. Inasmuch as the appearance of the times into which we have come are grievous (it was the time of the war with England), and inasmuch as party spirit has risen so high in the kingdom of this world, that men, and even the heads of government, are among themselves at variance, therefore it has been viewed in union, that it would be much better if no votes were given in at elections for such officers (by the brethren); for so long as there is such division of parties, we make ourselves suspicious and unpropitious on the one side, on whatever side we may vote. Thereby every one that desires to be defenseless (or non-resistant) may readily see what might be best (for him to do). Moreover, is (not only) our land and (but also) almost all empires engaged in war (in Europe especially); hence it was considered to be best to give in no vote, else we might perhaps assist in electing such that would afterward oppress us with war. To pray diligently for our government we believe to be our duty, and to call upon the Lord we think will be most acceptable.

Y. M. 1828. Art. 3 Whether brethren may go to the elections? It is the opinion of most of the brethren that we should keep ourselves free (clear) of them.

Y. M. 1835. (Miami.) Art. 7. Concerning going to elections and serving as jurymen. It was considered in both cases, that brethren should hold themselves loose as much as possible, or entirely, which is best. Particularly, no brother should take part in electioneering at an election, which is deemed very hurtful, and should not be among brethren, &c.

Y. M. 1837. Art. 7. How is it considered, if members go to the public election and vote, or even previously electioneer for the candidates of office? It is the advice of the old brethren to keep ourselves also in this respect as free as possible, and rather not go to the election; and as regards electioneering, it is the sense of the brethren, that according to the word no brother ought to interfere (or entangle himself) so far with the offices and government of this world.

Y. M. 1839. Art. 5. Whether a brother may give his house for holding a (political) election in it? The answer was, No; it should not be.

Y. M. 1849. Art. 33. Is it safe and proper for the humble followers of Jesus to go to the elections, and take an active part in the political affairs of the country? Considered, as it was always the advice of the older brethren, and as the anointing (1 John 2:27) will teach every sincere follower of Jesus, that it would be safest in regard to political elections to remain as neutral as possible, and rather than go to the election, to commit the matter in prayer to the care of Him who setteth up and removeth rulers.

Y. M. 1853. Art. 17. Concerning going to political meetings and elections. Considered best not to attend any such at all, inasmuch the true Christian belongs to another kingdom.

Y. M. 1863. Art. 18. Inasmuch as some brethren manifest a desire to prohibit brethren from voting at our common political elections, do not the brethren in yearly council see it the best to make no change differing from the counsel and practice of our ancient brethren in these days of trouble? In the present crisis we recommend that brethren abstain as much as possible from attending elections, according to John 18:36 2 Cor. 6:14–17.

Y. M. 1864. Art. 1. In no less than four papers the question is presented, whether it is right and proper for a brother to go to or take part in political elections, it being specially stated that it had caused hard feelings and disunion? Ans. We have been led to think that at all times it would be best and most consistent with our profession, and specially most proper and safe in the present critical state of things, to have nothing at all to do with politics, and entirely to abstain from voting. See 2 Cor. 6:14–17; also Min. of A. M. 1863, Art. 18.

ELECTIONS FOR OFFICERS IN CHURCH. See "*Choice.*"

EMANCIPATION OF SLAVES.

Y. M. 1782. Concerning the unchristian negro slave trade, it has been unanimously considered, that it cannot be permitted in any wise by the church, that a member should or could purchase negroes, or keep them as slaves. But concerning brother John Van L. who had bought a considerable time since a negro wench, and the same has given birth already during that time to four children by fornication, it is the united and cordial counsel of the brethren, that the said brother L. shall let the old negro wench go free from this time on, and shall tell her that she is free. But if she will not leave him, after he has given her liberty, then he may enter with her into a contract for her wages. But this setting free or emancipation shall be done before some brethren as witnesses of the transaction. Concerning the children, it is also unitedly considered, that he is to give the children free at the age of twenty-one years, and is to have them schooled and provided with (food,) raiment and bedding during the time, as it is just and proper; and when they are twenty one years old, he is to give them a free (new) dress. Still it is our cordial desire and counsel, that if the old negro wench would not like to go away, he (who was her master) should use all diligence to prevent such unchaste life, and lay it before her earnestly, and if she would be free, to give her her free papers, &c.

Y. M. 1797. (Virginia.) It was considered good and also concluded

unanimously, that no brother or sister should have negroes as slaves, and
in case a brother or sister had such, he (or she) has to set them free.
And in case a person is drawn by the grace of God, who has negroes,
and desires to be received into the church, then it is to be laid before
him (or her) before being received by baptism into the church, that it
is the brotherly and united counsel, that brethren and members having negroes for slaves, and thinking that they could not at once emancipate them, may hold them so long as the nearest church may deem that
they had earned the money, and then according to the counsel of the
church to let their slaves go out free with a good suit of wearing apparel
(frei kleid) as is given to a white serve. And if they (the slaves)
have children, they shall stay with the brother as servants, until they
are twenty-five years old; he is to have them taught reading and writing,
and bring them up in the fear of the Lord, and when they enter upon
their (26) twenty-sixth year, to let them go out free with a good suit of
clothing (frei kleid). Further it is considered, if a brother, contrary
to this conclusion, would purchase negroes, and would not emancipate
them, he would have to be considered as disobedient, and we could have
no fellowship with him until he sets them free.

Y. M. 1812. Art. 5. Concerning the slave trade and slaveholding,
it was considered, that it is a most grievous evil, and should be abolished
as soon as possible.

Y. M. 1813. Art. 1. With regard to the slave trade and slaveholding, it was unanimously considered, that it is wrong, and that it belongs
to the iniquities of Babylon, making merchandise of *souls of men* (Rev.
18 : 13), and that it is carried on by the spirit of this world, and is contrary to the good and holy Spirit of God, by whom all the faithful souls,
dedicated to God, are ruled, and led into all truth, and are to come out
according to the counsel of God, of Babylon, not touching the unclean
thing, that they be not partakers of her sins, and receive not of her plagues.
Hence it is unanimously and in union considered, that no member,
neither brother nor sister, shall purchase or sell negroes, and keep none
for slaves; members should also with all diligence restrain their children
from it, as far as it is possible, while they are yet out of the church.
Further it was concluded, if there were members having slaves, or persons who wish to be received into the church, and have slaves, that they
might hold them in a proper way so long as the church near which
they live may deem it necessary for the slaves to earn the money they
had cost, and then, with the counsel of the church, they are to be set
free, with a good suit of clothing; and if there are any who have not
bought, but inherited their negroes, they are to be liberated as soon as
the church consider it right and proper. And if members have negro
children under their care, or even as slaves, they shall bring them up in an
orderly manner, teach them also to read, and keep them, if males, to the
age of twenty-one years, and if females, to the age of eighteen years, and

then, with the counsel of the church, emancipate them, with a good suit of wearing apparel. Further it has been unanimously concluded, that if members having negro slaves, will not set them free, and thus oppose themselves to the order of God and the loving counsel of the old brethren, who are indeed servants and stewards of God, and even the united counsel of the whole yearly meeting, then after sufficient admonition they would have to be held bound (according to the word). We would have to deny such members the breaking of the bread of communion, the holy kiss and the brotherly counsel, yet according to the word of the apostle Paul to admonish them us brethren or sisters.

Y. M. 1837. Art. 10. How is it considered, if a brother buys and keeps slaves, and also sells them again? Considered, that it could in no wise be justified in a brother according to the gospel.

Y. M. 1853. Art. 9. Concerning slavery. How shall any branch of the church proceed in case an individual wishes to become a member who is in possession of a slave or slaves, and the law of the State in which they reside is such, that they cannot manumit them in safety without transporting them beyond its (the State's) limits, and as we are aware that the several States where slavery does not exist are contemplating and passing strenuous laws prohibiting their emigration thither, &c.? It seems indispensably necessary-for us to adopt some other plan than hitherto practiced, in order that the church should be kept clear from the evils of slavery, and that such persons may be enabled to come into Christ's kingdom. The questions involved were considered too important to be decided upon at once, and therefore (it was) concluded, to intrust this matter to a committee to report thereon as soon. as possible. The committee to consist of the following brethren: Joseph Arnold and B. Moomaw, of Va.; John H. Umstad, Sam. Lehman, Isaac Price and David Bosserman, of Pa., and D. P. Sayler and Henry Koontz, of Md. Art. 14. How is it considered for a man who is a brother to purchase a man or woman upon condition that such slave shall be free or emancipated after serving the purchaser a certain number of years, agreed upon by the slave and his purchaser without consulting the church? Considered, that no brother should do so without the counsel of the church, and we believe the better way would be to have nothing at all to do with slavery in any shape or form whatever.

Y. M. 1854. Art. 1. Report of the committee appointed last year on the subject of slavery (see Min. 1853, Art. 9). The question having been, How shall any branch of the church, &c.? (see above). Agreeably to the ninth query of Y. M. 1853, concerning slavery, the committee appointed to report on the same have had this subject under serious consideration in the fear of the Lord, and do report as follows:

First. Under no circumstances can slavery be admitted into the church.

Secondly. In all cases, where a holder of a slave or slaves wishes to become a member in the church, he be required to manumit all his slaves before baptism, upon the following conditions: the males to go out free at the age of twenty-one years, and the females at the age of eighteen years. All those over and above these ages when manumitted, are to be paid by their former owner such a sum, either in money or goods, as may be judged right by the church in which the case may occur, and which is considered as the best judge, being acquainted with all the circumstances, as a compensation for their services over age. This will enable the manumitted to emigrate to a land of liberty, and will relieve the conscience of the liberator from the burden of taking with him to the bar of God the wages of oppression. This report was adopted after a lengthy discussion by the meeting.

Y. M. 1857. Art. 6. As the subject of slavery has often been before the annual meeting, and as it has always been considered that no brother can, according to the gospel, hold a fellow-creature in bondage, to which we say, Amen—what then is to be done with brethren who do not observe the advice given by the yearly meeting in this or any other respect? Ans. That such churches or members should be visited, and if not willing to liberate their slaves, they shall be dealt with according to the gospel manner of dealing with all gross transgressions.

Y. M. 1862. Art. 15. How is it considered, if a minister defends and justifies slavery, even in a public debate? Ans. It is utterly wrong for any brother to do so, according to Matt. 7:12.

Y. M. 1863. Art. 5. What should be done with a brother who would preach that slavery was right according to the Scriptures, and cause discord among the brethren? Inasmuch as the brethren always believed, and believe yet, *that slavery is a great evil, and contrary to the doctrine of Christ,* we consider it utterly wrong for a brother to justify slavery either in public or private, and that he should be admonished, and if obstinate shall be dealt with according to Matt. 18.

ERRONEOUS DOCTRINES. See above, "*Doctrines, strange,*" &c.

EXCLUDING MEMBERS.

Y. M. 1848. (Indiana.) Art. 3. How is it considered, when a part, say a minority of a church, disowns the other part, or a majority of the members, without taking a legal or scriptural course, and without giving a legal notice to the body of the church, and not showing or informing the disowned members wherein they transgressed? The difficulties in this case occupied the greater part of Monday and Tuesday, and lastly were postponed for decision until Wednesday morning. See Art. 12. Art. 12. In regard to the third query or the difficulties of Batchelor's Run church with brn. Oyman and Patton and others, the brethren in general council considered, that there had been committed errors on both sides, in consequence of which many members on both sides made satisfactory acknowledgments before the meeting, and it was concluded, that with such all that is past should be forgiven and forgotten, and with as many as may yet come and make satisfaction, and that they all should be received into full fellowship, and brother David Fisher in his office as speaker. Furthermore, this meeting considers and counsels, that brn. Oyman and Patton, and such others that hold yet with them, should have still time to reflect, and should they come also in a reasonable space of time, and make satisfactory acknowledgment, the church should also be willing to forgive them. But if they should persist in their contrary course, going on in holding meetings in opposition to the church, and even become railers of the church, there would be no other way than to put them into full avoidance, according to 1 Cor. 5 : 11.

Y. M. 1852. Art. 17. How are churches to proceed in the following case? A brother being cut off from the church with an excluded party, and afterward becomes guilty of adultery. Considered, to hold him as the church does such party. See 1 Cor. 5 : 13, "But them that are without, God judgeth."—Art. 19. How is it considered, if a brother is legally expelled from the church, and afterward is taken sick, when he calls for the brethren and requests of them to be anointed, and the brethren do anoint him, knowing that he is excluded from the church? Considered, that according to gospel we have no right to anoint such as are not in fellowship with the church. The word (James 5 : 13, ff.) goes only to the faithful.

Y. M. 1859. Art. 29. Can a minister who is not ordained, with the counsel of the church, expel a member, or must there be an ordained elder present? Ans. It is not necessary for an ordained elder to be present, if the member to be expelled is a private member.

Y. M. 1862. Art. 40. Has a church a right to exclude a member before informing him of the charge they have against him; and if not, what course should a member pursue, that has been disowned that way? Ans. The church has no right to do so without duly notifying him, and if they do so, he is entitled to a rehearing, with the assistance of elders from other churches.—Art. 45. Is it in accordance with the gospel for the standing committee of the yearly meeting to send a committee into a church, if desired by such that are expelled from the church according to Matt. 18, the church having no knowledge of it? Ans. No; but the church which has expelled him should call a committee, if the expelled member requests it.—Art. 46. Is it according to the word of God, for such persons as are excommunicated from the church council, the salutation, and the communion, according to Matt. 18, to come before the committee, and can their complaints against members be received as evidence? Ans. No.—Art. 47. How is it considered, when two members of the church, a visiting brother and his wife, see another visiting brother intoxicated; afterward these two brothers visit the church and commune together, and some two months afterward, the first brother named and a private brother saw the same brother again, as they thought, with too much liquor. Still there is no complaint made to the church until some six or seven months after the first transgression, though there have been two or three church meetings held in the time. Then the first brother named lays in a complaint. What is now the duty of the church in this and like cases? Ans. We consider both parties are in fault, and they should be dealt with according to (the word). Matt. 18.—Art. 49. Should the hand be withheld or offered as connected with the admonition, in admonishing a brother? Ans. We consider that the right hand of friendship may be offered, supposing it to be included in the admonition. (The question is not very explicit, but was answered probably under the supposition that the question was referring to an excommunicated member.)—Art. 56. Is the testimony of one witness sufficient authority to expel a member under any circumstances, when the accused denies and objects to the testimony? [Ans. One witness is not sufficient in general, but we will not say that under no circumstances one is not sufficient.

EXCOMMUNICATION. See "*Avoidance,*" &c.

EXECUTORSHIP.

Y. M. 1821. Art. 2. Whether an ordained or private brother may serve as executor, where he knows beforehand that the law must be enforced, has been likewise considered, that it should not be according to the gospel doctrine. But inasmuch as many brethren are in such a position, the counsel is, to have patience with them, until they can get through with it, yet so as not to break the bread of communion with them. Since, however, an executorship is very difficult for brethren, it was deemed necessary to adopt measures to obviate or lessen the difficulties. And inasmuch as every parent (or other person of sound mind) has a right to make a will according to his own pleasure without being interfered with by the authorities, to divide and distribute his property, and also to select his executors, and to order them what they are to do, and how to do it (the testator may insert in his will the following clause), namely: "I nominate and appoint A. B. to be sole executor of my estate, to settle, pay off and collect, &c., as far as the·rules of our church and the gospel will admit of," &c.

Y. M. 1834. Art. 8. How is it considered, if a brother, being a minister, is, as executor of an estate, obliged to put the law in force? Considered, he should do nothing without the counsel of the church.

FAR WEST BRETHREN.

Y. M. 1850. Art. 25. There is a body of people or brethren in the far West, whose doctrine and practice is somewhat different from ours. Some of our brethren live near or almost among them. Now the question arises, are the brethren privileged, according to the gospel, to hold communion with them under existing circumstances? Considered, that according to the gospel and the constant practice of the church, it would not be advisable for brethren to commune with them until a union is effected, and they are agreed to practice according to the ancient order of the church, 1 Cor. 4:17.

Y. M. 1852. Art. 1. Proceedings of a council meeting, held Nov. 22, 1851, in Adams county, Illinois, by the brethren known as the Western brethren. with propositions for a re-union with the body of our brotherhood, represented in this meeting. After the differences having been stated, and considerable conversation had on the subject, it was finally concluded, that this meeting does not feel satisfied, how a full and true union can be obtained on the propositions made by the Western brethren, and that therefore th's matter should be postponed until the dear brethren in the West become better acquainted with the grounds of our practice, and meanwhile we should exercise charity and Christian love toward them.—Art. 2. A letter from Jefferson county, Iowa, referring to the differences existing between the brethren called the Western brethren, and those of our brethren settled around and among them from the East, and wishing to be guided in their intercourse with them by the council of this meeting. Considered, and answered by the foregoing decision.

Y. M. 1855. Art. 29. Request for a committee to (go to) Illinois to confer with the Far Western brethren or a committee of them, to investigate the differences in doctrine and practice existing between them and us, and report to next annual meeting. Granted, and brother A. Mass, Christian Long, John Metzger, Samuel Lehman, James H. Tracey, David Hardman, John Bowman, Daniel Fry, D. P. Sayler, John H. Umstad and James Quinter, appointed for this business.

Y. M. 1856. Art. 14. The committee appointed last annual meeting to visit and confer with the Far Western brethren or a committee of them, to investigate the differences in doctrine and practice existing between them and us, submitted the following

REPORT.

May 8, 1856. We, the brethren who constitute the committee appointed by the German Baptist church at our last annual meeting to visit the Western brethren (who recognize brother Wolfe, of Illinois, as their bishop), by the grace and favor of God, were permitted to meet at their meeting house, where we were received on the most friendly and Christianlike terms, and after different queries were proposed for our deliberation, the three (or four) following being considered the most important, we proceeded to make our report accordingly as follows.

1. The question concerning the reality of a devil (which seems to have been doubted by some of them) was considered, and after comparing opinions and sentiments on the subject of the reality of such a being and

his nature, we agreed upon the following view, that the Scriptures recognize a devil or an evil spirit, that manifests itself in the flesh.

2. On the doctrine of universal salvation, which denies punishment hereafter (a doctrine which never obtained foothold in our brotherhood, and while a good many of our ancient faithful brethren may have held the doctrine of *restoration*, and many of our dearly beloved brethren may still hold it, the preaching of such doctrine was, as far as our information extends, never countenanced in our church), we cordially agreed with brother Wolfe, "*that all men shall receive hereafter according to the deeds done in the body, whether they be good or bad.*"*

3. On the subject of feet-washing, brother Wolfe is firm in the opinion that one person should both wash and wipe the feet of a number of brethren (or among the female part of the congregation, one sister the feet of several sisters), and then another, and so on, until all are washed; but he is willing to conform to the practice of the brethren in general when in communion meeting with them, and begs for forbearance on the part of the brethren in general until they shall all come to see alike.

4. Brother Wolfe is likewise strongly of the opinion, that no time should be spent between the eating of the supper and the breaking of the bread in the communion, but that the whole ceremony should be prosecuted without intermission or delay.

It is the sincere desire of brother Wolfe, that however these sentiments may clash with the general practice of the brethren, they may not be considered a sufficient cause why they should not be received in communion and fellowship with the brethren, with which views we, the committee, unanimously agree, and present this our report to the brethren in general council met, for their deliberation and concurrence. Signed by David Hardman, J. H. Umstad, J. H. Tracey, A. Mass., John Metzger, S. Lehman, C. Long. (Thus it was entered upon the minutes without note or comment.)

Y. M. 1859. Art. 35. Several communications were sent to this annual meeting from the brethren hitherto distinguished as Western brethren. From these communications we shall give some extracts, as we have not room upon the minutes to give them entire.

---

* It is somewhat singular, that this report is so worded, that by it the fact cannot be ascertained on which side the error has been entertained, and which party stood up for the truth, as the Scriptures say. Indeed it would appear rather by the statement above, as if our committee had been in favor of Universalism (on the shady side of the truth), and finally had to agree with brother Wolfe in the express declaration of inspired light and truth. Now out of love to the truth, and to the church that has always professed to abide by the sure word of truth, and out of love to the brethren forming that committee, who would certainly not wish to leave their report to posterity open to misapprehension, also no less out of love to those Western brethren who have so nobly come forward to promote the cause of union among us, we must merely state, that the impression among our brethren, of the Western brethren holding and preaching Universalist doctrine and denying future punishment, was one of the causes that their re-union with us was somewhat retarded.

"Beloved brethren: We, the brethren in Adams county, Illinois, met together in council, to take into consideration the course we had best adopt in respect to the yearly meeting. On account of the great distance we are from the place of meeting, and none of us being in a situation suitable to take up such a journey, we have concluded to send you these lines, to inform you that after we received the minutes of last conference, held in Indiana, we called a church council, and we concluded for the sake of union in the brotherhood to adopt the minutes of the last Y. M., and we intend to carry them out as near as circumstances will admit of. . . . We further state, that we are willing to counsel and be counseled by the Y. M." Signed by elder George Wolfe and others, by order of the church.

The following extract is from a letter from Sugar Creek church, Sangamon county, Ill.: "We have unanimously agreed to be fully united with our beloved elder brethren, to counsel and be counseled. And we have put in practice the order of receiving and baptizing members, non-swearing, and non-conformity to the world." Signed by elder Isham Gibson and others, by order of the church.

From the brethren in Hurricane Creek district, Bond county, Ill.: "Dear brethren in the Lord: Considering your love and care for us as manifested by your kind forbearance and long-suffering to usward, we in love to you and all saints, thought it good to send to you this epistle, and also brother Daniel B. Sturgis, delegate from this district, witnessing that we desire full fellowship and union. And we unanimously agree to be counseled by the brethren, and submit to all the decisions of our beloved brethren in conference. We believe the best good of all is maintained by a full subjection to the decisions of the yearly meetings published in the minutes." Signed by Daniel B. Sturgis and others, by order of the church.

The following is the expression of this annual meeting upon the subject referred to in the above communications:

"Whereas, it is known that what have been called the Western brethren have not heretofore been in perfect union with our churches in observing the ordinances and regulations in the house of God; and, whereas, a number of communications have come before this council meeting from said brethren, expressing a strong desire to be in full fellowship with our brotherhood, and promising to submit to and to be governed by the rules by which we think the house of God should be governed, therefore, considered, that we have cause to thank God that the efforts made to bring about a union have been so successful, and we are now happy to recognize them as being in full fellowship with us."

FASHIONABLE GARMENTS, &c.

Y. M. 1804. Art. 8. Concerning the evil which grieves God and angels in heaven, and also the faithful souls on earth, namely, the new fashions which are in vogue in the world, and also here and there are believers who gratify too much the lust of the eye (Num. 15 : 39), and conforming therein themselves to the world, and especially our youth is corrupting itself herein so much, that the Lord has almost cause to complain, that all flesh has corrupted. its way; therefore it has been unanimously deemed good, that the bishops and ministers, as also all fathers and mothers of families, should use all diligence to counteract such things, that they might spread no farther, but rather be put out of the way; especially when persons desire to be received (in the church), it should be laid before them, that such things are contrary to the wholesome doctrine, and that it is their duty to deny themselves, and when they are willing to lay them aside, then they may be baptized in hope, that they will permit themselves further instructed, &c.

Y. M. 1822. Art. 6. How is it considered, when members will not receive the loving counsel of the brethren on account of high fashions of the world, which had been considered for the third time in the big meeting, that if a member had been admonished in love once and again (without effect), we could not break bread with them. But now at this meeting it was considered, that if they would not accept the loving counsel, we could not have full fellowship with such members according to the gospel. Also such who permit or approve the high fashions in their children, who are still under their control, especially housekeepers in the church, who should be examples of the flock (could not be fellowshipped in this).

Y. M. 1834. Art. 11. Concerning high fashions and conformity to the world. Considered, a great evil in many respects.

Y. M. 1840. Art. 7. About the more and more increasing evil, that members conform so much to the world in building, house-furniture, raiment, &c., and even to have a string of bells upon their horses at sleighing. Considered, that all the brethren and members, and especially teachers (ministers), ought to oppose and labor against this growing evil, and to avoid the tinkling of bells as improper for brethren.

Y. M. 1846. Art. 10. About pride in its various forms, which is creeping into the church, it is thought highly necessary that the yearly meeting instruct and urge it upon all the overseers of the churches, to see especially to that matter, and protest strongly against all manner of superfluity and vanity, such as building fine houses, and having paintings, carpetings and costly furniture, &c., together with the adorning of the body too much after the fashion of the world. We believe that we should deny ourselves and abstain from these things, especially the laborers in the word, who are called to be examples of the flock.

Y. M. 1847. Art. 9. How is it considered, if a brother or a sister should have two suits of clothes, one of them plain to go to meeting in, and one after the fashions of the world to go to other gatherings in? Considered by the brethren present, that it is very unbecoming for members to do so, and that it would be the duty of the teachers faithfully to admonish such brethren and sisters, again and again, if necessary, not to conform to the world in their dress and habits, as the apostles also have warned us. See Rom. 12:1, 2; 1 Tim. 2:9; 1 Pet. 3:3, 4.

Y. M. 1849. Art. 3. Can it be allowed for brethren to wear fur or cloth caps, and sisters to wear trimmed straw or leghorn bonnets? Considered to be inconsistent with the word of God, and therefore it ought not to be.

Y. M. 1858. Art. 6. How are we to proceed with members that come to our love-feasts from other congregations, and who when they leave home are dressed after the gay fashions of the world, and during the day change their dress several times, and put on in the evening a plainer dress to go to the communion table? Is it enough simply to admonish such members, or should the church in which they live be informed? And must we indeed commune with such members, when some of the members in the church are much grieved by their conduct? Considered, that it is wrong for members to do so, but they should not be debarred from the privilege of communing until the brethren of the district in which they live have been informed, and until they have been reproved, and afterward continue disobedient. (A new question might arise from the above questions, which should be deeply considered according to the word of God, namely: Can faithful and earnest members, who are grieved at such frivolous conduct as stated in the first question, having seen and noticed it during the day and before the communion, sit down in the evening at the Lord's table, and at the time of self-examination see such members at the same table; can those faithful members then say to themselves, that they have done their duty toward these failing members, without having given them a note of warning? Perhaps you think they are in danger of eating and drinking of the sacred emblems of a Saviour's dying love unworthily, and still you do nothing to prevent it.)

Y. M. 1861. Art. 3. Inasmuch as the brethren have decided in conference, that members who would not conform to the order in dress as generally practiced by the old brethren and sisters, that they could not have the privilege to the communion; but as this does not restrain them into the order, we wish to know whether the church has the right to deal with them as offenders, when they will not conform in dress or to wearing caps, and leave off wearing hoops? Considered, that such members should be admonished, and that warmly too, to lay aside all superfluities, and conform to the order of the church; otherwise they must and will be regarded as disobedient members. See Rom. 12.

Y. M. 1862. Art. 34. Can this annual meeting allow brethren, and especially the bishops and ministering brethren, to suffer their children while under their control, to follow all the foolish fashions of this world, such as wearing of hoops, and unnecessary ornaments of the body? Ans. We consider such things should not be tolerated by the brethren where they can reasonably be prevented.

Y. M. 1863. Art. 3. How are we to deal with sisters wearing hoops? They should be admonished once and again, and if they will not heed the admonition, they should be dealt with according to Matt. 18. See Min. 1861, Art. 3.

Y. M. 1864. Art. 7. When the apostles prohibit the wearing of gold and pearls, 1 Tim. 2:9, 1 Pet. 3:3, are gold watches to be included? Ans. As the carrying of gold watches may, and is likely to lead to pride, we think it advisable not to wear them.—Art. 8. How is it considered by the brethren in yearly council assembled, in relation to the members who do not conform to the order of the brethren in the wearing of apparel, and in the wearing of their hair, but follow the fashions of the world? Ans. We think that the ministering brethren should heartily admonish, and urge the members to conform to the order of the brethren, and set them a good example, and if those who are admonished again and again, and that by the church too as well as by the ministers, will not hear, the word of God directs us what to do with them, Matt. ch. 18th.—Art. 10. Is it considered right according to the gospel for a minister to wear a soldier's overcoat when in the pulpit, or at other times; and if it is not, how is such a brother to be dealt with, if he should continue to wear it after being admonished? Ans. It is considered not advisable for any brother, whether a minister or private member, to wear any military clothing; and if he is admonished, and still persists in being disobedient, he should be dealt with according to the 18th chapter of Matthew.

Y. M. 1866. Art. 27. Inasmuch as pride and an inclination to follow the fashions of the world are still increasing among us, in wearing fine apparel, frock and sack coats, dusters, shawls, &c., with the hair parted off to one side, or shingled and roached, mustaches, &c., the sisters also wearing fine apparel, going without caps, wearing hoops, hats, veils, overcoats, jewelry, &c., and as admonition in some cases has not effected anything, cannot this yearly meeting propose some plan by which this growing evil may be arrested? Ans. We think members of the church conforming to the fashions of the world as above stated, should be admonished again and again, and if they will not hear the church, the Saviour has given directions in Matt. 18, how to deal with them —Art. 47. The following resolution was proposed to the annual meeting by a district meeting, with a request that it be adopted: Resolved by this annual meeting, that the churches throughout the brotherhood enforce plainness of dress, and a plain manner of wearing the hair and beard, upon the preachers and officers of the churches. By plainness of dress we mean the common order of giving shape to dress as practiced by the old brethren and sisters generally, and by plainness of hair we mean the hair parted on the top of the head, or all combed back in a plain manner, or combed straight down all around the head, and not having the hair and beard trimmed according to the custom of the world. Considered, that the annual meeting unanimously adopt this resolution, according to Rom 12:2; 1 Pet. 1:14, 1 John 2: 15. 16; and that all preachers and officers that follow the fashions of the world in the foregoing particulars, violate the order of the gospel by doing so, and render themselves liable to be brought under the council of the church.

FAST DAYS.

Y. M. 1850. Art. 42. Is it consistent with the gospel for the brethren to recommend to the churches a day of fasting to be observed annually, and to have it published in the minutes of the annual meeting? Considered, inasmuch as the gospel teaches us to fast and pray, to always pray, and never faint; and the great Teacher says a certain species of evil spirits cannot be cast out but by fasting and prayer; we hope that every Christian shepherd will teach his flock to pray and fast oftener than once a year, as we do not know the time when he that goeth about as a roaring lion may tempt or deceive us. (The gospel does not appoint special times for meeting; but if we would not set a certain time, day and hour for meeting, how could the children of God meet at all? So if the perilous times into which we have come seem to require that all the children of God everwhere should unite in prayer and fasting, how could it be done with one accord and at the same time, unless the time is appointed and made known beforehand? Should the example of the king and people of Nineveh, and its gracious answer by God, have been in vain recorded for our learning? See Jonah 3:6–10.)

Y. M. 1853. Art. 20. Whether brethren should observe days of fasting appointed by the President of the United States, or by the Governors of the respective States in which we live? Considered, that brethren should pray always and not faint, and also to fast as often as practicable. But considering Rom. 13:1–7, and also 14:5, 6, it shall be left optional with the churches and members to observe such days or not, as they are "fully persuaded in their own minds." (When the Lord said by the prophet to his people Israel, "Seek the peace of the city whither I have caused you to be carried away captives, and pray unto the Lord for it: for in the peace thereof shall ye have peace," Jer. 29:7, it would certainly be no offense to God now to unite with the people generally in fasting and prayer for our country.)

FEASTING AT FUNERALS. See *"Funerals."*

FEET-WASHING.

Y. M. 1812. Art. 2. Concerning *feet-washing*, inasmuch as it has happened sometimes that members are permitted to have their feet washed by other denominations, who also practice feet-washing at their breaking of bread, yet not quite according to the word as we can understand it,

8

it is considered advisable that it should not be proper to take part in such imperfect exercises, &c.

Y. M. 1822. (Miami.) Art. 3. Whether there should be something of the supper on the table at *feet-washing*, it was the unanimous agreement in the council of the great meeting, that it should not be.

Y. M. 1833. Art. 5. Whether the supper must be on the table at *feet-washing?* Answered as before.

Y. M. 1841. Art. 2. Whether the brethren practice *feet-washing* strictly according to the gospel? Considered, after much conversation and reflection, that feet-washing as practiced hitherto by the brethren is according to the word, and that the mode as far as we could learn until now, could in nowise be improved.

Y. M. 1845. (Virginia.) Art. 12. About practicing *feet-washing* more according to the example of Christ, it was considered as in 1841, that our practice hitherto was according to the word, and that we could not improve it.

Y. M. 1846. (Tennessee.) Art. 8. Is it obligatory for all the members of the church *to wash feet*, to follow the example of Christ? Ans. That we should make no change in the observance of this ordinance; but that every member should as soon as possible fulfill this command, " Ye ought to wash one another's feet."

Y. M. 1848. (Ohio.) Art. 21. Whether it would not be more according to the word in St. John's gospel, 13 : 15, that a brother should both *wash and wipe his brother's feet?* Considered, that the brethren still think as they did seven years ago in this respect. See Min. of 1841, Art. 2 (above).

Y. M. 1849. Art. 39. Whether it would not be more according to the gospel in the observance of *feet-washing*, for the brother at the head of the table to wash and wipe the feet of the brother on his right hand, and that brother to wash and wipe the feet of the next, and so on around the table? Considered, that as this question has been so often before the council, and (decided) that the manner of its observance could not be amended, we are still of the opinion, that the command is fully obeyed if we wash our feet (inter einanden) among one another, as rendered by the German translation. But we would recommend to each brother and sister, at the earliest opportunity to obey the command to wash, and that in washing the members should change frequently.

Y. M. 1854. Art. 10. As there is some difference of opinion respecting John 13 : 5, the question arises, whether one and the same member shall perform the double act of washing and wiping the saints' feet? Considered in the same light as it was in 1849, Art. 39, that the manner of feetwashing could not be amended, inasmuch as the command is fully obeyed in the way we observe it. See about feet-washing under the heading, " *Far Western Brethren.*"

FORM OF AFFIRMATION.

Y. M. 1821.   Art. 4.   How far a brother is at liberty in giving testimony to speak the truth before the higher powers, inasmuch different forms are presented to brethren?   Considered, that a brother by no means should take the liberty to lift up his hand, but should obey simply the counsel of the gospel, saying yea, if it is yea, and nay, if it is nay; "for whatsoever is more than these cometh of evil."

Y. M. 1822 (Canton.)   Art. 5.   Concerning the form or proposing oaths in order to save one's conscience for the gospel's sake, whether we could answer with yea such a form, "And this you do under the pains and penalties of perjury;" it was considered, if a brother were grieved herein, let him counsel whether there was no other form for us.

FORM OF WORDS IN BAPTISM.   See "*Baptism.*"

FORM OF WORDS IN SOLEMNIZING MARRIAGES.

Y. M. 1858.   Art. 9.   Would it not be advisable for the annual meeting to make a form for the brethren to perform (solemnize) matrimony; Ans. It is thought not advisable.

.FREE-MASONRY, &c.

Y. M. 1804.   Art. 5.   What is to be done with brethren who join the Freemasons?   Though we are not sufficiently acquainted with this (secret) association to judge in the case, still there are revealed many trifling things, frivolities and unfruitful works, so that it is considered to be highly improper for brethren to be members in their association, or to have fellowship with their works.   Therefore it has been unanimously concluded, that in case there are brethren defiled therewith, they should be admonished in heartfelt love, and informed, that if they wanted to be (remain) in fellowship with these (masonic) brethren, we could not have fellowship with them; and if after such admonition they would not hear or receive counsel, we would have to avoid them, and could have no fellowship with them; but if one were contaminated with this, and would repent from the heart (and renounce all further fellowship with that association), in faith and hope, he might be received again in the name of Jesus Christ.

Y. M. 1828   Art. 1.   Whether a brother can belong to the Freemasons and still be a brother (in the church)?   Considered, that it cannot be.

Y. M. 1848.   (Indiana.)   Art. 5.   Whether brethren, and especially teachers (ministers) can consistently with the gospel and our holy profession attach themselves to the *Freemasons* and the society popularly called the Sons of Temperance; and if not consistent, how is the church to proceed in such a case?   Considered, that whereas the Holy Spirit testifies by the apostle Paul, 1 Cor. 11:39, "*He that eateth and drinketh unworthily, eateth and drinketh damnation to himself,* NOT DISCERNing the Lord's body,"—and, whereas, we are informed in holy writ, that the Lord's body is his church, of which we desire to be members, as he is the Head; from such and other considerations and declarations of the word of God, the brethren have always believed, and still believe, that it is not only unbecoming and wrong, but highly dangerous for brethren to attach themselves to such secret societies or any association of this world, and if they should do so, they should be visited in love, as the advice was forty-four years ago in a yearly meeting at Pipe Creek, and admonished to withdraw themselves from such; and if they should acknowledge their fault before the church, the members might bear with them. But in case of a minister of the word having gone so far as not only to attach himself to such secret societies, but also to act as their chaplain and orator, it was considered, that such a brother ought to be silent in the church, until the members should feel renewed confidence in him again.

Y. Y. 1852. Art. 27. Is it according to the gospel to receive a man into the church, belonging to the order of Odd Fellows? Considered, that it is not, unless he is willing to withdraw from and renounce that order.

Y. M. 1855. Art. 19. What to do with a person wishing to become a member, and confessing to be a Freemason, yet not willing to renounce them? Considered, that no person could or should be admitted into the church unless he shall previously renounce all connection whatever with Freemasonry, or any and every other secret society with which he may have been connected.

Y. M. 1859. Art. 4. As secret societies seem to be multiplying, and as many young men around us join them, and as some undertake a defense of them, it seems necessary that our minds need to be frequently stirred up upon this matter. Then as we profess to be followers of him who said, "In secret have I done nothing," will the yearly meeting through its proceedings come up to the side of our Lord? Ans. We consider that members should not participate in any secret or oath-bound societies whatever, and if after they have been duly admonished, they persist in such participation, we consider the church is justifiable in excommunicating them.—Art. 10. If a brother has held meetings according to the 6th article of the minutes of 1858—there being few members, and none of the ministers of the district in which the meeting was held. present—and would to his knowledge receive a person that is a Freemason into the church, without renouncing more of Masonry than just the wearing of the badge and the marching in parade, and the ministers and members of the district in which said member resides would afterward require a full renunciation, and he would refuse, and still claim the privilege of attending lodges, &c., justifying himself by saying he had made no such promise at his reception. What shall be done in such a case? Ans. If such a brother shall refuse to hear the church, he shall be dealt with according to Matt. 18:17.

Y. M. 1862. Art. 11. Inasmuch as there are so many secret societies, such as Freemasons, Odd Fellows, Sons of Temperance, &c., and as the members of Christ's church are not allowed to belong to any of them, would it not be best to ask all applicants for membership, whether they belong to any secret order, and if they do, to inform them that they must renounce all such before they are received into the church ? Ans. If there is a suspicion of any applicant for membership having fellowship with such societies, we think it not wrong to ask such question.

FUNERALS.

Y. M. 1819. Art. 6. Whether it is not displeasing in the sight of God, that there is so much conformity to the world at *funerals,* with the superfluity of drink as well as the superabundance of eatables, besides what is needful and proper ? Considered, that all superfluity in meat and drink, together with all extravagance in clothing, is an abomination in the sight of God, which we ought to avoid by all means, that the body of Christ may not be mixed up so much with the body of the world (especially at such solemn occasions as funerals).

Y. M. 1844. Art. 11. Whether our brethren have the liberty in cases of *funerals* to let preachers of other denominations preach in their houses ? Considering circumstances, such as a burying-ground on the farm of a brother, the weather being inclement, &c., such liberty could not be denied to brethren.

Y. M. 1851. Art. 19. How are the brethren, when called upon, to proceed in holding funeral services ? Considered, that according to the general and ancient practice of the brethren, we would advise, that in all cases the services should be begun and concluded by singing and prayer.

Y. M. 1856. Art. 8. How is it considered, when a brother of another district is solicited to preach a funeral sermon, and fails to attend, and the brethren who reside in the district attend and preach the funeral of the decease, and afterward the elder, who is a relative of the deceased, has the funeral preached over again ? Considered, that elders ought to be careful not to wound the feelings of their fellow-laborers by sending for others to do their work over again.

Y. M. 1859. Art. 29. Is it right to give liberty to other denominations to preach funeral sermons in our meeting-houses ? Ans. It is right, especially if preached on the day of the funeral.

Y. M. 1866. Art. 7. Is it according to the order of the gospel for brethren, being mourners, to keep their hats on in time of funeral services, at prayer, and preaching, &c.? And should brethren dress their dead after the fashion of the world ? Ans. We think not, for the apostle says, " It is a shame for a man to pray or prophesy having his head covered." 1 Cor. 11. And we think a white shroud becomes our dead the best.

GRAIN SELLING TO DISTILLERS.

Y. M. 1835. Art. 9. How is it viewed for brethren to sell grain to distillers? Considered, that it should not be, especially if grain is scarce and high in price. Besides, it was mentioned of the abuse and harm which comes from what is made by the distiller, and that brethren should take no part in it, and by no means use distilled liquors for a common beverage, nor offer it to those that work for them.

HIRING SLAVES.

Y. M. 1845. Art. 3. In regard to hiring slaves, it was considered, little better than purchasing and holding slaves, and that it would be best for a follower of Jesus Christ to have nothing at all to do with slavery.

HOOPS IN FEMALE GARMENTS. See "*Fashionable Garments.*"

HOUSE-KEEPING IN CHURCHES. See "*Difficulties in Churches*"

Y. M. 1799, 1803, &c., also, "*Order and Discipline of the Church.*"

Y. M. 1804. Our cordial and united greeting of love to our beloved brethren, especially to brothers C. L. and J. Z., and also to brothers Jacob H. and John G. We desire and wish you all that may tend to the glory of God, to the salvation of souls, and in the edification of the church. Inasmuch it appears that brother C. L. assumes more authority in the service of the church than it pleases us and the church, and brother J. Z. has given more out of his hands than is pleasing to us and the church, so that it causes pressure and offense, therefore it is our loving counsel to you, that you should keep house in the service of the church in union and concord, so that brother C. L. should make the commencement in meeting (preparatory) to prayer, and then it is all the same who is speaking first; and when the meeting is to be brought to a close, then the beloved brother John Z. is to make the conclusion. At the next meeting the loving brother J. Z. is to make the beginning, and it is immaterial who may speak first, and when the meeting is to be closed, the loving brother C. L. shall conclude, and so on. In important matters brother Z. should do nothing without counseling with brother L., and so likewise should brother L. do nothing without counseling with brother Z., so that union is preserved. But he who will not keep house thus, and give satisfaction to the church, and will not accept the apostolic counsel of love of the beloved old brethren, such should be silent, and cannot serve the church in his office. Further, if a person desires to be baptized, and makes known a preference by which brother he would like to be baptized, then that brother, with the counsel of the church, is to satisfy the candidate and forward him. With these lines we have given nothing new, but adhere to the conclusion which has been laid down already six years ago by the beloved old brethren. We have further to notice, that there were very rude expressions made by brother L., saying that there is gone forth a spirit of Satan, and rules in the church, and of this J. Z. is the head, &c., and even the church has been compared to the rebellious company of Korah. Such should be acknowledged and recalled by all means.

HYMN BOOK.

Y. M. 1849. Art. 38. Whether our hymn book now in use could not be improved by a better selection? Considered, that the hymn book we have answers our purpose very well.

Y. M. 1858. Art. 23. What does the annual meeting think of taking the preparatory steps for producing a new hymn book? Referred to next annual meeting.

Y. M. 1860. Art. 9. We the brethren assembled in general district council at the Valley meetinghouse in Botecourt Co., Va., desire that the brethren in the annual council meeting of 1860 devise some plan or way to remodel, or enlarge by appendix, our hymn book, so as to satisfy the wants of the brethren. Ans. To comply with the above request, this annual meeting appoints a committee of five to make a new hymn book, with the understanding that as many of the hymns in the present book as possible be retained. The following brethren constitute the committee: James Quinter, O., Samuel Garber, Ill., John Mezger, Md., John H. Umstad, Pa., John Kline, Va.

Y. M. 1861. Art. 14. That we are in favor of postponing the revision of our hymn book. Considered, since a committee was appointed by last yearly meeting to attend to this business, and circumstances preventing their action, we are in favor of extending the same committee to consummate the work assigned them at their earliest convenience.

INFARES.

Y. M. 1827. Art. 11. Whether we may be allowed to hold infares? Considered, that it (such things) belongs to pride, extravagance and vanity, and should not be among members.

INSTALLATION OF MINISTERS. See also " *Choice and Installation*," &c.

Y. M. 1846. Art. 9. (Pennsylvania.) Is a brother, that was a speaker or deacon, and has moved into another church, properly re-installed in his office, if an ordained brother takes the counsel of the church, and announces the same to him, without he being received by the members with hand and kiss? Considered unanimously by the elders, that inasmuch as he was properly received into his office by the church in which he was chosen, he would be sufficiently established.

INTEREST FOR MONEY TAKING.

Y. M. 1783.   Art. 2. Concerning taking interest, it is considered, that no member should take interest for his money, inasmuch in the law of God it was expressly forbidden, and Christ says that the Scripture cannot be broken (John 10 : 35); and inasmuch the dear and chosen vessel and faithful apostle Paul says, that Christ became the end of the law, and yet the word of God and also divine knowledge teaches, that in order to become partakers of Christ it is required to deny ourselves entirely of all those things which are contrary to the word and command of God : therefore, we exhort again heartily and unitedly, that such members, who might be involved in this point, should think of better things, and have more regard and respect for their denied Lord Jesus and his truth, and wish them faith and the grace of God heartily.

Y. M. 1822. (Canton.) Art. 10. Whether it be right for a follower of Jesus to take interest, was considered, that neither the law nor the gospel gives us such privilege, and that it should not be among the membership.

Y. M. 1834.   Art. 3. Whether we may take interest from a brother ? Considered somewhat differently, but our (charity) moderation should be known, and we should be willing to lend to the poor without interest.

Y. M. 1835. (Miami.) Art. 2. Concerning taking interest.   Considered not allowed by the gospel, and brethren should beware of usury (unlawful interest) especially.

Y. M. 1837.   Art. 9. How is it considered, if members take more than lawful interest ?   Considered, that this ought to be by no means, and if a brother should do so, he ought to be visited, and if he would not take advice, we could not be satisfied with him.

Y. M. 1845. (Virginia.) Art. 4. In regard to *usury* and *increase*, it was considered, that it was against the law of Moses, and could not be otherwise than against the gospel of Christ, which commands us "to lend where we hope for nothing again." We should be very careful not to ask or take more than lawful interest, and keep an open hand for the poor, and to lend them even without interest.

Y. M. 1850.   Art. 29. Is a member, brother or sister, not as justifiable in buying lottery tickets, as in purchasing bank stock, or taking 8 or 10 per cent. interest on money loaned to a brother ?   Considered, that buying lottery tickets is very wrong ; taking more than lawful interest is worse still ; and taking stock in a bank ought to be avoided also by brethren.   One wrong can never justify another.

Y. M. 1856.   Art. 1. What is to be done, according to the gospel, with brethren who take more than lawful interest, and are not willing to be subject to the decision of the annual meeting of 1836 ? The gospel directs the subjects of Christ's kingdom to be subject to the laws of the land ; therefore, no brother should take more than the law allows. If he doth, he should be dealt with according to Matt. 18, and required to restore what he has taken unlawfully.

Y. M. 1862. Art. 61. Is it consistent with the gospel and the order of the brethren, for wealthy brethren to make it a rule or custom, when they lend money to poor brethren or others, to make those who borrow the money pay the tax on the money, when they receive interest on the money? If not consistent with the gospel, what is to be done with such a brother? Ans. We think it is not consistent with the gospel to take more than lawful interest. See Luke 3 : 13. We think such a brother should be admonished by the church, and if he will not hear the church, he should be dealt with according to Matt. 18.

Y. M. 1863. Art. 9. If one brother should demand and receive more interest from another brother than the law allows, and the latter acquiesces for years, but finally becomes dissatisfied, must he make the complaint to the church, or commence in the ordinary way, by going first privately to the offending brother, &c.? Ans. The dissatisfied brother should proceed according to Matt. 18, and the offending brother should refund the lawful interest as far as the church in which both reside may judge equitable.

The different views expressed at different times on this subject of *"taking interest,"* requires a note of explanation. The circumstances of brethren and others prior to the settlement of the Western States of our country were similar to those of ancient Israel, that is, in both cases there was little occasion for borrowing money, except when the borrower was in absolute want and distress. In Canaan the land was distributed by Joshua among all the tribes and families of Israel, without money and without price, enabling every one to dwell under his own vine and fig tree, and possessing a nook of land sufficient to furnish all the necessaries of a simple and frugal life by proper cultivation. In our own country from its first settlement wild land could be bought at nominal prices of even a fraction of a dollar per acre, and at a long credit without interest, until the purchaser could raise the money out of the land itself. And not only wild land, but also well improved farms could be bought some fifty years ago in the Atlantic or old States, by making a first payment of perhaps the fourth, fifth or sixth part of the purchase money, and dividing the balance into twelve or more small annual payments, all without interest, at least until the bonds became actually due. This being the general custom of those primitive times, we can readily understand, why the brethren then discountenanced the taking of interest *in toto*, simply because in nine cases out of ten the cause of one's borrowing money was, as stated above, actual distress. But times, customs and circumstances have changed. Population and wealth have most wonderfully increased; towns and villages have grown into cities, and are multiplying daily; land and every other kind of property became more and more valuable, at least in the thickly settled parts of the country, and could no longer be bought on a long credit without interest. Even the public lands in the great Northwest could not be had any longer on credit, since it was found that many settlers in the new country, who had paid one-half of the purchase money, forfeited that by being unable to pay the balance of their dues, and lost eventually the land, with the improvements they had made thereon. Thus it came to pass that ready money became so valuable, that even farmers found it sometimes advantageous rather to pay interest than to do without the money. At any rate, with the increase of trade and commerce the custom of borrowing and lending money on interest became almost universal, and after brethren had been *paying* interest for years, when their circumstances became changed, so that instead of borrowing money they had money to lend, the question was seen in a different light, from what it was seen before, and the old saying became true in this matter, that circumstances alter cases. If it is wrong to take interest for money lent, it is wrong to pay or promise to pay interest for money borrowed, too; but it is more wrong still to break our promise, and refuse or neglect to pay or fulfil what we engaged to do, or on the other hand, to exact what is due to us too severely, and become oppressors of the honest poor, because we have a legal claim on them. God forbid that brethren should do either.

INTOXICATING DRINKS. See "*Ardent Spirits.*"

INVITING MINISTERS of other denominations. See "*Admitting Strange Ministers.*"

Y. M. 1846. (Tennessee.) Art. 5. Whether we should give liberty to preachers of other denominations to speak in our stated meetings? Considered, that it would not be allowed according to the gospel. See 2 John 9 : 10.

JEWELRY FOR MEMBERS TO WEAR.

Y. M. 1853. Art. 8. How shall we proceed in case we have a love feast, and a sister or sisters come from another congregation to our love feast who wear (gold) ear-rings or *jewels*, whether we have a right to take them in council, and if not willing to lay it (them) off, whether we are privileged to keep them from the communion-table? The committee was decidedly of opinion, that as it is positively forbidden by holy writ, see 1 Pet. 3 : 3, 1 Tim. 2 : 9, it should not be tolerated except in cases of actual necessity (for medical reasons); and that the church where such members propose to participate in the communion, has the right (if it is not the duty rather) to take them into council, and if they are not willing to be admonished, to advise them to withdraw until they are willing to sacrifice those forbidden things.

Y. M. 1864. Art. 7. When the apostles prohibit the wearing of gold and pearls, 1 Tim. 2 : 9, 1 Pet. 3 : 3, are gold watches to be included? Ans. As the carrying of gold watches may and is likely to lead to pride, we think it advisable not to wear them.

JUDGING HARSHLY.

Y. M. 1820. Art. 2. A brother had used hard expressions against a brother in presence of the brethren, such as " from the preaching of brother M. there was apparent a spirit of the Methodist and River-brethren and an Antichrist?" Considered, that the brother is to make proper acknowledgment for these harsh expressions, otherwise we would not be satisfied with him.

JURIES, SERVING ON.

Y. M. 1832. Art. 1. How is it considered, if a brother serves on a grand jury, and bears testimony against a brother, by which the latter is caused to suffer costs, and the testimony is not given from necessity or duty, but from want of love? Considered, that serving on juries was ever deemed improper for brethren ; but in this special case the church where it occurred, and who should know and weigh all the circumstances, should judge according to the law of Christ and according to the testimony.

Y. M. 1834.   Art. 13. Whether a brother can serve on a jury, where a man is tried for his life (as a murderer) ?   Considered, no, that it cannot be at all.

Y. M. 1835.   Art. 7. Concerning serving on juries at trials for life or death ?   Answered as before.

Y. M. 1841.   Art. 11. Whether it is becoming for a member of the church of Christ to act as a juror in the courts of our country ?   Considered, that it would be best not to serve at all even in civil cases, but by no means (can a brother serve) in criminal cases.

KEEPING THE LORD'S DAY.

Y. M. 1817.   Art. 7. Concerning working on Sunday, it was concluded, that members should do no work on Sunday except in cases of great necessity, inasmuch the apostle writes to "give none offense, neither to the Jews, nor to the Gentiles, nor to the church of God." 1 Cor. 10 : 32.   See also Y. M. 1810, Art. 6.   [See Sabbath Breaking]

Y. M. 1828.   Art. 4. Whether we may do labor on Sunday, it was deemed good that we should refrain from it.

Y. M. 1834.   Art. 2. Whether we may work on Sunday, such as sawing (on sawmills), shooting, moving, &c.   It was considered, that it should not be by any means, but that we ought to spend the Sunday in stillness and in the fear of God, in order to be offensive to no one.

Y. M. 1836.   Art. 6. Concerning work or moving on Sundays, it was considered improper to do so.

Y. M. 1863.   Art. 28. With regard to the question whether a brother minister was rightly dealt with who has taken the liberty to do servile work on the Lord's day repeatedly, and notwithstanding he has been admonished again and again, and continues to defend and pursue his course, to the offense of many in and out of the church, it appears that the church, with a chosen committee of elders, has decided that the brother has either to quit this practice, or the exercise of his ministry.   The standing committee unanimously confirms this decision.

Y. M. 1864.   Art. 15. How are we to hold a brother that keeps Saturday for the Sabbath, and works on Sunday, and strongly contends that he is right.   Ans. Inasmuch as the old brethren have always observed the first day of the week as a day of rest and public worship, we think such a brother should be heartily admonished to conform to the order of the brethren and the gospel, and if he does not do so, he should be dealt with according to the gospel.

Scriptural foundation for the same : Rom. 16 : 16, " Salute one another with an holy kiss." 1 Cor. 16 : 20, " Greet ye one another with an holy kiss." 2 Cor. 13 : 12, " Greet one another with an holy kiss." 1 Thess. 5 : 26, " Greet all the brethren with an holy kiss." 1 Pet. 5 : 14, " Greet ye one another with a kiss of charity."

Y. M. 1797. Art. 4. It was in union concluded, that the holy kiss and the kiss of charity should not be neglected, since in some places it is almost entirely omitted; but according to the words of the apostles, we should prove ourselves on all occasions as disciples of Jesus, and be st. adfast in brotherly love; and notwithstanding all disgrace, we should not be ashamed of the word and following of Christ.

Y. M. 1810. Art. 4. Concerning when brethren or members get at variance or in difficulty with one another, no one is allowed to refuse to the other the kiss for himself, without counsel of the church, unless there had been committed an obvious crime.—Art. 5. Concerning when a member has been put back from the communion, and some from kindness or relationship continue to salute such with the holy kiss, before they are received again by the church, was considered as a fault, and should be by no means.

Y. M. 1828. Art. 8. Whether the holy kiss should be observed at feet-washing and the breaking of bread? Considered, that it is right and proper.

Y. M. 1831. Art. 3. Whether it could be approved of when the brotherly kiss is so often omitted, even at meetings and love-feasts? Considered, no, not at all.

Y. M. 1832. Art. 4. Concerning the omitting of the holy kiss among members? Considered, that it should not be, and that it is an evidence of a want of love.

Y. M 1835. Art. 10. Ilow is it considered, when members wash the feet or salute with the holy kiss those who are not members of the church? Considered, we should not do so, if it gives offense.

Y. M. 1843. Art. 2. Whether a brother may refuse the kiss to a brother who has committed a fault, for instance, getting intoxicated. ere he has been brought before and judged by the council of the church? Considered, that though a member could not be required to salute a brother with the kiss, while in a state of intoxication, it is still our duty first to tell the fault unto the church, and to await its decision, before we withdraw ourselves from a member.

Y. M. 1845. (Indiana.) Art. 3. Whether a brother has a right to withdraw the kiss from a brother without the decision of the church? Considered, that inasmuch as our Saviour directs us in a case of offense to use all means to *gain* our brother (see Matt. 18), the gospel allows no brother to withdraw the kiss, until the church has so decided.

Y. M. 1849. Art. 4. Concerning the holy kiss, how often should it be practiced ? Considered, if we have love for one another, we should not dispense with it, especially at our meetings for worship.

Y. M. 1851. Art. 22. How do the brethren in general pass the kiss at the communion table; is it to the brother who sits at the administrator's right or left ? Considered, that we see no difference, but leave it to the administrator as he sees proper, or as circumstances will admit.

Y. M 1853. Art. 39. Would it not be more consistent with the gospel and the practice of the apostles, to extend the kiss, termed the holy kiss and the kiss of charity, to each other only when coming together and separating from each other, and not at feet-washing, and at the communion ? Or did our Lord and Master indeed institute such a thing in that night in which he was betrayed? Considered, that we feel perfect liberty in the gospel to continue as we always heretofore have done.

Y. M. 1856. Art. 27. Does Christian fellowship, according to the gospel, forbid, or require, or leave it optional for brethren, when meeting in cities, towns or at public gatherings, when extending the salutation of the hand, to accompany the same with the salutation of the holy kiss ? Considered, optional.

Y. M. 1857. Art. 29. The Marsh Creek church in Adams Co., Pa., requests a re-consideration of Art. 39 of Min. 1853, relating to the salutation of the kiss at baptism, the communion, and at ordination. Ans. It is neither expedient nor desirable to make any change in the aforesaid article of the Minutes.

Y. M. 1859. Art. 34. Is it according to the gospel and its principles for brethren of our fraternity to salute with the holy kiss those who do not stand in the faith with us, nor practice or keep the ordinances of the Lord as we do ? And is it according to the gospel to call such " brethren," and give them liberty to take part in our public worship ? Ans. As a general thing we think it is not expedient to do so.

KNOW NOTHINGS.

Y. M. 1855. Art. 3. How is it considered, if a brother or brethren belong to the party of " Know Nothings," so-called, and take an active part in it, trying to persuade brethren to join said party ? Considered, that no brother, who is a member of the so-called Know Nothings, or any other secret society, can be a member of our communion.

LAMB'S MEAT AT LORD'S SUPPER.

Y. M. 1853. Art. 21. Have we a right to put away the lamb at the Lord's supper, and use beef in the place thereof? Considered, that we would rather see a lamb prepared, but inasmuch as Christ has made us free from the ceremonial law, and as there is no command in the New Testament that it must be so, we should bear with each other in love in such matters.

Y. M. 1854. Art. 24. Is it more in unison with the gospel to use a lamb at our love-feasts instead of beef? Considered, that this query is answered by Art. 21 of Min. 1853.

Y. M. 1855. Art. 20. What is the advice of the general council to individual members, say four, five or more, who cannot commune with the church, because they have beef instead of a lamb at their love-feast? Considered as good advice for such members, to submit to the order of the church where they live, and to reflect on the admonition of the apostle, Col. 2 : 16, 17, " Let no man therefore judge you in meat, or drink, &c., which are a shadow of things to come, but the body is of Christ." Again, to learn of his example, Phil. 4 : 11, where he says, " For I have learned in whatsoever state I am, *with whomsoever I am*—according to the German translation—therewith to be content."

Y. M. 1863. Art. 4. Is it contrary to the gospel to have lamb's meat at the Lord's supper ? We think not; but since the gospel does not give a precept or example of what the supper did or shall consist, the members should try to be in union, love and forbearance in this matter. See Min. 1853, Art. 21, and 1855, Art. 20.

LANGUAGES, USING DIFFERENT, AT MEETINGS.

Y. M. 1841. Art. 4. Whether it is proper for teachers to speak both German and English in meetings, when there are only a few English members, the majority of the church being German ? Considered, that it is right and our duty to preach the gospel to every nation as far as we are able, yet so that in such a case not too much time ought to be taken up in English.

Y. M. 1845. (Indiana.) Art. 5. How is it viewed, when there are persons and members in a meeting, some not understanding the English, and others not the German (language), and there are some members still opposing the use of both languages ? Considered, that the commission of our Saviour, Matt. 28 : 19, commands us, and the love of Christ constrains us, 2 Cor. 5 : 14, to preach the gospel to *all* nations, and in every tongue as far as we are able. See also Y. M. 1841, Art. 4.

LAW, TAKING THE BENEFIT OF.

Y. M. 1822. (Miami.) Art. 2. Whether it is right for a brother to take the benefit of the law, was considered, that when a brother is so imprudent that he falls under the power of law, he is not to have privilege to take the benefit of the law, but to seek counsel from the church. Yet it would be always best to seek counsel before a member comes so far.

Y. M. 1841. Art. 5. Whether a brother, consistently with the gospel, can take the benefit of the law for insolvent debtors? Considered, that there may be cases, where the involving at first and the consequences thereupon are not at all compatible with the gospel, and where the church could not hold such as brethren; and that there may be cases, where a brother by misfortune may be brought to such extremity, and if he were honest in his declaration, his application for the benefit of the law might even be excusable.   In all such cases, however, the church has to investigate the matter, and judge accordingly; and if the church is at a loss, to call in, as in other cases, the assistance of elders from other churches.

LAW, USING IT AGAINST DEBTORS.

Y. M. 1810.   Art. 2. Concerning brethren who use the law for collecting debts, was considered, that it is unbecoming for brethren to do so, that it cannot be permitted, and if they should do such a disallowed thing, they are to be left over to the counsel of the church.

Y. M. 1821. (Pennsylvania.) Art. 1. Whether an ordained brother may collect debts by the power of the law?   Considered, that no brother, much less one that is ordained, has a right to do so, according to gospel doctrine, neither for himself nor for another.

Y. M. 1833.   Art. 2. Whether there is any difference in using the law for our own benefit or only as executors or administrators?   Considered, there is none in reality; it is wrong for ourselves, it is wrong if we do it for others.

Y. M. 1834.   Art. 8. How is it viewed when a ministering brother, as executor or administrator of an estate, is compelled to use the law?   Considered, he should do nothing without the counsel of the church.

Y. M. 1842.   Art. 11. Whether it be allowable for brethren to collect debts by force of law, and what is to be done with a brother who uses the power of the law, and justifies himself in the same?   Considered, as always was done by the brethren, that we have no right, according to the gospel, to use the rigor of the law in collecting debts, and that a brothe who has done so, falls into the judgment of the church.

Y. M. 1844.   Art. 7. Whether it be allowable for brethren to collect debts by force of law, it was again considered, that no brother has any right in the gospel to sue at law.   Luke 3 : 14, Matt. 5 : 38, 6 : 12, & c

Y. M. 1848. (Indiana.) Art. 9. Whether brethren can, according to the gospel, use the force of the law, and collect money from brethren, and thereby cause considerable costs, and whether brethren causing such costs should not at least pay the same?   Considered, that the gospel gives us no right to use the force of the law against a brother; and as to the other point in regard to the costs, the church can judge best in each individual case.

Y. M. 1849.   Art 28. Whether a brother, who considers himself injured by any public improvement, such as a turnpike or a rail road passing through his land, can without a violation of the gospel make use of the provision of the law, which government has enacted for the recovery of damages in such cases?   Considered, as the matter has been fully state d that it would not be a violation of the gospel to make use of the provisions of the law in such cases.

Y. M 1851.   Art. 24. With regard to the 28th query in 1849, a more definite answer is required, how far a brother may go in order to recover indemnification for losses sustained from a rail road, turnpike and the like passing through his land ?   Considered, that we might use the provision of the law, that is, petition court for what it will make at damages, but should use no violence by putting the law in force for recompense.

Y. M. 1852.   Art. 3. Have we a right to help making the political government, and to serve as officers; also, to put the law in force against any of our fellowmen in any case whatever ?   Considered, that the brethren should be careful, and not betray their profession in helping to make and serve the civil government, and if they give in their vote, they should do it in a quiet and peaceable manner, without taking part in electioneering, and return immediately from the ground : that brethren should hold no office under the civil government, that would cause them to betray their faith ; and as respects using the law against our fellow creatures, brethren should use lenity and Christian forbearance toward our fellowmen, and not compel them by the law, unless forced so to do by stern necessity.   But before so doing they should always take the counsel of the church.

Y. M 1853.   Art. 16. Concerning going to law.   Considered, that it should be left as it was decided last year.   See Min. of 1852, Art. 3.

Y. M. 1857.   Art. 16. Inasmuch as it is considered by the brethren, that we have no right, according to the gospel, to use the law in collecting debts, or to sue at law; would not a brother who has done so, or may do so, fall into the judgment of the church?   Ans. This subject has frequently been discussed in our annual meetings, and we cannot, we think, come to a better conclusion than our dear brethren came to in 1852 ; and as no brother should be his own judge in this matter, the brethren very *wisely* added the proviso, that in all cases the church should be consulted, and *if its counsel is disregarded,* those who disregard it will fall into the judgment of the church.

Y. M. 1858.   Art. 20. Is it right, according to the gospel, to enforce the law in any case whatever, and if so, where is the gospel authority ?   Concluded, to adopt the decision of the annual meeting of 1857.   See above Art. 16.—Art. 30. How is it considered, if a brother has a note against another poor brother, who cannot pay, and the brother who has the note sells it to his son, who is no member of the church, and he collects the debt by law, and causes the poor brother's property to be sold, the brother who sold the note justifying himself in doing as he did ?   What is to be done in such a case ?   Considered, that the brother who did so committed a great fault, and that he should make restitution to the poor brother to the satisfaction of the church.

Y. M. 1858.   Art. 32. If any man be in Christ, and Christ in him, can he institute and prosecute a process in law against any person or persons, and all the time still continue in Christ, and Christ in him? Considered, that he cannot, especially if gone into without the counsel of the church in which he lives. Art. 49. A brother buys a farm that is sold by executors that are not members of the church, and fails to make payment according to contract; the heirs being members of the church, who after waiting a long time and being in great need of the money, and living over one hundred miles distant from the brother who bought the farm, receive a letter from him stating that he will pay them $500, if they will throw off the interest. The heirs being unwilling to do so, send word to their executors to collect their money by law—now are the heirs under obligation to pay the cost of collection? Considered, that they are not under such obligation, (unless the church being acquainted with all the circumstances shall judge so.)

Y. M. 1862. Art. 62. Has a brother the right to put the law in force against his brother to collect money, in any shape or form whatever, without giving him notice before? Ans. In no case whatever.

LECTURING ON TEMPERANCE, &c.

Y. M. 1842. Art. 7. Whether it be right for a brother to deliver a lecture on temperance, if requested? Considered, as our commission is to preach the Gospel, that we should do so, and inculcate temperance as well as other virtues, but to hold lectures on the subject of temperance exclusively was considered not to be advisable for a brother.

LIGHTNING RODS.

Y. M. 1851. Art. 7. Should brethren have the privilege to put up lightning rods? Considered, that we would not advise brethren to do so, nor would we say to those who have them, to take them down; but advise all our dear brethren to bear with each other in such matters, and try to put their chief trust in God.

Y. M. 1856. Art. 25. Would it be proper to re-consider the 7th query of 1851, concerning the putting up of lightning rods? We would not advise brethren to put up those rods, but that the brethren should bear with one another in love in such matters.

LORD'S SUPPER.

By this we understand, not the communion of bread and wine as it is understood and used by many denominations, but we understand by it that meal immediately preceding the communion, called in the New Testament δεῖπνον—supper, the principal meal of the Hebrews, and taken by them in the evening; see Luke 14:12, &c., particularly 1 Cor. 11:21, or that feast of charity to which Jude, v. 12, is alluding.

Y. M. 1827. Art. 6. Whether there should be no other meat but mutton at the supper, was generally considered as most agreeable (to our feelings "gemüthlichste") to take mutton, as it has been always customary with the ancient brethren, yet to make no law herein, and to bear with one another.

Y. M. 1832.   Art. 2.· Whether such may participate in the (Lord's) supper who are not members, if there is room?   Considered, to leave it to the churches, when there is such room.   (N. B. This is not to be understood of the communion of bread and wine.) .

Y. M. 1833.   Art. 4. Whether a person may·be admitted to our (communion or) breaking of bread, who is not baptized according to Gospel (as we understand it)? Considered, No. Art. 5. Whether the supper must be on the table at feet-washing?—(No ; there is no such command in the Gospel, and if the example of Christ is urged, it is also a mooted, doubtful question on this point. It must be recollected that the translators of our modern version of the New Testament did not believe or practice feet-washing, or know any thing about the real Lord's supper, calling the communion of bread and wine the Lord's supper. We all believe, that John 13 : 2, is wrongly translated by saying, " Supper being ended" before feet-washing is mentioned, while it is evident from verses 26–30, that supper was not ended then.)

Y. M. 1834.   Art. 1. How it is considered to sing at or during the breaking of bread?   Considered, as not proper, but at the distribution of the cup very proper. It was also remarked, that there should be no drinking without necessity while the supper is served, until all is served up, and a blessing asked of God, because we are to " tarry for one another."

Y. M. 1839.   Art. 2. How the supper should be held?   Considered, as it was always observed.

Y. M. 1841   Art. 3. Whether the brethren have a right to admit friends, who are not members, to sit down with us at the Lord's supper, if there is room?   Considered, that making a proper distinction between the supper and the communion of the body and blood of Jesus Christ, there could be no objection to admit friends to the supper, when there is room.

Y. M. 1848.   Art. 24. Is the Lord's supper observed by the brethren according to the Gospel?   Doth the Gospel require a supper in holding communion meetings?   Considered, that we have ample testimony in the Gospel to enable us to conclude, that a supper was eaten by the Saviour and his disciples in the same night he instituted the communion. See Matt. 26 : 20; Mark 14 : 17, 18 ; Luke 22 : 20; John 13 : 1–30; Jude v. 12.   And the Apostle Paul, after reproving the brethren at Corinth for their disorder in observing the supper, and speaking of it as the LORD'S supper, expressly declares, that he had received of the

Lord what he had delivered unto them, telling them how to observe it in proper order. 1 Cor. 11 : 23–34.

Y. M. 1849.   Art. 14. Is the supper which the brethren eat in connection with the communion, sacred or common ?   As there seems to be some reason to believe that the Apostle Paul alludes to the supper with other means of grace in the term, "ordinances" used in 1 Cor. 11 : 2; and as we view it as a practice of the Apostolic church to promote the spiritual . edification of its members, we consider it a sacred institution, and as such it ought to be observed, especially as it is emphatically called "*the Lord's supper*." 1 Cor. 11 : 20.   Art. 19. Should the supper or part of it be on the table at the time of feet-washing, or not ?   Considered, to leave the matter as hitherto practiced by the brethren.   Art. 21. Is the Lord's supper a divine or sacred ordinance, and if so, have the children of God a right to invite such as are not members to eat of it with them at the same table and time ?   Considered, to be a divine and sacred ordinance, as all the Lord's ordinances are, and should be eaten by the members only.   (Is not preaching and praying also a divine ordinance, and should we therefore exclude all from our meetings but the members ?)   Art. 32. Is it material what the supper is composed of at communion?   Considered best not to deviate from the order of the old brethren.   (The word δεῖπνον, *deipnon* requires a full meal.)

Y. M. 1850.   Art. 34. Would it not be better and more corresponding with the Gospel, if the brethren would hold the Lord's supper more in unison with each other; for it appears that some have bread and cheese, and some have meat and soup, &c.   Considered, that uniformity would be better.

Y. M. 1856.   Art. 19. Would it not be nearer to the word to have the supper prepared and on the table before commencing to wash feet ?   Referred to Min. of 1849. Art. 19.

Y. M. 1857.   Art. 2. Is it according to the Gospel to have the supper on the table at the time the feet are washed ?   Answer. Inasmuch as it is not expressly declared that Jesus rose from the table, he may probably have risen from a prepared supper, and as the brethren have the supper prepared before they proceed to the washing of feet, with their past practices in relation to those things we are satisfied.

Y. M. 1858. Art. 33. Is it according to the word of God to make use of beef instead of lamb in eating the Lord's supper ? Answer. It is. (It should have been said, where ?)

Y. M. 1862. Art. 43. Is it in accordance with the word of God to have the supper on the table before washing feet ? Answer. We consider that it is (?) (See the next following.)

Y. M. 1863. Art. 21. Whereas, there has obtained of late years some difference in observing the Lord's supper among different churches, some setting the supper on the table before feet-washing, while some do not till after—the latter being the old universal practice;—and whereas, the proceedings of Annual Meeting of last year in the Art. 43, have grieved some of our brethren; and whereas, a conciliatory course should always be pursued when brethren have a preference as it regards the mode or way of observing an ordinance, so that it is properly observed— we therefore recall the decision of the Annual Meeting above referred to, and let the subject of the time of putting the supper on the table stand precisely where it stood previous to the decision of 1862, with the understanding that the churches may and should continue without making any change either way, until we have further light on the subject to bring about a more full union.

LOTTERIES.

Y. M. 1804. Art. 7. Concerning buying lottery-tickets with a hope of gain, it was unanimously concluded, that such cannot be approved in members, and parents should by all means prevent their children from it, because it cannot be viewed any better than other gambling for gain.

Y. M. 1841. Art. 1. Whether it would be right and allowable according to the Gospel for members to buy lottery-tickets? Considered, that as a species of gambling for gain's sake, whereby others must necessarily lose, it is wrong, and not allowable at all for a brother.

Y. M. 1850. Art. 29. Is a member, brother or sister, not as justifiable in buying lottery-tickets, as in purchasing Bank stock, or taking eight or ten per cent. interest on money loaned to a brother? Considered, that buying lottery-tickets is very wrong, taking more than lawful interest is worse still, and taking stock in a Bank ought to be avoided also by brethren. One wrong can never justify another.

Y. M. 1853. Art. 19. Concerning brethren purchasing and drawing lottery-tickets. Considered, that brethren should not have any thing at all to do with this or any other species of gambling.

LOVEFEASTS.

By these we understand those festivals celebrated from time to time in our churches, at which there generally assemble ministers and members from all the surrounding districts, and sometimes from far and near, and where most of the ordinances of the house of God are administered, viz: Baptism, when there are applicants, and always feet-washing, the Lord's supper and the communion, &c. These generally attract great crowds, hence the following queries.

Y. M. 1828. Art. 13. Whether we might hold small (private, not publicly announced) lovefeasts? Considered, in cases where there are but few members (or where a member is on a sick bed, desirous to partake once more), provided that one ordained brother would be present, and that everything would be done at the right time and in proper order, there could be no objection at all, and it would not be contrary to the (word of) truth; yet care should be taken that it may not cause grief (pressure) or loss of affection.

Y. M. 1842. Art. 3. Whether our lovefeasts could not be held more privately and more often? The advice (in connection with the foregoing) was to select such times and places as experience may teach to be most suitable for this purpose.

Y. M. 1849. Art. 5. Some members think there is too much feasting at our lovefeasts, in providing so much for those who come to feast and make disturbance at our meetings. Considered, that we are to feed the hungry, if we are led by Christ's example; and the apostle says, "Therefore if thine enemy hunger, feed him; if he thirst, give him drink: for in so doing thou shalt heap coals of fire on his head." Rom. 12 : 20. (Christ's example was to feed the hungry multitude: " Because they continued with me (Christ) now three days, and have nothing to eat." Matt. 15 : 32. There was no previous preparation, nor announcement what Christ was going to do.)

Y. M. 1862. Art. 52. Would it be against the order of the Gospel or of the brethren, for a church, if the members agree to do so, to hold a lovefeast without tendering an invitation to any of the members of the adjoining churches but the ministering brethren? Answer. We consider if a church for want of room, or for other good reasons, thinks it proper to hold a lovefeast without giving a general invitation, it may be permitted to do so.

MANUSCRIPT LETTERS OF OLDEN TIME.

Manuscript Letters of olden time, (the original hand-writing of part of them being in possession of the author of " Encyclopedia.")

Letter from Michael Frantz, in Conestoga, dated Dec. 9, 1747. Grace be with you, and peace from God our Father and the Lord Jesus Christ, who has loved us with his pure love, and loves us still and always with his fervent love; from him I wish you in his pure love peace, union, holiness, and steadfastness in faith, to persevere, and to continue laboring in the work of the Lord with all the laborers and warriors of Jesus Christ. Amen. All my very worthy and much beloved brethren,in God, old and young, together with the whole church, brethren and sisters, be heartily greeted with the love of Jesus. Amen.

Moreover, dear brethren, I would let you know, that I have duly received in love your loving letter and respectful inquiries by the dear brother Conrad Hartman, and since the brother was anxious to hasten away again, I could not counsel much with other brethren upon what you desired an answer, viz: Whether you would have authority according to the Gospel to break bread (of communion) or not without (the presence of) elders? My simple answer is not (intended) that it should stand conclusive or as an article of covenant, what I write, but I can well leave it over to other brethren, yet so that it is my understanding, mind and counsel, namely, when it happens from want of an elder (being present at a communion), it might well be allowed when there is a brother in a church, who has been put on trial by the church to serve in place of an elder (has been advanced to administer the ordinances, as we express it in the present day), after being approved, (that he should so serve). But if there is in a church no brother thus advanced, as stated just now, then the church may select two brethren, or as many as may be thought prudent, and then have it decided by lot in the name of the Lord, who is to serve, and let him upon whom the lot falls, serve in the fear of the Lord, as much as is required at that time—not as if he was confirmed (or ordained) for such service, but the same course would have to be repeated at another time. But when a brother is on trial for the office of an elder, let him "also first be proved; then let them serve—being without reproach," as Paul says, 1 Timothy, 3d chapter.

I let you know, dear brethren, from (my own) experience, that some years ago it came to pass once here with us in Conestoga, that baptism was to be performed; I was at that time sick, and could not attend to this work. Then two of the ministering brethren drew lots among themselves, and the one thus assigned did baptize at that time, and all passed off well. Then there was a brother who was proved in the office of providing for the poor. After some time there was a communion held, and it was entrusted to a brother without lot, and things went in a disorderly manner. Reference has been made to the ancient church at Corinth, that Paul permitted them to break bread without elders, and my belief is, that it was done for want of elders. For Paul charged Titus afterward, that he should appoint elders in each city. Titus 1 : 5. It is easily perceived that things with the Corinthians went on in a very disorderly manner, because they had no elder or overseer. But I hope concerning you for the best, and not for such things as occurred with the Corinthians. Therefore I wish you much peace and love, to be endeavoring to keep the unity of the Spirit, and "to continue steadfastly in the apostle's doctrine and fellowship, and in breaking of bread, and in prayer." Acts 2.

With this I close, and greet you with mine, and commend you to the word of his grace; yea to God and to the living word, to give to you and us through his Spirit, according to the counsel and word of God, to keep house in the love of Jesus. Amen.   MICHAEL FRANTZ.

Remaining by the grace of God yours in love, bound together as brethren and co-laborers according to the doctrine of Jesus Christ. Amen.

A LETTER dated December 28, 1758, written by Alexander Mack, jr., and others.

This day, the 28th December, 175⁴, we, the undersigned brethren, have consulted together in the fear of the Lord concerning the unreconciled difficulties between brother Schwartz and brother Peter, and have deemed it right and just, that brother Peter should give to brother Schwartz in money six pounds ten shillings, because it so happened that brother Schwartz could not keep his share in the contract about land which they had purchased together, and he had been a party concerned from the commencement. Afterward it turned out that the advantage of the cheap bargain slipped from his hand, and he had to pay for his field, comparatively with the other, too dearly, and brother Peter has not been quite guiltless, which he himself confesses. But in order that we may be satisfied with his acknowledgment, we have laid the above upon him, and give him time for reflection. If he can do it, and will then be at peace and reconciled with us and with brother Schwartz, all shall be forgotten and buried, and no man shall have a right to draw forth something of it again. Until then (that he shall do so) we will give him in hope the (salutation of the) kiss, but cannot break the bread (of communion) with him. But if he does so as stated above, then we can also break the bread of communion with him, if nothing else should be made manifest that would make him unfit for it. Yet with this proviso, that if it would go too long (before said Peter will do what is laid upon him), we will upon counsel of the church make again inquiry about this matter. On the other hand we have concluded, that if brother Schwartz will be able to be at peace with us, and make no (further) complaint or demand on brother Peter concerning those old matters, then we will be satisfied with him also. (Signed) Sander Mack, Lorentz Shweitzer, Christoph Saur, Henry Slingluff, Philip Weber, Anton Schneider, George Schreiber, Justus Fuchs, Philip Diehl, Henry Daumer, John Steiner.

CONCERNING THE VISIONS OF CATHARINE HUMMER, ABOUT ONE HUNDRED YEARS AGO.

In order to understand more fully to what the brethren had reference in the following conclusion, we give an extract of the report, taken from her own statements, and recorded in the "Chronicon Ephratense," page 131 ff. according to which it seems, that in the year 1762, the 3d of October, said Catharine Hummer, she had the first vision in the night, between 10 and 11 o'clock, while she was sitting in the kitchen by the fire. At first she heard a knocking at the door, upon which she looked out, but there was no person. Soon after she heard a second knocking, and went out again, but found nobody. At last it knocked the third time, and when she went out and looked around, an angel stood near her

on her right, who spoke : " Yes, my friend, it is midnight and late, &c."
and then sang, and thus a conversation and singing was continued, until
the angel disappeared.   From that night, Catharine relates herself, that
she was for seven days and nights most of the time in an ecstacy, that
her spirit was separated from her body, and was led about through
strange places, and saw and heard strange things.   Again, November
12, 1762, and December 6th and 13th of the same year, she had visions,
which are recorded at length in said " Chronicon," and it is stated
there these visions have continued until April of the year 1765, and
that the father of this person, who was, it appears, a minister among the
brethren, after the noise of these visions had brought people to his
house from a distance of sixty miles, finally went abroad with his daughter, and preached to the awakening of many souls.   But it appears that
these movements were also accompanied by disorder, confusion and
offenses, and hence the brethren wrote the following letter of

ADVICE.

CONESTOGA, May 28, 1763.

The undersigned brethren from their different places (of abode), have
been here assembled in the fear of the Lord, in order to see, in heartfelt and compassionate brotherly love, how we might advise our brethren,
in God beloved, concerning the many woundings and different transgressions that have occurred since the exercises, visions and doings of and
with the sister Catharine Hummer, in the White Oak country, have
happened.   After we have yesterday heard the accusations of the brethren
against one another, and their testimony, that they would not seek any
division, but were willing to hear our brotherly counsel of love—we have
(in the next place,) all, every one of us, carefully heard and considered
the mind of each and every one of us, the undersigned brethren has declared his mind and advice freely, one after the other, and then we have
further united in the fear of the Lord on this, that we would in union
counsel our brethren as follows :   First, we believe and judge, indeed,
that brother Hummer has brought too much of his humanity (or human
nature) into this movement, from which different fruits of disunion have
grown.   In the second place, however, we consider, that both sides have
gone too far in words and judgments against one another, and hence it
is our brotherly counsel that brother Peter Hummer should needs make
acknowledgments, where he might have offended with regard of brotherly
obedience, and if there are on both sides conviction and acknowledgment,
then we advise out of brotherly love, that on both sides all judgments
and harsh expressions might be entirely laid down, though we have not
the same opinion of that noted (singular) occurrence, so that those who
think well of it, should not judge those who are of the contrary opinion,

and those who do not esteem it, should not despise those who expect to
derive some use and benefit from it.   ·

For the rest, we advise you, beloved brethren, receive one another as
Christ has received us, and pardon one another as Christ has pardoned
us also, and let us everywhere consider, that all disputing, judging and
despising should be entirely laid aside, and thus remain, that every one
leave to the other his own opinion, in the fear of the Lord, and altogether for conscience' sake.   Moreover, it is our advice that all unnecessary and too frequent visiting should cease, and every one should earnestly abstain from all appearance of evil, and aim in all things after
truth and uprightness, in order that truth may make us free from all
that might still keep us in captivity, and prevent us from coming to a
oneness of mind in Christ Jesus according to the will of God.   If now
one or the other should think we have not sufficiently judged the occurrence, let him consider, that we cannot see the least cause of a separation for conscience' sake.   Hence, we have felt constrained not to criti-
cise or judge this (strange) affair, but rather to advise every one to a
godly impartiality and patience, that none may judge any thing before
the time until the Lord come, who both will bring to light the hidden
things of darkness, and will make manifest the counsels of the heart,
and then shall every man have praise of God according to his faith and
its fruits.   Signed by Jacob Meyer, Peter Dirdorff, Martin Urner,
Nicholas Martin, Lorenz Shrab, Henry Naff, George Schreiber,
Christopher Saur, George Etter, Joseph Rentsh, Jacob Stutzman, John
Shlipfer, Jacob Mohr, Mattes Schweitzer, Henry Raudenbush, Gideon
Rausser, Daniel Letterman, Daniel Arnold, Anton Hartman, Sander
Mack, Nicholas Letterman, Stephen Ulrich.

AN INTERESTING LETTER TO A BROTHER PRINTER.

In Jesus Christ, our only and true Saviour, much beloved brother
Christopher Saur. Love and a desire for the salvation of us all in
Christ causes us many inward afflictions in these dangerous days and
times. Our ever kind God would in mercy take care of our souls, that
we may not miss the right road, nor by a secret approval of commandments of men may get on the way of the murderer. Our souls are justly
prostrated to the dust, and cry for divine mercy: Spare, oh Lord, spare
thy inheritance, and take charge of thy scattered sheep!

Dear brother, it appears to us as if hidden and very politic powers
of the spirit of this world had laid a secret snare for thy soul, trying to
bring thee into their net by the well meant printing of Catechisms.
May God himself grant thy soul new strength, making thee young as an
eagle among those who hope in the name of the Lord, and put their
trust in the Lord of lords, who can save even from death. Yes, dear

brother, the Lord Jesus Christ make thee whole in the faith and in the love towards thy weak fellow-members; may He make thy feet like hart's feet to escape from all the snares of the enemy. Oh, how happy will our souls be, when we come with a good conscience to the end of our pilgrimage, and can hear the most blessed and glorious words: " Well done, thou good and faithful servant, thou hast been faithful over a few things, I will make thee ruler over many things: enter thou into the joy of thy Lord." Now the Lord still calls unto us: " Be thou faithful unto death, and I will give thee a crown of life !"

Dear brother, as it appears to us, thou hast committed a fault already, or (rather) hast been overtaken in a fault, which may often happen before we are aware of it, if we are not strictly attentive to the excellent and most perfect form of doctrine. According to our apprehension it was indeed already a fault, that thou hast ever printed a single H—catechism : for he who will teach the commandments of God, must teach no commandments of men; otherwise by the human commandments (or traditions), his whole religion will become a vain religion. So likewise thy printing-office, if it is to serve to the honor of God, must not honor human traditions; for God's commandments and human traditions do not agree together.

We had, however, some time since cause to hope, that by grace in the testimony of thy conscience, that fault was healed and amended, especially when thou "didst promise so willingly to members not to print any more of that catechism." But since we now see with grief that also the beloved brother Justus has been overtaken in the same fault with thee, and thou sayst that thou wouldst not promise any more what thou hadst promised formerly of your own accord. This matter has become to us very grave and serious; and we find ourselves constrained by our own consciences, to lay before you both, dear brethren, this matter according to our own view to your mature consideration, in hope that God and his grace· would awaken once more your consciences, to consider, and as it were address yourselves and say : What have we done ?

Christ has commanded to teach all nations and then to baptize, but you print (in said catechism) that infants should be baptized.

Christ has said that we should "swear not at all;" but you print we ought or might indeed swear an oath by the name of God in a godly manner.

Christ says, " He that loves me keeps my commandments;" and the Apostle John says, " His commandments are not grievous;" but you print that even a converted man could not keep God's commandments.

Christ says, " Not every one that saith unto me, Lord, Lord, shall enter into the kingdom of heaven; but he that doeth the will of my Father which is in heaven." You print that to him who has never kept any of the commandments of God, and is still inclined to every evil thing, to him the merits of Christ were imputed in such a manner as if he himself had fulfilled all obedience, if he only accepts such with a believing heart.

Dearly beloved brethren, the more we reflect on these things, the more inconsistent they appear to us. Oh do consider but once with us what James says: "Above all things, my brethren, swear not,   *   *   * (but let your yea be yea, and your nay, nay;) lest ye fall into condemnation!" Consider deeply what hypocrisy that little book contains! It teaches that we might swear in a godly manner, though He who is alone able to save has commanded we shall swear not at all? What kind of godliness was there ever found in disobedience? Christ, the eternal truth, calls those hypocrites who made the commandments of God of none effect, in order to observe their own traditions. Now, indeed, both repentance and baptism is made of none effect by their miserable infant sprinkling. It is, however, not our object to specify particularly all hypocrisy which is sown by this little book as a fruitful seed into the hearts of tender youths; yet we believe, as in ancient times, that, from false prophets in Jerusalem hypocrisy spread through the whole land; so from the seed of human commandments in Babylon comes up hypocrisy, and grows and blossoms among the great multitude of those who call themselves Christians. Oh that we might depart entirely from all hypocrisy!

Of course, you have not had that impression of this little book; for then it would have been impossible for you to print it. But we wish that none of you may have offended his own conscience in this matter, and that you might yet see how you have not at all obtained your well intended object by the printing of this little book. For as far as we have understood from thee, brother Christopher, you have to show no weightier reason than that we should not be offensive to any one, and indeed if this were correct, it would be nothing strange if you deemed that catechism a useful book; but oh far different is the case! You have already offended your members thereby, and the offense taken by the rude world on it is different; some say, the catechism must be right because Saur prints it; others say, Saur prints every thing for money. And oh how easily may we become offensive unto young babies in the truth, if they should learn that we are getting into difficulties among ourselves on account of that catechism. But unto peace we are called of God, and thus we are to follow "peace with all men, and holiness, without which no man shall see the Lord."

Therefore receive us, dear brethren; we will not require of you to make any special promise against your will, but this we desire, that if you or one of you in the future should undertake to print again that little

book, you would let us know in love, in order that we may call a big
meeting of all the Elders in the land to hear their mind, whether we
have done right or wrong in admonishing you on this matter, and
whether it be possible that after such admonition a follower of Christ
could print such a book or not?

Further, have we'understood thee to say to us, that it is thy desire to
know whether we could bid thee God speed in the good undertaking
with thy printing-office to make thyself useful among all sorts of men?
In reply, we bid thee from the heart, God speed; namely, that the word
of Christ dwell richly in thy heart, in thy house, and in thy printing-office;
but concerning the word of the serpent, which men want to be honored
instead of the commandment of God, in that we bid thee God speed,
that the Lord may deliver thee from it, and that also thy printing-office
may be purified from the same. "For whatsoever a man soweth, that
shall he also reap." Now, if thou wilt sow good seed by thy printing-
office, then thy children, and also thy fellow-believers who wish thee
well, may hope to reap a good harvest from it, according to the saying,
"One soweth, and another reapeth." Thus it is the will of the Lord
that we should reap a full harvest in truth and righteousness, that both
may rejoice together, he that soweth and he that reapeth.

Written in the month of August, Anno 1764. (Signed) Henry
Slingluff, Anthony Schneider, Alexander Mack, Philip Weber, George
Schreiber.

(Postscript in the same hand-writing.)

In consideration of my mortality, I testify that though I stand yet in
all points in the views as expressed above, still I will not insist that
for this cause by us the subscribers, or in our name, a big meeting should
be appointed, lest we might thereby with the good intention to seek
peace, indeed, cause dissension and distraction.

May 17, 1767.   SANDER MACK.

That we are united with the sentiments here expressed, we testify.
George Schreiber, Philip Weber, Henry Slingluff.

NOTE.

It is evident that the postscript, written nearly three years later
than the letter itself, modifies the latter considerably. Though both
the letter and the postscript breathe a spirit of the kindest love, and a
watchful care for the good of the individual members and the church at
large, the first seems to have been written under the pressure of a prevailing sentiment, while the last was the result of calm reflection.
Probably brother SAUR plead somewhat effectually, that as a man may
make a copy of a letter, agreement or any other instrument of writing,
without becoming personally concerned or responsible for the sentiments

or conditions contained therein, even so a printer may make hundreds and thousands of copies of a book without endorsing its contents in part or in the whole. Of course, profane or immoral publications would not be made by a printer who feels his responsibility to God and mankind, and is guided more by principle than self interest. We might multiply such letters to a considerable extent, but let these suffice as a fair sample of "Letters of olden times," expressing the views and sentiments of our brethren more than a hundred years ago.

MARRIAGE. See also *Divorce, Adultery, &c.*

Y. M. 1804. Art. 2. It was concluded, in concord and union, that ministers should be uniform in solemnizing marriage according to the law of our country, by publishing the bans of every couple three times, and this in the section where they live or reside, as near as possible, so that if there were any sufficient cause or impediment of such intended marriage, it might be brought to light, and all things might be conducted decently and in order.

Y. M. 1818. Art. 1. Concerning trouble arising in some churches on account of the marriage of young people, and their solemnization. Inasmuch some desire to hold fast to the counsel or conclusions of the old brethren, which was, that previous to marriage the bans were published three times, which they think is a good order and not at all inconsistent with the Gospel; but now some assert, that this publishing at the close of the meeting was against their conscience, and think that the effect of the word preached before was thereby interrupted; while on the other hand brethren think that there is danger in solemnizing marriage without publishing before, inasmuch we cannot know how matters stand with young folk, and there might be danger, even if they are neighbor's or brother's children; and we think, if we were so closely restricted by our conscience not to publish the bans, then we would also marry none. Yet we desire to control no man's conscience, provided he acts for peace, and as they say, for conscience' sake. We desire all housekeepers in churches might be united in one mind to hold fast to the counsel of the old brethren; for unto peace God has called us.

Y. M. 1819. Art. 4. How it is considered, that brethren receive other preachers (from other denominations) into their houses, in order to solemnize the marriage of their children after the manner of the world? Considered, that matrimony is a solemn matter, whether we commence it with or without a blessing, and hence we think we should have so much love for our children as to be concerned that they might enter upon that state with a blessing; and we believe no man can communicate such but he that is animated by the Holy Spirit, by whom he will also be led into all truths. Hence we should have our children married by a brother who is authorized to do it, with a blessing and brief exhortation; also without too great superfluity of meat and drink, so that we can believe to be pleasing to God; for all extravagance is sin. Art. 5. Whether a member is permitted to marry without counsel of the church, and without publishing the bans? Answer. We know that all who have entered into the covenant of grace, have promised also to receive counsel, and it seems to us, in such an important matter as marriage is, we should by all means seek counsel of our fellow believers. And concerning the publishing of the bans, it is our loving counsel, and daily experience teaches us, that it is very good to hold to a good order, inasmuch by the publishing the bans, many an accusation is cut off, while on the other hand much deception is prevented, which would have free course without the bans.

Y. M. 1848. (Ohio.) Art. 9. Whether a brother may be allowed, according to the Gospel, to take pay when offered for performing the ceremony of marriage? Considered, that this meeting cannot advise brethren to take a fee, and would leave it as a matter of conscience to the ministering brother, with the advice of the church in which he lives.

Y. M. 1849. Art 29. How is it considered, when a brother solemnizes a marriage contract between a sister, whose first husband is not known to be dead, and another individual? Considered, that under such circumstances a brother ought not to act. (Should he·not rather warn earnestly the sister from such a rash step?).

Y. M. 1850. Art. 16. What is the duty of a minister, when called upon to solemnize marriage, when one of the parties is the child of members, and these parents not consenting to the match, yet the minister knows of no other objection but the daughter's going from home to get married? Considered, as not advisable without the consent of the parents. Paul says, "If it be possible as much as lieth in you, live peaceably with all men." Rom. 12 : 18 ; Heb. 12 : 14.

Y. M. 1855. Art. 11. Is a speaker allowed to take any amount of money for solemnizing marriage that may be offered to him, and if so, how much? Referred to Y. M. 1848. Art. 9. (See above.)

Y. M. 1857. Art. 14. How is it considered if ministering brethren take as much as ten dollars as a fee for performing the marriage ceremony, and does the Gospel allow ministers a fee under any circumstances? Ans. The Gospel does not allow ministers to take a fee.

Y. M. 1858. Art. 18. Whereas, we are aware that the decision of the last annual meeting in relation to the subject presented in Art. 14, of said meeting, has given a great deal of dissatisfaction, and is to a great extent disregarded, thus bringing the decision of the annual meeting into disrepute; we therefore recommend that this meeting reconsider that subject, and if the decision of the last meeting is sustained, it is desirable that some scriptural authority should be given for it, as should be done in all cases. Reconsidered, and concluded to adopt the decision of the annual meeting of 1848. See above, Y. M. 1848. Art. 9.

Y. M. 1862. Art. 17. Is it considered right according to the Gospel for a brother to marry a woman, not a sister, that is divorced from her husband, when it is not known whether that divorced husband is dead; and the ordained elder, who performed the marriage ceremony, contends that all's right? Ans. We consider it wrong for any brother in the ministry to perform such a marriage, and also wrong according to the Gospel for any brother or sister to be married to any such party.

MARRIAGE OF TOO NEAR RELATIONS.

Y. M. 1789. Art. 5. Concerning marriages of near relations, especially cousins, was unanimously considered and deemed good, that such marriages should not at all be, and that parents should warn their children earnestly in this respect, so that offense and scandal might be prevented, which have been so often occasioned by it, and that our dear youth may not in ignorance be led into something, where, perhaps, afterwards their thoughts might be accusing one another about those things which cannot be altered any more, and therefore should be well considered previously in the fear of God.

Y. M. 1819. See Adultery, and also Matrimonial. Y. M. 1854. Art. 16. Is it allowed by the Gospel for a sister, after her husband is dead, to be married to her step-son? Considered, not to be allowed according to the following passages 1 Cor. 5: 1–12. Lev. 18: 8. Churches should be watchful to purge out such a leaven from among them.

See also Matrimonial. Y. M. 1858. Art 1.

MATRIMONIAL.

Y. M. 1812. Art. 4. Concerning a woman who was deserted by her husband, and being informed that he was dead, married again; when afterwards her first husband made his appearance again, he showed no concern about her and went away again; and now he is said again to be dead, and she makes application to be received into the church. Considered, that this cannot be done according to the word of God, before there is sure evidence that the first husband is dead, and then upon sincere repentance and acknowledgment she might be received.

Y. M. 1819. Art. 1. Concerning a woman who married a man who had deserted his wife because she had committed carnal intercourse with another man, as he says, proved by the time of her delivery. Considered, if there can be found no evidence as his (the husband's) assertion, it is not sufficient to decide that it was or is no true wedlock, consequently the woman he has now, with himself, will be considered as adulterers as long as the first wife lives, according to the declaration of the Apostle Paul, Rom. 7 : 2, 3. This is left over to further investigation. So we find no liberty to receive persons who live in adultery, into the church, as long as the first marriage is not dissolved by death, and then only upon sincere sorrow and repentance they may be received into the communion of the faithful. But if those who are in such case would resolve firmly for God's sake to live separate, and would also indeed do so, and lament sincerely their former state—then there might be mercy in store for them, and they might be thereby reconciled to God.

Y. M. 1830. Art. 2. Whether a brother may take a wife who has already a husband, but is deserted and set free by him? This has long since been considered that it cannot be according to the word and Gospel.

Y. M. 1842. Art. 8. Whether a person who was married, and whose partner broke the marriage vow by fornication, may marry again according to the Gospel, after obtaining a bill of divorce? Considered, that according to the word of God, Matt. 5 : 31, 32 ; 19 : 3–10; Mark 10 : 2–12; Luke 16 : 18; 1 Cor. 7, 10, 11, 39 — a person cannot marry again while the first companion lives ; and that the Gospel considers not only the person that would marry again after being divorced, but also the person who would marry the divorced party, as adulterers.

Y. M. 1847. Art. 2. Whether a brother or sister whose companion has broken the marriage-vow by fornication, may marry again according to the Gospel, after obtaining a bill of divorce? It was concluded by the brethren present that a brother or sister may not. See Min. of Y. M. 1842. Art. 8.

Y. M. 1848. Art. 15. If a sister married a man, and learns afterward that he had already a wife, and she immediately forsakes him— has she the liberty to get married to another man while the first man is yet living, according to the Gospel? Considered, that we submit the case to her own judgment, and advise her that in the future she should be cautious and take counsel of the church.

Y. M. 1850. Art. 4. How is it considered if a sister marries an unbelieving husband who afterwards does maltreat her by slandering and debauchery, and in many ways abuse and grieve her, so as to forbid and prohibit her from going to meeting or to any of her friends and relations ; she then upon the advice of her friends—members of the church—leaves him and tries to get rid of him by law, upon which he offers to give himself up to the church, and is willing to do what the church lays upon him, acknowledging that he has done wickedly, and promises to do better ; but he having made such promises before, and did not come up to them, the friends of the sister do not think it proper for her to unite with him again ? Considered, that we could not advise the sister to leave her husband; but if she did so, she ought to remain unmarried, according to Paul, 1 Cor. 7: 11, 12. Art. 10. Whether we can hold as members a man and wife that live together in strife, that have been parted on that account, and now live together, but not as man and wife should? Considered, that we could not hold such as members. Art. 17. How is it considered, when a sister has an unbelieving husband who gets drunk and abuses her, and attempts to kill her with an axe; she then leaves him, and returns to her father who then goes to the house-keeper in the church for advice, upon whose advice a bill of divorce is obtained? Considered, that a house-keeper has no right to give such advice without counseling the church, neither has a sister a right to get divorced without such counsel. See Matt. 19 : 6–9; 1 Cor. 7 : 11. Art. 23. If a woman leaves a husband for his extreme cruelty, and he obtains a bill of divorce and marries another woman, and his first wife afterward marries another man, both being unbelievers (at the time), can such persons be received into the church of Christ according to the Gospel? Considered, that we could not receive such according to the Gospel. Rom. 7 : 1–3; 1 Cor. 7 : 10, 11, 39.

Y. M. 1858. Art. 1. Can a person be received into the church who is uncle to his wife, or do the brethren think the Gospel will not allow of such person becoming a member of the church? Considered, that if he is uncle to his wife by marriage, he may be received; if by blood relation, he should not be. Art. 5. Is it required of those who are so unfortunate as to have their companions put in avoidance, not to accompany with them as man and wife? Considered, that as the apostle says, we are not to eat with them, we think his prohibition is sufficient. (Does he not expressly say "not to keep company?") Art. 10. How is it considered, when a difficulty arises between husband and wife, and the wife depart from her husband, is it the duty of the husband to pursue the course prescribed in Matt. 18 : 15–17? We consider it is.

Y. M. 1860. Art. 10. A brother has a wife who is not a member of the church, and she refuses to live with him peaceably, and having been living apart from him for more than two years, the brethren acquainted with the circumstances, believing the wife to be the cause of the trouble. She now demands a divorce. Now, brethren, we would be very glad if you will give us an advice in this case. *Ans.* We think a brother cannot grant or accept a divorce for any cause but that of fornication— "But I say unto you, that whosoever shall put away his wife, saving for the cause of fornication, causeth her to commit adultery: and whosoever shall marry her that is divorced, committeth adultery." Matt. 5: 32. (1 Cor. 7 : 15.)

Y. M. 1862. Art. 3. If a sister is married to a man, who after living

10

with her awhile, leaves her, and she not hearing from him for several years, marries again, can she be held as a member? *Answer*—No; she could not be held as a member. Art. 59. If a man and his wife leave one church and go into another, with a recommendation from the former, which is received by the latter—after awhile the sister leaves her husband, the brother, and returns to the church which she first left, charging her husband with crimes committed before the recommendation was given. Not bringing a recommendation from the church from which she last came, the former receives her or retains her as a member, and acts on the case of her husband, and expels him. Did this church do right? *Answer*—We consider that no church should receive a member from another without a certificate, or expel a member without a hearing.

Y. M. 1864. Art. 2. If a sister has a husband that is not a member in the church, and it is known that he is an adulterer, is it consistent with the gospel for her to live with him and be his wife? And if it is not consistent for her to do so, has she a right to get a bill of divorcement according to law? *Ans.* As to the first part of the query, we think it should be left to her choice whether to live with him or not. And as the second, we say with Paul, 1 Cor. 7 : 10, 11, "But and if she depart, let her remain unmarried."

MEETING-HOUSES.

Y. M. 1828. Art. 12. Whether we may build meeting-houses? Considered, to leave it over to every church to do as they deem good.

Y. M. 1855. Art. 14. Is it conforming to the world to build meeting houses? Ans. No; if built without unnecessary ornaments, and only for the worship (and service) of God.

MEETINGS, PROTRACTED.

Y. M. 1842. Art. 2. Whether it will be for the edification of the church of God, to hold protracted meetings, and to introduce mourning-benches, in imitation of the new measures adopted by different sects and denominations? The brethren generally considered that it was advisable to be very cautious, and at all times to keep good order, in accordance with the doctrine and example of the apostles, and not to introduce such innovations, like mourner's benches, &c.

Y. M. 1858. Art. 31. Is it contrary to the Gospel for brethren to hold meetings for a number of days in succession in one place, in order to preach the pure word of God, and to administer the ordinance of baptism to those who believe the word and receive it? Considered, not contrary to the gospel, if the believer is proceeded with according to the gospel, and the order of the brethren as given by the Y. M. of 1848.

Art. 3.   Art. 50. Is it agreeable to the gospel to hold a protracted meeting, say for one week or ten days in succession?   Ans. As to the phrase "protracted meetings," we know nothing of it in the gospel; but as touching the frequency of the saints meeting together, we find no limits in the gospel, so that they are held in the order of the house of God.

MEETINGS, REGULAR.

Y. M. 1849.   Art. 23. What should be done with such members as neglect attending our meetings for six or more months, and when the yearly visit is paid them they seem or feel satisfied with the church, and when there is a love-feast, they generally attend and commune? Considered, that the ministering brethren in the church, in which such members are, should (visit and) earnestly admonish them to adhere to the advice of the Apostle Paul, Heb. 10 : 25.

Y. M. 1862.   Art. 10. How are we to proceed with members who will neglect to attend council and public meetings, and that for months ? Answer—Such members should be admonished again and again, and their reasons for non-attendance ascertained, and the danger of living in such a manner set before them.   See Heb. 10 : 25.

Y. M. 1862.   Art. 41. What will the annual council advise in the following case, viz : A number of brethren in district A become prejudiced against the body of the church, and will not attend council and other meetings, after being cited frequently to do so ?   But they will attend meetings and councils in district B or the adjoining district, and they also will contribute means and money for the benefit of the said district B, to the entire neglect of their own district?   Also, what will annual council say of the brethren in district B, who encourage those brethren of district A to continue in such a practice?   Answer.—We consider it wrong for brethren to aid other districts and to neglect their own; and we also consider it wrong for a neighboring church to pursue such a course as district B is said to have done.

MINISTERS HOLDING MEETINGS, &c.

Y. M. 1848. (Indiana.)   Art. 2. Whether it is proper, if more than two or three ministers should rise in a common meeting to speak (preach)? Considered, that a due sense of order and propriety will teach us how to conduct our meetings, so as to edify and not to weary the congregation. See 1 Cor. 14 : 32, 33; 40.

MINISTERS MOVING FROM ONE PLACE TO ANOTHER.

Y. M. 1833.   Art. 3. Whether a brother, who was chosen to the (ministry of the) word, in one church, and moves into another with a good testimony, can be relieved from his office (or rather literally put back from it) ? It was always considered, when a ministering brother moves out of the church who chose him, he moves out of his office; that is, before he is fully ordained; and that it was at the option of the church into which he moves, to receive him with his office or not. If his life and conduct inspires love and confidence, it will not be long before he may be called to exercise his ministry again. Have patience!

Y. M. 1835. Art. 6. How is it considered, if ministers move into churches where there is no ordained elder, whether they can be received where no bishop is present? No; there ought to be one or more bishops invited for the occasion, or the matter postponed to another time. Meanwhile those new-comers may serve in their office as guests.

Y. M. 1838. Art. 7. Whether a teacher (minister) has the right to remove out of the church without the counsel of the same ? Considered, that it is right and good that a brother in such an important undertaking should seek the counsel of his church.

Y. M. 1848. (Indiana.) Art. 8. How is it considered, if a brother that is chosen for an office in the church, should move from one church and neighborhood to another without bringing a testimonial along, whether he can be received in his office before a testimony arrives? Considered, that if such brother moves only a little way into a church, where his standing is generally known, there would be no need of a written testimony, (still a sufficient testimony, by word of mouth of witnesses from his former church, and after council being held in that church, would be requisite.) But if a brother should move a considerable distance, it is right and proper to require a testimonial before such is received in his office.

Y. M. 1859. Art. 15. How is it considered when a bishop moves from his district into a third district, and takes no letter of recommendation along with him, but wants to retain the oversight of the church he has left, and says he will still keep his standing in that church during his life, although he is frequently absent from their regular meetings? Answer. He should have a letter of recommendation from the church from which he moved, and if the distance is not too great, he may still retain the oversight of that church, while his doing so may produce no difficulties.

Art. 30. If a brother in the ministry, or deaconship, move from one congregation to another, having a certificate of good standing in his office, has the congregation to which he moved, a right to refuse to receive him with his office ? Answer. We consider they have not.

Y. M. 1862. Art. 9. When official members move from one district to another, should they be received with hand and kiss, or is a letter sufficient? Answer.—Art. 9 of Min. of 1846, re-adopted, and here to be ep rinted.

["Is a brother that was a speaker or deacon, and has moved into another church, properly re-installed in his office, if an ordained brother takes the counsel of the church and announces the same to him, without he being received by the members with hand and kiss? Considered unanimously by the elders, that inasmuch he was properly received into his office by the church in which he was chosen, he would be sufficiently established."]

MINISTERS SERVING ON ARBITRATIONS, &c.

Y. M. 1842. Art. 6. Whether it be proper for a brother who is elected to speak the Word (chosen for the Ministry,) to serve at arbitrations or on juries, &c. Considered, as it has been often heretofore, that brethren would do best at all times, if it be avoidable, not to serve, except there is reason to hope that peace may be promoted thereby.

MINISTERS TAKING PAY.

Y. M. 1827. Art. 10. Concerning taking pay for solemnizing marriages and preaching funeral sermons. It was unanimously considered, that it should not be among brethren.
(See also *Marriages.*)

MINISTRY.

Y. M. 1845. Art. 7. How it is considered, if brethren will force themselves into the ministry without consent from the Elders, and some of the members encourage them in it? Considered, that inasmuch it appears by the words of James, chapter 3: 1, by the words of our Saviour, John, 10:1, and of Paul, Heb. 5:4 and 7; there is a right way, and also a wrong way, to enter into the ministry; the wrong way being, when one is taking this honor unto himself, and the right way, when one is called of God by the Church, which is the body of Christ; and the order of which calling to the ministry is found described in the Acts of the Apostles. Brethren ought to be very cautious, when they feel a desire to preach the Gospel, that they do not take the wrong way; rather humble than elevate themselves, and be fully assured, that if the Lord wants their services, he has all power in heaven and on earth to bring about their calling to it in the right order and in due time; but if such brethren would still go out of the way, appoint and hold meetings against the counsel of the church, the church will have to hold them as disobedient members according to Matt. 18; and members generally ought to be very careful not to encourage and support such brethren in their disorderly proceedings.

Y. M. 1848. (Indiana.) Art. 1. Whether a private brother has a right to speak in public? Considered, that inasmuch as there is a way appointed in the gospel to enter into the ministry, those who feel an inward desire or call to preach, (should exercise their gift faithfully in their own family, and at the family worship where they may happen to be, and in speaking privately to such individuals, as opportunity may offer to their soul's welfare, but) should wait patiently until (God by) the church sees fit to appoint them to the public ministry. See John's Gospel, 10 : 1, 2. Heb. 5 : 4, 5.

MINUTES OF Y. M.

Y. M. 1848. Art. 17. With regard to the printing of the Minutes of the Y. M., it was concluded to have as many printed as to supply each church with two copies, but that on no condition they should be sold to such as are not members.

Y. M. 1849. Art. 6. Would it not be well to have a committee appointed at this or some future annual meeting, whose duty it should be to collect all the (minutes) advice of councils, bearing on all points of duty, and put it in the form of a book, and bring it before the council of the following year for their approbation; and if approved of, get it printed, so that each member might have a copy, not as a creed, but as (a record of) advice, and as a testimony of the truths as we understand it? Considered, to let this matter lay over. Art. 43. Whether each elder, teacher, or visiting brother should not have the privilege of having a copy of the Minutes of the Y. M? Considered, that we are in favor for each ministering brother to have a copy, and they be advised to keep them if possible from coming before the world; and we will further recommend that they should be sent sealed (in letter form), as we know them to have been opened in Post Offices.

Y. M. 1850. Art. 2. How it is considered, inasmuch as our beloved brother, H. K., is not present at this meeting—for to appoint a com. mittee to have the Minutes of this meeting printed, and to receive all moneys appropriated to defray the expenses of printing. It has been agreed upon by this meeting, that bro. Benjamin Bowman, of Va., Daniel Summer, of Ohio, and David Hardman, of Indiana, be this committee.

Y. M. 1858. Art. 55. Would it not be well for the Standing Committee of this Y. M. to appoint a number of intelligent and pious brethren to collect all the minutes that can be still obtained of our yearly meetings, and have them printed in a volume, for the use and satisfaction of the churches? Considered, we think it not advisable so to do.

Y. M. 1861. Art. 6. Will this yearly meeting grant the privilege to re-print all the minutes of the yearly meetings (still extant), so that those wishing to have them may have a full copy? *Resolved,* By this annual meeting that this subject should be attended to, and we therefore recommend that a committee be appointed to gather up all the minutes as far

back as can be had, and bring them together in such a way and form as
may be thought best, and we hereby appoint brother Henry Kurtz, of
Ohio; Andrew Spanogle, of Pa.; John Kline, of Va.; Christian Long,
of Illinois, and Philip Boyle, of Maryland, to attend to said business.
and report to the next yearly meeting. (On account of the War and
other hindrances, this committee has not yet been able to meet or do any
thing, except individually.)

MISSIONARY.

Y. M. 1852. Art. 8. Whether the commission of our Lord and
Saviour Jesus Christ, Matt. 28 : 19, 20; Mark, 16 : 15, does not require of the church to send brethren to preach the Gospel, where the
name of Christ is not known? . Considered, that the brethren acknowledge the great commission of Christ to its full extent, and that it is the
duty of the church, the ministers and every private member, to do all
that is in their power to fulfill that commission in accordance with apostolic practice.

Y. M. 1856. Art. 22. A letter from Virginia urging that this Y. M.
devise a plan, how the church could fulfill the command of the Saviour,
Matt. 28 : 19, more effectually, so that the Article 8, on our Minutes of
1852, should not remain a dead letter. This meeting recommend the
subject to the serious consideration of *all* the churches.

Y. M. 1858. Art. 58. Whereas, there is a strong desire among the
brethren in various places to have a more general exertion made on the
part of the church to have the truth more universally spread; and,
whereas, the subject has been frequently talked of without any definite
plan being proposed; we, therefore, have concluded by way of introduction, to offer the following outlines of a plan, subject, however, to such
amendments as may from time to time be thought best. That is, let
each State where there is a respectable number of brethren, form a district; let the brethren then hold their annual meetings; let each
of these divisions (districts) have its treasury; let the churches that feel
favorable have their treasury; let the churches be called upon as often
as may be necessary to cast in their mite as a free-will offering. Then
let these contributions be put into the district treasury, and let the district meeting appoint ministering brethren, say two or more, if necessary
(such as are willing to go), to travel through the. respective States for
one year, their expenses being paid, and such provision made for their
families as may be thought necessary. What does the annual meeting
think of this proposition? Considered, that we think it not good to
adopt this proposition; but we believe it is a subject worthy the serious and prayerful consideration of the brotherhood, and we recommend
the brethren to give it such consideration.

Y. M. 1859.   Art. 28. Seeing the great necessity of having the gospel as held and practised by the brethren more extensively spread and known, we desire that the brethren in this annual council reconsider Art. 58 of Minutes of 1858, and adopt it with such amendments as in the fear of the Lord may seem best.

As it was recommended by the last annual meeting to make the subject of spreading the gospel one of prayerful consideration, it appears it was done; and several churches have expressed their wish to this annual council meeting, to have it take a favorable action upon the subject. The following is the conclusion this annual meeting has come to in relation to what is referred to in this article.

This meeting recommend and give liberty to any of the districts or States to make a move on the subject of spreading and sustaining the gospel as preached and understood by the brethren, so that the same may be done in the order of the gospel. And we recommend to those churches who may adopt this, to make a report to the next annual meeting upon their success. And in view of the importance of the subject, we appoint the following brethren as a committee, to propose some plan by which the brotherhood in general may take a part in this good work; said plan to be reported to the next annual meeting: DANIEL P. SAYLER, JOHN KLINE, JOHN H. UMSTAD, SAMUEL LAYMAN, JOHN METZGER, and JAMES QUINTER. DANIEL P. SAYLER is the corresponding member of the committee.

Y. M. 1860.   Art. 12. Whereas, the brethren in California and Oregon have earnestly desired and requested a delegation of two or three brethren to be sent by the Annual Council of the brethren, to encourage and strengthen them, and to "set in order the things needed" for a proper organization of churches, according to the Gospel of Christ, as well as to preach the Gospel where Christ is not known; the meeting, therefore, receiving with favor the request, came to the following conclusion concerning the subject:

It was decided that the standing committee of this Annual Meeting form a board for the purpose of corresponding with brethren, and of ascertaining if any seem to be called to the work, and of judging of their fitness for it, and for making the necessary arrangements for carrying out the purposes of this Annual Meeting to comply with the request from the brethren in California and Oregon.

And in order to obtain the necessary pecuniary aid, this meeting recommends to all the churches to make contributions for the purpose, and to report to the board the result of their operations. JAMES QUINTER, Columbiana, Columbiana Co., O., was appointed corresponding Secretary, and DANIEL P. SAYLER, Double Pipe Creek, Carroll Co., Md., Treasurer.

Y. M. 1861. Art. 7. Query 7. Contains a remonstrance from the Sugar Creek church, Allen Co., Ohio, as follows: "Having assembled in council, and having under consideration the Missionary question, we the church aforesaid enter our remonstrance against all plans that have been recommended through the Visitor, save the one on page 279, in September No. last.

All business upon this subject is referred to the next Yearly Meeting.

Art. 13. *Resolved*, That we are opposed to a treasury for the exclusive benefit of the ministry, but that every church should encourage their ministers to be active in their calling, and also to support them in all cases of necessity.

Considered, that we fully concur in the sentiments above expressed.

MORTGAGE, TAKING OF BRETHREN.

Y. M. 1825. Art. 2. Whether a brother may take a mortgage or judgment bond of another brother, was considered, that brethren should be as careful of the interest of their neighbor as of their own, and not be selfish; and inasmuch to take bail for large sums is deemed wrong, it is not improper to secure a debt by mortgage or judgment.

MOVING AWAY UNRECONCILED.

Y. M. 1849. Art. 13. When a member offends in a church, and then moves away without being reconciled, can he obtain a certificate by writing, without personally presenting himself? Considered, when a member removes under such circumstances, and is so far away, or unfavorably situated for coming back to make reconciliation, when he wishes to do so, if the church from which he removed is satisfied with his acknowledgments made in writing, it (the church) may signify this satisfaction in a letter to the church where he (now) resides.

MUSICAL INSTRUMENTS.

Y. M. 1852. Art. 11. Has a brother a right to have or keep in his house costly musical instruments? Considered, that members could lay out their money to better advantage. (Was it wrong, "that David took a harp and played with his hand, so Saul was refreshed, and was well, and the evil spirit departed from him?" (See 1 Sam. 16:23.)

Y. M. 1857. Art. 10. How is it considered for brethren, and especially ministering brethren, to adorn their children with ear-rings, breast-pins, finger-rings and jewelry in general, and send them from home to have them taught *music*, and to procure *pianos* for them. Answer. Brethren should not do so.

MUSTERING.

Y. M. 1785. See *"Erroneous Doctrines."* Y. M. 1789. Art. 5. Further it was discussed and unanimously considered, that no brother should permit his sons to go on the muster ground, much less that a brother go himself.

Y. M. 1815. Art. 2. See *"Non-resistance;"* also, *"Warfare."*

Y. M. 1817. Art. 5. Whether brethren or their children may go on the muster ground or not? The counsel was, that no member may go there, and prevent also their children from going on that ground, and not willingly permit it to them, as long as they are under parental authority; should a brother do so, he could not be in full fellowship with the church; for the Saviour said to Peter, "Put up thy sword into his place; for all they that take the sword, shall perish with the sword."

Y. M. 1822. (Miami.) Art. 6. Whether a brother may take the liberty to go on the muster ground or take part in the festivities of Independence-day? Considered, that no brother should take the liberty to go to such places.

Y. M. 1835. Art. 5. How it is considered when brethren go to muster and drill. Considered, that it is contrary to our baptismal vow, contrary to the Word of God, and contrary to the professed principle of the church, and can by no means be permitted or tolerated.

Y. M. 1840. Art. 9. Whether it could be permitted for brethren to attend a mustering in the militia? Considered, that mustering is a preparation for war; and since we by the gospel of Jesus are called unto peace and to a non-resistant state, it would in no wise be proper (consistent) or allowable for a brother to learn war. Isa. 2:4. Mic. 4:3.

Y. M. 1859. Art. 23. In those States where muster fines are high, and where the fines are the only means whereby the military musters are kept up, would it not be better for brethren to muster a few times, and thereby cause the military system to be abolished, than to pay an oppressive fine and thereby keep up the regimental muster? Ans. It would not, inasmuch as our Lord and Saviour teaches non-resistance in his gospel throughout. And when we go to musters, we there learn the art of war, and the most appropriate method of shedding our fellow-creatures' blood. See 2 Cor. 6:17, John 18:36.

NAME OF OUR FRATERNITY.

Y. M. 1836. Art. 6. What should be the name of our fraternity, when a title for a meeting-house is made and recorded in the public offices? Unanimously concluded to call ourselves the Fraternity of German Baptists.

NEAREST FRIENDS IN COUNCIL.

Y. M. 1817. Art. 3. Whether the nearest friends of a member, that fall under the censure of the church, or a candidate wishing to be received into the church, may be present at the council of the case ? Considered, necessary that the nearest friends should withdraw.

Y. M. 1832. Art. 13. Whether at a council concerning candidates for baptism, their nearest friends should withdraw? Decided as before.

Y. M. 1838. Art. 8 Whether in case a member falls into the judgment of the church, the nearest relations should withdraw while the counsel is taken? It has always been considered best to let such relations withdraw.

NON-CONFORMITY TO THE WORLD.

See *"Conformity,"* &c.; also, *"Fashionable Garments,"* and *"Our Three Principles,"* &c.

NON-RESISTANCE.

Y. M. 1845. (Virginia.) Art. 5. In regard to our being altogether *defenceless, "not to withstand the evil,"* but *"to overcome evil with good,"* the brethren consider, that the nearer we follow the bright example of the Lamb of God, who willingly suffered the cross, and prayed for his enemies; who, though " heir of all things," had on earth " not where to lay his head,"—the more we shall fulfill our high calling, and obtain grace to deny ourselves for Christ and his gospel's sake, even to the loss of our property, our liberty and our lives.

Y. M. 1855. Art. 4. Has a brother a right to defend himself with a deadly weapon at the appearance of his being in danger? Considered, that he has not, inasmuch as the Saviour says to Peter, " Put up thy sword into his place; for all they that take the sword, shall perish by the sword." Matt. 26 : 52:

(A more full exhibition of this principle, see Y. M. 1785, under the heading, *"Doctrines, Strange."* Also, Y. M. 1789. *Ibid.* See also *"Mustering"* and *"Warfare,"* and *"Our Three Principles."*)

OATHS, SWEARING OF.

Y. M. 1785. See *"Doctrines, Strange."* Y. M. 1790. See *"Doctrines, Strange."*

Y. M. 1821. Art. 4. How far a brother has liberty in giving testimony to speak the truth before a magistrate, since there are different forms presented to brethren, was considered, that by no means a brother should take the liberty to raise his hand (or kiss the book), but to obey the counsel of the Gospel; to affirm yea that is yea, and nay that is nay, " for whatsoever is more than these cometh of evil."

Y. M. 1822. Art. 5. Concerning the form or manner of swearing oaths to save our consciences for the gospel's sake, whether we could answer with yea such a form, viz: "And this you do under the pains and penalties of perjury." It has been considered, that if a brother were oppressed or troubled herein, let him consider or seek counsel, whether there is no other form for us.

OFFENSES, PUBLIC.

Y. M. 1797. Art. 2. It was in union concluded, that if a brother or sister should commit a fault or sin, that were not between brother and brother, but open before the world, then the church is to examine, and if the fault is not so criminal that the church is compelled to cut him off entirely, according to the word of the Lord, and the failing member acknowledges and repents for his sin, such should make a public acknowledgment in presence of believers and unbelievers. But if he should harden his heart, and would not be obedient to the counsel of the church, then the members could not have fellowship with him until such time he becomes willing to acknowledge and to obey, and then the whole church should heartily pardon and forgive him, in the name of the Lord and Saviour Jesus Christ. (See also "*Acknowledgments.*")

Y. M. 1821. Art. 8. What is to be done when a member commits a fault, which is not between brother and brother, but publicly against the gospel? Considered, that such a member (provided it is no crime, such as stated in 1 Cor. 5,) should always make acknowledgment before the church.

Y. M. 1828. Art. 11. Whether if a member sees another member commit sin publicly against truth, the first is in duty bound to speak privately to the failing member, or (at once to) present the case to one of the leading brethren? Considered (whether to do the first), it is as a member may choose (but to do the latter remains his duty, inasmuch public sins cannot be atoned for between member and member).

Y. M. 1840. Art. 10. Whether a public fault can be atoned for and forgiven, between brother and brother? Considered, that a fault publicly committed can only be settled before the church, and not between brother and brother, according to the word of the Lord.

Y. M. 1850. Art. 15. Whether it is according to the gospel, for a church to lay a public acknowledgment on a brother that has made a public offense? Considered, that the acknowledgment is to be made before the church alone, and before all the members present. See 1 Tim. 5 : 20. "*Them that sin, rebuke before all, that others also may fear.*" Art. 37. If it is proved by two or three brethren, that a brother has been drinking to excess, yet not so much as to disable him from keeping on his feet, but has often before been charged, and also before been set

back or put in avoidance, and still denies the charge—would he not
come under the class of drunkards; or would it be prudent to hold him
as a brother, or could he be expelled by the proof (evidence) of four or
five witnesses, though not members of the church? Considered, that no
member should be put in avoidance without positive proof from members,
that he or she has been guilty of one of those sins mentioned by Paul
in 1 Cor. 5 : 11.

[Love to truth and righteousness in Christ, and the prosperity of the church
and of the individual souls, constrains us to make a few serious remarks on a
very unpleasant subject. A question, such as the one given above, under Article
37 (the whole number of articles presented in that same year was sixty-four),
would alone require, in order to answer it rightly and scripturally, more space
and time than can be devoted at the Y. M. to the consideration of all the (64)
questions presented in this one year. If the case presented in the query has
actually occurred as presented, the sad fact is proved, that a brother may be
convicted again and again of drunkenness by two or three brethren, and may
have been dealt with by the church (according to the word of God), and he
still deny the charge, thus adding the sin of lying to the other sin, and still by
some means, but not by true repentance, for then he would confess instead of
denying his sins, he is still held as a member, and still continues to be a drunkard, only taking care that no brother shall see him drunk. Is there no remedy
for this?]

Y. M. 1855. Art. 24. If two brethren or members should raise a
quarrel before or in presence of others, so as nearly to come in bodily
conflict, or to fight, can such matters be settled between those members,
or ought it to be brought before the church? Considered, that such
public crimes must be settled before and by the church.

Y. M. 1858. Art. 27. Would it not be well for the brethren to
come upon some plan to acquaint all the bishops and housekeepers of
the various branches of the church with the rules and regulations concluded upon by the general council for the more perfect union and prosperity of the church? And if these rules and regulations be violated by
a minister, with some of the members composing his district, should they
not fall into the hands of the brethren of the adjacent districts as offenders, and he dealt with as such; and if the above should be considered
expedient, what plan should be devised to carry it into effect? Answer.
We are fully satisfied, that the means long had in practice by the brethren, namely, the Minutes of our Annual Meetings, are sufficient to give
the teachers and housekeepers, and members generally, the decisions of
our annual councils for the perfecting of love and union throughout the
brotherhood. And if it should so happen that a housekeeper, with a part
or all of the members of his district, could not be satisfied with the decisions of the general council, as we were advised and instructed by our
beloved elder brethren, and unanimously concurred in at the Annual

Meeting held in 1850, in Montgomery county, Ohio, they should bear with the annual council, and with one another, until the next annual meeting, and then bring their grievances to the annual council where they proceeded from, and we believe full satisfaction will be obtained.

[This article ought to have been inserted under some other heading, for instance—*"Minutes,"* or *"Opposition to Y. M."*]

OFFICES, HOLDING WORLDLY.

Y. M. 1779.　See *"Attest, taking the."*

Y. M. 1789. Art. 3.　Further it has been discussed and unanimously deemed good and evangelical, that all brethren in all places should shun all worldly offices, so as not to serve in any of them, provided it is possible to be relieved from them, such as Supervisor, Overseer of the Poor, Collector, Constable, Assessor, or also Juryman, &c.　Yet it is considered, with some difference, such as Supervisor or Overseer of the Poor, might be served perhaps with least objection; provided, there is no suing or something else contrary to the Word of the Lord.　If a brother should be elected to one of these offices contrary to his will, then only that what he would have to do contrary to the gospel, should be rebuked in love and compassion, according to the word of the Lord.

Y. M. 1812. Art. 6.　Concerning brethren who are sometimes prevailed upon to serve in the office of Constable, it was considered, that a follower of Jesus could not serve in such office, and if a brother should accept of it, take the oath of office, and serve in it, or by some person else as his substitute. such a brother would exclude himself from the breaking of bread, holy kiss, and brotherly council.

Y. M. 1822. (Canton, O.)　Art. 2.　Whether a brother might serve in a worldly office or as a juryman, was considered, that no follower of Jesus can serve in such, and if he could get relieved with money (by paying a fine), he should not serve herein.

Y. M. 1825. Art. 6.　Concerning a brother holding the office of Justice of the Peace, has been twice before the big meeting, and was always considered, that it was not at all consistent with the gospel; but as something more definite is requested, the counsel is now, if such an one has been admonished already before to give up that office, and is once and again admonished (in the name of the church) to do so, and will not give it up, such an one we could not hold as a brother.

Y. M. 1834. Art. 9.　Concerning the office of Supervisor and other worldly offices, was considered, that brethren should keep themselves clear of them as much as possible.

Y. M. 1837. Art. 5.　Whether a brother is at liberty to serve as cryer or clerk at public vendues?　It is the counsel of this meeting, that no brother should take the liberty to act as a cryer at vendues, because it is unbecoming for a brother so to serve. As to the clerkship at vendues, it would not be considered quite so unbecoming, yet so that brethren ought to refrain from such things as much as possible.

Y. M. 1839. Art. 1. Whether a brother could serve in the office of a Constable? No. (See above, Y. M. 1812.)

Y. M. 1841. Art. 11. Whether it is becoming for a member of the church of Christ to act as juror in the courts of our country? Considered, that it would be best not to serve at all (even) in civil (cases), but by no means in criminal cases.

Y. M. 1844. Art. 3. Whether a brother may go to the Legislative Assembly as a representative of the people, agreeably with the gospel? Considered, that though we look upon the higher powers of this world as being of God for the protection of the pious, &c., and desire to be thankful to God for the benefits we enjoy under our government, and feel it our duty to pray fervently and daily for the same, (still) we cannot see how a follower of the meek and lowly Saviour can seek or accept an office of this kind consistently with the gospel he professes. See Matt. 20 : 25–28 ; Mark, 10 : 42—46 ; Luke, 22 : 25 ; John, 17 : 16, &c.

Y. M. 1849. Art. 34. Whether a brother being elected to the office of Constable contrary to his will, would be justifiable in taking the obligations of the office, and (then) transfer it to another person, who will discharge the whole duty of said office? Considered, while the brother would have to be under oath, and responsible for all the acts of his substitute, it would not be safe for him to do so (not to repeat what has been testified so often already, that such office is improper and unbecoming for a brother).

Y. M. 1850. Art. 9. Is it allowed for a brother, especially one that holds an office in the church, to fill a worldly office, and if not, what is the proper course to pursue with such a brother? Considered, that we could not advise brethren to crave worldly offices ; but if the people of the world should impose an office on any of our brethren, they should, before acting in such office, lay the matter before the church, and act agreeably to the counsel of the same.

Y. M. 1852. Art. 3. Have we a right to help making the political government, and to serve as officers ; also, to put the law in force against any of our fellow men in any case whatever? Considered, (see *"Law, Suing against Debtors,"* page 106.)

Y. M. 1857. Art. 39. Is it consistent with the gospel for brethren to serve in the capacity of any of the civil officers under our government ; and is there any material difference as to state, county, or township officers? Answer. We consider it wrong for brethren to accept of any office which requires them to administer an oath, or to use physical force in performing the duties of that office.

OPPOSITION TO Y. M.

Y. M. 1805. Art. 2. Further, it has been considered, that when there is made a conclusion at the big yearly meeting, and there are members who would not heed, nor conduct themselves accordingly, it has been concluded unitedly, that when such persons cannot convince the church by evidence from holy scripture, and would or did rise up against such church conclusion, would not hear nor obey at all, in such case we could not well do otherwise, but after sufficient and friendly admonition to set them back from the breaking of bread until they learn to do better and become obedient.

Y. M. 1845. Art. 8. How is it considered, if brethren will rebel against the counsel held at council meetings, and say, it is an abomination to God? Considered, that such a brother should be visited and exhorted, and if he would not hear and obey the admonition, he could not be held as a brother.

Y. M. 1850. Art. 5. Whether it is right for brethren in different arms of the church, to go against the counsel of the Yearly Meeting? Considered, that it is wrong for brethren to go against the counsel of our great Annual Meetings; but should brethren not be satisfied with said counsel, they have liberty, with the consent of their church, to bring the matter before another Yearly Meeting for a reconsideration.

Y. M. 1853. Art. 30. How is it considered when brethren preach a doctrine which is not in accordance with the decisions of the Yearly Meeting, and speak privately to or with members against such decisions? Considered, that for love and union sake they ought not to do so.

Y. M. 1858. Art. 22. What should be done with a brother who holds the counsel of the annual meeting in disrespect, and who speaks lightly and disrespectfully of it? Considered, that he should be kindly admonished to do so no more, and if he will not hear the admonition (of the church) he should be dealt with according to Matt. 18.

Y. M. 1858. Art. 27. (That belongs specially to this place, but is inserted above, under the heading, " *Offenses, Public.*")

ORDER AT ANNUAL MEETINGS, &c.

Y. M. 1835. Art. 4. Concerning the commencement of Yearly Meetings on Saturday, or according to the ancient order. No change made at this time. (See further, " *Annual Meetings.*")

ORDER AT BAPTISMS.

See " *Baptism,*" especially Y. M. 1848.

ORDER AT CHOICES FOR MINISTERS, &c.

Y. M. 1843.   Art. 7.   When a large church, by common consent, has been divided into several districts, and in one of these districts it is found necessary to hold an election for teachers (ministers) and deacons, whether the members of such district alone are entitled to vote, or whether the members of the other districts have a right to vote also? Considered, that when such division takes place by common consent, for the greater convenience of members and of meetings, we understand that henceforth these several districts are to form so many particular churches, though they may be under the superintendence of but one bishop; and that, consequently, when one of these districts or one of these particular churches, stands in need of laborers, and has to hold an election, it would be as improper for the members of the other districts to vote at such election, as it would be for members from other churches that never formed a part of the old and large district.   In case there was no express word for such things, we think we may safely follow the Apostle Paul, when he says, 1 Cor. 11 : 14 : "Doth not nature itself teach you" what is proper.   Art. 8.   How it might be considered, when at the election for teachers and deacons, absent members do send their votes with other members?   Considered, that since the promise of our Saviour is given, "Where two or three are gathered together in my name, there am I in the midst of them." Matt. 18 : 20.   In such important church affairs, this promise belongs only to those that are assembled, and not to those that are absent; the brethren generally have acted upon that ground, and not taken any vote from absent members.

Y. M. 1853.   Art. 4.   Is it consistent with the gospel and its principles, as professed by our brotherhood, when a brother is chosen to the ministry only, not being authorized to baptize, that (afterwards) the ordained elder of the congregation should forward such brother without consulting the church?   Considered, that all the power under God is vested in the church, and that therefore the church should be consulted in all such cases.   Art. 44.   How it is considered, when choices are held for teachers or deacons in a different manner from the general usage, choosing by ballot in presence of all the church, and without ordained elders from other churches being present?   Considered, that a choice should be held by each and every member coming (one by one) before the elders, and giving their voice privately.   The presence of two or at least one ordained elder from another church, has been deemed necessary always, so as to avoid the least appearance of partiality, &c.

Y. M. 1856.   Art. 5.   Would it not be best, in holding elections for the purpose of choosing ministers or deacons, that none of the ministering brethren of such district should take any part, or even be in the room

11

where the votes of the members are received, but that brethren of other districts should be called for said purpose? Considered, that every member should have an equal privilege of giving their voices, and that the remainder of this query were best left to the control of the strange brethren.

Y. M. 1858. Art 24. When a church stands in need of speakers or deacons, should the bishop make it known to the members before, or only on the day of election? Considered, that we leave the churches to do as they have been accustomed to do, in relation to this subject. [But suppose a wrong custom has been introduced, such as voting by ticket, in imitation of the world, or such as invite and assist to electioneering practices, should such customs be continued?] .

Y. M. 1862. Art. 33. Would it not be advisable when an election is to be held for both a speaker and a deacon at the same time, to hold the election for the speaker first, and make the result known, and then hold the election for the deacon or deacons, as the case may be? Ans. We consider it would be advisable to do so.

ORDER AT COMMON MEETINGS FOR WORSHIP.

[The general order is: First, united prayer and praise by singing a hymn; then a brief exhortation to humbly worship God in spirit and in truth, followed by prayer upon our bended knees, two or three praying aloud, one after the other, the last repeating the Lord's prayer, each Amen repeated by the congregation. Then reading one or more portions of Scripture, followed by preaching, one, two or three speaking alternately; then, if candidates for baptism are presented, Matt. 18 : 10–22, is read and commented on, and every candidate is asked to assent to the rules laid down by the Saviour in that chapter; after that, the meeting is brought to a close, as it was commenced, by singing, exhortation and prayer. As meetings used to be held at the houses of members, the members would, out of love, prepare a refreshment for those who had come from a distance, and whoever would partake of the invitation. This latter particular was necessary to be mentioned for a better understanding of what follows.]

Y. M. 1822. (Miami.) Art. 9. Whether we might have two tables at lovefeast, and also at other meetings; that is, whether members might prepare something warm for the old brethren, and also elderly and weakly members, beside what is served up for all in general,—was considered, that members should be at perfect liberty to show their love toward their old brethren or weakly members, to set before them what they like; yet we would counsel in love to be careful that no bad distinction is made, so that friends and well-wishers are preferred to those that are weakly.

Y. M. 1840. Art. 12. How is it considered, when teachers at the beginning of meetings exhort so long, and consume so much time with speaking before prayer? Considered, that it would be more edifying to make the exhortation as brief as possible, since the Apostle teaches, that "first of all, supplication, prayers, intercession, &c., be made. 1 Tim. 2 : 1–4.

Y. M. 1841. Art. 4. Whether it is proper for teachers to speak both German and English in (one) meeting, when there are only a few English members, the majority of the church being German? Considered, that it is right and our duty to preach the gospel to every nation as far as we are able, yet so that in such a case not too much time ought to be taken up in English.

Y. M. 1842. Art. 2. Whether it will be to the edification of the church of God, to hold protracted meetings, and to introduce mourning-benches, in imitation to the new measures adopted by different sects and denominations? The brethren generally considered, that it was advisable to be very cautious, and at all times to keep good order in accordance with the doctrine and example of the Apostles, and not to introduce such innovations, like mourning-benches, &c. Art. 9. How is it considered, when brethren who are not ordained, in the presence of ordained brethren, without being requested, take the lead at public meetings, and at morning and evening worship, seat themselves at the head of the table, and call upon ordained brethren to be free. Considered, that order is an essential rule in the house of God, and that it would be most praise-worthy, if all the brethren id try in honor to prefer one another, and each one be faithful in his station, not seeking the uppermost seats, nor forgetting the advice of the Apostle, 1 Pet. 5 : 5 : "Ye younger, submit yourselves unto the elder."

Y. M. 1855. Art. 21. Is it according to the gospel, at the close of our meetings, to sing a hymn, and invite mourners to come forward; and if none will come, sing another hymn, and give another invitation; and lastly, to tell the congregation to rise upon their feet, and with raised hand speak a blessing over the people? Considered, that this is not agreeable with the gospel, and should not be done.

Y. M. 1858. Art. 8. Does the gospel convey the idea, that the public practical use of the spiritual gifts, such as prayer, exhortation, teaching, doctrine and prophesying, &c., is alone confined to the chosen officers of the church; or does it extend that privilege to every member, especially male members of the church, if the influence of the spirit of Christ so dictate to him? Answer. As it regards prayer, it is considered that private members may pray in public, if liberty be given by elder brethren; but exhortation, teaching and prophesying seem to be duties and privileges belonging to the officers of the church. See 1 Cor. 14:32. Art. 39. How should brethren proceed, after preaching, relative to getting members in the church? Shall the preacher, while singing a hymn, give an invitation to those who wish to join the church to come forward, or shall he leave it to them to make their own application? Considered, that it is best to let them make their own application, as in Acts 2 : 37, and 16 : 30.

Y. M. 1862. Art. 69. How is it considered when ministering brethren, after preaching, go into the congregation and invite persons to join the church? Answer. We consider it best to do as was done in Acts, 2d chap.

ORDER AT LOVEFEASTS.

(The order in general is, or was, as follows : If there is a day meeting, it is held as every other meeting: see "*Order of Common Meetings.*" The evening exercises commence in summer time about one hour before sunset by singing an appropriate hymn. Then, 1 Cor. 11th chapter, is read entirely or in part, chiefly from verse 17 to the end, from which scripture is spoken by two or three brethren, chiefly treating on self-examination; and this exercise closed with humble prayer, in which general liberty being given, private members, even sisters, sometimes join one by one to utter their hearts' desires for themselves, for the church, and for all mankind. In the next place, water is brought for feet-washing, and John's gospel, 13th chapter, is read, as far as time and the subject will permit and require. While the washing of feet is going on, in which work always two are engaged, two brethren to wash and wipe the brethren's feet, and two sisters to wash and wipe the sisters' feet, and those frequently relieved by other two, at large communions; the preaching is also going on upon that subject. Feet-washing being over, supper begins to be served on the table; and while the table servants are thus engaged, the ministering brethren in word and doctrine may speak something on the Lord's supper; and when all is ready, a verse or two are sung, and a blessing asked for this supper; and then all partake together of the frugal meal, consisting mostly of soup, boiled meat, bread and water; and after all have eaten, and thanks returned to God, the tables are cleared off. Now, the elements of the communion, bread and wine, are brought, and reverently set down at one end of the table, and a hymn to the praise of our once suffering and dying Redeemer is sung. Next, a part of the record of Christ's passion and death is read, such as Mark 15, or John 19, and spoken on according to the gospel and the injunction of Paul, 1 Cor. 11 : 26; during which the administrator prepares the bread (unleavened) for distribution, and then prepares the minds of the communicants still further for the solemn contemplation of what Christ has done for us, and what we ought to be willing to do and suffer also for his cause, and how we ought to be united as one in faithful love toward one another even unto death—which is sealed by the holy kiss going round in the whole congregation, among the sisters as well as among the brethren. Next, a blessing is asked over the bread, which is to be the emblem of the communion of the body of Christ, and then that bread is broken from brother to brother; and meanwhile by the administrator the same bread is administered to the sisters, each laying his or her portion before him or her on the table, until all are provided. Then all eat it at once in solemn silence, contemplating our Saviour's sufferings for our good. In the same manner thanksgiving is made and a blessing asked for the cup of the New Testament, which is the communion of the blood of Christ; then one cup is circulating among the brethren, and the administrator handing another cup to the sisters, while singing the praises of a Saviour's dying love is going on. And finally, the services are closed by singing a song of praise and prayer—all standing. This was written nearly thirty years ago in Germany, by request of God-fearing friends.)

Y. M. 1822. (Miami.) Art. 8. Concerning breaking up in the morning after lovefeast, it was considered, that members and their children, who stay till morning, should not separate and leave until prayer and thanksgiving to God is made.

Y. M. 1828. Art. 8. Whether the (holy) kiss should have a place at feet-washing (between those who serve and those who are served), and at (before) the breaking of bread? Considered, that it should be. (The new commandment, John 13 : 34, 35, brings it very near to both ordinances, and a *lovefeast* without this token of love would scarcely deserve the name.) Art. 13. Whether we might have small lovefeasts? See *"Lovefeasts."*

Y. M. 1854. Art. 11. If one or more churches would so choose to come together in the evening to observe the ordinances of the house of God as delivered unto us by the Saviour, and continue public worship next day, believing that thereby some of the evils might be obviated which too often accompany our lovefeasts, would it be considered a departure from the Word? Considered, No; but at the same time we would advise, that the churches should be careful to observe the ordinances of the Lord, at the proper time and in due order, and to avoid all unnecessary changes. Art. 22. A request that the oldest bishop choose or appoint twelve brethren to hold a communion or lovefeast at the time (and place) of yearly meeting, as a model to show us the right order according to the Gospel. Considered, that Christ with his Apostles in that doleful night, when he (the Saviour) was betrayed, has given a model, and showed us the right order.

Y. M. 1855. Art. 25. Concerning the difference in the time of coming together for holding lovefeasts. Does it not appear as if there was a division or disunion among us, when some churches meet and have public worship (according to the ancient order of the brethren) in the forenoon; others at one, two or three o'clock, and others again in the evening, about the time when the exercises immediately connected with the Lord's supper should begin? Could there not a uniform practice be adopted in this, as it used to be among the brethren in bygone years? Considered, to be left to the consideration of the churches, and to let them decide when their lovefeasts are to be held.

Y. M. 1855. Art. 28. How ought the church hold a member who argues and contends that Christ was eating the Jewish Passover with his disciples, and at the same time the Jews did eat it; and also contends that it is not binding on the followers of Christ to observe a supper, or anything more than the bread and wine; and that feet-washing ought to be observed after eating; neither can be satisfied with the brethren that preach otherwise? Considered, that as it appears evident from John 13 : 1–29; 19 : 14; 18 : 28, Christ's supper with his disciples was eaten before the Jewish Passover; and it appears from a comparison of Mark 14 : 20, and John 13 : 26, that the supper recorded by Mark and that recorded by John, are the same. Again, Luke calls the meal which Christ ate with his disciples, at which he instituted the communion, a supper; and a comparison of Luke 22 : 23, and John 13 : 25, will show that they were the same; now as it appears plain that the supper in John 13, was before the Jewish Passover, that of Luke 22 : 20, was likewise before it, and therefore not the passover itself. Further, from the Acts of the Apostles, and from the epistles, we find that there was in the church a feast of charity. See Jude 12; 1 Cor. 5 : 8; 2 Pet. 2 : 13; Acts 18 : 21. When we take all this evidence into consideration, we think it is sufficient to satisfy every sincere and candid mind that those who want to adhere to the practice of the church in the times of the Apostles, must have a feast of charity; and those brethren who oppose such a feast, oppose the gospel, and therefore should be admonished. And, concerning the washing of feet after the communion, we would say that it appears from the reading of the 13th chapter of John, that feet-washing was practiced before John leaned on the bosom of Christ (see John 13 : 23), but we find from John 21 : 20, that John leaned on the bosom of Christ at supper. Therefore, feet-washing was performed by Christ before supper, and certainly before the communion, as the communion was administered after supper.

Y. M. 1862. Art. 65. Would it not be more in accordance with the gospel, and the example of Christ, to omit returning thanks between the supper and the communion? Answer. We think it best to return thanks, according to 1 Thess. 5 : 18.

ORDER NECESSARY TO UNION.

Y. M. 1858. Art. 44. Is the gospel itself sufficient to preserve a union of practice throughout the brotherhood? Considered, that the gospel (being understood alike by and becoming a living principle in the members), with the practice or order consistent with the gospel, will preserve the union of the brotherhood.

ORDER NOT OBSERVED.

Y. M. 1850. Art. 28. How is it considered, when a district of church do not observe the ancient order of the brethren, and have new orders among them? Concluded, that no district church has any right to make changes in anything whatsoever, contrary to the ancient order, without a proper investigation before and the general consent of the annual meeting.

Y. M. 1856. Art. 21. How is it considered, when a branch of a church separates itself from the main body, forwards its ministers without a bishop being present, and pretends to act independent of the counsel of the church and the yearly meeting? Considered, that such proceedings are wrong and highly dangerous, so that love induces us to charge a committee to visit that church and branch.

Y. M. 1858. Art. 57. Can the brethren be in full communion with a brother or a community of brethren, who do not hold a church council in receiving applicants for baptism, and who do not ask those who are baptized, to renounce the devil and all the sinful practices of the world or flesh, and who do not practically follow the doctrine of self-denial? Considered, that we think such cannot be in full communion with us. Acts 10:47; Prov. 15:22; 1 John 2:15–17; Tit. 2:12.

ORDER OBSERVED DIFFERENTLY.

Y. M. 1858. Art. 34. Whereas, there is a diversity of opinion among the brethren concerning the mode of celebrating the Lord's supper; we therefore wish the brethren, at the annual meeting, to devise some plan that we may all be alike in our practices. Considered, that inasmuch as the difference is not stated, we recommend the practice heretofore recommended.

ORDER OF THE CHURCH IN GENERAL,

As we understand it, sometimes called "*the Order of the Brethren*," and by some, "*the Discipline of the Church.*" See APPENDIX.

ORDINATION.

Y. M. 1843. Art. 6. Whether the ordination of a brother can be frustrated, when the whole church is united on the subject, with the exception of one or a few members? Considered, that in case the ordination of a brother is judged as necessary and proper by the church and the ordained brethren from a distance, and there could be no weighty objection made by those that are of another opinion in this matter, they ought to acquiesce in it, and the ordination might go on according to the desire of the church.

PATENT RIGHTS.

Y. M. 1841. Art. 7. Whether members may be permitted to obtain and sell patent rights for their own inventions? Considered, that (inasmuch as patent rights will be of very little benefit, unless we enforce the law against all transgressors, and inasmuch this would be contrary to our professed principles,) it is not advisable for members to take out and sell patent rights.

Y. M. 1855. Art. 7. How it would be considered, if a brother obtains a patent for any invention? Considered, that it would be safest, in all cases, first to ask counsel of the church before obtaining a patent.

PENSIONS OF SOLDIERS.

Y. M. 1836. Art. 1. Whether a brother would have a right to take such money, which he had acquired as a soldier by war? Considered in union, that it cannot be according to the doctrine of Jesus. (It is uncertain whether this question has any reference to pensions at all, but if it had, it would need revision and reconsideration.)

PLEDGE OF TOTAL ABSTINENCE.

Y. M. 1842. Art. 4. How it is considered, if a brother or sister sign the pledge of total abstinence? Considered, that inasmuch our churches have always been testifying against intemperance, and even against the free use, the making and selling of ardent spirits. it is not advisable for members to put their hands to the pledge, or to meddle with the proceedings and excitement of the world on this subject.

POLITICS.

Y. M. 1840. Art. 10. Whether a follower of Jesus may attend political meetings? Considered, that it is not becoming at all for brethren who have renounced the world.

Y. M. 1852. Art. 3. (See above under " *Law*.")

Y. M. 1854. Art. 23. A request to reconsider Query 3, on the

Minutes of 1852, which read thus: "Have we a right to help making the political government, and to serve as officers, also to put the law in force against any of our fellow men, in any case whatever?" Considered, that this query was sufficiently and correctly answered in 1852. See Rom. 6 : 16; 10 : 1–3; 2 Pet. 1 : 19; 2 : 19; 1 John 3 : 8, 9; Matt. 6 : 24; 2 Cor. 6 : 5–8; John 18 : 36.

Y. M. 1863. Art. 18. Inasmuch as some brethren manifest a desire to prohibit brethren from voting at our common (political) elections, do not the brethren in yearly council see it to be best to make no change differing from the counsel and practice of our ancient brethren in these days of trouble ? In the present crisis, we recommend that brethren abstain as much as possible from attending elections according to John 18 ; 36; 2 Cor. 6 : 14–17.

Y. M. 1864. Art. 1. In no less than four papers the question is presented, whether it is right and proper for a brother to go to, or take part in political elections, it being specially stated that it had caused hard feelings and disunion ? Answer. We have been led to think that at all times it would be best and most consistent with our profession, and specially most proper and safe in the present critical state of things, to have nothing at all to do with politics, and entirely to abstain from voting. See 2 Cor. 6 : 14–17, also Minutes of the A. M. of 1863, Query eighteen.

Y. M. 1864. Art. 22. Is it right for a brother to go to an election, and there elect, or help to elect, a brother (who takes no part in elections,) to fill an office in which he must either serve or pay his fine ? Answer. We consider it utterly wrong for brethren to do so.

(OUR POSITION WITH REGARD TO GOVERNMENT.)

Y. M. 1864. Art. 35. As our national troubles consequent upon the Rebellion now existing in our country, have caused considerable difficulty in our church, and have tried our non-resistant principles, and have caused several questions concerning the paying of bounty money, voting, &c., to come before this council meeting, what counsel will this Annual Meeting give upon these subjects? Answer. We exhort the brethren to steadfastness in the faith, and believe that the times in which our lots are cast, strongly demand of us a strict adherence to all our principles, and especially to our non-resistant principle, a principle dear to every subject of the Prince of Peace, and a prominent doctrine of our fraternity, and to endure whatever sufferings, and to make whatever sacrifice, the maintaining of the principle may require, and not to encourage in any way the practice of war. And we think it more in accordance with our own principles, that instead of paying bounty money, and especially in taking an active part in raising bounty money, to await the demands of the government, whether general, state, or local, and pay the fines and taxes required of us, as the gospel permits and indeed requires.   Matt. 22 : 21; Rom. 13 : 7.

And lest the position we have taken upon political matters in general, and war matters in particular, should seem to make us as a body appear to be indifferent to our government, or in opposition ·thereto, in its efforts to suppress the Rebellion, we hereby declare that it has our sympathies, and our prayers, and that it shall have our aid in any way which does not conflict with the principles of the gospel of Christ.   But since in our christian profession we regard these gospel principles as superior or paramount to all others, consistency requires that we so regard them in our practices.

PORTRAITS.

Y. M. 1849.   Art. 17.   Whether brethren can be allowed to have their likeness or profile taken ?   Considered as not advisable.

Y. M. 1857.   Art. 15.   Is it really considered a sin according to the gospel, for members of the church to have their likenesses taken ? Answer. Members of the church should not have their likenesses taken.

Y. M. 1858.   Art. 52.   Is it right for a brother to go about taking likenesses with a Daguerrean apparatus ?   Considered, that it is not right.   See Rom. 1 : 23; Deut. 27 : 15.

PRAYER.

Y. M. 1805.   Art. 4.   Concerning praying (the Lord's Prayer) "Our Father," since some do not make the same expressions as given by the Evangelists from the mouth of Jesus, it was considered, that we should use the expressions according to the pattern of the doctrine of Jesus, our Master, and at the same time contemplate the meaning contained in these words, so that we may pray with the spirit and understanding of the heart, according to the mind of Christ and in truth.

PRAYER MEETINGS.

Y. M. 1851.   Art. 15.   How is it considered for brethren to appoint meetings for prayer exclusively?   Considered, that the brethren cannot recommend such meetings, as a general thing, except in cases of peril; but on the other hand they consider it a duty and privilege to pray in our families and in the closet and other secret places, as well as to join the public prayer in our regular meetings for worship.   Art. 16.   How is it considered for brethren that hold prayer meetings, and invite others that are of a different belief to take part in prayer, and call them brethren ?   Utterly wrong for brethren to do so.

Y. M. 1853.   Art. 25.   How is it considered, when brethren hold prayer meetings decently and in order? Considered, that every brother should meet daily with his family for worship in his own house; that when brethren meet together accidently or by appointment, they are at perfect liberty to sing and pray together, read the Scriptures, and exhort each other, which all should be done decently and in order; but we would advise our brethren to drop the name of Prayer Meeting, and call them simply—meetings.

Y. M. 1858. Art. 49. See " *Social Meetings.*"

Y. M. 1859. Art. 9. Is it considered to be right to call prayer meetings social meetings? Answer. It is considered right to do so. Art. 20. Is it agreeable with the gospel for ministers to hold prayer meetings, or what are sometimes called social meetings, and to invite members of other denominations to unite with us in prayer? Answer We consider it agreeable with the gospel to hold such meetings when they are strictly held in order; but as we do not call upon our own members individually to pray, it is not in our order of holding such meetings, to call on those of other denominations to pray. Art. 22. Is it according to the gospel and the rules of the brethren, for a brother in the second degree of the ministry to appoint a prayer meeting without the consent of the bishop and other brethren in the church? Answer. We think it is not. The Apostle Paul declares that God is a God of order, and such a course does not seem to be in order. And the Apostle Peter's language, 1 Peter 5 : 5, would likewise seem to disapprove of such a course.

Y. M. 1862. Art. 2. With regard to prayer meetings—how should they be conducted? Answer. All our meetings for divine service should be conducted according to the gospel, which requires all things to be done decently and in order.

PRAYER MEETINGS OF OTHER DENOMINATIONS.

Y. M. 1843. Art. 4. Whether members may take the liberty to go to prayer meetings, &c., of other persuasions, to take part in them, and to permit and invite ministers of other persuasions to hold meetings in their (the members') own houses? Considered, that as we have come into very perilous times, according to the word of our Saviour, Matt. 24 : 22–26, and of his Apostles, 1 Tim. 4 : 1; 2 Pet. 2 : 1; and we therefore have the greatest reason to be seriously on our guard; that prayer is an important part of worship, which must be performed in spirit and in truth, in order to be pleasing in the sight of God; that consequently, true inward union in prayer with such that are not in one spirit and in the same truth with us, cannot be thought of; that under these considerations it would be the safest course not to go to such places, nor to take part in such exercises, much less to invite or receive teachers of whom we may know beforehand that they will not bring the whole apostolic doctrine, in order to hold meetings in our houses. 2 John v. 10.

PREACHING.

Y. M. 1843. Art. 12. How is it considered, when one teacher commonly consumes as much time as two, three and four hours in one meeting, speaking continually? The unanimous opinion of the brethren was, that inasmuch as God is a God of order, and such long continued discourses must needs be fatiguing both to the teacher and the hearers, cause disorder, and deprive other teachers of the opportunity to speak to the edification of the church, this conduct is out of all order, and ought not to be; and it would always be best not to prolong our meetings beyond the usual time.

PRIDE.

Y. M. 1846. Art. 10. 1866. Art. 27. See "*Fashionable Garments.*"

PRONOUNCING A BLESSING.

Y. M. 1862. Art. 53. Is it in accordance with the gospel to pronounce a benediction over the people at the close of a funeral service at the grave, and if so, what should be the form? Answer. We have no authority in the gospel for doing so, and no such custom among the brethren to sanction it.

PROVIDING FOR THE POOR.

Y. M. 1812. Art. 8. Concerning a woman whose husband is dead, and having several children and no property, and her hands too weak to provide for them, was considered that the church should provide for her, and at the proper time to put out the children in good places, and to good people, and thus supply their wants.

Y. M. 1840. Art. 2. How is it considered when poor members are left over to the overseers of the poor in the township to provide for them? Considered, that the church to which such members belong, should investigate the case, and provide for their poor according to the gospel.

Y. M 1851. Art. 20. Whether it is according to the gospel to let any of our poor members go to the county poor house? Considered, that we know of no passage in the gospel authorizing this, but of many, where the duty of the church is expressly enjoined to support their poor members, and if not able, to ask aid from neighboring churches.

Y. M. 1852. Art. 18. Whether members have a right by the gospel to go begging for money through the different churches? Considered, that they have no right according to the gospel, and where there are poor members that are in a suffering condition, it is the duty of the church in which they live, to see to it and to supply their wants, and if that church is not able to support them, the church has a right to apply to the neighboring churches for help, and not the brother that is in want. See also, *" Alms, Collecting."*

Y. M. 1854. Art. 20. Is it not the duty of each church to keep their poor, and not let them become a county charge; or, is it right to send a brother to the poor house at the expense of the county? Considered, that this question was fully and correctly answered in 1851 and 1852. See Min. 1851, Art. 20, and of 1852, Art. 18.

Y. M. 1857. Art. 12. How is it considered if a poor brother becomes insane, and void of all reason, so much so as to become dangerous and very troublesome, and a place can scarcely be obtained for him in a private family upon any condition; a poor house being in the county, are the brethren bound to keep him according to the gospel, or are they permitted to deliver him to the trustees of the poor to take charge of him? Answer. A member of the church should not be put into the poor house if it can possibly be avoided.

Y. M. 1862. Art. 29. Is it right for a son to put his father on the county to be kept, both being members of the church; and if not right, where does the father belong, in the district where he is on the county, or in that from which he was taken? Answer. We consider it wrong for a son or brother to do so, and the father, under the circumstances stated, would of course belong to the district from which he was taken.

PUBLICATIONS.

Y. M. 1850. Art. 21. Whether there is any danger to be apprehended from publishing a paper among us? This subject to lay over till next annual meeting.

Y. M. 1851. Art. 8. What is the opinion of the Yearly Meeting with regard to having a paper published under the title, "The Monthly Gospel Visitor?" Considered at this council, that we will not forbid brother Henry Kurtz to go on with the paper for one year, and that all the brethren or churches will impartially examine the Gospel Visitor, and if found wrong or injurious, let them send in their objections at the next annual meeting.

Y. M. 1852. Art. 4. In regard to the continuation of the Gospel Visitor, it was concluded that inasmuch as there is a diversity of opinion upon the subject, some in favor and others opposed, we cannot forbid its publication at this time, and hope those brethren opposed to it will exercise forbearance, and let it stand or fall on its own merits.

Y. M. 1853. Art. 3. In regard to Query 4th, of last year's Minutes, concerning the Gospel Visitor. Inasmuch as the Visitor is a private undertaking of its editor, we unanimously conclude that this meeting should not any further interfere with it.

Y. M. 1854. Art. 14. Is it consistent with the example and doctrine of Christ and his Apostles, when brethren write and publish books, and afterwards revise and republish them, &c. Considered, that brethren should be careful in their publications, and especially of other men's books.

PULPIT OR STAND.

Y. M. 1847. Art. 3. Whether it is advisable for brethren who are teachers to occupy a stand three or four steps high, when they are invited to hold meetings in the meeting houses of the different persuasions or sects through our country. Considered advisable that (our) teachers should practice discretion and humility in taking their stands for speaking, and that members should also use forbearance, and not take offense in such matters, if circumstances would make it preferable for teachers to occupy such a stand.

Y. M. 1848. (Ohio.) Art. 2. Whether it be proper to reconsider Article 3, of last year's Minutes, relating to preaching from a stand? Reconsidered, that all our brethren should endeavor as much as possible to avoid (either) giving or taking offense.

Y. M. 1851. Art 23. Is it right for our teachers to enter up into pulpits in other denominations' meeting houses and teach there? Considered, that brethren should give no offense neither to Jew nor Gentile, nor to the Church of Christ; but we would advise brethren not to go up when they can avoid it, as the brethren had considered once before.

Y. M. 1863. Art. 15. Is it in accordance with the gospel to have stands or pulpits erected in our meeting houses? We have no direct gospel upon this subject, but we advise the brethren not to put pulpits, or stands in their houses of worship, when by so doing confusion and disunion may be produced.

QUESTIONS OF MISCELLANEOUS CHARACTER.

(These will mostly be found under other headings, or in the APPENDIX.)

RE-BAPTIZING.   (See also *"Baptism."*)

Y. M. 1827. Art. 3. Concerning receiving persons who have been baptized in the proper manner by other denominations. Considered, that those who have been received before with the laying on of hands (and prayer), we receive with hand and kiss; and those on whom the laying on of hands had not been observed, we should receive by the laying of hands, &c.

Y. M. 1832. Art. 11. How is it considered concerning persons who wish to be received, and had already been immersed but once by other baptists?. Considered, that some have been received without baptism. as we believe it ought to be performed, and they afterwards came of their own accord to receive the baptism according to the word.

Y. M. 1838. Art. 13. Whether persons that have been baptized formerly and elsewhere with a three-fold immersion, could be received among us as members without baptism or not? Considered almost unanimously, that when such persons are satisfied with their baptism having been performed in the right manner, they may be received as members without baptism, yet with stating to them the order (rules, principles,) of the brethren, and the laying on of hands (with prayer). If, however, they should desire baptism (by a brother), it might be granted to their satisfaction.

RECEIVING FALLEN MEMBERS.

Y. M. 1834. Art. 14. If a brother, who is a minister, should transgress so that the church has to set him back, and if he is afterwards received again upon his acknowledgment, whether he is to be received with or without his office? Considered, that depends upon the church, and also upon the nature of his transgression.

Y. M. 1838. Art. 6. Whether it be right to receive again, as a private member, a brother that was a teacher, and he had been put back, without entrusting him again with the office? Considered, that a (church) congregation has a right to do in such a case as it seemeth good to them.

Y. M. 1840. Art. 13. Concerning receiving again members that had been put back, in what manner it should be done? Considered, that it was hitherto *not* done in the same manner as newly elected ministers and deacons are received, where the members do advance toward those elected; but that it was and is the manner of the old brethren—the members to remain in their places, and the member that is to be received back again, to go from one to another, and thus to be received; if a brother, by the brethren with hand and kiss, and by the sisters with the hand, and *vice versa*.

Y. M. 1846. (Tennessee.) Art. 2. How, and whether a brother can be received who had been expelled from the church for selling and bill of saleing away his slaves, and afterwards wishes to be received again? Considered, that such a brother cannot be reinstated until he has used every exertion in his power to liberate them, and make full satisfaction to the church.

Y. M. 1852. Art. 22. If a member leaves the church and joins another denomination, and after awhile leaves that denomination and makes application to be received back into the church again, has the church a right to receive that member again? Considered, that by acknowledging his or her fault, and giving satisfaction to the church (of a more steadfast mind), he may be received again.

Y. M. 1858. Art. 47. How is it considered in case of a brother who has been expelled from the church, and then takes up with a woman that has a husband living, and lives with her fifteen years, then her husband dies, and the two get lawfully married, and now he has made application to be taken (again) into the church; and we desire the yearly meeting to give counsel what to do? Considered, that he may be received, provided he brings forth fruit meet for repentance.

Y. M. 1861. Art. 9. When expelled members upon application are re-admitted, how shall they be received by the church. Considered, that the applicating member be received by the hand of fellowship and the kiss of charity; but that the (reinstated) brother or sister go around to all the members, and (in order to) be received by them.

RECEIVING MEMBERS WITHOUT COUNSEL.

Y. M. 1845. Art. 1. How is it considered when a brother is excluded from the kiss, the communion and the council in the church where he lives, and the brethren in a neighboring church, with the knowledge of this fact, receive such an excluded brother in full fellowship? Considered, that whereas the whole Church of Christ is *one* body, of which we all are members, and which is to be directed by *one* Spirit, Ephes. 4 : 4, it seems to us as self-evident, if a particular church excludes a member from the church privileges according to Matt. 18, or from all communion according to 1 Cor. 5, the member ought to be so held in all the churches, until he has made satisfaction to that particular church where he has been excluded, otherwise the order of the house of God would be soon subverted, and discord, confusion and every evil would inevitably follow. Art 2. How would it be considered, when teachers go into other districts appointing and holding meetings, and even receiving members by baptism, without the counsel of the church in whose district such persons live. Considered, that teachers should be ever careful in the exercise of their office, to remember that it is appointed for the edification of the church, and that whatever might tend rather to disunion or dissatisfaction in the Church of Christ, ought to be carefully avoided. See 1 Cor. 14 : 1–4; 2 Cor. 10 : 8; Gal. 1 : 10; Phil. 1 : 15–17.

RECEIVING SICK PERSONS WITHOUT BAPTISM.

Y. M. 1827. Art. 4. Concerning receiving sick persons who cannot be baptized on account of their sickness and weakness, was considered, that they might be received, and if they should die, they might die as members, but if they should live and be well again, they should and would be baptized.

Y. M. 1837. Art. 12.   How it is viewed, to receive persons into the church without baptism in case of sickness and bodily infirmity? Considered, that we have no express word for it, and that it would be more advisable and more safe to direct them to the mercy of God in Christ.   Yet we would not set bounds in certain extraordinary cases, but advise all the teachers (ministers) to be careful to do nothing without the counsel of their fellow laborers, and if possible of their church.

REFRACTORY CONDUCT.

Y. M. 1848. (Indiana.)   Art. 10.   What is the proper course for a church to pursue with members that have been disowned by the church, and their office as teachers in the church taken from them, and yet, contrary to the counsel of the church, they still go on to hold meetings, and influence innocent members to go contrary to the rules and order of the church?   Considered, that such a brother should be still lovingly and faithfully admonished (in the name of the church), again and again, to desist from such a course, but if he would notwithstanding continue therein, we would have, as a last remedy, to put him in avoidance.   Art. 11.   When the church disowns a member so that it is set back from the salutation of the kiss, and from church fellowship, how is the proper way to do with such members, as come from other arms of the church, and knowing the standing of such disowned members, yet will still hold fellowship with such?   Considered, that inasmuch as the Church of Christ is one body all over the world, and the Word even says, " *What-soever ye shall bind on earth, shall be bound in heaven, and whatsoever ye shall loose on earth, shall be loosened in heaven ;*" then if one branch of this church (lawfully) disowns a member, members from other branches knowing this should hold them equally as disowned.

RESTORATION, THE DOCTRINE OF.

Y. M. 1858.   Art. 2.   Is it according to the gospel of Christ, for brethren, especially bishops, in speaking on the final destinies of the ungodly, to preach publicly that they shall be punished with everlasting destruction from the presence of the Lord, and privately teach that all will be restored everlastingly, whether they know God and obey the gospel of our Lord Jesus Christ or not; and if asked the question by an alien, whether the devil himself will be saved, make no reply?   Answer.—We think brethren should be careful not to contradict privately what they preach publicly.   Art. 3.   Is it consistent to preach eternal punishment, and at the same time to peddle Winchester's Dialogues on Restoration ?

Tell us how it is. Answer. If a brother preaches endless punishment, it would be inconsistent for him to distribute Winchester's Dialogues on Restoration.

SABBATH-BREAKING

Y. M. 1810. Art. 6. Concerning working on Sundays, inasmuch there are some members who are so easily brought to work on Sundays, it has been considered thus, that it should not be by any means, except in cases of necessity, for it is a transgression of the law of God, and that of our rulers.

Y. M. 1852. Art. 14. How is it considered, when brethren do any kind of servile work on the Sabbath or Lord's day? Considered, that brethren should by no means do any servile work on the Christian Sabbath day, nor engage in sporting, such as fishing, hunting, &c.; and in case members will do so, they should be visited in the name of the church, and heartily admonished to do so no more, and if they should persist in so doing, they should be dealt with as offenders. That necessary labor, such as feeding and watering our creatures, preparing food for the family, and the like, form an exception is obvious.

SCHOOLS, &c.

Y. M. 1852. Art. 12. How is it considered by the brethren, if brethren aid and assist in building great houses for high schools, and send their children to the same? Considered, that brethren should be very cautious, and not mind high things, but condescend to men of low estates. See Rom. 12 : 16.

Y. M. 1857. Art. 19. What are the views of the present annual council in regard to the contemplated school that was alluded to some time since in the Gospel Visitor? Answer. It is conforming to the world. The Apostle Paul says, "Knowledge puffeth up, but charity edifieth."

Y. M. 1858. Art. 51. We desire to know whether the Lord has commanded us to have a school besides our common schools, such as the one contemplated in the Gospel Visitor. If we are, ought we not to have one soon; and if it is not commanded of the Lord, ought we to have one; and is it right to contend for or against such an institution publicly through the press, since our different views may become stumbling blocks before the world; and if it is once decided, ought we not to keep forever silent about it? Answer. Concerning the proposed school in the Gospel Visitor, we think we have no right to interfere with an individual enterprise, so long as there is no departure from gospel principles.

Y. M. 1861. Art. 10. How is it considered, if brethren suffer their children to take an active part in school debates and exhibitions ? Considered, that there can be no objection if conducted in an orderly manner ; and we advise brethren (at the same time not to forget) to bring up their children in the nurture and admonition of the Lord.

Y. M. 1862. Art. 16. Inasmuch as the Yearly Meeting has allowed of brethren's children taking an active part in school exhibitions if properly conducted, is it wrong for brethren to go with them to investigate such exhibitions? Answer. We consider it best to leave the answer to Query 10 of last Yearly Meeting, as it is; and in answer to the additional question, whether the parents may go to school exhibitions, we would say we consider it best for them not to go, if their going would be likely to encourage anything that is of an evil character.

SECRET COUNCIL.

Y. M. 1866. Art. 3. Is it according to the gospel to hold church meetings in secrecy, or are we commanded to take Christ for our example and he said, "In secret have I said nothing?" John 18 : 20. Answer. It is according to the gospel, inasmuch as the Saviour only says, "In secret have I *said* nothing." Consequently, this does not prohibit us from transacting church business in secrecy, his language not applying to church meetings. In holding church meetings secretly, we act according to Matt. 18, where the Saviour says, " Tell it unto the church."

SELF-DEFENCE.

See " *Non-Resistance.*"

SELF-EXAMINATION.

Y. M. 1851. Art. 21. Whether a minister or any other member has a right, according to Paul's treating on self-examination, after being seated at the communion table, to order from the table any brother or sister ; or whether Paul's sentiment is to leave the member or members until after the communion, and then take them into the council of the church ? Considered, inasmuch as the Apostle Paul writes 1 Cor. 11 : 29 : " He that eateth and drinketh unworthily, eateth and drinketh damnation to himself," we think that no member should be permitted to remain at the communion table, when he is known to a member of the church to have been guilty of a violation of the order of the house of God.

Y. M. 1862. Art. 32. Where ministering brethren have difficulties in the church, and when they are not in full fellowship with the church in breaking bread, &c., may they still continue to appoint meetings ? Answer. We consider such brethren should be reconciled to the church before they make appointments to preach.

SINGING IN DIFFERENT VOICES.

Y. M. 1844. Art. 5. About singing in different voices at public meetings, it was considered that the singing of psalms, hymns and spiritual songs, is a part of divine worship, which we ought to perform always in the spirit and in truth, and with solemnity; to be watchful that nothing in our singing should detract our minds from the serious contemplation of what we sing; that we ought to avoid such light tunes which may make us merry rather than serious, and that our singing should always tend more to the glory of God than to the tickling of the outward ear. 1 Cor. 14 : 15; Ephes. 5 : 19; Col. 3 : 16.

SINGING SCHOOLS.

Y. M. 1825. Art. 4. Whether a brother may teach singing schools, was considered, that the musical schools, as they are generally conducted, have nothing to do with the service of God, and that a brother should teach none.

Y. M. 1838. Art. 2. Whether it is considered proper to hold singing schools in our meeting houses? Chiefly considered, that meeting houses are no proper places for holding singing schools therein.

Y. M. 1849. Art. 22. Can a brother be allowed to teach singing schools on Sundays, and take money for the same. Considered, that much as we are in favor of correct singing, we still think it best for a brother not to teach singing schools.

Y. M. 1857. Art. 22. Is it agreeable to the gospel for brethren to teach singing schools? Answer. We consider it best for brethren not to teach singing school on Sabbath or at night.

Y. M. 1862. Art. 7. Is it allowed by the brethren in annual council for the members of the church to attend singing schools on Sundays, or at night, or in the week? While we would caution our members, especially the young, against the abuses of singing schools, we would not absolutely forbid them if conducted orderly, and if they do not conflict with the time of preaching.

SISTERS COMMUNING.

Y. M. 1849. Art. 35. Whether it would not be more consistent with the word, if at the communion the administrator would give the bread and cup to the sisters, and they divide it like the brethren among themselves, and the administrator to pass along to keep order? Considered unanimously, to go on in celebrating the communion as heretofore.

[Observation of more than thirty years teaches the writer that a considerable number of the sisters are young mothers with babes on their arms, who claim their constant attention, and employ even their hands. Hence, when such a thought as expressed in the above query presented'itself, it was always dismissed by the reflection, that it would be next to impossible to preserve order and decency, by imposing on our dear sisters this additional duty, under their peculiar circumstan:es.]

Y. M. 1857. Art. 9. Why do not the sisters break the bread and pass the cup to each other in the same manner as the brethren do at the communion ? Answer. Man being the head of the woman, and it having been the practice of the church from time immemorial for the officiating brethren to break the bread to the sisters, we know of no scriptural reason for making a change in our practice.

[There is scarcely any church or society, beside our own, where the *rights and privileges of the female sex* are better regarded. Not to speak of those churches whose principles were established in the dark ages, when woman was considered as an inferior being, and even manhood groaned under the tyrannical sway of popes and priests. With us, the sisters are on a perfect equality with the brethren. The youngest sister's voice counts one, and the oldest bishop's vote does not count more, in any ordinary question before the church, or in a choice for ministers or deacons. In all things, rights and privileges, there is no difference between the male and female portion of the membership, and the only exception is the *service* of the church, from which the sisters are exempted by the gospel, though the wives of ministers and deacons are also presented to the church, and charged to be helpers to their husbands in their service.]

SISTERS; COVERING OF THE HEAD. See *"Covering of the Head."*

SLAVERY, SLAVE TRADING, &c. See *" Emancipation."*

SOCIAL MEETINGS.

Y. M. 1858. Art. 40. Is it according to the gospel for brethren to hold what is called social meetings, and to give liberty to all present to rise and speak, so that members of other societies feel themselves at liberty to admonish ? Considered, that social meetings should be strictly held in order, and to give liberty to all present to rise on their feet and admonish, is not in order.

Y. M. 1859. Art. 20. See *" Prayer Meetings."*

Y. M. 1861. Art. 1. QUERY 1. Are we to understand by the grant of social meetings, as decided in annual meeting of 1858, to make public appointments frequently, where there is an organized church and preaching every two weeks, and in conducting them liberty to be given to any brother or sister, or, if time admit, for all to rise to their feet by course, and to exhort; and if not so to be understood, what will the annual council say the order of social meetings shall be? Considered, that the order should be according to that rule laid down by the apostle, 1 Cor. 14 : 27—40. And to unite with other professors in worship in our meetings is inconsistent with the gospel and the practice of the church.

SOCIETIES, SECRET.   See also "*Freemasons*."

Y. M. 1847.   Art. 10.   Would it be proper for brethren to join the secret association of the "Sons of Temperance?"   Considered, inasmuch as we are to "prove all things, and hold fast that which is good," and as the nature of *secret societies* is such as to preclude the knowledge of them before a membership is obtained, we consider it improper for a member of the church to join such an order.

Y. M. 1859.   Art. 4.   As secret societies seem to be multiplying, and as many young men around us join them, and as some undertake a defence of them, it seems necessary that our minds need to be frequently stirred up upon this matter.   Then, as we profess to be followers of Him who said, "In secret have I done nothing," will the Yearly Meeting through its proceedings come up to the side of our Lord.

Answer.—We consider that members should not participate in any secret or oath-bound societies whatever, and if after they have been duly admonished, they persist in such participation, we consider the church is justifiable in excommunicating them.

SONS OF TEMPERANCE.   See "*Societies, Secret*," above.

SPIRITUAL KNOCKINGS.

Y. M. 1852.   Art. 10.   Has a brother, who is a speaker, a right to go to so-called "*spiritual rappings*," and ask such questions as these? "Are the ordinances of the gospel essential to salvation?"   "Are certain deceased relatives happy?" &c.—and to invite the so-called medium into his neighborhood, who thereupon calls at such brother's house, and neighbors, and also members attend there, asking and receiving information from such medium?—How is such a brother to be dealt with according to gospel?   Considered, that such rappings are a lying wonder and delusion, and that these things have been strongly forbidden both in the Old and New Testament, as the work of the devil.   See Deut. 18 : 9–16; Lev. 19 : 31;   20 : 6, 27;   Is. 8 : 19, 20;   Acts 16 : 16–18;   Luke 11 : 14; 2 Thess. 2 : 9–11; Rev. 13 : 13.   And where any brother goes so far as stated above, he should be admonished, and ought to make satisfactory acknowledgments to the church, and all the members should be earnestly admonished to have nothing to do with it, and totally to debar it from among them.

STOREKEEPING.

Y. M. 1832.   Art. 3.   Whether it would be approved, when brethren engage in storekeeping and selling of strong drinks?   Considered, the first might be allowed in cases of necessity, where a brother has no other way to make a living, but the latter in no case whatever.   See also "*Ardent Spirits*."

SUBSTITUTE MONEY.

Y. M. 1781.   Art. 1. Inasmuch at the big meeting in Conestoga last year it has been unanimously concluded, that we should not pay the substitute money; but inasmuch as it has been overlooked here and there, and some have not regarded it (said conclusion), therefore we the assembled brethren exhort in union all brethren in all places to hold themselves guiltless, and take no part in war and bloodshedding, which might take place if we would pay for hiring men voluntarily; or more still, if we would become agents to collect such money.   And inasmuch some brethren have received written orders to tell the people, and afterward collect (such money), accompanied by a threat of a heavy fine—we exhort heartily, not to be scared to do that which is not right.   Still, we exhort also heartily, that if a brother should be fined, there should provision be made for such brethren, and assistance rendered as far as concerns money.   In case a brother or his son should be drafted, that he or his son should go to war, and he could buy himself or his son from it, such would not be deemed so sinful, yet it should not be given voluntarily, without compulsion.   But where this has been overlooked, and the substitute-money has been paid voluntarily, and (the brother) should acknowledge his mistake from the heart, and repent it, the church might be satisfied with him.   But when a brother bears his testimony, that he cannot give the money on account of his conscience, and would say to the collector, "If thou must take it, then use your authority; I shall not be in your way,"—with such brother we should be also satisfied.   But concerning the tax*) it is considered, that on account of the troublesome times (1781, the fifth year of the Revolutionary War, and in order to avoid offense, we might follow the example of Christ (Matt. 17 :24–27) :—yet if one does not see it so, and thinks perhaps, he for his conscience' sake could not pay it, but bear with others who pay in patience, we would willingly leave it over, inasmuch we deem the overruling of the conscience as wrong.

[This tax was very likely something like what we had in the recent War (1861—5), where towns and townships are laying a tax for means to prevent a draft.]

SUNDAY-SCHOOLS.

Y. M. 1838.   Art. 10. Whether it be right for members to take part in Sunday-Schools, Class Meetings, and the like?   Considered, most advisable to take no part in such like things.

Y. M. 1857.   Art. 11. How is it considered for brethren to have Sabbath-Schools, conducted by the brethren?

Ans.—Inasmuch as we are commanded to bring upour children in the nurture and admonition of the Lord, we know of no scripture which condemns Sabbath-Schools if conducted in gospel order, and if they are made the means of teaching scholars a knowledge of the scriptures.

Y. M. 1862. Art. 1. Is it agreeable to the order of the brethren to hold Sabbath-Schools? And if so, how should they be conducted?

Ans.—The decision of the Annual Meeting of 1857, is re-admitted.

Art 31. Will the brethren at Annual Meeting consider it right to establish Sunday-Schools, and if they do consider it right, will they also consider it right for members of the church and their children to attend Sunday-School celebrations?

Ans.—We consider it right to have Sunday-Schools if conducted by brethren, but not to have celebrations.

SUPPER ON THE TABLE AT FEETWASHING. See "*Lord's Supper.*"

Y. M. 1844. Art. 2. Whether there must be something of the supper on the table when feetwashing is observed? This query has been likewise presented several times before this, and the brethren do still consider that they could not see a better way "to have all things done decently and in order," than the one hitherto followed. 1 Cor. 14:40.

SUSPENDING MEMBERS.

Y. M. 1858. Art. 12. Is it agreeable to the gospel for a church to grant the privilege to a member to do certain things, and at the same time debar him from the communion for so doing? Answer.—That no church according to the gospel has a right to do so.

SUSPENDING MINISTERS FROM THE MINISTRY.

Y. M. 1858. Art. 11. Is it according to the gospel to expel a brother from his office, whether deacon or minister, and yet leave him stand as a member? Answer.—We have a right—according to the gospel; inasmuch as he is put into office by the council of the church, by the council of the church the office can be taken from him. 1 Tim. 3.

SWEARING OF OATHS. See "*Oaths.*"

TAVERN-KEEPING.

Y. M. 1804. Art. 1. Whether it should or would be allowed to a brother or sister to keep public tavern by or with a license, was unanimously considered, that it could not be allowed, because we are convinced that it cannot be done without disorder, and is rather a hindrance to a godly life and quietness of spirit? It has been deemed good in union, that if a brother or sister should undertake to keep tavern, they should be visited in friendship, and in love and seriousness, and in the

name of the church be dissuaded and warned from it, and shown unto
them what disorder and harm is likely to result thereof. Further it was
concluded, that if a brother or sister would not hear, accept or obey such
counsel and admonition, then we would have to consider such as disobedient, and could not have fellowship with them. Yet the sisters, who
are bound in such matter by the urging of their husbands, and would
gladly be relieved from it, but cannot without the consent of their husbands, they should be held less guilty.

Y. M. 1835. (Miami.) Art 11. How it is considered, when brethren
keep tavern ? Considered, as entirely unbecoming for brethren.

TAXES.

Y. M. 1781. Art. 1. See *"Substitute Money."*

TEACHING BY A PRIVATE BROTHER.

Y. M. 1836. Art. 3. What is to be done with a brother who professes and claims to be urged by the spirit of God to preach the gospel,
and who is not chosen by the church for it? He is counselled and allowed, after the elect brethren have spoken, to make known by exhortation, if there is anything on his mind; he may also use liberty in public
prayer, when necessary, or in reading the scriptures, provided he is
acceptable by the church.

Y. M. 1838. Art. 4. Whether a common (private) brother has the
right to go out, to appoint or let others appoint meetings for himself, or
generally to teach publicly without the counsel of the church? Considered, that a brother, who is not entrusted with the office, is not justified
so to do. James 3 : 1.

 Y. Y. 1839. Art. 4. What is to be done with a brother who wants
to preach, and forces him into it without or contrary to the counsel of
the church? Considered, that such a brother, having been admonished
once and again, cannot be held as a member in full fellowship, if he is
disobedient.

Y. M. 1845. Art. 7. How it is considered, if brethren will force
themselves into the ministry without consent from the elders (and the
church), and some of the members encouraging them in it? Considered, that inasmuch it appears by the words of James, 3 : 1;—by
the words of our Saviour, John 10 : 1;—and of Paul, Heb. 5 : 4-7—
there is a right way, and also a wrong way to enter into the ministry;—
the wrong way being when one is taking this honor unto himself,—and the
right way, when one is called of God by the church, which is the body
of Christ, and the order of which calling to the ministry is found described in the Acts of the Apostles; brethren ought to be very cautious,
when they feel a desire to preach the gospel, that they do not take the

wrong way; rather humble than elevate themselves, and be fully assured,
that if the Lord wants their services, he has all power in heaven and on
earth to bring about their calling to it in the right order and in due
time;—but if such brethren would still go out of the way, appoint and
hold meetings against the counsel of the church, the church would have
to hold them as disobedient members according to Matt. 18; and members generally ought to be very careful not to encourage and support
such brethren in their disorderly proceedings.

Y. M. 1848. (Indiana.) Art. 12. In regard to the third query on
the difficulties of Bachelor's Run church with bro. O., P., and others,
the brethren in general council considered that there had been committed
errors on both sides, in consequence of which many members on both
sides made satisfactory acknowledgments before the meeting, and it was
concluded that with such all that is past should be forgiven and forgotten,
and with as many as may yet come and make satisfaction ; and that they
all should be received into full fellowship, and brother David Fisher in his
office as a speaker. Farthermore, this meeting considers and counsels,
that bro. O., P., and such others that hold yet with them, should have
still time to reflect, and should they come also in a reasonable space of
time, and make satisfactory acknowledgments, the church should also be
willing to forgive them. But if they should persist in their contrary
course, going on holding meetings in opposition to the church, and even
become railers of the church, there would be no other way than to put
them into full avoidance, according to 1 Cor. 5 : 10.

TEACHING BY SISTERS.

Y. M. 1834. Art. 17. Concerning a sister's preaching. Not approved of; considering such sister being in danger, not only exposing her
own state of grace to temptation, but also causing temptations; discord
and disputes among other members.

Y. M. 1859. Art. 7. Does the gospel admit of female preaching?
And if it does, shall they not have authority from the church under
whose jurisdiction they are ?

Answer.—As Paul recognizes a distinction, in Rom. 12 : 6, 7, between
teaching, ministering, and prophesying, and as he evidently approves of
females prophesying, 1 Cor. 11 : 5—we then think that a female cannot
teach or preach, according to 1 Cor. 14 : 34; 1 Tim. 2 : 12, in the ordinary acceptation of those terms, yet we cannot under all forbid them
to prophesy.

TESTIMONY OF OUTSIDERS.

Y. M. 1817. Art. 4. Whether testimony against a member may be
received from outsiders (persons not members), in case of a crime being

laid to the charge of the member? Considered, that we could not pass judgment on a member upon testimony from outsiders; but in case one single member could testify with truthful outsiders, then we could and might judge according to the word of God, for *" in the mouth of two or three witnesses every word may be established "*

Y. M. 1837. Art. 2. How it is viewed, if a member is accused of a crime only on testimony from (such as are) out of the church? Whether it would be right, to take a member into judgment (before the church) on such testimony? The counsel is, to make a strict investigation, and if there should be nothing found, and the member continue to deny the charge, it could not be judged on testimony (from) out (siders) of the church alone.

Y. M. 1841. Art. 6. Whether members may be brought before the council of the church, and be judged for a crime, only on testimony from without (the church); *i. e.* from persons that are not members of the church? Considered, that when there is some report abroad of a brother walking disorderly, or having committed a crime, it is the duty of the church, to send some brethren to the place where the report has originated to investigate the matter. If nothing be found establishing the charge, and the member denying the same after a close examination, nothing more can be done. If there should, however, some suspicion be created in the members by the general conduct of the accused, the church may advise such a member not to approach the Lord's table until the matter is cleared up to the satisfaction of the church. But to disown entirely (put in avoidance) a member on (outside) testimony only from without, was not considered right and just according to the gospel.

Y. M. 1845. Art. 9. How is it considered, if brethren are accused by the mouth of two or three witnesses of honest moral character, but not being members, and their testimony against those members agrees, that they were guilty of drunkenness or any other crime, and the church has cause to believe such testimony from other circumstances—but the brethren so accused deny the charge? Considered as in the year 1841, Art. 6, that such members might be advised not to approach the Lord's table until the matter is cleared up to the satisfaction of the church; but to judge a brother on testimony from without alone, and without his own confession, would not be just according to the gospel.

Y. M. 1862. Art. 5. In case a complaint is found against a brother because he was sued at court for an honest debt, and then took the stay, and when he is visited he denies the charge and says that he was not sued. But the brethren having evidence to the contrary, agree to send two brethren to the county clerk's office, and the clerk shows by his record that the brother was sued, and took the stay for nearly six months, and then paid the debt together with the costs. Now the question is, which is to be taken as truth, the brother's word, or the record in the clerk's office? And have the brethren a right, or have they not, to send brethren to the world to investigate church matters?

Answer.—It is not wrong for brethren to have such matters closely investigated, and to obtain all the light possible.

Art. 56. Is the testimony of one witness sufficient authority to expel a member under any circumstances, when the accused denies, and objects to the testimony?

Answer.—One witness is not sufficient in general, but we will not say that under no circumstances one is not sufficient.

Art. 57. Can a member who is accused of some fault, give testimony before the church?

Answer.—While a person is a member of the church, his testimony cannot be altogether set at naught by the church.

THEATRE AND SHOWS.

Y. M. 1835. (Miami.) Art. 3. How it is considered when brethren go with their children to shows? Considered, it should not be.

Y. M. 1838. Art. 11. How it is considered, when members go to public shows, and even take their children along? Unanimously considered, that members ought to avoid such places, and to warn their children therefrom.

Y. M. 1848. Art. 28. Whether church members have a right according to the gospel to go to public shows? Considered far better for members to avoid all such places.

Y. M. 1859. Art. 14. What shall we do when brethren, and even speakers and bishops, attend yearly the county fairs?

Answer.—Such brethren should be admonished not to attend such places, and if they still persist in doing so, they should be dealt with according to Matt. 18.

TOBACCO.

Y. M. 1817. Art. 1. Concerning the abuse of Tobacco, it was in union considered, that if a member should be contaminated with it, such should be admonished to quit it, and if it would not be told, such a member could not be elected to any office in the church. (But what is to be done with one already in the ministry?)

Y. M. 1822. (Miami) Art. 5. Concerning the abuse of Tobacco. This has been before the meeting already before this, and was always considered a shamefully bad habit (*German, Untugend*)—and every thing bad, says the apostle, is sin, and sin defileth the body; and another apostle says, that your bodies together with soul and spirit shall be holy.

Y. M. 1827. Art. 12. Concerning members who engage in the raising of Tobacco? Considered, that members should have nothing to do with such things, by which so much mischief is done, and so many men (and women too) are led captive, as is the case with Tobacco.

Y. M. 1839. Art. 7. Whether a brother may be intemperate with strong drink or tobacco? No.

Y. M. 1864. Art. 9. Inasmuch as all that our annual meetings has hitherto done to suppress the excessive or intemperate use of Tobacco in smoking and chewing, has virtually proved a failure, could not this meeting adopt some method by which the excessive use of this growing evil could be suppressed in our brotherhood?

Answer —As the use of Tobacco is offensive to some brethren and sisters, and the excess of it an evil, we advise and counsel brethren not to use it in time of worship so as to be either filthy, or offensive to others; and we think our ministering brethren should admonish their members not to indulge in the excessive use of it in any way, because it is wrong to do so.

TOMBSTONES.

Y. M. 1855. Art. 8. Whether it is agreeable with the word of God to erect tombstones? Considered, that it would not agree with the principles of the gospel, such as humility, non-conformity to the world, &c. to erect large and expensive tombstones.

TRADITIONS.

The question is sometimes asked: You profess to have no law or discipline, no rule of faith or practice but the Bible, and more especially the New Testament of our Lord Jesus Christ. But are not the Minutes of your Yearly Meeting, to which you so often refer, something like the traditions of the elders of the Jews, something beside, and over and above the Word of God. To this we reply, No, no. The traditions of the Jewish elders caused transgressions of the commandments of God, and therefore our Saviour told the Pharisees, "Thus have ye made the commandments of God of none effect by your traditions." Matt. 15 : 3, 6. On the contrary, the counsels of the brethren, or if you please, the traditions of our brethren, have the very opposite tendency, namely to assist in keeping the commandments of God. There is a kind of traditions, which we are to keep according to the express command of the New Testament. Thus we read, "Now I praise you, brethren, that ye remember me in all things, and hold fast the *traditions*, as I delivered them to you." 1 Cor. 11 : 2. Revised version according to the Greek text. Again: "Therefore, brethren, stand fast, and hold the *traditions*, which ye have been taught, whether by word, or our epistle." 2 Thess. 2 : 15. Again: "Now we command you, brethren, in the name of our

Lord Jesus Christ, that ye withdraw yourselves from every brother that walketh disorderly, and not after the *tradition* which ye received of us." 2 Thess. 3 : 6.

Y. M. 1842. Art. 12. Whether a church has the right to make resolutions framed by men, binding on its members? Considered by the elders and answered thus : If the resolutions are founded upon and in accordance with the gospel to which we are all bound, they are binding;—but if they are not according and even contrary to the gospel, we cannot be bound to observe them, and no church can make them binding.

UNION OF THE CHURCH.   See *Appendix.*

UNIVERSALISM.

Y. M. 1849.   Art. 30. Whether it is advisable for a brother to preach *universal redemption* publicly; that is, that all men, however vile they may have been, shall share alike in the fruition of happiness with the saints?   Considered, that we could not approve, by any means, of such proceeding.

Y. M. 1856.   Art. 14. (2) See " *Far West Brethren,*" page 108.

VANITY IN DRESS.   See " *Fashionable Garment.*"

VISITING BRETHREN.   See "*Deacons.*"

VISITING THE CANDIDATES FOR BAPTISM.

Y. M. 1837.   Art. 8. When persons desire to be received by baptism into the church, if it be necessary to instruct them before baptism (of our not being able) of the taking of oaths, going to war, and the like, that according to our view it is forbidden in the gospel? The advice is that such persons ought if possible be visited before their baptism, and by all means ought to be previously instructed on the following points, to wit : on the taking of oaths, going to war and muster, on not using the power of the law contrary to the gospel, and on not conforming to the fashions of this world in apparel and the like ; and that they ought to state before their being received their willingness to refrain from all such things.

Y. M. 1840.   Art. 5. How it is considered about the visiting of such persons who apply for baptism, whether they must be visited in all cases before baptism ?   Considered, that this is a good order, and should be introduced and observed every where if possible, without debarring however (brethren or churches) from making in certain cases an exception. But where this order is yet unknown, it would be proper to inform the members thereof, and by them such as wish to be received by baptism. See also " *Baptism.*"

VISITING OF MEMBERS YEARLY.

Y. M. 1858. Art. 4. Is it according to the gospel of Christ, in paying our annual visit, to collect from twenty to thirty of the brethren together in one place, and then the bishops pay the visit to them openly when they are all together, and then send them out two or three together and visit those that were not thus collected? Or is the duty restricted to the visiting brethren exclusively, and should the visit be made from house to house?

Answer.—As we have no direct rule in the gospel for making the visit, we think it best for the visiting brethren to go from house to house.

VISITING THE CHURCHES.

Y. M. 1848. Art. 8. Would it not be right for the brethren in council at the annual meeting to appoint several brethren that are experienced and sound in the faith, and send them two and two with the decisions of the annual meeting, and let them visit all the congregations in the United States, and establish them all in the same order according to example in Acts 15 : 22? Considered, to leave this over for further consideration.

Y. M. 1851. Art. 18. Would it not be advisable for the brethren assembled in annual meeting to establish (appoint) certain well established ordained elders, and send them two by two to visit certain districts appointed to them, &c.? The decision to lie over till next year.

Y. M. 1853. Art. 27. Would it not be well for the brethren to come upon some plan to acquaint all the bishops and housekeepers of the various branches of the church with the rules and regulations concluded upon by the general council for the more perfect union and prosperity of the church? And if these rules and regulations be violated by a minister, with some of the members composing his district, should they not fall into the hands of the brethren of the adjacent district as offenders, and be dealt with as such, and if the above should be considered expedient, what plan should be devised to carry it into effect? Answer.—We are fully satisfied that the means long had in practice by the brethren, namely, the Minutes of our Annual Meetings—are sufficient to give the teachers and housekeepers, and members in general, the decisions of our annual councils for the perfecting of love and union throughout the brotherhood. And if it should so happen that a housekeeper, with a part or all the members of his district could not be satisfied with the decisions of the annual council, as we were advised and instructed by our beloved elder brethren, and unanimously concurred in at the annual meeting held in 1850, in Montgomery county, Ohio, they should bear with the annual council and with one another until the next annual meeting, and then bring their grievances to the annual council where they proceeded from, and we believe full satisfaction will be obtained.

VOTING, (POLITICAL.)   See *"Electioneering."*

Y. M. 1866.   Art. 1. A number of questions being presented upon the subject of voting and some asking for a repeal of former minutes, the following resolution as an answer to the questions, was adopted :

Resolved, That we think it most expedient not to repeal any minutes touching voting ; that this Annual Meeting recommends to the members of the church to refrain from voting, fearing that by voting we may compromise our non-resistant principles.   But we recommend forbearance towards those who vote, not making voting a test of fellowship, hoping that in time they will see with the body of the brethren upon this subject.

Art. 2. Inasmuch as the Annual Meeting has frequently decided against the brethren voting, is it not inconsistent, and even injurious to the brotherhood, for brethren to write and editors to publish any thing in opposition to those decisions?   Answer.—We think that our brethren who write and print articles, should be very careful not to promote strife and divisions in the church, but peace, love, union, and holiness.

VOTING OF THE ABSENT AT CHURCH ELECTIONS.

Y. M. 1843.   Art. 8 How it might be considered when at an election for teachers (ministers) and deacons, absent members do send their votes with other members?   Considered, that since the promise of our Saviour is given : "Where two or three are gathered together in my name, there am I in the midst of them."   Matt. 18 : 20. In such important church affairs this promise belongs only to those who are assembled, and not to those who are absent, the brethren generally have acted upon that ground, and not taken any vote from absent members.

WANT OF UNION AMONG MINISTERS.

· Y. M. 1799.   Art. 1. See *Difficulties in Churches.*
Y. M. 1815.   (See *ibid.*)   That there is still a sad want of union among our preachers and members, became evident in the " Deacon question," "the Supper question," the question about " the Avoidance," &c., &c.

WARFARE.   See also *Non-resistance, Substitute-money,* &c.

Y. M. 1790.   At a (large and) numerous meeting of brethren on the Schuylkill, at (the place of) brother John Bach, May 22d, 1790, the following was unanimously concluded by the brethren, viz : We wish and desire, that the dear brother V. . . B. . . . would desist from his strange notion, because he has renounced with us before God, angels and men every thing which is contrary to wholesome doctrine, and we believe and profess that Christ has prohibited to his followers the swearing of oaths and the partaking in war. Hence we must hold fast to His truth and word, and withdraw ourselves from every such brother who will justify swearing of oaths and warfare. It is impossible for us to break the bread of communion with such a brother, even if he would allege that the powers that be require us to do so. For our rulers could not do it, if they would, because we must obey God more than men. But now, thanks be to God, we have such a government that will not require of us such contrary to (the dictates of) our conscience. But if there should be some one among us that had such a conscience, that he could fight and swear oaths, such a one would not be of us.

Likewise, we could not break the bread of communion with a ministering brother who would, contrary to our views, baptize backward.

Signed in the great meeting, in the name and with the consent of all the assembled brethren.

George Preiss, Martin Meyer, Michael Frantz, Daniel Bollinger, John Landes, Christian Lawshe, Justus Fuchs, Martin Gaby, Peter Keyser, Sander Mack, Nathaniel Schreiber, David Kuntze, Martin Urner, Peter Leibert, Jacob Boeshor, Jacob Danner, Abraham Lawshe.

WASHING OF FEET. See also *Feetwashing*.

WILLS, MAKING.

Y. M. 1846. Art. 8. About brethren making a will, and treating their children very unequally without a cause. Considered, that though we would not by any means infringe upon the right of a parent to make a free disposition of his worldly goods in his last will—it would be advisable for a christian father not to make a too great difference among his children without a good cause, and that it would be best to treat children as much alike as possible, so that love and peace may be preserved among them.

WINE AT COMMUNIONS.

Y. M. 1858. Art. 36. Is it right to use at our communion meetings the article of wine frequently used and known by those who are judges of the article to be an adulterated article, and hence cannot properly be called the fruit of the vine? Considered, that it is (desirable) advisable to procure the purest article.

WITHDRAWING FROM THE CHURCH.

Y. M. 1837. Art. 1. How it is considered, if a member desires (to withdraw from or) to be no more with the church, and yet has committed no other offense? The counsel is, since circumstances are so differ-

13

ent, there is also a difference (in judging such a case). If a member is desirous to be off, and does not commit any other offense, we could have patience somewhat longer with such a member, than if a member would speak contemptuously of the church. Then the church can judge best, how soon to let it withdraw, and place it according to its desire; yet there should be used all possible diligence to bring back again such souls to the flock. But if they will not hear (the church,) nor heed the admonitions, then there would be just cause to put them as they desire.

WIVES, OF MINISTERS OR DEACONS.

Y. M. 1862. Art. 36. Is the practice good and sustained in the gospel, for the church enjoining on the believing wives of teachers the duty of aiding by their humble example and chaste conversation, their husbands in the solemn duty laid upon them?

Answer.—We consider such a practice in perfect harmony with the spirit of the gospel.

Y. M. 1862. Art. 37. Why are not the sisters who become wives of ministers after they are appointed to the ministry, called upon in the church to promise the same duties as the sisters who are wives at the time their husbands are appointed to the office?

Answer.—We consider they should be, according to the practice of the church touching those who are wives of brethren when the latter are appointed to office.

YEARLY MEETING. [See Note.] See *Annual Meeting.*

Y. M. 1861. Art. 15. Would it not be better and give more satisfaction to the brotherhood at large, if the brethren serving or composing the standing committee at our annual meetings would be changed every year, so as to have at least two thirds of the same fresh members? Considered, that we do not think it advisable to make any change in the manner of choosing the standing committee, and are still satisfied with the decision of the Yearly Meeting of 1853. See Art. 1, in the Minutes of said year.

Y. M. 1863. Art. 6. Would it not be expedient and consistent, that the brethren forming the standing committee of the Annual Meeting of the brethren should open and examine all questions sent in by the several churches, and assort them, and thereby save an amount of unnecessary labor and time spent, as there are frequently two, three, and even more queries of the same import and meaning sent in, and acted upon and separately reported hitherto by different committees at the same conference, which we think could be avoided in a great measure? Considered, it is expedient.

Y. M. 1864. Art. 36. It having been agreed upon at a former time

that our Yearly Meetings should be held alternately in the East and
West, the Allegheny Mountains being considered the dividing line, it is
requested that this meeting change the line to the Ohio River. This
request was granted. Art. 37. Would it not be good to make some
change in holding our Yearly Meetings, for the purpose of preventing so
great a multitude of people from being present. And would it not also
be better to have the conference more private, and not to name on the
Minutes who were chosen on the standing committee, or who was clerk,
&c. Answer.—We think it not expedient to make any change at this
time.

Y. M. 1865. Art. 1. Could not this Annual Meeting make some
change in the manner of holding our Annual Meetings, which would be
advisable and acceptable to the brotherhood? Answer.—This meeting
feels the importance of a change, but not to make any change too hastily,
it appoints the following committee to take this matter into consideration, to propose the result of their wisdom and labor to the next Annual
Meeting for its acceptance or rejection. D. B. Sayler, Philip Boyle,
Benjamin Moomaw, Andrew Detrick, J. H. Umstad, John Wise, H. D.
Davy, Jacob Hershey, John Miller, Hiel Hamilton, Christian Long,
John Metzger, David Brower, and Frederick P. Lochr. Art. 34. Does
the Annual Council make laws, or give advice only, in case where it has
no direct gospel on the subject? Answer.—It gives advice only.

Y. M. 1866. Page 1–3.—The deferred business of last Annual
Meeting being the first business in order before the council, the commit
.tee appointed at that meeting to devise some plan for holding our Annual
Meetings which will be more satisfactory to the brotherhood, was called
upon for its report, and submitted the following :

INTRODUCTORY REMARKS.

The authority for holding General Conference Meetings is founded on
the 15th ch. of the Acts of the Apostles, and a strict compliance with
the example therein is advisable. By reference to said scripture, we
learn that the question in dispute, and upon which the disciples differed,
was not referred to a general council until all efforts had failed to settle
it in the church in which it originated. The following language occurs
in the chapter above referred to : " When therefore Paul and Barnabas,
had no small dissension and disputation with them, they determined that
Paul and Barnabas, and certain others of them, should go up to Jerusalem unto the apostles and elders about the question." Here seems to
be authority to send questions upon which the brethren differ in their
judgments to a General Council, and that the bishops ought to go, and
also to have certain others with them. It is further said : " And being
brought on their way by the church, they passed through Phœnice and

Samaria, declaring the conversion of the Gentiles : and they caused great joy unto all the brethren." Here we see that those who were sent were brought on their way by the church. So should we do. That is, help such to go that we send. It is said further, that " the apostles and elders came together to consider this matter." Hence we see that the Council Meeting should be for conference only.

The Annual Meeting.

We recommend that the Annual Council be formed by the delegates sent by the District Meetings, and by all the ordained elders present; that the Meeting be held at the place designated by the Council the preceding year, to commence on the first Tuesday after Whitsunday, the previous Lord's day (Whitsunday) to be spent as it has hitherto been by the brethren, in worship at such places in the vicinity in which the meeting is to be held, and shall be desired, and as may be judged most profitable; that there be no public meeting for worship where the Council Meeting is held, though the meeting should be opened with devotional exercises, and the reading of the 15th ch. of Acts, and likewise closed with devotional exercises ; that the Meeting shall be held alternately in the East and in the West.

The District Meetings.   [See above, page 88]

The church holding the meeting shall make arrangements to receive and entertain all the brethren and sisters privately. There shall be no boarding tent put up at the place of meeting to entertain and feed a mixed multitude as heretofore.

All churches shall have the privilege to call on the General Council Meeting for committees to investigate grievances, and it shall be its duty to appoint such committees as heretofore.

The Organization of the Annual Meeting.

The bishops and elders of the church holding the Annual Meeting, shall select from among the bishops present the standing committee. Virginia, Maryland, Pennsylvania, Ohio, Indiana, and Illinois, shall each be entitled to three, if present, and two, if present, from each of the remaining states in which churches are established , and whenever said states shall contain ten bishops each, they also shall be entitled to three. The standing committee shall choose its own officers, and these shall be a moderator, two clerks, and a door keeper. It shall be the duty of the moderator to keep order among the members of the committee, and also in the public meeting. He shall not permit two brethren to speak at the same time, and he shall decide who is entitled to the floor. He shall also keep the speakers to the question, and declare the query passed, after general consent, by silence. It shall be the duty of the first clerk to keep a faithful record of all the queries and answers, and prepare them for publication. It shall be the duty of the second clerk to read distinctly all papers as often as requested. It shall be the duty of the door keeper to take charge of the room in which the committee meet for business, and shall allow no intrusion in time of session.

As soon as the standing committee has been named, they shall retire to a private room for organization, and the reception of the queries presented by the delegates from the District Meetings (or churches), after which all proper queries shall be read by the General Council Meeting for adoption or amendment, and sub-committees be dispensed with.

The proceedings of the Annual Meetings shall be published, and it is earnestly recommended that all the overseers of churches, whether ordained or not, have them faithfully read and observed in their respective charges. And if it be represented to the Annual Meeting, that this recommendation is disregarded, it shall be the duty of the standing committee to appoint faithful brethren, whose duty it shall be to visit said churches, and see that the Minutes are properly read and observed, and to set in order things that are lacking. The above is unanimously recommended to the Annual Meeting by the Committee.

Signed by the Committee. D. P. Sayler, Henry Koontz, of Md., Benj. Moomaw, of Va ; David Derick, of Tennessee ; John H. Umstad; John Wise, of Pa.; H. D. Davy, James Quinter, John Hershey, of Ohio ; Jacob Miller, Hiel Hamilton, of Indiana; Christian Long, John Bowman, of Illinois; David Brower, of Iowa.

(Three members of the committee not being present, John Bowman, Henry Koontz, and James Quinter were appointed to fill their places.)

This report being read before the General Council, was adopted by the following resolution :

Resolved, That we try the committee's report for at least a sufficient length of time to give it a fair trial.

[YEARLY MEETING.—The first people we know that assembled themselves together annually, and calling it " Yearly Meeting,'' were the Friends or Quakers.. In their history we find the following account of its origin : " In the beginning of this year (1666), the members of this Society held a general YEARLY MEETING at London, which since that time hath been used to be held there annually, in the week called Whitsun-week, because at that time of the year it is commonly best traveling, &c. Several are deputed from all places to this meeting, and what concerns the church in general is there treated on."—SEWELL'S *History of the Rise, Increase and Progress of the Christian People called Quakers*, &c. Vol. 2, page 168.

What Dr. THOMAS CLARKSON says in his "*Portrait of Quakerism*" about the Yearly Meeting : " As deputies were chosen by each monthly meeting to represent it in the quarterly meeting, so the quarterly meetings chose deputies to represent them in the yearly meeting   These deputies are commissioned to be the bearers of certain documents—which contain (in part) answers in writing to a number of the queries (following):

"I. Are meetings for worship and discipline kept up, and do Friends attend them duly, and at the time appointed; and do they avoid all unbecoming behavior therein?

"II. Is there among you any growth in the truth; and hath any convincement appeared since last year?

"III. Are Friends preserved in love towards each other; if differences arise, is due care taken to speedily end them; and are Friends careful to avoid and discourage tale-bearing and detraction?

"IV. Do Friends endeavor, by example and precept, to train up their children, servants, and those under their care, in a religious life and conversation, consistent with our Christian profession, in the frequent reading of the Holy Scriptures, and in plainness of speech, behavior and apparel?

"V. Are Friends just in their dealings, and punctual in fulfilling their engagements; and are they annually advised carefully to inspect the state of their affairs once in the year?

"VI. Are Friends careful to avoid all vain sports and places of diversion, gaming, all unnecessary frequenting of taverns and other public houses, excess in drinking, and other intemperance?

"VII. Do Friends bear a faithful and Christian testimony against receiving and paying tithes, priests' demands, and those called church-rates?

"VIII. Are Friends faithful in our testimony against bearing arms, and being in any manner concerned in the militia, in privateers, letters of marque, or armed vessels, or dealing in prize-goods?

"IX. Are Friends clear of defrauding the King of his customs, duties and excise, or of using or dealing in goods suspected to be run?

"X. Are the necessities of the poor among you properly inspected and relieved; and is good care taken of the education of their offspring?

"XI. Have any meetings been settled, discontinued, or united, since last year?

"XII. Are there any Friends prisoners for our testimonies; and if any one has died a prisoner, or been discharged, since last year, when and how?

"XIII. Is early care taken to admonish such as appear inclinable to marry in a manner contrary to the rules of our Society; and to deal with such as persist in refusing to take counsel?

"XIV. Have you two or more faithful Friends, appointed by the monthly meeting, as overseers in each particular meeting; are the rules respecting removals duly observed; and is due care taken, when any thing appears amiss that the rules of our discipline be timely and impartially put in practice?

"XV. Do you keep a record of the prosecutions and sufferings of your members; is due care taken to register all marriages, births, and burials; are the titles of your meeting-houses, burial-grounds, &c. duly preserved and recorded; and are all legacies and donations properly secured and recorded, and duly applied?"

These questions, properly modified, might serve as a guide also to our local church meetings, as well as to our district and yearly meetings, inasmuch we are apt to forget and overlook our duties, or at least some of them. The answers to these questions would undoubtedly give a practical view of the condition of the church. But let the said author speak:

"These answers are made up from the answers received by the several quarterly meetings from the respective monthly meetings. The deputies are generally four in number for each quarterly meeting—to exercise the power of deputies, judges and legislators in turn, and to investigate and settle the affairs of the Society for the preceding year."

"Among the subjects introduced at this meeting may be that of any new regulations for the government of the Society. The Quakers are not so blindly attached to antiquity, as to keep to customs merely because they are of ancient date. But they are ready, on conviction, to change, alter and improve. Such regulations or alterations may be, and sometimes are proposed by individuals, except in cases of removals and settlements, when it is expected that they should come through the medium of one of the quarterly meetings."

"I may mention here two circumstances, that are worthy of notice on these occasions."

"It may be observed that whether such business as that which I have just detailed, or any of any other sort, comes before the yearly meeting at large, it is decided, not by the influence of numbers (as by a vote), but by the weight of religious character. With the brethren the weight of the express word of God or religious principle founded in the gospel, will decide questions. As most subjects afford cause for a difference of opinion, so individuals at this meeting are found taking their different sides of the argument as they believe it right. Those, however, who are in opposition to any measure, if they perceive by the turn the debate takes, either that they are going against the general will, or that they are opposing the sentiments of members of high moral reputation in the Society, give way. But in whatever way the question before them is settled, no division is ever called for. No counting of numbers (votes) is allowed. No protest is suffered to be entered. In such a case there can be no ostensible leader of any party; no ostensible minority or majority. The Quakers are of opinion that such things, if allowed, would be inconsistent with their profession. They would lead, also, to broils and divisions, and ultimately to the detriment of the Society. Every measure, therefore, is settled by those who are present at this meeting in the way I have mentioned, in brotherly love, and, as the name of the Society signifies, as Friends."

"The other remarkable circumstance is, that there is no ostensible president or head (Christ is supposed by the Quakers to be the head, under whose guidance all their deliberations ought to take place,) of this great assembly, nor any ostensible president or head, of any of its committees; and yet the business of the Society is conducted in as orderly a manner as it is possible to be among any body of men, where the number is so great." See CLARKSON'S *Portraiture of Quakerism.* Vol. 1. Pages 162, 164, 167–173.

Another remarkable circumstance about the Yearly Meetings of the Friends, which the above named author did not notice, is this: that the way and manner of holding their Yearly Meeting is essentially the same as it was two hundred years ago. There was no material change or alteration in conducting said meetings from A. D. 1666, to this A. D. 1866. The reason of this seems to be: First, these people acted from the outset from and upon correct principles; and, secondly, there must have been among them from the first, men of business who understood the forms, proprieties and amenities in conducting public business, and who also were able to give a reason for every step they took; and the members generally were thus enabled to understand and acquiesce in it, and go along contentedly.

If one would say, What is all this about the Quaker Yearly Meeting to us, we would answer: Just as the great prophet Moses could learn something of his father-in-law, Exod. 18: 14–24.—and as Christ taught the lawyer a lesson from the example of the Samaritan, Luke 10: 33–37, telling him, "Go and do thou likewise;—even so, we might learn something from these people, and follow their example, in whatever they followed Christ and his gospel, and tried to do right.

Having been asked what plan we considered best to follow in conducting Yearly Meetings, we will in humility repeat what we said to the committee a year ago in substance when on the subject: " Finding that the committee, as all the brethren from the earliest period of their history in this country, were inclined to follow the example of the apostles in their first general council at Jerusalem (see Acts 15), in the conduct of our Yearly Meetings, with which we were most cordially agreed, we merely suggested, that by observing as strictly as possible that illustrious example and the principles inculcated by the gospel, such as 1, SIMPLICITY; 2, LIBERTY; 3, ORDER; 4, SUBORDINATION of our reason TO THE WORD OF GOD in its letter and spirit in all matters of difference; 5, A DUE REGARD to the conclusions of former Yearly Meetings; 6, A SINCERE LOVE OF THE BRETHREN consistent with the love of God, and Truth and Righteousness; 7, A CONSTANT AIM FOR UNION in the body of Christ, the church, &c., &c.;—that these items would suffice without any lengthy plan, or many particular rules and regulations, which would only tend to curtail the liberty with which the committee that conducted the meeting, and the church that received the meeting, ought to act.]

YOUTH, DISCIPLINE OF. See above, *Discipline of Children*, page 86.

INDEX.

INDEX.

Kurze und einfältige Vorstellung

der äußern, aber doch heiligen

Rechte und Ordnungen

des

Hauses Gottes,

Wie es der wahre Haus=Vater Jesus Christus befohlen, und in seinem
Testament schriftlich hinterlassen.

Vorgestellt

in einem Gespräch zwischen

Vater und Sohn,

durch

Frag und Antwort,

nebst

Grundforschende Fragen

beantwortet von dem Autor

Alexander Mack

einem Mitberufenen zu dem großen Abendmahl.

Begleitet

mit einer neuen Uebersetzung ins Englische,

kurtzen Lebensbeschreibung des Autors ꝛc. ꝛc.

Columbiana, O.
1860.

A SHORT AND PLAIN VIEW

OF THE OUTWARD, YET SACRED

RIGHTS AND ORDINANCES

OF THE

HOUSE OF GOD,

AS COMMANDED BY THE TRUE STEWARD JESUS CHRIST,

AND LEFT ON RECORD IN HIS LAST WILL AND TESTAMENT.

ARRANGED

IN A CONVERSATION BETWEEN A

FATHER AND SON

IN QUESTIONS AND ANSWERS.

ALSO

GROUND SEARCHING

QUESTIONS

ANSWERED BY THE AUTHOR

ALEXANDER MACK.

A NEW ENGLISH TRANSLATION ACCOMPANIED WITH THE

ORIGINAL GERMAN,

MEMOIR OF THE AUTHOR &c. &.

COLUMBIANA,

1860.

Ankündigung der gegenwärtigen Ausgabe.

Die Schriften von Alexander Mack dem Aeltern, welche zwar nicht viel weniger als 150 Jahre alt sind, wir aber nun in einer neuen Ausgabe verlegen, sind von bleibendem Werth, in so fern die Wahrheit von solchem gediegenen Gehalt ist, der durchs Alter nicht herabgesetzt wird, sondern vielmehr kostbarer wird, als sie bei jedem nachfolgendem Geschlecht ihre Kraft und wohlthätige Wirkungen beweißt. Ueberzeugt, daß die Grundsätze und Gesinnungen, wie sie in gegenwärtigem Werk anerkannt und erklärt, und von den Brüdern überhaupt angenommen und geübt werden, wenn sie allgemein bekannt und herrschend würden, die Welt viel weiser, besser und glücklicher machen könnten, als sie nun ist, scheint es sehr wünschenswerth zu seyn, ihnen die weiteste Oeffentlichkeit zu geben.

Wiederum—da die Presse des Gospel-Visitors ausschließlich gewidmet ist der Publication solcher Werke, und da von Zeit zu Zeit Application gemacht wurde an die Herausgeber für das Werk, das jetzt wieder dem Publikum vorgelegt wird, aber schon seit Jahren nicht mehr zu haben war,— so fingen wir an auf Erstattung des offenbaren Mangels zu denken. Indessen erhoben sich verschiedene schwierige Fragen, die ziemliche Zeit und Ueberlegung erforderten, um zu einem vergnüglichen Schluß zu kommen.

Unser Hauptzweck war, dieses einfache Zeugniß, das unser Bruder für die Wahrheit ablegte, wie sie in Christo ist, so vielen unserer Mitmenschen, sonderlich in diesem Lande erreichbar zu machen, als wir möglicher Weise könnten, sonderlich solchen, die gelegentlich mit unsern Brüdern in Berührung kommen. Indem wir das Buch

ADVERTISEMENT OF THIS Present Edition.

The writings of ALEXANDER MACK, sen. though not much less than a century and a half old, which we here present in a new edition, are of an abiding value, inasmuch truth is of such intrinsic worth, which is not depreciated by age, but is becoming rather more precious as it may prove through every successive generation its efficacy and beneficial tendency. Persuaded that the principles and sentiments, as avowed and explained in the present work, and as adopted and practized by the Brethren generally, should they become known and prevalent, would make the world much wiser, better, and happier, than what it is, it seems very desirable to give them the utmost publicity.

Again—the Press of the Gospel-Visitor being exclusively devoted for publications of that character, and frequent applications having been made to the Editors for copies of the work, which is now presented again to the public, but had been out of print for years,—we began to think of supplying the apparent want. However various difficult questions arose, which required considerable time and reflection in order to come to a satisfactory conclusion.

Our main object was, to bring this simple testimony of our brother to the truth as it is in Jesus, within the reach of as many of our fellowmen, especially in this country, as we possibly could, chiefly those that come in contact occasionally with our brethren, By reprinting the book in only one

wieder druckten nur in einer besondern Sprache, wären alle die von dessen Gebrauch abgeschnitten gewesen, welche diese Sprache nicht lesen und verstehen konnten. Andererseits durch Veröffentlichung des Werks in denen zwei Sprachen, welche vorzüglich in unserer Brüderschaft und in diesem Lande herrschend sind, fühlten wir befriedigt es für Alle oder beinahe so zugänglich zu machen. Aufgemuntert zu diesem Plan durch die Popularität der deutsch-englischen Testamente, und einiger anderer Bücher seit kurzem auf gleichem Plan publicirt, entschieden wir uns endlich, die gegenwärtige Form anzunehmen; und wir hoffen, daß sie auch Beifall finden werde bei allen Freunden des Buchs.

particular language, all those would be cut off from its perusal, who could not read and understand that language. On the other hand by publishing the work in those two languages, chiefly prevailing in our fraternity and in this country, we felt satisfied to make it accessible to all, or nearly so. Encouraged in this plan by the popularity, of the German—English New Testaments, and of some other books published lately on the same plan, we finally decided to adopt the present form, and we hope, that it will find favor with all the friends of the book.

Noch Eines. Als wir dazu kamen, die frühere englische Uebersetzung, gedruckt Philadelphia 1810, also vor fünfzig Jahren etwas näher zu untersuchen, so fanden wir nöthig, um dem Werk Gerechtigkeit widerfahren zu lassen, eine ganze neue Uebersetzung zu machen, welche zuerst so wörtlich als möglich gemacht wurde durch Schreiber dieses, und dann durch seinen englischen Mitarbeiter übersehen und in gutes Englisch übertragen ward, so daß keine Mühe gespart wurde, um unsern Bruder, ob er wohl schon lange todt ist, so verständlich reden zu lassen zu Allen, so viel als möglich.

One thing more, When we came to examine into the former english translation published Philadelphia 1810, consequently fifty years ago, we found in order to do justice to the work that we would have to make an entirely new translation, which was first made as literal as possible by the writer of this, and then revised by his english colaborer to make good English, so that we spared no pains, to make our brother, being dead long ago, speak yet as intelligibly to all as possible.

Nun möge der Herr dieses Werk segnen zu seiner eigenen Verherrlichung, zur Erbauung seiner Gemeinde, und zum Heil Vieler theuren Seelen.

Now may the Lord bless this work to his own glory, to the building up of his church, and the salvation of many souls.

H. K.

Geschrieben im August 1860.

H. K.

Written August, 1860.

MEMOIR
of
ALEXANDER MACK, SEN.

Although there may be some persons found that have thought that Luther and his coadjutors completed the great work of giving to the world a pure form of Christianity, this was by no means the case with all those who lived at the time of the great reformation, or in the times which immediately succeeded that memorable event. The spirit of inquiry had been awakened. The liberty of thought and the liberty of speech had been asserted. And there were those who by their investigations of the oracles of divine Truth, ascertained that, whatever good work the previous reformers had done to redeem the world from error, and to restore to it a purer form of Christianity, still all error had not been detected, nor all truth discovered; and they were resolved to make the Christian tabernacle after the pattern showed them on the mount—not on Mount Sinai, but on Mount Zion, according to the pattern taught and exemplified in the doctrines and lives of Christ and his apostles.

Of this number was the faithful little band of eight persons, a number between which and that which peopled the world after the deluge, a striking coincidence is observable. And one of

Aus dem Leben
von
Alexander Mack, d. ältern.

Obschon es Leute gegeben haben und noch geben mag, die da denken, daß Luther und seine Mitgehülfen das große Werk vollendeten der Welt eine gereinigte Form des Christenthums darzustellen, so war dieses keineswegs der Fall bei allen denen die zur Zeit der großen Reformation, oder zu den Zeiten unmittelbar darnach lebten, welche auf dieses denkwürdige Ereigniß folgten. Der Geist der Forschung war erwacht. Die Freiheit des Gedankens und die Freiheit der Rede war behauptet worden. Und es gab solche, die durch ihre Untersuchungen der Urkunden göttlicher Wahrheit überzeugt wurden, daß was immer Gutes an dem Werk der vorigen Reformatoren war, um eine reinere Form des Christenthums wieder herzustellen, dennoch nicht aller Irrthum entdeckt, noch alle Wahrheit ans Licht gestellt worden sey; und diese waren entschlossen, das christliche Heiligthum zu bauen nach dem Muster, das ihnen gezeigt worden auf dem Berge—nicht auf dem Berge Sinai, sondern auf dem Berg Zion, nach dem Vorbild der Lehre und dem Beispiel Christi und seiner Apostel.

Von dieser Zahl war die treue, kleine Schaar von Acht Seelen, eine Zahl, deren auffallendes Zusammentreffen mit derjenigen, welche die Welt nach der Sündfluth wieder bevölkerte, bemerkenswerth ist.—

those eight persons, and one, too, who was prominent among them, was Alexander Mack sen., the subject of the following memoir.

It is said of Abel, that though he is dead, he yet speaketh. And how does he speak? One way in which he speaks, is by his life recorded upon the imperishable pages of the Bible. And the church of Christ has on her calendar a list of instructive names. Not only are the lives of her divine Founder and his apostles, and her early martyrs replete with instructive lessons, but she has also had in different ages, and in different countries, distinguished members and devoted friends, whose memories are cherished and honored by those who live long after them. And what member of the Christian family does not love to think of those of his brethren who have blessed the world by their example and influence, and to whom as the chosen of the Lord, we feel ourselves indebted for the precious legacy of divine truth which they have contended for, and which they have suffered for, and which they have handed down to us? And though they are dead, they yet speak, and the tongues which give utterance to the wisdom of their experience, their lessons and their admonitions, and the different traits of character by which we may profit, are heard through their biographies.

Such considerations have led the writer of the following Memoir to give a short notice of the life of Alexander Mack, sen., thinking that many of our brethren will be pleased to learn all they possibly can of one who took such an important part in the organization of the Christian community of which they are members. We regret much

Und eine von diesen acht Seelen, und zwar eine hervorragende unter ihnen, war Alexander Mack, der ältere, der Gegenstand folgender Notizen.

Es heißt von Abel, daß wiewohl er gestorben sey, er noch rede; und wie redet er?—Eine Weise, in welcher er redet, ist es, daß sein Leben aufgezeichnet ist auf den unvergänglichen Blättern der Bibel. Und die Kirche Christi hat in ihrem Calender ein Verzeichniß von lehrreichen Namen. Nicht nur sind die Lebensläufe ihres göttlichen Stifters und seiner Apostel, und der ersten Märtyrer voll belehrender Lectionen, sondern die Kirche hat auch in verschiedenen Zeitaltern und unterschiedlichen Ländern ausgezeichnete Mitglieder u. selbstaufopfernde Freunde gehabt, deren Andenken aller Ehren werth gehalten wird von solchen, die lange nach ihnen lebten. Und welches Glied der christlichen Familie liebt nicht an solche seiner Mitbrüder zu denken, welche der Welt durch ihr Exempel und ihren Einfluß zum Segen wurden, und welchen als den Auserwählten des Herrn wir uns Schuldner fühlen für das kostbare Vermächtniß göttlicher Wahrheit, um welches sie gekämpft, und für welches sie gelitten, und welches sie uns hinterlassen haben? Und obschon sie todt sind, so reden sie noch, und die Zungen, welche Ausdruck geben der Weisheit ihrer Erfahrung, ihrer Unterweisungen und Ermahnungen, und die verschiedenen Charackterzüge, von welchen wir Nutzen schöpfen mögen, werden vernommen durch ihre Lebensbeschreibungen.

Dergleichen Betrachtungen haben den Schreiber folgender Denkwürdigkeiten bewogen, eine kurze Beschreibung des Lebens von Alexander Mack, dem ältern zu geben, indem wir denken, daß es vielen von unsern Brüdern angenehm seyn wird alles Mögliche von Einem zu vernehmen, der einen so wichtigen Antheil nahm an der Bildung der christlichen Gesellschaft, von

that we do not possess materials for a more complete Memoir. We went to considerable trouble and expense to obtain materials for the memoir, but we obtained but few. There were no doubt incidents in his life, which it would have been both interesting and profitable to know; but at this distance of time after his death they cannot be collected. We must therefore be satisfied with the very few materials we possess. Br. Abraham Cassel of Montgomery Co. Pa. furnished us with the documents containing the principal facts upon which the memoir is written.

Alexander Mack sen., author of the following work was born in 1679, in Schreisheim, in the Electoral of Palatia, between Manheim and Heidleberg, in Germany. We may, in our want of genealogical knowledge, take some consolation from the sentiment, that whatever regard is due to ancestry in forming an estimation of a person he is to stand or fall mainly by his own personal character, and not by that of his ancestors.

Although we know but little of his ancestors, it appears he descended from a very respectable and wealthy family. He was a Presbyterian, and educated in the Calvinistic faith. Of his literary acquirements we know nothing but what we can gather from his writings; and from these it does not appear that he had a classical education. His occupation was that of a miller, and he possessed a very profitable mill, and a handsome patrimony, and several vineyards at Schreisheim.

welcher sie Mitglieder sind. Wir bedauern sehr, daß wir nicht Materialen besitzen für eine vollständigere Lebensbeschreibung. Wir wandten nicht geringe Mühe und Unkosten an, um Materialien habhaft zu werden; aber wir konnten nur wenige erlangen. Ohne Zweifel ereignete sich in seinem Leben Manches welches, sowohl interessant als auch nützlich seyn würde, wenn wir es wüßten; allein die Entfernung der Zeit, die seit seinem Tod verflossen ist, macht ein Mehreres unerreichbar, und wir müssen uns deswegen mit dem Wenigen begnügen, was wir haben.— Bruder Abraham Cassel von Montgomery County, Pa. versorgte uns mit den Notizen enthaltend die hauptsächlichsten Thatsachen, auf welche das Folgende gegründet ist.

Alexander Mack, der ältere und der Verfasser des folgenden Hauptwerks war geboren in 1679 zu Schrießheim in der Chur-Pfalz, zwischen Mannheim und Heidelberg in Deutschland. Bei unserem Mangel an Nachrichten des Herkommens können wir uns trösten mit dem Gedanken, daß obwohl wir den Vorfahren gehörige Achtung schuldig sind, in der Hauptsache bei der Würdigung eines Mannes ein Jeglicher steht oder fällt nach seinem eigenen persönlichen Character, und nicht nach dem seiner Vorfahren.

Obschon wir nur wenig wissen von seinen Vorfahren, so scheint er doch von einer sehr achtbaren und wohlhabenden Familie abzustammen. Er war der Reformirten Kirche zugethan, und auferzogen im Calvinischen Glauben. Von seiner Schulbildung wissen wir nichts, als was wir aus seinen Schriften zu schließen vermögen, woraus erhellet, daß er zwar keine gelehrte Erziehung genossen. Seine Beschäftigung war die eines Müllers, und er besaß eine sehr einträgliche Mühle, nebst einem schönen väterlichen Erbgut und verschiedene Weingärten in Schrießhem.

In 1700 he was married to Anna Margaretha Klingin, a native of the same place that he was, and about his age. As the fruits of their union, there were born unto them five children, three sons and two daughters. Their names were as follows: John Valentine, John or Johannes, Alexander, Christina, and Anna Maria. The daughters both died young. There is a large number of his descendants still living and in membership with the Christian community which their worthy ancestor did much as an humble instrument in the hands of God to organize and establish. Elder Fox of the Philadelphia church is a descendant of his; elder Jacob Mack of Fayette Co. Pa. is a descendant; the Holsinger family in Bedford Co. Pa. of which there are several worthy ministers, is also a descendant of his; and several of his descendants are members of the Jonathan's creek church in Perry Co. Ohio, as elsewhere.

Becoming dissatisfied with the religious system in which he had been brought up, and being anxious to ascertain the mind of the Lord as revealed in the scriptures, to this source was his attention directed in searching for the old paths. He became convinced by his reading of the scriptures that an immersion in water was the New Testament baptism, and a believer the only proper subject for the ordinance, and that the doctrines and practices defended in the following work are such as believers should receive and obey. Accordingly, he and his wife and six others, in the year 1708, were immersed in the river Aeder, and covenanted together to walk in all the commandments and ordinances of the Lord.

Im 1700 verehlichte er sich mit Anna Margaretha Klingin, gebürtig aus dem nämlichen Ort, und fast gleichen Alters mit ihm. Als Früchte dieser Verbindung wurden ihnen geboren fünf Kinder, drei Söhne und zwei Töchter. Ihre Namen waren wie folgt: John Valentin, Johannes, und Alexander; Christina und Anna Maria. Die Töchter starben beide jung. Es ist noch immer eine große Nachkommenschaft von seinen Söhnen vorhanden, und in Gemeinschaft mit der Brüderschaft, zu deren Bildung und Begründung ihr würdiger Vorfahr so Vieles that als ein demüthiges Werkzeug in der Hand Gottes. Der Aelteste Fox von der Philadelphia-Gemeinde ist ein Nachkomme von ihm; der Aelteste Jacob Mack von Fayette Co. Pa. ist ebenfalls ein Abkömmling; die Holsinger-Familie in Bedford Co. Pa. von welcher verschiedene würdige Lehrer sind, stammt gleicher Weise von ihm ab; und verschiedene seiner Nachkommen sind Glieder der Jonathans Creek Gemeinde, Perry Co. Ohio und sonstwo.

Als das religiöse System, in welchem er aufgebracht worden war, ihm nicht mehr Genüge that, und er darüber bekümmert wurde den Sinn des Herrn zu erforschen, wie er geoffenbaret ist in der Schrift, so wurde seine Aufmerksamkeit auf diese Quelle gelenkt, um sich nach den alten Wegen zu erkundigen. Er wurde überzeugt durch sein Forschen in der Schrift, daß eine Eintauchung in Wasser die neutestamentliche Taufe sey, und daß nur ein Gläubiger einzig tauglich sey, dieselbe zu empfangen; und daß die Lehren und Uebungen, welche in folgendem Werk vertheidigt sind, von der Art seyen, welche Gläubige anzunehmen und zu beobachten sich bestreben sollten. Demgemäß wurde er und sein Weib und sechs Andere im Jahr 1708 in dem Strom Aeder getauft, und verbanden sich miteinander zu wandeln in allen Geboten und Satzungen des Herrn.

Although considerable liberty of conscience was at first granted to persons at Schwartzenau to those who had resorted there, to enjoy the liberty of practicing whatever they thought the Scriptures required, yet this liberty did not continue long. The same spirit which actuated the great red dragon with seven heads and ten horns, that stood ready to devour the man child which the woman clothed with the sun was to bring forth, Rev. 12 : 1—6, manifested itself at Schwartzenau to devour the infant community which the truth had conceived and brought forth But God protected it, although there was much to be endured and sacrificed by the faithful. And Alexander Mack sen. had a large share of persecution to endure. But he was prepared by the grace of God for the emergency. The truth was more precious to him than any thing else, and while he would buy it at any price, he would sell it at no price.

Although he was rich, yet out of love to his brethren he became poor, like his Master before him. The cruel hand of persecution frequently arrested the brethren and shut them up in prison. By paying the money which the laws required as fines, they had a temporary releasement. By paying these fines, his handsome patrimony, fine vineyards, and profitable mill, were all taken from him. He with his brethren sought refuge in different places from persecution, but could find none. A sad state of things, this, and painful to reflect upon. With all the Christian profession of the times, this community, with its non-resistant principles, with its self-denying doctrines,

Obschon anfänglich ziemlich Gewissens-Freiheit den Leuten zu Schwartzenau gewährt worden war, namentlich solchen die sich eben deßwegen dahin gewandt hatten um die Freiheit zu genießen, zu üben alles was nach ihrem Gedenken die Schrift forderte, so währte diese Freiheit doch nicht lange. Derselbe Geist, welcher den großen rothen Drachen antrieb, der sieben Häupter und zehn Hörner hatte, und bereit stand das männliche Kind zu fressen, welchen das Weib gebären sollte, bekleidet mit der Sonne, Offenb. 12, 1—6. offenbarte sich auch in Schwartzenau, um das neugeborne Gemeinlein zu verschlingen, welches die Wahrheit empfangen und hervorgebracht hatte. Allein Gott beschützte es, obschon Vieles von den Gläubigen erduldet und aufgeopfert werden mußte. Namentlich hatte der ältere Alexander Mack einen großen Antheil an der Verfolgung zu erdulden. Die Gnade Gottes hatte ihn aber vorbereitet für jedes Vorkommniß. Die Wahrheit war ihm köstlicher als irgend etwas sonst, und während er sie zu kaufen suchte um irgend einen Preis, wollte er sie zu keinem Preise verkaufen.

Obschon er reich war, wurde er aus Liebe zu seinen Brüdern arm, gleich seinem Meister vor ihm. Die grausame Hand der Verfolgung nahm öfters die Brüder gefangen, und verschloß sie in Gefängniß. Durch Bezahlung von Geld, welches die Obrigkeit als Strafe forderte, konnten sie eine zeitweilige Befreiung erlangen. Durch Bezahlung solcher Strafen wurde ihm nach und nach sein schönes Erbgut, seine Weingärten, seine einträgliche Mühle, alles entrissen. Er suchte Zuflucht mit seinen Brüdern an verschiedenen Orten der Verfolgung zu entgehen, konnte aber keinen finden. Mit allem christlichen Bekenntniß damaliger Zeit konnte diese Gemeinde mit ihren wehrlosen Grundsätzen, mit ihren selbstverleugnenden Lehren, und

and with the sole object in view of glorifying God in bringing forth the fruits of obedience to his commandments, was not tolerated!

When requisition for blood is made, woe to the persecutor. "Whoso shall offend one of these little ones which believe in me, it were better for him that a mill-stone were hanged about his neck, and that he were drowned in the depth of the sea." "Saul, Saul, why persecutest thou me?"

But he had domestic afflictions to endure, as well as those arising from persecution. In 1720, twenty years after they were united in the bands of matrimony, and twelve years after they were united to Christ by a living faith and gospel obedience, his companion was taken from him by death. She is said to have been a meek Christian and virtuous wife. She found in death, what she and her husband had sought in vain for on earth, a calm retreat from the storm of persecution. Within one week of the death of his wife, his oldest daughter then about six years old, also died. It is said the child was uncommonly fond of its mother. And out of regard perhaps to the fondness which existed between the mother and child, as well as out of regard to the circumstances of persecution under which the father and child were placed, the Lord, in his wisdom and goodness may have taken the little daughter to the quiet home of the mother where it could enjoy her fond caresses, rather than leave it where it must endure the hardships and troubles of persecution in common with its father. Thus in about one week, in addition to the troubles consequent upon the great persecution which was then raging, he had to bear the loss of a kind and Christian wife, and a dear little daughter.

mit ihrer einzigen Abſicht, Gott zu verherrlichen durch Hervorbringung der Früchte des Gehorſams gegen ſeine Gebote, keine Duldung finden! Wenn einmal der groſße Tag der Rechenſchaft kommt, wehe dem Verfolger! "Wer der Kleinen einen ärgert, die an mich glauben, dem wäre es beſſer, daß ihm ein Mühlſtein an den Hals gehänget würde, und er in das Meer geworfen würde." "Saul, Saul, was verfolgeſt du mich?"

Allein er hatte auch häusliche Trübſal zu erleiden ſowohl als ſolche von Verfolgung. In 1720, zwanzig Jahre nach ihrer Verehlichung, und zwölf Jahre nachdem ſie ſich Chriſto verlobt hatten in einem lebendigen Glauben und evangeliſchen Gehorſam, wurde ſeine Gefährtin von ihm genommen durch den Tod. Es wird von ihr geſagt, daß ſie eine ſanftmüthige Jüngerin und tugendſame Gattin war. Sie fand im Tode, was ſie und ihr Mann vergeblich auf Erden geſucht hatten, einen ſtillen Ruheort vor dem Sturm der Verfolgung. Innerhalb einer Woche vom Tode ſeines Weibes, ſtarb auch ſein älteſtes Töchterlein, damals ungefähr 6 Jahre alt. Man ſagt das Kind habe ſeine Mutter ungemein zärtlich geliebt, und vielleicht geſchah es um der Neigung willen die zwiſchen Mutter und Kind Platz hatte, ſowohl als aus Rückſicht auf den Stand der Verfolgung, unter welchem Vater u. Kind ſich befanden, daß der Herr es in ſeiner Weisheit u. Güte in die ruhige Heimath der Mutter verſetzte, wo ſie ihre zärtliche Liebkoſungen genießen konnte, ſtatt es da zu laſſen, wo es die Mühſeligkeiten und Bedrängniſſe der Verfolgung in Gemeinſchaft mit ihrem Vater leiden mußte. So hatte unſer Bruder in einer Woche, zuſätzlich zu den Leiden, die die große Verfolgung verurſachte, welche damals wüthete, den Verluſt eines liebenden, chriſtlichen Weibes, und einer lieben kleinen Tochter zu ertragen.

After seeking unsuccessfully for a retreat from persecution in his native country, he with his three sons, and a number of his brethren, emigrated to America in 1729, and settled as a poor man—poor in this world's goods, but rich in faith, on a small lot of ground near Germantown in the vicinity of Philadelphia. Here he found rest from persecution, and assisted Peter Baker in ministering in the word to the church at Germantown.

He, however, did not live long to enjoy the quietude of a home under the mild government of Pennsylvania. In 1735, six years after he came to America, he closed his labors on earth. He was buried in the Brethren's public burying ground in Germantown, and the following brief inscription in the German language, marks the place: "Here rest the remains of A. M. born 1679, and died 1735, aged 56 years."

His christian character appears to have been that of a primitive follower of Christ. Humility, zeal, self denial, and charity were conspicuous among the graces that adorned his character. The high estimation in which he was held by his brethren, is seen in the circumstance that he was chosen by them to be their minister. He was the first minister in the little Christian community organized at Schwartzenau in 1708, and labored zealously and successfully to enlarge the borders of their Zion. Of his private character as a christian father we may infer favorably from the circumstance that all his sons became pious and were united to the church before they had completed their seventeenth year. And what seems somewhat remarkable, they all made a pub-

Nachdem er erfolglos einen Bergungs-Ort in seinem Vaterlande gesucht hatte, wanderte er mit seinen drei Söhnen, und einer Zahl von seinen Brüdern nach Amerika aus in 1729, und siedelte sich als ein armer Mann an—arm an Gütern dieser Welt, aber reich am Glauben, auf einem kleinen Grundstück unweit Germantown in der Nachbarschaft von Philadelphia. Hier fand er Ruhe von der Verfolgung, und stand dem Bruder Peter Becker im Dienst des Wortes bei an der Gemeinde zu Germantown.

Er lebte indessen nicht lange, um die Ruhe zu genießen einer Heimath unter der milden Regierung Penns. In 1735, sechs Jahre nach seiner Ankunft in Amerika, beschloß er sein Werk auf Erden. Er wurde begraben in der Brüder Begräbniß Platz in Germantown, und die folgende kurze Inschrift in deutscher Sprache bezeichnet sein Grab:

"Hier ruhen die Gebeine A. M. (der Name ist nicht völlig gegeben,) geboren 1679, gestorben 1735, seines Alters 56 Jahre."

Sein christlicher Character scheint der eines ursprünglichen Nachfolgers Christi gewesen zu seyn. Demuth, Eifer, Selbstverleugnung und Liebe waren die hervorragenden Züge, die seinen Wandel zierten. Die hohe Achtung, in welcher er bei seinen Brüdern stand, ist aus dem Umstand ersichtlich, daß er ihr erster erwählter Lehrer war, und in diesem Ansehen als der erste unter seinen spätern Mitarbeitern blieb, und auch bei Gegnern mit gebührender Achtung behandelt wurde. Von 1708 an arbeitete er eifrig, unermüdet und erfolgreich an der Erweiterung der Gränzen unseres Zions. Von seinem Privat Character als christlicher Vater dürfen wir günstige Schlüße machen aus dem Umstand, daß alle seine Söhne sich frühzeitig bekehrten zu einem gottseligen Leben, und einer nach dem andern sich der Gemeinde an

lic confession of religion in the seventeenth year of their age.

His writings show that he was well acquainted with the Scriptures, and very anxious to adhere to the form of doctrine contained therein.

Such are the brief Memoirs we have collected of Alexander Mack, sen. And while we venerate his character, may we honor the system of faith and practice which he and his coadjutors have handed down to us.

J. Q.

August, 1860.

schloß, ehe jeder sein siebenzehntes Jahr vollendete, (welches etwas sonderliches zu seyn scheint, daß sie alle in dem siebenzehnten Jahr ihres Alters ein öffentliches Bekenntniß der Religion ablegten, wozu sie kein herkömmlicher Gebrauch noch auch irgend eine ungebührliche Autorität nöthigte.)

Seine Schriften beweisen, daß er wohl vertraut war mit der Schrift, und daß es ihm sehr darum zu thun war, bei der darin enthaltenen Form der Lehre unverrückt zu bleiben.

Dieß sind die wenigen Nachrichten die wir gesammlet haben von Alexander Mack, dem ältern, und während wir seinen Character hochachten, mögen wir das System des Glaubens und der Uebung in Ehren halten, das er und seine Mitgehülfen uns hinterlassen haben.

J. Q.

CONTENTS.

Inhalt,

# Erste Vorrede.	# First Preface.

Geliebter Leser,

Weilen Gott ein allmächtiger, allgewaltiger, ja auch allen Ungehorsamen jederzeit ein sehr schröcklicher Gott gewesen ist, der den Ungehorsam der ersten Menschen im Paradies, und nachmals den Ungehorsam seines eigenen Volkes unter dem Gesetz hart gestraft hat, so daß wann jemand das Gesetz Mosis gebrochen, der mußte ohne Barmherzigkeit auf zweier oder dreier Zeugen Munde, sterben. Ja es hatte Gott seinem Volk durch seinen Knecht Mosen im 5ten Buch Capitel 4 sagen lassen: Und nun höre Israel die Gebote und Rechte die ich euch lehre, daß ihr sie thun sollet, auf daß ihr lebet und hinein kommt, und das Land einnehmet, das euch der Herr eurer Väter Gott giebt; ihr sollt nichts zu thun, das ich euch gebiete, und sollt auch nichts davon thun, auf daß ihr bewahren möget die Gebote des Herrn eures Gottes, die ich euch gebiete."

Hier siehet man, wie Gott so eifrig befohlen, dasjenige zu halten, was er durch seinen Knecht Mosen an sein Volk hat reden lassen. So kann man vielleicht glauben: Daß Gott vielmehr alle dasjenige ganz gewiß wird gehalten haben wollen, was er in der letzten Zeit durch seinen Kn-

Dear Reader:

Inasmuch as God has at all times been an omnipotent, yea, and to all the disobedient a most dreadful God, who punished the disobedience of the first human beings in Paradise, and afterward the disobedience of his own people under the law with such severity, that when any man had broken the law of Moses, he had to die without mercy on the testimony of two or three witnesses;—yea, God has said to his people through his servant Moses, Deut. 4: 1, 2, "Now therefore hearken, O Israel, unto the statutes and unto the judgments which I teach you, for to do them, that ye may live, and go in and possess the land which the Lord God of your fathers giveth you. Ye shall not add unto the word which I command you, neither shall you diminish aught from it, that ye may keep the commandments of the Lord your God which I command you."

Hence we see how strictly God commanded his people to observe the laws which he had made known by his servant Moses. So we may very readily believe, that God will be still more strict to have observed all that he has in these latter times revealed to all the world by

ben Sohn der ganzen Welt hat kund und offenbar machen laſſen, nemlich: Alle die ſich Chriſten nennen, ſollen als Kinder in einem Hauſe wandeln, und denen hat der gute Hausvater Riegel und Geſetze gegeben, die ſie wohl und weißlich halten und in acht nehmen ſollen, und hat ihnen dabei ein ewiges Leben verheißen, wann ſie ihm in allem werden gehorſam ſeyn, ſowohl im Kleinen als im Großen, wiewohl in der Lehr und Ordnung des Herrn Jeſu gar nichts als Klein darf angeſehen werden, weilen es gar ein großer und allgewaltiger Monarch und König befohlen und geordnet hat.

Und darum wegen der Größe des Geſetzes, muß auch die Waſſertauf, welche von Jeſu in ſeinem Namen zu thun befohlen worden, nebſt allen ſeinen andern Geboten, groß angeſehen werden. Wie nun der Gebieter im neuen Bunde groß iſt, ſo auch ſeine Geſetze, Rechte und Verheiſſungen, welche er dazu gethan hat, ſehr groß, nemlich: Ein ewiges Leben, ſammt allen andern Gnaden-Gaben des Heiligen Geiſtes, welche die Glaubigen beſitzen.

Alſo wird auch ohnfehlbar die Strafe an den Ungehorſamen, welche gegen das Evangelium Jeſu Chriſti gehandelt haben, groß und ſehr erſchröcklich ſeyn. Dann Paulus ſpricht an die Theſſalonier im 2. Brief im 1. Cap. daß der Sohn Gottes kommen werde mit Feuerflammen, Rache zu üben an denen die ſeinem Evangelio ungehorſam geweſen ſind. Ja es wird in der Offenbarung Johannes Cap. 22, V. 18. 19. gezeuget: So jemand davon thut von den Worten dieſes Buchs der Weiſſagung, (womit ſonderlich die Lehre Jeſu verfaſſet iſt,) von dem werde Gott abthun ſein Theil vom Buche des Lebens. Und wer dazuthun würde, zu dem würde Gott thun die Plagen, die in dieſem Buche geſchrieben ſind.

his beloved Son, that all who profess to be Christians, may live together as children of one family. And to them the good Father of the house has given rules and laws, which they are to observe well and wisely; and has promised them at the same time eternal life, if they will obey him in all things, in small matters as well as in great, though nothing at all should be deemed as small in the doctrine and ordinances of the Lord Jesus, because such a great and all-powerful Sovereign and King has commanded and ordained them.

And hence, on account of the greatness of the Sovereign, water baptism, which has been commanded by Jesus to be performed in his name, together with all his other commandments, are to be considered great. And as his laws and statutes are also great, so likewise, are the promises which he has given, great, namely, life everlasting, with all the gracious gifts of the Holy Spirit, which believers possess. So also will the punishment of the disobedient, who have opposed the gospel of Jesus Christ, certainly be great, and very dreadful. For Paul says to the Thessalonians, 2 Ep. 1: 7, 8. that "the Lord Jesus shall be revealed from heaven with his mighty angels in flaming fire, taking vengeance on them that know not God, and that obey not the gospel of our Lord Jesus Christ. And, it is declared in the Revelation of John 22: 18, 19, "If any man shall add unto these things, God shall add unto him the plagues that are written in this book. And if any man shall take away from the words of the book of this prophecy, (by which the doctrine of Jesus is especially included) God shall take away his part out of the book of life &c."

Also haben wir aus Liebe dem geneigten Leser wollen vor die Augen stellen: Den wahren und rechtmäßigen Gebrauch derer Dingen, welche Christus den Seinigen in seine Haushaltung zu thun befohlen hat. Wie auch ein wenig den großen Mißbrauch welcher unter dem ganzen Christenhaufen eingerissen, abbilden wollen. Und wollen es dann einem jeden zu seiner Prüfung überlassen. Und dieses wird in einem Gespräch zwischen einem Vater und Sohn in Frag und Antwort vorgestellet werden, welche als Reise-Gefährten mit einander wandeln.

We have, therefore, felt moved by love, to present to the consideration of the kind reader, the true and lawful use of those things, which Christ has commanded his (disciples) to do in his house, and also to show him a little of the great abuse, which has been introduced among the whole multitude of christian professors, leaving it to the judgment of every one to decide for himself. We shall give our work the form of a dialogue between a father and son, who are supposed to be traveling together as companions on a journey.

Vorrede oder Einleitung.

Geneigter lieber Leser, wer du auch bist, dem dieses Büchlein in die Hand kommt:

Gleichwie es vieles beitragen kann den rechten Sinn eines Tractätleins nützlich zu faßen, wann man mit unpartheyischem Gemüthe in redlicher Liebe zu der Wahrheit, die darinnen vorkommende Zeugniße beherziget, und mit Anrufung der göttlichen Barmherzigkeit neben die Zeugniße der Apostel und Propheten hält, und also mit demüthigem Geiste prüfet; also ist es auf der andern Seite sehr schädlich, wann man mit Vorurtheil eingenommen, sich durch ein unzeitiges richterliches Wesen unvorsichtiger Weise dahin reißen läßet; als wodurch sich der rechte Adel eines christlichen Prüf-Geistes gleichsam zuschließet, und mit der edlen Weisheit in ihre Kammer gehet, da dann nichts als Dunkelheit und Verwirrung aus dem Grunde menschlicher Eigenheit offenbar wird; und verursachet eine wesentliche Nacht, so daß, wer darinnen wandelt, der stößet sich, ja Christus selbst und das Zeugniß seiner ewigen Wahrheit wird dem Menschen zum Stein des Anstoßens und zum Fels der Aergerniß.

Wer nun etwan solcher Art wäre, daß er durch ein disputiersüchtiges Wesen, an diesen einfältigen und doch wohlgegründeten Wahrheiten sich wollte suchen groß zu machen, der sey in christlicher Liebe gewar-

PREFACE OR Introduction.

Kind and dear reader, whoever thou art, into whose hand this little book may come:

Just as it may contribute much to apprehend usefully the true sense of a treatise, when a person is considering the testimonies contained therein with an impartial mind and with a sincere love for the truth, to compare them prayerfully (invoking divine mercy) with the testimonies of the apostles and prophets that he may examine them in an humble spirit;—so it is on the other hand very hurtful, when one prepossessed with prejudice, permits himself to be carried away inconsiderately by a prematurely judging spirit; as by so doing the truly noble spirit of investigation is in a manner locked up, and real wisdom remains hid, and then nothing but darkness and confusion are revealed from the fountain of human selfishness, and these cause such a state of moral night, that he who walketh in it, stumbleth, and Christ himself and the testimony of his everlasting truth become to such a man a stone of stumbling and a rock of offence.

Now, if there should be any one, who prompted by a passion for disputation and a spirit of contradiction against those simple, yet wellfounded truths (which are here presented) would seek

net, und es sey ihme hiermit auf das
freundlichste zu Gemüth geführet, daß er
doch aus Mitleiden zu sich selbst solche
Mühe spare, und solche Arbeit nicht vor-
nehme, damit er nicht einen Streit anfan-
ge, den er doch nicht vermag auszuführen,
denn ob ihm auch kein Mensch auf Erden widersprechen thäte, so würde einem
solchen sein eigen Gewissen zu einem stren-
gen Richter werden; dann die Wahrheit
ist stark genug, in eines jeden Menschen
Gewissen sich hinlänglich zu verantworten.
Wer aber in der That ein unpartheyischer
geneigter Leser ist, oder seyn will, dem können nachfolgende Zeilen dienen an statt
eines freundlichen Vorberichts.

Es hat dem guten Gott gnädiglich wohlgefallen, gleich bei dem Eingang in dieses
gegenwärtige Seculum oder Jahrhundert,
seine allen Menschen erschienene heilsame
Gnade durch manche Buß- und Erweck-
ungs-Stimme zu unterstützen, und hat dadurch viele Menschen aus dem Tod und
Schlaf der Sünden aufgewecket, welche sich
nach einem rechtschaffenen Wesen in Christo umgesehen, da sie dann sogleich mit be-
trübten Augen den großen Verfall fast an
allen Orten sehen mußten; dahero ihnen
auch manch redliches Zeugniß der Wahrheit ausgepresset wurde, und entstunden
hin und wieder privat Versammlungen neben dem gemeinen Kirchen-Wesen, worinnen die neuerweckten Seelen ihre Erbauung sucheten, bis der geistliche Priesterneid
die Herzen der Obrigkeiten erbitterte, und
hin und wieder Verfolgungen entstanden:
Nemlich in der Schweiz, in dem Würtem-
bergerland, in der Churpfalz, in dem Hessenland, und mehr andern Orten.

Diesen verfolgten Exulanten zeigte nun
der Herr einen Zufluchts-Ort, oder ein
kleines l. Pella in dem Wittgensteinerland,
allwo dazumal ein geliebter Graf und etliche erweckte Gräfinnen wohneten, da wur-

to make himself great, we would in
christian love advise him to have a proper regard to his eternal welfare, and to
desist from his present course, and not
to undertake such labor, lest he might
enter into a contest, which he would
not be able to carry out. For though
no man on earth should contradict him,
his own conscience would become to
him a severe judge, for truth is powerful enough in every man's conscience to
defend itself successfully. But he, who
is, or who will be, indeed, an impartial,
candid reader, may find the following
sketch of the revival of evangelical
truth to serve instead of a more for-
mal introduction.

It pleased the good God in his mercy, early in the beginning of this (last)
century, to support his "grace, that
bringeth salvation, and which hath appeared to all men," by many a voice
calling them to awake and repent, so
that thereby many were aroused from
the sleep and death of sin. These
then began to look around them for the
truth and righteousness, as they are in
Jesus, but had soon to see with sorrowful eyes the great decay (of true christianity) almost in every place. From
this lamentable state of things they
were pressed to deliver many a faithful
testimony of truth, and here and there
private meetings were established beside the public church-organization, in
which newly awakened souls sought
their edification. Upon this, the hearts
of the rulers were embittered by an en-
vious priesthood, and persecutions were
commenced in various places, as in
Switzerland, Wurtemberg, the Palatinate, Hesse and other places.

"To those persecuted and exiled persons the Lord pointed out a place of
refuge, or a little "*Pella*" in the land
of WITGENSTEIN, where at that time
ruled a mild count, and where some

be Gewissens-Freiheit gegeben zu Schwarzenau, ohngefehr eine Stunde von Berlenburg, dahero, ob wohl das Witgensteiner-land ein armes und rauhes Land ist, so kamen döch viele und mancherley Menschen in Schwarzenau zusammen, und wurde gar bald der sonst wenig geachtete Ort in eine ganz andere Gestalt verändert, so daß es in wenig Jahren ein weit und breit berufener Ort wurde.

Die aber aus der Verfolgung daselbst zusammen kamen, ob sie wohl durch mancherley Meinungen unterschieden, und auch in Sitten und Gebräuchen unterschiedlich waren, so wurden sie doch zuerst alle Pietisten genannt, sie selbst nenneten sich aber untereinander Brüder. Doch zeigte sich gar bald, daß die Worte Christi Matth. 18. wo er spricht: Sündiget aber dein Bruder, so strafe ihn zwischen dir und ihm allein, und so ferner, nicht zu einem recht christlichen Gebrauch kommen konnten, weil keine geschlossene christliche Gemeine da war; dahero auch einige wieder zurück in die Religionen, wovon sie ausgegangen waren, giengen, weilen sie sich nämlich zu einer näheren christlichen Zucht nicht verstehen konnten, und die allzugroße Freigeisterey schiene manchem noch gefährlicher zu seyn, als die Religionen so sie verlassen hatten.

Da funden sich einige kräftig angezogen, die Spuren der ersten Christen wieder aufzusuchen, und sehneten sich herzlich, die befohlene Zeugniße Jesu Christi nach ihrem rechten Werth im Glauben zu ergreifen; so wurde ihnen dann zu gleicher Zeit mit Nachdruck inwendig aufgeschlossen, wie nothwendig der Gehorsam des Glaubens ist einer Seelen, die da selig werden will, und solcher Aufschluß brachte sie auch zugleich an das Geheimniß der Wasser-Taufe, welche ihnen vorstunde als eine Thüre in die Gemeinde, nach welcher sie sich sehne-

pious countesses dwelt. Here liberty of conscience was granted at SCHWARTZENAU, which is within a few miles of Berlenburg. And from this cause, though Witgenstein is a poor and rough country, many people, and those of various kinds collected at Schwartzenau, and this place, which had been but little esteemed, became so much changed, that in a few years it became a place extensively known.

Those who were brought together there from the persecution, though they were distinguished by different opinions, and also differed in manners and customs, were still, at first, all called Pietists, and they among themselves called each other Brother. But very soon it appeared, that the words of Christ, Matt. 18, where he says: "If thy brother shall trespass against thee, go and tell him his fault between thee and him alone, &c." could not be reduced to a proper christian practice, because there was no regular order yet established in the church. Therefore some returned again to the religious denominations, from which they had come out, because they would not be subjected to a more strict christian discipline; and to others it appeared, that the spiritual liberty was carried too far, which was thought to be more dangerous, than the religious organizations they had left.

Under these circumstances some felt themselves drawn powerfully to seek the footsteps of the primitive christians, and desired earnestly to receive in faith the ordained testimonies of Jesus Christ according to their true value. At the same time, they were internally and strongly impressed, with the necessity of the obedience of faith to a soul that desires to be saved. And this impression also led them at the time to the mystery of water-baptism, which appeared unto them as a door into the church,

ten. Von der Taufe aber wurde unter den Pietisten sehr unterschiedlich geredet, welches zwar manchesmal den wahrheitlieben-den Seelen wehe that.

Bis in dem Jahr 1708 sich 8 Personen miteinander verbunden, einen Bund eines guten Gewissens mit Gott aufzurichten, und alle Befehle Jesu Christi als ein sanf-tes Joch aufzunehmen, und also dem Herrn Jesu, ihrem guten und getreuen Hir-ten, in Lieb und Leid als treue Schäflein nachzufolgen, bis zu einem seligen Ende.

Diese 8 Personen waren wie folget: nemlich 5 Brüder und 3 Schwestern: Die fünf Brüder waren G e o r g G r e b i, von Hessen-Cassel, der erste; L u c a s W e t t e r, gleichfalls aus dem Hessenland, der 2te; der dritte war A l e x a n d e r M a c k, aus der Pfalz von Schrießheim zwischen Manheim und Heidelberg; der 4te war A n d r e a s B o n e y, von Basel aus der Schweiz; der 5te, J o h a n n e s K i p p i n g, von Bareit aus dem Wür-tembergerland; die 3 Schwestern waren J o h a n n a N ö t h i g e r i n, oder B o-n i s i n, die Erste; A n n a M a r g a-r e t h a M a c k i n, die Andere; und J o-h a n n a K i p p i n g e n, die Dritte: Diese 8 Personen verbunden sich miteinan-der als Brüder und Schwestern in den Kreutzes-Bund Jesu Christi zu einer christ-gläubigen Gemeinde.

Und als sie in bewährten Historien fun-den, daß die ersten Christen in dem ersten und zweiten Jahrhundert, sich nach dem Befehl Christi, durch ein dreimaliges Ein-tauchen in das Wasser-Bad, der heiligen Taufe, haben pflanzen lassen in den Kreu-tzes-Tod Jesu Christi; so forscheten sie fleißig in dem neuen Testament, und fun-den alles vollkommen damit eintreffende, dahero bekamen sie ein sehnliches Verlan-gen, durch dieses von Christo selbst geübte und befohlene Mittel, nach seinem so hell-

which was what they so earnestly sought. Baptism, however, was spoken of among the Pietists in very different ways, and the manner in which it was sometimes spoken of, caused pain to the hearts of those that loved the truth.

Finally, in the year 1708, eight per-sons consented together, to enter into a covenant of a good conscience with God, to take up all the commandments of Jesus Christ as an easy yoke, and thus to follow the Lord Jesus, their good and faithful shepherd, in joy and sorrow, as his true sheep, even unto a blessed end. These eight persons were as follows: namely, five brethren and three sisters. The five brethren were GEORGE GREBI from Hesse Cassel, the first; LUCAS VETTER, likewise from Hessia, the second; the third was ALEX-ANDER MACK from the Palatinate of Schriesheim between Manheim and Heidelberg; the fourth was ANDREW BONY of Basle in Switzerland; the fifth JOHN KIPPING from Bareit in Wurtem-berg. The three sisters were, JOHAN-NA NOETHIGER or BONY the first; AN-NA MARGARETHA MACK, the second; and JOHANNA KIPPING the third.

These eight persons covenanted and united together as brethren and sisters into the covenant of the cross of Jesus Christ to form a church of christian be-lievers. And when they had found in authentic histories, that the primi-tive Christians in the first and second centuries, uniformly, according to the command of Christ, were planted into the death of Jesus Christ by a threefold immersion into the water-bath of holy baptism, they examined diligently the New Testament, and finding all perfect-ly harmonizing therewith, they were anxiously desirous to use the means ap-pointed and practiced by Christ him-self, and thus according to his own

samen gegebenen Rath, zur Erfüllung aller Gerechtigkeit ge fördert zu werden.

Da war dann nun die Frage, wer dieses Werk äußerlich an ihnen bedienen sollte? Einer unter ihnen, der in Versammlungen das Wort führete, hatte unterschiedliche Versammlungen der Tauf-Gesinnten in Deutschland hin und wieder in herzlicher Liebe besucht; von welchen die meisten zugaben, daß das Eintauchen in das Wasser zwar recht sey, wann man es aus Liebe zu Christo in der heiligen Taufe gebrauchen wolle; wollten aber darneben auch gern beweisen, daß das Begießen mit einer Handvoll Wassers auch gut genug seyn könnte; wann es nur sonst in allem recht dabei zugienge.

Allein solches wollte ihrem Gewissen kein Genüge thun. Dahero begehrten sie von dem, der das Wort führete, nach dem Exempel der ersten und besten Christen auf ihren Glauben eingetaucht zu seyn. Weilen er aber sich selbst als einen Ungetauften ansahe, so begehrete er zuerst von ihnen getauft zu werden, ehe er einen andern taufen sollte, dahero wurden sie Raths, sich mit Fasten und Beten zu vereinigen, um ein gutes Auskommen, in dieser Sache von Christo, dem Stifter seiner heiligen Ordnungen, selbst zu erlangen: Dann er wollte von der Gemeinde Christi getauft seyn, und die andern hatten auch ein solches Verlangen in sich.

In diesem Unvermögen nun wurden sie gestärket durch die Worte Christi, welcher so treulich gesprochen hat: Wo zwei oder drei in meinem Namen versammlet sind, da bin ich mitten unter ihnen. In solchem Vertrauen auf Gottes theure und gewisse Verheissung, wofeten sie bei Fasten und Beten, welcher von den vier Brüdern den Bruder taufen sollte, der so sehnlich begehrete von der Gemeine Christi getauft zu seyn. Sie gaben aber untereinander ihr

salutary counsel, g
fulfillment of all righ

Now the question
administer the wor
them? One of thei
a leader, and speake
their meetings, had
love, different con
tist (Tauf gesinnten)
of which admitted, t
when performed by
water and out of love
deed right; but the
sides this, maintain t
handfull of water mi
well, provided all else

The conscience ho
brethren) could not
this. They theref
him, who led in pre
to immerse them acc
ample of the primitiv
tians, upon their fai
sidering himself as u
first to be baptized of
before he should ba
they concluded to un
prayer, in order to
himself, the founder
nances, a direction ar
matter. For he who
baptize the other, w
tized by the church
rest had the same de

In this their diff
encouraged by the
who has said so faith
or three are gathered
am I in the midst
such confidence in
sure promise of God,
ing and prayer cast
four brethren should
er, who so anxiously
tized by the church

Wort von sich, daß es niemand verrathen sollte, welcher der erste Täufer unter ihnen gewesen, damit niemand Ursache nehmen möchte, sie irgend nach einem Menschen zu nennen, weilen sie solche Thorheit schon von Paulo an den Corinthern bestrafet funden.

Als sie nun dazu bereitet waren, so giengen sie des Morgens in der Einsamkeit selb achte hinaus an das Wasser genannt die Aeder, und der Bruder, auf den das Loos gefallen war, taufte zuerst den Bruder, der von der Gemeine Christi wollte getauft seyn, und als er getauft war, taufete er den, der ihn getauft hatte, und die übrigen 3 Brüder und 3 Schwestern; und so wurden sie alle 8 getauft in der frühen Morgen-Stunde.

Nachdem sie aber alle aus dem Wasser herauf gestiegen waren, und sich wieder angekleidet hatten, so wurden sie auch zugleich inwendig mit großer Freudigkeit angezogen, und wurde ihnen durch die Gnade wesentlich eingedruckt dies nachdenkliche Wort: Seyd fruchtbar und mehret euch! Dieses ist geschehen, in dem oben gemeldeten Jahr 1708. Von dem Monat aber des Jahrs, oder von dem Tag des Monats oder der Woche, haben sie uns keine Nachricht hinterlassen.

Nach diesem wurden die obengemeldete 8 Personen in dem einmal angetretenen Gehorsam des Glaubens mehr und mehr kräftiglich gestärket, auch öffentlich in den Versammlungen von der Wahrheit zu zeugen, wozu ihnen der Herr seine Gnade sonderlich mittheilete, daß ihrer mehr dem Glauben unterthänig wurden; also daß in 7 Jahrenzeit, nemlich bis in das Jahr 1715, nicht allein in Schwarzenau eine große Gemeinde wurde, sondern auch hin und wieder in der Pfalz funden sich Liebhaber der Wahrheit, und sonderlich zu Marienborn sammlete sich auch eine Gemeinde, dann als sich in der Pfalz eine Ge-

mutually pledged their word, that no one should ever divulge, who among them had baptized first (according to the lot,) in order to cut off all occasion of calling them after any man, because they had found, that such foolishness had already been reproved by Paul in his writing to the Corinthians.

Being thus prepared, the Eight went out together one morning, in solitude, to a stream called the *Aeder*, and the brother, upon whom the lot had fallen, baptized first, that brother, who desired to be baptized by the church of Christ, and when he was baptized, he baptized him, by whom he had been baptized, and the remaining three brethren and three sisters. Thus these Eight were all baptized at an early hour of the morning.

And after all had come up out of the water, and had changed their garments, they were also at the same time made to rejoice with great inward joyfulness, and by grace they were deeply impressed with these significant words, "Be ye fruitful and multiply!" This occurred in the year above mentioned, 1708. But of the month of the year, or the day of the month or week, they have left no record.

After this, said eight persons were more and more powerfully strengthened in their obedience to the faith they had adopted, and were enabled to testify publicly in their meetings, to the truth; and the Lord granted them his special grace so that still more became obedient to the faith, and thus, within seven years time, namely, to the year 1715, there was not only in Schwarzenau a large church, but here and there in the Palatinate there were lovers of the truth, and especially was this the case in MARIENBORN where a church was gathered; for the church in the Palati-

meinde sammlen wollte, so wurden sie ver=
folgt, und kamen nach Marienborn, und
als die Gemeinde daselbst groß wurde,
wurden sie da auch verfolgt, und sammle=
ten sich zu Creyfeld unter dem König von
Preußen, da fanden sie Freiheit.

Es hat aber der Herr in denen sieben
Jahren hin und wieder unterschiedliche
Mitarbeiter erwecket, und in seine Erndte
ausgestoßen, unter welchen waren Jo=
hann Henrich Kalklöser, von
Frankenthal; Christian Libe und
Abraham Duboy, von Ebstein;
Johannes Naas und mehr andere
von Norten, Peter Becker von Dils=
heim. Und zu diesen geselleten sich auch
Johann Henrich Traut und seine Brüder,
Henrich Holzapfel und Stephan Koch, die
meisten von diesen kamen in diesen 7 Jah=
ren noch Creyfeld; Johann Henrich Kalk=
löser aber und Abraham Duboy kamen
nach Schwarzenau, dahin kam auch Georg
Balser Ganß von Umstatt, und Michael
Eckerlin von Straßburg.

Wie sie aber auf der einen Seite Gna=
de hatten bei Gott und den Menschen, so
funden sich auch Feinde der Wahrheit,
und entstunden hin und wieder Verfolgun=
gen um des Wortes willen, da dann zwar
einige den Raub ihrer Güter mit Freuden
erduldet, andere aber mußten auch Bande
und Gefängniße erdulden; einige zwar ha=
ben nur einige Wochen, andere aber auch
unterschiedliche Jahre in den Gefängnißen
zugebracht. Christian Libe hat etliche
Jahre auf der Gallee angeschlossen unter
den Uebelthätern müssen am Ruder ziehen;
doch sind sie alle durch Gottes sonderbare
Fügung mit gutem Gewissen wieder loß
worden.

Weilen sie nun durch die Verfolgungen,
Armuth, Trübsal und Gefängniße, womit
sie gedrücket wurden, nur desto freudiger
wurden, so machten sich einige gelehrte
Männer an sie, und suchten sie mit schar=

nate was persecuted and its members
then came to Marienborn. And when
the church here became large, it was
also persecuted. Then those that were
persecuted, collected in Creyfeld, where
they found liberty, under the King of
Prussia.

Moreover, the Lord called during
those seven years, several laborers, and
sent them into his harvest, among whom
were JOHN HENRY KALKLESER, of
Frankenthal; CHRISTIAN LIBE and
ABRAHAM DUBOY from Ebstein; JOHN
NASZ and several others from Norten;
PETER BECKER from Dillsheim. And
to these were added also JOHN HENRY
TROUT and his brothers, HEINRICH
HOLSAPPLE and STEPHEN KOCH. The
most of these came during those seven
years to Creyfeld; JOHN H. KALK-
LESER, however, and ABRAHAM DUBOY
came to Schwartzenau; so did also
GEORGE B. GANSZ from Umstatt;
and MICHAEL ECKERLIN from Stras-
burg.

But as they found favor with God
and men on the one hand, so (on the
other hand) there were also enemies
of the truth, and there arose here and
there persecutions for the word's sake.
There were those who suffered joyfully
the spoiling of their goods, and others en-
countered bonds and imprisonment some
for a few weeks only, but others had to
spend several years in prisons. Christian Libe was some years fastened to a
galley, and had to work the galling oar
among malefactors; yet, by God's
special providence, they were all delivered again with a good conscience.

Since the persecutions in the form of
poverty, tribulation, and imprisonment,
by which they were oppressed, made
them only the more joyful, they were
tried in another manner by men of

fen Disputationen und spitzfindigen Fragen irre zu machen, wovon die 40 Grundfor-schende Fragen die diesem Tractätlein bei-gefüget sind, mit ihrer Antwort, den Leser sattsam berichten können.

Um diese Zeit nun, wurde es von der Gemeinde des Herrn in Schwarzenau vor gut angesehen, dieses Büchlein herauszu-geben, zum Unterricht vor die einfältigen Gemüther, in welchem ein jeder unpar-theyischer Leser, wann er es ohne Vorurtheil sammt diesem Vorbericht lieset, selbst fin-den kann, was sie dazumals veranlaßet solches Büchlein dem Druck zu übergeben.

Da aber nunmehr diejenigen, welche da-mals in dem Werk des Herrn so freudig ge-standen, und in großer Einfalt und Red-lichkeit die Wahrheit bekannt haben, alle im Frieden entschlafen sind; so ist ein Ver-langen entstanden in den Gemeinden, so hier in America solches Zeugniß tragen, und in der Wahrheit zu wandeln sich gleich-falls dem Herrn ergeben haben, dieses ein-fältige Zeugniß wiederum zum Druck zu befördern, vor erst zwar sonderlich vor die liebe Jugend, damit sie einen einfältigen und gewissen Grund haben mögen von der Wahrheit, in welcher sie unterrichtet sind; vornemlich aber zur Ehre Gottes, der seine Wahrheit so wunderbarlich geschützet bis in diese allerletzte Zeit.

Demselbigen guten Gott, der allein wei-se ist, sey dann auch dieses einfältige Zeug-niß seiner Wahrheit nochmals zu seinen Gnaden-Füßen geleget, und in seinen mächtigen Schutz anempfohlen. Dem ge-neigten Leser aber wünschet man eine Gottgefällige, wahrheitsliebende Gemüths-gestalt, in welcher allein der recht göttliche und nutz- und heilbringende Prüfgeist her-für tritt, und die Schäflein Christi in alle Wahrheit zu leiten geflissen ist. Wohl dem Menschen, der ihm nicht widerstehet;

learning, seeking to confound them with sharp disputations, and subtile questions, of which the forty searching Questions of Eberhard Ludwig Gruber, which with their answers will be an-nexed to this treatise, will sufficiently inform the reader.

About this time it was deemed ex-pedient by the church of the Lord in Schwartzenau, to issue this publication, for the instruction of those pure mind-ed persons who are seeking after truth: And in this work every impartial read-er, if he will read it with these intro-ductory remarks, and without prejudice, can find, what has been the cause and object of publishing it.

But in as much as those, which then stood in the work of the Lord so cheer-fully, and confessed the truth with great simplicity and honesty, have now all departed in peace, the desire has arisen in those churches, who bear the same testimony here in America, and who have likewise given themselves to the Lord to walk in the truth, to have this simple testimony again published, more especially for the benefit of our dear youth, that they may have a plain and simple exposition of the truth, in which they are instructed, and chiefly for the glory of God, who has so won-derfully preserved his truth even to these latter times.

This simple testimony of truth we commend to the good and wise God for protection, and as an offering, we lay it at his feet of mercy. And may he give to the kind reader such a state of mind that will cause him to love the truth, and be acceptable to him, for it is only when we are in such a state that the truly divine Spirit, who will ena-ble us to prove all things, and hold fast that which is good and useful, will come forth and lead us as the lambs of

den wird er erinnern alles deſſen, was Jeſus die ewige Wahrheit, ſelbſt geredet und gelehret hat.

Nun demſelbigen unſchuldigen Lamme Gottes, welches die Sünden der Welt wegnimmt, ſey Ehre, Lob und Anbetung in der Gemeinde der Erſtgebornen in dem Himmel und auf Erden, in der Gemeinſchaft des Vaters und des H. Geiſtes, Amen.

N. B. Dieſer einfältige Bericht iſt zum Theil aus etlichen Papieren, welche von 2 Brüdern, nemlich Alexander Mack, und Peter Becker hinterlaſſen worden, ausgezogen, welche nun ſchon eine geraume Zeit in dem Herrn entſchlafen ſind; zum Theil iſt auch hier und dar etwas eingerückt von dem was mir meine Aeltern mündlich erzählet haben, nebſt etlichen anderen Brüdern, die nun auch in dem Herrn entſchlafen ſind, und ſelbſt Augenzeugen mitgeweſen, von dem was ſie uns zum Troſt und Ermunterung bezeuget haben. Solches bezeuget, der dieſes geſchrieben, den 30ſten Januar 1774, als ein Mitberufener zu der Hochzeit des Lammes, und zu dem, zu ſolcher herrlichen Hochzeit zubereiteten großen

Abend-Mahl.

Christ into all truth
man, who does not o]
will bring all things t
whatsoever Jesus,
himself has said and
Now to that innoc
which taketh away tl
be glory, honor, and
congregation of the
and on earth, in t
the Father and the I

N. B. This simj
in part from some]
left by two brethren,
Mack and Peter Bec
ready some considera
asleep in the Lord;
things were inserted
ted to me orally by 1
as by some other br
also fallen asleep in {
were themselves ey
which they have tes
consolation and en
he witnesseth who l
30th. January 1774
the marriage of the
great supper prepare
marriage.

Ein Gespräch

zwischen

Vater und Sohn,

in Frag und Antwort.

Sohn. Lieber Vater, weil wir hier in diese Wüste so alleine sind, so will ich dir doch erzählen, wie mirs, als ich nicht bei dir war, in einer Gesellschaft ergangen ist: Ich wurde angegriffen wegen der Tauf, und wurde ein Wiedertäufer geheissen, weilen wir diejenigen taufen, welche schon in ihrer Kindheit getauft sind. Ja ich wurde auch sehr hart angegriffen von denen, welche zwar in ihren erwachsenen Jahren getauft, doch nur besprenget sind, und wir sie doch auch taufen, wann sie in unsere Gemeinde wollen. Ferner auch vom Abendmahl halten, und vom Bann, und daß wir so gesetzlich wären im Fußwaschen, auch wegen des süßen Brods im Brodbrechen. Ich wurde durch allerley vernünftige Reden so angefochten, daß ich nicht genugsam Grund geben konnte. Darum bitte ich dich, lieber Vater, daß du mich doch in allen diesen Dingen, welche jetzund im Streit liegen, und man am meisten darüber angefochten wird, nach dem Zeugniß der H. Schrift und auch der ersten Christen, willst besser unterrichten, damit ich in meinem Glauben möchte gestärket werden, und auch andern Menschen einen rechten schriftmäßigen Grund geben könn=

A Conversation

BETWEEN A

FATHER AND SON,

IN QUESTIONS AND ANSWERS.

Son. Dear father, as we are quite alone here in this wilderness, I will relate to thee, how I was treated by a certain company, when I was away from thee. I was attacked on account of baptism, and was called an Anabaptist, because we baptize such as have already been baptized in their infancy. I was also very severely attacked by those, who in their riper years baptized, only by sprinkling (or pouring), and whom we baptize afterwards by immersion when they desire to become members of our church; also, concerning our manner of keeping the Lord's Supper and of excommunicating persons, our strict observance of feet-washing, and our using unleavened bread at our communion. By divers specious reasonings, I was so disturbed, that I was not able to give sufficient answers. Therefore, I entreat thee, dear father, to give me still better instructions in all those matters, which are yet controverted, and on account of which we are assailed, so that with the testimony of the holy Scriptures, and of the primitive Christians, I might be established in my faith, and be enabled to give others a true scriptural account, for

te; ich will mich gegen dich dankbar dafür mein ganzes Lebenlang erzeigen.

Vater. Liebes Kind, ich will dir hievon ganz einfältig genugsam Unterricht geben, darum höre fleißig zu, und frage mich wegen denen Dingen, die du nicht beantworten konntest, so wollen wir eine einfältige Unterredung halten.

Sohn. Lieber Vater, ich freue mich daß du geneigt bist mich zu unterweisen, ich will nun fleißig fragen und hören: Sage mir doch, wo die äußerliche Wasser-Taufe gegründet sey in heiliger Schrift?

Vater. Der ewige und allmächtige Gott ist der eigentliche Stifter der Wasser-Taufe. Er hat schon zu Noah Zeiten angefangen, im Vorbild der Wasser-Taufe im Neuen Bund zu offenbaren: Dann als die Menschen so gottlos wurden, so ließ Gott der Herr eine Sündflut kommen, daß alle gottlose Menschen im Wasser ersaufen mußten. Davon spricht nun der Apostel Petrus: 1 Pet. 3, 20. 21. Welches nun auch uns selig machet in der Taufe die durch jenes Wasser bedeutet ist, nicht das Abthun des Unflaths am Fleisch, sondern der Bund eines guten Gewissens mit Gott, durch die Auferstehung Jesu Christi.

Ja merket ferner, als Gott der Herr durch seinen Knecht Mosen ein Fürbild machen wollte, zum Zeugniß dessen was durch den Sohn sollte geoffenbaret werden. Hebr. 3. So mußte Moses von der Tochter Pharao aus dem Wasser gezogen werden, darum sprach sie auch: Er soll Moses heißen, dann ich habe ihn aus dem Wasser gezogen 2 Mose 2. Ja als Gott eben durch diesen Mosen den Saamen Abraham durch eine mächtige Hand aus Egypten führete, und sie den Egyptern entrinnen thäten; so geschahe das Entrinnen durch das Meer, welches ein kräftiges Fürbild auf die Taufe im neuen Bund war. Wie es auch Paulus eine Taufe nennet:

which favor, I shall try to prove grateful unto thee all my life.

FATHER. Dear son, I am willing to give thee as plain and satisfactory instruction as I can; therefore, hear me diligently, and ask me about those things which thou couldst not answer, and thus will we hold a plain conversation.

SON. Beloved father, I rejoice that thou art willing to instruct me. I will therefore diligently ask and hear. Tell me then, where outward water-baptism is founded in the holy Scripture?

FATHER. The eternal and almighty God is the proper author of water-baptism. Already in the days of Noah, he began to reveal a figure or type of water-baptism in the New Covenant; for when men became very wicked, the Lord God sent a flood of water, in which all ungodly men were drowned. Of this the apostle Peter speaks 1 Pet. 3 : 20, 21. The like figure whereunto, even baptism, doth also now save us, (not the putting away of the filth of the flesh, but the answer of a good conscience toward God,) by the resurrection of Jesus Christ."

Observe further, when the Lord God by his servant Moses intended to give a figure in testimony of what afterwards should be revealed by his Son, Heb. 3, Moses therefore had to be drawn out of the water by the daughter of Pharaoh. "Therefore said she, he shall be called Moses, because I drew him out of the water." Exod. 2 : 10.

Again, when God by this same Moses led Abraham's seed out of Egypt, and when by a mighty hand they were delivered from the Egyptians, their escape was through the Red Sea, which prefigured strongly the baptism of the New Covenant. Hence Paul calls it,

Unter Mosen mit der Wolken, und mit dem Meer. 1 Cor. 10, 2.

Ja als Gott der Herr eine Stifts=Hütte durch Mosen ließ aufrichten, welche ein Fürbild war auf das Haus oder Gemeinde des Herrn Jesu; so mußte Moses nach dem Befehl des Herrn vor der Hütten einen großen Becken oder Kessel machen, darinnen der Priester Aaron und seine Söhne sich vorher waschen mußten, ehe sie in die Hütte des Stifts gehen durften. 2 Mos. 30, 18. 19. 20. C. 40, 12. Dieses ist auch ein kräftiges Fürbild gewesen auf die Wasser=Taufe, welche Jesus befohlen: Daß keiner in des Herrn Gemeine kommen noch darinnen dienen kann, er muß dann auch vorhero auf seinen Glauben an Jesum, im Wasser getaufet werden.

Ja ferner kannst du sehen, was Gott der Herr im Gesetz geboten hat: Wann ein Aussätziger war rein geworden, so mußte er seinen Leib im Wasser waschen. 3 Mos. 14, 8. 9. Ja wann die Weiber sich reinigen wollten, so mußten sie sich im Wasser baden, oder waschen. Ferner sind mancherley Wasser=Tauffen im Gesetz geboten gewesen, welche alle auf die Wasser=Taufe im Neuen Testament gezielet.

Nun will ich dich auch berichten, wie es mit der Wasser=Tauf im neuen Bund beschaffen ist: Merke es wohl. Als Gott der Vater seinen lieben Sohn in der Welt offenbaren wollte, so mußte ein Vorläufer vorher gehen, nemlich Johannes, der kam auf göttlichen Befehl in das Jüdische Land und predigte: Die Menschen sollten Buße thun, und taufte auch die Menschen im Wasser zur Buße, daß sie an den glauben sollten, welcher nach ihm kommen würde, das ist: An Jesum den Sohn Gottes. Er taufte zu Enon nahe bei Salem, weil viel Wasser daselbst war.

a baptism "unto Moses in the cloud and in the sea." 1 Cor. 10 : 2.

Again, when the Lord God caused Moses to erect a tabernacle, it was a figure of the house or church of the Lord Jesus. Thus had Moses to make according to the command of the Lord, a large laver or vessel before the tabernacle wherein Aaron the priest and his sons, had to wash themselves, before they were permitted to enter into the tabernacle. Exod. 30 : 18—20. ch. 40 : 12. This was also a powerful figure of water-baptism which Jesus commanded, since none can enter or serve in the church of the Lord without previously being baptized in water upon the confession of their faith in Him.

Again, thou mayest see what the Lord God commanded in the Law: namely, this: if a leper had been cleansed of his leprosy, he had to wash himself in water. Lev. 14 : 8, 9. Likewise the women, in order to fulfill the law concerning their purification, had to bathe or wash themselves in water.

Further, there were many washings commanded in the law, all of which pointed to water-baptism in the New Testament.

Now I will also inform thee, how it is with the water baptism in the New Covenant; and mark it well. When God, the Father, was about manifesting his beloved Son in the world, a forerunner had to precede him, namely John, who came by a divine command into the land of Judea, and preached to the people, that they should repent. He also baptized them in the water unto repentance, directing them to believe in Him who should come after him; that is, in Jesus the Son of God. "He baptized at Aenon near to Salim, because there was much water there."

Sohn. Ey, gab es dann nicht einen großen Aufstand unter dem Volk, weilen der Johannes so ein ungewöhnlich Werk that, daß er die Leute im Wasser taufte?

Vater. Es war zu selbiger Zeit die Wasser-Taufe kein so sehr fremdes Werk unter den Juden, dann es war schon vorhin gebräuchlich im Gesetz, zur äußerlichen Reinigung, darum gab es in Ansehung der Taufe kein großes Wunder, aber in Ansehsehung seiner Predigt war ihnen diese Taufe was neues, weilen er die Menschen zur Buße gewiesen, und von dem Sohn Gottes geredet, daß er kommen würde, und daß die Menschen an ihn glauben sollten.

Sohn. Ließen sich dann die Schriftgelehrten und die Großen der Welt auch taufen?

Vater. O nein! Es war ihnen ein allzuverächtlich Werk, sie verachteten den Rath Gottes wider sich selbst, und ließen sich nicht taufen, wie du es lesen kannst beim Luc. 7, 30. Aber Jesus der Sohn Gottes war seinem Vater hierinnen gehorsam, weilen er wußte: daß die Taufe Johannes vom Himmel war; darum gieng er auch einen ziemlichen weiten Weg aus Galilea zu dem Johannes an den Jordan, und ließ sich taufen. Matt. 3, 13.

Sohn. Das war doch ein großes Wunder und eine große Demuth von dem Herrn Jesu, daß er sich von seinem Knecht Johannes im Wasser hat taufen lassen.

Vater. Ja wohl! war es ein großes Wunder, und eine große Demüthigung von dem Sohn Gottes. Welches er uns und allen seinen Nachfolgern hinterlassen, als ein kräftiges Vorbild, das ...

Son. Did not this occasion a great commotion among the people, since John did such an extraordinary work as to baptize people in water?

Father. Water baptism at that time was not such a strange work among the Jews, for it had previously been used under the Law for external purification. Hence, there was no great surprise concerning baptism. But in connection with his preaching this baptism, there was something new, because men were directed to repent; and they were likewise told of the Son of God that he would come, and that they should believe in him.

Son. Did then the scribes, and the great ones of the world, suffer themselves to be baptized too?

Father. Oh no! to them it was a thing entirely too contemptible. "They rejected the counsel of God, against themselves, and were not baptized," as thou mayest read in Luke 7: 30. But Jesus the Son of God was herein obedient to his Father, because he knew that the baptism of John was from heaven. He therefore came a considerable distance from Galilee to Jordan, unto John, in order that he might be baptized of him. Matt. 3: 13.

Son. This was a wonderful thing, and a great humiliation of the Lord Jesus, to permit himself to be baptized in water by his servant John.

Father. Indeed, it was truly wonderful, and a great condescension of the Son of God, which he has left as a strong example for us, and all his fol-

gar wohl, darinn er auch zu dem Jor-
... es ...: Es gebühret uns alle
... zu erfüllen. Weilen nun der
... Gottes seiner ganzen Gemeinde auch
... Wasser-Bad, stiften und ordnen wollte,
; es ein kräftiges Siegel und äußerliches
... sollte, allen denen, die an ihn
...uben würden, so hat der Sohn Gottes
... den Willen seines Vaters erfüllet,
... die Taufe Johannes von Gott be-
...len hat, und hat zugleich einen Anfang
Wasser-Taufe gemacht, die nicht mehr
Buße seyn sollte, sondern eine solche
...ufe, die Denen gehöret, die schon Buße
...gan, und an Jesum den Sohn Gottes
...uben, und auf diesen ihren Glauben
...o bekenntniß sie getauft werden sollten,
dem Namen des Vaters, des Sohnes,
...d des heiligen Geistes. Dann als der
...er Jesus getaufet war, und aus dem
...asser herauf stieg, so wurde eine Stim-
...e von Himmel gehöret, die sprach:
es ist mein lieber Sohn, an dem ich
...ohlgefallen habe. Und der heil. Geist
...r als eine Taube auf den Herrn Jesum.
...st also dieser Anfang der Wasser-
...ufe des Neuen Testaments gar einen ge-
...altigen Erster und Einsetzer hat, nem-
...: Gott den Vater, Gott den Sohn,
...d Gott der Heiligen Geist. In welchen
...y allerhöchsten Namen der Herr Jesus
...ch die Taufe zu thun befohlen hat.

Sohn. Als nun der Herr Jesus ge-
...aufet war, hat er denn auch sogleich die
...assertauf gelehret und getrieben?

Vater. Ja, der Herr Jesus fieng
...ch sogleich an Lehr-Jünger zu machen,
...d zu taufen. Wie du solches lesen
...nst im Joh. 3, 26. 4, 1. "Es kamen
... Jünger zu Johannes und sagten:
...eister, der bei dir war jenseit des Jor-
...ns, von dem du zeugetest, siehe, der tau-
..., und es kommt jedermann zu ihm. Jo-
...nnes sagte: Er muß wachsen, und ich
...uß abnehmen. Der von oben kommt, ist
...er alle, und er zeuget was er gehöret

---

er, that he said to John, "For this it
becometh us to fulfil all righteousness."
As it was the design of the Son of God,
to ordain and institute a water-bath for
his whole church, that it should be an
efficacious seal and outward sign to all
those who should believe in him,—he
in the first place fulfilled his Father's
will because the baptism of John was
commanded of God. He at the same
time made a beginning of that water-
baptism, which should not be any more
unto repentance, but such a baptism,
which belongs to those, who have already repented, and believed in Jesus,
the Son of God, and are to be baptized
upon this their faith and confession, in
the name of the Father, and of the
Son, and of the holy Ghost. For when
the Lord Jesus was baptized, and arose
up out of the water, a voice from heaven
was heard, which said, "This is my beloved Son, in whom I am well pleased."
And the holy Ghost, like a dove alight-
ed upon the Lord Jesus." Thus, then,
this beginning of the water baptism of
the New Testament has a most powerful author and ordainer, namely, God,
the Father, God the Son and God the
holy Ghost. In which three most exalted names, Jesus commanded baptism
to be administered.

SON. When Jesus was baptized, did
he immediately after also teach and administer baptism?

FATHER. Yes, he immediately began to make disciples and to baptize, as
thou mayest read John 3: 26; 4: 1.
"The disciples of John came to him,
and said, Rabbi, He that was with thee
beyond Jordan, to whom thou barest
witness, behold, the same baptizeth,
and all men come to him. John answered and said, He must increase, but
I must decrease. He that cometh from
heaven, is above all, and what he has

und gesehen hat, und sein Zeugniß nimmt niemand an, wer es aber annimmt, der versiegelt daß Gott wahrhaftig sey." Ja es zeuget auch Johannes in seinem ersten Brief 5, 6. daß der Sohn Gottes kommen sey mit Wasser und Blut, und mit dem Heiligen Geist, und dieses wären die drey Zeugen auf Erden.

Sohn. Findet man denn auch, daß Christus nach seiner Auferstehung, die Wasser-Taufe befohlen habe?

Vater. Ja, dieses will ich dir zeigen; Erstlich als der Herr Jesus seine Jünger wollte aussenden in alle Welt, sein Evangelium zu predigen, so gab er ihnen diesen ausdrücklichen Befehl: Sie sollten lehren, und taufen in seinem Namen, alle die an ihn glauben werden. Matth. 28, 19. 20. Und lehret sie halten alles, was ich euch befohlen habe. Wie du auch dieses ferner sehen kannst, in der Apostel Geschicht, im 2 Cap. V. 37. 38. "Als das Volk fragte was sie thun sollten; antwortete Petrus: Thut Buße, und lasse sich ein jeglicher taufen auf den Namen Jesu, zur Vergebung der Sünden, so werdet ihr empfahen die Gabe des heiligen Geistes."

Sohn. Liesset man auch noch mehr von andern daß sie getauft haben?

Vater. In der Apostel Geschicht C. 8, V. 5–12. stehet: "Daß Philippus zu Samaria von Christo geprediget, und die da glaubten, ließen sich taufen, beyde Männer und Weiber."

Sohn. Ey Vater, weilen hier stehet: Es ließen sich taufen Männer und Weiber, haben sich denn keine Kinder taufen lassen?

Vater. O nein! Davon liesset man im neuen Testament kein einziges Exempel, sondern die Apostel tauften nur solche: Die durch wahre Buße öffentlich den Glauben an Jesum haben bekennet, weil Jesus ihr Meister es ihnen nicht anders befohlen,

seen and heard he testifieth; and no man receiveth his testimony. But he that hath received his testimony, hath set to his seal, that God is true." In confirmation of this, John says in his first epistle, 5 : 6. "that the Son of God came with water and blood, and with the holy Ghost; and that these were the "three that bear witness on earth."

SON. Do we find also, that Christ after his resurrection commanded water-baptism?

FATHER. Yes, this will I shew thee. In the first place, when the Lord Jesus was about sending his disciples into all the world, to preach his gospel, he gave them this express charge: "That they should teach and baptize in his name all such who should believe in him." Matt. 28 : 19, 20. "Teaching them to observe all things whatsoever I have commanded you." See also in the Acts of the Apostles, 2 : 37, 38. When the people asked Peter, what they should do, he answered, "Repent, and be baptized every one of you, in the name of Jesus Christ, for the remission of sins, and ye shall receive the gift of the holy Ghost."

SON. Do we also read of others, who administered baptism?

FATHER. Yes, we find Acts 8 : 5—12, that "Philip preached Christ to the people of Samaria, and those who believed were baptized, both men and women."

SON. But, father, since it says here, that both men and women were baptized,—were then no children baptized?

FATHER. Oh no, in the New Testament we do not find a single instance of the kind, for the apostles baptized only such as upon true repentance, publicly confessed faith in Jesus, because he, their Master,, did not command any

als solche zu taufen, die vor und nach der Tauf können gelehret werden.

Sohn. Ey hat denn Christus auch nicht befohlen die Kinder zu taufen, und haben die Apostel solches nicht gethan?

Vater. Christus hat nur befohlen die Gläubigen zu taufen, und gar nicht die Kinder.

Sohn. Ey stehet dann nicht geschrieben Matth. 19. Da Christus spricht: "Lasset die Kindlein zu mir kommen, und wehret ihnen nicht, denn solcher ist das Reich Gottes?"

Vater. Merke wohl, es stehet dabey: "Jesus legte die Hände auf sie, und segnete sie." Aber von der Taufe stehet nicht geschrieben.

Sohn. Ich habe auch hören sagen: Daß die Apostel ganze Häuser getauft hätten, darunter wären ja auch Kinder gewesen.

Vater. Nur die Vernunft saget solches, daß Kinder darunter gewesen sind. Die Heil. Schrift spricht hiervon gar nichts mit keinem einzigen Wort.

Sohn. Weil nun die Wasser-Taufe ein so großes Gebot ist, wie du mir gezeiget aus dem alten und neuen Testament. Wann denn nun ein Kind stirbt, ehe daß es getaufet wird, leidet es nicht Schaden an seiner Seligkeit, wann es ohne Taufe stirbet, weilen doch viele sagen: Die Tauf sey eingesetzt anstatt der Beschneidung, und wann ein Knäblein am 8ten Tag nicht beschnitten wurde, so mußte es ausgerottet werden?

Vater. Es ist mir lieb daß du mich dieses fragest. Aber merke wohl den Sinn und die Meynung Gottes. Jederzeit, wann Gott was geboten, so hat er es wollen gehalten haben, so wie er es geboten. Die Beschneidung nun im alten Testament, wurde nur den Knäblein geboten, am 8ten Tag. Wann nun ein Kind vor der Zeit wäre gestorben, so hätte es ja das Gebot

others to be baptized than those who are capable of being taught both before and after baptism.

Son. Why, did not Christ then command to baptize children, and did not the apostles do it?

Father. Christ only commanded to baptize believers, and not children at all.

Son. But is it not written in Matt. 19, where Christ said, "Suffer little children, and forbid them not to come unto me, for of such is the kingdom of heaven?"

Father. Note well, what is added; —"Jesus laid his hands on them, and blessed them." But of their baptism, there is nothing written

Son. I have also heard it asserted, that the apostles baptized whole families, among whom there must have been also children?

Father. Only reason says that there were children in those families; but the holy Scripture says not one single word about it.

Son. Since then water-baptism is such a great command, as thou hast shown me from the Old and New Testament, supposing a child should die before it is baptized, will such not suffer loss in their salvation, because they die without baptism, as there are many who say, that baptism was instituted in the place of circumcision; and when a male child was not circumcised on the eighth day, it was to be cut off from God's people?

Father. I am pleased with this thy question. Only mark well the design and mind of God. Whenever God commanded something, he would have it observed just as he commanded. Circumcision in the Old Testament was only required of male children, on the eighth day. Suppose a child died before that day, the law of God would not

Gottes nicht übertreten, wie ohn allen Zweifel viele vor dem 8ten Tag werden gestorben seyn, dieselbige sind nicht verworfen worden, wie auch die Mägdelein, die waren gar nicht beschnitten, und haben doch mit zum Segen gehöret. Also wann ein Kind stirbt ohne die Wasser-Taufe, so schadet es ihm gar nichts, weilen ihm dieselbe nicht befohlen ist, und das Kind den 8ten Tag noch nicht erlebet hat. Das ist: Den Tag worinnen es hätte können Buße thun, und glauben an den Herrn Jesum, und auf diesen seinen Glauben hätte können getauft werden. Worauf der 8te Tag in der Beschneidung gezielet hat. Und darum ist die Taufe nur vor die Erwachsenen und Gläubigen befohlen, und gar nicht vor die Kinder. Und die Kinder sind in Gnaden um des Verdienstes Jesu Christi willen; und werden aus Gnaden selig. Und bey solchen wichtigen Glaubens-Sachen müssen ausgedrückte Befehle seyn.

Sohn. Findet man denn nicht in Historien, daß die ersten Christen ihre Kinder getauft haben?

Vater. Man findet in Gottfried Arnold's Abbildung der ersten Christen: daß die Kinder-Tauf erst angefangen hat, in dem Ausgang des zweiten hunderten Jahrs nach Christi Geburt. Und anfänglich thäten sie es in der Freiheit, wer da wollte, und dann wurde nur auf die Ostern getauft, endlich hat ein Pabst einen Befehl daraus gemacht, daß man kein Kind ohne Tauf sollte sterben lassen, und das ist durch langwierige Gewohnheit so eingerissen, daß jetzund fast jederman meint, die Kindertauf sey von Christo befohlen.

Sohn. Du hast mir schon vieles von der Wasser-Tauf gesagt, und von deren Wichtigkeit. Nun dünkt mich zu fragen, ob denn in dem Wasser was besonders sey, weil Gott im alten Testament schon so viele Reinigungen im Wasser befohlen, und auch im neuen Testament wiederum seinen

have been transgressed, as undoubtedly many died before the eighth day. They were not rejected (for the want of circumcision), nor the female children, who were not circumcised at all, and had still a part in the blessing. Thus when a child dies without water-baptism, it will suffer no harm, because the command did not apply to it, and the child had not yet reached that eighth day; that is, that day, wherein it might have repented, and believed in the Lord Jesus, and been baptized upon its own faith, unto which the eighth day of circumcision had pointed. Baptism is commanded only to believers and adults, and not at all to children. But children are in a state of grace, and will be saved by grace through the merits of Jesus Christ. In matters of faith and of such importance, we must look to the express and positive commands.

Son. Do we not find in histories, that the primitive Christians did baptize their children?

Father. We find in Godfrey Arnold's Portraiture of primitive Christians, that infant baptism began to be practiced in the end of the second century after the birth of Christ. In the beginning it was done at the request of those who wished it, and at any time; afterward baptism was only performed at Easter; finally a certain pope made it a law, that no child should be suffered to die without baptism, and thus by a long continued custom it has become so established, that a great many now believe infant-baptism to be commanded by Christ himself.

Son. Thou hast told me already a great deal about water-baptism and its importance; now I would ask, whether there is any particular virtue in water, since God already in the Old Testament commanded so many purifications in water, and also in the New Testament

Gläubigen ein Wasserbad verordnet und ge=
stiftet hat?

Vater. Merke wohl: Das Wasser ist ein Element von Gott geschaffen, und alle Dinge werden durchs Wasser gezeuget, ja die ganze Erde bestehet im Wasser, und ist darauf gegründet, und der Mensch selbst wird in Mutterleibe im Wasser geboren, ja der Geist Gottes hat anfänglich auf dem Wasser gewohnet, und darum ist in dem Wasser eine göttliche Barmherzigkeit: Und Christus hat auch noch durch seine Taufe das Wasser geheiliget. Darum er auch gesprochen: Joh. 3. Daß man müßte aus dem Wasser und Geist wiedergeboren werden, wann man in das Reich Gottes eingehen wolle, anders sey es ohnmöglich. Dannoch aber sehen die Gläubigen gar nicht auf die Kraft des Wassers in der Tauf, sondern sie sehen auf die Kraft des Worts, welches es also befohlen hat. Weilen nun Christus seiner Gemeinde ein Wasserbad geordnet hat, und dieselbige durch das Wasserbad im Wort reinigen will, wie Paulus spricht Ephes. 5, 26. So glauben denn die Gläubige: daß der Gehorsam gegen das Gebot der Wasser= Tauf dieselbe reiniget, und sie befreyet von den zukünftigen Strafen, wenn nur der Mensch nach dieser Schwemme sich nicht wieder in den Koth wälzet, durch sündigen und übertreten gegen das Wort, denn Gott siehet nur auf den Gehorsam, und sind die Gläubigen verpflichtet dem Wort zu folgen, und dann erlangen sie in dem Gehorsam ein ewiges Leben.

Sohn. Wann nun ein Mensch in allem sich verläugnen thäte, sein Gut den Armen gäbe, viel betete und fastete, er wollte aber nicht getauft seyn, weil es ein äußerliches Werk ist, könnte ein solcher Mensch Gott nicht gefallen?

Vater. Merke wohl: Wann ein Mensch dieses thäte aus wahrem Glauben und Liebe zu Gott, so wären es gute und heilsame Dinge, und solcher Mensch

---

again ordained and instituted a water bath for his believers?

FATHER. Observe well, Water is an element created by God, and all things are generated by water. Yea the whole earth subsists in water, and is founded thereon. Man himself in the womb is formed in water. The Spirit of God in the beginning moved on the water, and hence in the water is represented divine mercy. Christ, also, by his baptism has sanctified the water. Hence he said, John 3: 5 "Except a man be born of water and of the Spirit, he cannot enter the kingdom of God;" otherwise it would be impossible. Nevertheless, believers do not consider the power of baptism to be in the water, but, in the word, in which baptism is commanded. Now since Christ has ordained for his church a water-bath, and will "purify it by the washing of the water by the word," as Paul says Ephes. 5: 26, the faithful believe, that the obedience to the command of water-baptism purifies and delivers them from future punishment, provided they, after this ablution, do not wallow again in the mire by transgressing and sinning against the word. For God looks only upon the obedient; and believers are bound to obey the word, and in obedience they obtain life everlasting.

SON. Suppose a man would deny himself in all things, would give his goods to the poor, would pray and fast a great deal, but would not be baptized; because it is an outward work, would such a man not please God?

FATHER. Mark well! If a man were to do these things from true faith and love to God, then they would be good and useful; and such a man could cer-

könnte auch ganz gewiß diesem Gebot der Wasser-Taufe sich willig unterwerfen, denn das ist eben die wahre Liebe zu Gott, daß man seine Gebote hält, und seine Gebote sind nicht schwer. 1 Joh. 5, 4. Ferner spricht Paulus: 1 Cor. 13. daß wenn man "seinen Leib brennen ließe, und alle sein Gut den Armen gäbe, und hätte die Liebe nicht, so wäre es nichts," und dann beschreibet er der Liebe Art, daß sie alles glaubet was Gott geboten hat. Ja Christus spricht: Joh. 14, 23. 24. "Wer mich liebet, der wird meine Gebote halten, wer aber mich nicht liebet, der hält meine Gebote nicht." Darum kann ein Mensch wohl in eigner Heiligkeit viel thun, und sich dennoch nicht in der Liebe an Jesum als das Oberhaupt halten, gleichwie es zu Pauli Zeiten solche Menschen gegeben hat. Wie er schreibet in dem Brief an die Col. 2, 18. die in Geistlichkeit der Engel einher gehen. Paulus nennet es aber einen fleischlichen Sinn. V. 19. Weil sie sich nicht an dem Haupt gehalten haben.

Sohn. Kann dann ein Mensch Gott nicht lieben, wenn er gleich in Einem nicht wollte gehorsam seyn, und sonst in den andern allen?

Vater. Kannst du denn noch nicht merken was Jacobus spricht: Cap. 2, 10. "So jemand das ganze Gesetz hält, und sündiget an einem, der ist's ganz schuldig." Dann bedenke nur bei dir selbsten: Wenn du mir 10 Jahr und noch mehr, wärest in allem gehorsam gewesen, und ich thäte dich jetzund nur heißen einen Strohhalm aufheben, du wolltest dieses aber nicht thun, und thätest es auch nicht, so müßte ich dich ja vor ein ungehorsames Kind halten, und wenn du tausendmal sprechen thätest: Vater ich will alles thun, ich will fleißig arbeiten; wo du mich hinsendest, will ich hingehen, aber den Strohhalm aufzuheben dünket mich sey nicht nöthig, es nützet ja dir und mir nichts. So thäte ich zu dir sprechen: Du bist ein ungehorsamer Bösewicht.

tainly not refuse to submit himself willingly to this command of water-baptism. For this is the true "love of God, that we keep his commandments, and his commandments are not grievous." 1 John 5 : 3. Again, says Paul 1 Cor. 13. "Though I give my body to be burned, bestow all my goods to the poor, and have not love,*) it profiteth me nothing." He describes the nature of love as believing all what God has ordained. Christ also said, John 14 : 23, 24: "If a man love me, he will keep my word; but he that loveth me not, keepeth not my sayings." Therefore a self righteous man may do a great deal, and not cleave to Christ in love as his head, for there were such men in Paul's time. See his epistle to the Colossians, 2 : 18, where he speaks of such as had "a voluntary humility and spirituality of angels," but whom he speaks of as being vainly puffed up by a fleshly mind, because they did not adhere to the Head.

Son. Can then a man not love God, if he will not obey in one thing, though he would be obedient in all others?

Father. Canst thou not understand what James says 2 : 10. "For whosoever shall keep the whole law, and yet offend in one point, he is guilty of all." Reflect upon thyself, if thou hadst been obedient to me for ten years or more in every thing, and I were to command thee now merely to pick up a straw, but if thou wouldst not do it, nor even try to do it, I would have to consider thee as a disobedient child, though thou wouldst say a thousand times, "Father, I will do every thing; I will work industriously; wherever thou sendest me, I will go; but to pick up that straw, I consider unnecessary; it will be of no use to thee or me." Would I not justly call thee a disobedient fellow.

Sohn. Vater, du sprichst zwar dieses von dir, ist aber Gott der die Liebe ist, auch so gesinnet gegen seine Kinder, und wie wollte man dieses erweisen?

Vater. Ja, ich will dir es aus Heil. Schrift ganz wohl erweisen, daß Gott eben so gesinnet sey: Betrachte nur was der erste Mensch im Paradies gethan hat. Gott sagte zu ihm; Er sollte von allen Bäumen essen, aber nur von einem sollte er nicht essen. Siehe, sobald er von dem verbotenen Baum gegessen, da verlor er alle seine Glückseligkeit, und wurde als ein Ungehorsamer zum Paradies hinaus gestoßen. Ja betrachte ferner was Gott im Gesetz gethan und geboten hat; 4 Mos. 15, 30. 31. da heißt es: "Wenn eine Seele mit Vorsatz sündiget, und des Herrn Wort verachtet, und sein Gebot fahren läßet, die soll ausgerottet werden." Siehe ferner, als die Söhne Aarons fremdes Feuer vor den Herrn brachten, so mußten sie des Todes sterben. 3 Mos. 10, 1. 2. Und der König Saul ward wegen seines Ungehorsams von dem Herrn verworfen. 1 Sam. 15, 22. 23. Ingleichen Achan mußte mit seinem ganzen Hause sterben, weil er dem Befehl Gottes war ungehorsam gewesen, indem er bei der Eroberung der Stadt Jericho etwas von dem Verbanneten genommen, welches Gott verboten hatte. Jos. 7, 20. Ja es wären noch viele dergleichen Zeugniße aus der Heil. Schrift anzuführen, aber dieses sey genug. Woraus du sehen kannst; daß Gott von allen seinen Geschöpfen einen unumgänglichen Gehorsam fordert.

Sohn. Ich merke nun wohl: Daß der Mensch nicht nur sehen soll auf das was geboten ist, sondern auf den Gebieter selbsten, und vornehmlich um der Größe des Gebieters, darum sollen auch alle Gebote des großen Gottes groß gehalten werden.

Vater. Ja, das ist jederzeit der wahre Glaube und die wahre Liebe aller Heiligen und Gläubigen gewesen. Sie

Son. Father, thou sayest this of thyself; but is God, who is love, of the same mind toward his children? and if he is how can it be proved?

Father. Yes, I will prove it unto thee from holy Scripture very clearly, that God is just so minded. Only consider what the first man did in Paradise. God said to him, Thou shalt eat of every tree but one; of that thou shalt not eat. Now see! As soon as he had eaten of the forbidden tree, he lost all his happiness, and was expelled from the garden of Eden for his one disobedient act. Again, see what God has done and commanded in the law, Numb 15 : 30, 31, where it is said, "If a soul doeth aught presumptuously, and despises the word of the Lord, and breaks his commandments, it shall be cut off." See further, that, when the sons of Aaron brought strange fire before the Lord, they died," Lev. 10 : 1, 2. And King Saul was rejected by the Lord on account of his disobedience. 1 Sam. 15 : 22, 23. Thus also Achan had to die with his whole family, because he disobeyed the command of God in taking of the accused thing at the downfall of Jericho, which God had forbidden. Josh. 7 : 20. Thus many testimonies of the same import might be adduced from the holy Scriptures, but let these suffice to show thee that God requires a strict obedience from all his creatures.

Son. I apprehend now, that man ought not to look only at the commandment, but also at the lawgiver, and especially at his greatness Therefore all the commandments of the great God should be esteemed great.

Father. Yes, that was always the true faith and the true love of all the saints and believers. They did what

haben gethan, was ihnen Gott geboten hat, und haben allen ihren Verstand und Willen gebeuget unter den Willen ihres Gottes. Und man kann von keinem Gläubigen hören oder merken, daß er sich in einem einzigen Gebot hätte Gott widersetzet.

Sohn. Wann nun so viel ja alles daran gelegen ist an Haltung der Gebote Gottes, wie kommt es dann, daß Gott allezeit den Menschen lauter einfältige Dinge geboten hat, wie man sehen kann im Alten und Neuen Testament?

Vater. Merke wohl, Gott ist an sich selbsten ein einfältiges gutes Wesen, und hat der Menschen ihren Dienst gar nicht nöthig, denn er hat viel tausend mal tausend Engel und Geister, die ihm dienen. Die Gebote nun, die Gott jederzeit denen Menschen gegeben hat, sind nur um des Menschen willen gegeben, daß der Mensch dadurch auch soll klein und einfältig werden, weil der Mensch durch den Fall Adams in die Höhe gestiegen ist, und gerne will groß, mächtig und heilig in seinen eigenen Augen seyn. Um nun den Menschen von diesem seinem Verderben zu erlösen, hat Gott durch seinen Sohn einfältige Dinge zu thun befohlen. Und wenn sie der Mensch in wahrem Glauben thut, und seine Vernunft in den Gehorsam gefangen nimmt, so wird er auch nach und nach einfältig und kindlich, und eben in dieser Einfalt findet die Seele wieder Ruhe, Friede und Sicherheit. Darum auch Christus spricht: Wahrlich ich sage euch: Wann ihr nicht werdet wie die Kinder, so könnet ihr nicht in das Himmelreich eingehen.

Sohn. Nun hab ich wohl verstanden, daß alle Gebote nur auf den wahren Gehorsam zielen. Wie auch das Gebot der Wasser-Taufe, welches Christus seinen Aposteln befohlen hat, daß sie taufen sollen, und sie auch getauft haben. Ist aber dieses Gebot nur alle Gläubige ergangen, daß sie sollen getauft werden, und daß dieses

God commands them, and subjected all their own will and understanding to the will of God. Neither can we find the case of a single believer, that refused obedience to God in any commandment.

SON. If so much, and especially if all depends upon the keeping of God's commandments, why did God always command men nothing but simple things, as we can see both in the Old and New Testament the did?

FATHER. Consider well, that God is a simple and good being, and does not stand in need at all of any services from man: for he has many thousands of angels and spirits, who serve him. Now the commandments, which God gave at any time to man, were given only for man's sake, to make him lowly and simple, because by Adam's fall he became exalted in his own conceit, and desired to be great, mighty and holy by his own devices. Now to rescue man from this perilous condition, simple things were required of him by God through his Son. And when man does them in true faith, and if his reason yields to the obedience which is required of him, he will then by degrees become simple and childlike, and in this very simplicity the soul will find again rest, peace and security. Hence Christ also says, "Verily, I say unto you, that unless ye become as children, ye cannot enter the kingdom of heaven."

SON. I have now well understood, that all commandments point only to true obedience. The same is the case with the command of water-baptism, which Christ has commanded his apostles to administer, and which also they did. But was this command intended for all believers, that they should be

bleiben — — bis an das Ende der Welt?

Vater. Dieses ist ganz klar ausgesprochen, wie er Matth. 28, 19. 20. da der Heiland spricht: "Lehret alle Völker, und taufet sie 2c. Und lehret sie halten alles, was ich euch befohlen habe. Und siehe, ich bin bey euch alle Tage, bis an der Welt Ende."

Sohn. Haben denn nach der Apostel Tod auch andere Menschen taufen dürfen, die eben nicht so wie die Apostel dazu gesandt waren?

Vater. Merke wohl, die Haushaltung und Ordnungen Gottes, schon unter dem Gesetz. Als Gott durch Mosen ein Haus machen ließ, worinnen Priester zum Dienste seyn mußten; so hat Gott den Stamm Levi dazu erkohren, und aus diesem Stamm hat Gott selbst Aaron und seine Söhne erwählet, die das Priesteramt pflegen sollten. Als nun oftmals der Tempel und alles zerstöret und verderbet wurde, und sie wiederum den Gottesdienst pflegen wollten, so durfte es kein anderer thun, als der aus dem Stamm Levi war. Aber der gottlose König Jerobeam machte solche zu Priester, die nicht aus dem Stamm Levi waren, diese konnten auch den falschen Gottesdienst verrichten. 1 Kön. 12, 31. Wann sie aber aus dem Stamm Levi Priester erwählten, so nahmen sie solche, die in dem Gesetz Mosis wohl erfahren waren, und diese durften keine Fehler noch Gebrechen am Leibe haben. 3 Mos. 21. 21.

Merke wohl: Es hat der Sohn Gottes selbsten unter seine Gemeinde, vors erste Apostel, und hernach Lehrer, und andere dergleichen gesetzt. Die Apostel nun, haben zugleich auch andere erwählet zu dem Dienst in der Haushaltung Gottes, als zum Taufen, den Bann zu führen und dergleichen, damit die göttlichen Ordnungen wohl unterhalten würden. Sie haben aber jederzeit nur solche erwählet, die aus

---

baptized, and was it designed to extend to the end of the world?

FATHER. This is very clearly expressed in Matt. 28; 19, 20, where the Savior says, 'Teach all nations, and baptize them, and teach them to observe all things, whatsoever I have commanded you; and lo, I am with you always, even unto the end of the world.'

SON. After the apostles were dead, had also other men permission to baptize, though they were not sent like the apostles?

FATHER. Mark well God's ceremony and ordinances as they already had been given under the law. When God caused a tabernacle to be raised by Moses, in which the priests were to serve, he chose the tribe of Levi, and from this tribe God himself selected Aaron and his sons, that they should minister in the priest's office. Now, as it often happened that the temple and all were destroyed and ruined, when divine service was to be observed again, no others would do it, but those from the tribe of Levi. But the wicked King Jeroboam made such priests, who were not of the tribe of Levi, and who would only administer false worship. 1 Kings 12: 31. When however, priests were chosen from the tribe of Levi, they took such, as were well instructed in the law of Moses, and whose bodies were free from blemishes and infirmities. Lev. 21: 21.

Note well, that the Son of God himself first appointed in his church apostles, and then teachers and others. Now the apostles also soon chose others for the service in the house of God, namely, to baptize and administer discipline &c. in order that the divine ordinances might continually be sustained. But they always chose only such, who descended from the royal priesthood;

dem hohenpriesterlichen Geschlecht waren. Das ist: die den Geist Jesu hatten, und durch denselben Geist durften sie auch taufen und andere Dinge thun. Nun haben die Apostel schon bey ihren Zeiten solche Menschen gemerket, die zwar unterm Schein Christen waren, aber den Geist Christi nicht hatten. Von denen sagt Paulus zu den Aeltesten von Epheso; in der Apost. Gesch. 20, 29. 30. "Aus euch selbst werden Männer aufstehen, und verkehrte Dinge reden." Sie werden sich selbsten aufwerfen und vor tüchtig achten.

Und dieses ist jederzeit ein Kennzeichen des falschen Geistes gewesen. Denn wann der Mensch sich selbst in Ehre setzen will, so ist er nicht der Art Christi. Der hat sich nicht selbst in das Priesterthum gesetzt, sondern sein Vater. Und daß die ersten Lehrer und Aeltesten der Gemeinden von dem Heil. Geist sind eingesetzet worden, das lieset man in der Ap. Gesch. 20, 18. 28. Da der Apostel Paulus die Aeltesten und Lehrer von der Gemeinde zu Epheso zu sich fordern ließ, gab er unter andern ihnen auch diese Vermahnung: "Habt acht auf euch selbst, und auf die ganze Heerde, unter welche euch der Heil. Geist gesetzt hat zu Bischöfen." 2c.

Wie aber die Menschen sich selbst durch ihren eigenen Geist, und eigene Ehre in den Dienst der Kirchen gesetzet, so ist daraus der große Mißbrauch und alles Verderben eingerissen und entstanden. Nun sind so viel tausend Prediger in der Welt, und die wenigsten sind von dem königlichen Priesterthum, von dem heiligen Volk. 1 Pet. 2, 9. Die wenigsten haben den Geist Christi. Die wenigsten sind von dem heil. Geist eingesetzt zu Bischöfen. Darum predigen sie auch nur um ihre eigene Ehre und

Aber die Gläubigen Gemeinden nach der Apostel Tod, die noch rein und lauter geblieben, die haben jederzeit solche Männer unter sich erwählet, die den Geist Jesu hat-

that is, such as had the spirit of Jesus, and in this spirit they were also permitted to baptize and do other things. But the apostles already in their time noticed such men, as indeed appeared to have become christians, yet they had not the Spirit of Christ. Of these Paul said to the elders of Ephesus, Acts 20 : 29, 30, 'Of your ownselves shall men arise, speaking perverse things, to draw away disciples after them.'

This has been at all times a sign of the false spirit. For where a man will 'take this honor unto himself,' he is not of the mind of Christ; for He did not place himself into the priesthood, but (was made an high priest by) his Father. That the first teachers and elders of the churches were appointed by the Holy Ghost, appears from Acts 20 : 18, 28. When the apostle Paul had called to him the elders and teachers of the church at Ephesus, be gave them among other charges this also; 'Take heed, therefore, unto yourselves, and to all the flock over which the Holy Ghost hath made you overseers, &c.

But whenever men pleased themselves in the service of the church by their own spirit, and to their own honor, from this great abuse and corruption originated, and spread. Thus there are now many thousand preachers in the world, but by far the smallest number are of the royal priesthood, of the holy people. 1 Pet. 2 : 9. The smallest number have the Spirit of Christ. The smallest number were made overseers by the Holy Ghost. Therefore they preach also for their own glory and emolument.

But the churches of believers, after the death of the apostles, which did still continue pure and uncontaminated, always chose such men among themselves, who

ten, und sich selbst verleugneten. Und wie Christus äußerlich seine Apostel erwählet hat, so hat auch jederzeit die Gemeinde des Herrn, als der Leib Christi, wieder erwählet solche, die sie vor tüchtig erkannten, die haben denn auch getauft, und ist der Befehl des Herrn Jesu nach seiner Lauterkeit niemals ausgeblieben noch aufgehöret, da er spricht: »Lehret sie halten alles was ich euch befohlen habe.« Matth. 28, 20. Sondern dieser Befehl wird bleiben, bis daß Christus wird wieder kommen Rechnung zu halten wegen seiner Lehr, mit seinen eigenen Knechten und auch mit seinen Feinden.

Cyprianus, und andere fromme Männer der ersten Kirchen, forderten von einem der da taufen wollte, den wahren gesunden Glauben an Christum, und wann nemlich die Gemeinde ihn dazu erwählet hatte. Eben so schreibet auch das Concilium zu Jlibris und fordert von einem der da taufen will und soll: Daß er zuerst seine Taufe solle richtig haben, und nach seiner Taufe nicht wieder in Sünden gefallen seyn, dadurch er die Gnade verloren habe. Und wie auch Gregorius meldet: halte du einen jeden würdig und geschickt genug zum Amt des Taufens zu verwalten; wann er unter die Gottseligen kann gezählet werden.

Sohn. Ich versteh nun gar wohl von der Tauf, daß es ein Befehl von Christo an seine Gläubigen ist, bis an das Ende der Welt. Nun möcht ich auch Gewißheit haben von der Art des Taufens, ob man im Wasser taufen soll, und ob man auch in einer Stube mit einer Hand voll Wassers taufen kann, und den Gehorsam gegen das Gebot erfüllen?

Vater. Merke wohl, ich will dir auch dieses aus Heil. Schrift wohl zeigen, erstlich): Christus als der wahre Vorgänger seiner ganzen Gemeinde, ist von Johanne im Jordan getaufet worden. Matth.

had the Spirit of Jesus and who denied themselves. And as Christ himself chose the apostles, so likewise the church of the Lord, as the body of Christ, ever since chose such, as they thought fit, and these also baptized, and thus the command of the Lord in its purity has never ceased nor been discontinued, for he said, 'Teach them to observe all things whatsoever I have commanded you.' Matt. 28 : 20. Yes, this command will remain in full force, until Christ shall come again to call to account concerning his doctrines, not only his own servants, but also his enemies.

CYPRIANUS and other pious men of the primitive church required of one who would baptize, a true sound faith in Christ, and a proper appointment by the church to that office. The same was required also by the council at Ilibris of one who would baptize, that first he should have received his baptism regularly, and after his baptism should not have fallen again into sin, by which he might have lost grace. GREGORY also says, "Consider thou every one worthy and sufficiently qualified to administer baptism, if he be numbered among the pious.

SON. I understand now very well about baptism, that it is a command of Christ to believers, even unto the end of the world. Now I would wish also to have some assurance about the mode of baptism, to know whether we are to baptize in the water, or whether we may also baptize in a room with a handful of water, and thereby fulfil the commandment?

FATHER. Observe well; I will point out to thee also this clearly in the holy Scripture. First, Christ, as the true leader of his whole church, "was baptized of John in the river of Jordan." Matt.

3, 12—10. Johannes taufte an einem Ort nahe bei Salim, denn es war viel Waſſer daſelbſt. Joh. 3, 23. Siehe aus dieſen zweien Zeugen ſollteſt du ſchon genug merken können, daß wenn man das Gebot der Tauf an einem trockenen Ort hätte erfüllen können, ſo würde Johannes nicht hingegangen ſeyn, wo viel Waſſer war, denn es iſt ja viel gemächlicher in einer Stube als im Waſſer ſolches zu thun, denn das Waſſer iſt oftmals kalt, und greift die Natur ein wenig an.

Nun will ich dir zum Ueberfluß noch mehrere Zeugniße ſagen: Es heißet der Befehl von der Taufe eigentlich nach dem Griechiſchen Wort, Eintauchen. Wie es denn von Jeremias Felbinger, ſo iſt überſetzt worden. Seitdem aber das Beſprengen aufgekommen iſt, und die Gelehrten wegen Zärtlichkeit ſich für dem Waſſer geſcheut haben, ſo meynen ſie, man könne das griechiſche Wort auch. Beſprengen, Begießen oder Naßmachen, nehmen. Dennoch müſſen ſie gelten laſſen, daß es Eintauchen heißet.

Siehe ferner, als dorten Philippus den Kämmerer taufte, da hieß es, "ſie ſtiegen hinab in das Waſſer, und Philippus taufte ihn." Ap. Geſch. 8, 38. 39. Hiervon findet man auch noch vieles in den Hiſtorien von den erſten Chriſten, daß ſie in Strömen, Flüſſen und Brunnen getauft haben. Wie auch im blutigen Tonel der Taufgeſinnten zu leſen pag. 265. daß im Jahr Chriſti 980 viele Perſonen in dem Fluß Euphrates getauft worden. Ferner ſtehet, pag. 207 daß Anno 1620. Paulinianus an dem Mittag bei der Stadt Truvolſinga in dem Waſſer-Fluß Trentho getauft, und daß dieſes Taufen bei denen Alten, Eintauchen oder Unterdumpfung geheißen. Ferner ſtehet, pag. 220. daß Engländer im Fluß Schwalbe und im Rheinſtrom getauft worden ſind. Und daß es auch auf keine andere Art und Maßier geſchehen könne. Ja die Menſchen

3 : 13—16. — John baptized in a place near to Salim, because there was much water there." John 3 : 23. Behold, from those two testimonies thou shouldst be able to see sufficiently, that if the command of baptism could be performed in a dry place, John would not have gone to places where there was much water; for it is certainly much more convenient to perform this in a room, than in the water, which is often cold and disagreeable to nature.

But I will give thee out of many testimonies we have, some more. The command to baptize properly signifies, according to the greek word *to immerse*, and it has been so translated by Jeremias Felbinger, (and many others). But since sprinkling has been introduced, and the learned from an effeminate weakness have become afraid of the water, the opinion has been held, that the Greek word might also signify to sprinkle, pour, or make wet. Yet all must admit, that it signifies to immerse.

Again, when Philip baptized the eunuch, it is said, "They went down both into the water, and Philip baptized him. Acts 8 : 38. We also find yet a great deal in the histories of primitive Christians showing that they baptized in streams, rivers, and fountains. As we read in the bloody Tonel of the Doopsgesind page 255, that in the year of Christ 980, many persons were baptized in the river Euphrates. Again, page 207, that in the year 620, Paulinianus baptized at noon near the city Truvolsinga in the river Trenth, and that this baptism was called by the Ancients an immersion or dipping. Again page 220, we find, that some Englishmen were baptized in the river Schwalbe and in the Rhine, and that it could not be done in any other way or manner. Indeed people must be very

müssen recht blind und verstockt seyn, weil es auch in der Schrift so hell und klar geschrieben stehet.

Röm. 6. 4. heißt es, eine Begrabung der Sünden. Ferner nennet es Paulus ein Wasser-Bad. Ephes. 5, 26. Und Christus spricht, Joh. 3. 5. Man müsse aus Wasser und dem Heil. Geist wiedergeboren werden.

Die ersten Christen haben von der Tauf also geredet: Die fleischlichen Kinder Adams (sagten sie), steigen in das Wasser, und müssen alsobald aus dem Wasser aufsteigen, nachdem sie geistliche Kinder Gottes worden sind. Justinus hat es dem Kaiser selbsten also vorgestellet: "welche überzeuget sind und glauben daß es wahr sey, was von uns gelehret wird, und das bey versprechen, daß sie durch die Gnade Gottes also leben wollen, die unterweiset man, wie sie beten und fasten und von Gott Vergebung der Sünden suchen sollen. Darnach führen sie sie hin, wo Wasser ist, und sie werden wiedergebohren, gleich wie wir wiedergebohren sind. Dann werden sie im Wasser abgewaschen, im Namen Gottes des Vaters, und Herrn aller Dinge, und unsers Herrn Jesu Christi, und des Heil. Geistes."

Obgemeldeter Justinus setzte noch hinzu, "diese Weise haben wir von den Aposteln empfangen." Hiervon zeuget auch Beda, lib. 2. Cap. 14. daß das Volk bey den Engländern im Anfang der ersten Gemeinden hin und wieder in den Wasserflüssen wäre eingetaucht worden. Wallfried Strabo schreibet in Lib. de Rebus Eccles. Cap. 26. Man soll wissen, daß die Gläubigen anfänglich in fließenden Wassern oder Brunnen getauft worden sind, denn unser Herr Jesus selber, damit er uns dieses Bad heilige, ist von Johanne im Jordan getauft worden, wie man auch lieset: Johannes taufte zu Enon bey Salim, denn es war viel Wasser daselbst. Joh. 3, 23.

blind and much prejudiced not, to see it, since it is written so plainly, and clearly in the holy Scriptures.

In Rom. 6: 4. it is called a burial of sin; again Paul calls it a washing of water. Eph. 5: 26. And Christ says, John 3: 5, that we must be born again of water and of the Spirit.

The primitive Christians have thus spoken of baptism. The carnal children of Adam go down into the water, and soon rise up again out of the water, after they have become the spiritual children of God.

Justinus gave this account to the emperor himself: "Those who are convinced of, and believe in the truth, which is taught by us, and also promise that by the grace of God that they will live thus, are then taught by us how they are to pray and fast, and seek the forgiveness of their sins of God. Then they are led to a place, where there is water, and they are regenerated, as we were regenerated. Then they are washed in the water in the name of God, the Father and Lord of all things, and of our Lord Jesus Christ, and of the Holy Ghost."

Said Justinus further adds, 'This form we have received from the apostles.' Of this Beda testifies, Lib. 2. chapt. 14. that in the beginning of the first churches among the English, the people were immersed here and there in streams of water.

Wallfried Strabo writes in Lib. de Reb. Eccles c 26. 'Be it known, that the believers were originally baptized in running streams and fountains; for our Lord Jesus himself in order to sanctify this bath unto us was baptized of John in Jordan. And we also read, 'John baptized at Enon near Salim, because there was much water there." John 3: 23.

Sohn. Mich dünket, du hast mir hievon Zeugniße genug gezeiget, daß Christus, Johannes, die Apostel, und so viele der ersten Christen in den Waffern getauft haben.

Vater. Dieses wäre freilich genug gewiesen, aber ich will dir noch mehrere Zeugniße anweisen aus den Historien der ersten Christen. Honorus Aug. schreibet im Buch Gemma Anima Lib. 3. pag. 106. Man soll wissen: "daß die Heil. Apostel und ihre Jünger vor Zeiten in fließenden Waffern und Brunnen getaufet." Tertullianus meldet in seinem Buch Lib. de Corona militis: Die, so zur Tauf gehen, bekennen eine Zeitlang zuvor in der Gemeinde vor dem Lehrer, daß sie absagen dem Teufel seinem Pomp und Engeln, darnach werden sie dreymal eingedunket und getauft, und solcher Brauch sey gehalten worden bis 801, da Ludovicus Kaiser worden ist.

Sohn. Ey sage mir doch auch, ob die Apostel den ganzen Menschen eingetaucht haben, oder nur eine Hand, oder das Haupt, oder wie es geschehen. Denn ich habe schon von etlichen hören sagen: Man könne wohl merken in der Schrift, daß man in das Waffer gehen soll, aber wie man in dem Waffer taufen soll, das wiffe man nicht?

Vater. Du gibst damit zu verstehen, daß es dir fehle an dem inwendigen Licht, und diejenigen die das sagen: Man wiffe nicht wie man taufen solle, die geben zu verstehen, daß sie einen elenden Lehrmeister haben. Sollte Jesus ein solcher Meister seyn, der die Seinigen etwas in seinem Namen sollte thun heißen, nämlich ein solches wichtiges Werk wie das Taufen ist, und sie müßten nicht, auf was für Art sie solches thun sollten. So müßten sie den Lehrmeifter fragen, wie sie es thun sollten, und es lieber unterlaffen, ehe sie solches so in der Ungewißheit thäten. Dann bedenke nur einmal, wenn solche die über die Ge-

Son. Methinks thou hast given me sufficient testimony to prove that Christ, John, the apostles and many of the primitive Christians have baptized in the water.

Father. Truly this might suffice; but I will add some more testimonies from the histories concerning primitive Christianity. HONORUS AUG. writes in his book *Gemma Anima* Lib. 8 pag. 106 "It is to be known, that the holy apostles and their disciples in early times baptized in flowing streams and fountains." TERTULLIANUS mentions in his book, *Delorona Militis*, "That the candidates for baptism profess sometime previous in the church before the teacher, to renounce the devil, his pomp and angels, and then they are plunged in the water three times and baptized." This custom prevailed until 801, when Ludovicus was made emperor,

Son. Please do tell me also, whether the apostles did immerse the whole person, or only a hand, or the head, or how it was done. For I have already heard some say, 'We can plainly perceive in the scriptures, that we ought to go into the water, but how we are to baptize in the water, we do not know.'

Father. By this thou givest me to understand, that thou art in need of inward light, and those who say, that they do not know how baptism is to be performed, give us to understand that they have a bad teacher. Is Jesus such a Master as to command his people to do something in his name, especially such an important act as baptism is, and they not know in what manner it is to be done? Of course they would ask the Master, how they should do it, and they would rather leave it undone, than go about it in such uncertainty. Consider only for a moment about such, who want

heimniße in dem Haufe Gottes Haußhalter feyn wollen, und nicht wiffen wie man im Waffer taufen foll; woher oder bey welschem Lehrmeister haben fie denn diefes gelernet, daß fie an einem trocknen Ort, in einer Stube, oder im Verfammlungs-Platz, mit einer Handvoll Waffers das Haupt befprengen oder naß machen follen, weil man diefes an keinem einzigen Ort der Heil. Schrift findet, fondern ganz das Gegentheil an Jefu und feinen Apofteln fiehet?

Weil du mich nun hiervon gefraget haft, fo will ich dir es ferner kürzlich fagen: Du haft gehöret von Chrifto, feinen Apofteln, und von fo vielen Zeugnißen der erften Chriften: Daß fie in Strömen, in fließenden Waffern und Brunnen getauft haben. Und taufen ift nichts anders denn im Waffer eintauchen. Wie das Wort und der Befehl alfo lautet. Denn Chriftus hat ja gefaget zu feinen Apofteln: Matth. 28, 19. Lehret die Völker (die Menfchen) und taufet fie (tauchet fie ein) und nicht die Glocken, wie im Pabftthum gefchiehet. Der Herr Jefus hat ja nicht gefaget: Taufet an den Menfchen das Haupt, oder etwas anders, machet den Menfchen ein wenig naß mit Waffer in meinem Namen. Nein, fo hat der Herr Jefus nicht befohlen, fondern den ganzen Menfchen follten fie ins Waffer eintauchen. Wie ich dir auch fchon vorher von der Bedeutung der Tauf gefaget habe: Daß fie eine Bedeutung von dem Inwendigen feyn müffe.

Sohn. Kann man denn nicht mit einer Handvoll Waffers ein Waffer-Bad, oder eine Begrabung der Sünden abbilden, oder dergleichen?

Vater. Das ift unmöglich, denn dasjenige fo etwas äußerliches abbilden foll, das muß nicht anders als wie es im Wefen, feyn.

Sohn. Wenn nun das Wefen inwendig wäre, und die äußere Abbildung deffelben wäre eben nicht fo wie das innere Wefen, follte denn diefes etwas fchaden?

to be stewards over the mysteries in the house of God. and do not know how we are to baptize in the water! Where then, or from what teacher, have they learned this, that in a dry place, in a room, or at a place of meeting, they should sprinkle or make wet with a handfull of water the head, since there is not a single passage in holy Scripture alluding to such a practice, but the very reverse is seen in Jesus and his apostles?

On thy question upon this, I will yet say in brief: Thou hast heard of Christ, his apostles, and of so many witnesses, that they and the first Christians baptized in rivers, in flowing streams and fountains. And to baptize is nothing else than to immerse in water, as the word and command require. For Christ said to his apostles, Matt. 28 : 19. 'Teach all nations, (mankind) baptizing them, (immersing them) and not the bells, as is done in Papal countries. The Lord Jesus has not said, Baptize the head or some other part of man, or sprinkle a man a little with water in my name. No, thus the Lord Jesus did not command, but that they should immerse the whole person in water. I have already told thee before of the signification of baptism, that it signifies an inward purification.

Son. Can a water-bath or a burial of sin, not be represented by a handfull of water, or the like?

Father. This is impossible; for any thing that is to be represented outwardly in its true light, must exactly correspond with the inward substance.

Son. Suppose the inward substance was right, and the outward representation did not exactly correspond with the inner substance, would there be any harm?

Vater. Merke wohl: wenn ein großer Herr zu seinem Diener oder ein Mahler seyn wollte, sagen wäre: Er solle ihn abmahlen, damit auch Andere die ihn außerhalb nicht sehen, doch in dem Bilde seine Gestalt betrachten, und erkennen könnten. Und der Diener, der solches thun wollte, gäbe nicht genau Achtung auf seinen Herrn, sondern sein Gemüth wäre mit andern Dingen beschäftiget, thäte auch seinen Herrn nicht recht lieben, dennoch aber wollte er das Gebot erfüllen, und thäte dann mit solcher Leichtsinnigkeit seinen Herrn abmahlen, mahlete ihm aber nur ein Aug, oder einen Fuß, oder eine Hand, und das Bild würde also ganz verstümmelt, daß es also ganz keine Gleichheit hätte von dem Körper selbsten. Was sollte nun wohl der Herr zu solchem Diener sagen? Er würde ihn als einen unnützen Knecht aus seinem Dienst wegjagen.

Also sind leider viele unnütze Mahler in der Welt, sonderlich wegen der Wasser-Tauf, und allen andern Geboten Christi, weil der Meisten ihre Gemüther mit Welt, Eigenliebe und dergleichen angefüllet sind. Und weil die Liebe zu JEsu dem Gekreuzigten, und die Liebe zur Verleugnung ihrer selbst nicht in ihnen ist, so haben sie auch das Bild JEsu in seiner Lehre und kräftigem Vorbild vergessen, und haben also die Lehre JEsu ganz verstümmelt. Da mahlet ein Jeder nach seinem fleischlichen Sinn, wie er will, oder wie es hie oder da im Gebrauch ist, und sehen nicht einzig und allein auf ihren Herrn und Meister. Etliche besprengen die kleinen Kinder ein wenig auf das Haupt. Andere die etwas näher gekommen sind, besprengen die Erwachsenen mit einer Handvoll Wassers auf das Haupt, etliche nehmen 3 Hände voll, andere nur eine, und sagen alle: Ich taufe dich. Und dieses soll nun ein Wasser-Bad seyn,

FATHER. Mark well! Suppose a great Lord would tell to his servant, who pretended to be a painter, to draw him a good likeness, as that others, who could not see him personally, might be enabled to contemplate and know his outward form in the picture. But supposing the servant, who should do this, would not pay strict attention to his Lord; on the contrary, if he would permit his mind to be engaged in other things, and would have no true regard for his master, still he would try to comply with the command. Suppose further, then, he would draw his master with such carelessness, as to give him but one eye, or only one foot, or one hand, and thus mar the picture so entirely, that it should be no likeness at all of the person of his master; what would the master say to such a servant? Would he not dismiss him from his service as an useless servant?

Alas, there are many such useless painters in the world, especially concerning water-baptism and all other commandments of Christ, because the minds of most of them are filled with the world, self love and the like. And since the love of Jesus the crucified one, and the love to deny themselves is not in them, they have also forgotten the image of Jesus in his doctrine and his powerful example, and thus disfigured his whole doctrine. Every one of course paints according to his carnal mind, as he pleases, or as it is here and there customary, and does not look only and altogether on his Lord and Master. Some sprinkle little children with a few drops of water on their head. Others, who have come a little nearer sprinkle (or pour) grown persons with a handfull of water on their head. Some take three handfulls, others only one, and all say, *I baptize thee.* And this is

ober eine Begrabung der Sünden bedeuten.

S o h n. Ich merke nun wohl daß die Lehre Jesu sehr verstümpelt ist, und man kein rechtes Bild mehr davon sehen noch spüren kann.

Vater. Ja es hat jetzund alle Völker sammt der ganzen Erden eine große Finsterniß bedecket, wird aber gar bald wieder erleuchtet werden, wie es geweissaget ist. Zach. 14, 7. Offenb. 18, 1.

Von dem Abendmahl des Herrn.

S o h n. Ich danke dir, lieber Vater, daß du mir solches alles erzehlet hast, und kann mich nicht genugsam wundern über den großen Mißbrauch wegen der Tauf bei diesen Zeiten, es muß wohl eine große Finsterniß die Völker bedecket haben; aber ich muß dich auch noch ferner fragen wegen dem heil Abendmahl, wie es Christus habe eingesetzet, und wie es gehalten werden soll, ob dieses denn auch so im Verfall sey, als wie die Taufe?

Vater. Ja du kannst wohl denken: Wann man in einem so weit fehlet, daß man auch in allen fehlet, wie du wohl sehen wirst an der Einsetzung Christi, und an dem heutigen Gebrauch: Erstlich heißet es ein Abendmahl, welches der Sohn Gottes seinen lieben Jüngern zu einem Gedächtniß eingesetzet, und befohlen hat, daß sie dabey seinen Kreutzes-Tod verkündigen, das Brod der Gemeinschaft brechen, und den Kelch der Gemeinschaft trinken, und sich in der Liebe als Glieder Jesu mit einander verbinden, ihrem Herrn und Meister immer treuer zu werden, im wahren Gehorsam des Glaubens, bey ihm auch im Kreutz beständig zu bleiben, auf daß sie denn auch am Ende der Welt mit ihm das große Abendmahl halten können.

S o h n. Sollen und dürfen sonst keine andere Menschen des Herrn Abendmahl halten, als nur allein die wahre

to signify a water-bath or a burial of sin !

Son I perceive right well that the doctrine of Jesus is greatly mutilated, so that its true form is scarcely discernible.

Father. Yes, at this time a great darkness covers all nations upon the whole earth, but we trust there shall soon be more and more light again, as it is prophesied, Zech. 14: 7. Rev. 18 : 1.

OF THE SUPPER OF THE LORD.

Son. I thank thee, dear father, for all that thou hast related to me, and I cannot sufficiently express my wonder over the great abuse of baptism in our times; truly, a great darkness must have covered the nations. But further, I must enquire of thee concerning the Lord's Supper, how it was instituted by Christ, how it should be observed now, and whether it is in the same state of decay as baptism?

Father. Yes, one may easily think so, for if a person is so far in error in one point, he will likely be in error in other points also, as thou mayest well perceive by comparing the institution of Christ with the present g neral practice. First, it is called a supper, which the Son of God has instituted for his beloved disciples as a memorial, and has commanded, that they should show forth his death on the cross by breaking the bread of communion, and by drinking the cup of the New Testament; and unite together in love as his members to become more faithful, to be steadfast in the true obedience of faith with him even under the cross, so that they may be enabled to partake with him of the great supper at the end of this world.

Son. May there none others be permitted to partake of the Lord's supper, but such only, who are the true follow-

Nachfolger des Herrn Jesu, die da seine Gebote halten, und sein Kreuz tragen helfen?

Vater. Der wahre Hausvater Jesus Christus hat es nur allein seinem Hausgesinde befohlen, welche durch wahre Buße, Glaube und die Taufe in das Reich Jesu Christi eingegangen sind, und denn ferner alle Regeln des Hausvaters in Gehorsam des Glaubens willig halten. Eben so wie es Gott der Herr im Gesetz befohlen hatte: Wer von dem Osterlamm essen wollte, mußte vorhero beschnitten seyn. 2 Mos. 12, 48. Also wer des Herrn Abendmahl würdiglich halten will, der muß vorhero abgeschnitten seyn von dem Leibe des Satans, der Welt, ja von allen Ungerechtigkeiten, und von allen falschen Secten und Religionen, und muß als ein wahres Glied, Jesu dem Oberhaupt anhangen im Glauben und in der Liebe, und muß bereit seyn, um Jesu und seiner Lehre willen, auch sein Leib und Leben willig in den Tod hin zu geben, wenn es Evangelischer Weise, nach dem Willen Gottes von ihm gefordert würde. Wer aber noch wissentlich in Sünden und Ungehorsam gegen Gott lebet, und nicht will in der Verleugnung seiner selbsten und aller Dinge dieser Welt Christo nachfolgen, nach dem Rath Jesu, Luc. 14, 26. 27. Der ist noch unwürdig, und isset und trinket ihm nur das Gericht, darum, daß er nicht Unterschied machet an dem Leib des Herrn, und an dem Leib der Sünden. 1. Cor. 11, 29.

Sohn. Ey Vater, wie kommt es denn, daß es ein Abendmahl heißt, und es wird doch gemeiniglich des Morgens oder zu Mittag gehalten, und nicht des Abends?

Vater. Wie ich dir schon oben von der Taufe gesagt habe, wie dieselbe in großen Verfall und Zerrüttung kommen sey; also ist es auch mit dem Abendmahl. Einige halten es des Morgens, andere zu Mittage, und bey keinem ist es ein Abendmahl, denn wo ein Abendmahl oder ein

ers of the Lord Jesus, who keep his commandments and help bear his cross?

Father. The true Father of the house, Jesus Christ, has commanded this only to his family and his servants, who have entered into his kingdom by true repentance, faith and baptism, and who keep all the rules and ordinances of the house of God willingly, and in in the obedience of faith. Just as God had commanded in the law, that whoever would eat the passover, must previously be circumcised, Exod. 12: 48; so, whoever wishes to partake of the Lord's supper in a worthy manner, must be separated from the body of Satan, the world from all unrighteousness, and from all false sects and religions; he must adhere to Jesus the head, as a true member in faith and in love, and be ready, if it should be required according to the will of God, in an evangelical manner to yield up his body, and even his life for the sake of Jesus and his doctrine. But he that lives, knowingly in sin, and in disobedience to God, and will not follow Christ in denying himself of every evil thing of this world, according to the counsel of Jesus, Luke 14: 26, 27—is still unworthy, and eateth and drinketh damnation to himself, not discerning the Lord's body from the body of sin. 1 Cor. 11: 20.

Son. Why, father, how is it that it is called a supper, and yet it is generally taken in the morning, or at noon, and not in the evening?

Father. As I have told thee already of baptism, that great abuses and confusion have taken place concerning it; so it is also with the Lord's supper. Some observe it in the morning, others at noon, and with none of them it is a supper. For where there is to be a sup-

Mittagsmahl gehalten werden soll, da muß auch etwas zu essen seyn! Aber da gehen die Menschen zu ihrem vermeinten Abendmahl, und kommen wieder hungrig und durstig davon, etliche bekommen nicht einmal einen Bissen Brods, und andere nicht einen Tropfen Wein, wieder andere bekommen zwar einen Bissen Brods, und ein wenig Weins, und dabey seynd sie mit großem Kleider-Pracht, Wohllust, eigener Ehre und dergl. angefüllet, wie denn dieses bey denen größten Haufen in allen Religionen zu sehen ist, wann sie ihrem Vorgeben nach des Herrn Abendmahl halten.

Sohn. Muß es denn am Abend gehalten werden, und eine Mahlzeit dabey seyn, oder ist es auch nicht gut, ohne des andern Essens solches des Morgens oder des Mittags zu halten?

Vater. Merke wohl, wie die wahren Gläubigen und die Liebhaber des Herrn Jesu allezeit gar genau und einfältig auf ihren Herrn und Meister in allen Dingen alleine sehen, und ihm gerne so nachfolgen in allen seinen Befehlen, wie er es ihnen geboten hat, und mit seinem eigenen Exempel gezeiget hat, und dann lernen sie auch in ihrer Einfalt den Sinn ihres Meisters wohl verstehen, auch in den einfältigsten Vorstellungen, dann erstlich heißt es in der Schrift: ein Abendmahl, 1 Cor. 11, 20. welches damals die Gläubigen gehalten, und von Paulo diese Weise gelernet, wie in eben diesem Cap. v. 1. stehet, und Paulus hat es von seinem Herrn Jesu selbst empfangen, was er denen Corinthern gegeben hat, v. 23. und nun haben sie ja dazumal ein Abend-Essen oder ein Abendmahl gehalten; Und kann die blinde Vernunft (wenn sie nur wollte) wohl merken und einen Unterschied machen, daß ein Abendmahl nicht ein Mittagsmahl bedeuten kann.

Es sind auch schon zu Pauli Zeiten die Menschen zusammen gekommen und haben Abendmahl gehalten. Paulus aber saget:

per or a dinner, there must be also something to eat! But people generally go to their supposed supper, and come away again hungry and dry. Some do not get even a bit of bread, and others not a drop of wine. Again others do get a bit of bread, and a little wine; but, as is the case with the greatest number of all denominations, when they do come to their Lord's table, as they call it, they come with great extravagance in dress, with pride, vain glory, &c. &c.

SON. Is it then necessary to keep it in the evening, and must there be a real meal, or may it not as well without a meal, be taken in the morning or at noon?

FATHER. Observe well, how the true believers and lovers of the Lord Jesus always have their eye singly and strictly directed to their Lord and Master in all things; they wish to follow and obey him in all his commands, that he has given them, and shown them with his own example; and thus they learn in their simplicity to understand the mind of their Master, even in the very smallest matters. For, first, it is called in the scripture a supper; 1 Cor. 11 : 20, which believers observed at that time, and had learned of Paul the manner, as it is said in the same chapt. v. 1. And Paul declares that he had received of the Lord that which also he delivered to the Corinthians v. 23. We thus see that they truly kept a supper, or evening meal; and even blind reason might see (if she would) and distinguish, that a supper cannot mean a dinner.

Even as early as the days of Paul, Christians came together, and had a supper. But Paul said, they did not eat the

Sie hielten nicht des Herrn Abendmahl. 1 Cor. 11, 20. Wann aber die Gläubigen in vereinigter Liebe und in Gemeinschaft sind versammlet gewesen, und haben ein Abend-Essen gehalten, und dabey des Herrn Jesu seinen Befehl in acht genommen, daß sie sich die Füße gewaschen, nach dem Befehl ihres Meisters. Johannes 13, 14. 15. Ja wenn sie das Brod der Gemeinschaft dabey gebrochen, und den Kelch (den Trinkbecher) der Gemeinschaft getrunken, den Tod und das Leiden Jesu verkündiget, seine große Liebe gegen sie gelobet und gepreiset, sich untereinander zum Kreutz und Leiden ermahnet, und ihrem Herrn und Meister nachzufolgen und treu zu bleiben in allen seinen Geboten, und wider alle Sünden bis auf das Blut zu streiten, einander herzlich zu lieben, und im Frieden und Einigkeit beisammen fort zu wandeln, das hat denn geheißen des Herrn Abendmahl, die können sich denn des Herrn Jesu seines Leidens freuen und trösten. Und bilden durch solches Abendmahl ab: Daß sie Hausgenossen und Glieder des Herrn Jesu seyn. Welche denn auch endlich am Ende der Welt mit dem Herrn Jesu das große Abendmahl halten und der ewigen Freuden genießen werden.

Von diesem obbemeldeten Abendmahl saget Paulus: Wer unwürdig von diesem Brod isset, und von dem Kelch des Herrn trinket, der isset und trinket sich selbst das Gericht, darum, daß er nicht unterscheidet den Leib des Herrn. Wo aber ein Morgens- oder Mittagsmahl gehalten wird von solchen Menschen, die nicht wahre Buße gethan, die dem Herrn Jesu in seinen Be-

Lord's supper. 1 Cor. 11: 20. But when believers met in union and love, and had a supper, and were attentive at the same time to the command of washing feet, which Jesus their Master had given them, John 13: 14, 15; and likewise broke the break and drank the cup of communion, and spoke of the sufferings and death of Christ, and praised his great love towards them; exhorted each other to bear the cross, and suffer patiently, to follow their Lord and Master, and be faithful in all his commands, to resist earnestly all sin, to love each other fervently, and to live together in peace, and union;—this alone could be called the Lord's supper, and in this manner they could truly rejoice in the Lord Jesus, and be comforted by his sufferings. And by such a supper, they would represent, that they are of the family of Christ, and members of his body. And then in the end of the world, they will keep with him that great supper, and enjoy eternal felicity.

Of this supper says Paul, ''He that eateth and drinketh unworthily, eateth and drinketh damnation to himself, not discerning the Lord's body.'' But where people eat a breakfast or dinner, who have not truly repented, who do not believe the Lord Jesus in his commandments, and are not baptized upon a true repentance, and a true 'faith, and

welcher in die Vernunft durch den Welt-Geist eingeführet ist, und durch die falsch berühmte Kunst der Gelehrten und ihre vielen vernünftigen Schluß-Reden, und durch die langwierigen Gewohnheiten in denen einfältigen Menschen rest gemachet worden. Daß nun jedermann meynet: Er gehe zu des Herrn Abendmahl, da es doch solches in der That nicht ist.

Sohn. Gehören denn die offenbaren Sünder nicht zu des Herrn Abendmahl?

Von der Absonderung.

Vater. Es gehören solche offenbare Sünder, wann auch nur ein einziges Werk des Fleisches an ihnen offenbar wird (wovon Paulus schreibet: Galat. 5.) nach geschehener Vermahnung und nicht darauf erfolgender Buße oder Besserung, nicht nur nicht zu des Herrn Abendmahl, sondern auch gar nicht in das Reich Gottes, und gehören nicht in die Gemeinde des Herrn! denn wie sie von dem Reiche Gottes durch ihre Sünden ausgeschlossen sind, so müssen sie auch von der Gemeinde des Herrn ausgeschlossen werden.

Sohn. Ey Vater, ich meynte es müßte ein jeder Mensch vor sich selbst Rechenschaft geben, was thäte es mir denn schaden, wenn mein Nebenglied etwas Böses an sich hätte, ich aber wäre für mich fromm, thäte es ihm aber dennoch in der Liebe sagen, er sollte davon abstehen, er aber wollte nicht, so könnte ich ja dennoch in der Liebe mit ihm umgehen, und in seiner Gemeinschaft bleiben, er möchte dann vor sich selber Rechenschaft geben.

Vater. Höre und merke wohl: Es hat zwar solche Vorstellung einen gar guten Schein der Liebe, aber es ist nur eine gefärbte Liebe, und gar nicht die Art der Liebe Gottes! denn die göttliche Liebe muß ja nicht anders gesinnet seyn wie Gott. Ja sie kann auch nicht anders lieben, als so, wie es Gott die ewige Liebe befohlen und geordnet hat: Sie kann nicht anders glauben, als so, wie es Gott die Liebe befohlen hat zu glauben. Die wahre göttli-

established by the supposition of science falsely so called, and by the vain philosophy of the learned, and by long continued practice of the simple men led by those, so that every body now thinks, he is going to the Lord's supper, though indeed such is not the fact.

SON. Are then open sinners not to be permitted to go to the Lord's supper?

OF EXCOMMUNICATION.

FATHER. Such open sinners, though only one single work of the flesh of which Paul writes Gal. 5. becomes manifest in them, after having been admonished, and they have not repented or reformed thereupon, have no right to the Lord's supper, and do not belong at all to the kingdom of God, nor to the church of the Lord. For as they are excluded from the kingdom of God by their sins, they must also be excluded from the church of the Lord.

SON. Why, father, I thought, every man was accountable for himself. What harm then would it do to me, if my fellow-member had done something bad, and I being pious, were to tell him in love that he should abstain from it, but he would not. Might I not still continue to associate with him in love, remain in fellowship with him, and leave him to give his account for himself?

FATHER. Hear and observe well! True, such an idea has a very charitable appearance; but it is only a feigned love, and not at all according to the manner of the love of God. For divine love must not be otherwise minded than God himself. Yea, it can not love in any other manner than God, who is eternal love, has commanded and ordained; it cannot believe otherwise than God, who is love, has commanded to

che Liebe kann und darf auch dem Geist Gottes in Sinn, Weisheit, und Rathgebungen gar nichts vorschreiben. Nun siehet die wahre Liebe Gottes allein auf Gott, ihren ewigen Ursprung. Und der Mensch in welchem die Liebe Gottes wahrhaftig ist, der siehet auf Gott, und lernet von Gott seine Eigenschaft und Natur.

Weilen nun ein wahres Kind Gottes (wegen des Ausschließens wie oben gemeldet) von seinem himmlischen Vater jederzeit eine Scheidung und Absonderung gelernet, nemlich: Zwischen den Reinen und Unreinen, zwischen Licht und Finsterniß, zwischen seinem Volk und den Heiden. Wie dieses an der Schöpfung wohl zu ersehen ist: Als Gott Himmel und Erden geschaffen hat, da war Licht und Finsterniß, Erden und Wasser untereinander. Da scheidete Gott das Licht von der Finsterniß, und nennete das Licht Tag, und die Finsterniß Nacht.

Ferner: Als Gott ein Paradies gepflanzet, und darin allerley Ergötzlichkeit aus Liebe erschaffen, so hat er auch den Menschen aus Liebe nach seinem Bilde erschaffen, und ihn so würdig gemacht, daß er in dem Paradies wandeln durfte, und durfte essen von den Früchten des Paradieses, die ihm Gott geboten hatte. Sobald aber der Mensch seinem Gott ungehorsam wurde, so wurde er unrein, und konnte als ein Unreiner nicht mehr im Paradies bleiben, sondern mußte hinaus, bis er durch Christum den andern Adam gereiniget wurde, da durfte er wieder in das Paradies eingehen, und mußte Adam viel hundert Jahr harren, bis auf Christum den verheißenen Weibes-Saamen, der ihn alsdann wieder in das Paradies einführte, und mit Adam noch viele Heiligen stunden auf, nach der Auferstehung des Herrn Jesu, und er führete sie mit sich in sein Reich. Wie solches zu merken: Matth. 27, 52. Hie kann man sehen, wie die Sünde und der Ungehorsam uns scheidet von Gott und seinem Reich.

believe. True divine love can and dare not dictate to the Spirit of God in mind, wisdom and counsel; but looks alone upon God, as her eternal origin. And the man in whom the love of God truly exists, looks upon God, and learns of God his nature and character.

Now, since a true child of God, concerning excommunication, as above stated has learned of his heavenly Father a distinction and separation between the clean and unclean, between light and darkness, between his own people and the Gentiles. This may be plainly seen in the Creation. When God made the heavens and the earth, light and darkness, earth and water were all mixed together. Then God divided the light from darkness, and called the light day, and darkness night.

Again, when God planted a paradise, and created therein out of love many pleasant things, then he created also out of love man after his own image, and made him worthy to dwell in the paradise, and he was permitted to eat of the fruit of paradise, which God had commanded him. But as soon as man became disobedient to his God, he became unclean, and as such could no longer remain in paradise. Yea, he had to leave it; until he was purified by Christ, the second Adam, he could not re-enter paradise. Thus Adam had to wait many hundred years until Christ, the promised seed of the woman, introduced him again into paradise. And with Adam, many saints rose again, after the resurrection of the Lord Jesus, and he conducted them into his kingdom, as we infer from Matt. 27: 52. Here we may see, how sin and disobedience separate us from God and his kingdom.

Ferner hat Gott dem Abraham als dem Vater aller Gläubigen eine Scheidung und Absonderung in Ansehung der Beschneidung geoffenbaret, daß nemlich sein Saame ein von den Heiden abgesondertes Volk seyn sollte. Welches er denn auch mit mächtiger Hand aus Egypten geführet, und ihnen ein gelobtes Land zu geben verheißen. Welchem Volk Gott der Herr in der Wüsten auf dem Berg Sinai ein sonderliches Gesetz gegeben, wodurch sie gänzlich sollten abgesondert werden nicht allein von den unreinen Heiden, sondern auch von den unreinen Thieren, Fischen und Vögeln, darum hat Gott zu ihnen gesagt, 3 Mos. 20, 24. 25. 26. Ich bin der Herr euer Gott, der euch von den Völkern abgesondert hat, daß ihr euch absondern sollt, das reine Vieh vom Unreinen, und unreine Vögel von den Reinen, und eure Seelen nicht verunreiniget am Vieh, an Vögeln, und an allem, das auf Erden kriechet, das ich euch abgesondert habe, daß es unrein sey, darum sollt ihr mir heilig seyn, denn ich der Herr bin heilig, der euch abgesondert hat von den Völkern, daß ihr mein wäret. Da siehest du, wie Gott seinen Sinn und Willen auch hierin geoffenbaret: In der Absonderung des Reinen von den Unreinen, des Herrn Volk von den Heiden, welche zwar auch Geschöpfe Gottes waren, durften aber kein Theil und Gemeinschaft mit dem Volke Gottes haben.

Sohn. Ja lieber Vater, ich habe wohl von dir verstanden: Die Absonderung unter dem Volke Gottes im Alten Testament unter dem Levitischen Priesterthum, welches solche äußerliche ceremonische Dinge gelehret. Weil aber Christus als ein ewiger hoher Priester, das Gesetz erfüllet, und kein äußerliches Canaan verheißen, sondern ein ewiges Reich, welches geistlich ist verkündiget, darum auch alle seine Gesetze geistlich sind. Wie verstehet man denn nun die Absonderung im Neuen Testament, oder ist auch eine Absonderung nöthig. Davon möchte ich noch wohl gründlich berichtet seyn.

Again God revealed to Abraham, as the father of the faithful, a distinction and separation in the circumcision; that his seed, which he conducted by a mighty hand from Egypt should be a people separate from the heathen, and he promised them a goodly land. To this people the Lord God in the wilderness, upon mount Sinai, gave a peculiar law, by which they were to be kept entirely separate not only from the unclean heathens, but also from unclean beasts, fishes and birds. Therefore God said to them, Lev. 20: 24—26. "I am the Lord your God, who have separated you from other people; you shall therefore, put a difference between clean beasts and unclean, and between unclean fowls and clean; and ye shall not make your souls abominable by beast, or fowl, or by any manner of living thing that creepeth on the ground, which I have separated from you as unclean. And ye shall be holy unto me: for I, the Lord, am holy, and have severed you from other people, that ye should be mine." Observe here, how God revealed his mind and will in the separation of the clean from the unclean, the Lord's people from the heathens, who truly were also the creatures of God, but should have no part or communication with the people of God.

Son. Yes, beloved father, I have indeed understood of thee about the separation among the people of God in the Old Testament, under the Levitical priesthood, where such external ceremonies were taught. But since Christ, the eternal High priest fulfilled the law, and promised no earthly Canaan, but an everlasting kingdom, which is spiritual, as also all his laws are spiritual. How then must we understand separation in the New Testament, or is one necessary? Of this I wish to be more fully informed.

Bater. Höre, merke, und gieb wohl Achtung auf die Reden des Herrn Jesu und seiner Aposteln, so wirst du wohl eine unumgängliche nothwendige Absonderung im neuen Bunde, zwischen Glaubigen und Unglaubigen erkennen. Es redet der Herr Jesus: Matth. 13, 24. daß die gegenwärtige Welt ein Acker sey, auf welchem Gute und Böse gesäet werden: Den guten Saamen säet der Herr Jesus durch sein Evangelium, und das sind die Kinder seines Reichs, die durchs Wort der Wahrheit von oben her geboren werden. Jac. 1, 18. Das Unkraut aber, ist der böse Saame, den säet der Teufel und pflanzet ihn durch sein falsches, kluges, und lügenhaftes Wort, nach menschlicher Weisheit. Nun die Ernde von diesem Saamen, ist das Ende der Welt. Da wird der Herr der Ernde den guten Saamen in seine Scheuern sammlen, das böse Unkraut aber wird er mit ewigem Feuer verbrennen.

Nun merke wohl, wie oben gemeldet von der Absonderung im Alten Testament durch Mosen geboten, welches alles von dem Knecht Mosen geredet worden, zu einem Zeugniß auf den Sohn und seine Haushaltung. Hebr. 3, 5. 6 Gleichwie nun dorten kein Unbeschnittener, kein Aussätziger, keiner, der sich an einem Todten verunreiniget hatte, in den Tempel gehen durften: Eben also hat Jesus der Sohn Gottes, wieder durch seinen Kreuzes-Tod, durch seinen heiligen Geist, einen Tempel, eine Gemeinde und Haushaltung gestiftet und geordnet. Welcher Tempel oder Gemeinde, in heiliger Schrift der Leib des Herrn Jesu genennet wird. Röm 12, 5. 1 Cor. 12, 27. Eph. 1, 22. 23. c. 4, 12. c. 5, 30. Colof. 1, 18.

Zu diesem Leib, Tempel oder Gemeinde, werden alle Glieder Jesu gepflanzet und getaufet, spricht Paulus: 1 Cor. 12, 13. Wir sind durch einen Geist alle zu einem Leibe getauft. Diesen Leib, Tempel, oder Gemeinde, welches alles eines ist, reiniget

FATHER. Hear, mark, and attend well to the discourses of the Lord Jesus and his apostles, for then thou wilt easily discover, how absolutely necessary a separation is in the New Covenant between believers and unbelievers. The Lord Jesus says Matt. 13 : 24, that the present world is a field sown with good and bad seed. The good seed is sown by the Lord Jesus through his Gospel, and these are the children of the kingdom, born from above by the word of truth. James 1 : 18. But the tares are the bad seed, sown and planted by the devil through his false, cunning and lying word, agreeably to human ingenuity. Now the harvest of these is the end of the world. Then the Lord of the harvest will gather the good seed into his garners, but the bad tares he will burn with everlasting fire.

Now, take notice of what has been said above of the separation in the Old Testament, commanded by Moses. This was all said by the servant Moses as a testimony unto the Son, and concerning his economy. Heb. 3 : 5, 6. For just as then, no one uncircumcised, no leprous or unclean person who became unclean by touching a corpse was permitted to enter the temple; even so Jesus the Son of God, has built and established a temple, a church and household by his death on the cross, and by his Spirit. This temple or church in holy writ is called the body of the Lord Jesus. Rom. 12 : 5. 1 Cor. 12 : 27. Eph. 1; 22, 23. 4 : 12. 5; 30. Col. 1: 18.

Into this body, temple or church, all the members of Jesus are planted and baptized, says Paul 1 Cor. 12 : 13. "For by one Spirit are we all baptized into one body." This body, temple or church, which is all one and the same,

Christus als das Oberhaupt, durchs Wasser-Bad im Wort. Eph. 5, 26. Dieser Leib oder Gemeinde ist abgesondert von der Welt, von den Sünden, von allem Irrthum, ja von dem ganzen alten Adams-Haus, verstehe nach dem inwendigen Theil im Glauben.

Diese Gemeinde wird in heil. Schrift genennet: Das auserwählte Geschlecht, das königliche Priesterthum, das heilige Volk, 2c. 1 Petr. 2, 9. Weil nun dieser Leib nach Röm, 6, 2. 4. der Sünden abgestorben, und begraben durch die Taufe in den Tod, und auch wieder auferstanden zu einem neuen Leben in Christo Jesu, und in demselben als eine fruchtbare Rebe bleibet und wächset; doch aber dieser Leib oder die Gemeinde Christi nach dem auswendigen Theil noch in dieser argen Welt, im Stande der Erniedrigung wandelt, so geschiehet es durch göttliche Zulassung, daß der Satan Tag und Nacht um ein jegliches Glied darf herum gehen mit Sünden, und mit mancherley Irrthümer, und allerley bösen und schädlichen Saamen, es in seinem Glauben und Liebe zu prüfen; darum heißet der Herr Jesus und seine Apostel die Gläubigen zu wachen, beten, ringen und kämpfen.

Dennoch aber geschiehet es gar leicht, daß ein solches Glied, so einmal der Sünden abgestorben, und den Herrn Jesum als das neue Leben angezogen hat, wann es nicht beständig im beten und wachen bleibet, wiederum etwa an seinem Neben-Glied, oder gar an den Wegen und Rechten des Herrn sich versündiget. So lehret denn der Herr Jesus, als das wahre Oberhaupt seines Leibes: Matth. 18, 15. Wann dein Bruder sündiget an dir, so strafe ihn zwischen dir und ihm allein. Höret er dich, so hast du deinen Bruder gewonnen. Höret er dich nicht, so nimm noch einen oder zween zu dir, auf daß alle Sache bestehe in zweier oder dreier Zeugen

is sanctified and cleansed by Christ, who is the head, "with the washing of water, by the word. Eph. 5 : 26. This body or church is separated from the world, from sin, from all error, in a word from the whole house of old Adam, understand, according to the inward part in faith.

This church is called in holy writ, "the chosen generation, the royal priesthood, the holy nation &c. 1 Pet. 2 : 9. Now as this body according to Rom. 6 : 2, 4. is dead to sin, and buried by baptism into death, and raised again to a newness of life in Christ Jesus, and abideth and groweth in the same as a fruitful branch; yet this body or the church of Christ is still walking outwardly in this evil world, in a state of humiliation. Hence it happens by divine permission, that Satan goes about every member day and night tempting him with sins, and with manifold errors, and with all kinds of bad and pernicious seed, to try him in his faith and love. Therefore the Lord Jesus and his apostles call upon the faithful to watch and pray, to wrestle and to strive.

Nevertheless, it will come to pass very easily with such a member, who has once died unto sin, and put on the Lord Jesus in newness of life, if he is not constantly engaged in watching and prayer, that he may again offend, perhaps, against his fellow-member, or even against the ways and statutes of the Lord. Concerning such then, the Lord Jesus, as the true head of his body, teaches, Matt. 18 : 15. "If thy brother shall trespass against thee, go and tell him his fault between thee and him alone: if he shall hear thee, thou hast gained thy brother. But if he will not hear thee, then take with

Munde. Höret er die nicht, so sage es der Gemeinde; höret er die Gemeinde nicht, so halte ihn als einen Heiden und Zöllner.

Siehe, hier siehest du nun, wer der Stifter ist der Absonderung und des Bannes im Neuen Testament, nemlich: Der Herr Jesus, der wahre Hausvater; dieses ist nun eine Absonderung über solche Sünder, deren Sünden ohne die Absonderung können vergeben werden, wann nemlich der Sünder hören will: Höret er aber nicht, so wird er nicht um der Sünde willen abgesondert, sondern um seines verstockten und hochmüthigen Herzens willen. Weil er den Rath des Geistes Gottes verwirft, eine ganze Gemeinde betrübet und verachtet, da er doch verpflichtet wäre, aus Liebe zu sterben für seine Mitglieder eher als sie zu betrüben, und ihren guten Rath zu verachten.

Von solchen frevelhaften Menschen hat auch schon das Gesetz geredet. 4 Mos. 19, 13. "Wann jemand einen todten Menschen anrühret, (welches eine geringe Sache ist) und sich nicht wieder reinigen wollte, der verunreiniget die Wohnung des Herrn, und solche Seele soll ausgerottet werden aus Israel, 2c. Was nun im Gesetz das Spreng-Wasser war, wodurch die Unreinen gereiniget wurden, das ist im neuen Bunde, die brüderliche Bestrafung.

Wenn nun ein Glied sündiget, und thut todte Werke der Sünden und verachtet die brüderliche Bestrafung, so hat schon die Betrüglichkeit der Sünden ein solches Herz verstocket. Wie Paulus saget, Hebr. 3, 13. und die Gläubigen vermahnet: "Sehet zu, daß nicht jemand unter euch verstocket werde durch Betrug der Sünde; denn wir sind Christi theilhaftig worden, so wir anders das angefangene Wesen bis ans Ende fest behalten." Das ist: wir sind des neuen Lebens aus Christo Jesu

thee one or two more, that in the mouth of two or three witnesses every word may be established. And if he shall neglect to hear them, tell it unto the church : but if he neglect to hear the church, let him be unto thee as an heathen man and a publican."

Behold, and see here, who has ordained separation and excommunication in the New Testament, namely the Lord Jesus, the true father of the house.

Now this is a separation of such sinners, whose sins may be forgiven without their being disowned, namely, if they will hear. But if they will not hear, they are disowned, not on account of their sin, but for their pride and obstinacy; because they reject the counsel of God's Spirit, despise and grieve the whole church, while it would have been their duty rather to die for their fellow-members, than to grieve them and despise their good counsel.

Of such frivolous persons, notice was taken already in the Law. Numb. 19 : 13. "Whosoever toucheth the dead body of a man, (which in itself is of no great consequence,) and purifieth not himself, defileth the tabernacle of the Lord; and that soul shall be cut off from Israel, &c." Now, what in the Law was the water of separation, by which the unclean were made clean, that is in the New Testament the brotherly admonition.

Now if a member trespasses, and touches a dead work of sin, and despises brotherly admonition, his heart is already hardened by the deceitfulness of sin. Hence Paul exhorts the faithful, Heb. 3 : 13; "Take heed, lest any of you be hardened through the deceitfulness of sin. For we are made partakers of Christ, if we hold the beginning of our confidence steadfast unto the end." That is, we are become partakers of a new life from Christ Jesus. Therefore,

theilhaftig worden. Lasset uns auch nur beständig drinnen bleiben bis an das Ende, und ja nicht durch das alte sündliche Leben wieder abtreten von dem wahrhaftigen Leben in Christo, und von dem lebendigen Gott.

Sohn. Wann nun ein Mensch wegen einer geringen Sünde (die leicht könnt vergeben werden, so er höret,) aus des Herrn Leib und Gemeinde, ja gar aus dem ewigen Reich Gottes kann ausgebannet werden. Wie gehet es denn, wenn ein Glied eine vorsetzliche wissentliche Sünde thut, eine Lügen, und dergleichen, ja gar wider des Herrn Recht und Gesetze streitet?

Vater. Merke wohl den Sinn des Geistes Gottes in allen Dingen. Der ist der beste Rathgeber, der hat alles zuvor gewußt, und darum alles in seiner Haushaltung sehr weißlich geordnet. Gott hat schon im Gesetz befohlen: 4 Mos. 15, 27. 30. "Wann eine Seele oder eine ganze Gemeinde unwissend sündiget an einem Gebot des Herrn, so soll sie dafür Opfer bringen dem Herrn, und die Sünde soll vergeben werden. Wenn aber eine Seele aus Frevel sündiget an des Herrn Gebot und Ordnung, dafür ist kein Opfer, sondern eine solche Seele soll schlecht ausgerottet werden, die Schuld soll auf ihr seyn, denn sie hat des Herrn Wort verachtet, und seine Gebote fahren lassen."

Ja wenn eine ganze Gemeinde oder Stadt also sündigen würde, und andern Göttern dienen, das ist: Solche Dinge thun, die ihr Herr und Gott ihnen verboten hat, so soll solche ganze Stadt verbannet seyn. 5 Mos. 13, 12. Nun siehe, wie dieses nach dem Geist im Neuen Testament unter des Herrn Gemeinde muß in acht genommen werden, damit die Pforten der Höllen, welches die Sünde ist, sie nicht möge überwältigen. Nun weiß ein jegliches Glied an dem Leibe Jesu gar wohl, daß es durch die Taufe in den Tod begraben

let us remain constant therein until the end, and by no means go away again from the true life in Christ, and from the living God, through the old life of sin.

Son. If now a person may be excluded from the Lord's body and church, yea, even from the everlasting kingdom of God for a small sin, (which could easily be forgiven, if he would hear;) how will it be, if a member commits a wilful, known sin, a lie, an the like, yea even contends against the statutes and Laws of the Lord?

Father. Attend well in all cases to the mind of the Spirit of God. He is the best counselor, who has forseen every thing, and therefore has ordained every thing very wisely. God has commanded in the law, Numb. 15 : 27, 30. "If any soul, or a whole congregation sin through ignorance, then he shall bring unto the Lord a sin-offering, and the sin shall be forgiven him. But the soul that doth ought presumptuously against the Lord's commands and ordinances, for such there is no sacrifice, but such a soul shall be cut off; his iniquity shall be upon him, for he despised the word of the Lord, and let slip his commandments."

Yea, if a whole congregation or city should thus sin, and serve other gods, that is, do such things, which the Lord their God had forbidden them, the whole city shall be utterly destroyed. Deut. 13 : 12. Now behold, how this, according to the Spirit in the New Testament, must be observed in the Lord's church, so that the gates of hell, which are sin, may not prevail against it. Now every member in the body of the Lord knows full well, that he is buried by baptism into death, Rom. 6 : 4. and

ist. Röm. 6. Und daß es in einem neuen Leben wandeln soll. Es wird ihm auch bey seiner Tauf vorgehalten, allen Sünden und dem Teufel ganz abzusagen, sammt seinem eigenen Willen, und daß es dem Herrn Jesu unter allem Kreuz beständig in allen seinen Befehlen müßte gehorsam nachfolgen, bis in den Tod hinein.

Nun sind ja die Werke des Fleisches offenbar, nach dem Zeugniß Gal. 5, 19. Als da ist: "Ehebruch, Hurerey, Unzucht, Unreinigkeit, Abgötterey, Zauberey, Feindschaft, Hader, Neid, Zorn, Zank, Zwietracht, Rotten, Haß, Mord, Saufen, Fressen und dergl." Allen solchen Menschen ist das Reich Gottes durch den Heil. Geist ganz und gar abgesprochen, wenn nemlich ein einziges von diesen bösen Werken in einem Glied herrschend wird.

Wenn nun an dem Leibe des Herrn an einem Glied ein solches Werk offenbar wird, daß es die Gemeinde wohl erkennen kann, so muß ja billig ein solches Glied aus der Gemeinde gethan werden, nach 1 Corinth. 5, 13. bis es durch wahre Reu und Buße wieder davon gereiniget wird, und also nicht der ganze Leib oder Gemeinde dadurch versäuret oder verunreiniget werde. Wie böß und verdorben muß nun ein solches Glied worden seyn, wenn es noch mit den Werken des Fleisches wollte Recht haben.

Sohn. Ich merke wohl hierinnen den Sinn Gottes. Aber das Werk Zwietracht kann ich noch nicht recht erkennen, was dieses sey, möchte es also gerne wissen?

Von Uneinigkeiten.

Vater. Es ist ein solcher Geist, welcher denen Menschen, so noch nicht genugsam erleuchtet seyn in den Wegen des Herrn, begegnet, gleichwie die Schlange im Paradies der Eva begegnet ist, die gesprochen: Ihr werdet nicht sterben, sondern eure Augen werden aufgethan werden, und

that he should walk in newness of life. He has also been required at his baptism to renounce all sin, the devil and his own (corrupt) will, and that he must obediently follow the Lord Jesus under all crosses, and constantly in all his commandments, even unto death.

Now the works of the flesh are indeed manifest, according to the testimony, Gal. 5 : 19. They are 'adultery, fornication, uncleanness, lasciviousness. idolatry, witchcraft, hatred, variance, emulations, wrath, strife, discord, heresies, envyings, murders, drunkenness, revellings and such like. To all such the kingdom of God is utterly denied by the holy Spirit; that is, in case if any one of these evil works should become manifest in a member.

Now, if in the body of the Lord, any member should actually manifest such a work, so that the church is enabled to discern it clearly, then such a member must necessarily be separated from the church according to 1 Cor. 5 : 13. until he shall be purified again by a true repentance and reformation, in order that the whole body or church may not be leavened or contaminated thereby. How evil and corrupt must such a member have become, if he would justify himself in doing the works of the flesh.

SON. I seem to understand the mind of God in this. But what is meant by discord, I cannot rightly apprehend, and therefore I would like to know?

OF DISSENSIONS (OR SCHISMS.)

FATHER. This is such a spirit meeting those, who are not yet sufficiently enlightened in the ways of the Lord, like the serpent meeting Eve in Paradise, saying, 'ye shall not surely die; for your eyes shall be opened, and ye shall be as gods, knowing good and

werdet seyn wie Gott, und erkennen, was gut und bös ist, wenn ihr von der verbotenen Frucht essen werdet. Welches auch zum Theil geschehen: Nemlich, so bald sie gegessen hatten, sind ihrer beyder Augen geöffnet worden, daß sie gesehen haben, daß sie nackend seyen. Darum rufet Paulus den Corinthern zu: Ich fürchte, daß nicht wie die Schlange Eva verführete mit ihrer Schalkheit, also auch eure Sinne verrücket werden von der Einfältigkeit in Christo. 2 Cor. 11, 3. So lange nun ein gläubiges Glied Jesu in diesem Streit bleibet, daß es alle seine Vernunft unter den Gehorsam des Herrn Jesu gefangen nimmt, und verstöret alle Höhe und Anschläge, die sich in der Vernunft erheben wider das göttliche Erkenntniß. 2 Cor. 10, 5. So lange kann solcher fleischlicher Geist des Zwietrachts die Seele nicht gefangen nehmen. Sondern der Mensch wandelt in der Einfalt, im Gehorsam des Glaubens im Frieden und in der Einigkeit mit seinen Mitgliedern. Was er nicht verstehet, das lässet er im Frieden und in der Einfalt williglich seinen Mitgliedern über, und demüthiget sich unter seine Mitglieder, nach dem Rath Petri. 1 Petr. 5, 5.

Sobald aber dieser Geist, nemlich der Geist des Zwietrachts, Meister wird bey denen, die ihn nicht kennen, so wird der Mensch innerlich nach und nach von dem Frieden und der Liebe gegen seine Mitglieder getrennet, gehet in Aergerniß, bald gegen dieses und jenes, und verlieret nach und nach die wahre Kraft des Glaubens! Es werden ihme auch die Versammlungen seiner Mitglieder, womit er sich billig erbauen sollte, zu einer Last. Wenn man nun solches merket und er in Liebe darüber gefraget wird, so kann er leichter ein eiteles unerbauliches Gespräch anhören, als die Liebes-Anredung seiner Mitglieder, die solches wohl merken und gewahr werden.

evil," if ye will eat of the forbidden fruit. This in part so happened, for as soon as they had eaten thereof, their eyes were opened, and they knew, that they were naked.

Hence, Paul says to the Corinthians, 'But I fear, lest by any means, as the serpent beguiled Eve through his subtilty, so your minds should be corrupted from the simplicity that is in Christ." 2 Cor. 11 : 3. As long therefore as a faithful member of Jesus continues in this conflict, 'bringing into captivity every thought to the obedience of Christ, and casting down imaginations, and every high thing that exalteth itself against the knowledge of God," 2 Cor. 10 : 5—so long the fleshly spirit of discord cannot bring the soul into captivity; but the member walketh in simplicity, in obedience of faith, in peace and union with his fellow-members. What he does not understand, he leaves willingly, simply and peacefully to them, and humbly submits himself unto these his fellow-members, according to the advice of Peter 1 Ep. 5 : 5.

'But as soon as this spirit, i. e. the spirit of discord, obtains the mastery over those that know him not, they inwardly and gradually are separated from the peace and love toward their fellow-members; they take offence now against one, and then against another, and lose by degrees the true power of faith. To them even the religious meetings of their fellow-members, which should be to their edification, become burdensome. If this is observed, and they are questioned on the subject in love, it seems to be more easy for them to listen to a vain, trifling conversation, than to the affectionate address of their fellow-members, who notice and discern their coldness.

Wenn nun der Mensch nicht hören will die Liebes-Zurufungen seiner Mitglieder, sondern er höret den falsch betrüglichen Geist, der sich als ein Engel des Lichtes verstellet, und solche Seele so klug und weiß machet, daß sie auf alle Fehler ihrer Mitglieder genau siehet, sich daran stößet und ärgert, und fänget darnach an, dieselbe zu tadeln nebst der ganzen Gemeinde, und arbeitet ein solcher Geist der Zertrennung stets dahin, durch solches Glied alle Glieder an der Gemeinde in die Zerreißung zu bringen, alle Ordnung aufzuheben, und vor sich ein eigener Herr zu seyn; bekommt auch gemeiniglich einen Anhang. Und solches wird von dem Geist Gottes Zwietracht und Rotten genennet.

Und ist ein offenbares Werk des Fleisches, und gehöret nicht ins Reich Gottes, auch nicht in die Gemeinde des Herrn, sondern in des alten Adams Haus und Reich, welches lauter Zertrennung ist und darum nicht bestehen wird, sondern fallen muß, denn Zertrennung ist jederzeit ein Anfang alles Uebels gewesen, und kann, wo Zertrennung ist, keine irdische, noch vielweniger eine göttliche Haushaltung im Segen bestehen.

Darum müssen solche Geister bei den wahren Gläubigen in sich, und auch solche Menschen äußerlich gemeidet werden, welche auf solche und andere Art Aergerniß und Zertrennung anrichten. Wie Paulus dazu vermahnet Röm. 16, 17. das ist ein solches Werk des Fleisches, und ein fleischlicher Sinn, und fleischlicher Mensch, wenn er schon in einer englischen Demuth sich äußerlich im Schein verstellen thäte. Wie Paulus auch solche Menschen nennet und meinet: Col. 2, 18. Ja er nennet es eine Ketzerey, welche man meiden soll. Tit. 3, 10.

Fr. Was für Menschen würdig seyn, die Ordnung des Banns zu führen.

Sohn. Ich habe wohl verstanden den Geist des Zwietrachts, und derer die

---

Now if they will not hear the loving admonitions of their brethren, but rather give ear to that false and deceitful spirit, who transforms himself into an angel of light, and causes such members to think themselves very wise and discreet, so that they look with scrutinizing eyes upon all faults of their fellow-members, stumble and are offended at them, commencing to censure them and the whole church. Such a spirit labors constantly to the end, to bring about by these members a total rending apart of all the members in the church, to abolish all order, and to rule by his own authority; and he frequently succeeds to find some adherents. This is called by the Spirit of God "seditions and heresies."

Such is a manifest work of the flesh, not belonging to the kingdom of God, nor to the church of the Lord, but to the kingdom and house of old Adam, which is all division, and therefore cannot stand, but must fall. Disunion has been at all times the beginning of every evil, and wherever it exists, there no earthly house and family, much less a divine economy, can prosper.

Hence true believers must avoid such a spirit in themselves, and also put in avoidance outwardly such persons, who in this or any other manner cause offence and division, as also Paul admonishes, Rom. 16 : 17. They are works of the flesh, proceeding from a carnal mind, even though such a carnal person would appear in a voluntary, angelic humility. Col. 2 : 18. Paul also calls such, "heresies," who are to be rejected. Tit. 3 : 10.

QUERY. *What kind of men are qualified to conduct the office of excommunication?*

SON. What was said of the spirit of discord, and of those, who are to be

man meiden soll; Aber lieber Vater ich bitte dich, sage mir doch was müssen das für Menschen seyn, die solche Ordnung des Bannes treiben und führen, denn wir fehlen ja alle mannigfaltig, und mangeln des Ruhms, und wer nicht an einem Worte fehlet, sagt Jacobus, der ist ein vollkommener Mann. So wir nun alle fehlen, welche sollen denn die andern um ihrer oder andern Sünden willen meiden?

Vater. Es ist gar gut, daß du mich in allem fragest, damit du in keinem Ding unwissend bleibest, welches ein großer Schaden der Seelen ist. So merke nun wohl, und gieb Achtung: Vors erste, wird keinem andern Menschen die Seligkeit verheißen, als nur allein den Glaubigen. Die nun glauben an den Sohn GOttes, die sollen ein ewiges Leben haben. Welche aber nicht glauben, über denen wird der Zorn GOttes bleiben.

Nun merke die Art und Eigenschaft des Glaubens, wie es JEsus der Sohn GOttes ausgesprochen hat, Marc. 16, 17. Da saget der HErr JEsus zu seinen Jüngern: "Das werden die Zeichen seyn denen die an mich glauben: Sie werden in meinem Namen, (das ist: in seiner Lehr, Wort, und Geboten) Teufel austreiben," erstlich aus sich, und denn auch aus andern, die an ihn glauben und durch ihr Wort an Christum glaubig werden. "Sie werden mit neuen Zungen reden, Schlangen vertreiben, und so sie was tödliches trinken, wirds ihnen nicht schaden, sie werden auf die Kranken die Hände legen, so wird es besser mit ihnen werden."

Solchen Glaubigen ist ein ewiges Leben verheißen, und solchen Glaubigen ist von Christo befohlen: Die sündliche, ärgerliche, eigenliebige Geister zu vertreiben, aus ihrer Gemeinschaft auszuschließen; und was solche Glaubige auf Erden binden, das wird ganz gewiß auch im Himmel gebunden seyn, und was sie auf Erden lösen, das wird auch im Himmel loß seyn.

avoided, I have well understood. But, dear father, I beg you to tell me, what kind of men they must be, who are to conduct and execute such office of excommunication. For we all are liable to faults, and have come short of the glory of God, and James says, "If any man offend not in word, the same is a perfect man." Now since we all have come short, who then shall avoid others on account of their own sin, or that of others?

FATHER. It is indeed well that thou inquirest of me concerning every thing, so that thou mayest not remain ignorant in any thing, for ignorance is a great disadvantage to the soul. Therefore take notice, carefully. First there is no promise of salvation to any man but the believer. 'Whosoever believes in the Son of God, shall have eternal life; but they that believe not, will remain under the wrath of God, or it abideth on them.'

Now observe the nature and quality of faith as pronounced by Jesus, the Son of God. Mark 16 : 17. Here the Lord Jesus says to his disciples, 'And these signs shall follow them that believe in my name, i. e. in his doctrine, word and commandments. 'They shall cast out devils;" first out of themselves, and then also out of others who believe in him, and by their word are converted. 'They shall speak with new tongues, and take up serpents, and if they drink any deadly thing, it shall not hurt them: they shall lay hands on the sick, and they shall recover." To such believers eternal life is promised, and to such believers it is commanded by Christ, to exclude from their communion all sinful, offensive and self-loving spirits; and what they bind on earth, that will most certainly be bound in heaven, and what they shall loose on earth, shall be loosed also in heaven.

Solche Gläubigen führen ihres Königes Rechte und Ordnungen seines Hauses, und wandeln unter vielen Anfechtungen, durch eine große Freudigkeit des Glaubens, nach der Regel ihres HErrn und Meisters, und wann sie schon als Boßhaftige von denen Menschen darüber verworfen werden. Und obgleich solche glaubige Glieder JEsu durch eine Uebereilung auch fehlen und sündigen, so thun sie es ja nicht mit Vorsatz, sondern es ist ihnen von Herzen leid. Sie sind solche, die Leid tragen über ihre Schwachheit. Und wenn sie durch ihre Mitglieder erinnert werden, so hören sie gar gerne, lassen sich sagen wo sie fehlen, und seyn solche wovon Johannes spricht: "Meine Kindlein ob jemand sündiget, so haben wir einen Fürsprecher bey dem Vater, JEsum Christum, der gerecht ist." 1 Joh. 2, 1.

Und solche stehen in sich durch den Glauben in einem beständigen Kampf und Streit wider die Sünde, und tödten stets in sich die sündliche Glieder, die auf Erden sind, ja sie wollten lieber aus des HErrn Gemeinde seyn, als sündigen, und nicht abstehen wenn sie bestraft werden. Und solche Glaubige können dann mit einem guten Gewissen auch ihre allerliebste Mitglieder ausschließen helfen, und sie meiden, wenn sie sündigen und die Liebes-Bestrafung nicht mehr hören wollen, weil sie in sich selbst einen solchen Sinn und Geist schon verworfen und ausgebannet haben.

Und diese Glaubigen können auch in der Gewißheit des Glaubens sagen, was Johannes sagt: 1 Joh. 4, 6. "Wir sind von GOtt, und wer GOtt erkennet, der höret uns, wer GOtt nicht erkennet, der höret uns nicht, daran erkennen wir den Geist der Wahrheit und den Geist des Irrthums." Solche Glieder können denn mit gar gutem Gewissen ein solches Glied welches sich nicht mehr in der Liebe will bestrafen und erbauen lassen, von sich absondern, denn wann ein Glied sündiget und

Such believers carry into effect the statutes and ordinances of the house of their King, and walk under many tribulations in great cheerfulness of faith, according to the rule of their Lord and Master, though they are rejected of men as evil doers. And though such believing members of Jesus should be overtaken by a fault or sin, they do it not designedly, and are truly sorry for it in their heart. They are such who mourn over their frailty. And if they are reminded of it by their fellow-members, they hear it very willingly, when they are told of their fault. They are such of whom John says, 'My little children, if any man sin, we have an advocate with the Father, Jesus Christ the righteous." 1 John 2: 1.

Such stand by faith in a continual war and combat against sin, and constantly mortify the sinful members, which are of the earth; they would even rather be excluded from the church of the Lord, than sin, and will not resist, when they are rebuked. Such believers then can assist with a good conscience in excommunicating and withdrawing from their most beloved fellow-members, when they do commit sin, and and will not hear any more the reproof of love, because they have already banished and rejected the mind of the Spirit.

Such believers, in assurance of faith' can say with John, 1 John 4: 6. 'We are of God: he that knoweth God, heareth us; he that is not of God, heareth not us. Hereby know we the Spirit of truth, and the spirit of error." Thus, with a very good conscience, can they separate from their communion such a member, that will not receive correction or reproof in love. For if a member transgresses, and will not hear; then it is a sin unto death, for

nicht mehr höret, so ist "solche Sünde zum Tode," wovor man nicht bitten kann. Wie Johannes meldet, 1 Joh. 5, 16.

Da siehest du nun den großen Unterschied im sündigen: Denn es könnten zwei Menschen einerlei Sünden thun, der eine könnte verloren werden, der andere könnte zu Gnaden kommen, wie du solches an denen Uebelthätern die mit Jesu gekreutziget wurden, sehen kannst. Denn es kam der eine mit Jesu ins Paradies, weil er seine Sünde erkennete, und an den Herrn Jesum glaubete. So kann es eben seyn unter einer Gemeinde, daß zwei Glieder einerlei Sünde thun, das eine höret und lässet ihm seine Sünde leid seyn, so wird ihm alles vergeben; das andere kann die Liebes-Bestrafungen nicht hören, und sich in Hochmuth und Eigenheit setzen, und verloren werden. Es ist ein großer Unterschied unter den Sünden, darum auch David gesprochen: "Wohl dem Menschen, dem der Herr die Missethat nicht zurechnet, in deß Geist kein Falsch ist." Ps. 32, 2.

Das sind eben die aufrichtigen Seelen, die da Leide tragen, wenn sie etwa übereilt worden sind, und gefehlet haben, hören aber gar gerne die Liebes-Bestrafungen ihrer Mitglieder. Von denen alleine saget Jacobus: "Wir fehlen alle mannigfaltig." Jac. 3, 2. Sind aber dennoch in Christo Jesu, und ist nichts verdammliches an ihnen. Röm. 8, 1. Denn sie wandeln nicht nach dem Fleisch, sondern nach dem Geist. v. 4. Die können auch nicht zur Verdammniß sündigen, denn sie sind aus Gott geboren, und der göttliche Saame erhält sie. 1 Joh. 3, 9.

Diese sind der gesegnete Weibessaamen, welche in einem täglichen Streit wider die Sünde als des Teufels Saamen liegen, und ist zwischen ihnen und der Schlangensaamen eine beständige Feindschaft, müssen auch ihre Fersenstiche fühlen, ob ihr schon der Kopf, das ist die Herrschaft, zertreten

which we are not commanded to pray, 1 John 5 : 16.

There we may see the great difference in sin; for there might be two persons committing the same sin, and the one may be lost, while the other finds grace, as thou canst see in the case of the two malefactors, who were crucified with Jesus. The one entered with Jesus into Paradise, because he acknowledged his sins, and believed in the Lord Jesus. The same may be the case in a church, where two members sin alike. The one hears, is sorry for his sins, and all is forgiven to him. The other, not able to bear correction in love, becomes hardened in pride and self-love, and will be lost. There is a great difference in sins, therefore David said, "Blessed is the man unto whom the Lord imputeth not iniquity, and in whose spirit there is no guile." Psalms 32 : 2.

These are the upright souls, who mourn, when they have been overtaken in committing a fault, but bear most willingly the loving admonitions of their fellow members. Of such alone James speaks, 'For in many things we offend all." James 3 : 2. And Paul says, 'There is therefore now no condemnation to them which are in Christ Jesus, who walk not after the flesh, but after the spirit.' Rom. 8 : 1, 4. Such cannot sin unto condemnation, for they are born of God, and the Divine seed preserves them. 1 John 3 : 9.

These are of the blessed seed of the woman, who are in daily warfare against sin, as the seed of the devil; and there is between them and the seed of the serpent, continual enmity. They must still feel its bruises in their heels, although its head, that is, its dominion,

und genommen ist. Darum werden die Gläubigen, so lange sie im Stande der Erniedrigung leben, die streitende Kirche genennet. Aber sie überwinden durch des Lammes Blut. Apoc. 12, 11.

Sohn. Ich habe nun ein wenig den Unterschied unter den Sünden verstanden, wie auch die Meidung und deren Ursachen; aber ich habe von etlichen, wenn sie in der Meidung sind, sagen hören: Es wäre ihnen gar wohl, sie fühlten keinen Bann. Auch von andern hab ich gehöret, der Bann hätte ja keine Kraft und Wirkung, weilen die, die darinnen sind, es nicht fühleten, sondern sprechen: Sie wären gutes Muths.

Vater. Merke auch hierin wiederum den Sinn Gottes, so wirst du wohl sehen, wie solche arme Seelen, die sich und ihren Gott nicht kennen, von der Schlangen List betrogen werden. Denn siehe: Wenn sie anfänglich über ihre Sünde Buße thun, und der Lehre Jesu glauben, so gehen sie ja durch den Glauben in die Gemeinde und göttliche Ordnungen ein, u. helfen selbsten durch den Glauben eine Zeitlang den Bann führen, und glauben: Was des Herrn Gemeinde bindet auf Erden, das wird auch im Himmel gebunden seyn.

Weil aber solche arme Seelen nicht über den Glauben kämpfen wollen, nach dem Rath des Apostels Judá v. 3., sondern treten wieder ab vom Glauben, und hängen sich in ihrem Gemüth an die verführischen Geister, welche sie für gute Engel ansehen, wie Paulus klar davon schreibet, 1 Tim. 4, 1. Und geben solchen Geistern Gehör, welche ihnen lauter Gutes verheissen, und lauter Freiheit predigen. Wie auch schon der Apostel Petrus hiervon geschrieben: 2 Pet. 2, 18. 19.

Wenn nun solche arme Seelen vom Glauben abgetreten, so bekommen sie zwar Brandmahle in ihrem Gewissen, weil sie aber den Glauben verlassen, so fühlen sie den Bann nicht, bis an den Tag der Of=

is trod down and broken. Hence the faithful, as long as they live in the state of humiliation, are called the church militant; but they shall overcome through the blood of the Lamb. Rev. 12 : 11.

Son. I have now understood a little of the difference in sins, as also of avoidance and its causes. But I have heard some, who are in avoidance, to say, they were quite at ease, and did not feel any ban. Again, of others I heard, that the ban (avoidance) had no power and effect, because those, who were in that state, did not feel it, but would say, they were in good spirits.

Father. Observe also in this again the mind of God, and thou shalt easily see, how such poor souls, who know not themselves nor their God, are deceived by the subtlety of the serpent. For behold, when at first they repent for their sins, and believe the doctrine of Jesus, they enter by faith into the church and the divine ordinances, and by faith themselves assist for a time in carrying out the ban, believing that what the church of the Lord will bind on earth, "shall also be bound in heaven."

But since such poor souls will not contend for the faith according to the advice of the apostle, Jude 3; but depart again from it, and in their minds give heed to seducing spirits, whom they take for good angels, as Paul clearly writes, 1 Tim. 4 : 1; and give ear to such spirits, who promise them nothing but good, and preach to them nothing but liberty, &c. as Peter wrote to the believers, 2 Pet. 2 : 18, 19.

Now when these poor souls have apostatized from the faith, their conscience becoming seared as with an hot iron on account of their departing from the faith, they do not feel the anath-

fenbarung; Ja sie können zu des Herrn Gemeinde stolziglich sprechen: Ihr möget mich ausbannen wie ihr wollet, ich will doch bei Gott in Gnaden kommen. Die andern aber, die um der Sünden willen in den Bann gethan werden, und nicht von dem Glauben abtreten, die fühlen den Bann wohl, und thun Buße und gehen wieder ein durch den Glauben.

Nun merke aber, die große Blindheit derer Menschen, die deffentwegen eine Gemeinde tadeln, weilen diejenigen so von ihrem Glauben abtreten, wie oben gemeldet, sagen: Sie fühlten keinen Bann, sondern könnten noch wider des Herrn Gemeinde streiten. So merke, daß Gott selbsten mit den allermeisten Menschen einen solchen Bann führet; denn alle unwiedergeborne Menschen liegen unter dem Zorn Gottes, und wartet auf sie mit ewiger Verdammniß, wenn sie nicht wahre Buße thun und durch den Glauben an Jesum wiedergeboren werden, nach dem Willen Gottes zu leben.

Nun sehe man diese Menschen an: Sie sind lustig und fröhlich, haben in ihnen eine Hoffnung zur Seligkeit, welche Hoffnung durch das falsche Evangelium in sie gepflanzet ist, und sind solche Art Menschen wovon der Herr Jesus spricht: Matth. 24, 38. 39. "Wie sie waren in den Tagen vor der Sündfluth: Sie aßen, sie tranken, ic. sie waren fröhlich, bis die Sündfluth kam, und nahm sie alle dahin.' Sie haben den Noa predigen und den Kasten bauen lassen, und ihn dabei verspottet, und nicht geglaubet.

Eben so werden die Menschen seyn, in den Tagen, wenn des Menschen Sohn soll offenbaret werden. Sie werdens nicht glauben daß es mit ihnen so übel stehet, darum haben sie auch kein Gefühl in ihnen von dem göttlichen Bann der schon auf ihnen lieget, denn der Unglaube hat ihre Herzen verstocket und hart gemacht, wie des Lots Weib, die zu einer harten Salz-

ema until the day of revelation. Such can even proudly say to the church of the Lord, "ye may excommunicate me as you please, but I shall still find grace before God." Those others however, who are excommunicated for their sins, but do not depart from the faith,— such feel the power of the ban well, and therefore repent, and are restored again by faith.

Consider then the great blindness of those, who still find fault with a church, because such, as become apostates from their faith, as stated above, say, that they felt no ban, and could even contend against the church of the Lord. For remember, God himself carries out such a ban with the greater part of mankind. All unregenerated men are under the wrath of God, waiting on them with everlasting condemnation, unless they repent truly, and by faith in Jesus are born again to live according to the will of God.

Now if we look upon these men, we see, they are merry and cheerful, and have even a hope of salvation, which hope however is planted into them by a false Gospel. They are such of whom Jesus says, Matt. 24: 38, 39; "For as in the days, that were before the flood, they were eating and drinking &c., in a word, they were rejoicing until the flood came and took them all away." They cared nothing for Noah's preaching, and his building the ark, but mocked him and did not believe.

Even so will it be with mankind in the days of the coming of the Son of man. They will not believe their condition to be so bad, because they have no feeling in them of the divine ban that rests already upon them, for unbelief has hardened their hearts. Even as Lot's wife, who became a s a hard pillar of salt, so likewise the poor souls,

Seule worden. Eben also auch die armen Seelen, die einmal aus dem sündlichen Sodom ausgegangen sind, und auf dem Wege wieder zurücksehen, die werden solche Salz=Seulen, die dem Evangelio nicht mehr glauben.

Der Apostel Petrus saget: "Es wäre solchen Seelen besser daß sie den Weg der Wahrheit nicht erkennet hätten, denn daß sie ihn erkennen, und sich kehren von dem heiligen Gebot das ihnen gegeben ist." 2 Pet. 2, 21. Darum rufet der Herr Jesus seinen Nachfolgern mit einer starken Stimme also zu: "Gedenket an des Lots Weib." Luc. 17, 32.

Ja wenn man ferner die Engel betrachtet, die gesündiget haben, die hat Gott ausgebannet, und mit Ketten der Finsterniß zur Höllen verstoßen, und übergeben, daß sie zum Gericht behalten werden." 2 Pet. 2, 4. Nun siehe, wie halten sich diese ausgebannete Engel? Sie streiten eben auch wider die guten Engel; wie zu sehen in dem Brief Judä v. 9. und Offenb. 12, 7. Ja merke den Streit mit dem Satan, und mit dem Herrn Jesu selbsten. Matth. 4.

Hier könnten nun solche arme und blinde Menschen auch zu Gott sagen: Daß sein Bann keine Wirkung hätte; dürfen die von Gott ausgebannete Engel noch wider die guten Engel streiten, so wundere du dich nicht mehr, wenn die ausgebannete Menschen, welche vom Glauben abgetreten, und solchen verbanneten Geistern anhangen, noch gegen die Gläubigen streiten können, und ihnen viele Mühe machen, aber nur zur Vergrößerung ihrer Verdammniß, und Prüfung derer Gläubigen, um ihre Seligkeit zu vermehren.

Darum bekümmere dich nicht was Menschen reden, denn gemeiniglich ist ihr Zeugniß falsch, und gehet wider den Sinn Gottes. Und ob auch jemand solcher Menschen Zeugniß annimt, so ist doch das göttliche Zeugniß viel größer. 1 Joh. 5. Denn Gott hat von seinem Sohn gezeuget, und

---

who once departed from sinful Sodom, and on their way look back again, they will become such pillars of salt, not believing any more the gospel.

The apostle Peter says, 'For it had been better for them not to have known the way of righteousness, than after they have known it to turn from the holy commandment, delivered unto them." 2 Pet. 2: 21. Therefore the Lord Jesus calls upon his followers with a powerful voice: 'Remember Lot's wife!" Luke 17: 32.

Again, if we consider the angels who have sinned, and whom God has excommunicated, 'and cast down to hell in chains of darkness, to be reserved unto judgment." 2 Pet. 2: 4, we shall observe how these cast out angels act. Why, they contend even against the good angels, as we see in the epistle of Jude verse 9, and Revel. 12: 7. Remember even the combat our Lord Jesus himself had with Satan. Matt. 4.

Here now such poor, blind men might say to God, that his ban had no effect. But if those angels which God rejected are still permitted to contend against the good angels, then be not surprised, if those excommunicated persons, who have departed from the faith, and are adherents of those fallen spirits, can contend yet against the faithful, and make them much trouble, but only to augment their own condemnation, and to try the faithful to the promoting of their salvation.

Therefore be not concerned about what people say, for in most cases their testimony is false, and contrary to the mind of God. And though one would receive such human testimony, still the divine testimony is much greater. 1 John 5: 9. 'For God has

wer an den Sohn Gottes glaubet, der hat das göttliche Zeugniß in ihm, welches gewisser ist als aller Menschen Zeugniße, es mag scheinen wie es will. Nun siehe, hier hast du den Grund und die Ursache wegen der Ausgebannten und deren Art, die da streiten wider die Gemeinde Gottes, genugsam gehöret.

Sohn. Wenn nun eine Gemeinde vor sich einen Mann und Absonderung führet, leidet auch solches die weltliche Obrigkeit?

Vater. Merke wohl, daß solche gute Ordnung gar nicht wider die Obrigkeit streitet, sondern vielmehr dem Stand der Obrigkeit beförderlich ist. Und auch die Gläubigen dieses gelehret werden durch Paulum, Röm. 13, 1. 7. Daß man solle um des Herrn willen denen menschlichen Ordnungen, die durch die Obrigkeit geordnet sind, sich unterwerfen, und der Obrigkeit Zoll, Schoß, Ehre und Furcht geben, weil alle Obrigkeiten von Gott gesetzet sind, darum daß sie das Böse strafen sollen, das Gute aber beschützen helfen, wann sie anders ihr Amt nach Gottes Willen führen wollen.

Und sollten sich billig die Obrigkeiten freuen, wann sie viele ja lauter solche Unterthanen hätten, die also in einer göttlichen Furcht wandelten, daß sie unter ihrer Gemeinschaft keine offenbare Sünder duldeten, und in solcher göttlichen Furcht der Obrigkeit das Ihrige williglich hingeben, und dem Herrn ihrem Gott auch das, was Ihm gehöret. Und der Herr hat verheißen von einer solchen Zeit: Daß die Könige werden Säugammen seyn der Gemeinde des Herrn. Es. 60, 16.

Vom Eidschwören.

Sohn. Ist die Obrigkeit auch zufrieden, wann man nach der Lehre Christi, keinen Eid schwöret?

Vater. Wenn die wahre Gläubigen nach der Lehre Christi, mit Ja bejahen was Ja ist, und mit Nein beneinen was

borne witness of his Son," and whosoever believes in the Son, has that divine witness in himself, which is more certain, than the testimony of all men, be it ever so bright. Let this suffice about the foundation and cause of excommunication, and of those who contend against the church of God.

Son. In case a church would establish such an order of excommunication within itself, would the civil government allow it?

Father. Mark well, that such good order is not at all opposed to the civil government, but on the contrary, conducive to the same. And believers are also taught by Paul, Rom. 13 : 1, 7, that every soul shall be subject for the Lord's sake, to human regulations, made by those in authority, and to render them all their dues, tribute, custom, fear and honor : for all governments are ordained of God to punish evil doers, and protect the good, i. e. if they will fulfil their office according to the will of God.

And governments should indeed rejoice, if they had many, yea no other than such subjects, that would truly walk in the fear of God, and not suffer in their communion any public transgressors, and in such fear of God render to their rulers their dues, and also to the Lord their God, what is due to him. And the Lord has foretold of such a time, when Kings shall be the tender nurses of the church of the Lord. Isai. 60 : 16.

OF TAKING OATHS.

Son. Will magistrates be satisfied, if we take no oath according to the doctrine of Christ?

Father. If true believers agreeably to the doctrine of Christ, affirm with yea, what is yea, and deny with nay,

Nein ist, das ist viel besser, als viele Eide, welche meistentheils geschworen und nicht gehalten werden. Und kann also eine Obrigkeit viel ruhiger und gewisser bei solchen Unterthanen seyn, welche ihnen in der Furcht Gottes mit Ja und Nein Wahrheit sagen, und bei der Wahrheit bleiben, als bei den andern, die Eide schwören, und ihnen doch nicht zu glauben und zu trauen ist.

Von der Prüfung.

Sohn. Lieber Vater, ich danke dir daß du mich in allem unterweisest, und merke nun wohl, wenn man einen gewissen Grund in göttlichen Dingen haben will so muß man auf Gott sehen, so wie er sich jederzeit in seinem Wort geoffenbaret, und allein im Glauben dabei bleiben, so wird das Herz durch die Gnade veste: Ich will dich aber noch etwas fragen, welches ich auch habe sagen hören, und davon gerne Gewißheit haben möchte, nemlich: Warum man die Menschen nicht vorher prüfen thäte, ehe man sie taufete, und in die Gemeinde aufnimmt, als daß man sie taufet, und darnach wieder in den Bann thut: Man gebe hierdurch zu verstehen, daß man den Geist der Prüfung nicht habe, welcher doch zu solchem Werk allerdings vonnöthen sey?

Vater. Lieber Sohn, höre und merke auch dieses wohl: Wie die Menschen den göttlichen Sinn und seine Art noch nicht merken und verstehen, u. nur nach menschlichen Meinungen ein Ding richten und verwerfen, welches sie nicht verstehen. Ich will dich aber auch hierinnen deutlich berichten, daß du es wohl wirst fassen und begreifen können: Denn erstlich dürfen die Gläubigen nicht anders gesinnet seyn in der Haushaltung Gottes, als so, wie sich Gott jederzeit in seiner Haushaltung geoffenbaret hat, ja sie dürfen sich nicht klüger als Gott zu seyn einbilden, und sollten sie vor den Menschen für lauter Narren angesehen werden, so müssen sie dennoch allein bei der göttlichen Weisheit bleiben.

---

what is nay,—this is far better than many oaths, which mostly are sworn, and not regarded after all. And indeed a government can be much more at ease, and more sure of the truth with such citizens, who tell them the truth in the fear of God with yea and nay, and who abide by the truth, than with others, who swear oaths, and still deserve not to be believed and trusted.

OF EXAMINATION.

Son. Dear father, I thank thee for all thy instruction, and perceive clearly, that in order to have a sure ground in divine things, we must look upon God, as he has always revealed himself in his word, and remain stedfast in faith, and then the heart will be established with grace. But I would still ask thee something more, which I have also heard, and of which I desire also correct information, namely, this: why are men not examined previously, before they are baptized and received into the church, instead of being baptized first, and then afterwards excommunicated by the church? By this, it is said, people are given to understand, that such have not the spirit of examination, which undoubtedly is necessary to qualify one for baptism.

Father. Dear son, hear & observe well, that mankind do not yet apprehend and understand the mind and character of God, and consequently judge and reject a thing only according to human opinions, without understanding it. But I will inform thee also in this matter, so plainly, that thou wilt be able to comprehend. For in the first place, the believers must not be otherwise minded in the household of God, than what God has always himself required of those therein; neither dare they imagine themselves wiser than God; though they should be accounted by the world as fools; they have still to abide by the divine wisdom.

Darum spricht Paulus: „Wer will weise seyn, der werde ein Narr in dieser Welt, denn dieser Welt Weisheit ist Thorheit bei Gott." 1 Cor. 3, 18. 19. Nun siehe: Weil die Glaubigen in allen Dingen nur allein auf Gott sehen müssen, so sehen sie auch billig in Ansehung der Prüfung derer Menschen, auf Gott. Nun kann man nicht anders von Gott sehen und lernen, als auf diese Art: Wenn er einen Menschen oder ein Volk hat prüfen wollen, so hat Gott solchen Menschen oder einem ganzen Volk seine Rechte und Gebote aufgeleget, und alsdann erst unter seinen Rechten und Gesetzen ist der Mensch recht geprüfet worden, wie dieses die Art der göttlichen Weisheit also jederzeit gewesen und noch ist. Sir. 4, 19. Cap. 6, 22.

Daß dieses also wahr sey, so merke: Erstlich Adam mußte ja nicht ausser dem Paradies, sondern in dem Paradies geprüfet werden. Unter dem Willen Gottes, ob er von der Frucht die ihm Gott verbot, essen oder nicht essen wollte. Zweitens: muste Noah in seinem Glauben geprüfet werden in Erbauung des Kastens oder der Archen, und im Hineingehen in dieselbe. Ferner, wurde ja Abraham der Vater aller Glaubigen am allermeisten geprüfet, indem ihm von Gott befohlen wurde aus seinem Vaterland und von seiner Freundschaft auszugehen. Und die allerhärteste Prüfung geschahe an ihm, da er schon den Bund der Beschneidung hatte, wie er seinen Sohn Isaak opfern sollte, 1 Mos. 12, 1. Cap. 22, 1.

Ja ferner siehet man, daß Gott den ganzen Saamen Abrahams recht prüfete, in Egypten, und auch da sie schon durch eine mächtige Hand ausgeführet waren, da fing Gott an sie zu versuchen und zu prüfen in der Wüsten, da sie schon die Verheissung von Gott von dem gelobten Land hatten, da wurden sie erst in der Wüsten geprüfet, damit kund würde, was in ihrem Herzen wäre, ob sie Gottes Gebot halten

Hence Paul says, 'If any man among you seemeth to be wise in this world, let him become a fool, that he may be wise. For the wisdom of this world is foolishness with God.' 1 Cor 3 : 18, 19. Now since believers are to look in all things alone upon God, they justly look to him also with regard to the trying of men. In this however we can see and learn of God nothing else but that when he intended to try or prove a person or nation, he gave such person or nation his laws and commandments, and under these laws and commandments men were properly tried. That this has been the method of divine wisdom always, and that it is still so, see Sirach 4 : 19 ch. 6 : 22.

That this is even so, observe that even Adam had to be tried, not outside of Paradise, but in it, according to the will of God, to see whether he would eat of the fruit which God had forbidden him, or not. Secondly, Noah was to be tried in his faith by building an ark, and entering into it. Again, Abraham, the father of all the faithful, was severely tried, when God commanded him to go out from his own country, and from his own kindred. But the most severe trial came upon him after he had already received the covenant of circumcision, when he was to sacrifice his son Isaac. Gen. 12 : 1. 22 : 1.

Further, we see that God tried well the whole seed of Abraham in Egypt, and also after being delivered by a mighty hand, God began to try and prove them in the wilderness, even after they had already received the promise of God of the holy land, that it might be made manifest, what was in their hearts, whether they would keep God's commandments or not. See Deut.

würden oder nicht. Wie zu sehen 5 Mos. 8, 2. In dieser Versuchungs-Wüsten sind die allermeisten um ihres Unglaubens willen darnieder geschlagen worden, und an ihrer vielen hatte Gott keinen Gefallen, ob sie schon unter Mosen mit der Wolken und dem Meer getaufet, und alle einerlei Speise, ja Engel Speise, wie es das Buch der Weisheit nennet, Cap. 16, 20. gegessen hatten. Ja sie haben alle einerlei geistlichen Trank getrunken von dem geistlichen Fels, der mit folgete, welcher war Christus. 1 Cor. 10, 3. 4. Diese sind nun in der Prüfung nicht bestanden, da Gott vor seine erwiesene Liebe und Wohlthaten und gegen seine Befehle, Ordnungen und Gesetze, Gehorsam forderte.

Nun siehe und merke auf den Sinn Gottes im neuen Bunde: Erstlich lieset man vor der Taufe des Sohnes Gottes selbsten, von keiner Prüfung und Versuchung. Als er aber von Johannes im Jordan getaufet war, und die Stimme vom Himmel gehöret worden: Dieß ist mein lieber Sohn, an dem ich Wohlgefallen habe. Matt. 3, 16. 17. Da ging erst die Versuchung an; da versuchte ihn der Teufel, da versuchten ihn die Schriftgelehrten und Pharisäer, da mußte er Gehorsam lernen. Hebr. 5, 8. Ja er wurde gehorsam bis zum Tode am Kreuz, Philip. 2, 8.

Gleichwie nun der Herr Jesus der Sohn Gottes von dem Vater ist geführet und versuchet worden; eben also u. nicht anders führet Jesus seine Nachfolger. Da ist das Himmelreich verglichen einem Netze, das gute und böse Fische fänget, die Faulen aber werden weggeworfen. Matt. 13, 47. 48. Da berufet der Herr Jesus gar viele, und werden durch den Glauben und die Taufe, seine Jünger. Joh. 4, 1. Aber durchs Kreuz werden sie erst geprüfet und in seiner Lehre auserwählt gemacht. Der Herr Jesus hat die Menschen niemalen

---

8 : 2. In this wilderness of temptation, most all of them were laid in the dust, on account of their unbelief, for God had no pleasure in them, though they had been already baptized unto Moses in the cloud and in the sea, and had all eaten of the same meat, yea of the food of angels, as it is called in the book of wisdom, ch. 16 : 20. Yes, they all drank of the same spiritual drink of that spiritual rock that followed them, which was Christ. 1 Cor. 10 : 3, 4. These, therefore, did not hold out in their trial, when God for his goodness and favors shown to them required obedience to his commandments, ordinances and laws.

Now see and observe the mind of God in the new covenant. In the first place, we read of no trial and temptation of the Son of God himself before his baptism. But as soon as he was baptized by John in Jordan, and the voice from heaven had been heard, 'This is my beloved Son in whom I am well pleased," Matt. 3 16, 17, then temptations began ; then was he tempted of the devil; afterwards he was tempted of the Scribes and Pharisees; thus had he to learn obedience. Heb. 5 : 8. Yea he became obedient unto death, even the death of the cross. Phil. 2 : 8.

In the same manner now as the Lord Jesus, the Son of God, was led and tried by his heavenly Father, so likewise Jesus tries his followers. Therefore the kingdom of heaven is compared to a net, by which good and bad fishes are caught, but the bad are cast away. Matt. 13 : 47, 48. For the Lord Jesus calleth a great many, and many became his disciples by faith and baptism. John 4 : 1. But by the cross they are tried, and made his chosen ones by and in his doctrine. The Lord

außer seiner Lehre und Evangelium geprüfet, sondern alle die zu ihm kamen und an ihn glaubten, die nahm er an als Jünger, er sagte aber zu ihnen: Wenn ihr bleiben werdet an meiner Rede oder Lehre, so seyd ihr meine rechte Jünger, und werdet die Wahrheit erkennen, und die Wahrheit wird euch frei machen. Joh. 8, 31. 32.

Ferner saget der liebe Jesus zu seinen Aposteln: Wenn ihr in mir als eine Rebe an dem Weinstock bleibet, so werdet ihr viele Früchte bringen wo ihr aber nicht in mir bleibet, so werdet ihr als eine dürre Rebe weggeworfen. Joh. 15, 4. 6. Solchen und keinen andern Sinn, muß die Gemeinde des Herrn Jesu haben: Daß wenn ein Mensch Buße thut, dem Teufel, der Welt, und allen Sünden öffentlich abschwöret, und in die Lehre des Herrn Jesu eintreten will; und gesetzt, man könnte muthmaßen, daß etwa dieser Mensch nicht würde beständig bleiben, man wüßte aber gegenwärtig nichts Böses von ihm, so könnte dieser Mensch auf sein öffentliches Bekenntniß nicht von der Gemeinde ausgeschlossen werden, sondern unter der Nachfolge Jesu wird der Mensch erst geprüfet, da sich denn offenbaret, ob er die Lehre Jesu als den rechten Prüfstein, von sich wirft, wie die Weisheit zeuget. Sir. 6, 22.

Und die göttliche Weisheit ladet alle Menschen ein, zu ihr zu kommen, ja auch gar die Narren: Spr. Salom. 9, 1. 4. und schließet keinen Menschen aus, welcher der Einladung folget, den Weg der Thorheit verläßt, und auf den Weg der Weisheit tritt; darnach wird der Mensch in der Haushaltung Gottes geprüfet, da muß er seine Füße begeben in die Fesseln, und seinen Hals in ihre Halseisen. Sir. 6, 25. Bleibet er alsdann nicht getreu, so ist die Schuld allein auf ihm: Und dieses ist der göttliche Sinn, daß der Mensch, wenn er mit seinem Gott in die Verbindung eingetreten, alsdann hernach erst geprüfet wird, nämlich in den Geboten Gottes.

Jesus never did try men without his doctrine and gospel, and all that came to him and believed on him, he received as disciples. But he said to them, "If ye continue in my word, then are ye my disciples indeed, and ye shall know the truth, and the truth shall make you free." John 8 : 31, 32.

Again says Jesus to his apostles, 'If ye abide in me, as the branches do in the vine, ye shall bring forth much fruit; but if ye will not abide in me, ye will be cast forth as a withered branch." John 15 : 4, 6. Such, and no other mind must govern the church of Christ, that when a man does repent, publicly renouncing the devil, the world and all sins, and is willing to submit to the doctrine of Jesus, the Lord, and though it might be presumed, that he would not remain constant, but while we know nothing evil of him at present, such a man, making a public profession, could not be excluded from the church ; but by his following Jesus, afterwards he would be tried when it would become manifest, whether he would reject the doctrine of Jesus, which is the true test, as wisdom testifies Sir. 6 : 22.

Divine wisdom invites all men to come to her, even the simple and foolish. Prov. 9 : 1, 4. It excludes no man, who obeys the invitation, forsakes the way of foolishness, and enters upon the way of wisdom. Then a man is tried in the household of God, when he must commit his feet to the fetters, and his neck to the yoke. Sir. 6 : 25. If then he does not remain faithful, the fault is only in him. And this is the divine mind, that after man has entered into connection with his God, he should be tried and proved by the commandments of God.

Sonsten könnte man auch Gott selbsten vielfältig beschuldigen, im alten Testament, daß er nicht hätte prüfen können die Menschen, so er in seine Verheissung habe angenommen, welche nicht beständig geblieben seyen. Ja man könnte auch den Herrn Jesum beschuldigen, daß er habe Jünger angenommen, die ihm nicht getreu geblieben, warum er nicht lauter solche Jünger habe gemacht, die ihm wären beständig geblieben. Denn es stehet, daß viele seiner Jünger wieder hinter sich gegangen sind. Joh. 6, 66. Ja man könnte auf solche Art alle Apostel beschuldigen; wie aus ihren Schriften zu ersehen, daß sie durch die Predigt des Evangelii viele Jünger gemacht, u. jederzeit viele auf mancherlei Art und Weise wieder abgewichen sind.

Nun merke noch ein einfältiges Gleichniß: Wann zwei Personen sich einander liebten, daß sie sich miteinander verehlichen wollten, wann können sie sich wohl unter einander am besten prüfen? Vor der Verehlichung sind sie noch frei von der Last der Haushaltung, das Weib ist noch frei von dem Gehorsam gegen den Mann, der Mann ist noch frei von der Sorge und Schwachheit des Weibes, da wissen sie nichts als von lieben.

Sobald sie aber eine öffentliche Eheverbindung miteinander machen, und in die Haushaltung eintreten, da gehet die rechte Prüfung an: Da darf das Weib um keinen andern Mann mehr buhlen, da muß sie ihrem eigenen Mann gehorsam seyn, da wird der Mann gewahr die Schwachheiten des Weibes und dergleichen, da verlieret sich denn die erste Buhlerliebe, und wird eine göttliche Liebe erfordert, wenn sie im Frieden bei einander wohnen wollen. Da wird eine Liebe erfordert, die auch bis in den Tod beständig bleiben muß. Lieb und Leid, Süß und Sauer mit einander gleich zu haben, und bis in den Tod einan-

---

Otherwise we might also accuse God himself often in the Old Testament, for not proving men, whom he had accepted in his promises, and who did not prove constant. Yea, we might also accuse the Lord Jesus, that he chose and received disciples, who did not remain faithful to him, and we might ask, why did he not make only such his disciples, who would continue steadfast? For it is written, that 'many of his disciples went back, and walked with him no more.'' John 6 : 66.

Thus, too, we might blame all the apostles, inasmuch we read in their writings, that they made many disciples by the preaching of the gospel, and that many of them at all times and in different ways apostatized again.

Consider a simple comparison. Suppose two persons love each other, so that they desire to enter into a state of matrimony with each other; now when will they be able best to prove each other?—Before marriage they are yet free from the burden of housekeeping; the woman is yet free from the obedience towards the man; the man is still free from the cares and infirmities of the woman: they yet know nothing but to love.

But as soon as they enter publicly into the matrimonial connection, and go to house keeping, then the proper trial commences. Then the wife may not have a familiar intercourse with any other man; she must be subject to her own husband. Then the husband will discover the weakness of the wife, and so forth. Then the passionate love will subside, and a divine love is required, if they wish to live in peace together. Then a love is necessary, which is to remain constant until death. Then they must partake equally of joy and grief, sweet and bitter, and not

der nicht verlaſſen. Das iſt der Eheſtand unter den Gläubigen, welcher abbildet den Herrn Jeſum und ſeine Gemeinde. Epheſ. 5, 32.

Gleich wie nun gemeiniglich die Welt=menſchen thun, wenn ſie ſich verehlichen wollen, und noch keine Verbindung ge=macht, da hängen ſie ſich bald an dieſe, bald an jene, und iſt lauter Unbeſtändig=keit, können auch wohl Geehlichte urtheilen, und meinen, wenn ſie in den Eheſtand kä=men, ſie wollten viel beſſer leben; wenn ſie aber in denſelben kommen, ſo müſſen ſie auch erſt in der Haushaltung lernen, und werden wohl manchesmal gar Ehebrecher, haben nicht ſo viel Liebe und Geduld, daß ſie in der Prüfung aushalten könnten.

Nun merke wohl, wie es auf ſolche Wei=ſe auch im Geiſtlichen ergehet; wie viel Seelen ſind nicht erwecket, daß ſie die gro=ße Hure verlaſſen haben, ſind aus dem gro=ben äuſſern Babel ausgegangen, und buh=len nun auf vielerlei Art an und mit der Lehre Jeſu. Einer nimmt ſich hie einen Spruch aus dem Teſtament, der andere dorten, damit buhlen ſie, ja geben auch ei=ne große Liebe unter einander vor, heißen ſich einander Brüder und Schweſtern, und können mit einander in dieſer Liebe wan=deln, ſind aber nicht verbunden, oder zu einem Leibe durch einen Geiſt getauft. 1 Cor. 12, 13. Darum haben ſie Frei=heit unter einander, ein jegliches ſich wo und wie es will anzuhängen.

Das eine hänget ſich an ſolche, das an=dere an eine andere Meinung, das eine an dieſen, das andere an einen andern Geiſt, und können dabei immer in der Buhler=Liebe bleiben, da heißt es unter ihnen: Die Liebe decket alles zu. Sie ſtrafet nicht. Welches wahr iſt, die ungebunde=ne Buhler=Liebe decket alles zu, denn es iſt kein Eheſtand mit Chriſto und ſeiner Ge=meinde, zu wandeln nach ſeinen Regeln,

leave each other until death separates them. This is the state of matrimony among believers, which represents the Lord Jesus and his church. Eph. 5 : 32.

Worldly men however, when they wish to get married, and are yet free, are very inconstant, profess love now to one, and then to another and are full of fickleness. They are apt to find fault with married people, and imagine, if they should marry once, they would do much better. But upon their actu-al entrance into that state, they have to learn yet the first lessons of a mar-ried life, and often get divorced again, because they have not love and patience sufficient to hold out in the trial.

Now mark well, how it comes to pass in like manner in a spiritual sense. How many souls have not been awak-ened, and have abandoned the great whore; have come out of gross, outward Babylon, and fallen in love in various degrees with the doctrine of Christ? One takes a passage out of the New Tes-tament here and another there, which they love and embrace; they pretend also great love toward each other, call one another brother and sister, and can thus walk together in such love. But they are not united or baptized by one spirit into one body. 1 Cor. 12 : 13. Hence they have and grant liberty to each one to attach himself to whatever body he pleases, and in whatever man-ner.

Thus one holds to one opinion, the other to another; one is led by this spirit, the other by that; still they can remain in that species of love, which comes before marriage. Then the say-ing is among them, Love covers all, and condemns none. This is true, the unconfined love in courtship covers all, for there are no sacred ties yet to bind the soul to Christ and his church, to

allwo kein Buhler=Liebe mehr statt hat, sondern eine Liebe die das Arge, Böse, und Sündliche hasset, wenn sie nicht falsch ist. Röm. 13, 9.

Siehe, solche Buhler können denn diejenigen richten und urtheilen, welche in den Ehestand mit Christo getreten, und verbunden sind, wenn sie sich einander erbauen, arbeiten, und bestrafen, und so sichs ereignet, daß auch unter ihnen einer sich an einen andern Geist hänget, mit demselben buhlet, daß sie solchen als einen Ehebrecher richten, und so er nicht hören will, von der Gemeinde ausschließen. Da kommt denn ein solcher gleich wieder unter die Gesellschaft der Buhler, da darf er denn mit allen falschen Geistern auffer dem Hause und der Gemeinde des Herrn buhlen.

Das muß denn eine große Freihet des Geistes heissen; und ist es auch in der That. Aber auffer dem Hause Gottes, auffer seiner Gemeinde, und auffer seinem Reich; denn in dem Reiche Gottes ist keine Unordnung uud falsche Freiheit, sonder lauter Ordnung und Einigkeit. Und müssen alle Engel und Geister im Himmel wollen, was ihr Gott will; so sie anderst wollen als Gott will, so können sie in seinem Reich nicht bestehen. So bald als die Engel anders gewollt als Gott, sind sie verstoßen, und mit Ketten der Finsterniß gebunden, und zum Gericht behalten worden. 2 Pet. 2, 4.

Siehe das ist die Art der wahren Liebe Gottes. Und so müssen alle Glaubigen gesinnet seyn, gleich wie auch ihr Herr und Meister ihnen solches lehret; und auch in diesem Verstande solches abgebildet. Nemlich, so eines deiner Glieder an deinem Leibe dich ärgert, so reiß es aus, und wirf es von dir. Matth. 18. Diesen Befehl hat Jesus sonderlich seiner Gemeinde, welche sein Leib ist, gegeben, daß sie alle sündliche ärgerliche Glieder abschneiden sollen, damit nicht der ganze Leib verderbet werde.

walk according to his statutes, where no blind, passionate love finds a place, but such a love, which hates all that is evil, wicked and sinful, provided it be not false. Rom. 13 : 9.

Behold such freelovers may undertake to judge and condemn those that have entered into covenant with Christ, and are united to him; these endeavor to edify, admonish and rebuke one another, and if it so happens, that one among themselves is affected by a strange spirit, and is in love with it, and the church considers him as an adulterer, and if he will not repent, the church must exclude or disown him. Then such a one will readily go back to that society of free lovers, where he may enjoy his unbridled love with all the false spirits, yet without the house and church of the Lord.

This, then, is called a great liberty of the spirit, and indeed it is. But where? Why, out of the house of God, out of his church and kingdom. For in the kingdom of God no disorder or false liberty exists, but it is all order and union. All the angels and spirits in heaven must subject their will to the will of their God; for if they would do otherwise, they could not exist in his kingdom. So soon as the angels went contrary to the will of God, they were cast down to hell, and delivered into chains of darkness, to be reserved unto judgment. 2 Pet. 2 : 4.

Behold, this is the true nature of the love of God. And all believers must be thus minded, even as also their Lord and Master teaches them, and in this he has said "If one of the members of thy body offend thee, pluck it out and cast it from thee." Matt. 18. This commandment Jesus gave particularly to his church, which is his body, that all sinful and offensive members should be cut off, in order that the whole body may be preserved from destruction.

Solche Lieb ist auch schon im Gesetz von Gott geboten worden: Wenn dir dein Freund, der dir ist wie dein Herz, Aergernisse giebet, und dich ablocken will, andern Göttern zu dienen die Gott nicht befohlen, so gehorche ihm nicht, und dein Auge soll seiner nicht schonen. 5 Mos. 13, 6. Siehe, von solcher Liebe wissen alle Buhler nichts, so lange sie nicht mit Christo in seinen Ehestand, in seine Lehr und Ordnung treten. Meinen dennoch Wunder, was das vor eine unparteyische Liebe sey, die sie haben und vorgeben, werden auch von den ungeübten Seelen angesehen als Menschen, die in einer großen göttlichen Liebe und guten Glauben wandeln.

Aber es wird noch offenbar werden, daß es nur eine falsche Buhler-Liebe gewesen, welche durch prächtige und kluge Reden wohl gefärbet war, dadurch manches unschuldiges Herz betrogen wird. Darum saget die Schrift: Die Liebe sey nicht falsch. Röm. 12. Und die Haupt-Summa des Gebots ist: Liebe von reinem Herzen und gutem Gewissen, und von ungefärbtem Glauben. Welcher aber etliche gefehlet, und sind umgewandt zu unnützem Geschwätz. 1 Tim. 1, 5. Hie siehest du nun, daß ein gefärbter Glaube, und also auch eine gefärbte Liebe seyn kann.

Von der Liebe.

Sohn. Ja, woran aber prüfet man die wahre Liebe, und den wahren Glauben, oder die falsche Liebe, und den gefärbten Glauben?

Vater. Der wahre Glaube, welcher gültig, und vor welchen ein ewiges Leben verheissen ist, muß ein schriftmäßiger Glaube seyn, gleich wie der Herr Jesus spricht: Wer an mich glaubet, wie die Schrift saget, von deß Leibe werden Ströme des lebendigen Wassers fließen. Joh. 7, 38. Und ein schriftmäßiger Glaube wirket auch die wahre Liebe nach der Schrift. Denn das ist die Liebe zu Gott daß wir seine Gebote halten. 1 Joh. 5, 3. Und der Herr

Such love was already required in the Law of God. 'If thy friend, who is as thine own soul, entice thee secretly to serve other gods not commanded by God, thou shalt not hearken unto him; neither shall thine eye pity him.'' Deut. 13 : 6. See, of this love all those free lovers know nothing as long as they do not enter with Christ into his covenant, in his doctrine and ordinances. Still they are in great conceit, that they possess and profess a remarkably impartial love; they are also looked upon by inexperienced souls as men walking in a great and divine love and in true faith.

But it will yet become manifest, that it was only a false, pretended love, well painted and varnished with fine speeches and pompous words, by which many innocent souls are deceived. Therefore says the Scripture, 'Let love be without dissimulation!'' Rom. 12 : 9. 'Now the end of the commandment is CHARITY out of a pure heart, and of a good conscience, and of faith unfeigned. From which some having swerved have turned aside unto vain jangling.'' 1 Tim. 1 : 5, 6. Thus we see that there may be a feigned faith, and also a feigned love.

OF LOVE.

SON. But whereby do we prove and distinguish true and false love, a true and a feigned faith?

FATHER. True faith, which is genuine and has the promise of eternal life, must be a scriptural faith, as the Lord Jesus says, 'He that believeth on me as the scripture hath said, out of his body shall flow rivers of living water.'' John 7 : 38. And a scriptural faith will also produce a true love according to Scripture. 'For this is the love of God, that we keep his commandments.'' 1 John 5 : 3. And the Lord Jesus

Jesus spricht von der wahren Liebe: Liebet ihr mich, so haltet meine Gebote. Wer meine Gebote hat, und hält sie, der ist es der mich liebet. Und wer mich liebet, der wird mein Wort halten. Joh. 14, 21—23.

An welcher schriftmäßigen Liebe man auch seine Jünger erkennen soll. Joh. 13, 34. 35. Denn gleich wie der Herr Jesus nach der Schrift geboren worden, auch nach der Schrift gekreuziget und auferstanden. 1 Cor. 15, 3. 4. So hat er auch allen den Seinigen einen schriftmäßigen Glauben gelehret, und verheisset ihnen nach der Schrift ein ewiges Leben. Aber ein gefärbter Glaube und gefärbte Liebe kann sich nicht auf die Schrift, sondern nur auf menschlich Gutdenken gründen; Da wird einer, wie er von den Schriftgelehrten gelernet hat, glauben, der andere, wie er etwa durch dieses oder jenes Buch ist überzeuget worden. Der Dritte, gar nach seines Herzens Gutdünken und eigenem Willen. Da doch die Schrift ausdrücklich spricht: Daß nur ein Herr, ein Glaube, und eine Taufe sey. Ephes. 4, 5.

Wenn zehn Menschen seyn, die noch in einem gefärbten Glauben stehen, und man sollte sie nach der Schrift examiniren, so würde man erfahren, daß alle Zehen ein jeder einen eigenen Glauben haben würde, und sollte keiner nach der Schrift seyn.— Denn es ist nur ein einiger ungefärbter Glaube, und alle die nun den wahren Glauben nach der Schrift haben, die sind auch alle nach der Schrift einig, was Glaubens-Regeln anbetreffen.

Von dem Glauben.

Sohn. Ich habe aber auch sagen hören, daß alle Secten sich auf die Schrift berufen, und darum man seinen Glauben nicht mit der Schrift behaupten könne.

Vater. Wer dieses spricht, weil alle Secten sich auf die Schrift berufen, so dürfte ein wahrer Gläubiger solches nicht thun; das muß nothwendig ein elender und unwissender Mensch seyn. Denn das

speaks of true love, 'If ye love me, ye will keep my commandments. He that hath my commandments, and keepeth them, he it is that loveth me, and if a man love me, he will keep my words.' John 14 : 21, 23.

By this scriptural love Christ's disciples shall also be known. John 13 : 34, 35. For as Christ was born according to Scripture, and also crucified and raised again according to Scripture, 1 Cor. 15 : 3, 4. So he taught all that are his, a scriptural faith, and promised them according to Scripture, an everlasting life. But a feigned faith and a feigned love are not founded on Scripture, but only on human conceit. There one believes, because he has learned so from some learned scribe; another, because he has been convinced by this or that book. A third one will be guided only by his own opinion and selfwill, whereas the Scripture says expressly, that there is but 'One Lord, one faith, one baptism.' Eph 4 : 5.

Should there be ten persons, who stand yet in a feigned faith, and they were all examined according to Scripture, it would appear, that every one would have a peculiar faith of his own, and that not one was altogether according to Scripture. For there is only one true and unfeigned faith, and all those who possess that true faith according to Scripture, are also all of one mind as to the rules and practice of faith.

OF FAITH.

Son. But I have heard it asserted, that all sects appeal to Scripture, and hence one could not maintain his faith by Scripture?

Father. Whosoever says this, because all sects appeal to Scripture, that therefore a true believer should not do the same, such must necessarily be a miserably ignorant person. For it is

dienet einem Gläubigen gar sehr zur Stär-
kung seines Glaubens, weil alle Secten
die heilige Schrift vor göttlich erkennen und
sich darauf berufen, ob sie derselben schon
nicht glauben. Denn auf die Schrift sich
zu berufen, und der Schrift zu glauben,
das ist gar ein großer Unterschied. Welches du aus der Rede des Herrn Jesu
merken kannst, da er zu den Juden sagte:
Wenn ihr Mosen glaubetet, so glaubetet
ihr auch mir, denn er hat von mir geschrieben. Joh. 5, 46. Nun haben die
Juden sich auch alle auf Mosen berufen,
aber sie haben ihm in seinen Schriften
nicht geglaubet.

Also berufen sich alle Secten nicht nur
allein auf die Schrift, sondern auf den
Herrn Jesum selbsten, aber wie sie dem
Herrn Jesum glauben, also, und nicht anders glauben sie auch der Schrift; könnte
nun wohl ein wahrer Gläubiger also blind
seyn, und denken oder sprechen: Ey alle
Secten berufen sich ja auf einen gekreutzigten Heiland, darum kannst und darfst du
dich nicht darauf berufen; das wäre dem
Teufel eben recht.

Aber nein! die wahre Gläubige haben
von ihrem Herrn und Meister mehr und
bessere Klugheit gelernet. Denn als der Teufel in der Versuchung des Herrn Jesu sich
auch auf die Schrift berief, da antwortete
ihm Jesus im Glauben aus der Schrift,
und berief sich auf dieselbe. Matt. 4, 6. 7.
So mag dann der Teufel und alle falsche
Geister sich auch auf die Schrift berufen,
darum glauben sie aber derselben nicht. Und
du wirst erfahren, daß eben diese Menschen, die einen Gläubigen irre machen
wollen, wenn sie sprechen: Alle Secten
berufen sich auf die Schrift; so werden sie
dennoch sich auch selbsten auf dieselbigen
berufen.

Und darum siehet ein gläubiges Kind
Gottes nur auf seinen himmlischen Vater,
und glaubt, und folget ihm in seinem geof-
fenbarten Wort, weilen es gewiß ist, und
glaubet, daß Gott und sein ausgesproche-

to a believer a strong
faith to know that all
edge the holy scripture
appeal to it, though the
in it (scripturally).
great difference betwe
the Scriptures and belic
This we can perceive b
the Lord Jesus, when h
Jews, "For had ye beli
would have believed me
of me." John 5 : 46.
true, all appealed to Mo
writings they did not b

Thus all sects appea
Scripture but to Jesus
as they believe in Jesus
in the Scripture. Can
then be so stupid or bli
or say, "Because all sc
crucified Savior, therefo
appeal to him." Th
please the devil very m

But no! true believe
of their Lord and Ma
better wisdom. For whe
temptation of the Lord J
the Scriptures, Jesus a
from the Scripture, and
unto, Matt. 4 : 6, 7.
devil and all false spiri
Scripture, still they beli
wilt discover, that these
want to mislead a belie
that all sects appeal to
yet always will appeal to
themselves.

Hence the believing
look only to their heav
believe and follow him
word, because they are
lieving, that God and h

ift, denn fonft müßte
unterlaffen, wenn er
n thun wollte, was
glaubigen im Unglau=

Beten, nicht Singen,
Schlafen, und der=
Gottlofen alles Sün=
or Gott ift. Denen
en aber ift es alles
n &er ift nichts rein.
lerne in allen Din=
fchied nach der Schrift
nicht in Verwirrung
ele Seelen bei diefer
rrung gerathen, wenn
Gottlofen auch gottes=
errichten, als Beten,
ing halten, Taufen,
und dergleichen.

erleuchtete Vernunft:
diefes thun, fo ift
du willft es gar blei=
en folche Menfchen in
daß fie endlich nicht
meinen oder glauben.
ch einen Weg machen
n die Schrift nicht leh=
meinen fie auf fol=
n weiter geftiegen als
auch keinen Rath
ten der Apoftel an.—
inen Zeiten viele folche
und gehöret habe, aber
daß das Ende ihres
rderben nach fich ge=
gar bald gefallen und
n, daß fie endlich gar
en, fondern find der
ten Weg wieder heim
alle in Chrifto ein=
n Gnaden bewahren
fo hoch zu fteigen be=
herunter zu den Nie=
12, 16.

are altogether one, otherwise a believer
would have to omit much, if he would
not do in faith, what the wicked and
infidels do in their unbelief.

He would not be allowed to pray, to
sing, to labor, eat and sleep and the
like, because to the wicked it is all
sin and an abomination before God.
But unto believers and those that are
pure, all things are pure; while unto
unbelievers nothing is pure. Tit. 1:
15. Therefore learn well to distinguish
in all things according to Scripture,
that thou mayest not get into confusion,
as it is the case, alas! with many souls
at this time, who are greatly confused
when they see the ungodly wicked performing acts of worship, such as praying, singing, holding meetings, baptizing, going to sacrament and the like.

Then unenlightened reason may
think, "If the wicked do this, then it
is of no account, and I will omit it
altogether," and thus such people are
confounded so much, that at last they
know no more what to think or believe.
Thus they will be led to make or invent
a way, which the Scripture did not
teach, and to imagine when on this
way, that they have risen higher than
the apostles, and hence receive no counsel any more from the apostolic writings. Already have I known and heard
in my time many such persons, but
have also noticed, that the end of their
way has produced a deep ruin; for
soon, very soon, they fell so low, that
at last they believed nothing at all, but
fell back to the world and to the broad
road. May God in mercy preserve
all simple believers in Christ, that they
may not desire to mount so high, but
to condescend to those of low estate
and humble mind. Rom. 12: 16.

Und Paulus rufet seinem Timotheum also zu: Weil du von Kindheit auf die heilige Schrift weisest, kann dich dieselbige unterweisen zur Seligkeit, durch den Glauben an Christo Jesu. Denn alle Schrift von Gott eingegeben, ist nütz zur Lehre, zur Strafe, zur Besserung, zur Züchtigung in der Gerechtigkeit, daß ein Mensch Gottes sey vollkommen, zu allen guten Werken geschickt. 2. Tim. 3, 15—17.

Sohn. Kann und darf man in allem dem Zeugniß der heiligen Schrift glauben, und ist ein Gläubiger dazu verbunden, eben der Schrift zu glauben und zu folgen, oder führet nicht der Geist Gottes dieselbe andere Wege, wovon eben der äußere Buchstabe der Schrift nichts weiß?

Vater. Es darf niemand einem Gläubigen sagen, er solle und müßte der Schrift glauben und folgen, denn es kann niemand ohne den heiligen Geist gläubig seyn, welcher den Glauben wirken muß; Nun ist die Schrift nur ein äußeres Zeugniß derer Dinge, welche ehemalen durch den heiligen Geist gelehret und befohlen sind, und durch denselbigen sind auch die Verheissungen und Bedrohungeu ausgesprochen worden.

Wenn nun ein Mensch durch wahre Reue und Buße aus Gnaden den heiligen Geist erlanget, von Gott dem Vater aller Geister, so ist es eben der Geist des Glaubens, der vor viel hundert Jahren in Petro, Paulo und Johanne gewesen und gewirket hat, obschon der heilige Geist in den Aposteln in einem größeren Maaß war, zur Ausbreitung des Evangelii, dennoch aber ist eben derselbe heilige Geist in allen Gläubigen; was nun Paulus, Petrus und Johannes dazumal geschrieben, geordnet und befohlen, damit waren dazumal alle Gläubigen eins, so fern sie noch gesund im Glauben waren. Weilen denn nun nur ein Gott, und ein einiger Geist ist, so kann eben derselbe einige heilige Geist nicht anders wollen, als was er zur Heiligung vor

And Paul says to his son Timothy, 'Because thou hast known the holy Scriptures from a child, they are able to make thee wise unto salvation through faith, which is in Christ Jesus. All scripture is given by inspiration of God, and is profitable for doctrine, for reproof, for correction, for instruction in righteousness; that the man of God may be perfect, thoroughly furnished unto all good works.'' 2 Tim. 3: 15, 17.

Son. Can or may we believe in all things the testimony of the holy Scripture, and is a believer bound to believe and obey that Scripture, or does the Spirit of God lead him other ways sometimes, of which the external letter of the Scriptures knows nothing?

Father. It is not necessary to tell a believer, that he shall and must believe and obey the Scriptures. For no man can be a believer without the Holy Ghost, who is to bring forth faith. Now the Scripture is only an external testimony of those things, which have been taught and commanded by the Holy Ghost in former times, and by whom also were pronounced the promises and threatenings. If therefore a person, being truly sorry and repentant of his sins, through grace obtains the Holy Spirit from God, the Father of all spirits, it is that same Spirit of faith, who worked many hundred years ago in Peter, Paul and John. And though the Holy Spirit was given to the apostles in a greater measure, for the spread of the gospel, yet he is that same Holy Spirit in all believers. Now whatsoever Paul, Peter and John have then written, ordained and commanded, all believers then were agreed to, so far as they are sound in the faith.

Now since there is but one God, and but one Spirit, this same one, Holy Spirit can will nothing else, but what

gewollt. Was nun
Glaubigen geordnet,
geschrieben, und damit
eins, denn der heilige
ndig eben so, wie es
lehret.

chen mit ihrer Weis-
Sinn über die Schrift
e in ihnen keinen Geist
m können sie auch äu-
der Schrift nicht glau-
m des Glaubens nicht
auch nicht an sie ge-
b sie auch frei von de-
rinnen enthalten sind;
König seinen Unter-
Befehle schreiben lässet,
heissung thut, wenn si-
kommen werden, auch
venn sie dieselbe nicht

auch andere Menschen,
önigs Unterthanen sind
iel Redens davon ma-
eine Unterthanen sind
, so achten sie seine
glauben auch seinen
, und beugen sich auch
ebote, Rechte und Ge-

it der heiligen Schrift
Welcher Mensch es
, was Jesus, der Kö-
en Menschen die wahre
glauben, und ihm ge-
wollen in allen seinen
hat; man kann auch
hen und lesen, was der
nbußfertigen Sündern
ht Buße thun wollen,
um glauben, auch nicht
nit seinen Befehlen, die
ssen, durch seinen Geist
ll.

his will was many hundred years ago,
namely, our sanctification. And again,
what the Holy Spirit has ordained for
believers to observe, that is externally
written and recorded, and with this
agree all believers, because the Holy
Spirit teaches us inwardly just the
same, as the Scripture teaches outwardly.

But whenever men come upon the
Scriptures with their own wisdom and
carnal minds, they have not within
themselves the spirit of faith; hence
they cannot believe the external testimony of the Scriptures, nor exercise
the obedience of faith. And indeed
it is not written for them; the commandments contained therein, do not
concern them. Even as if a King gave
his subjects written laws, with great
promises to those, who should obey
them, and also great threats against
those, who should not observe them.
Now there might other men, who are
not that King's subjects, read those
laws, and talk about them a great deal.
But since they are not, nor wish to
become subjects, they do not regard
his threats, nor believe his promises,
nor bow themselves under his laws,
statutes and commandments.

Just so it is with the Holy Scripture
of the New Testament, whosoever
reads it, may see what Jesus, the King
of kings has promised to all men, who
truly repent, believe in him, and are
willing to follow him obediently in all
his commandments. They can likewise see and read in holy writ, what
the Lord Jesus has threatened to all
impenitent sinners, who will not repent,
and who will not believe his gospel, nor
are they willing that Jesus with his
commandments, which he has left to us
in writing, through his Spirit should
reign over them.

Es kann ein Mensch die Schrift zwar äusserlich lesen, davon reden und schreiben, wenn aber in dem Menschen der Geist des Glaubens nicht ist, so wird er sich um die Gebote so darinnen stehen, wenig bekümmern, wird auch wenig vor den Drohungen, so darinnen enthalten sind, erschrecken.— Das machet weil die inwendige Ohren noch nicht geöffnet sind.

Darum sagte der Herr Jesus zu dem Volk, so ihn selbsten predigen hörete: Wer Ohren hat zu hören, der höre. Matth. 11, 15. Cap. 13, 43. Und in der Heil. Offenbarung St. Johannes, rufet der Geist Gottes an alle sieben Gemeinden: Wer Ohren hat zu hören, der höre, was der Geist den Gemeinden saget. Offenb. 2, 7.

Also wenn ein Mensch die heilige Schrift äusserlich lieset, wenn's ein Gläubiger ist, dem seine innere Ohren geöffnet sind, so höret er was der Herr Jesus in seiner Lehre haben will, er höret was die Aposteln in ihren Schriften haben wollen, und durch das inwendige Gehör wird er getrieben, zu dem wahren Gehorsam auch äusserlich zu folgen. Er lieset äusserlich die Schrift im Glauben, und höret das innere Wort des Lebens, das gibt ihm Kraft und Stärke zur Nachfolge Jesu, wo es aber am Glauben fehlet, da kann wohl ein Mensch äusserlich hören und lesen, und sprechen: Es ist ein todter Buchstabe dem ich nicht folgen kann, ich bin es ja inwendig nicht so überzeuget, wie es äusserlich geschrieben stehet, er weiß aber nicht das es ihm am Glauben fehlet, und an der wahren göttlichen Liebe. Joh. 14.

Von der äußern und innern Schrift.

Sohn. Ich habe aber auch schon von vielen sagen hören, daß die Christen im neuen Bund stünden, u. das Gesetz Gottes sey in ihrem Herzen geschrieben, hätten also nicht nöthig sich nach der äußern Schrift zu richten, und derselben zu folgen.

A man may read indeed outwardly the Scriptures; he may talk and write about them, but if he has not the spirit of faith in him, he will concern himself but little about their commandments, nor be much terrified by the threats contained therein. The reason is plain, his inward ears are not yet opened.

Therefore the Lord Jesus said unto the people, who heard himself preach: 'He that hath ears to hear, let him hear.' Matt. 11 : 15; 13 : 43. And in the Revelation of St. John the Spirit of God calleth upon all and each of the seven churches, 'He that hath an ear let him hear, what the Spirit saith unto the churches. Rev. 2 : 7 &c.

Thus when a person reads externally the Holy Scripture, and is a believer, whose inward ears are opened, he hears, what the Lord Jesus in his doctrine enjoins; he hears what the apostles require in their writings, and by this inward hearing he is urged on to observe a true obedience also outwardly; he reads externally the Scripture in faith, and hears the internal word of life, which gives him power and strength to follow Jesus. But where faith is wanting, a man may indeed outwardly hear and read, and say, 'It is a dead letter, which I cannot obey,' because I am not internally convinced, of what is outwardly written.' But he knows not, that he is wanting faith, and the true love of God. John 14 : 15.

OF THE EXTERNAL AND INTERNAL WORD.

SON. But I have been told by many, that Christians stood in the new covenant, and had the law of God written in their hearts, and consequently it was not necessary for them to obey and follow the external Scripture?

Vater. Es ist mir lieb, daß du mich auch dieses fragest, nun merke aber gar wohl auf den lautern Sinn Gottes, so wirst du wohl sehen daß diese Reden einestheils Wahrheiten, aber auch sehr mit Lügen vermenget sind. Dann als Gott der Herr ehemalen seinem Volk durch Mosen sein Gesetz offenbaren ließ, so schrieb es Gott auf zwei steinerne Tafeln, und gab sie Mosen, welcher sie in die Lade des Bundes legen mußte. 5 Mof. 10, 1—5. Hebr. 9, 4. Sie mußten eine Abschrift davon nehmen, und an ihre Thürpfosten schreiben. 5 Mof. 6, 6—9. stehet: Sie sollten die Worte des Gesetzes zu Herzen nehmen, sie sollten zu ihren Kindern davon reden, sie sollten sie binden zum Zeichen auf ihre Hand, und sie über ihres Hauses Pfosten schreiben.

Nun hat das äußere Abgeschriebene nicht anders, noch vielweniger wider dasselbe seyn müssen, das Gott selbsten auf die steinerne Tafeln geschrieben hatte und in dem Allerheiligsten in der Bundes-Lade verborgen lag; also, daß das äußere und innere Gesetz einerlei Sinn hatte. Was nun die Lade des Bundes in dem Allerheiligsten darinnen die Tafeln des Gesetzes lagen, war, das ist nun im neuen Bund eines jeden Gläubigen sein Herz, in welchem auch ganz unfehlbar die Tafeln des Gesetzes seines Gottes liegen werden, und in ihren Herzen nicht durch Menschen Hände sondern durch den heiligen Geist geschrieben seyn.

Und dieses Gesetz welches inwendig durch den Geist Gottes geschrieben ist, das ist in allem ganz eins mit dem, das im neuen Testament äußerlich aufgeschrieben stehet, welches alles aus dem Inwendigen herausgeflossen, und ein ausgedrücktes Ebenbild von dem inwendigen lebendigen Wort Gottes ist. Wo aber der Mensch nur aus Hochmuth spricht: Das Gesetz seines Gottes wäre in seinem Herzen, und

FATHER. I an glad that thou hast started this question. Now attend well to the pure mind of God, and thou wilt easily see, that such sayings contain some truth, which however is very much mixed with lies. For when the Lord God formerly manifested to his people his Law by Moses, he wrote it upon two tables of stone, and gave them to Moses, who was to put them into the ark of the covenant. Deut. 10 ; 1, 5. Heb. 9 : 4. They were to make a copy of the laws and place them upon the posts of their houses. Deut. 6 : 6, 9. It is said, 'that the words of the commandments should be in their hearts; of which they should talk to their children, bind them for a sign upon their hands, and write them upon the posts of their houses and gates.''

That external copy now was to be nothing else, much less any thing to the contrary, but a faithful transcript of that which God himself had written on the tables of stone, and which were laid up in the Holy of holies, hidden within the ark of the covenant, so that the external and internal Laws were of the same import. Now what the ark of the covenant was in the Holy of holies, in which the tables of the Law were kept, that is now in the new covenant, every believer's heart, in which also most surely will be found the tables of the Law of his God, with the law written on their hearts, not by the hand of man, but by the Holy Ghost.

And this law, which is internally written by the Spirit of God, is altogether one and the same with that externally written in the New Testament, which has proceeded entirely from the internal, and is an express image of that internal living word of God. But where a person proudly says, that the law of his God is in his heart, while he still opposes the commandments,

er doch wider die Befehle, Rechte und Gesetze welche der Sohn Gottes und seine Aposteln befohlen, und wovon die Schrift äußerlich zeuget—streitet, so glaube ganz gewiß daß solcher Mensch noch fleischlich ist, und daß sein Gesetz wovon er spricht daß es in seinem Herzen stünde, noch von dem Geist des Irrthums und der Lügen geschrieben sey.

Ferner ist das ein klares Kennzeichen des Gesetzes Gottes, und des Gesetzes des verführischen Geistes; denn alle, in welche das Gesetz Gottes in die Herzen geschrieben ist, die sind eins in dem einigen Glauben, in der einigen Taufe, in dem einigen Geist, nach Jesu Christo. Welches also der vollkommene Wille des wahren Gesetzgebers ist, daß die Seinigen alle eins seyn sollen, so wie der Vater und der Sohn. Joh. 17, 21. Aber das Gesetz, das der Irrthumsgeist durch sein falsches Evangelium in die Herzen schreibet, das ist von solcher Art, daß es erstlich ganz ungewiß in den göttlichen Zeugnissen ist, Pf. 5, 10. (2) Trennet es die Menschen von Gottes Geboten und Ordnungen ab, und zertrennet sie in so vielerlei Glaubens-Bekenntnisse, und Meinungen.

Ich habe dieses von vielen erfahren, die da gesprochen: Sie wären freie Leute, dürften sich der Schrift neues Testaments als dem Buchstaben nicht unterwerfen, denn das Gesetz Gottes sey in ihre Herzen geschrieben. Haben aber gesehen und erkannt, daß ihrer auch nicht zwei in dem Anfang christlichen Lebens, nach der Schrift eins seyn, sondern viel Menschen als in solchem hohen Sinn stehen, so viele Gesetze haben sie auch, und ist mir öfters gewesen, als ob dieses ein wunderlicher Geist seyn müßte, der so vielerlei Gesetze in die Herzen der Menschen schreiben thäte.

Darüber hat Gott der Herr auch schon bei dem Propheten Jeremia geklaget: Daß das Volk Israel durch die falsche Propheten verführet, das einige Gesetz Gottes,

statutes and laws, which the Son of God and his apostles have instituted, and whereof the Scriptures externally testify, then we may safely believe, that such a person is yet carnal, and that the law, which he says is in his heart, has been written there by the spirit of error and falsehood.

Again, herein is a clear token of the law of God, and of the law of the deceiving spirit. For all in whose hearts the law of God is written, are all united in the one faith, in the one baptism and in the one Spirit according to Jesus Christ. For it is the perfect will of the true Lawgiver, that his own should all be one, even as the Father and the Son are one. John 17: 21. But the law, which the spirit of error, by his false gospel writes in the hearts, is of such a kind, that it is in the first place quite uncertain concerning divine testimonies, Psalm 5: 10. In the second place, it separates men from the commandments and ordinances of God, and divides them into a multitude of different confessions and opinions.

I have observed this in many, who said, they were a free people, they needed not subject themselves to the Scripture of the New Testament in the letter; for the law of God was written in their hearts. But likewise have I seen and known, that not two of them were agreed concerning the beginning of a christian life, or the principles of the doctrine of Christ according to scripture, but that as many were the men that had such a haughty disposition, so many were the laws, which they had, and I was often led to think, what a curious spirit that must be, who would write such different laws into the hearts of men.

Of this the Lord God complained already through the prophet Jeremiah, that the people of Israel were led astray by false prophets, forsook the

und den einigen Altar des Herrn verlassen, und in ihrer falschen Freiheit, wie's ihnen gut dünket, sich andere Götter und Altäre machten. Jerem. 11, 13. Eben so gehet es auch denen Menschen bei dieser Zeit, welche sich großer Freiheit rühmen, und dem göttlichen Rath und Geboten nach der heiligen Schrift nicht folgen. Da heißt es auch wohl recht: So mancher Mensch, so mancher Geist, und so manches Gesetz.

Aber es bleibt Babel, Verwirrung und Uneinigkeit, bei allem großen geistlichen Vorgeben, und dennoch wollen solche Bauleute von ihrem Sinn nicht nachlassen, ohngeachtet sie selbsten sehen, daß der Herr ihre Sprache verwirret hat. Ja sie sehen, wie schon so viele gelehrte und weise Leute auf solche Art, außer des Herrn Jesu seiner Ordnung gebauet, und zu Schanden, ja manche zu Narren worden sind; dennoch fangen immer wieder neue Bauleute an solchen verwirreten Bau fortzusetzen. Und wird immer verwirreter und greulicher, und wenn sie nicht bald davon ablassen werden, so giebts endlich Menschen von zerrütteten Sinnen, die untüchtig zum Glauben sind. Und wird dennoch endlich solche Thorheit jedermann offenbar werden, wie auch jener. 2 Tim. 3.

Nun siehe, da kannst du merken von dem wahren und falschen Gesetz, welches alle beide in den Herzen der Menschen geschrieben ist; das falsche Gesetz wird durch den Geist des Irrthums in die Herzen der Ungläubigen geschrieben. Das wahre Gesetz des Lebens wird durch den heiligen Geist der Wahrheit geschrieben in die Kinder des neuen Bundes, in den wahren Gläubigen, und ist in allem ganz eins, was Christus äußerlich befohlen und was die Apostel geschrieben haben.

Sohn. Ich habe es nun genugsam verstanden, und ist mir sehr nützlich und bächtig, daß ich in vielen Dingen wohl bin unterrichtet worden, weil es bei dieser Zeit

---

only law of God, and the only altar of the Lord, and in their false liberty made for themselves other gods and altars, according to their own notion. Jerem. 11 : 13. The same is the case with people in our times, who boast of great liberty, without obeying the divine counsel and commandments according to holy Scripture. Truly, it may be said, 'As many men, as many spirits, and as many laws.''

But however great the spiritual pretentions are, it still continues to be Babylon, confusion and discord. Yet such builders will not desist from their intentions, though they see themselves, that the Lord has confused their language. Yea, they see how to many learned and wise people have built in this manner, contrary to the order of the Lord Jesus, and have been brought to shame, and become fools; still new builders begin again and again to prosecute this building of confusion. Things become more and more confused and abominable, and if they shall not soon cease, there will be at last 'men of corrupt minds, reprobate concerning the faith. Yet at last their folly shall be manifest unto all men, as theirs also was." 2 Tim. 3 : 8, 9.

Now here you may see and know of the true and false law, how both may be written into the hearts of men. The false law will be written by the spirit of error into the heart of the unbelieving; the true law of life is written by the holy spirit of truth into the children of the New Covenant, in the true believers, and is altogether one and consistent with what Christ externally commanded, and with what the apostles have written.

Son. I have now sufficiently understood what you have said, and find it very useful and necessary to be well instructed in many things, since in

wohl gute Augen erfordert, das Wahre und Falsche zu erkennen und zu unterscheiden. Nun muß ich auch noch etwas fragen: Ich habe in der Apostel Geschicht Cap. 15, 29. gelesen, daß die Apostel zu Jerusalem denen Gläubigen aus den Heiden verboten haben, das Blut und Erstickte zu essen; ob dieses jetzt auch noch müsse gehalten werden?

Vom Erstickten und vom Blut.

Vater. Merke wohl, weil das Blut im Alten Testament zur Versöhnung war, darum hat Gott, sobald er Noa und seinen Söhnen erlaubete Fleisch zu essen, zu ihnen gesagt: Esset das Fleisch nicht, das noch lebet in seinem Blut. 1 Mos. 9, 4. Ferner hat Gott durch Mosen seinem Volk dieses sagen lassen: Ihr sollt auch kein Blut essen, weder von Vieh noch von Vögeln, und welche Seele Blut isset, die soll ausgerottet werden von ihrem Volk. 3 Mos. 7, 26. 27.

Dieses hat Gott noch klärer ausgedrückt, da er spricht: Welcher Mensch, er sey vom Hause Israel, oder ein Fremdling, unter euch Blut isset, wider den will ich mein Antlitz setzen, und will ihn mitten aus dem Volk rotten, denn des Leibes Leben ist im Blut, und ich habe es euch zum Altar gegeben, daß eure Seelen damit versöhnet werden, denn das Blut ist die Versöhnung für euer Leben, darum habe ich euch gesaget, keine Seele unter euch soll Blut essen. 3 Mos. 17, 10—12.

Da siehest du, warum Gott seinem Volk im alten Testament das Blut zu essen verboten hat; weil nun zu der Apostel Zeit diejenige, so aus den Juden waren gläubig geworden, schon aus dem Gesetz gelernet hatten kein Blut zu essen, die Gläubigen

these times we need good discerning eyesight, to know and distinguish the true and false. Now I must ask something yet; I have read in the Acts of the apostles, C. 15: 29, that the apostles at Jerusalem have forbidden the believers from the Gentiles to eat blood, and things strangled. Is this to be observed still?

OF THINGS STRANGLED AND OF BLOOD.

FATHER. Mark well! Since blood in the Old Testament was appointed for atonement, God, as soon as he permitted Noah and his sons to eat flesh, said to them, 'But flesh with the life thereof, which is the blood thereof, shall ye not eat." Gen. 9 : 4. Again, by Moses, God commanded his people thus: 'Moreover ye shall eat no manner of blood, whether it be of fowl, or of beast, in any of your dwellings. Whatsoever soul it be, that eateth any manner of blood, even that soul shall be cut off from his people." Lev. 7 : 26, 27.

This God has expressed still more clearly, when he said, 'And whatsoever man there be of the house of Israel, or of the strangers, that sojourn among you, that eateth any manner of blood, I will even set my face against that soul that eateth blood, and will cut him off from among his people. For the life of the flesh is in the blood, and I have given it to you upon the altar to make an atonement for your souls: for it is the blood that maketh an atonement for the soul. Therefore I said unto the children of Israel, No soul of you shall eat blood." Lev. 17 : 10—12.

Here thou seest, why God has forbidden his people in the Old Testament, to eat blood. Since then in the time of the apostles, those who had come to the faith from the Jews, had already learned from the Law, not to eat blood,

aber aus den Heiden davon nichts wußten, so hat es dem heiligen Geist gefallen, durch die Apostel ihnen solches als ein nothwendiges Stück zu befehlen, sich vom Blutessen zu enthalten, eben als wie von der Hurerei. Act. 15, 29.

Und weil auch den Christen das Blut des Sohnes Gottes ihre Versöhnung ist, darum essen sie billig kein Blut, weil es auch sowohl im alten als neuen Testament verboten ist. Die ersten Christen haben zu den Heiden also gesaget: Wir sind nicht so bestialisch wie die Thiere, wenn wir der Thiere Fleisch essen, daß wir auch ihr Blut essen sollten, und darnach begierig seyn; ja sie haben einen Bann darauf geleget, wann einer Blut gegessen hat. Wie in Gottfried Arnolds Abbildung der ersten Christen zu sehen ist.

S o h n. Ich habe aber hören sagen: Weilen der Herr Jesus spricht, Es ist nichts ausser dem Menschen das ihn könnte gemein machen, so es in ihn gehet. Marc. 7, 15. Und der Apostel sagt: Alles, was feil ist auf dem Fleischmarkt, das esset. 1 Cor. 10, 25.

V a t e r. Die Menschen so dieses sagen verstehen noch nicht die Einigkeit des Geistes, sondern wie sie in der Uneinigkeit stehen, so meinen sie die Schrift und der Geist Gottes wären auch so uneins, daß an einem Orte was verboten, und am andern wieder erlaubet wäre. Denn wann Christus die verbotene Dinge gemeinet hätte, so dürfte man sich getrost vollsaufen, welches aber eine große Sünde ist.

Und wenn Paulus ohne Unterschied alles gemeinet zu kaufen, was auf dem Fleischmarkt feil wäre zu essen, so sind noch sonst viele Dinge feil, die man gar nicht essen kann, und so wenig Paulus andere Dinge als natürliche Speise so man essen kann, gemeinet, so wenig hat er auch das Blut kaufen und essen gemeinet. Einmal bleibt also das Blut und Erstickte eben wie die Hurerei von dem heiligen

the believers from the Gentiles, however, knowing nothing of this, it pleased the Holy Ghost to command by the apostles those necessary things, namely, to abstain from blood, as well as from fornication. Acts 15 : 29.

And since, to the Christians, the blood of the Son of God is their atonement, they should certainly eat no blood, because it is forbidden both in the Old and New Testament. The primitive Christians said to the Heathens thus: 'We are not as brutal as the beasts, when we eat the flesh of animals, that we should also eat their blood, and long after it." They have even laid the ban upon such, as should eat blood, as may be seen in Godfrey Arnold's Portraiture of the Primitive Christians.

SON. But it has been said, because the Lord Jesus declares, 'There is nothing from without a man, that entering into him, can defile him." Mark 7 : 15. And the apostle says, Whatsoever is sold in the shambles, that eat." 1 Cor. 10 : 25.

FATHER. Men who say this, do not understand the unity of the Spirit, but as they stand in disunion, they think, the Scripture and the Spirit of God were as discordant as they are, just as if that which was forbidden in one place, was allowed again in another place. For if Christ had meant the forbidden things, we might go to drinking to excess, which however is a great sin.

Again, if Paul had meant to buy all without distinction, whatsoever is sold in the shambles, and to eat it, then remember, that there are many things still in the shambles, which cannot be eaten, and as little as Paul would mean other things, besides what was natural food, and which can be eaten, so little he meant to buy and eat blood. Thus it is a settled point, that the eating of

Geist durch die Apostel allen wahren Christen verboten.

Von dem Ehestand.

Sohn. Sage mir doch auch, was es für eine Bewandniß habe mit dem Ehestand im neuen Bund, ob die Glaubigen auch heirathen dürfen, oder wie der Ehestand soll gehalten werden.

Vater. Es hat Gott der Herr den Ehestand im Paradies selber eingesetzt, wie es auch der Herr Jesus zu den Pharisäern gesprochen: Habt ihr nicht gelesen, daß der, im Anfang den Menschen erschaffen, hat gemacht, daß ein Mann und Weib seyn sollte, und daß sie nicht zwei, sondern ein Fleisch seyen. Siehe solcher Ehestand zweier Personen, die in der Furcht Gottes und im Glauben an Gott eins seyn, ist von Gott selber eingesetzet, und gesegnet. Wie man an Abraham, Isaak, Jacob, und den Heiligen im alten Testament wohl merken und sehen kann.

Wie aber der Ehestand in der Einigkeit geführet werden soll, davon ist schon im Gesetz etwas ausgedrücket. Erstlich ist dem Volk Israel von Gott verboten gewesen, auffer dem Saamen Abrahams nicht zu heirathen. 5 Mos. 7, 3. Und als Gott der Herr das Volk Israel sein Gesetz wollte hören laffen, ließ er durch Mosen dem Volk sagen: seyd bereit auf den dritten Tag, und keiner nahe sich zum Weibe. 2 Mos. 19, 15. Ferner hat Gott im Gesetz geboten, wenn ein Weib ein Mägdlein gebiehret, so soll sie 66 Tage daheim im Blut ihrer Reinigung bleiben, 3 Mos. 12, 5. Und in der Zeit mußten sie sich gänzlich enthalten. Und wenn ein Weib ihre ordentliche Krankheit hatte, so war die Enthaltung scharf geboten. 3 Mos. 20, 18.

Aus allen diesen Befehlen Gottes kann man wohl merken, daß der Ehestand rein und in der Enthaltung geführet werden

blood, and things strangled, as well as fornication, are forbidden to all true Christians by the Holy Ghost, through the apostles.

OF MATRIMONY.

Son. Do tell me also, how the case stands with regard to matrimony under the new covenant, whether believers are permitted to marry, or how is that matter to be regarded?

Father. The Lord God himself instituted matrimony in Paradise, as the Lord Jesus said to the Pharisees, 'Have ye not read, that he who made them in the beginning, made them male and female, and that they should be no more twain, but one flesh.'' Behold such union of two persons, who are one in the fear of God and the faith in God, is ordained and blessed by God himself, as may be seen in the case of Abraham, Isaac, Jacob, and the saints of the Old Testament.

But how the marriage-relation should be conducted in unison, has been expressed in part already in the Law. First the people of Israel were forbidden to marry any other except of the seed of Abraham. Deut. 7 : 3. And when God was about to give them his Law, he told them by Moses, 'Be ready against the third day; come not at (near) your wives!'' Exod. 19 : 15. Again, God commanded in the Law, 'If she (a woman) bear a maid-child, then she shall be unclean two weeks, as in her separation, and she shall continue in the blood of her purifying three-soore and six days.'' Lev. 12 : 5. And during this time they had to abstain entirely. And if a woman had her ordinary sickness, abstinence was strictly commanded. Lev. 20 : 18.

From all these commandments of God, it is clear, that marriage should be conducted in purity and abstinence,

soll, und nicht in der Lustseuche wie die Heiden, die von Gott nichts wissen, also kann man wohl sehen, daß Gott den Ehestand seines Volks in der Reinigung und Enthaltung geführet haben wollte. Nun im neuen Testament soll und muß der Ehestand nicht unheiliger sondern billig heiliger geführet werden.

Und von den ledigen Personen sagt der Apostel Paulus: Es wäre ihnen gut, wenn sie blieben wie er, nemlich wie Paulus. Denn so der ledige Stand wird in der Reinigkeit des Geistes und des Fleisches in wahrem Glauben an Jesum geführet, und in wahrer Demuth bewahret, so ist es besser und höher, auch dem Bilde des Herrn Jesu ähnlicher, so zu bleiben. Wenn aber ein Lediges heirathet, so sündiget es nicht, wann es nur in dem Herrn Jesu geschiehet, das ist, in wahrem Glauben an Jesum Christum, daß sie einig nach der Lehre Jesu und nach seinen Befehlen seyn. Das heisset, Ein Fleisch seyn, gleich wie Christus und seine Gemeinde. Ephes. 5, 30.

Dann anders kann kein Mensch ein Fleisch seyn mit Christo, oder von seinen Gebeinen, als wann er das Wort, welches Jesus war, und was er gelehret, im Glauben annimmt, und ihm im Gehorsam folget. So ist er Fleisch und Bein von seinen Beinen, dieses kann ja nicht von der Gläubigen verwesentlichem Fleisch verstanden werden, dann das Fleisch Christi ist ja unverweslich. Also muß auch der wahre Ehestand welchen Gott eingesetzet hat, in dieser Einigkeit bestehen, auf daß sie nicht nur nach dem äußerlichen Fleisch und verwesentlichen Theil ein Fleisch seyn sollen, sondern vielmehr nach dem inwendigen Theil, in dem Willen ihres Gottes müssen sie ein Fleisch seyn, und einerlei Glauben an Christo Jesu haben.

Auf keine andere Art ist der Ehestand eingesetzet oder gesegnet, ausser solchem wie gemeldet nach der heiligen Schrift. Wo

and not in concupiscence like the heathens do, who know nothing of God. Thus we can easily see, that God would have his people to live pure and chaste in matrimony. Now under the New Testament, matrimony should not be less, but rather more sacredly observed.

And of unmarried persons, says the apostle Paul, 'it would be good for them if they abide even as he," i. e. as Paul himself. For if the single state be conducted in purity of the spirit and of the flesh, in the true faith in Jesus, and kept in true humility, it may be deemed better and higher, and more in accordance with the pattern of the Lord Jesus. But if a single person marries, he commits no sin, provided it be done in the Lord Jesus; that is, in true faith in Jesus Christ, and in union according to the doctrine and commandments of Christ. This is to be 'One flesh even as Christ and his church are one body. Eph. 5 : 30.

For no man can be one flesh with Christ, or of his bones, in any other way than by receiving the word, which was Jesus himself and what he taught, in faith, and following him in obedience. The words, 'He is flesh of his flesh, and bone of his bones, cannot be understood of the corruptible flesh of the believer, for the flesh of Christ is incorruptible. Thus also must the true marriage consist in true union, that they may not only be one flesh according to the outward flesh and corruptible part, but much more according to the inward part, in the will of their God must they be one flesh, and have one faith in Christ Jesus.

In no other manner has matrimony been instituted and blessed, than has been stated according to holy writ.

aber Menschen sind die sich um Augenlust, Fleischeslust, und Reichthums wegen heira=then, und nicht auf die Einigkeit des Glau=bes in Christo sehen, solcher Ehestand lieget unter dem Fluch, und muß billig von den wahren Glaubigen verworfen werden, ist auch nicht gültig in des Herrn Haus oder Gemeinde, und ist jederzeit von Gott ge=straft worden. Wie zu sehen, da die Kinder Gottes von Gott abfielen und fleischlich wurden, sich umsahen nach den Töchtern der Menschen wie sie schön wa=ren, und zu Weibern nahmen, welche sie wollten, da mußte eine Sündfluth kom=men und sie alle umbringen.

Die Schrift nennet diejenige Kinder Gottes welche vom Geschlecht Seths waren, der ein Sohn Adams und nach seinem Bilde gezeuget war. 1 Mos. 5, 3. Die Kinder der Menschen aber waren von dem Geschlechte Kains, welchen der Herr ver=fluchte, um seines Bruder=Mords willen. Diese beiderlei Geschlechte sollten sich nicht vermischen, aber sie wollten Gott nicht fol=gen, darum mußten sie alle beide vertilget werden. Aus dem Geschlechte Seth aber wurde ein Saame übrig behalten, nemlich Noa und seine Söhne. Aber der Teufel brachte sogleich auch den Ham als des Noa Sohn unter den Fluch, daß ihn sein Va=ter Noa verfluchte. 1 Mos. 9, 25.

Und aus dem Geschlecht Hams hat sich Gott niemand erwählet, sondern aus dem Geschlecht Sems, Noa's Sohn, von die=sem ist Abraham der Vater aller Glaubi=gen geboren. Nun erkannte Abraham schon den Sinn Gottes, da er seinem Sohn Isaak wollte ein Weib nehmen, da sprach er zu seinem ältesten Knecht: Er sollte ja seinem Sohn kein Weib nehmen, von den Töchtern des Landes Kanaan, als von dem Geschlecht Hams. Sondern er sollte zu seines Vaters Haus ziehen und ihm daselbst ein Weib nehmen. Eben diesen Sinn hatte auch Isaak, der befahl seinem Sohn Jacob, als er ihn segnete, und sprach zu

But where there are people, who marry for the lust of the eye, the lust of the flesh, or for the sake of riches, and do not look upon the unity of faith in Christ, such matrimony is under the curse, and is justly to be rejected by true believers, it is also not legitimate in the house or church of the Lord, and always has been punished by God, as may be seen, when the children of God turned away from God, and became carnal, and saw the daughters of men, that they were fair, and took to them wives as they pleased, then a flood came, and destroyed them all.

The Scripture represents those as children of God, who were the descend-ants of Seth, who was a son of Adam, begotten after his image Gen. 5: 3. But the children of men were descend-ants of Cain, whom the Lord had cursed for the murdering of his brother. These two generations were not to be mixed; but they would not obey God, and so they all perished. From the family of Seth, a seed was preserved, namely, Noah and his sons. But the devil soon brought Ham, one of the sons of Noah, under the curse, for even his father Noah cursed him Gen 9: 25.

From the family of Ham, God chose no one, but from the family of Shem, the son of Noah. From him descend-ed Abraham, the father of all the faith-ful. Now Abraham understood the mind of God, and when he wished to get a wife for his son Isaac he told his eldest servant, 'that he should not take a wife unto his son of the daughters of the Canaanites, or of the family of Ham, but that he should go to his father's house, and there get a wife for him. Of the same mind was Isaac, who com-manded his son Jacob, when he blessed him, and said unto him, 'Thou shalt

ihm: du sollt nicht ein Weib nehmen von den Töchtern Kanaan, sondern zeuch zu deiner Freundschaft, zu deiner Vater (Mutter) Haus, und nimm dir ein Weib daselbst.

Aber Esau, auch Isaaks Sohn, war ein wilder u. von Gott verhaßter Mensch, dann er achtete nicht auf den Sinn Gottes im Heirathen, sondern er freiete nach Lust und Gefälligkeit, und nahm zwei Weiber unter den Hethitern, ausser seinem Geschlecht, und diese machten dem Isaak und der Rebecca lauter Herzeleid. Ja man siehet an dem weisen Könige Salomon, als ihn die Lust und Gefälligkeit gegen die fremden Weiber überwunden, und wider das Gesetz geheirathet, wie er dadurch bei Gott in Ungnaden gekommen, und sein ganzes Reich zerrissen worden. Dahero siehet man, als dorten die Juden sich bekehrten, und den Tempel zu Nehemia Zeiten wieder baueten, wie sie sich von allen fremden Weibern, die sie genommen hatten, und deren einige auch schon schwanger waren, scheiden mußten, wie du solches im 10ten Capitel im Buch Esra lesen kannst.

Sohn. Wenn aber Menschen ohne Glauben heirathen, und das eine Theil bekehret sich, und wird gläubig, darf es denn bei dem Unglaubigen bleiben?

Vater. Unter den ersten Christen muß dieses wohl zum öftern geschehen seyn, daß das eine gläubig worden ist, und das andere nicht, darum lehret Paulus: Wann es dem Unglaubigen gefallen thäte, bei dem Glaubigen zu bleiben, so sollte sich der Glaubige nicht scheiden, wollte sich aber der Unglaubige scheiden, so möchte er solches thun, und das glaubige Theil wäre gar nicht gebunden in solchen Fällen. 1 Cor. 7, 12–15. Und ist wohl zu merken, was Paulus in den vorhergehenden Versen vom Ehestand der Glaubigen saget, nemlich, der Herr sage es, daß das Weib sich nicht vom Manne scheiden soll,

not take a wife of the daughters of Canaan, but go to thy mother's father, and take thee a wife from thence.

But Esau, also a son of Isaac, was a wild man, and hateful to God, because he did not regard the mind of God in marrying, but followed his own lust and pleasure. He took two wives, not of his kindred, but of the Hittites, and this caused much grief to Isaac and Rebecca. We see also in the wise king Solomon, when overcome by his love and lust towards strange women, and marrying contrary to the law, how he thereby fell under the displeasure of God, and finally his kingdom was torn apart. Further we see, when afterwards the Jews were converted, and built again the temple in the time of Nehemiah, how they had to separate themselves from all strange wives, whom they had taken, some of whom were even with child, as we may read in the book of Esra, ch. 10.

Son. But if people marry without faith, and one part should be converted and come to the faith, may he who is converted still remain with the unbelieving partner?

Father. Among the first Christians this must have happened frequently, that one of the parties became faithful, while the other did not. Paul therefore teaches, 'If the unbelieving party be pleased to dwell with the believing one, this should not leave the other. But if the unbelieving depart, let him depart. A brother or sister is not under bondage in such cases.' 1 Cor. 7 : 12, 15. And it is well to take notice, what Paul says in the foregoing verses concerning the marriage of believers, namely, that the Lord commands, 'Let not the wife depart from

so sie sich aber scheidet, daß sie ohne Ehe bleibe. Den andern aber sage ich, nicht der Herr, daß das Gläubige sich nicht vom Unglaubigen scheiden soll, so es dem Letztern beim Erstern zu wohnen gefällt.

Hierdurch hat man zu verstehen: Daß das ungläubige Theil kein Wolf oder Bestie seyn muß, gleich wie es Menschen gibt, die wie Hunde, Löwen und grimmige Thiere seyn, zanken, lästern, und das Gute mit Gewalt verderben und vertilgen wollen, aber wenn das Ungläubige in allerlei Schand und Ehebrecherei ausbrechen thäte, daß das Gläubige nur sein Schanddeckel seyn sollte, auf solche Art sollte durchaus ein Gläubiges nicht gebunden seyn, bei einem solchen wilden Menschen zu bleiben.

Von dem Ehebruch.

Sohn. Wenn nun unter Eheleuten eines sich durch den Teufel zur Ehebrecherei verführen ließe, es wollte aber dennoch bei seinem Ehegatten bleiben, dürfte solches zugelassen werden?

Vater. Vors erste ist im Gesetz befohlen die Ehebrecher zu tödten, dann es hat keiner unter des Herrn Volk seyn sollen; wann aber ein Mann sein Weib durch einen Scheidebrief losgelassen hatte, so war sie keine Ehebrecherin ob sie gleich einen andern Mann genommen, wann aber der andere Mann gestorben, so hat sie der Erste nicht wieder nehmen dürfen, denn sie ist unrein worden, und solches ist dem Herrn ein Greuel gewesen. 5 Mos. 24, 3. 4.

Nun kann man ja leicht merken, wenn das Weib so unrein worden ist, weil es der Mann nach dem erlaubten Gesetz von sich gelassen hat, wie viel mehr wird ein Weib unrein wenn sie gar in Ehebrecherei fället, und wie viel weniger darf alsdann ein Gläubiger, welches Leib heilig seyn soll, sich wieder vermischen mit einem ehebrecherischen Huren-Leib, welches gewiß ein

her husband: but and if she depart, let her remain unmarried. But to the rest speak I, not the Lord, that a believer should not depart from the unbelieving part, if the latter be pleased to dwell with the former.''

By this we are to understand, that the unbelieving part must not be like a wolf or other brute, for there are some people, who are as dogs, lions or other wild beasts, who scold and chide continually, and try to oppose and destroy violently all that is good. But if he, the unbelieving part, should break out into shameful and adulterous acts, so that the believing part should be only to serve as a cloak to hide the other's shame, then and in that case a believer should not be bound to remain with such a vicious person.

OF ADULTERY.

Son. But among married people, should one be seduced by the devil to commit adultery, and the innocent party would be willing to remain with the guilty, may this be permitted?

Father. In the first place, it is commanded in the Law, to kill the adulterers; for there were none such to remain among the people of God. But if a man had set his wife at liberty by a letter of divorcement, she was no adulteress, though she married another man. Yet if that second husband died, the first was not allowed to take her again to be his wife, for she had become unclean, and such is an abomination before the Lord. Deut. 24 : 3, 4.

Now it is easily to be conceived, if the woman became unclean, because she was set free by her first husband by a law of permission, how much more will she become unclean, if she should fall into adultery; and much less then may a believer, whose body should be holy, connect himself again with an adulterous whorish body, which certain-

großer Greuel in den Augen Gottes ist, und in des Herrn Gemeinde durchaus nicht zugelassen werden kann, dann es würde hierdurch eine ganze Gemeine verunreiniget. Es wäre denn daß ein solches Weib oder Mann wahrhaftig Buße thäte, dann könnte es wohl bei dem reinen Theil wohnen, aber sich wieder miteinander zu vermischen, das wäre unrein nach dem lautern Sinn Gottes.

„Er sprach zu ihnen: Moses hat euch erlaubet zu scheiden von euren Weibern, von eures Herzen Härtigkeit wegen; von Anbeginn aber ist es nicht also gewesen. Ich sage aber euch: Wer sich von seinem Weibe scheidet (es sey denn um der Hurerei willen) und freiet eine andere, der bricht die Ehe. Und wer die Abgeschiedene freiet, der bricht auch die Ehe. Matth. 19, 8. 9.

Wegen dem Bann.

Sohn. Wenn aber unter den Gläubigen ein Theil sündiget, es sey Mann oder Weib, so daß es von der Gemeinde in den Bann gethan wird, muß dann auch das andere Theil dasselbige meiden, und sonderlich in ehelichen Beiwohnungen?

Vater. Merke hierin wieder auf den Sinn Gottes. Es hat Gott im alten Testament geboten, „wenn dich dein Bruder, oder Sohn, oder Tochter, oder das Weib in deinen Armen, oder dein Freund der dir ist wie dein Herz, heimlich überreden wollte, und sagen: Laß uns andern Göttern dienen die du nicht kennest, so bewillige nicht, und dein Auge soll ihn nicht schonen, du sollt ihn auch nicht verbergen, und du sollt dich seiner nicht erbarmen, sondern deine Hand soll am ersten über ihm seyn, daß man ihn tödte, darnach die Hand des ganzen Volks." 5 Mos. 13, 6—9.

Nun siehe wie hier alle Freundschaft nichts dürfte helfen demjenigen, so nach dem Gesetz getödtet werden mußte.

---

ly is a great abomination in the sight of God, and can by no means be permitted in the church of the Lord; for by this the whole church would be defiled. But if it be, that such a man or woman would truly repent, then such might indeed continue to live with the innocent party; but to cohabit together, would be unclean, according to the pure mind of God.

'He saith unto them, Moses, because of the hardness of your hearts, suffered you to put away your wives: but from the beginning it was not so. And I say unto you, whosoever shall put away his wife, except it be for fornication, and shall marry another, committeth adultery: and whoso marrieth her which is put away, doth commit adultery." Matt. 19 : 8, 9.

OF AVOIDANCE (BAN.)

Son. But if among believers one party, either husband or wife, sins so as to be put in avoidance by the church, is the other party also to avoid and have no communication with the party put in avoidance?

Father. Take notice again of the mind of God. He had commanded in the Old Testament, 'If thy brother, the son of thy mother, or thy son, or thy daughter, or the wife of thy bosom, or thy friend, which is as thine own soul, entice thee secretly, saying, let us go and serve other gods, which thou hast not known, thou, nor thy fathers :— thou shalt not consent unto him, nor hearken unto him : neither shall thine eye pity him, neither shalt thou spare, neither shalt thou conceal him :—thy hand shall be first upon him to put him to death, and afterward, the hand of all the people. Deut. 13 : 6, 8, 9.

Now see here, how all the friends could not help him, who was to be put to death according to the Law. This

Dieses hat schon nach dem neuen Bund den Bann in der Gemeine des Herrn abgebildet. Da hat der Herr Jesus gesaget: "Wann dein Bruder an dir sündiget (hierunter ist Mann und Weib, Kinder und Eltern, wenn sie mit einander in dem Bund Gottes stehen, verstanden) und er will dich und die Gemeinde nicht hören, so halte ihn als einen Heiden und Zöllner." Matt. 18, 17. (Und noch sonderlicher redet der Apostel von solchen, "mit welchen wir n i ch t s sollen zu schaffen haben, auch nicht einmal mit ihnen zu essen." 1 Cor. 5, 9—11.)

Dies ist nun eine Meidung sowohl in geistlicher als fleischlicher Gemeinschaft, und müssen billig diejenige am ersten in die Meidung thun, die am nächsten bei ihm seyn, wie schon oben gemeldet, wollen sie nicht beflecket werden, und dieses ist noch kräftig abgebildet, 5 Mos. 17, 7. Wenn einer sich versündiget hatte, daß er sterben mußte, und gesteiniget wurde, so mußte die Hand der Zeugen am ersten über dem Verbrecher seyn, darnach die Hand des ganzen Volks. Und als Israel sich am güldenen Kalb versündiget hatte, so mußten die Leviten nach des Herrn Wort, am ersten erwürgen im Lager, von einem Thor zum andern seinen Bruder, Freund und Nächsten, alsdann wurde durch Mosen der Segen über sie gebracht. 2 Mos. 32, 27–29.

Also ist es am allernothwendigsten im Christenthum, das allerbeste zu verleugnen um des Herrn willen. Dahin gehet auch insonderheit die Lehre Jesu in der Verleugnung. Aber manche Unerleuchtete können wohl einen Bann führen helfen gegen jemanden, da es ihnen keine Verleugnung kostet, aber wenn es an sie selbsten kommt, daß sie sich oder ihre liebste Freunde, Mann, Weib und Kinder verleugnen sollen, da ist leider manchmal die natürliche Liebe viel stärker als die göttliche Liebe,

already prefigured the avoidance in the church of the Lord according to the New Testament. Here the Lord Jesus said, 'If thy brother shall trespass against thee, (by which husband and wife, children and parents, if they are included in the covenant of God, are understood,) and if he shall neglect to hear thee and the church, let him be unto thee as an heathen man, and a publican." Matt. 18 : 17. (And more especially the apostle speaks of such, 'with whom we are not to keep company, and not even to eat with them." 1 Cor 5 : 9—11.)

This is indeed an avoidance not only of spiritual, but also of carnal connection, and it is no more than proper, that those should be first, in avoiding such, who are nearest connected with him, as above stated, if they do not wish to be defiled. This is yet strongly prefigured in Deut. 17 : 7, namely, if one had transgressed, so that he must suffer death, 'the hands of the witnesses shall be first upon the transgressor, and then the hands of all the people." And when Israel had sinned with the Golden Calf, the Levites had according to the word of the Lord first to slay from gate to gate throughout the camp every man his brother, companion and neighbor, and then the blessing was restored upon them by Moses. Exod. 32 : 27—29.

Thus in Christendom it is most necessary to renounce all, even the very best, for the Lord's sake. The doctrine of Jesus has the same tendency of self-denial. It is, however, an easy matter for many that are unenlightened to assist in putting in avoidance one, where it costs them no self-denial. But when it comes to themselves, that they are to deny themselves, or their dearest friends, husband, wife or children, then alas! is their natural love often much

und kommen solche Seelen ins Verderben. Darum bleibet es fest was der Herr Jesus saget: "Wer etwas lieber hat als mich, der ist mein nicht werth."

Vam äußern Gottesdienst.

Sohn. Du hast mir nun von mancherlei Dingen gesaget, ich höre aber von vielen, daß solche Dinge gar nicht nothwendig wären in acht zu nehmen, weilen die Glaubigen ins Himmlische Wesen versetzt wären, so gingen sie auch mit lauter Himmlischen Dingen um, und hätten nicht mehr nöthig sich in solchen Dingen aufzuhalten.

Vater. Ja ich habe selbst genug solche Menschen gesehen die solches sagen, lehren, und davon schreiben, aber sie irren gar sehr, und fehlet ihnen nur an einem demüthigen Herzen, welches sich gar gerne dem göttlichen Rath und Ordnungen unterwirft, und lernet in den geringen Dingen treu seyn, alsdenn wird es auch gesetzt über hohe und große. Es ist eine Zeit der Erniedrigung und eine Zeit der Erhöhung; es ist der Herr Jesus vorerst ganz klein und niedrig erschienen in dieser Welt, in einer demüthigen und willigen Unterwerfung gegen den Willen seines Vaters. Zum andernmal aber wird er in großer Kraft und Herrlichkeit als ein erhöheter Christus erscheinen.

Alle Seelen nun, die gerne bei seiner Erhöhung bei ihm seyn wollen, die müssen ihn auch erst als einen erniedrigten Christum annehmen, ihn bekennen vor den Menschen in allen seinen Geboten, und sich dieses nicht schämen, damit sie auch klein werden in den kleinen Geboten, so werden sie auch endlich zu seiner Zeit erhöhet werden, sonsten wird es unmöglich seyn. Darum ist jederzeit des Herrn Gemeine in dieser Welt klein und verachtet gewesen, sie hat immer müssen unterliegen, als ein Auskehrsel.

stronger than their love to God, and such souls may thereby be brought to ruin. Hence what the Lord Jesus says, stands fast, namely, this, 'Whosoever loveth any thing more than me, is not worthy of me."

OF OUTWARD WORSHIP.

Son. Thou hast told me now of many things; but I hear of many (who say) that such things are not at all necessary to be attended to, because believers are made to sit together in heavenly places, and are to converse about heavenly things alone, and have no more need to be perplexed in such things.

Father. Indeed, I have seen myself enough of such men, who talk, teach, and write in this way. But they err greatly, and they are wanting of that humble mind, which is very willing to submit to the divine counsel and ordinances, and to learn to be faithful in small things, so that they may afterwards also be made stewards of high and great things. There is a time for humiliation, and a time for exaltation. The Lord Jesus first appeared in this world humbly and lowly, in a voluntary submission to the will of his Father. At another time he will appear in great power and glory, as an exalted Christ.

All those souls now, who desire to be with him in his exaltation, must also first receive him as an humble Christ, must confess him before men in all his commandments, and not be ashamed to become little in little commandments, so that they, also, finally, in due time may be exalted. Otherwise it will be impossible for them to become exalted. Thus the church of the Lord in this world has always been small and despised. Indeed it was ever considered as the filth of the earth by the unbelieving world.

Darum irren solche Menschen mit ihren Gedanken gar sehr, die da vorgeben, die Gläubigen hätten nicht nöthig mit elementischem Wasser getauft zu werden, sie hätten auch nicht nöthig, irdischen Wein der Gemeinschaft, zur Verkündigung des Todes Jesu, zu trinken, sondern sie trinken geistlichen Wein, und seyen getauft mit geistlichem Wasser, und was dergleichen ihr hohes Vorgeben mehr ist, wider die klare Zeugnisse der heiligen Schrift; darum ist es sehr gut, daß man nur einig allein siehet auf des Herrn Jesu seine ausgesprochene Worte, und auf sein eigenes vollkommenes Exempel, und folget dem nur im Gehorsam des Glaubens einfältig nach, und nimmt gefangen alle Vernunft unter den Gehorsam des Herrn Jesu, so wird man nicht von denen hochsprechenden Menschen irre geführet.

Von Ausflüchten der Ungläubigen.

Sohn. Ich habe aber auch viele sich hören berufen auf die heilige Männer, als Tauleri, Thomä a Kempis, und dergleichen. die schöne geistreiche Bücher geschrieben, und von Haltung der äuserlichen Lehre nichts gemeldet.

Vater. Solche Menschen, die sich auf Menschen Zeugnisse berufen, die geben zu verstehen, daß sie das göttliche Zeugniß von Jesu nicht haben; darum spricht der heilige Johannes: So wir der Menschen Zeugniß annehmen, so ist Gottes Zeugniß viel größer, denn Gott hat gezeuget von seinem Sohn, und wer da glaubet an den Sohn Gottes, der hat solches Zeugniß in ihm. Wer Gott nicht glaubet, der macht ihn zum Lügner, denn er glaubet nicht dem Zeugniß, das Gott zeuget von seinem Sohn. 1 Joh. 5, 9. 10. Solches Zeugniß ist nothwendig zur Seligkeit, und haben es alle Heiligen gehabt.

Aber ein solches Zeugniß von den Menschen, so noch unter dem groben Babel sind stehen blieben, ist leider gar gefähr-

---

Hence such men err very much in their thoughts, who pretend that it is needless for believers to be baptized with elementary water; that they needed not to drink the earthly wine of communion to shew forth the death of Jesus, but say that they drink spiritual wine, and that they were baptized with spiritual water, and make other like high pretensions against the clear testimony of the Holy Scriptures. It is therefore very good to look wholly and alone . to the express words of the Lord Jesus, and to his own perfect example, and to follow that only in obedience with faith and simplicity, and bringing every thought into subjection to the Lord Jesus. We shall not be likely then to be led astray by these high talking people.

OF THE EXCUSES OF UNBELIEVERS.

SON. But I have also heard many, who appeal to holy men such as TAULERUS, THOMAS a KEMPIS and others, who have written such fine spiritual books, and mentioned nothing of the observance of the outward doctrine of Jesus.

FATHER. Such men, who appeal to human testimony, give us to understand that they are in want of the divine testimony of Jesus. Hence St. John says, "If we receive the witness of men, the witness of God is greater: for this is the witness of God which he has testified of his Son. He that believeth on the Son of God hath the witness in himself: he that believeth not God hath made him a liar, because he believeth not the record that God gave of his Son." 1 John 5: 9, 10. Such testimony is necessary to salvation, and all the saints had it.

But, alas! it is very dangerous to appeal to such testimony of men, who still remain under the obviously

lich sich darauf zu berufen, und sind gemeiniglich alle die sich auf solche berufen, dennoch mit selbigen Menschen nicht eins. Dann wer sollte wohl können eins seyn mit solchen, die noch unter dem Kloster, und unter des Pabstes Lehre gestanden seyn, und vielleicht aus Menschenfurcht nicht bekannt, was sie mögen erkannt haben. Aber solche Berufung auf heilige Menschen ist eben so blind, als die ganze Welt, welche sich auf Christum und seine Apostel berufet, und sind doch gar nicht mit Lehre und Leben eins.

Darum sind solche arme Seelen wohl zu bedauern, die ihren Glauben auf einen so blinden Grund bauen wollen, welches doch zur Zeit der Anfechtung immer wieder einfällt. Der Sohn Gottes aber hat gelehret: "Wer diese meine Rede höret, und thut sie, den vergleiche ich einem klugen Mann." Matth. 7, 24. Ferner spricht der Heiland: "Wahrlich ich sage euch, wer mein Wort höret, und glaubet dem der mich gesandt hat, der hat das ewige Leben, und kommt nicht in das Gericht." Joh. 5, 24. Ferner: Wer an mich glaubet, wird nimmermehr sterben. Das sind gewisse Zeugnisse dem, der da glaubet.—

Aber, o wie elend ist dies, sich auf Menschen Zeugnisse zu berufen, und auf Menschen zu sehen, die man vor heilig und klug ansiehet, daß man denkt oder spricht: ja wenn diese es so lehrten und glaubten nach der Schrift, so wollte man es auch glauben. Dagegen aber spricht der Apostel Paulus: So auch wir, oder ein Engel vom Himmel euch ein ander Evangelium predigte, anderst, dann das wir euch geprediget haben, der sey verflucht. Gal. 1, 8. Siehe, das ist das einige Evangelium, worauf Moses und alle Propheten gewiesen, daß man es hören solle, und welches von Christo und seinen Aposteln uns geoffenbaret ist.

seductive power of Babylon, and commonly all those who do appeal to these very men, do not agree with them. For who indeed would or could agree with such as still continued to be in monasteries, and under the popish doctrine, and who perhaps for fear of man, would not confess what they knew to be the truth. But such an appeal to holy men is just as inconsistent as the whole world professing Christ and his apostles, and still not agreeing with them at all in doctrine and practice.

Such poor souls therefore are to be pitied, who wish to ground their faith upon such a blind (slender) foundation, which in times of tribulation will always fail. But the Son of God has taught, that "whosoever heareth these sayings of mine, and doeth them, I will liken him unto a wise man, who built his house upon a rock." Matt. 7 : 24. Again, says the Savior, "Verily, verily, I say unto you, he that heareth my word and believeth on him that sent me, hath everlasting life, and shall not come into condemnation." John 5 : 24: Again, "Whosoever believeth on me will never die." These are sure testimonies to him that believeth.

But oh! how wretched is it to appeal to men's testimonies, and to look to men, whom we deem holy and wise, thinking and saying, yes, if these had taught and believed that this was according to Scripture, then we would believe it. But on the contrary, the apostle Paul says, 'Though we, or an angel from heaven, preach any other gospel unto you, then that which we have preached unto you, let him be accursed." Gal. 1 : 8. Behold, this then is the only gospel, to which Moses and the prophets have pointed in order that we should listen to it; for it has been revealed to us by Christ and his apostles.

Dieses Evangelium kann keine Heiligs keit der Engel noch viel weniger der Mens schen, ja auch weder Macht noch Gewalt der ganzen Welt verändern noch kränken, und weder dazu oder davon thun, ohne der großen Ungnad Gottes, dann es stehet fest wie der Berg Gottes, und ist ein solcher Stein, wie Christus redet: "Wer auf diesen Stein fället, der wird zerschellen, auf welchen er aber fället, den wird er zers malmen." Matth. 21, 44.

Von Belohnung der Glaubis gen.

Sohn. Weilen du mir nun vieles von der Lehre Jesu Christi gesagt, und daß man nothwendig unter allem Kreutz und Trübsal darinnen wandeln soll; was hat nun ein Mensch zu gewarten, wann er sich verleugnet und Christo nachfolget, und dabei ausharret unter allem Kreutz und Leiden, bis an das Ende?

Vater. Es sind solche Güter und Herrlichkeiten durch Christum zu erlangen, die von solcher großen Würde seyn, daß es keine menschliche Zunge aussprechen kann, und nicht kann beschrieben werden, was Gott bereitet hat denen, die Ihn lieben. Dennoch will ich dir so viel sagen, wie es der Geist Gottes in Heil. Schrift ausges drucket hat. Es zeuget der Sohn Gottes selbst: Wer an mich glaubet, der wird ein ewiges Leben haben. Joh. 3, 15. Das ist schon ein großer Ausspruch der ewigen Herrlichkeit.

Und dieses ist kein solches Leben, wie die Könige und große Monarchen in dieser

This gospel cannot be altered or injured by any holiness of angels, much less by that of men, or even by the power and dominion of the whole world. To add any thing to it, or take away from it, would bring upon us the great displeasure of God. For it stands as firm as the mountain of God, and Christ says, when referring to it as a stone, "Whosoever shall fall on this stone shall be broken; but on whomsoever it shall fall, it will grind him to powder." Matt. 21 : 44.

OF THE REWARD OF THE BELIEVERS.

SON. Since thou hast told me a great deal of the doctrine of Jesus Christ, and that it was necessary for us to walk according to it under all crosses and tribulations,—what then has a man to expect, if he denies himself, follows Christ, and perseveres therein under every trial and affliction, even unto the end?

FATHER. There are such blessings and glories to be obtained through Christ, and of such great dignity, that they cannot be expressed by any human tongue, nor can it be described what God has prepared for those who love him. Yet I will tell thee so much as the Spirit of God has expressed in holy writ. The Son of God himself testifies, "Whosoever believeth in me, shall have eternal life." John 3 : 15. This is already a great expression of eternal glory.

And this is not such a life, as kings and great monarchs have in this world,

Schmerzen, keine Furcht, kein Mangel noch Ungemach, kein Kampf noch Streit, kein Weinen noch Klagen, wird mehr zu finden seyn, denn gleichwie das Leben ewig, so wird auch die Freude ewig seyn, wie Gott durch den Propheten saget: Ewige Freude wird über ihrem Haupte seyn, Freude und Wonne wird sie ergreifen, Schmerzen und Seufzen wird weg müssen. Jes. 35, 10.

Ja hier wird ein lauterer Strom des lebendigen Wassers von dem Stuhl Gottes und des Lammes ausfließen, und auf beiden Seiten wird Holz des Lebens stehen. Das wird die allerköstlichsten Früchte tragen. Apoc. 22, 1. 2. In diesem Freudenleben wird die Stadt Gottes sich offenbaren. Apoc. 21. Welche Stadt und Gassen wird von lauter Gold und Edelgestein seyn und die Gläubigen werden in den Gassen der Stadt das freudenreiche Halleluja singen. Tob. 13, 22. Sie werden Kronen auf den Häuptern tragen, und Siegespalmen in ihren Händen. Apoc. 7. Ja singen und klingen, und für gutem Muth jauchzen, und das Lamm wird sie leiten zu den lebendigen Wasserbrunnen, und werden Früchte der Unsterblichkeit genießen.

Ja über dieses wird das die Freude immer vergrößern, wenn sie sehen den Herrn Jesum in seiner großen Herrlichkeit und Majestät, mit seinen viel tausendmal tausenden Heiligen und Engeln, die um seinen Thron herum stehen, und mit großer Heiligkeit und Freuden das Halleluja singen, daß Himmel und Erden davon erschallen wird, und dadurch auch die freigemachten Creaturen bewogen werden, dem erwürgten Lamm Lob, Ehr und Preiß, und Gewalt von Ewigkeit zu Ewigkeit, zu sagen. Apoc. 5, 13.

Ueber dieses alles wird dieses die höchste Lust seyn, den Herrn Jesum in seiner verklärten Menschheit anzuschauen. Ja sie

dispute, no weeping nor complaint will be found any more, for just as the life will be everlasting, so the joy will also be eternal. As God says by the prophet, "Everlasting joy will be upon their heads; they shall obtain joy and gladness, and sorrow and sighing shall flee away." Is. 35. 10.

Yes, there will proceed "out of the throne of God and of the Lamb, a pure river of life, and on either side thereof will be the tree of life," bearing the most delicious fruit. Rev. 22: 1, 2. In this life of joy, the city of God will be manifested. Rev. 21: The streets of the city will be of pure gold and precious stones, and there in the streets of the city will the faithful sing their gladsome Hallelujahs. They will have crowns on their heads, and palms in their hands. Rev. 7. They will sing and make melody, yea, even shout for joy, and the Lamb will lead them unto living fountains of water, and feed them with immortal food.

Yes, it will make their joy still greater, when they shall behold the Lord Jesus in his great glory and majesty, with his many myriads of myriads of angels and saints, surrounding his throne, and singing with great and holy fervor and joy, Hallelujah, so much so that heaven and earth shall be filled with the sound, and even the liberated creatures shall be induced to cry out, "Blessing, and honor, and glory, and power, be unto him that sitteth upon the throne, and unto the Lamb, for ever and ever." Rev. 5: 13.

More than all, will this be their highest delight, to behold the Lord Jesus in his glorified humanity. Indeed

werden sich verwundern, daß so wenige
Menschen diesen allein gewaltigen und
herrlichen Jesum geliebet und ihm gefolget
haben. Ja die Gläubigen werden sich ver=
wundern, daß sie in dieser Welt nicht wil=
liger gewesen sind, Leib und Leben und al=
les was sie hatten, zu lassen, aus Liebe zu
diesem Himmels=König und seiner Heil.
Lehre.

Ja sie werden erkennen, daß der Herr
Jesus aus Liebe zu ihnen diese Herrlichkei=
ten verlassen hatte und in das Jammer=
thal gekommen, ja gar aus Liebe für sie
gestorben, damit sie diese Seligkeit erlangen
könnten: dieses wird dennoch mehr Lob,
Preiß und Dank erwecken in alle Ewigkei=
ten.

Da wird seyn das Freuden=Leben,
Da viel tausend Seelen schon,
Sind mit Himmels=Glanz umgeben,
Stehen da für Gottes Thron,
Da die Seraphinen prangen,
Und das Hohe Lied anfangen:
Heilig, Heilig, Heilig heißt,
Gott der Vater, Sohn und Geist.

Von der ewigen Qual.

Sohn. Wenn nun die wahre, gläu=
bige Seelen solche große und wohl unaus=
sprechliche Seligkeiten genießen werden,
wie wird es denn denen Ungläubigen ge=
hen, welche dem Herrn Jesu in seinen Be=
fehlen nicht gehorsam gewesen, und ihn
und sein Reich nicht geliebet, sondern die
Welt und dero Herrlichkeit, und die in ih=
ren Sünden gestorben sind?

Vater. Gleich wie die Herrlichkeit
der Gläubigen unaussprechlich seyn wird,
eben so ist auch die Qual der Verdamm=
ten und Ungläubigen unaussprechlich.—
Denn die Schrift saget: Daß der Sohn
Gottes werde kommen in großer Kraft
und Herrlichkeit, da werden ihn sehen alle
Menschen und werden heulen alle ungläu=
bigen Geschlechte der Erden. Apoc. 1, 7.
Und werden vor lauter Angst und Furcht

they will wonder, why so few men did
love and obey such an all-powerful and
glorious Lord. Yes, believers will then
wonder why they themselves, while in
this world, were not more willing, to
give body, life and all they had, out of
love to this heavenly King and his
holy doctrine.

They will know then, that the Lord
Jesus out of love to them forsook those
glories and came into this world of
affliction, yea died even out of love for
them, in order that they might obtain
this great salvation. And this view of
his love will still more move them to
praise, honor and thank him to all eternity.

Then what a life of jubilee,
Will there in that period be,
To the thousands whose happy home,
Is before, and near to God's throne.
With rays of glory surrounded,
With the seraphic host joined
In the heavenly song, thrice holy,
Are th' THREE unit'd in testimony.

OF EVERLASTING TORMENT.

SON. But if the truly believing
souls shall enjoy such great and even
inexpressible blessedness, what will be
the fate of those unbelievers, who would
not obey the Lord Jesus in his commandments, who did not love him nor
his kingdom, but loved the world and
its glory, and died in their sins?

FATHER. Just as the glory of the
faithful will be inexpressible, so likewise will be the torment of the unbelieving and condemned. For the Scripture says, that the Son of God shall
come with great power and glory, "and
every eye shall see him, and all kin-
dreds of the earth (that did not believe)
shall wail." Rev. 1 : 7. And full of
fear and anguish, they shall say "to the

zu den Bergen und Hügeln sagen: "Fal=
let auf uns, und verberget uns, denn wir
können nicht stehen für dem, der auf dem
Stuhl sitzt, und für dem Zorn des Lam=
mes." Apoc. 6, 16.

Das wird ihnen aber nun nichts mehr
helfen, sondern sie werden von Christo hö=
ren müssen: "Gehet hin, ihr Verfluchten,
in das Höllische Feuer, das bereitet ist dem
Teufel und seinen Engeln." Matth. 25,
41. "Denn die das Thier und sein Bild
anbeten, sollen gequälet werden mit Feuer
und Schwefel, vor dem Lamm und allen
heiligen Engeln, und der Rauch ihrer
Qual wird aufsteigen von Ewigkeit zu
Ewigkeit, und sie werden keine Ruhe haben
Tag und Nacht." Apoc. 14, 10. 11.

Denn so jemand nicht wird gefunden im
Buch des Lebens, der wird geworfen wer=
den in den feurigen Pful, da ihr Wurm
nicht stirbet, und ihr Feuer nicht verlöschen
wird. Apoc. 20, 15. Marc. 9, 44. Jes.
66, 24. Ja sie werden allem Fleisch ein
Greuel seyn; und denn in dieser Qual
wird das die Schmerzen um noch so viel
mehr vergrößern, wenn sie erkennen, wie
sie solche große Seligkeiten und Herrlich=
keiten, die sie an den Kindern Gottes se=
hen, so leicht verscherzet haben, da sie noch
in der Gnadenzeit gelebet, und dieselbe
nicht geachtet, sondern in allen Sünden zu=
gebracht haben.

Wenn alsdann die Gerechten stehen wer=
den mit großer Freudigkeit gegen die, so sie
geängstiget, und ihre Arbeit (ihre Lehre
und Glauben an Jesum Christum) ver=
worfen haben. Da werden denn die Ver=
dammten solches sehen, und grausam er=
schrecken für solcher Seligkeit, und werden
unter einander reden mit Reu, und für
Angst des Geistes seufzen: "Das ist der,
welchen wir etwa für einen Spott hatten.
Wir Narren hielten sein Leben für unsin=
nig, ꝛc. Wie ist er nun gezählet unter die
Kinder Gottes, und sein Erbe ist unter den

mountains and rocks, Fall on us, and
hide us from the face of him that sitteth
on the throne, and from the wrath of
the Lamb." Rev. 6 : 16.

But that will not avail them any
thing, for they will have to hear the
sentence of Christ, "Depart from me,
ye cursed into everlasting fire, prepared
for the devil and his angels." Matt.
25 : 41. For they that worship the
beast and his image, "shall be torment-
ed with fire and brimstone in the presence of the holy angels, and in the
presence of the Lamb, and the smoke
of their torment will ascend up forever
and ever: and they will have no rest
day nor night." Rev. 14 : 10, 11.

"And whosoever was not found written in the book of life was cast into the
lake of fire, where the worm dieth not,
neither will the fire be quenched."
Rev. 20 : 15. Mark 9 : 44. Isai. 66 :
24. Yes, they will be an abhorring to
all flesh; and their pain amidst all this
torment will be still more aggravated,
when they become aware how they
have so wantonly neglected such great
salvation and glory, which they now
see in the children of God, while they
lived in the time of grace, and did not
regard the same, but continued heedlessly in sin.

When then the righteous shall stand
with great gladness opposite to those
who have troubled them, and rejected
their labor, their doctrine and faith in
Jesus Christ, the damned shall see it,
and will be dreadfully dismayed at such
blissfulness, and will say to one another
with remorse, sighing with anguish of
spirit: "This is he whom we fools
deemed as an outcast, and his life as
that of an insane person. How is he
now counted among the children of God,
and his inheritance is among the saints!

Heiligen. Darum so haben wir des rechten Weges gefehlet. Was hilft uns nun
der Pracht, was bringt uns nun der
Reichthum sammt dem Hochmuth." B.
Weish. 5, 1. Wann sie nun alle diese
Dinge bedenken werden, wie sie ihr Leben
in Sünden zugebracht, wie sie Gott als
das höchste Gut nicht geliebet, und dadurch
alle solche große Seligkeit verscherzet haben;
so wird eine solche Qual, Jammer und
Elend in ihnen sich befinden, die keine
Zunge aussprechen kann. Denn sie sind
von Gottes Angesicht und allen Heiligen
verstoßen.

Sohn. Es sind diese Dinge sehr
schrecklich anzuhören. Aber sage mir:
Sollen denn solche Qualen und Marter
ewig und ohne Ende seyn?

Vater, Nach dem Zeugniß der heiligen
Schrift siehet man, daß der Rauch ihrer
Qual wird aufsteigen von Ewigkeit zu
Ewigkeit, Apoc. 14, 11. Daß es aber
gar unendlich sollte währen, das stehet in
heil. Schrift nicht, aber davon ist nicht viel
zu reden, und nicht noth darnach zu fragen: denn die freudenreiche Seligkeit ist
einmal bei ihnen verscherzet, daß wenn
auch schon die Qual aufhöret nach den
langen Ewigkeiten, so wird nimmermehr
dasjenige, was die Gläubigen hier in der
Gnadenzeit durch Jesum Christum erlangen, wenn sie ihm gehorsam seyn, erlanget
werden. Und ist wohl bei vielen eine große Thorheit, weil sie gehöret haben von einer Wiederbringung, so achten sie es nicht,
daß sie sich gänzlich verleugnen, sondern
hoffen schon auf die Wiederbringung, welche Hoffnung ganz gewiß ihnen dann
entfallen wird, wann sie in die Qual kommen und derselben kein Ende sehen, und
der leidige Trost wie ein Rauch verschwin-
den wird.

Darum ist viel besser, man übe sich in
diesem einfältigen Erkenntniß: Daß man
in der Gnadenzeit möchte würdig werden,
dem Zorn Gottes und der höllischen Qual
zu entfliehen, als daß man sich lange beden-

Therefore have we missed the right
way. What profiteth us now our splen-
dor, and what availeth us our riches
and pride?" Sap. 5 : 1. Now when
they consider all these things, how they
have spent their lives in sin, how they
did not love God as the chief good, and
thereby have forfeited all that great salvation, then such a torrent of pain and
misery will overwhelm them, which no
tongue can express. For they are banished from the presence of the Lord,
and from all the saints.

Son. These things are most horri-
ble to listen to. But tell me, will this
torment and torture last forever, and
be without end?

Father. According to the testimony of holy writ it appears, that 'the
smoke of their torment will ascend up
forever and ever." Rev. 14 : 11.
But that it should continue altogether
without an end, is not sustained by the
scriptures. But of this not much is to
be said, and it is not necessary to enquire after it. 'For the joyful salvation
being by them once forfeited, if even
the torment should terminate after long
ages of eternity, they will never, never
obtain that, which the believers do obtain here in this time of grace by Jesus
Christ, if they are obedient to him. It
is indeed a great folly with many, that
because they have heard of a restitution, put their trust in it, and do not
consider, that they must entirely deny
themselves. This hope will most certainly be lost, when they come into the
place of torment of which they see no
end, and their miserable confidence will
vanish like smoke.

Hence it is much better to exercise
ourselves in the simple truth, that in
the time of grace we may be made worthy to escape from the wrath of God
and the torment of hell, than to delib-

ket, wie oder wann man aus derselben wieder kommen könne. Eben als wann ein Dieb sich damit trösten wollte: Ey wann du schon über dem Diebstahl ergriffen wirst, deine Strafe nimmt doch wieder ein Ende. Würde das nicht ein elender Trost seyn? Also ist das Evangelium viel besser und seliger, welches lehret, wie man dem Zorn Gottes entfliehen kann, als solches Evangelium, welches lehret, daß die ewige Qual ein Ende hat, welches zwar eine Wahrheit ist, gehöret aber gar nicht als ein Evangelium denen Gottlosen zu predigen.

Aber es ist leider bei dieser Zeit alles durch die hohe Einbildung derer Menschen die von der Wiederbringung lehren und Bücher davon schreiben, ganz verkehret. Und gibt wenig solche treue Haushalter, welche der Herr Jesus über sein Hausgesinde gesetzet, die ihnen zu rechter Zeit die gebührende Speise geben. Luc. 12, 42. "Den Kindern die Milch, den Jünglingen stärkere, und den Vollkommenen starke Speise." Aber es gibt so viel treulose Haushalter, welche der Herr nicht selbst über sein Hausgesinde gesetzet, sondern laufen nach ihrer eigenen Gefälligkeit durch menschliche Weisheit, wollen kluge Leute seyn, verkehren aber nur des Herrn Sinn und Meinung, denen sie sollten Milch geben, legen sie starke Speise vor.

Dorten sagt der Apostel Paulus zu den Korinthern: "Milch habe ich euch zu trinken gegeben und nicht starke Speise, darum weil ihr noch junge Kinder in Christo, und noch fleischlich seyd." 1 Cor. 3, 2. Denn es verhält sich auf diese Art in dem geistlichen, als wie im natürlichen Leben.— Wann nun einer einem jungen Kindlein die Milch entziehen thäte, und stellte ihm einen köstlichen Braten vor davon zu essen, man sollte wohl erfahren, daß ein solches Kind bald sterben würde, obgleich der Braten an sich selbst ganz gut und köstlich wä-

erate long, how or when we may bo permitted to come out of it again. Suppose a thief would comfort himself thus: Well if I am caught in the act of stealing, my punishment will still come to an end again. Would that not be a miserable consolation? But that gospel is much better and more blessed, which teaches us, how we can escape from the wrath of God, then such a gospel which teaches, that eternal torments will have an end, which though it be true, is not proper at all to preach as a gospel to the wicked.

But alas! at this time, all things have been entirely perverted by the high imaginations of those men, who teach and write books about the restoration. There are indeed but few faithful stewards, whom the Lord Jesus has set over his household, to give them their portion of meat in due season. Luke 12 : 42. To the children, it is proper to give milk, more nourishing food to the youth, and to the perfect, strong meat. There are so many faithless stewards whom the Lord himself has not put over his household, but who run according to their own pleasure in human wisdom, wishing to appear as wise men, and who only pervert the Lord's mind and word, and give meat to those who should have milk.

So saith the apostle Paul to the Corinthians: "I have fed you with milk, and not with meat: because ye are still babes in Christ, and carnal." 1 Cor. 3 : 1, 2.

For it is the same in the spiritual life as in the natural. For if one would withdraw from a young babe its milk, and present in its place a fine piece of roasted meat for the child to eat, we should soon see that such a child could not live, though the meat in itself was very good and excellent. Unfortunate-

re. Eben so gehet es leider auch bei diesen verwirrten Zeiten, da viele Seelen durch die Gnade zur Buße erwecket worden, und noch wohl gar junge Kinder im Glauben seyn: Daß billiger Weise ihnen sollte der Anfang des christlichen Lebens, als die rechte Milchspeise vorgelegt werden, worauf auch Petrus weiset: Daß sie sollten dadurch zunehmen, als die jetzt geborne Kindlein. 1 Pet. 2, 2.

Aber solche lautere Milch wird ihnen durch allerlei Verdacht, und Vorlegung anderer starken Speise entzogen, und was dieses vor Nutzen bringet ist nicht genug zu bejammern. Weilen es lauter Schaden bringet, lauter Sterben und Verderben, Zerstreuung und Zertrennung. Und wann ein solcher Lehrer und Haushalter, lange starke Speise vorgeleget hat, dann gehet er wieder fort, da wissen denn die arme Menschen nicht was es gewesen sey, sind zwar lange durch seinen schönen Klang, aber undeutlichen Ton geführet worden. Dadurch hat sich dann niemand recht können zum Streite rüsten, wider den Teufel und seinen Anhang. Und solche Menschen sind von Paulo verglichen: Einem tönenden Erz, und klingenden Schelle. 1 Cor. 13. Weil sie die Lehre und die Liebe nicht haben, wodurch man die Ordnungen und Gebote Gottes halten kann. Joh. 14, und 1 Joh. 5, 3.

Sohn. Lieber Vater, ich danke nochmals für deine gute Unterweisung, u. weil nun unsere Reise bald zum Ende ist, so will ich dich noch dieses fragen: Weil ich von dir wohl verstanden, und es auch glaube, daß der Weg zum Leben sehr eng und schmal, und die Verführung in der Welt sehr groß ist, und so viel falsche Geister, falsche Lehrer und falsche Propheten gibt; wie soll ich mich dann in diesem allem verhalten, damit ich die ewige Seligkeit erlange, und nicht verführet werde?

ly, the same is the case in these corrupt times, where many souls by grace have been awakened unto repentance, and are still but very young children in the faith, to whom properly should be presented the first principles of the doctrine of Christ, as the true milk, as Peter recommends, that they may grow thereby, as new born babes. 1 Pet. 2: 2.

But this sincere milk is taken from them, by making them suspicious, and by laying before them other strong meat; and the consequences of this cannot be sufficiently lamented, because it brings nothing but harm, nothing but death and corruption, schism and division. And when such a teacher and steward, for a long time has presented to them strong meat, he goes away again, and the poor people know not what it was, but have been led astray by his fine voice and false teaching, by which no one could prepare himself for the warfare against the devil and his host. Such men are compared by Paul to 'a sounding brass or a tinkling cymbal.' 1 Cor. 13 : 1, because they have not the doctrine and love, by which we are enabled to keep the ordinances and commandments of God. John 14; 15, and 1 John 5: 3.

Son. Dear father, I thank thee again for thy good instruction, and since our journey will soon be at an end, I would ask thee yet this question: understanding well, and believing also that the way to life is extremely narrow and straight, and the deception in the world very great, being full of false spirits, false teachers, and false prophets; how, under all these circumstances, should I conduct myself in order to obtain everlasting salvation, and avoid being deceived?

Ein Väterlicher Rath.

Vater. Ich will dir dennoch einen guten und gewiſſen Rath aus väterlicher Liebe mittheilen, u. an den gedenke dein Lebenlang, laß es aus deinem Herzen nimmermehr kommen, ſondern gedenke daran wo du geheſt und ſteheſt, wann du dich niederlegeſt und aufſteheſt, ſo laß dieſes deine größte Sorge ſeyn, daß all dein Seufzen und Verlangen dahin gehe, wie du deinen Gott der dich erſchaffen, und Jeſum Chriſtum der dich mit ſeinem theuren Blut erlöſet hat, von ganzem Herzen, von ganzer Seele, und von ganzem Gemüth lieben mögeſt über alle Dinge in der Welt, es ſey Schönheit oder Reichthum, ja was dir für deine Augen und Ohren kommen möchte.

Und in dieſer Liebe fürchte Gott mit kindlichem Herzen, betrachte alle ſeine Gebote Tag und Nacht, halte ſie mit reinem Herzen, laſſe dieſelben deine Rathgeber ſeyn und bitte beſtändig um den Heil. Geiſt, welcher dich in alle Gebote Gottes in der Wahrheit leiten wird.

Laſſe dieſes beſtändig in deinen Ohren erſchallen, was David ſagt: "Wie wird ein Jüngling ſeinen Weg unſträflich gehen: Wann er ſich hält nach deinen Worten." Pſ. 119, 9. Ferner: Die Rede des Herrn iſt lauter, wie durchläutert Silber im erdnen Tiegel, bewähret ſiebenmal. Pſ. 12, 7. Ferner: Das Geſetz des Herrn iſt ohne Wandel und erquicket die Seele, das Zeugniß des Herrn iſt gewiß und macht die Albern weiſe, die Befehle des Herrn ſind richtig und erfreuen das Herz, die Gebote des Herrn ſind lauter und erleuchten die Augen, ja ſie ſind köſtlicher denn Gold und viel feines Gold, ſie ſind ſüßer denn Honig und Honigſeim. Pſ. 19, 8—11.

Laß daneben in deinem Gemüthe ſtets die Worte des Herrn Jeſu erſchallen: Wer

A Paternal Advice.

Father. I will yet give thee a good and sure advice out of paternal affection, and mayest thou remember it all thy life-time. *Let it never pass from thy mind, but think of it wherever thou goest, and wherever thou art; when thou dost lie down and rise up, let this be thy greatest care that all thy sighs and desires may be for this, to love thy God, who created thee, and Jesus Christ, who redeemed thee with his precious blood, with all thy heart, with all thy soul, and with all thy mind, yea above all things in the world, whether they be beauty, or riches, or whatever may come in sight or hearing.

And in this love, fear God with a childlike heart; contemplate all his commandments day and night; keep them with a pure heart, let them be thy counsellors, and pray continually for the Holy Spirit, who will guide thee into all the commandments of God, and into all truth.

Let it always be resounding in thy ears, what David said: 'Wherewithal shall a young man cleanse his way? By taking heed thereto according to thy word." Ps. 119 : 9. Again: 'The words of the Lord are pure words; as silver tried in a furnace of earth, purified seven times." Ps. 12 : 6. Again: 'The law of the Lord is perfect, converting the soul: The testimony of the Lord is sure, making wise the simple. The statutes of the Lord are right, rejoicing the heart. The commandments of the Lord are pure, enlightening the eyes. More to be desired are they than gold, yea, than much fine gold; sweeter also than honey, and the honey-comb." Psalm 19 : 8, 10.

Moreover, let the words of the Lord Jesus be always in thy mind: 'If a

mich liebt, der wird meine Gebote halten, wer aber mich nicht liebet, der hält meine Worte nicht. Joh. 14, 23. 24. Ferner: Meine Schaafe hören meine Stimme, und sie folgen mir, und ich gebe ihnen das ewige Leben. Joh. 10, 27. Und darneben bedenke mit Fleiß, was der Herr Jesus von seinen Geboten saget, da er spricht: Ich habe nicht von mir selbst geredet, sondern ich habe geredet, was mir der Vater befohlen hat, und ich weiß, daß seine Gebote sind das ewige Leben. Joh. 12, 49. 50.

Und behalte stets den theuren Rath des Herrn Jesu, den er den Seinigen giebet, da er spricht: Sehet euch für, für den falschen Propheten, die in Schaafs-Kleidern kommen, inwendig aber sind sie reißende Wölfe. Matth. 7, 15. Ferner: Sehet zu daß euch nicht jemand verführe, denn es werden viele kommen unter meinem Namen und sagen, Ich bin Christus. Und werden viele verführen. Matth. 24, 4. 5. Trage deine Seele als deinen allerbesten Schatz immerdar in deinen Händen. Und wandle zu allen Zeiten in Heiliger Furcht. Sprich wie David mit aufrichtigem Herzen zu Gott: Ich bewahre mich in dem Wort deiner Lippen, vor Menschenwerk auf dem Wege des Mörders. Pf. 17, 4.

Und wenn dir alsdann schon Menschen begegnen, und unter sie kämest, die da viel heiliger als Johannes, viel feuriger als Elias, viel wunderthätiger als Moses, viel sanftmüthiger, demüthiger, und geistlicher als Christus selbst und seine Apostel scheinen sollten, und sie wandelten nicht in der Lehre Jesu des gekreutzigten Heilandes, so wie in dem neuen Testament geschrieben stehet, und wollten dich abführen von diesen einfältigen Geboten des Herrn Jesu, so denke und glaube in deinem Herzen: Es sind falsche Apostel, und betrügliche Arbeiter, stopfe deine Ohren zu vor ihrem Evangelio, sey klug wie eine Schlange, welche die Ohren verstopfet vor dem Beschwörer,

man love me, he will keep my words: but he that loveth me not, keepeth not my sayings." John 14 : 23, 24. Again : 'My sheep hear my voice, and they follow me, and I give unto them eternal life." John 10 : 27. 28. And at the same time remember diligently, what the Lord Jesus spake of his commandments, when he said, 'I have not spoken of myself; for I speak even as the father gave me a commandment, and I know that this commandment is life everlasting." John 12 : 49, 50.

Bear continually in mind also the precious advice of the Lord Jesus, which he gave to his (disciples,) saying: 'Beware of false prophets, who come to you in sheeps' clothing, but inwardly they are ravening wolves." Matt. 7 : 15. Again : 'Take heed that no man deceive you; for many shall come in my name, saying, I am Christ, and shall deceive many." Matt. 24 : 4, 5. Always carry thy soul, as thy most precious treasure, in thine own hands, and at all times walk in holy fear. Say like David with an upright heart to God: 'Concerning the works of men, by the words of thy lips I have kept me from the paths of the destroyer." Ps. 17 : 4.

Shouldst thou then meet with men, and converse with them, who seem to be much more holy than John, much more zealous than Elias, performing more miraculous deeds than Moses, and appearing more meek, more humble, and more spiritual than Christ himself and his apostles, but should they not walk in the doctrine of Jesus, our crucified Redeemer as it is written in the New Testament, and would they try to lead thee away from those simple commandments of the Lord Jesus;— then thou mayest think and believe in thy heart, that they are false apostles, and deceitful workmen. Close

und rufe und schreie nach Jesu, als wie ein Schaaf nach seinem Hirten.

Sohn. Ich muß noch etwas fragen, welches mir in etwas hart vorkommt, daß ich solche Menschen, die in einer solchen Heiligkeit und Wunderthätigkeit sich zeigen, für falsch halten solle, wenn sie nicht in der Lehre Jesu wandeln, und darwider seyn, wie es äußerlich im Testament geschrieben stehet.

Vater. Ich habe gemeinet du solltest den göttlichen Grund wohl verstanden haben, durch das lange Gespräch, so will ich es dir hierinnen nochmals sagen nach dem Zeugniß der heiligen Schrift, alten und neuen Testaments. Als Gott durch Mosen sein Gesetz dem Volk Israel offenbaren ließ, welches ein solches vestes Wort war, daß, wer es brach, sterben mußte. 4 Mos. 15, 35. Hebr. 10, 28. Wenn eine Seele aus Frevel sündigte und des Herrn Gebot fahren ließ, die wurde schlecht ausgerottet, und die Schuld war auf ihr. So veste war das Wort des Herrn, durch Mosen gegeben. Nun waren das alle falsche Propheten welche im Gesetz etwas dazu oder davon thaten.

Die wahren Propheten aber richteten sich alle nach dem Gesetz, so wie es der Knecht Moses geredet hatte. Die falschen wandelten nach ihres Herzens Gedanken, und sagten zwar dem Volke: Der Herr habe es gesagt. Aber es waren lauter Lügen. Nun merke wohl, was das für eine Lehre, Recht und Gesetz sey, das durch den Sohn Gottes selber in die Welt eingeführet, und mit Zeichen, Wundern, und Austheilung des heiligen Geistes wohl bekräftiget ist. Hebr. 2. 4. Durch den Sohn Gottes, durch welchen der Vater am letzten zu uns geredet hat. Hebr. 1, 1. 2. Durch welchen der Vater die ganze Welt gemacht hat. Er ist das lebendige Wort, welches Fleisch worden ist. Joh. 1, Wel=

thy ears against their gospel; be as wise as the serpent, which stoppeth its ears to the charmer; and call and cry after Jesus, as a sheep after its shepherd.

Son. One query more. It appears to me somewhat hard, to consider such men as false, who manifest so great holiness and power, because they do not walk in the doctrine of Jesus, but are opposed to it, as it is written externally in the (New) Testament?

Father. From the long conversation we have had, I thought thou mightest have well understood the divine mind; but still I will repeat unto thee again some things according to the testimony of the holy scriptures, both of the old and new Testament. When God revealed his law through Moses unto the children of Israel, it was such a sure and steadfast word, that every one who transgressed it had to die. Numb. 15 : 35. Heb. 10 : 28. 'And the soul that doeth ought presumptuously, and breaketh the Lord's commandment, that soul shall utterly be cut off; his iniquity shall be upon him.', Thus firm was the word of the Lord, given by Moses. Now those were all false prophets, who added any thing to the law, or diminished it by taking aught away.

The true prophets indeed all adhered to and observed the law, as it was made known by the servant Moses. The false ones walked after the thoughts of their own hearts, still they said unto the people, 'The Lord has spoken." But it was all falsehood. Now ponder well of what character the doctrines, laws and ordinances must be, which were introduced into the world by the Son of God himself, and so well confirmed "by signs, miracles and the gifts of the Holy Ghost;', Heb. 2 : 4,—by the Son of God, by whom 'the Father has spoken unto us in these last days;" Heb. 1 : 1, 2,—by whom the Father 'made the whole world;" who is that

chem der Vater alle Gewalt gegeben hat, im Himmel und auf Erden. Matth. 28, 18. Welches Gesetz über alle Macht, Gewalt, Herrschaften, und Obrigkeiten, nicht allein in dieser sondern auch in der zukünftigen Welt ist. Ephes. 1, 21. Es ist der Sohn-Gottes: Welcher aufgefahren ist, und sind ihm unterthan die Engel, und die Gewaltigen, und die Kräfte. 1 Pet. 3, 22.

Nun bedenke, daß die Lehre des Sohnes Gottes viel besser, viel unbeweglicher und unveränderlicher wird müssen gehalten seyn von allen, die dem Sohn Gottes in seiner Lehre, Gebote, guten Rath und Gesetzen glauben. Hieraus kannst du ja leicht merken, wie gottlos, wie hochmüthig, wie blind und finster eine Seele seyn muß, die einen einzigen Befehl des Herrn Jesu verachtet. Und wie viel gottloser müssen nicht solche Lehrer und Propheten seyn, die mit ihrer Weisheit die Weisheit Jesu verachten, die einen andern Weg, als Jesus geordnet, machen wollen. Die die Seelen, welche Jesum in seinen Geboten einfältig nachfolgen wollen, davon abzuführen suchen, einige durch süße und prächtige Reden im Schaafs-Pelz verkleidet, andere dräuen gar mit Gefängniß, und suchen durch Drohen und allerlei Verfolgung die Seelen von dem guten Rath Jesu abzuhalten.

Wie meinest du? sollen das nicht Verführer, falsche Propheten, ja Diebe und Mörder seyn, die da allezeit über die Mauer hinein steigen und nicht durch die Thür, welche Jesus selber ist, eingehen wollen. Joh. 10. Es ist nichts greulicher und sündlicher in den Augen Gottes, als wenn ein sterblicher Mensch seinem Gott nicht glaubet, in allen seinen Geboten und Verboten. Und du wirst auch sonsten von keiner andern Heiligkeit nichts im alten und neuen Testament finden, als nur allein

---

living 'word which was made flesh;" John 1:—to whom the Father has given all power in heaven and on earth." Matt 28 : 18. Which law is 'far above all principality, power, might, and dominion, not only in this world, but also in the world to come." Eph. 1 : 21. It is the Son of God, who has ascended again into heaven, and to whom 'angels, authorities and powers are made subject." 1 Pet. 3 : 22.

Now consider how much better, more unmovable and unchangable the doctrine of the Son of God is to be observed by all those who believe him in his doctrine, commands, counsels and laws.—From this thou mayest easily conclude, how wicked, how proud, how blind and dark a soul must be, who despises a single command of the Lord Jesus; and how much more wicked must not such teachers and prophets be, who with their own wisdom despise the wisdom of Jesus, and point out another way than Jesus ordained;—who endeavor to lead astray souls, who desire to follow Jesus simply in his commandments, some by their smooth and ingenuous discourses under the garb of sheep's clothing, and others by their threatening with prison and manifold persecutions, trying to prevent souls from adhering to the good counsels of Jesus?

How thinkest thou? Should those not be deceivers, false prophets, nay thieves and robbers, who always climb up some other way, and refuse to enter the door, which is Jesus himself? John 10.—There is nothing more abominable and sinful in the sight of God, than for a mortal man not to believe his God in all his commandments and prohibitions. Thou wilt find nothing of any other holiness at all in the oln and new Testament, than in doing

ist der Wille Gottes die Heilung der Seelen gewesen, und jederzeit bleiben wird.

Und dieses ist der Weg zu Gott, wenn eine Seele thut was Gott haben will, thut sie es aber nicht, und widersetzt sich ihrem Gott in seinem Willen, aus Geringschätzung denkt und spricht: Dieses und jenes ist mir nicht nöthig, ob es gleich Gott geboten hat. So ist eine solche Seele ein Feind Gottes. Und wie der heil. Johannes spricht: Wer übertritt, und bleibet nicht in der Lehre Christi, der hat keinen Gott. 2 Joh. v. 9. Wer aber in der Lehre Christi bleibet, hat beide, den Vater und den Sohn.

Darum will ich dir dieses noch zum Beschluß rathen: Daß du allein auf Jesum deinen Erlöser und Seligmacher sehen sollt. Hebr. 12, 2. Und wenn du von ihm seine Lehre so wie sie äußerlich im Testament befohlen, gelernet hast, daß du alsdenn beständig dabei bleibest, und dich resolvirest viel lieber dein Leib und Leben, deine Güter, Freundschaft, ja alles was du hast in der ganzen Welt, fahren zu lassen, als von der Lehre Jesu zu weichen. Und must dich gewöhnen täglich das Kreuz Jesu auf dich zu nehmen, mit Verleugnung deines Willens, sonst kannst du kein Jünger des Herrn Jesu seyn, noch viel weniger ein Erbe seines Reichs. Luc. 14, 27.

Nun der Herr Jesus segne deine Seele, und stärke dir den Glauben, und lasse diese einfältige Ermahnung in dir wachsen und Früchte tragen, die in das ewige Leben bleiben, so wollen wir unsern Gott ewig mit einander loben und preisen, Amen.

the will of God. This has always been, and it will ever be the salvation of the soul.

This then is the way to God for every soul, namely, to do and act agreeably to the will of God. But to refuse doing so, and to oppose him in his will, and disregarding him one thinks and says, 'This and that I do not find necessary for me, though God has commanded it;'—such a soul is an enemy of God, and as St. John said, 'Whosoever transgresseth, and abideth not in the doctrine of Christ, hath not God.' 2 John 9. 'But he that abideth in the doctrine of Christ, he hath both the Father and the Son.'

Hence, in conclusion I will advise thee to look only unto Jesus, our Redeemer and Savior. Heb. 12 : 2. And when thou hast learnt from him his doctrine, as literally commanded in the (new) Testament, then try to continue steadfast therein, and to resolve firmly within thyself, much rather to lose thy liberty, property, the friendship and all that thou hast in this world, and even thy life, than to fall away from the doctrine of Jesus. Thou must accustom thyself to take up thy cross daily, denying thine own will, or else thou canst not be a disciple of the Lord Jesus, much less be an heir of his kingdom. Luke 14 : 27.

Now, may the Lord Jesus bless thy soul, increase thy faith, and let this simple exhortation grow in thee, and bear fruit, which remaineth unto eternal life, and then we will praise and glorify our God in unison for evermore; Amen.

Der Sünden austilgende Jesus.

Mel. In dich hab ich gehoffet.

Ich bin ein Herr, der Sünd vergiebt,
Ich bin, der unverändert liebt,
Ich, Gott und Menschen=Sohne!
　　Es ist vollbracht,
　　Mein Opfer macht,
Daß ich nun deiner schone.

Die Sünde werf ich in das Meer,
So daß sie nimmer wiederkehr,
Und ich nicht mehr gedenke.
　　Mein theures Blut
　　Macht alles gut,
Nur darum ich dirs schenke.

Doch wandle vor mei'm Angesicht,
Sey fromm, getreu, und weiche nicht
Zur Linken noch zur Rechten;
　　Gieb acht auf dich,
　　Und liebe mich,
Man wird dein Recht verfechten.

JESUS,

.A SIN EXTINGUISHING SAVIOR.

A pard'ning Lord I am,
In love I will be found;
The Son of God and man,
To heal the sinful wound.
　　All is now gain'd,
　　My death has bought,
　　And pardon wrought
　　That thou be spar'd.

Thy sin I cast away,
It shall return no more;
Thy debt I had to pay,
And suffer'd for it sore.
　　My blood I· gave,
　　My life I spent,
　　Through death I went
　　For thee to save.

This have I done for thee;
Be faithful then, and true,
Do not depart from me,
I shall be faithful too.
　　Then watch and pray,
　　And love me too,
　　Who first lov'd you
　　And am thy stay.

Eberhard Ludwig Gruber's Grundforschende

Fragen,

welche denen Neuen Täufern

im Witgensteinischen, insonderheit zu beantworten, vorgelegt waren.

Nebst

beygefügten kurzen und einfältigen Antworten auf dieselben, vormals schriftlich herausgegeben von einem

Aufrichtigen Mitglied

der Gemeinde zu Witgenstein,

Und nun auf vieles Verlangen zum öffentlichen Druck befördert.

EBERHARD LUDWIG GRUBER'S

GROUND-SEARCHING QUESTIONS,

PROPOSED

TO THE NEW BAPTISTS

OF WITGENSTEIN, TO BE ANSWERED EACH SEPARATELY:

ALSO

BRIEF AND PLAIN REPLY

TO THE SAME, FORMERLY GIVEN OUT IN MANUSCRIPT

BY A MEMBER OF THE CHURCH IN

WITGENSTEIN,

AND NOW BY THE REQUEST OF MANY, PUBLISHED

THROUGH THE PRESS.

In Gott geliebte Freunde, und Mitpilgrime.

Es haben bishero manche etwas näheren Grund und Bericht von eurer neuen Taufe und Gemeinde zu haben verlangt, dieweilen dasjenige, so etwa hin und wieder davon geredet oder auch geschrieben worden, sie annoch in vieler Ungewißheit gelassen. Um nun eure Meinung so viel gründlicher u. pünktlicher hiervon zu vernehmen, und damit außer allem weiterem Zweifel diesfalls gesetzet zu werden, hat man euch gegenwärtig offenherzige und nun vorgestellte Fragen vorlegen wollen, worüber man eurer deutlichen und aufrichtigen Antwort hiernächst gewärtig ist.

Geliebte Freunde.

Weilen ihr in Liebe von uns Grund fordert, und auch der Apostel Petrus die Gläubigen in 1 Pet. 3, 15. lehret, daß sie allezeit bereit seyn sollen zur Verantwortung gegen jedermann, welcher Grund fordert der Hoffnung, die in ihnen ist: So haben wir auch nicht vorbei gekonnt, sondern euch in Liebe offenherzig und in Gewißheit des Glaubens, nach unserer Einfalt, auf diese vorgelegte Fragen, ganz kürzlich geantwortet, und es dann eurer Prüfung vor Gott überlassen wollen.

1. Fr. Ob sie nicht davor halten, daß über tausend Jahre keine rechte und wahre Taufe, u. folglich auch keine wahre Kirche mehr, auf Erden gewesen seye?

Antw. Wir halten und glauben, daß Gott jederzeit seine Gemeinde gehabt welche die wahre Tauf und Ordnung gehalten, so aber jederzeit vor den Unglaubigen verborgen gewesen, und auch manchmal in wenigen Gliedmaßen bestanden, dennoch hat die Pforten der Höllen niemalen die Gemeinde des Herrn Jesu überwinden können; Ja es ist auch zu erweisen aus den Historien, daß Gott jederzeit seine Ordnung den Unglaubigen zu einem Zeugniß hat offenbaren lassen.

Beloved in God, friends and fellow pilgrims.

There are many, who have hitherto desired to have a more direct account and report of your new baptism and church, since that what has been said, or even written here and there on the subject, has left them still in much uncertainty. In order now to obtain your opinion more fully and authentically, and to be relieved from all further doubt on this subject, we have come to the conclusion to propound to you the present frank, and simply stated questions, upon which we expect your plain and candid answers as early as possible.

(Reply.) Dear friends.

Since you ask in love our opinion, and since also the apostle Peter teaches believers, 1 Pet. 3 : 15 'to be ready always to give an answer to every man that asketh you a reason of the hope that is in you;'—we could not avoid giving you in love and candor, and with assurance of faith, according to our simplicity, very brief answers on those proposed questions, and to leave them to your examination before God.

QUERY 1. Whether you do not suppose, that for more than one thousand years there had been no true, genuine baptism, and consequently also no true church on earth?

ANSWER. We hold and believe, that God at all times had his church, which observed the true baptism and order, but which was always hidden from the unbelievers, and consisted often also in but few members; still the gates of hell could never prevail against the church of the Lord Jesus. Yea, it is evident from history that God has caused his order to be revealed to unbelievers in all ages, as a testimony or witness.

2. Fr. Ob die Kirche Gottes zu keiner Zeit, und auf keinerlei Weise, in irgend einigen Gliedmaßen, ohne die erste und äußere Tauf-Ordnung bestehen könne, wie etwa die Israelitische Kirche nach Jos. 5, 5. 7. eine geraume Zeit in der Wüsten ohne die Beschneidung bestanden?

Antw. Die Kirche Christi ist nicht anders geordnet, von dem rechten Baumeister Jesu Christo, als daß sie solle halten seine Tauf und Ordnung, ja Christus hat in seiner Gemeinde oder Kirche alles gar wohl geordnet durch Apostel und Lehrer, und mit Zeichen und Wundern genug befestiget, und ist deswegen unwahrscheinlich, daß jemalen eine Kirche Christi oder Gemeinde hat seyn können, ohne die Tauf und Ordnung wie es der wahre Stifter befohlen.

Daß aber nicht sollten Seelen gewesen seyn, die etwa im verborgenen sind gezogen worden zu der Kirche Christi, leugnen wir nicht; ob sie aber gefolget und Christum öffentlich bekennet, oder ob sie die Ehre der Welt lieber gehabt als die Ehre Gottes, lassen wir an seinen Ort gestellet seyn.

Was aber anlangt die Israelitische Kirch, so siehet man klar daß die Kinder mußten in der Wüsten die Schande Egypti tragen, und auch die Missethat ihrer Väter! So daß sie aber in das verheißene Land wollten, und ehe sie die erste Stadt Jericho einnahmen, mußten sie vorher alle beschnitten werden, und Gott sagte zu Josua 5: "Heute habe ich die Schande Egypti von euch gewendet:" Und da durften sie erst das Pascha halten, zuvor aber nicht, welches dann auch ein Vorbild ist gewesen auf uns; dann so lange wir in der Wüsten und großen Unordnung und Ungewißheit wandeln, ob wir schon aus Egypten wären ausgegangen u. von den großen Sünden durch eine mächtige Hand Gottes erlöset, so könnten wir doch nicht in das

QUERY 2. Whether it be impossible for the church of God to exist at any time, in any manner, and even with but few members, without the primitive and outward order of baptism, as perhaps was the case with the Israelite church according to Josh. 5 : 5, 7, which continued a considerable time in the wilderness without circumcision?

ANSWER. The church of Christ is in no other way ordered by the great master-builder Jesus Christ, but that it should observe his baptism and order. Yea, Christ has ordained every thing in his congregation or church perfectly well by apostles and teachers, and which is sufficiently confirmed by signs and miracles. It is therefore improbable, that there could ever have been a church or congregation of Christ without the baptism and order as the true founder (or author) has appointed.

But that there should have been souls, who were secretly drawn to the church of Christ, we do not deny. However, whether they obeyed and publicly professed Christ, or whether they loved the honor of the world more than the honor that cometh from God only, (John 5 : 44,) we will not determine. Concerning the church of Israel, we clearly see that the children in the wilderness had to bear the reproach of Egypt, and also the transgression of their fathers! But as soon as they were about to enter the land of promise, and before the taking of the first city, Jericho, they were all to be circumcised. God said therefore to Joshua (ch.) 5 "This day have I rolled away the reproach of Egypt from off you."

Then they were permitted to keep the passover, but not before, and this also was intended as a figure for us. For so long as we walk in the wilderness, in great disorder and uncertainty, although we have gone out already from Egypt,

Haus Gottes eingehen, und in der Gemeinschaft Jesu und seiner Glieder das Brod brechen: sondern Gott forderte auch von uns, wir sollten getauft seyn, und wird es auch wohl, obschon im Verborgenen, von einem jeden fordern, wann die Menschen nur auf die inwendige Stimme merkten, und mit ihrer Selbstverleugnung folgen thäten.

3. Fr. Ob dann die Kirche Gottes hier auf Erden, in solcher Zeit, da die erste Tauforbnung nicht mehr beobachtet worden, ganz und gar aufgehöret habe?

Antw. Wenn die erste Tauforbnung aufgehöret hätte, so hätte auch freilich die Kirche Christi aufgehöret, und wann schon Seelen gewesen wären, die unter dem grossen Verfall hin und her geseufzet hätten, so hätte man es noch keine Kirche nennen können; weilen wir aber glauben, und es auch wohl aus den alten Historien zu erweisen wäre, daß die erste Taufe niemalen aufgehöret nach der Ordnung Christi, so hat auch niemalen die Kirche aufgehöret, und sollten nur wenige gewesen seyn.

4. Fr. Wie sie solches mit der Verheissung Christi Matth. 16, 18. daß die Pforten der Höllen seine Gemeinde auch nicht überwältigen sollen, u. Cap 28, 20. daß er bei ihnen seyn wolle alle Tage bis an der Welt Ende, und dergleichen; zu reimen getrauen?

Antw. Dieses ist beantwortet, weilen wir glauben, daß die Pforten der Höllen die Gemeinde Christi nicht überwältiget hat; sondern sie ist geblieben, und wird bleiben bis an der Welt Ende.

5. Fr. Was sind dann von den unleugbaren Zeugen der Wahrheit nach der Gottseligkeit halten, die sich auch unter sol-

and have been saved from gross sins by the mighty hand of God, yet we could not enter the house of God, nor break bread in the communion of Jesus and his members. For God requires of us, that we should be baptized, and will require it also by the calls of his spirit, if men will listen to that inward voice, and obey it by denying themselves.

QUESTION 3. Whether the church of God here on earth at such time had ceased to exist altogether, when the primitive order of baptism was observed no longer?

ANSWER. Had this primitive order of baptism ceased, then of course the church of Christ had ceased to exist, and though there had been souls, who here and there lamented the great apostacy, they could not have been called a church.

But since we do believe, and think it may be shown also from ancient history, that primitive baptism, as ordained by Christ, never has ceased to be practiced, it follows as a consequence, that the (true) church never ceased to exist, though it should (at some periods) have consisted of but few members.

QUESTION 4. How would you undertake to reconcile this with the promise of Christ, Matt. 16 : 18, 'That even the gates of hell should not prevail against it;' and ch. 28 : 20, 'That he will be with them (his disciples) always, even unto the end of the world,' and similar declarations?

ANSWER. This is (already) answered, because we believe, that the gates of hell have not prevailed against the church of Christ, but it has remained, and will remain even unto the end of the world.

QUESTION 5. What then do you think of the undeniable witnesses of truth according to godliness, who have

cher Zeit, von Jahrhundert zu Jahrhundert annoch hervorgethan: Und ob solche nur deswegen, daß sie nicht nach der ersten Ordnung getauft worden, keine Gliedmaßen Christi, und seiner im dem Wesen des Geistes vereinigten Gemeine oder wahren Kirche, gewesen seyen?	appeared at such time, from century to century; and whether simply because they were not baptized according to the primitive order, they were not members of Christ and of his true church and congregation, united essentially in the spirit, simply because they were not baptized according to the primitive order?
Antw. Christus spricht Matth. 7. Man solle den Baum an den Früchten erkennen; weilen wir nun glauben, daß das schöne Bücherschreiben oder auch Weissagen, nicht eben die Früchte eines guten Christen seyn, wobei man ihn allein erkennen soll, und darum können wir einen Menschen nicht vor einen Christen halten, dennoch wollen wir niemand richten, und weil wir diese Leute in ihrem Leben nicht gekannt, so lassen wir sie ihrem Gott stehen; und kann all ihr Schreiben oder auch Weissagen, uns das Evangelium Jesu nichf verdächtig machen: und wir können sie wegen dem Weissagen allein nicht vor die Kirche Christi halten, wann sie nicht in der Lehre Jesu, in der Tauf und übrigen Ordnungen, so er befohlen, gewandelt haben.	**Answer.** Christ says, Matt. 7: "By the fruits ye shall know the tree." Now since we believe, that the writing of fine books, or even prophesying, are not the proper fruits of a good christian, by which we shall know him, and on this account cannot consider a person as a christian. Yet we will judge no man, and since we did not know these men in their lives, we leave them to their God; and all their writings and prophesying cannot make us to suspect the gospel of Jesus. And on account of their prophesying alone we cannot deem them to be the church of Christ, if they did not walk in the doctrine of Jesus, in baptism and other ordinances, as he has commanded.
6. **Fr.** Ob sie nicht der Meinung seyen, daß die so lang verfallene Taufceremonie in der letzten Zeit allerdings wieder aufgerichtet werden müsse, und mit was Grund? oder ob nicht vielmehr der allweise Gott diese zum christlichen Wesen des Christenthums eben nicht gehörige Ceremonie darum so sehr verfallen lassen, daß er auch dieselbige, wie die Beschneidung im alten Bund, als annoch unvollkommen, und noch nicht vollkommen machend, ganz und gar aufheben, und eine neue Oeconomie und Haushaltung des lautern Geistes, wie alle	**Question 6.** Were they not of the opinion, that the ceremony of baptism, which had been so long in decay, is, by all means, to be established again in the latter times, and if so, for what purpose? Or did not an all-wise God permit this ceremony, which like circumcision in the old covenant which covenant was neither perfect itself, neither could make any thing perfect, to be put entirely away, that in its room a new economy and dispensation of the pure Spirit should be established for

darf verändert werden; dann so lang das Levitische Priesterthum gestanden, so lang hat niemand das Gesetz oder die Beschneidung aufheben dürfen, ohne große Strafe und Ungnade bei Gott: Als aber Christus gekommen, hat er, als der ewige Hohepriester und Sohn Gottes, ein Gesetz des Lebens eingeführet, und das erste, weil es zu schwach war und nicht vollkommen machen konnte, anfzehoben, und eine ewige Erlösung funden, den Weg in das Allerheiligste geoffenbaret, und lauter Gesetze des Lebens gegeben, seinen Willen oder Testament mit seinem Blut fest gemacht, daß wir glauben und bekennen, daß wenn ein Engel vom Himmel käme, und ein anderer oder besser Evangelium vermeinte zu offenbaren, daß auch solcher Engel müsse verflucht seyn; nach dem Zeugniß Pauli Galat. 1, 8. Und darum glauben wir daß die Lehre Jesu des Gekreutzigten solle gehalten werden, bis er selbsten wird wiederkommen, und mit Feuerflammen Rach üben, an denen so seinem Evangelium nicht gehorsam sind gewesen; nach dem Zeugniß Pauli 2 Theff. 1, 8. Weßwegen dann die Lehre Jesu von den Gläubigen auch in diesen Tagen wird billig müssen gehalten werden, den Unglaubigen aber ist nichts befohlen.

7. Fr. Ob sie in jenem Fall nicht erkennen und bekennen müssen, daß zu derer Wiederaufrichtung sowohl als zu deren ersten Einsetzung, ein unmittelbarer göttlicher Beruf gehöre und erfordert werde, dergleichen nach dem Zeugniß der Schrift und allgemeinen Bekenntniß, jederzeit bei solchen großen Kirchen Reformationen ergangen?

Antw. Wir glauben dieses gar wohl, daß zu der Ausrichtung der Lehre Jesu ein unmittelbarer Beruf und Trieb des Geistes Gottes erfordert wird: daß aber dieser Beruf mit Zeichen und Wundern vor

law may not be changed." For as long as the Levitical priesthood was standing, so long no body was permitted to abolish the law, or circumcision without incurring severe punishment, and the displeasure of God. But when Christ was come, he as the eternal High Priest and Son of God, introduced a law of life, and the first, because of its weakness and not being able to make perfect, was abolished. Christ 'having obtained eternal redemption for us," revealed the way to the Holy of Holies, gave none but laws of life, and has established his will or testament by his blood, so that we believe and confess, should an angel from heaven come, and would intend to reveal another or better gospel, that even such an angel must be accursed, according to the testimony of Paul. Gal. 1 : 8. Hence we believe, that the doctrine of Jesus the Crucified, is to be observed, until he himself shall come again in flaming fire, and take vengeance on them, that have not been obedient to his gospel in accordance with the testimony of Paul, 2 Thess. 1 : 7, 8. Therefore, the doctrine of Jesus is justly to be observed by the believers in these (our) days, but to the unbelievers nothing seems to be commanded.

QUESTION 7. Whether in that case, they are not compelled to acknowledge and confess, that to the re-establishment of the same, as well as to its first institution an immediate divine calling is necessary and required, such as according to the testimony of scripture, and to general confessions have occurred at all times in such great reformations of the church?

ANSWER. We believe indeed, that for the establishing of the doctrine of Jesus an immediate calling and incitement of the Holy Spirit is required. But whether this calling is to be con-

den Menschen soll befestiget und geoffen-baret werden, hierinnen wollen wir dem allwissenden Gott nichts vorschreiben, es wird genug seyn so er von Gott ist, die Menschen mögens glauben oder nicht: hierin muß man gelassen seyn.

8. Fr. Ob dann einer unter ihnen auf-treten könne, der vor Gott auf seine Seele und Verantwortung in der Stunde seines Todes, und am Tage des Gerichts zu sagen getraue, daß er einen solchen unmittelbaren Beruf, die so lang verfallene Tauforbnung, und damit eine ganz neue Kirche Christi hier auf Erden (dergleichen seit der Apostel und der ersten Christen Zeiten nicht mehr gewesen seyn solle) wieder aufzurichten, von Gott empfangen habe?

Antw. Als die Pharisäer von Jerusa-lem sandten und ließen den Johannem fragen: Ob er Christus oder ein Prophet seye, weilen er taufete? so antwortete er: ich taufe euch mit Wasser zur Buße, aber er ist mitten unter euch getreten, den ihr nicht kennet, der wird euch mit Feuer und mit dem Heiligen Geist taufen. Also sa-gen wir auch in der Einfalt, wir taufen ja nur im Wasser auf den Glauben an Chri-stum, welcher in diesen Tagen seine Stim-me in den Herzen der Menschen hören läßt; O! thäte man nur folgen und ihn recht kennen, so sollte ers allein seyn, und würde es auch allein bleiben, der sich in dieser Zeit eine Gemeinde wird aufrichten und sie heiligen und reinigen durchs Was-serbad im Wort Ephes. 5, 26. und dieses wird sich kein Mensch dürfen zueignen, oder vor Menschen sagen er wäre gesandt von Gott eine Gemeinde aufzurichten, son-dern er wird gerne Gott die Ehre lassen, u. wann schon Gott einige als sonderbare Werkzeuge hiezu brauchen wird, so muß man sie nur darin prüfen, ob sie von Gott gesandt seyen wie Johannes sagt Cap. 3, 34. Dann welchen Gott gesandt, der re-det Gottes Wort.

firmed and manifested before men by signs and miracles, in this we would not prescribe any thing to the all know-ing God. If the calling is of God, let that suffice, whether men will believe or not; in this we must be resigned.

QUESTION 8. Whether any one of them could rise up, and venture to de-clare before God in the hour of death, and in the day of judgment, on his con-science and in view of his accountabil-ity that he had received from God such an immediate call to re-establish that order of baptism so long neglected, and thereby form an entirely new church of Christ here on earth, such as had not been since the time of the apostles and primitive Christians?

ANSWER. When the Pharisees sent from Jerusalem, and propounded the question to John, whether he was Christ or a prophet, because he baptized,—he answered, "I indeed baptize you with (in) water unto repentance; but there standeth one among you, whom ye know not, who shall baptize you with (in) the Holy Ghost and with (in) fire." Thus we say also in our simpli-city. We indeed baptize only in water upon the faith in Christ, who in these days causes his voice to be heard in the hearts of men. Oh that they would only obey and know him truly, then He would be it alone, and would also abide with us, who at this time will build up, sanctify and cleanse his church "with the washing of water by the word." Eph. 5 : 26. Then no man would undertake to appropriate this to himself, or declare before men, that he was sent from God to establish a church, but willingly he would give the glory to God; and though God may employ some as peculiar instru-ments, we must nevertheless try them, whether they are sent of God, as John said, ch. 3 : 34. "For he whom God hath sent, speaketh the words of God."

9. Fr. Worin doch solcher sein unmittelbarer Beruf bestehe, und wie er denselben an die Herzen und Gewissen, sowohl derer, die noch unter den Secten, als auch derer, die bereits außer denenselben sind, zu ihrer äußerlichen oder innerlichen Ueberzeugung rechtfertigen und darthun könne oder wolle?

Antw. Der unmittelbare Beruf bestehet ja darinn daß es der Mensch innerlich kräftig durch den Geist Gottes gewiß ist, und sich nicht bekümmert, die Menschen mögens glauben oder nicht; gleichwie nun Christus selbst spricht: Joh. 6, 43. 44. Murret nicht, es kann niemand zu mir kommen, es sey dann, daß ihn ziehe der Vater der mich gesandt hat: Eben also ist es noch, es kann niemand zur Lehre Christi kommen, er muß sich dann vom Vater ziehen lassen, und wer dem Zug des Vaters folgen wird, der wird wohl erkennen, wo die berufenen und auserwählten Gläubigen seyn.

10. Fr. Ob nicht nach der Wahrheit billig davor zu halten, daß, wann dies Werk aus Gott, u. sie einen solchen unmittelbaren göttlichen Beruf hierzu empfangen hätten, sich gutwillige Seelen alsofort bei tausenden dazu würden eingefunden haben, wie in der ersten Pfingsten neuen Testaments, auf die damalige Beweisung des Geistes, und der Kraft Jesu Christi in und an den Aposteln des Herrn geschehen?

Antw. Christus spricht Matth. 24. zu den Seinigen, insonderheit bey dieser Zeit, sie sollen sich nur vorsehen daß sie nicht verführet werden, er spricht ja nicht, daß in solcher trübseligen Zeit (worin wir leider jetzt seyn, da die Liebe in vielen Herzen erkaltet ist,) die Menschen tausendweise zu seinem Evangelio laufen werden; ja selbst die gutwilligen Seelen laufen eben nicht so gerne in die Nachfolge Jesu, wobei man alles verläugnen muß, so man anders Christo recht folgen will.

QUESTION 9. Wherein then does his immediate calling consist, and how could or would he justify and prove the same to the outward or inward conviction in the hearts and consciences of those who are still belonging to sects as well as to those, who are already withdrawn from the sects?

ANSWER. The immediate calling indeed consists in this, that a man feels inwardly and powerfully assured by the Spirit of God, and is not concerned about it whether men believe it or not. Even as Christ himself says, John 6 : 43, 44. 'Murmur not among yourselves. No man can come to me, except the Father which hath sent me draw him." Thus it is also at this time: No man can come to the (true) doctrine of Christ, except he is willingly drawn by the Father, and he that will obey the Father's drawing, will easily know, where the called and chosen believers are.

QUESTION 10. Whether we may not readily and in truth suppose that if this work proceeded from God, and they had received such an immediate divine call to it, thousands of souls would willingly and at once have come, as at the first Pentecost of the New Testament upon the demonstration of the Spirit and of power, which then occurred in and about the apostles of the Lord?

ANSWER. Christ says, Matt. 24, to his disciples, referring especially to these latter times, that they should "take heed, that no man may deceive them." He says not indeed, that in such troublesome times, (in which, alas! we are now, since love has grown cold in so many;) men would run by thousands to his gospel. Nay, even upright souls do not walk so readily in the footsteps of Jesus, whereby all is to be denied, if indeed we wish to be true followers of him.

Christus spricht vielmehr von dieser Zeit da der große Greuel der Verwüstung sich offenbaren wird, und ist nur gesagt, man solle auf die Berge fliehen, das ist, die Lehre Jesu des Gekreutzigten, ist erhöhet bei allen Gläubigen, und ist die Stadt Gottes und der Berg Zion, wovon Hebr. 12, 22. 23. stehet: Wohin jederzeit alle wahre Gläubige geflohen sind, und kann mancher sein Weib und Kind nicht einmal mitbringen, wie es dem Loth ergangen, ob er schon durch einen göttlichen Beruf, durch Engel ausgeführet ward, dem Verderben zu entfliehen, seinen Freunden war es dennoch lächerlich, ja er muste sein eigen Weib auf dem Wege stehen lassen. Weswegen dann Christus gar kurz zu einem tiefen Nachdenken Luc. 17, 32. zu den Seinen spricht: Gedenket an Loths Weib!

11. Fr. Ob die Wassertauf dergestalt absolut nothwendig, daß schlechterdings niemand ohne dieselbe selig werden könne, er glaube und lebe auch sonsten so heilig und unsträflich als er immer wolle?

Antw. Wir glauben und bekennen, daß im alten und neuen Testament, nur den Gläubigen Segen und Seligkeit verheißen ist: Und wie die Gläubigen jederzeit gesinnet und geartet gewesen sind, sehen wir an dem gläubigen Abraham, dem Vater aller Gläubigen, wie er in allem Gott gehorsam gewesen u. die Verheißung erlanget, wegen seines Glaubens, der lebendig war, und hat also Werke des Gehorsams gewürket. Also glauben wir, wann ein Mensch heilig und unsträflich lebet, und das Leben gewürket wird durch den wahren Glauben an Christum, so wird dem Glauben der Gehorsam zur Wassertauf ja leichter seyn,

Christ is rather speaking of such a time, where the abomination of desolation shall be revealed, and we are only told to flee to the mountains, i. e. to the doctrine of Jesus the crucified, which is exalted with all believers, and is the city of God and mount Sion, of which we read Heb. 12 : 22, 23. To this all true believers have taken refuge, and many could not even bring along their wives and children, as it happened to Lot, though he was led out through a divine call by angels in order to escape from destruction. To his friends it still seemed ridiculous, and even his own wife he had to leave behind on the road. Therefore Christ speaks very briefly and emphatically the solemn words to his disciples, Luke 17 : 32. *"Remember Lot's wife."*

Question 11. Whether baptism in water be so absolutely necessary, that no one can, by any means be saved without it, however faithful, holy and irreproachable he might be?

Answer. We believe and confess, that in the Old and New Testament, a blessing and salvation is promised only to the believers; and how the believers at all times were minded and disposed, we see in faithful Abraham, the father of all the faithful, being obedient in all things to God, and obtaining the promise on account of his living faith, by which he also wrought works of obedience. Thus, we believe, when a man lives holy and piously, and this life is produced by true faith in Christ, then it will be easier to faith to be obedient in water baptism, than it was to

der Röm. 10, 9. 10. Und solcher eigenen Heiligkeit ist keine Seligkeit verheißen, sondern Christus ist des Gesetzes Ende, wer an den glaubet, der ist gerecht, und der Glaube an Christum wirket Gehorsam, und Unterthänigkeit gegen alle seine Worte und Gebote.

12. Fr. Ob die Hauptstelle Marci 16, 16. nicht vielmehr das Gegentheil erweise, da Christus so bedächtlich sagt: Wer nicht glaubt, (und nicht getauft wird,) der wird verdammt werden?

Antw. Wir glauben ja und bekennen dieses daß nicht um der Tauf willen, sondern nur dem Glauben an Christum das ewige Leben verheißen ist: Joh. 3, 15—18. Warum sollt nun ein Gläubiger nicht wollen, was der will, an den er glaubt; weil nun Christus will der Gläubige soll getauft werden, so wird dieses der Gläubige auch wollen, und wann er so will, und glaubt wie Christus will, so ist er selig: und wann er schon aus Noth nicht die Tauf erlangen könnte: Eben wie Abraham, der wollte seinen Sohn Isaak opfern, und es geschahe nicht, der Sohn wurde nicht geopfert, aber der Gehorsam wurde erfüllet, und erlangte den Segen; also auch ein Gläubiger, der da will getauft seyn, und aus Noth nicht erlanget, wie der Schächer am Kreutz, so ist er selig: will aber ein Mensch nicht getauft seyn so wird er billig als ein Ungläubiger und Ungehorsamer gerichtet werden, nicht wegen der Tauf, sondern wegen seines Unglaubens und Ungehorsams. Und ist gar recht, wann Christus spricht, wer glaubt: sonsten wann Christus die Seligkeit an das Wasser gebunden hätte, so sollten die Menschen wohl eher getauft seyn wollen, und den eigenen Willen sonsten behalten, gleich wie der Antichrist thut und die Seligkeit nur dem Wasser zuschreibet, der Mensch mag sonsten leben wie er will.

to such self-righteousness no salvation is promised; but he that believeth in Christ, who is the end of the law, he is justified; and faith in Christ produces obedience and submission to all his words and commandments.

QUESTION 12. Whether the principal passage, Mark 16 : 16. does not prove rather the contrary, when Christ so emphatically says, "He that believeth not, (and not, he that is not, baptized,) shall be damned."

ANSWER. We believe indeed and confess this, that not on account of baptism, but only to the faith in Christ, eternal life is promised. John 3 : 15, 18. Why then should a believer not be willing to do what is the will of him, in whom he believeth? Now since it is the will of Christ, that a believer should be baptized, it is also the will of the believer, and thus believing and willing, as Christ willeth, he is saved, although he should by necessity be prevented from obtaining baptism. Just as Abraham, who was willing to sacrifice his son Isaac, and it was not done;—the son was not sacrificed, but the obedience was fulfilled,—obtained the blessing;—so likewise a believer, being willing to be baptized, and from necessity not being able to obtain it, as the thief on the cross could not, is still saved. But if a person will not be baptized, he will be righteously judged an unbeliever and as disobedient, not on account of baptism, but on account of his unbelief and disobedience. Hence it is quite right, when Christ says, "He that believeth! Else; if Christ had confined salvation to the water, men would be much more willing to be baptized, and retain their self-will in other things; as Antichrist is doing, ascribing salvation only to the water, though a person may do in other things as he pleases.

13. Fr. Wann die Wassertauf so absolut nöthig, warum Christus in seiner
Bergpredigt von denen Seligkeiten Matth.
5. so gar keine Erwähnung davon gethan:
auch in seiner Gerichtsbeschreibung Matth.
25. da er doch sonderlich von denen, die da
selig oder verdammt werden sollen, handelt,
nicht die geringste Meldung davon thut?

Antw. Es ist wunder, daß man doch
den lautern Sinn Gottes nicht merket;
Christus spricht freilich Matth. 5, von vielen Seligkeiten, wäre aber wohl zu fragen,
wo man solche Seligkeiten doch erlangen
kann; Christus spricht, selig sind die Sanft-
müthigen, nun merket man wohl wie
Christus ruft Matth. 11, 28. 29. Kommt
her zu mir u. lernet von mir, also bekennen
wir, daß Christus allein der Seligmacher ist,
und wer so selig werden will wie er Matt.
5, prediget, der muß nothwendig ihn annehmen in wahrem Glauben, und muß
sich ihm in dem Gehorsam unterwerfen,
als ein Thon seinem Töpfer, und er ist der,
so alles neu und selig machen muß, worauf alle Propheten gewiesen haben: und
Gott selbsten weiset auf den Sohn; weilen nun Christus der Seligmacher, ja der
gute Arzt, auch die Taufe nöthig achtet
den Gläubigen, so ist auch der Gehorsam
gegen dies Gebot der Taufe nöthig zur Seligkeit; obschon Christus Matth. 25, selig
preiset die ihn gespeiset und gekleidet haben,
und meldet auch nichts von der neuen
Creatur oder Wiedergeburt, wovon er gesprochen Johanni 3, daß Niemand ohne
Wiedergeburt ins Reich Gottes kommen
könne, und hat dorten nichts gelehret von
Besuchen, wann er gefangen sey, oder von
Speisung seiner Glieder: wer wollte nun

QUESTION 13. If baptism "in water
be absolutely necessary, why has Christ
made no mention of it in his sermon
on the mount, when speaking of the
blessings; Matt. 5; nor in his description of the (last) judgment, Matt. 25,
does he intimate the least of it, though
he treats especially of those who shall
be saved or damned?

ANSWER. It is astonishing, how
little men attend to the pure mind of
God! Christ indeed speaks, Matt. 5,
of many blessings; but we might do
well to enquire, whence may such blessings be obtained? Christ says, 'Blessed are the meek;" and we should notice well, how Christ calleth, Matt. 11:
28, 29: 'Come unto me and,— learn of
me!" Hence we confess, that Christ
alone is the Savior, and whoever wishes
to be blessed, as he preaches, Matt. 5,
must necessarily accept him in true
faith, and submit to him in obedience
as clay in the hands of the potter, and
He it is, who must make all things
new, and save all, and to him all the
prophets have pointed. Now since
Christ the Savior, and good physician,
deems baptism also necessary for the
believer, obedience to this command of
baptism is also necessary unto salvation.
Although in Matt. 25. Christ calls
those blessed who fed and clothed him,
without saying anything about the new
birth or regeneration, of which he had
spoken, John 3, when he said 'Except
a man be born again, he could not come
into the kingdom of God." Here he
said nothing of visiting him in prison
or of (feeding) giving meat to his mem-

nicht ein einziger Verächter der Wasser=
taufe darunter wird gefunden werden,
wohl aber Ungetaufte, die etwan aus Noth
und nicht aus Verachtung nicht getauft
waren.

14. Fr. Woher sie erweisen wollen, daß
Johannes der Täufer auch selbsten getauft
worden, nachdem er gleichwohl Matth, 3,
14. zu Christo von sich gesagt: Ich bedarf
wohl daß ich von dir getauft werde, und du
kommst zu mir, oder ob der etwa durch ei=
ne sonderliche Ausnahme, ohne die Wasser=
tauf selig worden sey?

Antw. Eben so könnte man noch vieles
fragen, wo Petrus und Johannes wären
getauft worden, oder wo dieser oder jener
Heilige im alten Bund beschnitten worden,
und könnte mehr Fragen aufbringen dann
Besserung zu Gott im Glauben wo Paulus
1 Timoth. 1, meldet, auch Menschen gewe=
sen seyn, die nach dem Geschlechtregister ge=
fragt haben; jedoch wollen wir auch hier=
in in Gedult antworten: Johannes wollte
sich ja gerne taufen lassen von Christo und
begehrete es, welchem Glauben wir ja die
Seligkeit nach der Schrift zuschreiben, und
nicht der äussern Tauf, ob es nun in der
Schrift äusserlich nicht stehet daß er ge=
tauft worden sey; so stehet doch in der
Schrift daß er kein Verächter der Tauf
war, und wird Johannes gar nicht unter
denen gefunden werden, die da sagen: Ei
was kann mir das Wasser helfen, sondern
er hat seinen Gehorsam gegen Christum er=
wiesen, wie Abraham den Gehorsam er=
wiese gegen Gott in Aufopferung seines
Sohnes; der Sohn wurde nicht geopfert,
und der Gehorsam wurde doch erfüllet.

15. Fr. Ob dann alle diejenige, so nach
den Zeiten der ersten Christen, außer der
ersten Tauordnung gestanden, und gestor=
ben, da sie schon im übrigen allen Grund=
regeln Christi und des wahren Christen=
thums getreulich nachgekommen, auch zum
Theil ihr Blut und Leben darüber gelas=

a single despiser of water baptism will
be among them, though there may be
some unbaptized ones, who were such
out of necessity, and not from scorn.

QUESTION 14. How would you
prove, that John the Baptist himself
was baptized, when he said to Christ,
Matt. 3 : 14. 'I have need to be baptized of thee, and comest thou to me?"
or whether, by a particular exception,
he was saved without water-baptism?

ANSWER. In the same manner we
might enquire after a great deal, (for
instance,) where Peter and John were
baptized, or where this and that saint
of the old covenant was circumcised, and
more questions might be raised, than
would tend to edification torward God
in faith, as Paul mentions 1 Tim. 1 :
that there were men who gave heed to
fables and endless genealogies. Yet we
will also herein reply in patience. John
was indeed willing to be baptized of
Christ, and desired it, and to such faith
we ascribe salvation according to scripture, and not to external baptism. Now
though it is not literally stated in scripture, that he was baptized, still we find
so much written, as to show, that he
was no despiser of baptism, and John
will not be found at all among those,
who say: Why, what can water help
me? But he has proved his obedience toward Christ, as Abraham proved
his toward God in offering up his son.
The son was not sacrificed, and yet
obedience was fulfilled.

QUESTION 15. Whether, then all
those, who lived and died after the
time of the primitive Christians, and
who had not received baptism in the
original manner, must be absolutely
lost and damned, though they have
faithfully observed in other respects all

fen, nur darum daß sie entweder aus Un=
erkenntniß, oder auch an Mangelung hö=
heren Triebs, bei ihrer in der Kindheit
empfangenen Tauf geblieben, schlechter=
dings verloren und verdammt seyen?

Antw. Wann es ihnen ergangen wie
Abraham in Aufopferung seines Sohnes,
nemlich, daß sie den wahren Glauben hat=
ten an Jesum, welcher der Grund ist al=
ler Regeln des wahren Christenthums, so
sind sie gewißlich selig, wann sie schon die
äußere Taufe nicht erlanget, etwan zu Zei=
ten der Verfolgung, oder um anderer Um=
stände willen: Wann sie aber gemeint,
ihre Kindertauf wäre gut, so sind sie frei=
lich noch unwissend gewesen im Anfang der
Christlichen Religion, und werden also
wenig oder gar nicht den Grundregeln des
wahren Christenthums nachgelebet, und die
neue Creatur, so allein vor Gott gilt,
schwerlich erlanget haben; wir aber wollen
dennoch die nicht richten, so vor langen
Jahren gelebt, sondern sie ihrem Gott ste=
hen lassen. Und wird derselbigen Unwis=
senheit denen heutigen Menschen, die sich
der Tauf auch etwan aus Unwissenheit
widersetzen, gar nichts am Tage der Offen=
barung helfen können.

16. Fr. Ob das Taufgebot nicht auch,
wie das Gebot der Beschneidung in dem
alten Bund, die Kinder angehe; und sol=
che demnach, so lang sie nicht getauft, in
Gefahr der Seligkeit seyen; auch, wo sie
ohne die Taufe dahin sterben, verdammt
werden?

Antw. So wenig als die Beschneidung
vor dem achten Tag die Kinder etwas an=
gieng, sondern wäre vielmehr eine Ueber=
tretung der Beschneidung gewesen; so
wenig gehet die Taufe, so den Gläubigen
befohlen die Kinder an, ehe sie ihren Glau=
ben bekennen können, worauf eben der
achte Tag der Beschneidung im Vorbild ge=
zielet.

the fundamental rules of Christ and
true christianity, and in part have sacrificed their blood and life for it, merely
from ignorance, or from want of a higher motive, they remained satisfied with
that (so called) baptism received in
their infancy?

ANSWER. If it happened to them
as to Abraham in the offering up of his
son, namely, that they had that true
faith in Jesus, which is the foundation
of all the rules of true Christianity,
then they are surely saved, though they
did not obtain the outward·baptism, as
may have been the case in times of persecution, and from other causes. But
if they thought their infant baptism to
be right, it shows that they were still
ignorant of the first principles of the
christian religion. Hence they lived
out few, perhaps none of the fundamental rules of Christianity, and will scarcely become partakers of the nature of
the new creature, which alone is acceptable to God. However, we will not
judge them, who lived many years ago,
but leave them to their God. But
their ignorance will not help those of
our day, who refuse baptism, and who
will then plead ignorance, at the great
day of accounts.

QUESTION 16. Is not the commandment of baptism as binding on children,
as the command of circumcision in the
old covenant was, and are they not
therefore in danger of being lost if they
die without being baptized?

ANSWER. As little as circumcision
concerned children before the eighth
day, (and to have circumcised them before that time would have rather been
a transgression of the law;) so little
does baptism concern children before
they are able to confess their belief;
and to this age of belief, the eighth day
in the law of circumcision, seems to
point as a figure.

17. Fr. Ob die Kinder welche im alten Bund ohne die Beschneidung und vor Erlangung derselbigen dahin gestorben, verdammt seyen? und wie man dann die getroste Worte Davids, 2 Sam. 12, 23. von seinem mit der Bathseba gezeugten und am siebenten Tag verstorbenen Kind anzusehen habe?

Antw. Die Kinder so vor dem achten Tag gestorben, haben ja das Gebot der Beschneidung so wenig übertreten als die Mägdlein, welche gar nicht beschnitten worden, welches sie doch an ihrer Seligkeit nichts gehindert. Enoch führete ein göttlich Leben, erreichte viel hundert Jahr, und wurde nicht beschnitten, und dennoch war er Gott gehorsam; es ward ihm nicht befohlen. So geht's mit den Geboten Gottes, wo kein Gesetz ist da ist auch keine Uebertretung, wo keine Uebertretung ist, da ist auch keine Strafe.

18. Fr. Wann die Kinder eigentlich zu taufen? Und ob man nicht allen Fleiß anzuwenden habe, dieselbige, so bald immer möglich, und sollte es auch in ihrer Kindheit noch geschehen können, zur Taufe zu befördern?

Antw. Die Kinder soll man durchs Gebet dem Herrn Jesu aufopfern, mit der Taufe aber warten bis sie Glauben erweisen, und bekennen können, welches eben der achte oder erste Tag der neuen Schöpfung im Menschen ist. Taufe man sie aber eher in ihrer Unwissenheit, so wäre es eben als wann die Juden vor dem achten Tag beschnitten hätten, welches vielmehr eine Uebertretung der Beschneidung, als ein Gehorsam gewesen wäre.

19. Fr. Ob die Kinder nicht, wie des Glaubens, nach Luc. 1, 41—44. Matth. 18, 3—6. Luc 18, 16. 17. 1 Cor. 7, 14. 2c. also auch der Taufe fähig seyen, ob sie schon solchen eben nicht, wie die Erwachse-

QUESTION 17. Were children which were under the old covenant, and which died before the eighth day without circumcision, lost? And how are the words of comfort by David, 2 Sam. 12 : 23, to be regarded with regard to his child, begotten of Bathsheba which died on the seventh day?

ANSWER. Male children which died before the eighth day, transgressed the law of circumcision as little as girls, which were not at all circumcised, yet the want of circumcision interfered in no wise with their salvation. Enoch led a godly life for some hundred years, and was not circumcised, for it was not commanded to him; yet he was obedient to God. Thus it is with divine commandments; where there is no law, there is no transgression, and where no offence is committed, there is no punishment.

QUESTION 18. When is it proper to baptize children? And are we not to use all diligence to bring them to baptism as soon as possible, even in their infancy?

ANSWER. Children are to be offered up to the Lord Jesus in prayer, but as to their baptism, we are to wait until they can show their faith, and make confession, which may be called the very eighth day, or their first day of the new creation in man. If they were baptized sooner, in their ignorance, it would be just as if the Jews had circumcised before the eighth day, which would rather have been a transgression of (the law of) circumcision, than an obedient act.

QUESTION 19. Are not children susceptible of faith, according to Luke 1: 41—44, Matt. 18 : 3, 6. Luke 18: 16, 17. 1 Cor. 7 : 14, &c. and consequently of baptism, though incapable of

ne, mit vielen Worten zu bekennen wissen: Nachdem es gleichwohl, auch Kraft der Worte Marci 16, 16. mit der Taufe nicht so wohl auf die leicht betrügliche Wortbekenntniß, als auf die Wahrheit des Glaubens selbsten, ankommt?

Antw. Dieses einzige Exempel hat man in der Schrift mit Johanne, daß er in Mutterleibe beweget worden durch den heiligen Geist, weilen er ein Kind der Verheißung und der Vorläufer des Herrn seyn sollte, dennoch siehet man daß sie ihn in Mutterleibe nicht haben beschneiden können, sondern nachdem er zur Welt geboren war, warteten sie dennoch mit der Beschneidung bis auf den achten Tag, und konnte also die Bewegung des heil. Johannes die Ordnung Gottes in der Beschneidung nicht aufheben, sondern er mußte eben wie die andern Kinder am achten Tag beschnitten werden; eben so ist es mit der Tauf, daß wann schon der glaubigen Eltern ihre Kinder in Mutterleibe bewegt werden sollten, so müßte man doch mit der Tauf warten, bis sie zur Welt geboren, und wenn sie zur Welt geboren, so müßte man wieder warten bis sie bewegt würden vom heiligen Geist die Taufe mit äußern Worten zu begehren; und dann dürfte man sie taufen, weilen die äußere Wassertaufe ein äußeres Begehren erfordert, wie an Christo selbsten zu sehen ist: Matth. 3, 13. und solches Begehren muß gewürket werden durch den wahren Glauben an den Herrn Jesum, sonsten ist nicht erlaubt ein Kind zu taufen, weilen die Seligkeit nicht an das Wasser gebunden ist, sondern allein an den Glauben, der durch Liebe und Gehorsam muß erwießen werden.

20. Fr. Ob es nicht wider die Evangelische Art des neuen Bundes laufe, daß man eine äußere Ceremonie zur Seligkeit unumgänglich nöthig mache: Und mit der Lehre der alten Gesetztreiber übereinkomme, wider welche Paulus in seinen Briefen an die Galater und Colosser so ernstlich geschrieben hat?

confessing the same by as many words as the adults; for agreeably to Mark 16 : 16, a mere easily, deceptive confession in baptism by words, is less essential, than the reality of faith?

ANSWER. The only circumstance in Scripture, which we have about John, that he was moved in the womb by the Holy Ghost, was because he was to be a child of promise, and a forerunner of the Lord; and yet we see, that in his mother's womb he could not have been circumcised. But after he was born, they still deferred circumcision until the eighth day, and thus the motion of St. John did not occasion a change in the order of God with respect to circumcision, but he was to be circumcised like other children on the eighth day. Just so it is with baptism, for if even the children of believing parents were moved in their mother's womb, they would have to wait for baptism, until they were born into the world, and even then to wait, until they were moved by the Holy Ghost to desire baptism with express words. Then they might be baptized, because outward baptism requires an outward demand, as we may see in Christ himself, Matt. 3 : 13. And such demand must be awakened by true faith in the Lord Jesus; otherwise it is not allowable to baptize a child, since salvation is not connected with simple water, but only with faith, which is the proved by love and obedience.

QUESTION 20. Does it not militate against the evangelical spirit of the new covenant, to make an outward ceremony as absolutely necessary unto salvation; and would this not correspond with the doctrine of the old law-zealots, against whom Paul has written so severely in his epistles to the Galatians and Colossians?

Antw. Wir machen die äußere Taufe nicht anders als wie sie die Schrift befohlen; weilen sie nun sagt die Glaubigen sollen getauft seyn, so halten wir es vor einen Ungehorsam, wann man sich dem widersetzet was Gott befohlen; und wer sich Gott auch nur in einem widersetzt, und sollte es auch noch so wenig seyn als die äußere Taufe, so würde ein solches billig um des Ungehorsams willen gestraft; ich wüßte auch nicht ob man ein einzig Gebot des Herrn Jesu durfte vor klein ansehen, wann man ohne Widerwillen auf die Gewalt und Macht des Gebieters siehet: Was Paulus aber an die Galater und Colosser geschrieben, das gehet ja nur die Gesetze des Knechtes Mosis an, weilen sie zu schwach waren, und die Galater sie halten wollten, um dadurch von dem Kreutz Christi befreiet zu seyn, und die Lehre Jesu hintan zu setzen. Aber Paulus erinnerte sie vielmehr der Tauf, wann er schreibet: Wie viel euer getauft sind, die haben Christum angezogen, Gal. 3, 27. und ist also der Sinn Pauli gar nicht wider, sondern vielmehr vor die Taufe.

21. Fr. Ob nicht damit daß man die Taufe als ein Gebot zur Seligkeit unumgänglich nöthig machet, ein neues Pabstthum eingeführet, und die Seligkeit aus den Werken hergeführet werde?

Antw. Es ist oben genugsam gezeuget, daß wir die Seligkeit nicht suchen zu verdienen mit solchen einfältigen Werken, sondern allein durch den Glauben an Jesum, welcher muß Werke des Gehorsams würken, so es ein seligmachender Glaube seyn soll, und wo ein solcher Glaube nicht ist der Gehorsam würket, (nicht nach des Pabstes Lehr und Befehl, sondern nach dem Befehl Jesu des Gekreutzigten) so ist auch keine Seligkeit auf kein einziges Werk das ohne Glauben gethan wird, verheißen.

22. Fr. Ob der äußere Bann ein wesentliches zu der Kirche Christi gehöriges

Answer. We do not make any thing more of baptism than what is commanded in scripture. Now since it is there said that believers should be baptized, we deem it a disobedience to oppose that which God has ordained. And he who resists God only in one thing, and should it be so small as outward baptism, would be justly punished for his disobedience. I do not know however, whether we may consider any single command of the Lord Jesus, as small, if we have no aversion to the power and authority of the Lawgiver. Concerning what Paul wrote to the Galatians, and Colossians, that relates only to the laws of the servant Moses, because they were too weak, see Heb. 7 : 18. And the Galatians wanted to observe those laws in order to escape the cross of Christ, and to lay aside the doctrine of Jesus. But Paul rather reminded them of baptism, when he writes, "As many of you as have been baptized, have put on Christ." Gal. 3 : 27. Consequently, the mind of Paul is not at all against, but rather in favor of baptism.

Question 21. Is there not, by making baptism an absolutely necessary command unto salvation, a danger of introducing a new system of popery, and a salvation by works?

Answer. It has been sufficiently testified, that we do not endeavor, to obtain salvation by such simple things, but alone by faith in Jesus, which must produce acts of obedience, if indeed it is to be a saving faith. Where, however, no such faith exists, which produces obedience, (not after the doctrine and commandment of the pope, but) according to the command of Jesus the Crucified, there is no salvation promised.

Question 22. Whether the external ban (excommunication) is an essen-

Stück seye: Da doch Christus solchen selbsten an dem grundbösen Juda nicht einmal practiciret und ausgeübet?

Anwt. Der Bann ist ein wesentliches und nothwendiges Stück in der Kirche Christi, so lange sie hie auf dieser argen Welt im Streit unter den Wölfen und bösen Geistern lieget: und kann keine Gemeine Christi seyn ohne den Bann; es sollte der Teufel bald mit seinem bösen Sauerteig alles Gute verderben: Und die wahre Gläubigen haben sich auch dessen niemalen, so sie im Glauben geblieben, weigern können; sondern haben es als eine göttliche Gnade, und große Liebe und Vorsorge Gottes angesehen, und ihn als eine feste Mauer um die Gemeine des Herrn gebrauchet. Was aber von Juda gefraget wird, so sagen wir, daß Christus den Bann genugsam an ihm ausgeübt hat, und dem Satan so übergeben, daß er sich selbst erhänget hat, daß er aber vor der äußern That von Christo nicht in den Bann gethan ist, so ist solches nicht wider den Bann, sondern vielmehr davor; welches der Sinn Gottes allezeit gewesen ist, gleich wie man an Adam merket, der auch wohl wird vorher mit dem Versucher umgegangen seyn, er ward aber nicht aus dem Paradies gejagt, bis er von der verbotenen Frucht äußerlich gegessen: Eben so hatte Judas mit dieser Verrätherei schon lang vorher umgegangen. Aber die Langmüthigkeit Jesu hat ihn getragen, geduldet und zur Buße gelocket, bis das Böse endlich die Ueberhand hatte, und in der That ausbrach, da kam er ja genugsam in den Bann von Christo: Und ist wohl an Juda der Bann recht practiciret worden.

23. Fr. Ob das Binden und Lösen der Apostel auf Erden nicht ein ihnen ins be-

tial part of (the constitution of) the church of Christ, since he himself did not enforce and exercise it, even upon the very wicked Judas?

ANSWER. The ban is an essential and necessary thing in the church of Christ, as long as it is at war in this wicked world with wolves and evil spirits. No church of Christ could exist without it. The devil with his leaven of wickedness would soon destroy all that is good. True believers, while they were stedfast in the faith, never could refuse (the salutary restraints appointed in the gospel). They have always viewed them as divine means of grace, appointed by the great love and provident care of God, and used them as a strong tower and wall round about the church of the Lord.

With respect to Judas we say, that Christ has executed the ban sufficiently upon him, giving him over to Satan, for he hanged himself. But that he was not excommunicated, before he committed the outward act, is not against excommunication, but rather in its favor. That this was the mind of God at all times, as we perceive in Adam, who may have had probably some intercourse with the tempter previously (to his fall); but he was not driven out of Paradise until he had actually eaten of the forbidden fruit. So Judas may have entertained traitorous thoughts long before he carried them out; but the longsuffering of Jesus had borne with him, and patiently tried to bring him to repentance, until the evil obtained the supremacy, and became manifest in the deed. Then he was sufficiently excommunicated by Christ, and we think the ban was fully executed upon him.

QUESTION 23. Was not the binding and loosening a peculiar prerogative of

sondere anvertrauetes Vorrecht seye, dessen sich heut zu Tag niemand dergestalten anmaßen könne?

Antw. Daß das Lösen und Binden an den Aposteln ein besonderes Vorrecht sey, ist wahr; aber auf diese Art, gleich wie es ein besonderes Vorrecht war an Moses, daß durch ihn das Gesetz offenbaret ward dem Hause Israel: Dennoch aber war es kein solches Vorrecht, daß bey Absterbung Mosis das Gesetz sollte abgestorben seyn, sondern die Nachkömmlinge so Gott treu waren, unterwarfen sich dem in Gehorsam, was durch Moses im Hause Gottes geoffenbaret war: Also hat Christus der wahre Hausvater ihme eine Gemeinde und Haushaltung gestiftet, und seinen Aposteln als den vorerwählten Zeugen dieses Vorrecht gegeben, daß sie alle Ordnungen im Hause Gottes anrichteten, und mit Zeichen und Wundern befestiget, und daß alle Nachkömmlinge sich ja nicht überheben sollten, etwan aus Vorwitz, oder aus Hochmuth andere Ordnungen einzuführen; sondern sich willig denen Ordnungen unterwerfen, wo durch die Apostel, als Haushälter über Gottes Geheimniß im Haus Gottes befohlen sind; weil nun der Bann von Christo, und seinen Aposteln, befohlen, so wird ihnen das Vorrecht billig gelassen: Aber die Gläubigen müssen sich im Glauben unterwerfen, und ihn ohne Ansehung der Person brauchen.

24. Fr. Ob Christus mit den Worten Matth. 18, 17. ein allgemeines Gesetz für die Kirche Neuen Testaments gegeben: oder nicht vielmehr nach der Beschaffenheit der Jüdischen davon redet: Und denen Seinigen im übrigen, in gleichfolgendem 21 und 22sten Vers ganz eine andere Lection gegeben habe?

Antw. Daß Christus mit den Worten Matth. 18, 17. ein allgemeines Gesetz für seine Kirche gegeben, ist oben erwiesen; Und keines Weges durch die nachfolgende

the apostles, which no one at this day should arrogate to himself?

Answer. That the loosening and binding with the apostles was a peculiar prerogative, is true; but only in this manner, aa it was a peculiar prerogative of Moses, that by him the law should be promulgated to the house of Israel. Yet it was not such a prerogative, that at the death of Moses the law itself should have died, but the posterity, that was faithful to God, submitted to that in obedience, which was revealed through Moses in the house of God. Thus has Christ, the Father or Lord of the house himself, instituted a church and dispensation, and given to his apostles as the witnesses chosen before, this prerogative, that they should introduce all the ordinances in the house of God, and confirm them by signs and miracles; and in order that none of their successors should presume from either forwardness or pride, to introduce other ordinances, but should be willing to submit to those commanded by the apostles as stewards over the mysteries of God's house. Now since excommunication is commanded by Christ and his apostles, this prerogative properly belongs to them; but to believers it belongs to submit to it in faith, and to observe it without respect to persons.

Question 24. Did Christ in the words Matt. 18 : 17, institute a universal law for the church of the New Testament; or, did he not rather speak of it with regard to the condition of the Jewish church, and give to his disciples moreover in the following 21st. and 22nd. verses, quite a different lesson?

Answer. That Christ instituted a universal law for his church in the words of Matt. 18 : 17, has been shown above; the verses 21st. and 22nd. in

Verse 21. und 22. aufgehoben, sondern vielmehr befestiget; und werden diese Vers Luc 17, 4. recht ausgedruckt, wann Christus spricht: Wann dein Bruder siebenmal an dir sündigen würde, und käme siebenmal wieder und spräche: Es reuet mich, so sollt du ihm vergeben; denn ohne Erkenntniß der Sünde ist keine Vergebung, auch bei Gott: Eben so müssen die Gläubigen auch gesinnet seyn, wann der Sünder seine Sünden erkennet, so muß man vergeben;* Erkennet er aber nicht, so muß der Bann billig gehalten werden, weil Christus Matth. 28 saget: lehret sie halten, alles was ich euch befohlen habe, und siehe, ich bin bey euch, bis an der Welt Ende.

25. Fr. Ob die Apostel jemal verboten, einem von denen Gebannten die nöthige geist- oder leibliche Handreichung der Liebe zu leisten?

Antw. Die Apostel haben niemal geboten, den Gebanneten die nöthige geist- oder leibliche Handreichung zu verhalten; sondern den Gebanneten soll man zur Buße rufen, und wann ers nicht höret oder annimmt, so ist man frey. Eben so auch mit den leiblichen Dingen, wann man Ueberfluß hat, und der Gebannete hat Mangel, so soll man ihme nach Nothdurft mittheilen.

26. Fr. Ob ihr, der neuen Täufer, Bann, jemalen, wie der Apostel, bei eini-

* Hier möchte ein Mißverständniß entstehen, wenn wir das Wort nicht recht theilen. Bey Privat-Beleidigungen müssen wir vergeben, wenn der Beleidiger seinen Fehler erkennt, und gut zu machen sucht. Aber bei solchen Sünden, wie 1 Cor. 5, 11. Gal. 5, 19—21. ꝛc. ꝛc. wäre eine bloße Erkenntlichkeit und Bekenntniß nicht hinreichend für eine Gemeinde zu vergeben, sondern das Wort müßte beobachtet werden wie Paulus anweißt 1 Cor. 5.

no wise disannul that law, but rather confirm it. This is still more plainly expressed in Luke 17 : 4, where Christ says, "If thy brother trespass against thee seven times in a day, and seven times a day turn again to thee saying I repent, thou shalt forgive him." Without a confession therefore, no remission of sin is granted, not even by God. So believers must be likewise minded. If the sinner acknowledges his sins, we must forgive.* But if he does not acknowledge then we have to deal with him even to excommunication, since Christ says, Matt. 28, "Teach them to observe all things whatsoever I have commanded you, and lo, I am with you alway unto the end of the world."

QUESTION 25. Did the apostles ever prohibit the necessary spiritual and temporal assistance of charity from being rendered to the excommunicated?

ANSWER. The apostles have never commanded to withhold from the excommunicated necessary spiritual or temporal assistance; moreover, they are to be admonished to repentance, and though they do not hear or receive it we are clear. So likewise in worldly things, if we abound in the things of this world, and the excommunicated is in want, we are to communicate according to his need.

QUESTION 26. Whether the excommunication of the New Baptists, ever

*Here some misapprehension might occur by not rightly dividing the word. In private offences we must forgive, when the offender confesses his fault, and makes proper amends. But in offences, such as are described in 1 Cor. 5 : 11. Gal, 5 : 19—21. &c. &c. a mere acknowledgement or confession would not be sufficient for a church to forgive, but the word would have to be observed as Paul directed in 1 Cor. 5.

gen von ihnen Gebannten einen göttlichen Effect und Würkung gehabt?

Antw. Wir glauben gewiß, daß der Bann an allen, die wir nach des Herrn Wort darein thun, einen Effect und Wirkung schon am inwendigen allhier habe, und wird am Tage der Offenbarung erst äußerlich offenbar werden, so sie nicht, in der Gnadenzeit, Buße thun. Daß die Menschen aber gleich todt sollten niederfallen, wie Ananias, ein solches ist noch nicht geschehen, und auch von den Aposteln nur einmal zu lesen; Und sind wohl viel in den Bann gethan worden von den Aposteln, und keiner mehr so äußerlich gestorben; Dennoch aber wird die Kraft des Bannes an ihnen genug in die Erfüllung gegangen seyn.

27. Fr. Ob die wahre und wesentliche Wiedergeburt mit der Wasser-Tauf unzertrennlich verbunden seye?

Antw. Die wesentliche Wiedergeburt ist nichts anders als wahr- und wesentlicher Gehorsam gegen Gott, und gegen alle seine Gebote, und wird ein Wiedergeborner ja auch mit Christo sprechen: Matth. 3, 15. Also gebühret uns alle Gerechtigkeit zu erfüllen; und können wir also antworten: Daß der Wille oder Gehorsam gegen die Wassertauf unzertrennlich ist, mit der wahren Wiedergeburt; sollte nun aus Noth, aber nicht aus Verachtung oder Ungehorsam, die Wassertauf ausbleiben, könnte es der Wiedergeburt nichts schaden.

28. Fr. Ob alle von ihnen Getaufte zugleich auch in der Wahrheit aus Gott neu geboren werden?

Antw. Dieses wäre wohl eine gute Tauf, wann alle die, so wir im Wasser taufen, neugeborne Menschen wären; welches man aber weder an Christo, noch seinen Aposteln erweisen kann, daß nemlich alle ihre Täuflinge wohlgerathen seyen:

had in any of their subjects upon whom it was practiced such a divine effect and result, as that of the apostles?

ANSWER. We firmly believe that all those we excommunicate according to the word of the Lord will feel an internal effect, and an impression already here, and if not repented in this time of grace, it will become manifest in the great day of judgment. But that men should immediately fall dead to the ground like Ananias, such has not happened yet, and is only once recorded of the apostles, and how ever many were excommunicated by the apostles, no more died thus literally, yet we believe the power of excommunication was fully realized in them.

Q. 27. Is true and genuine regeneration inseparably connected with water-baptism?

ANS. Genuine regeneration is nothing else but real and genuine obedience towards God and all his commandments, and a regenerate person will readily say with Christ, Matt. 3 : 15. "Thus it becometh us to fulfill all righteousness." Hence we can answer, that the will or obedience with regard to water-baptism is inseparably connected with true regeneration. Should, however, water-baptism be omitted from necessity, and not from contempt or disobedience, then, and in that case, the omission would not injure regeneration.

QUES. 28. Whether all those they baptized, were at the same time truly born again of God?

ANS. That would indeed be a good baptism, if all those, whom we baptize in water, were truly regenerate men. It however cannot be proved that all those that Christ and the apostles baptized, turned out well. But where

Wann aber der wahre Glaube da ist, und durch den Glauben das Wort im Wasser-bad gefasset oder angenommen wird, so ge-schiehet eine wesentliche Wiedergeburt oder Reinigung durchs Wort im Wasserbad. Ephes. 5, 26.

29. Fr. Ob einer nicht wahrhaftig wiedergeboren seyn könne, auch noch ehe er getauft worden: Nachdeme die Wassertau-fe, wie sie selbsten nicht in Abrede seyn können, die wahre und wesentliche Wieder-geburt nicht giebet?

Antw. Adam war im Paradies ge-schaffen nach dem Bilde Gottes, als er aber seinem Gott ungehorsam war, so verlor er alle seine schöne Gestalt, und mußte, um seines Ungehorsams willen, in Fluch und Tod: Also kann freylich ein Mensch, vor der Wassertauf, ein gut Theil der Wiederge-burt erlanget haben, wird er aber nicht im-mer gehorsamer und kleiner, so kann er gar leicht wieder verlieren was er erarbeitet hat. Und ist also der neuen Creatur ihre Speise, zur Unterhaltung und Wachsthum, der wahre Gehorsam gegen den Herrn Je-sum: Isset sie diese Speise nicht (welches doch der neuen Creatur ihre Speise war. Joh. 4, 34.) sondern isset der Schlangen Speise, welches ist Ungehorsam, in allerley Weisheit und Klugheit gegen das Wort, so gehts ihr wie Adam im Paradies: weil nun die Wassertauf befohlen von Christo, muß auch der wiedergeborne Mensch sich im Gehorsam biegen, und diese Gerechtig-keit erfüllen.

30. Fr. Ob sich die wahre Brüder-schaft der Christen nicht vielmehr auf die Wiedergeburt, als auf die Wassertaufe, gründe?

Antw. Die wahre Brüderschaft der Christen hat sich jederzeit auf den wahren Glauben, und Gehorsam gegen den Herrn Jesum, und gegen sein Evangelium gegrün-det. Darum haben niemalen die wahre

there is true faith, and where by faith the word in the water-bath is received and taken hold of, a true regeneration or purification takes place in the wash-ing of water by the word. Eph. 5 : 26.

QUES. 29. May not one really be regenerated, even before he is baptized, inasmuch as water-baptism, as you will not be able to deny, cannot impart true and genuine regeneration?

ANS. Adam was created in Para-dise after the image of God. But when he was disobedient to his God, he lost all his divine beauty, and incurred on account of his disobedience, the curse and death. Thus a person may be re-generated to a considerable degree, be-fore he is baptized in water. But un-less he becomes more and more obedi-ent and humble, he may easily lose again, what he had previously obtained. Hence the food of the new creature, for its sustenance and growth is true obedi-ence to the Lord Jesus. Should he refuse to eat this meat, (so necessary for the new creature, John 4 : 34.) and eat the food of the serpent, which is disobedience, in manifold cunning and crafty excuses against the word, his fate will be the same as that of Adam in Paradise. Since, therefore, water-baptism is commanded by Christ, the regenerate man must submit to it in obedience, and fulfill this righteous-ness.

QUES. 30. Does not the true brother-hood of Christians, ground itself upon regeneration much more than upon water-baptism?

ANS. The true brotherhood of Christians, has been always founded upon true faith and obedience to the Lord Jesus and his gospel. Hence the true brethren of Christ could never re-

Brüder Christi sich der äußeren Wassertauf weigern können; weil sie es an ihrem erstgebornen Bruder gesehen, und derselbige es ihnen auch befohlen; und er, Christus selbst, die nur für seine Brüder hält, so den Willen Gottes thun. Matth. 12, 50.

31. Fr. Ob man diejenigen, welche ihre Wiedergeburt in der That vor Gott und Menschen erweisen, nicht mit allem Recht für Brüder zu halten habe, ob sie schon nicht aufs neue getauft worden? besiehe Matth. 12, 49. 50.

Antw. Diejenigen, so ihre Wiedergeburt in der That vor Gott und Menschen erweisen, halten wir vor Brüder, aber die werden sich der Wassertauf auch nicht widersetzen, sondern sich nach ihrem Glauben und inwendigen Trieb taufen lassen. Dann Christus hat ja die auch nur vor seine Brüder gehalten, welche seine Jünger, und getauft waren. Besiehe recht, Matth. 12, 49. 50.

32. Fr. Ob sie vor dem Angesicht Jesu Christi, des allwissenden Herzenkündigers und Richters der Lebendigen und der Todten, sagen könne, daß ihrer selbsten allerseits ein Herz und eine Seele seye?

Antw. Dieses wird nicht von Gott gefordert; daß wir schon sollten, in der Vollkommenheit, ein Herz und eine Seele seyn: Und darum wir auch nicht sagen können, daß wirs im Wesen seyen, im Willen aber müssen wir es seyn: Nemlich, daß wir an einander arbeiten wollen, bis wir alle zu einerley Glauben hinan kommen, und zur Einigkeit des völligen Glaubens. Wovon Ephes. 4, 11. 12. 13. stehet. Es wird auch niemand sagen können, daß die Gemeinde zu Jerusalem in der Vollkommenheit ein Herz und eine Seele gewesen, sondern im Anfang waren sie eins, Christo nachzufolgen mit Verleugnung alles Irdischen: Daß sie aber in Erkenntniß noch ganz uneins waren, ist zu merken Apostel

fuse outward water-baptism, because they saw it in their first-born brother, who also commanded them so to do, and because he declared them only his brethren, who do the will of God. Matt. 12 : 50.

Ques. 31. Are not such, who prove themselves as being regenerated indeed before God and men, to be deemed rightfully as brethren, although they are not baptized again or anew? See Matt. 12 : 49, 50.

Ans. Those who prove their regeneration indeed before God and men, we hold as brethren; but such will not oppose themselves to water-baptism, but will suffer themselves to be baptized according to their faith and inward desire. For Christ verily acknowledged only those as his brethren that were his disciples, and had been baptized, as you will discover by examining closely Matt. 12 : 49, 50.

Ques. 32. Can you declare before the face of Jesus Christ, the omniscient searcher of hearts and the Judge of the quick and the dead, that you yourselves are all of one heart and of one soul?

Ans. This, God has not required, that we should at this time, be of one heart and one soul in a perfect state. Hence we cannot say, that we are so in reality. But in will, we must be it, namely, this far, that we labor together until we all come to the unity of faith and fulness in Christ, as written in Ephes. 4 : 11—13. No person can say that the church at Jerusalem were in perfection, and all of one accord. But in the beginning, they were unitedly willing to follow Christ in renouncing their earthly all. However, that they afterwards differed in knowledge, we may perceive in Acts 15 : 5 &c. We know, that from this very church

Gesch. 15, 5. ıc. Da eben von der Ge=
meinde zu Jerusalem ausgegangen sind,
und anders gelehret, als es die Apostel leh=
reten wegen der Beschneidung; Und muß=
ten die Apostel noch große Mühe haben, an
der Einigkeit zu arbeiten. Und ist also
Wunder, daß man von uns, in diesen
greulichen Tagen, da Finsterniß und Dun=
kelheit alle Völker bedecket haben, so gleich
eine solche vollkommene Einigkeit fordert:
Da doch Diejenigen, so sich der innern
Geistestauf rühmen, so uneins seyn, daß
auch in den hell und klaren Befehlen von
der Wassertauf, lauter Ungewißheit und
Uneinigkeit unter ihnen hervorkommt, wie
auch in andern vornehmsten Glaubens=
Punkten.

at Jerusalem there went out some, who
taught differently from the apostles concerning circumcision, and that the
apostles had a great deal of trouble in
laboring for union. Hence it is remarkable that it should be required of us,
in these dreadful times, where darkness
and obscurity covers all nations, that
there should be such a perfect union
among us, while those who boast of an
inward spiritual baptism, still disagree
so much, that even in the plain and
clear commandments about water bap.
tism, there is nothing but uncertainty
and discord among them, as well as in
other principal points of faith.

33. Fr. Ob sie nicht ihre Gemeinden
besser halten, dann aller andern Taufge=
sinnten dieser oder voriger Zeiten? und
worin dann? und warum?

Antw. Daß wir unsere Gemeinde bes=
ser halten als der jetzund zerfallenen Täu=
fer, die wir wissen und kennen, das ist
wahr: und zwar darum, weilen sie in
Lehr und Leben verfallen, und weit von
der alten Täufer Lehr und Leben abgegan=
gen seyn. Welches viele unter ihnen mer=
ken und sehen. Von den vorigen Täufern
aber können wir nicht antworten, weilen
wir sie im Leben nicht gekannt. Was
aber die Lehr betrifft, sind wir mit denen
ganz eins, welche nichts wider das Evan=
gelium gelehret.

QUES. 33. Do you not regard your
church as superior to all other Baptists
of this or former times; and if so, in
what respect and why?

ANS. That we do esteem our church
better, than those now decayed Baptists,
whom we know and are acquainted with,
is true, and it is for this reason, because they have fallen away in life and
doctrine, and departed far from the old
Baptist's life and doctrine, which even
many among themselves see and acknowledge. For former Baptists we
cannot answer, since we did not know
them in their lives. But we are entirely united in what concerns their doctrine, with those, who taught nothing
con trary to the gospel.

34. Fr. Mit was Grund sie davor
halten, daß ihre neu aufgerichtete Gemein=
de, Tauf= und Bannes=Uebung, ıc. der
Apostolischen gleich komme; Da sie weder
gleich göttlichen Beruf, noch Gaben, noch
Würkung, an sich erweisen?

QUES. 34. With what propriety do
they hold, that their newly established
church, baptism, excommunication &c.
agreed with the practices of the apostles, since they cannot prove a similar-
ity neither in divine calling, nor gifts,
nor results?

Antw. In Ansehung der Kraft Wun=
der zu thun, halten wir uns gar weit, und
noch unwürdig gegen die Apostel. In
Ansehung der Lehr und des Sinnes, müs=

ANS. With regard to the power of
performing miracles, we consider ourselves still as much inferior to, and as
unworthy of any comparison with the

sen wir Gott bitten, daß er uns dem Sinn der Apostel ja gar seinem Sohn Jesu wolle ähnlich machen.

35. Fr. Ob ihre Lehrer und Vorsteher das Zeugniß ihres Gewissens vor Gott bringen können und dürfen, daß sie der heil. Geist zu Bischöffen in ihren Gemeinden eingesetzet habe, dieselbe als Gemeinden Gottes zu weiden: Und ob sie die 2 Cor. 6, 2c. dazu erforderte und gehörige Geistes-Gaben an sich haben und beweisen?

Antw. Vor Gott müssen sie es freylich bringen können, anders sind es keine rechte Hirten. Daß es aber die Menschen nicht glauben, solle sie nicht bekümmert noch betrübt machen, sondern vielmehr erfreuen; wann ihr Name als boßhaftig von den Menschen verworfen wird. Luc. 6, 22.

36. Fr. Ob sie nicht vor Gott auf ihre Seelen gestehen müssen, daß viele unter ihnen vor ihrer Taufe weit liebreicher, sanft- und demüthiger, und so fort gewesen seyen, als nach derselbigen?

Antw. Hierzu sagen wir nein. Es wäre dann von denen, so als dürre Reben abgeschnitten sind, oder auch, wann die übertünchte Liebe gemeint wird, da man einander nur, etwa ums Brod, oder Gunst willen geheuchelt, die Sünde und Irrthümer nicht bestrafet, und es hieße: Laß mich in meinem eigenen Willen, Meinen und Thun, ich will dich auch so lassen, wir wollen einander lieben und Brüder seyn; Wann dieses gemeint wird, so bekennen wir daß es wahr ist, und daß wir leider! lang genug unter dieser verderblichen Heuchel-Liebe gestanden, da wir noch unter den Pietisten waren. Aber nun haben wir eine solche Liebe gelernet, und müssen noch daran lernen, die das Böse und Arge hasset und strafet.

37, Fr. Ob sie ihre neue Taufe nicht mit vieler Ungewißheit und Veränderlichkeit angefangen, und bis dahero fortgeführet; Auch solche in andern Dingen erwie-

apostles. Concerning the doctrine and the mind, we must pray God to make us resemble the mind of the apostles, and even of his Son Jesus.

QUES. 35. Can your teachers and elders bring the testimony of their conscience before God, and say that the Holy Ghost has made them overseers in their churches, to feed them as the churches of God; and do they possess the spiritual gifts required 2 Cor. 6 &c.

ANS. Before God they must be able to bring it, or else they are no true shepherds. But if men do not believe it, that must not disturb or grieve them; on the contrary, they should rather rejoice, if their names are cast out as evil. Luke 6 : 22.

QUES. 36. Must they not on the testimony of their consciences before God confess, that many of them were much more loving, meek and humble &c. before their baptism than afterwards?

ANS. To this we say, No; unless you allude to those who like dry branches were cut off or unless you mean that feigned love, by which people deceive one another, for the sake of bread or favor, and where sin and error is not rebuked, but where it is said, leave me alone in my own self-will, opinion and doing, and I will let theo alone likewise; we will love one another, and be brethren." If such is the meaning, we confess, that it is true; and that, alas! we have but too long stood in such pernicious hypocritical love, while we were yet among the Pietists. But now we have learned such a love, and have yet to learn it, which hates and reproves evil and wickedness.

QUES. 37. Have they not begun and continued until now, their new baptism with a great deal of uncertainty and mutability, and shown the same

sen; da sie, zum Exempel, bald den Ge=
brauch der Ehe verworfen, bald wiederum
gebilliget; bald die Arbeit abgeschaffet,
bald wiederum hervorgesuchet haben?

Antw. Die Tauf des Herrn Jesu,
nach seinem Befehl, haben wir in großer
Glaubens=Gewißheit angefangen, und hat
uns der liebe Gott bisher unter vielen Wi=
dersprechen darinnen erhalten und fest ge=
macht durch seine Gnade, daß wir wohl in
Gewißheit sagen können, die da glauben,
sollen getauft werden. Daß wir aber nach
der Taufe, noch Unterredung mußten ha=
ben, wegen derer Punkten des Ehestandes,
Arbeitens, ja noch anderer mehr, ist wahr;
Dann wir, vor unserer Tauf, als wir noch
unter den Pietisten, nicht anders von denen
so man vor große Heilige gehalten hat, ge=
lehret waren. Hatten also viel Streit,
bis wir den eingesogenen Irrthum fahren
ließen.

38. Fr. Woran man dann die unge=
zweifelte Göttlichkeit ihrer neuen Gemeinde
vor allen andern in der ganzen Welt erken=
nen solle?

Antw. Wir haben ja keine neue Ge=
meinde, auch keine neue Gesetze; Sondern
wollen nur in der Einfalt und wahren
Glauben bey der alten Gemeinde bleiben,
welche Christus gestiftet durch sein Blut;
Und wollen dem Gebot folgen, welches im
Anfang war. Und wir verlangen ja
nicht, daß man an unserer Gemeinde die
ungezweifelte Göttlichkeit erkennen soll;
sondern wir wünschen, daß die ungezwei=
felte Göttlichkeit doch möchte erkannt wer=
den an Christo selbst, und dann an der Ge=
meinde zu Jerusalem. Und wann dieses
sollte erkannt werden, und derselben Gött=
lichkeit der Lehre, Worten und Geboten,
die sie gehabt, und dann müßte gesehen
werden, ob eine Gemeinde eben dieselbige
göttliche Lehr unter sich hat, und wann die=
ses erkannt wird, so meinen wir, das wäre
genugsam, eine Gemeinde zu erkennen, vor

also in other things, having for instance,
at one time rejected the marriage-state,
and at another approved it again;
sometimes desisted from labor, and then
again took it up?

Ans. The baptism of the Lord Jesus, according to his commandment we
have commenced in great assurance of
faith, and to this day our God has sustained and confirmed us therein, under
much opposition, through his grace, and
we can say with great confidence, those
who believe are to be baptized. That
we however, after baptism, had difficulties to overcome concerning marriage,
labor and many other points, is true;
for before our baptism, while we were
yet among the Pietists, we were not
otherwise taught by those, who were
deemed as great saints. Hence we had
much contention, until we gave up our
imbibed errors.

Ques. 38. Whereby then may we
know the undoubted divinity of your
new church, before all others in the
whole world?

Ans. We have indeed no new
church, nor any new laws; but in simplicity and true faith, we desire to remain with the old church, which Christ
instituted through his blood, and to
follow the commandment which was
from the beginning. And we demand
not at all, that an undoubted divinity
should be acknowledged in our church,
but we desire that such an undoubted
divinity might be known in Christ himself and the church at Jerusalem.
Should this be perceived, and the divinity of the doctrine, words and commandments, which they had, then it
can be seen, whether a church has that
same divine doctrine, and if this is
known, we think it to be sufficient to
prefer that church before all other
churches in the whole world, if like

allen andern Gemeinden in der ganzen Welt, wann sie als ein treues Weib ihrem Mann Christo unterthan ist in seinen Befehlen, ja noch dahin arbeitet immer unterthäniger zu werden. Wer aber Christum selbsten nicht erkannt in der Göttlichkeit seiner Befehlen: O! der wird auch gewiß seine Gemeinde nicht erkennen, und wann die 12 Apostel schon darunter Bischöffe und Lehrer wären.

39. Fr. Ob sie selbsten auch versichert, und die unbewegliche Versicherung dessen in der göttlichen Feuerprobe allbereits durchgehends empfangen, daß sie Gott auch selber dafür erkennen und erkennet haben wolle; und wie sie solches beweißlich und glaubwürdig zu machen getrauen?

Antw. Die Versicherung muß zwar vor Gott seyn, so wie es Paulus beschreibet, Röm. 5. Nun wir dann sind gerecht worden, durch den Glauben, so haben wir Friede mit Gott durch unsern Herrn Jesum Christum, durch welchen wir auch einen Zugang haben, im Glauben, zu dieser Gnade darinnen wir stehen. Und rühmen uns der Hoffnung der zukünftigen Herrlichkeit. Diese Gewißheit aber hat nicht länger die Verheissung, auch zu den Aposteln durch den Herrn Jesum geschehen, Joh. 15, 7. als so lange sie in Ihm, und seine Worte in ihnen bleiben, so wären sie seine rechte Jünger, und was sie bitten werden, soll ihnen widerfahren. Und so bleibets: Wer beharret in der Lehre Jesu bis ans Ende, der wird selig werden.

Dies sind die angelegensten Fragen, so man euch, geliebte Freunde! von eurer neuen Taufe und Gemeinde, so wohl um Eurer selbst, als auch um Anderer willen, dermalen vorzulegen nöthig erachtet: Worüber ihr euch nun bedenken, und eure gemeinschaftliche, deutliche und aufrichtige Erklärung, mit euren beygefügten Gründen, dergestalten thun könnet, wie ihr es in einer so wichtigen Sache vor dem Angesichts-

a faithful wife, she is obedient to her husband, Christ, in all his commandments, and labors to become still more so. But whosoever has not known Christ in the divinity of his commandments, would undoubtedly not acknowledge his church, if even the twelve apostles should be there serving as bishops and teachers.

Ques. 39. Whether they themselves were assured, and had received already the immoveable assurance of the same in the divine trials as by fire, that God himself also acknowledges and owns them, and would have them acknowledged; and how would they undertake to prove this and make it credible?

Ans. Truly, the assurance must be before God, as Paul describes it. Rom. 5. "Therefore being justified by faith, we have peace with God, through our Lord Jesus Christ: By whom also we have access by faith into this grace wherein we stand and rejoice in hope of the glory of God." But this assurance is no longer promised even to the apostles by the Lord Jesus, John 15: 7. then they would abide in him, and his words abide in them. Then they would be his true disciples, and they should ask what they will, and it should be done unto them. And so it is: He that is faithful in the doctrine of Jesus to the end, shall be saved.

These are the most important questions, dear friends, which we deemed necessary to lay before you at this time concerning your new baptism and church, as much for your own sake as for the sake of others. On which you will now reflect, and make your united, plain and candid declarations, together with your reasons assigned, in such a manner as you may be willing to ren-

te Jesu Christi, und aller seiner heiligen Engel und Auserwählten, an dem unaus= bleiblichen Tage der genauesten Durchprü= fung dieses eures angefangenen Werkes, ohne Widerspruch seines ritterlichen Gei= stes in eurem oder anderer Gewissen, zu verantworten getrauet.

Geliebte Freunde.

Auf euer Begehren und scharfe Fragen, die ihr uns in diesen 39 Punkten vor Gott, auf unser gut Gewissen habt vorge= legt, haben wir in Liebe diese Antworten auf jeden Punkt herausgegeben, nach un= serm Glauben und guten Gewissen, vor dem Gott der seinen Sohn aus Liebe da= rum in die Welt gesandt, daß wir ihn hö= ren, und an ihn glauben, und durch den Glauben an ihn, das ewige Leben haben sollen. Ist euch nun auch euer Heil und Seligkeit lieb, so eilet und bieget auch euren Hals unter dieses großen Königs Scepter; glaubet, daß seine Lehr wahrhaftig, und seine Tauf den armen Sündern heilsam und selig ist. Sprecht nicht, was kann mir das Wasser helfen, und tröstet euch ja nicht mit eurer Kindertauf, welche wider Gottes Wort in die Welt eingeführet ist; sonsten soll auch euch dieses einfältige Zeugniß (welches auf dringendes Begehren herausgegeben von den Täufern in Schwar= zenau) müssen seyn ein Zeugniß, nebst eu= rem eigenen Gewissen, an dem großen Ge= richtstage des Herrn Jesu, welcher kommen wird mit Feuerflammen, Rache zu üben an allen, die seinem Evangelio ungehorsam worden seyn. Nun dem erwürgten Lamm, welches allein Macht und Gewalt hat, im Himmel und auf Erden, dem seye Lob, Ehre und Preis, von Ewigkeit zu E= wigkeit, ja Amen. Er kommt in den Wolken und werden ihn sehen alle Augen, und die ihn gestochen haben, Amen.

(Herausgegeben zu Schwarzenau, im Monat July, im Jahr Christi 1713.

der an account of before the face of Je- sus Christ and all his holy angels, and the elect, without contradiction from his Holy Spirit in your own consciences and those of others, in the great day when this weighty matter or work which you have commenced will be strictly scrutinized.

Beloved friends:

Upon your request and sharp ques- tions, which you have proposed unto us in these thirty nine points, we have tried to answer in love upon every point according to our faith and good conscience before that God, who out of love sent his Son into the world to that end, that we should hear him, believe in him, and by faith in him have life everlasting. Now if you also regard your own welfare and salvation, then hasten and bow also your neck under the scepter of this great king; believe, that his doctrine is true, and his baptism wholesome and blessed for poor sinners. Say not, what good will water do me? and do not try to com- fort yourselves with your infant bap- tism, which has been brought into the world contrary to the word of God. Else this simple testimony (given out upon urging request by the Baptists in Schwartzencau) must be a testimony together with your own conscience, at the great judgment day of the Lord Jesus, who will come "in flaming fire taking vengeance on them that know not God, and that obey not the gospel of our Lord Jesus Christ."

Now to the Lamb that was slain, who alone has power and dominion in heaven and on earth, to him be glory, honor and praises for ever and ever Amen. "Behold he cometh with clouds; and and every eye shall see him, and they also which pierced him, &c. Amen.

Done at Schwartzenau in the month of July in the year of Christ 1713.

Beilage,

(von dem jüngern
Alexander Mack.)

Gnade und Friede von Gott dem
Vater, durch Jesum Christum
vermehre sich in euch allen, Amen.

Geliebte Brüder!

Weilen wir vernommen, daß einige
Brüder was Schwierigkeit haben,
wegen dem Fußwaschen, welches Jesus
den Seinigen befohlen hat, als ob solches
geschehen wäre zwischen dem Abendmahl
und Brodbrechen, und meynen, es seye
nicht recht gethan, so man die Füße wascht
vor dem Abendmahl; So bin ich in mei=
nem Gemüthe bewogen worden, aus einfäl=
tiger Liebe die Ursach zu schreiben, warum
wir vor dem Abendmahl die Füße waschen,
sage aber dieses dabey, daß unser Glaube
und Erkenntniß so ist, daß wann ein Bru=
der oder anderer Mensch uns in Liebe und
Bescheidenheit kann gründlicher nach des
Herrn Wort anweisen anders als nun an=
gewiesen wird, daß wir bereit seyn, nicht
allein in diesem Punkte des Fußwaschens
es anzunehmen, sondern auch in andern
Dingen, und wollen gar nicht beruhen auf
lange Gewohnheiten, sondern des Herrn
Wort soll allein unsere Regel und Richt=
schnur seyn.

Vor erst sehen wir, wie die alten from=
men Väter das Fußwaschen im Brauch
hatten, vor dem Gesetz, 1 B. Mosis 18, 4.
Cap. 24, 32. und Cap. 19, 2. Nun sie=
het man hier ganz klar, daß die fromme
Väter das Fußwaschen gethan vor der
Mahlzeit, und siehet man unter dem Ge=
setz im bildlichen Gottesdienst, daß Moses
mußte ein groß Handfaß machen, und
Wasser darein thun, und Aaron und seine
Söhne, ja die nachfolgende Priester, muß=
ten sich vorher Händ und Füße waschen,

APPENDIX.

By the younger
ALEXANDER MACK.

May grace and peace from God the
Father through Jesus Christ be multiplied unto you all, Amen.

Beloved brethren :

Inasmuch as we have understood, that
some brethren have difficulties with regard to feetwashing, which Jesus has
commanded to his disciples, as if it had
been performed between the supper and
breaking of bread, and think it not rightly
done, if feet are washed before supper;
—we felt moved in our mind in sincere
love to give the reasons, why we wash
feet before supper. At the same time
we would say, that it is our belief and
view, if a brother or any other person
can in love and moderation instruct us
according to the word of the Lord more
fully, and otherwise than is here pointed out, we should be ready to accept
of it not only in this point of feet-washing, but also in other matters, and not
at all rest upon long usage, but let the
word of the Lord be our only rule and
guide.

In the first place, we will see, how
the old pious fathers before the law
practiced feet-washing, Gen, 18 : 4.
24 : 32. and chap. 19 : 2. Now here
we see quite clearly, that the pious fathers performed feetwashing before the
meal : we see also under the law in the
levitical service, that Moses had to
make a great laver, to put water therein,
and that Aaron and his sons, yea the
succeeding priests washed their hands
and their feet thereat, when they went

wann sie im Tempel dienen sollten, wie zu sehen 2 Mose 40, 31 und 32. ja man kann merken daß unter dem Gesetz das Fußwaschen gebräuchlich war, wie zu sehen im ersten Buch Samuel im 25. Capitel im 41. Vers.

Nun war noch bey des Herrn Jesu Zeiten, als er selbst das Evangelium geprediget, eine gebräuchliche Sach das Fußwaschen, wann Freunde einander Liebesdienste erweisen wollten, ja so war der Gebrauch allzeit vor der Mahlzeit; wie zu sehen im Evangelio Lucas Cap. 7, 44. Da hielte der Herr Jesus dem Pharisäer vor, über der Mahlzeit, daß er Ihme, als er in sein Haus kommen, kein Wasser gegeben zum Fußwaschen. Nun auf die Sache selbst zu kommen, so siehet man vorerst, als das Osterfest herbey kommen, so sendete der Herr Jesus die zwei Jünger, nemlich, Petrum und Johannem, eben den Jünger welcher das Fußwaschen beschrieben, bey Johanne im 13 Capitel, den sandte der Herr Jesus das Osterlamm zu zubereiten: Wie der Evangelist Lukas meldet Cap. 22, 8. als es nun Abend war, da kam der Herr Jesus mit den Jüngern, und satzte sich. Wie der Evangelist Markus meldet Cap. 14, 17. und Matth. Cap 26, 20.

Nun schreiben die andern Evangelisten nichts vom Fußwaschen, sondern der Evangelist Johannes beschreibet es Cap. 13. Nach dem Griechischen Text, wie es Reitz, ja auch die holländische Uebersetzer, ja auch Felbinger gegeben. Im 2. Vers sagt Johannes welcher selbsten das Abendmahl bereitet hat, der sagt: als das Abendmahl gethan war, haben die Holländer, der Felbinger setzt, als das Abendmahl geschehen war; ja der Reitz druckt es noch klärer aus, und setzt darzu, bereitet war. Andere setzen es nach dem Griechischen, wie es auch im griechischen Wörterbuch stehet; als das Abendmahl gemacht worden, oder als das Abendmahl entstanden war.

into the tent, as may be seen Exod. 40 : 31, 32;—yea, we may notice, that under the law feetwashing was customary, as we find 1 Sam. 25 : 41.

Still in the time of the Lord Jesus when he himself preached the gospel, feetwashing was a common thing; when friends would show each other acts of kindness, it was the custom always before the meal, as we see in the gospel of Luke ch. 7 : 44. Here the Lord Jesus reproached the Pharisee, while at the table, that he had given him no water for his feet, when He (the Savior) entered his (the Pharisee's) house. Now to come to the point itself, we see in the first place, when the feast of the passover was come nigh, that the Lord Jesus sent two of his disciples, namely, Peter and John, the very disciple, who has recorded feetwashing, John 13th. chap. These were sent by the Lord Jesus to prepare the passover, as Luke the evangelist mentions, ch. 22 : 8. 'And in the evening he cometh with the twelve, and sat down,' as Mark (chap. 14 : 17.) and Matthew (chap. 26 : 20) relate.

Now the other evangelists say nothing of feetwashing, but the evangelist John describes it ch. 13. According to the Greek text, as REITZ, the Dutch translators, and also Felbinger have given it, John, who himself prepared the supper, says, 'when the supper was *done*," according to the dutch version: when the supper was *made*," according to Felbinger, and REITZ expresses it still more clearly, by saying, 'when the supper was *prepared*.' Others say according to the Greek, as it is in the Greek Lexicon, 'when the supper had been made," or 'had come into existence."

Das Wort, nun, wie es Lutherus setzet: nach dem Abendessen, stehet nicht so im Griechischen. Sondern so schreibet Johannes Cap. 13, 2. Als das Abendmahl gethan war, das ist alles bereitet, so stunde Jesus vom bereiteten Abendmahl auf, wie im 4. Vers folget, er stund vom Abendmahl auf, wusch seinen Jüngern die Füße, und siehe ferner, daß sie auch in Niedrigkeit, Demuth und Liebe. einander sollten die Füße waschen. Dann daß Jesus nach dem Fußwaschen sich gesetzt mit den Jüngern, schreibet nicht allein Johannes daß er gegessen habe, wie klar im 26. Vers zu sehen, da er den Bissen vom Osterlamm* eintauchte, und gab ihn dem Judas, sondern der Evangelist Matthaus schreibet Cap. 26, 23. daß Jesus gesagt: Der mit der Hand mit mir in die Schüssel tauchet, der wird mich verrathen, so schreibet es auch Markus Cap. 14, 20. der mit mir in die Schüssel tauchet.

Hier kann man sehen, daß wenn Johannes solches schreibet, dem ich den Bissen eintauche, daß solches geschehen über dem Essen des Osterlamms, und daß die Füße schon gewaschen waren, siehet man auch noch dieses mit an, wann Johannes saget im 21sten Vers, wahrlich, wahrlich ich sage euch, einer unter euch wird mich verrathen; nun waren damals die Füße gewaschen, als Jesus dieses. gesagt, und Judas war noch mit dabey, nun siehe man wieder bey Matth. 26, 21. und bey Marci Cap. 14, 18. Da zeigen nun die zwey Evangelisten, daß Jesus solches gesagt habe über dem Essen, als sie aßen.

Nun sagen die andern Evangelisten gar nichts vom Fußwaschen, hingegen Johannes schreibet nichts von der Einsetzung des Brodbrechens, so muß nothwendig die Schrift mit einem geistlichen Auge der Liebe und Gelassenheit angesehen und verstan-

---

*Dieses sollte billig "vom Abendmahl" heißen, denn der Evangelist Johannes sagt nichts vom Osterlamm.

Now the word, as given by Luther, we do not find in the Greek; for thus writes John, ch. 13 : 2. 'When the supper was done," that is, all ready, Jesus arose from the prepared supper, as follows in the 4th. verse, 'He riseth from supper," washing his disciples' feet. See further, how they (the disciples) should wash one another's feet in lowliness, humility and love. That Jesus sat down after feetwashing with the disciples, and that he then did eat, is not only recorded by John, as may be seen clearly in verse 26, 'when he dipped the sop,* and gave it to Judas." But the evangelist Matthew also states, chap. 26 : 23. 'He that dippeth his hand with me in the dish, the same shall betray me." And Mark also writes, chap. 14 : 20, of the one, 'that dippeth with me in the dish.'

Here we can see, that when John writes thus, 'To whom I shall give a sop when I have dipped it; this was done while eating the (pascal, see note) supper; and that the feet were already washed, we see also, when John says, verse 21. 'Verily, verily, I say unto you, that one of you shall betray me." The feet then were washed, when Jesus said this, and Judas was yet present. Now look again at Matt. 26 : 31. and Mark 14 : 18. Here the two Evangelists show, that Jesus said this at the meal, 'as they did eat."

Now these other Evangelists say nothing at all about feetwashing, and on the other hand John writes nothing about the institution of breaking bread; therefore scripture must be understood and looked upon with a spiritual eye

---

*Here are added the words "of the pascal lamb" in the German which are not in the text alluded to.

den werden. Und wann auch alle Uebersetzer geschrieben hätten, wie Lutherus geschrieben, nach dem Abendessen, so müßte
man billig verstehen, und nachdem das
Abendessen gethan oder bereitet war; nun
aber geben sie es genug zu erkennen, daß,
als das Abendmahl fertig, oder gemacht,
oder geschehen, oder bereitet war, so stunde
Jesus von dem zubereiteten Abendmahl
auf, und wusch auch Judas mit die Füße,
dann sobald Jesus ferner über dem Essen
anfing zu sagen: Einer unter euch wird
mich verrathen. So war dann keine Ruhe
oder Aufhören mehr, bis daß Judas hinaus war.

Nun setzten drey Evangelisten, daß über
dem Essen Jesus den Verräther Judas geoffenbaret, der Evangelist Lukas aber setzet
das Wort hinten an, nach dem Brodbrechen, wann er Cap. 22, 21. setzet nach dem
Brodbrechen, doch siehe die Hand meines
Verräthers ist mit mir über Tisch; nun
höret auch solches Wort nach den andern
drey Evangelisten nicht nach dem Brodbrechen, sondern unter das Essen des
Osterlamms, und dazu war Judas nach
dem Gesetz rein, am äußern Leibe, darum
konnte auch Jesus ihme die Füße waschen,
nemlich vor dem Abendmahl.

Hätte aber Jesus nach dem Abendmahl
eine besondere Vorbereitung wollen stellen,
durch Fußwaschen zu dem Brodbrechen,
und dem Judas auch die Füße gewaschen,
und das Brod gebrochen, auch dem Verräther Judas, welchen Jesus wohl gekennet,
so dürfte man auch einem wissentlichen
Sünder das Brod der Gemeinschaft brechen und geben, nemlich wenn man müßte
daß einer hätte sich schon angeben bei einer
Diebsrott oder Mörderrott, er wollte noch
denselben Abend stehlen oder morden, so
dürfte man, wann man es wüßte, dennoch
mit ihme gemeinschaftlich Brodbrechen,
weilen Jesus selbst so gethan hätte, welches aber ferne seyn soll von allen wahren

of love and calmness. And though all
translators had written like Luther,
'after supper," yet we would have to
understand, 'after the supper was done
or prepared. However it is even by
them made sufficiently plain, that when
the supper was ready, or done, or made,
or prepared, Jesus arose from the prepared supper, and washed even Judas'
feet with the rest, and then while they
were eating Jesus commenced saying,
'One of you shall betray me." Here
then there was no pause or stop any
more until Judas went out.

Three Evangelists stated, that while
they were eating Jesus made known
the traitor Judas. However the evangelist Luke puts the declaration back,
even after the breaking of bread, when
he says chap. 22: 21. 'But behold,
the hand of him that betrayeth me is
with me on the table." But according
to the other three evangelists this word
does not belong after the breaking of
bread, but (was spoken) while eating
the meal (paschal lamb, see Note;) and
for this Judas was legally purified in
the outward body; hence Jesus could
also wash his feet, namely, before supper.

But if Jesus after the supper had intended to institute a special preparation
by the washing of feet unto the breaking of bread, and thus had washed also
the feet of Judas, and even broken the
bread to that traitor, whom Jesus knew
well;—then we might also break and
give the bread of communion to a known
sinner, even if we knew that he had
joined a gang of robbers or murderers,
and that he would that very night commit robbery or murder; I say, we might,
knowing all this, still break with him
the bread of communion, because Jesus
had done so himself. But this should
be far from us; yea, I on my part

Gläubigen, ja ich wollte auf meiner Seite lieber kein Brod mehr brechen, als mit solchen.

Nun sagen die blinden Schriftgelehrten, der Judas hätte mit Jesu das Brod der Gemeinschaft gebrochen, und bleiben auf dem Buchstaben so steif stehen, weilen es Lucas gesetzt: als Jesus erst nach dem Brodbrechen gesagt, die Hand meines Verräthers ist mit mir über Tisch, und wollen die andern Evangelisten nicht dazu gebrauchen; auf solche Art müssen wahre Liebhaber der Weisheit nicht gesinnet seyn; sondern die wahre Weisheit und ihre Liebhaber müssen so geartet seyn, gleich wie Jacobus lehret in Cap. 3, 1?. und spricht: Die Weisheit aber von Oben her, ist auf's erste keusch, darnach friedsam, darnach gelind, lässet ihr sagen.

Aber gemeiniglich ist es also, daß wann der Mensch nur etwas fasset in eigenem Erkenntniß, und führet dann solches Erkenntniß in eigenem Willen, so wird er sich nicht gerne sagen lassen, der Mensch wird mit eigener Weisheit um die Schaale disputiren und den Kern fahren lassen, u. darum lieben Brüder lasset uns alle klug seyn, auch insonderheit in Ansehung von dem Fußwaschen, lasset uns darauf merken wie man gesinnet seyn soll, in Liebe, und Friede und Demuth soll man sich unter einander beugen.

Dann Christus hat ja kein absonderlich Gebet gegeben, wann man solches sollte thun, vor oder nach der Mahlzeit, sondern er hat befohlen daß man's thun soll, und aber auch einander lieben; dann Christus hat nicht gesagt, daß man am Fußwaschen, oder am Brodbrechen, seine Jünger sollte kennen, sondern er sagte: Dabei wird Jedermann erkennen daß ihr meine Jünger seyd, wann ihr Liebe unter einander habt. O! wie sollte der Satan uns billig ausspotten, wann wir thäten um die Zeit mit einander zanken, wann die Füße sollten gewaschen werden, und die

would rather never break bread any more, than with such.

Now say the blind scribes, that Judas did break with Jesus the bread of communion, and abide stubbornly in this idea that Luke states, how Jesus did not till after the breaking of bread say, 'The hand of him that betrayeth me, is with me on the table, and will not consult the other Evangelists on the subject. Such ought not to be the manner and mind of the true lovers of wisdom; but true wisdom and her lovers must be minded, as James teaches ch. 3: 17. and says, "But the wisdom that is from above, is first pure, then peaceable, gentle, and easy to be entreated."

But commonly it is thus, that when a person receives some knowledge in selfishness, and maintains it in self-will, he is not willing to be instructed, but will dispute in his own wisdom about the shell, and drop the kernel. Therefore, dear brethren, let us all be wise, and let us especially concerning feet-washing be careful, how we are to be minded, in love, in peace and humility to submit to each other.

For Christ indeed has given no special command, when or what time it should be performed, before or after supper; but he has commanded, that it should be done, and also that we should love one another, since Christ has not said, that his disciples should be known by washing feet, or by the breaking of bread; but he said, "By this shall all men know, that ye are my disciples, if ye have love to one another." O how should Satan mock us justly, if we were to quarrel with each other about the time, when the feet

Liebe würde zerstöret, ja selbsten das Fuß-waschen und Brodbrechen würde gar zer-nichtet werden, und der Friede verstöret, das sollte dem Satan eben recht seyn, und die Lehre Jesu sollte verspottet werden von den andern Menschen.

Darum ist es die allerhöchste Nothwen-digkeit, daß man sich in Liebe und Friede fasset, und bei sich denket, man wolle den lieben Gott bitten um immer mehrere Weisheit; dann ich kann in Wahrheit aus Erfahrung dieses schreiben, daß als wir im Anfang der Tauf, da haben wir im Segen und Liebeserweckung einander die Füß gewaschen, nach dem Essen und nach dem Brodbrechen; darnach sahen wir näher und haben im Segen einander die Füße gewaschen, nach dem Essen und vor dem Brodbrechen; darnach als der Reitz das Neue Testament heraus gegeben, und ein Bruder unter uns kam der Griech-isch konnte und es uns ordentlich angewie-sen, daß Jesus vor dem Abendessen die Fü-ße gewaschen, so waren wir einfältig und thaten es seither, allezeit vor dem Essen; nun wird uns kein Bruder verdenken daß wir nicht noch einmal wollen hinten an-fangen, sondern so lang uns niemand kann gründlicher anweisen, so wird uns niemand verdenken daß wir so thun, wie wir es verstehen. Doch sage ich dieses, daß wenn ich zu einer Brüderschaft käme, die wollten Brodbrechen, und die Vorste-her von derer Brüderschaft erkenneten es noch nicht anders, als die Füße müßten gewaschen seyn nach dem Abendessen, so wollte ich es ganz einfältig mithalten in Liebe und Friede, und wollte es dennoch ihnen vorhalten nach der Schrift, wollte aber in Liebe warten und mit ihnen Ge-dult haben, bis sie es auch so erkenneten; dann ich bin es gewiß, daß wann man die Sach ganz unpartheiisch wird ansehen, und in Liebe und Friede bleiben, so wird man es wohl merken und sehen können,

ought to be washed; and love were de-stroyed, and even feet-washing and breaking of bread were altogether neg-lected. If our peace were thus disturb-ed, it would please Satan right well, and the doctrine of Jesus would be scoffed at by other men.

Therefore it is of the utmost neces-sity, to maintain love and peace, and to conclude to pray our dear Lord for still more wisdom. For I can say, in truth and from experience, that in the beginning we have washed one another's feet after supper, and after the break-ing of bread, yet accompanied by a blessing and awakening of love. Af-terward we saw a little nearer, and washed one another's feet after supper, and before the breaking of bread, also with a blessing. Then, when *Reitz* published the New Testament, and a brother came among us, who under-stood Greek, and pointed out to us properly, how Jesus washed feet before supper, in single heartedness we did do it ever since and at all times before supper.

Now no brother should take it amiss of us, that we do not wish to begin again at the wrong end. For so long as no one can instruct us any better, no one should find fault with us, if we do, as we understand it. Yet I say this, if I should come to a fraternity, who would break bread, and the leaders of that fraternity did not yet understand it otherwise, but that the feet ought to be washed after supper, I would par-take with them in great simplicity and love, yet I would lay my views before them according to the scripture, and wait in love, and have patience with them, until they could see it so likewise.

For I feel assured, that when the matter is examined quite impartially, and love and peace are preserved, it will be easily seen and understood, that it is so, as we have shown above, that Je-

daß es also ist, gleichwie oben angewiesen, daß Jesus vor dem gemachten oder zubereiteten Abendmahl ist aufgestanden, und hat seinen Jüngern die Füße gewaschen, und habe sich dann gesetzt und gegessen, und über dem Essen hat Jesus den Verräther geoffenbaret, der ist dann hinaus gegangen, dann hat Jesus erst das Brodbrechen eingesetzt, und so schicket sich die Schrift auf einander, und die Vorbilder der frommen Väter vor dem Gesetz, und unter dem Gesetz stimmt alles mit überein, und man wird mit einem guten geruhigen Gewissen bestehen können vor Gott und Menschen; so man aber würde meinen, man müßte die Füße waschen erst nach dem Essen, so getraute ich gar nicht solches mit einem verständigen Sinn der Schrift zu behaupten, und würde es schwerlich jemand können thun, dann wann man nur die zwei Evangelisten Matthäus und Markus ansiehet so schreiben sie alle beide, erstlich Matth. 26, 26. da sie aber assen, nahm Jesus das Brod, dankete und brach es; so schreibt auch der Evangelist Markus Cap. 14, 22. und indem sie assen, nahm Jesus das Brod, und dankete und sprach: Nehmet, esset, das ist mein Leib. Nun siehet man ja hier klar, daß zwischen dem Osterlammessen und Brodbrechen gar keine Veränderung geschehen ist, dann wann das Fußwaschen dazwischen geschehen wäre, so hätten sie es gewiß auch geschrieben, weilen es aber vor dem Essen geschehen ist, so haben sie es nicht geschrieben sondern ausgelassen.

Johannes aber hat beschrieben das Fußwaschen u. hat hingegen die Einsetzung des Brodbrechens ausgelassen, darum erfordert die Schrift geistliche Augen, Sinn und Verstand, dann sonst würde man durch den Buchstaben lauter Elend und Zerreißung kriegen, wann man ohne wahre Erleuchtung würde meinen an einem Ort den Buchstaben fest zu halten, aber am

---

sus arose from the ready made or prepared supper, and washed his disciples' feet, and then did sit down, and eat, and while eating Jesus revealed the traitor, who thereupon went out. And then after this Jesus instituted the breaking of bread, and thus the scriptures are brought in harmony, and the types of the patriarchs before the law, and those under the law all correspond with it, and we can stand with a good, quiet conscience before God and men.

But if we were of the opinion, that the feet must be washed just after supper, then I would not undertake to maintain it with a rational sense of the scriptures, and scarcely any person would be able to do it. For if we look only to the two evangelists Matthew and Mark, they write both, first Matt. 26 : 26. "And as they were eating, Jesus took bread, and blessed it, and brake it." So likewise writes the evangelist Mark (14 : 22.) 'And as they did eat, Jesus took bread, and blessed, and brake it, saying, 'Take, eat, this is my body.'' Now here we see clearly, that between the eating of the passover (supper) and the breaking of bread, there occurred no change. For if feet-washing had been performed between, they would certainly have mentioned it too; but since it was done before supper, they have not written about it, but left it out.

But John has described feet-washing, and on the other hand left out the institution of breaking bread. Hence the Scriptures require spiritual eyes, mind and understanding; otherwise by the letter we would have nothing but trouble and division, if without true illumination one would think to hold fast to the letter in one place, but would act

andern würde man darwider thun, und es nicht achten.

Darum lieben Brüder, lasset uns wachen und vorsichtig seyn und über alles die Liebe bewahren, so bewahret man das Licht, dann der Geist der Wahrheit bezeuget im ersten Brief Johannes Cap. 2, 10. daß wer seinen Bruder liebet, der bleibet im Licht, und ist keine Aergerniß bei ihm, dann auch der gute Gott, der, welcher die lautere unpartheiische Liebe ist, der kann und wird nach und nach ersetzen, was an diesem oder jenem Erkenntniß fehlet. Nun schließe und bitte nochmalen alle Brüder, solches in Liebe, mit stillem Gemüthe zu lesen und zu betrachten, ich bin dann Euer schwacher Bruder,

Alexander Mack.

contrary to it in another place, and not regard it.

Therefore, dear brethren, let us watch, and be careful, and above all preserve love; for then we will preserve light. For the Spirit of truth testifies in the first epistle of John 2: 10. 'He that loveth his brother abideth in the light, and there is none occasion of stumbling in him.'' Then our good God, who is love purely and impartially, can and will add by degrees, what may be wanting in this or that knowledge (of truth).

I now conclude, begging again all my brethren to read and consider this in love and with a calm spirit. And so I am your weak brother,

ALEXANDER MACK.